# General Nathanael Greene

*Nathanael Greene by Thomas Sully,*
*after the original by C. W. Peale*
(Courtesy of Bernard Nightingale)

# THE PAPERS OF
# General Nathanael Greene

---

**VOLUME I**
*December 1766—December 1776*

---

*Richard K. Showman*
**EDITOR**

*Margaret Cobb and Robert E. McCarthy*
**ASSISTANT EDITORS**

*Assisted by Joyce Boulind, Noel P. Conlon, and
Nathaniel N. Shipton*

THE UNIVERSITY OF NORTH CAROLINA PRESS
*Chapel Hill*

*Published for the*
RHODE ISLAND HISTORICAL SOCIETY

Library of Congress Cataloging in Publication Data

Greene, Nathanael, 1742–1786.
  The papers of General Nathanael Greene.

  Includes bibliographical references.
  CONTENTS: v. 1. December 1766–December 1776.
  1. Greene, Nathanael, 1742–1786. 2. United States—History—Revolution, 1775–1783—
Sources. I. Showman, Richard K. II. Rhode Island Historical Society.
E302.6.G77A33          973.3'3'0924          76-20441
ISBN 0-8078-1285-4

# TABLE OF CONTENTS

---

# ILLUSTRATIONS

# MAPS

# FOREWORD

Perhaps the principal incentive for the formation of the Rhode Island Historical Society in 1822 was an alarming realization that the relics and records of the state's colonial past were being lost, destroyed, and scattered. Of particular concern among the society's founders— all of whom were members of the postrevolutionary war generation— was the increasing loss of contact with the events and personalities of the struggle for American independence to which Rhode Island had contributed in truly heroic and spectacular proportions.

It was no accident, therefore, that one of the first relics to be gathered into its collections was a British grenadier cap found at the base of Bunker Hill and that among its earliest recruits and the second president of the society was the venerated veteran of the Revolution, John Howland. Almost at once the society set about rescuing materials of historical interest. Howland, himself, reportedly recovered a packet of Roger Williams's letters from a rubbish heap on Market Square in downtown Providence.

The seeking out of significant documents has been a practice of the society for the last century and a half. In 1893 J. Franklin Jameson, Brown University history professor and vice-president of the society, tried to rally the historical society's members and the state of Rhode Island to purchase a large collection of General Nathanael Greene's letters then being offered for sale by a descendant of the General's in Georgia. The effort was unsuccessful, but the natural interest in one of this state's great heroes has been an abiding one as the pages of our publications of the last fifty years will testify.

It is not surprising, therefore, that impetus for the current project to publish the general's letters derived from the Rhode Island Historical Society, although its own collection of his letters is not the largest. Fittingly, too, the project grew out of a conversation at Potowomut, Nathanael Greene's birthplace, where nine generations of Greenes have lived. Mrs. Thomas Casey Greene, her son Thomas, and a nephew, Carlos Greene of Chile, were the earliest adherents one snowy morning early in 1971.

Just as one of Nathanael Greene's achievements was the successful welding together of diverse forces to make an effective fighting organization for the southern campaign, so the project to publish the documents detailing his efforts has drawn upon the support of many sources. To obtain the necessary quarter of a million dollars to finance

[xi]

such a project required the nearly simultaneous agreement of half a dozen funding organizations. The ease and eagerness with which they responded could only be explained by the universal recognition of the compelling need to tell the general's story. After nearly two centuries and a number of frustrated attempts, the conditions were for once favorable. The collaborating institutions and groups are the Rhode Island Historical Society, the William L. Clements Library at the University of Michigan, the National Historical Publications and Records Commission, the General Nathanael Greene Memorial Association, the Rhode Island Bicentennial Commission, and the Rhode Island Society of the Cincinnati. We are now delighted to have, in addition, The University of North Carolina Press.

Among the individuals who participated in creating this partnership are Mrs. Thomas Casey Greene; Howard H. Peckham, director of the Clements Library; United States Senator Claiborne Pell; Dr. Oliver W. Holmes and Berkeley Tompkins, former directors of the National Historical Publications and Records Commission; members of the General Nathanael Greene Memorial Association—Stuart H. Tucker, George E. C. Allen, the late Clarkson A. Collins III, Lee Remington, and M. Randolph Flather; George F. McDonald, former chairman, and Dr. Patrick T. Conley, present chairman, of the Rhode Island Bicentennial Commission; and Frank Mauran of the Rhode Island Society of the Cincinnati. For assistance rendered from the inception of this project, we extend our gratitude to the society's presidents, Joseph K. Ott and Duncan A. Mauran; Stuart C. Sherman, chairman of the society's publication committee, and its members; Frank Burke and the National Historical Publications and Records Commission staff; James B. Rhoads, archivist of the United States; Matthew Hodgson and the staff of The University of North Carolina Press; and most of all to our own hard-working editorial staff, Richard K. Showman, Margaret Cobb, Robert E. McCarthy, Joyce Boulind, Noel P. Conlon, Nathaniel N. Shipton, Debra Read, and David Shields.

*Providence, R.I.*                                    A L B E R T  T .  K L Y B E R G
*4 May 1976*                                                      *Director*

# INTRODUCTION

If *The Papers of General Nathanael Greene* were to be dedicated to any individual, a fitting person to be so honored would be Nathanael Greene's grandson, George Washington Greene, who undertook 130 years ago the task of collecting and publishing six volumes of the selected papers of his grandfather.

George Washington Greene was born in Rhode Island in 1811, twenty-five years after his grandfather had died at Mulberry Grove near Savannah, Georgia. His father, Nathanael Ray Greene, had moved with his wife and oldest child to East Greenwich, Rhode Island, just a year before. As a boy George had greatly revered his grandfather, hearing from Nathanael's two surviving brothers—then in their late seventies—stories of his grandfather's early years and his exploits during the war.

In 1846, while serving as consul in Rome, he wrote a short biography of his grandfather for Jared Sparks's *American Biography* series. When he returned to Rhode Island the following year, he had decided to devote himself to collecting and publishing selections of Nathanael Greene's papers. He was encouraged in the undertaking by Sparks, who had come across many Greene letters in his indefatigable search for documents of the period.[1]

Unfortunately he was without sufficient funds to carry on such a work. An amiable, well-loved, scholarly man—he numbered among his friends Henry W. Longfellow, James Russell Lowell, and Charles Sumner—he was never able fully to support himself and family, much less to subsidize a book. Although he received financial help from his father, a successful doctor, and from Longfellow (who contributed to his support for twenty some years), eight years after starting this undertaking he found himself without funds.

Regarding his project as a "national work," as he later wrote, "I asked from the national government the assistance which it had given to other works of the same character."[2] His request had the strong support of his friend Senator Charles Sumner of Massachusetts and Senator James A. Pearce of Maryland, a friend to scholars and of the Library of Congress. Pearce asked that Congress authorize the librarian to "purchase one thousand copies of the works of Gen-

---

1. Greene's earlier years are thoroughly covered in the introduction to Frederick Charles Harrison, "Early Letters of George Washington Greene, 1827–1846," (Ph.D. diss., University of Washington, 1966).
2. Greene, *Greene*, 1: viii.

eral Nathaniel [sic] Greene, to be published by George Washington Greene" at $2.25 per volume. Speaking on the Senate floor about the contribution that Washington's papers had made to the history of the war in the North, he said, "The papers of General Greene will furnish us with a similar authentic account of the operations of the army of the South. I need not say, sir, that he held the place in the Army next to that which General Washington held." He ended by saying that such a purchase would at last fulfill the spirit of a resolution passed by the Continental Congress, 8 August 1786, which had committed Congress to erect a monument to Greene's memory.[3]

Although Senator Sumner spoke eloquently in support of the project, calling his friend, "one of the most accomplished scholars and most cultivated gentlemen whom it has ever been my fortune to meet in this country," he did not count on the stonewall opposition of Senator Robert Toombs, an opposition based on a solid footing of misinformation. Toombs agreed that a history of Greene's life by his descendants would be a national contribution, that no honor was too great for his fellow Georgian (many of whose descendants were his constituents), but declared that, since General Greene "has no male descendants by the name of Greene," this man must be an interloper. Senator Sumner assured Toombs that Greene was not an interloper, but Toombs insisted it would be "a mistake to suppose that he [General Greene] left a son." Sumner could have agreed it would be a mistake since Nathanael Greene left not one but two sons, the eldest of whom, George Washington Greene, was drowned in the Savannah River six years after his father's death; but Charles Sumner, the abolitionist, was not the best man to support Greene's proposal in opposition to a proslavery man such as Toombs. When Senators Butler and Dawson joined Toombs in assuring the Senate that Greene had no male descendants, Pearce withdrew his amendment.[4] Unreasonable as the opposition was, it seems to have set a pattern of congressional inaction.

The following year Greene issued a hopeful prospectus for a six-volume work to be published "at intervals of from three to six months, to be sold only to subscribers at $2.50 per vol."[5] Although Longfellow and Lowell were the first two subscribers, their names attracted few others, and the venture never got started. Another ten years were spent in appealing to government and publishers before he gave up, writing bitterly "of the false hopes, broken promises, and heartless delays by which I was led on from year to year, till the best years of life were passed and other cherished plans gone with them,

3. *The Congressional Globe*, 33d Cong., 2nd sess., 3 March 1855, p. 1105.
4. Ibid., p. 1106.
5. George Washington Greene Papers, printed prospectus, RPB.

it is humiliating to speak and painful even to think." By this time (1867) he had found a publisher for a three-volume biography of his grandfather, in which he printed a good many letters, but as for publishing an extensive collection of the general's papers, he said that "after a full trial both of publishers and of Congress . . . the letters . . . must still be left to the chances of fire and damp, of moth and mice, of autograph fanciers, and descendants too full of themselves to remember their duty to their ancestors."[6] He died in 1883, his ambition still unrealized.

The "national government" has at last made good on the 1786 resolution of Congress calling for a monument to Greene. It has made possible the publication of these volumes through the generous support of the National Historical Publications and Records Commission. George Washington Greene could only be pleased.

The present volume is the first of several that The University of North Carolina Press will publish for the Rhode Island Historical Society. Something less than a fourth of the documents will be printed in full; the rest will be briefly calendared in their proper chronological order. When the series is completed, a microfilm of all the collected letters is planned. It will be made from the opaque copies (mostly xeroxes) that have been collected for the project from originals located in many places. Since the copies are often difficult to read—because of a faded original, a poor reproduction, or both—it is planned to accompany each document with its typed counterpart.

In collecting and editing the papers of Nathanael Greene, the editors have assigned themselves several goals. The first and most fundamental of these is to transcribe a document as faithfully as possible within the guidelines given below under Editorial Method. Anyone familiar with two-hundred-year-old manuscripts will agree that this is no mean achievement. In such painstaking work the editor/transcriber has the advantage over the casual researcher through familiarity with the handwriting and modes of expression common to the period, as well as with the particular styles of the individuals involved.

The remaining goals they have set for themselves are concerned with annotation. The most important of these is to explain a document sufficiently to make it intelligible to the modern reader who may be unfamiliar with the subject. In a sense the editor puts the reader in the place of the eighteenth-century recipient. He may, at times, give the reader an advantage over both author and recipient of a document by alluding to facts that were unknown or unknowable to them. Another goal is the correction of errors in a document, since many a myth has found its source in "documentary evidence" that

6. Greene, *Greene*, 1: ix

was false or inaccurate. Then, too, for the reader's convenience, the editor should relate the document at hand with other documents or notes in the series by the use of cross-references. And there is the final goal, where it is possible, to provide continuity and understanding to the reader by filling gaps in the documents before him.

The most serious gaps to be filled in Greene's life are in the early years when documents are sparse or nonexistent. In this respect Greene was no John Quincy Adams. The first document in his handwriting to have survived was written when he was twenty-four; the first letter, when he was twenty-eight. Since he wrote no memoir and seldom reminisced about those years, scholars have been largely dependent upon Justice William Johnson's two-volume biography of Greene written in 1822.

From a brief visit that Johnson made to Rhode Island in 1818, he gathered material for his first chapter by talking to Greene's surviving brothers and a few friends. Johnson undoubtedly learned a great deal about his subject's early life but unfortunately he was often uncritical of his sources and careless with facts. He reported, for example, that he had talked to General James Varnum, who, according to Johnson, was one of those who "passed their youth in habits of unrestrained intimacy" with Greene.[7] It is true that Varnum was a friend, but Greene did not meet him until he was twenty-seven, and Varnum, moreover, had died in Marietta, Ohio, in 1789.

Johnson was no less confused over several important aspects of Greene's early years: his suspension by the Quakers, his early friendship with Ezra Stiles, the role played by HMS *Gaspee* in his attitude toward England—to name some that are discussed in appropriate notes below (see index).

The editors have succeeded in filling gaps in Greene's early life by combing the repositories in Rhode Island. More than a hundred documents concerning Greene have been found among town and county records, the State Records Center, or the vaults of the Rhode Island Supreme Court, the State Archives, and Brown University Archives. In addition to documents concerning Greene, they have come across several signed or written by him during the years before 1775. These are printed below.

A document or documents that they have never found, despite diligent search, concerns his supposed place in the Rhode Island legislature. It is from Johnson's colorful account that biographers have described that role:

As a member of the legislature, he had taken a decided part against the royal government, and the firmness, public spirit, and great good sense

7. Johnson, *Greene*, 1: vi.

which he displayed on all occasions, had acquired for him a highly respectable standing in that body. He seldom spoke, for a consciousness of his want of early education hung upon him, and rendered him diffident. But when he did, his manner was bold, commanding, and unembarrassed, and he was listened to with marked attention. Yet he was often employed on important committees. And on one occasion, when envoys were to be sent to Connecticut to concert measures preparatory to arming for defence, he was one of the delegates selected. This was a delightful opportunity to Greene to visit his early and venerable friend, Stiles, then President of Yale, and he gladly embraced it. An entry on the minutes of the legislature shows, that his expenses on this mission amounted to ten pounds, about thirty-three dollars. Such were the frugal habits of the men of that day.[8]

From the explicit description of the "bold, commanding, and unembarrassed" manner in which Nathanael Greene addressed his fellow legislators and from other details, one might suppose that Johnson wrote from explicit primary sources. It seems more likely that he fleshed out his account from the bare-bones listing in the legislative records on one "Nathaniel Greene Jr" as a deputy from the town of Coventry in the years 1770, 1771, 1772, and 1775 and as a member of a committee sent to Connecticut in 1775.[9] Accounts since then of Green's legislative experience have been largely based on Johnson's account—sometimes corroborated by a reference to the same listing in Bartlett, *Records*. Or they have used George Washington Greene's account based on Johnson.

A study of Greene's letters, however, as well as other contemporary records, raises considerable doubt as to whether it was the future general that represented Coventry in the Assembly. It has seemed strange indeed that in the eighteen letters that he wrote Samuel Ward, Jr., between 1770 and 1774 (printed below), there is not a single mention of his sitting in the legislature—although he was not averse to impressing his young friend. Nor is there a reference to it in the hundreds and hundreds of later letters that have been examined. His attitude toward legislators increases one's doubts even further. He was critical of the Assembly as a body at the very time he was supposedly part of it. His impatience with the Continental Congress during the early war years contrasts sharply with Washington's tolerant dealings with that body—a patience that no doubt grew out of his experience with the legislative process during twenty years in the Virginia House of Burgesses.

Other evidence—though inconclusive—can be adduced. For example, the designation of "Jr" after his name in the legislative rolls is found nowhere else after his father's death in 1770. In May 1775 the Coventry deputy is listed as simply "Nathaniel Greene Jr, Esq." although a deputy holding a commission as brigadier general would

8. Johnson, *Greene*, 1: 20.
9. The lists of deputies are now located in R-Ar. Many have been reprinted in Bartlett, *Records*.

be far more likely to be so titled than the captains, majors, and colonels sitting in the chamber who were listed as such.[10]

Early in the present project, the editors became aware of more than one Nathanael Greene. There were, it turned out, four Nathan*ae*l and three Nathan*ie*l Greenes living within fifteen miles of each other at the same time. To further complicate the picture, "our" Nathanael (as he is distinguished from others by the staff) was almost invariably spelled "Nathaniel" in the public records—even on his military commissions. Most of the seven, furthermore, signed their names as "Nathl."

One of the leading citizens of Coventry during the period was Nathaniel Greene, Jr., who had served on the town council before "our" Nathanael moved to Coventry in the summer of 1770, and continued to serve into the war years. He seemed a likely candidate for the post of Coventry deputy. His candidacy was strengthened with the discovery that two months after "Nathaniel, Jr" was elected at the Coventry Town meeting in the spring of 1770 to represent the town in the legislature,[11] "our" Nathanael was listed in the Warwick town records as still serving on a Warwick town road committee.

Perhaps some time a document will be found that settles the matter. It could be a simple document—a list of signatures of the deputies for any one of the four years or a letter from Greene reading in part "When I served in the Rhode Island Assembly. . . ."

One gap that remains in Greene's early life is the mystery surrounding his military appointment. When he was commissioned brigadier general of the Continental army on 22 June 1775, he was, at thirty-two, not only the youngest general in the army, but he was also the only one who had never held a military commission. Six weeks earlier, when Rhode Island had named him to command the newly created Army of Observation, his total military training had consisted in having served for eight months as a private in the Independent Military Company of East Greenwich and its successor company, the Kentish Guards, meeting a few hours weekly.

Because of a slight limp, he had been passed over when the Guards elected officers—to his great mortification, since he had been a prime mover in organizing the group. He hid his injured pride during the winter of 1774–75 by the intensive reading of all the military treatises he could lay his hands on, by persuading a former English soldier to teach the "manual of exercises," and by faithfully attending the meetings of the Guards.

That he acquired considerable military expertise in the months before Lexington and Concord is undeniable, but it remains a mystery

10. Bartlett, *Records*, 7: 313–14.
11. Minutes of Council and Annual Town Meeting, Coventry, R.I.

why the Assembly chose him over a number of other contenders—including his friend James Mitchell Varnum (captain of the Kentish Guards) and several veterans of the French and Indian War with the rank of colonel or general of the militia. Certainly, in part, he owed his appointment to his connection with Samuel Ward, then a delegate to the Continental Congress, for he was a friend of Samuel Jr.'s, and related to the Wards through his brother Christopher's marriage to one of Ward's daughters. His appointment also owed something to his brother Jacob, who was a deputy in the legislature from Warwick, chairman of the Kent County Committee of Safety and a member of the five-member Committee of Safety for the colony. There were men with military experience, however, who had even better political connections with the dominant Hopkins faction, but none, it would appear in retrospect, possessed Greene's military genius. Perhaps by some miracle the leaders of the Rhode Island Assembly recognized his hidden genius; it is more likely that like the winner of a lottery they simply picked the right number.

However many gaps the editors might fill in Greene's life, *The Papers of General Nathanael Greene* are no substitute for a biography or a history of the times. The reader who makes sustained or repeated use of these volumes would do well to have a small reference shelf nearby. It should include Theodore Thayer's scholarly biography of Greene, as well as a few general works on the revolutionary war. After twenty-five years, Christopher Ward's two-volume history is still the best study of the "war on land," although there are areas in which recent scholarship supplements his study. An excellent brief history is Willard M. Wallace, *Appeal to Arms: A Military History of the American Revolution* (New York: Harper & Bros., 1951). Don Higginbotham's more recent *War of American Independence* admirably fulfills its objective, which, in the author's words, is "more an effort to examine military policy and attitudes toward war than it is an exercise in battles and campaigns."[12] The war as seen by a modern English scholar is Piers Mackesy's *War for America*—an excellent book. The editors have made constant use of all these works. But the workhorse on their reference shelf has been the *Encyclopedia of the American Revolution* by Mark Mayo Boatner III, a carefully wrought compendium with excellent bibliographical sources.[13]

*Providence, R.I.*
*4 May 1976*

RICHARD K. SHOWMAN
*Editor*

---

12. Higginbotham, *War*, p. xv.
13. For full bibliographical information on the books cited above, see Short Title List below.

# ACKNOWLEDGMENTS

The names on the title page of this first volume of *The Papers of General Nathanael Greene* constitute but a fraction of the people who have made this series possible. Some are omitted here because they are acknowledged in the Foreword. It is the editor's sincere hope that none of those who are known to him have been omitted through inadvertence or last-minute shuffling of cards.

The editor is grateful to a number of people whose works guided him at the beginning of this project. He would like to pay special tribute to Samuel Eliot Morison, Wilmarth Lewis, Julian Boyd, and Leonard Labaree—all of whom have left an indelible influence on the art of historical editing.

He is equally indebted to many other editors for the time they have given him in person or by letter and telephone. The list includes: Lyman H. Butterfield, Adams Papers; W. Edwin Hemphill, Calhoun Papers; William B. Willcox and Whitfield Bell, Jr., Franklin Papers; George C. Rogers, Jr., Laurens Papers; Robert A. Rutland, Madison Papers; E. James Ferguson and John Catanzariti, Morris Papers; Albert E. Van Dusen and Glenn Weaver, Trumbull Papers; Donald Jackson and Dorothy Twoig, Washington Papers.

Special thanks are due a number of people who have made important contributions: Professor Don Higginbotham of the University of North Carolina at Chapel Hill, who in his capacity of consultant has read the entire manuscript, sharing his expertise by criticism and encouragement; Carl Bridenbaugh, professor emeritus of Brown University, who has offered sound editorial advice over the past four years; Mark Carroll, director of publications for the National Park Service, for his advice on the publication of the papers; Grant Dugdale of Brown University Press, for help on the editorial guidelines; Elizabeth Drew of New York City, whose admiration for Nathanael Greene has led her as volunteer to spend many hours in New York City repositories checking documents for the project; Helen Cripe and staff of the Index to the Manuscripts of Prominent Americans; Phillips D. Booth, for his maps; Lawrence Tilley for his photographs; the Reverend David H. Coblentz of Raphine, Va., who has not only made his collection of Greene letters available but, as former president of the Manuscript Society, has helped to find other individual owners of Greene documents; and Dr. Patrick T. Conley, whose encouragement to the Greene Papers preceded his chairmanship of the Rhode Island Bicentennial Commission.

It would be difficult to acknowledge all of the help we have received from the staff of the National Historical Publications and Records Commission. In addition to the directors, who are acknowledged in the Foreword, our thanks go to Fred Shelley, who, as acting director of the commission in 1972, got the Greene Papers project off to a good start; to Roger A. Bruns, assistant to the director, who has never failed to respond to calls for help; and to H. B. Fant, Sara Dunlap Jackson, and Richard N. Sheldon.

Besides those listed on the title page, our warmest appreciation is extended to the following staff members of our own Rhode Island Historical Society for their unfailing patience and cooperation: Virginia Catton, Nancy F. Chudacoff, Clifford Cone, Pamela Fox, Lisa Krop, Nancy E. Peace, and Marsha Peters.

Libraries that have contributed documents are listed below, but we owe a debt to many librarians for other help they have extended: the staffs of Providence Public Library; Dinand Library, College of the Holy Cross; and Bapst Library, Boston College. We would like to give special thanks to Madeline F. Gross, John D. Rockefeller, Jr., Library, Brown University; Phyllis Peloquin, Rhode Island State Archives; and Alan Fox, George Fingold Library, Commonwealth of Massachusetts.

We wish to thank Doubleday & Company for permission to adapt four maps from Richard M. Ketchum's *The Winter Soldiers*. Acknowledgment is made with each map.

A very special vote of thanks to Mary Mac Showman, who has contributed many hours of her time in the search for Greene papers and other editorial chores. Her suggestions have improved many of the annotations; her patience and encouragement have helped to bring this first volume to completion.

To the following individual owners of Greene documents who have made them available, we are most grateful: Harry Ackerman, Burbank, Calif.; Francis F. Brooks, East Weymouth, Mass.; David H. Coblentz, Raphine, Va.; Sol Feinstone, Washington Crossing, Pa.; Mrs. Thomas Casey Greene, Warwick, R.I.; Helen Roelker Kessler, Cambridge, Mass.; Albert E. Lownes, Providence, R.I.; Richard Maas, White Plains, N.Y.; Mary Lynn McCree, Chicago, Ill.; Mr. and Mrs. Gene E. Miller, Nutley, N.J.; Bernard Nightingale, Brunswick, Ga.; John F. Reed, Valley Forge, Pa.; Nancy Lyman Roelker, East Greenwich, R.I.; Emily Taussig Sherman, Newport, R.I.; Leander W. Smith, Princeton, N.J.; Nathaniel E. Stein, New York, N.Y.

We also wish to thank the following repositories for making documents available, and their staffs for research assistance and for locating and copying documents: Marcus A. McCorison and William

L. Joyce, American Antiquarian Society; Whitfield J. Bell, Jr., and Murphy D. Smith, American Philosophical Society; J. Richard Phillips, Amherst College Library; Biblioteek der Universiteit van Amsterdam; Boston Public Library; Frederick Bogert, Albert B. Dearden, and Adrian C. Leiby, Bergen County Historical Society; Thomas Adams, Richard Boulind, Laurence C. Hardy, and Diana E. Steimle, John Carter Brown Library; Stuart C. Sherman and John Stanley, John Hay Library, Brown University; R. W. Constantue, Buffalo and Erie County Historical Society; Virginia Rugheimer, Charleston Library Society; Travis Coxe, Chester County Historical Society; Archie Motley, Chicago Historical Society; John D. Kilbourne, Society of the Cincinnati; Curtis Carroll Davis, Society of the Cincinnati, North Carolina; Howard H. Peckham and John C. Dann, William L. Clements Library, University of Michigan; Susan C. Finlay, Colonial Dames, Wethersfield, Conn.; Kenneth A. Lohf, Columbia University Library; Marcia E. Moss, Concord (Mass.) Free Public Library; Mary A. McKenzie, Connecticut College Library; Thompson R. Harlow and Doris E. Cook, Connecticut Historical Society; Robert Schnare and Eunice Gillman, Connecticut State Library; Ellen B. Wells and Mary F. Daniels, Cornell University Library; Kenneth C. Cramer, Baker Memorial Library, Dartmouth College; Mollie Somerville, National Society Daughters of the American Revolution; Delaware Hall of Records; Bernice C. Sprenger, Detroit Public Library; Roberta A. Vincett and Martha C. Slotten, Dickinson College; Mattie Russell, Sue McHale, Paul I. Chestnut, and Sharon E. Knapp, Perkins Library, Duke University; Martha McPartland, East Greenwich (R.I.) Free Library; Mary F. Riley, Fordham University Library; Howell J. Heaney, Free Library of Philadelphia; Carroll Hart, Georgia Department of Archives and History; Lilla M. Hawes, Georgia Historical Society; Magdalena Houlroyd, Savitz Library, Glassboro State College; William J. Moore, Greensboro Historical Museum; Rodney G. Dennis III, Houghton Library, Harvard University; Edwin B. Bronner, Haverford College Library; Jean F. Preston and Harriet McLoone, Henry E. Huntington Library; Paul Spence, Illinois State Historical Library; Leona T. Alig, Indiana Historical Society; Elfrieda Lang, The University Libraries, Indiana University; Jane Katz, John Work Garrett Library, Johns Hopkins University; Clyde L. Haselden and Ronald E. Robbins, Skillman Library, Lafayette College; Lee A. Walck, Lehigh County Historical Society; Library Company of Philadelphia; Paul Sifton, Paul H. Smith, and Carolyn Hoover Sung, Library of Congress; John H. Lindenbusch, Long Island Historical Society; Gerald E. Morris, Maine Historical Society; Jane H. Wilson, Dawes Memorial Library, Marietta College; Morris L. Radoff and Phebe R. Jacobsen, Maryland Hall of Records; Richard J. Cox and Alice Chin,

Maryland Historical Society; John Cushing, Malcolm Freiberg, and Gertrude A. Fisher, Massachusetts Historical Society; Helen Ball, King Library, Miami University; Sue E. Holbert, Minnesota Historical Society; Herbert Cahoon and Evelyn W. Semler, Pierpont Morgan Library; Bruce W. Stewart, Morristown National Historical Park; National Archives; Lawrence W. Towner, Newberry Library; Robbin Murray and Jean G. Johnson, New Hampshire Historical Society; William T. Kerr, Don Skemer, and Sharon Pugsley, New Jersey Historical Society; David C. Munn, New Jersey State Library; Gladys E. Bolhouse, Newport Historical Society; Thomas J. Dunnings, Jr., New-York Historical Society; Paul R. Rugen and Richard M. Salvato, New York Public Library; Sylvia C. Hilton, New York Society Library; James Corsaro, New York State Library; Paul P. Hoffman, North Carolina Division of Archives and History; Catherine Mead, State Library of Ohio; Nicholas B. Wainwright, Peter Parker, and Gary Christopher, Historical Society of Pennsylvania; the Reverend Donald Bilinski, Polish Museum of America; Alexander P. Clark and Wanda M. Randall, Princeton University Library; Richard L. Champlin, Redwood Library and Athenaeum; Rhode Island Governor's Office; Phyllis Peloquin, Rhode Island Archives; Howard Presel and Frank Conti, Rhode Island State Records Center; Antone P. Roderick, Rhode Island Supreme Court Vault; Richard B. Talbot, Rosenbach Foundation; Roy L. Kidman and Donald A. Sinclair, Rutgers University Library; Daniel M. Lohnes, Society for the Preservation of New England Antiquities; Ruth S. Green, South Carolina Department of Archives and History; Mary B. Prior, South Carolina Historical Society; Patricia J. Palmer, Stanford University Libraries; Eleanor Mayer, Friends Historical Library, Swarthmore College; Peter J. Knapp, Trinity College Library; Jean F. Butt, Tufts University Library; Edwin K. Tolan, Schaffer Library, Union College; Robert Schnare and Marie T. Capps, United States Military Academy Library; Albert M. Tannler, Joseph Regenstein Library, University of Chicago; Royce McCrary, University of Georgia Libraries; Isaac Copeland and Richard A. Shrader, University of North Carolina Library; Allen H. Stokes, South Caroliniana Library, University of South Carolina; Edmund Berkeley, Jr. and Gregory A. Johnson, Alderman Library, University of Virginia; Richard C. Berner, University of Washington Libraries; John F. Reed, Valley Forge Historical Society; Howson W. Cole, Virginia Historical Society; Donald R. Haynes and Louis H. Manarin, Virginia State Library; David M. Parrish, Wadsworth Atheneum; Mary Anne Burns, West Chester State College; Kermit J. Pike, Western Reserve Historical Society; William C. Pollard and Margaret C. Cook, Earl Gregg Swem Library, College of William and Mary; Elizabeth B. Scherr, Williams College; Edward Riley and N. M. Merz, Colonial Williamsburg; Josephine L. Harper, State Historical Society of Wisconsin; Judith Schiff, Sterling Library, and Dorothy W. Bridgwater, Franklin Collection, Yale University.

# HISTORY OF
# GREENE'S PAPERS

The search for the papers of Nathanael Greene began in the summer of 1972 and has not yet ended. By May 1976 the editors had assembled photocopies of some nine thousand letters to and from Greene and more than seven hundred documents originated by him, including military orders. More than 90 percent of the total were written during the War for Independence, constituting—aside from Washington's—the largest body of papers of a Continental army general.

The Clements Library, with over four thousand documents (plus many concerning Greene), has by far the largest collection. The National Archives, the Library of Congress, and the American Philosophical Society Library account for another twenty-five hundred, while the remainder (except for sixty some items in private hands) are scattered among a hundred repositories. At least five hundred are copied from nineteenth-century transcripts or printed versions of originals that have since disappeared.

A large proportion of the documents have variant copies. It is not uncommon to have a draft, an autograph copy, and a contemporary copy of the same letter. Nineteenth-century transcripts of Greene letters are numerous. Copies of more than four thousand have been received, twenty-six hundred of them collected by Greene's grandson and biographer, George Washington Greene, and now in Huntington Library; the rest are found principally among the papers of Jared Sparks, Harvard College Library; Peter Force, Library of Congress; George Bancroft, New York Public Library; and Lyman Draper, State Historical Society of Wisconsin. Copies of three dozen transcripts of Greene's letters to his wife have been made available by Bernard Nightingale of Brunswick, Georgia. Transcripts have often proved invaluable in the transcribing of damaged originals.

Of the almost ten thousand documents that have been photocopied, the vast majority—perhaps four-fifths—have been fairly accessible to the diligent researcher. The remainder have been difficult or even impossible to locate through conventional finding aids. These have offered the greatest challenge—and the greatest reward. As Leonard W. Labaree once wrote: "Editors are psychologically much like the biblical shepherd who rejoices far more over the one lost sheep that is found than over the ninety and nine that never strayed from the fold."[1] Many such strays have turned up in institutions where one would not ordinarily expect to find revolutionary war manuscripts, such as the Polish Museum of Chicago, the Western Reserve Historical Society in Cleveland, the Detroit Public Library, or the Savitz Library of Glassboro (N.J.) State College. Some have rested, unknown to scholars, in such unsuspected places as the New Jersey Department of Defense.

Most, however, have hidden uncataloged—and sometimes unseen—in the major repositories. One of the first things an editor learns is that few institutions have had the staff or funds to keep abreast of cataloging manuscripts. The countless hours the editors have spent in leafing through catalog cards or manuscript pages of Greene's principal correspondents have been rewarded by the addition of several hundred documents. Equally rewarding, though even more laborious, has been the task of looking at reels of microfilm, frame by frame. At the Library of Congress and the National Archives, the editors have been aided in such searching by staff members of the National Historical Publications and Records Commission.

Occasionally an entire parcel of uncataloged Greene letters has been turned up. One of the most valuable of such discoveries was made by William Joyce of the American Antiquarian Society, who came across thirty some letters from Greene to his brothers that had lain uncataloged since they were donated in 1917. Transcripts of a dozen letters from Greene to his brother Jacob were similarly found among the papers of Theodore Foster in our own Rhode Island Historical Society Library.

Hundreds of documents continue to be held by individuals. Where they are known, a direct appeal has almost always elicited a favorable response, but general appeals have failed to reach most of the unidentified owners of manuscripts. Some of those who have been reached have failed to respond—perhaps from inertia or from the mistaken notion that printing a document diminishes its value. The editors can only hope that this volume will bring out more copies of letters still in private hands.

The sheer number of Greene's correspondents is impressive (three hundred persons with four or more documents from each), but even more impressive are the number of revolutionary leaders who are represented. Included are all of the presidents of the Continental Congress, the War Board, almost all of the state governors, and most of the major generals of the Continental army, as well as men of lesser rank who served under him. His correspondence with Washington is by all odds the most voluminous, with over six hundred

1. Leonard W. Labaree, "In Search of 'B. Franklin'," *William and Mary Quart.* 3 Ser., 16 (1959): 189.

letters between them, including those written for Washington over an aide's name.

The southern campaign accounts for well over half of the total. Much of the correspondence was with partisan leaders and the Continental officers who served with him. A hundred letters to and from Francis Marion have survived; over a hundred and thirty of Thomas Sumter, and two hundred of "Lighthorse Harry" Lee. From the year 1781 alone more than twenty-four hundred documents have come down to us. And finally there are personal letters—five hundred of them between 1770 and 1786, including eighty to his wife.

That so many documents should have survived the rigors of war, not to mention the vicissitudes of two intervening centuries, is little short of miraculous.

The chief hazard confronting wartime documents was the mobility of the army. During the eight and a half years that Greene served, he had a total of twenty-four separate headquarters from Massachusetts to South Carolina. From each one, moreover, he made innumerable excursions, operating out of a saddlebag and field desk. Most of his correspondents were equally mobile. Some—especially the partisan leaders in the Carolinas—were constantly on the move. Even the Continental Congress moved six times during his tenure.

Greene's own collection of his papers must have had many narrow escapes as they were periodically boxed and shipped either by water or by wagon along backcountry roads. Some of the near disasters are documented. When, for example, his brigade was en route from Boston to New York in April 1776 the transports out of New London encountered a storm that swept baggage from the deck of one vessel and turned several back to port.[2] When Cornwallis made a surprise landing near Ft. Lee in November that same year, Greene had only minutes to gather up his possessions and to evacuate the fort.[3] Near the war's end, he came close to losing all his records; on returning to his quarters in Charleston he found his room ablaze, some thirty books already burned.[4] Fortunately the fire was extinguished before any papers were destroyed.

Many papers escaped destruction through sheer good fortune; others—especially official letters—often survived through some form of duplication, which amounted in effect to survival insurance: these included drafts, file copies, copies made of incoming mail, circular letters, and letters printed in newspapers. When Greene was in enemy territory, he often sent two copies of a letter via two different riders to ensure that one got through. At least one such letter has

2. See below, note 1, NG to Commanding Officer of the sloop *Gale*, 10 April 1776.
3. See below, note 2, NG to Nicholas Cooke, 4 Dec. 1776.
4. NG to Benjamin Lincoln, 28 Dec. 1782, NcD.

come down to us from the British Public Records Office. It did not get through.

Good fortune, however, did not always ride with his papers. Those that he had accumulated between May 1775 and April 1778 have disappeared. No positive evidence of the disappearance has ever turned up, but the negative evidence is persuasive. For the three-year period, for example, there are no drafts or file copies of his letters; after April 1778 there are almost two thousand. Of the hundreds of letters that he received in the three-year period, only twenty five recipients' copies have reappeared, and they seem in each case to have survived only because he sent them on to other persons—nine of them now being in the Washington papers. There are, of course, many retained copies of letters to him kept by the senders.

Not all of the missing letters were victims of accident. He once wrote brother Christopher: "I make it a constant rule to burn all [letters from the brothers] that contain family secrets, as soon as I have read them."[5] He did save business letters from Jacob (which contained some family secrets), but only three letters from his other four brothers have survived. Fortunately his brothers did not follow his rule, since his letters to them are the most revealing we have.

He did not destroy his wife's letters to him, but someone apparently did. Mrs. Greene is the most likely suspect since she had both motive and opportunity. Her motive could well have been embarassment over her poor grammar and spelling (which he once criticized), and she had ample opportunity to destroy the letters during the twenty-eight years his personal papers were in her possession. Fortunately, unlike Martha Washington, she did not destroy her husband's letters to her.

During the last months of the war, Greene put his papers in some order, filling two trunks with six thousand documents—divided into personal and official papers. Since much of the quartermaster correspondence had been left with his deputy, Charles Pettit, the bulk of the official papers in his possession concerned the southern campaign. He had given some thought to writing an account of the campaign based on the papers, for he had told John Adams that the "measures which led to important events and the reasons for these measures must lay in the dark, untill a more leisure hour."[6]

He was also concerned that Congress have copies of the papers. On his return north in the autumn of 1783, he stopped at Princeton, where Congress was then meeting, and there, at the suggestion of President Elias Boudinot, he wrote the following letter:

5. NG to Christopher Greene, 22 April 1778, MWA.
6. NG to John Adams, 28 Jan. 1782, MiU-C.

The letters and miscellaneous papers containing a history of the most material parts of the Southern operations may contain some things which Congress or their officers may hereafter have occasion to refer to. Loose files are easily disordered and where recourse is often had to them papers often get lost.

If Congress should think it an object worthy the expence and would indulge my wishes, I should be glad to get the whole papers transcribed into bound books. Having taken the liberty of suggesting my wishes I shall be happy to take the trouble of directing the business if Congress will be at the expence of a Clerk to do the writing.[7]

On the same day, Congress ordered Secretary Thomson to furnish him with a clerk, but it is not recorded that it appropriated money to pay his salary.[8] In 1785, as Greene prepared to move his family to Georgia, he hired Phineas Miller, a young Yale graduate, to tutor his children and transcribe the papers. Beset as he was by financial troubles, he had undoubtedly been assured by Thomson that Congress would pay part of Miller's salary. On Greene's death in June 1786, Miller had barely started the copying.

Before Catharine Greene returned to New England in 1786, she left the two trunks of papers with Greene's friend and executor, Edward Rutledge of Charleston, S.C., a distinguished lawyer and signer of the Declaration of Independence.[9] It was Miller's plan to spend a year with Catharine and her family in Connecticut, copying the documents, but he did not receive the two trunks from Rutledge until shortly before he was ready to return to Georgia.[10] Catharine Greene kept the personal papers, taking them with her to Cumberland Island; but she returned the official papers to Rutledge's office, where they sat for twelve years. It is doubtful if Miller ever touched them again; it is possible that Rutledge oversaw the copying of the three bound volumes that are now in the Library of Congress. Several of the transcriptions appear to be in Rutledge's hand. When he died in 1800 (while governor), his son Henry took the papers. They probably were in Henry's possession for some years, since he later wrote that he had had "full leisure to examine" them. Before moving to Tennessee he placed the bulk of the official papers with his uncle, General Charles Cotesworth Pinckney, who had been his father's law partner.[11] Young Rutledge kept some letters (perhaps inadvertently); they showed up a century later in the hands of a descendant who was unaware "how they came into the possession of the family."[12]

In 1796 Catharine Greene married Phineas Miller. She died in 1814, leaving the estate on Cumberland Island and Nathanael

7. NG to Boudinot, 1 Nov. 1783, PCC (DNA).
8. JCC, 25: 788–89.
9. Jeremiah Wadsworth to Charles Thomson, 1 Oct. 1786, and Wadsworth to Edward Rutledge, 29 July 1787, CtHi.
10. Phineas Miller to Henry Knox, 24 July 1790, MHi.
11. Henry M. Rutledge to William Johnson, 26 June 1822, MiU-C.
12. "Letters to General Greene and Others," *S.C. Hist. and Gen. Mag.* 16 (1915): 97.

Greene's personal papers to her youngest daughter, Louisa Shaw. In 1817 Louisa turned over the papers to Justice William Johnson of South Carolina to use in writing a biography of her father. At the same time, she asked General Pinckney to let Johnson use all of the official papers.[13] The status of those papers was undetermined. General Pinckney may have planned to send them to the War Department, but when he died eight years later, they were still in Johnson's possession. When Louisa pressed Johnson two years later to return the personal papers to her, he apparently responded by also sending her the official papers he had received from Pinckney.[14] Considering Johnson's careless handling of the documents, it is remarkable that after ten years they were relatively intact.

At some point Louisa turned over several hundred letters to her sister Cornelia. The remainder—almost six thousand—were left on her death to her nephew, Phineas Miller Nightingale, along with her estate on Cumberland Island. In 1847 his cousin, George Washington Greene, then living in New York, asked to borrow the papers with a view to publishing selections in a proposed six-volume collection of his grandfather's papers. Nightingale agreed and sent them to a lawyer in New York for inventorying. When Greene received the two trunks there were 5597 documents, two-thirds of them original letters addressed to the general and the other third, drafts or file copies— many in his grandfather's hand.[15]

George Washington Greene kept the papers for many years, returning, in the meantime, to Rhode Island to live. Before he sent them back to Georgia, he showed them to the trustees of the Rhode Island Historical Society, who indicated they would be glad to have the collection—as a gift. But times were hard in postwar Georgia, and the letters constituted an asset the heirs could not afford to give away (there were forty-seven letters signed by Washington, fourteen of them written in his hand). After twenty years Phineas M. Nightingale's widow offered to sell them to the Rhode Island Historical Society. Professor J. Franklin Jameson of Brown University, an officer of the society, tried unsuccessfully to raise funds to purchase them.[16] Two years later the family sold them to Joseph Sabin, the New York autograph dealer. There were still more than 5,500 documents in the

13. Johnson, *Greene*, 1: v, and Alexander Garden to Charles C. Pinckney, 11 Feb. 1817, GHi.

14. Jared Sparks recorded in his diary, after seeing Louisa Shaw in Providence, that she said she would reclaim the papers from Johnson. Sparks Diary, 12 Oct. 1827, MH.

15. A. H. Richards to P. M. Nightingale, 8 May 1848. Letter in possession of Bernard Nightingale, Brunswick, Ga. A receipt for the documents, signed by Greene, is on the back of the inventory.

16. J. Franklin Jameson, "The Papers of Major-Gen. Nathanael Greene," RIHS, Pub. 3 (Oct. 1895): 159–67.

collection. The price: $5,000. Between 1894 and 1920, Sabin or his son sold approximately a third of the collection at one time or another, hundreds of which have never reappeared. The remaining two-thirds were kept together until they were purchased in the 1920s by William L. Clements. Today they constitute the core collection of the Greene papers at Clements Library.[17]

The rest of the papers in Greene's possession at the time of his death—those given by Louisa Shaw to her sister Cornelia and consisting of several hundred items—have had a more charmed existence. Cornelia bequeathed them to her son Peyton Skipwith of Oxford, Miss., who some time before the Civil War lent them to his cousin, George Washington Greene, in Rhode Island. Some years later they were en route back to Skipwith when the vessel carrying them was wrecked off the Carolina coast. They were retrieved by a gunboat and eventually found their way back to Mississippi. All were water-damaged, some severely. In 1920 they made a final passage to a safe resting place in the Library of Congress.[18] Fortunately some of the most severely damaged letters had been copied by Greene before shipping them back.

We have mentioned one other set of papers that were once part of General Greene's files—the so-called quartermaster papers that he left in 1780 with his deputy, Charles Pettit. When Pettit left the department a year later, he apparently took the papers with him. After his death in 1806, according to William Johnson, they were sold as wastepaper and retrieved by Robert DeSilver, a Philadelphia publisher, who made them available to Dr. Charles Caldwell for a biography of Greene that was subsequently (1819) published by DeSilver.[19] The following year, some thirteen hundred items of DeSilver's collection were given to the American Philosophical Society, where they have been cared for ever since.

In 1835 the State Department acquired the rest of Greene's quartermaster papers that had been found, according to DeSilver, "in an old Barrel of rubbish and arranged and bound by him (DeSilver)."[20] Whether they were the letters Johnson speaks of as being sold for wastepaper cannot be ascertained.

It is not impossible that Greene's missing collection of letters from the 1775–78 period might also show up in a "barrel of rubbish" sometime, but lacking such a near-miracle, it is fortunate that copies of many of them have reappeared from other collections—as can be seen by the number that are printed in the latter half of this volume.

17. Joseph Sabin's correspondence with the Nightingales and William L. Clements is found in the New York Public Library.
18. See the Introduction to the Skipwith Collection in the Greene Papers, DLC.
19. Johnson, *Greene*, 1: viii.
20. L. B. Clarke to George Templeman, 4 Dec. 1833, PCC (DNA).

# EDITORIAL METHOD

---

### Arrangement of Material

Letters and documents are arranged chronologically. If two or more related items are dated the same day they are arranged in sequence; if unrelated to each other, they are arranged as follows:

1. Military orders and documents (as opposed to letters)
2. Letters from NG, alphabetically by recipient
3. Letters to NG, alphabetically by sender

### Undated Items

If a date omitted by the writer can be determined, it is printed in brackets, and the item takes its place chronologically. A doubtful conjecture is followed by a question mark.

If a precise day cannot be established, the shortest conjecturable time span is placed in brackets and the item arranged as follows:

| Conjectured Time Span | Chronological Arrangement |
| --- | --- |
| Sept. [10–18] 1776 | Placed at 10 Sept. 1776 |
| [April] 1776 | Placed at end of April |
| [Nov. 1775–Feb. 1776] | Placed at end of Nov. 1775 |
| [1775] | Placed at end of 1775 |
| [1776–78] | Placed at end of 1776 |
| [before 12 Dec. 1776] | Placed at 12 Dec. 1776 |

All such conjectures are explained in footnotes. If no time period can be conjectured, the item will be placed at the end of the last volume of the series.

### Misdated Items

If a correct date can be determined for a misdated item, it follows the incorrect date in brackets; if the correct date cannot be established, a question mark in brackets follows the incorrect date. Misdated items are explained in footnotes.

### Form of a Letter

The form of a letter is rendered as follows, regardless of the original:

1. Place and date is at top right.

2. Complimentary close is set continuously with the body.
3. Paragraphs are indented, and paragraphing is sometimes introduced to relieve long, unbroken segments.
4. Author's interlineations or brief additions in the margin are incorporated into the text silently.
5. Scored-out or erased passages are ignored unless mentioned in a footnote.
6. Address sheet and docketing are normally omitted.

## Calendared Items

Less important items may be calendared, with an abstract of the contents set within brackets. The item is arranged according to date. If the writer's original wording is included, it is set off by quote marks.

## MANUSCRIPT TEXTUAL POLICY

Following the practice established by Julian Boyd, Leonard Labaree, and other modern editors, manuscripts are rendered in such a way as to be intelligible to the present-day reader while retaining as much as possible the essential form and spirit of the writer. The following guidelines reflect this compromise.

## Spelling

Spelling is retained as written. If a misspelled word or name is not readily recognizable, the correct spelling follows in brackets. Names are correctly spelled in notes and index.

Slips of the pen and inadvertent repetition of words are corrected silently.

## Capitalization

The only instance in which an author's capitalization is always followed is the eighteenth-century practice of capitalizing words within sentences—usually, but not confined to, nouns. In other cases an author's capitalization is changed where necessary to conform to the following rules:

1. All sentences begin with initial capitals.
2. Personal names and titles used with them, honorifics (such as "His Excellency"), geographical names, and days of the week and months are capitalized.

## Abbreviations and Contractions

1. Shortened word forms still in use or those that can easily be understood (as "t'was" or "twixt") are rendered as written.
2. Those no longer readily understood are expanded silently, as in "dn" to "deacon."
3. Abbreviations of names or places—forms known only to the correspondents or their contemporaries—are expanded in brackets, as in S[amuel] A[dams] or Chsn [Charleston].

## Symbols Representing Letters and Words

When any of the following symbols are expanded they are done so silently.

1. The ampersand is expanded to "and" except in "&c," "&ca.," and "& Co." in business firms.
2. The thorn, which by 1750 had been debased to "y" as in "ye," is expanded to "th." Such abbreviations as "yt" or "ym" are rendered as "that" or "them." ("Ye," of course, is rendered "the.")
3. The tilde is replaced by the letter(s) it represents.
4. The ꝑ sign is expanded to the appropriate letters it represents (e.g., per, pre, or pro).
5. Superscript letters are brought down to the line as in 9th to 9th.

## Punctuation

Where necessary, punctuation is changed to conform to the following rules:

1. A period or question mark is placed at the end of every sentence.
2. Within a sentence, punctuation is sparingly added or deleted in order to clarify a confused or misleading passage.
3. Dashes used in place of commas, semicolons, periods, or question marks are replaced with appropriate punctuation; dashes are retained when used to mark a suspension of the sense or to set off a change of thought.
4. No punctuation is used after a salutation.

## Missing or Indecipherable Passages

If such passages cannot be conjectured, they are indicated by italicized editorial comments in brackets, such as [*mutilated*], [*indecipherable*], [*remainder of paragraph (or letter) missing*].

If missing or indecipherable portions can be conjectured they are treated in one of the following ways:

1. If no more than four letters are missing they are supplied silently.
2. If more than four letters are conjectured they are inserted in brackets. If there is some doubt about the conjecture, it is followed by a question mark: Ch[arleston?].
3. If such portions can be supplied from a variant version of the manuscript they are set in angle brackets: ⟨Washington⟩.
4. A blank left by the author is so depicted and the fact mentioned in a footnote.

## PRINTED MATERIAL

In reprinting documents from printed sources the capitalization, spelling, punctuation, and paragraphing have been faithfully followed—except for obvious printer's errors.

The earlier practice of italicizing names, however, is dropped.

## SOURCE NOTE

An unnumbered source note directly follows each document. For manuscript material it consists of a symbol describing the type of manuscript, followed by the symbol or name of the repository that owns the document, or the name of an individual owner. Pertinent facts or conjectures concerning the manuscript are added when required. A list of manuscript symbols and a list of the Library of Congress repository symbols follow the section on annotation below.

## ANNOTATION

A few points need emphasis:
1. Identification of persons is usually made at the first appearance of their names and is not repeated. References to these biographical notes are found in the index. Identifications are omitted for such leading figures as Washington or Franklin, as well as for obscure persons who played an insignificant role in NG's career.
2. Cross-references in the notes are to documents rather than to

page numbers, as in "See below, NG to Washington, 9 Nov. 1776." If a cross-reference is to a document within the same year, the year is often omitted: "See above, 13 Sept." Cross references may refer to dates found in an earlier or later volume.

3. When a page number does not appear in a citation, the reader can assume the work is in dictionary form.

## DESCRIPTIVE SYMBOLS FOR MANUSCRIPTS

Following are the symbols employed in source notes to describe the kinds of manuscripts used in the texts.

| | |
|---|---|
| AD | Autograph document |
| ADS | Autograph document signed |
| ADf | Autograph draft |
| ADfS | Autograph draft signed |
| AL | Autograph letter |
| ALS | Autograph letter signed |
| D | Document |
| DDf | Document draft |
| DS | Document signed |
| Df | Draft |
| DfS | Draft signed |
| LS | Letter signed |
| LB | Letter book copy |
| FC | File copy |
| Cy | Copy (made contemporaneously with original) |
| ACy | Autograph copy |
| ACyS | Autograph copy signed |
| Tr | Transcript (later copy made for historical record) |
| [A] | Indicates some uncertainty about the autograph |
| [S] | Indicates signature has been cropped or obliterated |

(No symbol is given to printed letters or documents)

## LIBRARY OF CONGRESS SYMBOLS OF REPOSITORIES

The following institutions have provided copies of manuscripts which are printed or calendared in volume one:

CSmH   Henry E. Huntington Library, San Marino, Calif.
Ct   Connecticut State Library, Hartford, Conn.

DLC      U.S. Library of Congress, Washington, D.C.
DNA      U.S. National Archives, Washington, D.C.
DNDAR    Daughters of the American Revolution, Washington, D.C.
MH       Harvard College Library, Cambridge, Mass.
MHi      Massachusetts Historical Society, Boston, Mass.
MWA      American Antiquarian Society, Worcester, Mass.
MeHi     Maine Historical Society, Portland, Me.
MiU-C    William L. Clements Library, University of Michigan, Ann Arbor, Mich.
N        New York State Library, Albany, N.Y.
NHi      New-York Historical Society, New York, N.Y.
NN       New York Public Library, New York, N.Y.
NhHi     New Hampshire Historical Society, Concord, N.H.
NjMoW    Morristown National Historical Park, Morristown, N.J.
NjP      Princeton University, Princeton, N.J.
OClWHi   Western Reserve Historical Society, Cleveland, Ohio
PHi      Historical Society of Pennsylvania, Philadelphia, Pa.
R-Ar     Rhode Island State Archives, Providence, R.I.
RHi      Rhode Island Historical Society, Providence, R.I.
RPB      Brown University Library, Providence, R.I.
RPJCB    John Carter Brown Library, Providence, R.I.

Repositories that have not been assigned a Library of Congress symbol are credited at the pertinent documents, as are individuals.

Those repositories that have supplied documents for later volumes are listed in acknowledgments above.

## SHORT TITLES FOR WORKS FREQUENTLY CITED

Adams, *Works*

Adams, John. *The Works of John Adams, Second President of the United States: With a Life of the Author.* Edited by Charles Francis Adams. 10 vols. Boston, 1850–56.

Alden, *Gage*

Alden, John Richard. *General Gage in America: Being Principally a History of His Role in the American Revolution.* Baton Rouge: Louisiana State University Press, 1948.

Alden, *Lee*

Alden, John Richard. *General Charles Lee: Traitor or Patriot?* Baton Rouge: Louisiana State University Press, 1951.

Allen, *Naval History*

Allen, Gardner W. *A Naval History of the American Revolution*. 2 vols. Boston and New York: Houghton Mifflin Co., 1913.

Amer. Antiq. Soc., *Proc.*

American Antiquarian Society, *Proceedings*, 1843–.

Arnold, *R.I.*

Arnold, Samuel Greene. *History of the State of Rhode Island and Providence Plantations*. 3rd ed. 2 vols. New York and London, 1878.

Bakeless, *Turncoats*

Bakeless, John. *Turncoats, Traitors, and Heroes*. Philadelphia and New York: J. B. Lippincott Co., 1959.

Bartlett, *Records*

Bartlett, John Russell, ed. *Records of the State of Rhode Island and Providence Plantations in New England*. 10 vols. Providence, 1856–65.

Baurmeister, *Revolution*

Baurmeister, Carl Leopold. *Revolution in America: Confidential Letters and Journals 1776–1784 of Adjutant General Major Baurmeister of the Hessian Forces*. Translated and edited by Bernhard A. Uhlendorf. New Brunswick, N.J.: Rutgers University Press, 1957.

Bell, *Morgan*

Bell, Whitfield J., Jr. *John Morgan: Continental Doctor*. Philadelphia: University of Pennsylvania Press, 1965.

Bezanson, *Prices*

Bezanson, Anne. *Prices and Inflation during the American Revolution: Philadelphia, 1770–1790*. Philadelphia: University of Pennsylvania Press, 1951.

Billias, *Glover*

Billias, George Athan. *General John Glover and His Marblehead Mariners*. New York: Henry Holt & Co., 1960.

Billias, *GW's Generals*

Billias, George Athan, ed. *George Washington's Generals*. New York: William Morrow & Co., 1964.

Boatner, *Encyc.*

Boatner, Mark Mayo, III. *Encyclopedia of the American Revolution*. New York: David McKay Co., 1966.

Bronson, *Brown Univ.*

Bronson, Walter C. *The History of Brown University, 1764–1914*. Providence, R.I.: Brown University, 1914.

Burnett, *Letters*

Burnett, Edmund C., ed. *Letters of Members of the Continental Congress*. 8 vols. Washington: Carnegie Institute of Washington, 1921–36.

Callahan, *Knox*

Callahan, North. *Henry Knox: General Washington's General*. South Brunswick, Me., and New York: A. S. Barnes & Co., 1958.

Clark, *GW's Navy*

Clark, William Bell. *George Washington's Navy: Being an Account of His Excellency's Fleet in New England Waters*. Baton Rouge: Louisiana State University Press, 1960.

Clark, *Naval Docs.*

Clark, William Bell, ed. *Naval Documents of the American Revolution*. Washington: United States Government Printing Office, 1964–. Vols. 1–5, 1964–70. Vol. 6 edited by William James Morgan.

Clarke, *Greenes*

Clarke, Louise Brownell. *The Greenes of Rhode Island, with Historical Records of English Ancestry, 1534–1902*. New York: Knickerbocker Press, 1903.

Commager and Morris, *Spirit of '76*

Commager, Henry Steele, and Morris, Richard B., eds. *The Spirit of 'Seventy-Six: The Story of the American Revolution as Told by Participants*. 2 vols. Indianapolis and New York: Bobbs-Merrill Co., 1958.

*DAB*

Johnson, Allen, and Malone, Dumas, eds. *Dictionary of American Biography*. 21 vols. New York: Charles Scribner's Sons, 1928–36. 3 supplements, 1944, 1958, and 1973.

*DAR Lineage*

*Lineage Book: National Society of the Daughters of the American Revolution, 1893–*.

Dickerson, *Navigation Acts* — Dickerson, Oliver M. *The Navigation Acts and the American Revolution*. Philadelphia: University of Pennsylvania Press, 1951.

Dupuy and Hammerman, *People* — Dupuy, Trevor N., and Hammerman, Gay M., eds. *People & Events of the American Revolution*. New York and London: R. R. Bowker Co., 1974; Dunn Loring, Va.: T. N. Dupuy Associates, 1974.

Field, *Long Island* — Field, Thomas W. *The Battle of Long Island (Long Island Historical Society Memoirs*, Vol. II). Brooklyn, 1869.

Field, *R.I.* — Field, Edward. *State of Rhode Island and Providence Plantations at the End of the Century: A History*. 3 vols. Boston and Syracuse: Mason Publishing Co., 1902.

Fitzpatrick, *GW* — Washington, George. *The Writings of George Washington, from the Original Manuscript Sources, 1745–1799*. Edited by John C. Fitzpatrick. 39 vols. Washington: United States Government Printing Office, 1931–44.

Fleming, *1776* — Fleming, Thomas. *1776: Year of Illusions*. New York: W. W. Norton & Co., 1975.

Force, *Archives* — Force, Peter, ed. *American Archives*. Fourth and Fifth Series. 6 vols. and 3 vols. Washington: 1837–53.

Fortescue, *British Army* — Fortescue, J. W. *A History of the British Army*. 2nd ed. 13 vols. London: Macmillan & Co., 1910–30.

Freeman, *GW* — Freeman, Douglas Southall. *George Washington*. 7 vols. The last volume by John C. Alexander and Mary W. Ashworth. New York: Charles Scribner's Sons, 1948–57.

French, *First Year* — French, Allen. *The First Year of the American Revolution*. Boston and New York: Houghton Mifflin Co., 1934.

Frothingham, *Boston*

Frothingham, Richard, Jr. *History of the Siege of Boston and of the Battles of Lexington, Concord, and Bunker Hill.* Boston, 1849.

Gordon, *History*

Gordon, William. *History of the Rise, Progress and Establishment of the Independence of the United States of America.* 4 vols. London, 1788.

Graydon, *Memoirs*

Graydon, Alexander. *Memoirs of His Own Time, with Reminiscences of the Men and Events of the Revolution.* Philadelphia, 1846.

Greene, *Greene*

Greene, George Washington. *The Life of Nathanael Greene, Major-General in the Army of the Revolution.* 3 vols. 1871. Reprint. Boston and New York: Houghton Mifflin Co., 1897–1900.

Gruber, *Howe Brothers*

Gruber, Ira D. *The Howe Brothers and the American Revolution.* New York: Atheneum, 1972.

Hall, "Ft. Lee"

Hall, Edward Hagaman. "Fort Lee, New Jersey." *Fourteenth Annual Report.* New York: American Scenic and Historical Society, 1909.

Hammond, *Sullivan*

Sullivan, John. *Letters and Papers of Major-General Sullivan, Continental Army.* Edited by Otis G. Hammond. 3 vols. Concord: New Hampshire Historical Society, 1930–39.

Hatch, *Administration*

Hatch, Louis Clinton. *Administration of the American Revolutionary Army.* New York, London, and Bombay: Longmans, Green & Co., 1904.

Hawke, *Rush*

Hawke, David F. *Benjamin Rush: Revolutionary Gadfly.* Indianapolis: Bobbs-Merrill Co., 1971.

Heath, *Memoirs*

Heath, William. *Heath's Memoirs of the American War.* Edited by Rufus Rockwell Wilson. New York: A. Wessels Co., 1904.

Hedges, *Browns*

Hedges, James B. *The Browns of Providence Plantations: Colonial Years*. Cambridge, Mass.: Harvard University Press, 1952.

Heitman, *Register*

Heitman, Francis B., comp. *Historical Register of Officers of the Continental Army during the War of the Revolution*. 1914. Reprint. With addenda by Robert H. Kelby. Baltimore: Genealogical Publishing Co., 1967.

Higginbotham, *War*

Higginbotham, Don. *The War of American Independence: Military Attitudes, Policies, and Practice, 1763–1789*. New York: The Macmillan Co., 1971.

Jensen, *English Docs.*

Jensen, Merrill, ed. *American Colonial Documents to 1776*. English Historical Documents, vol. 9. London: Eyre and Spottiswoode, 1955.

JCC

Ford, Worthington C., and others, eds. *Journals of the Continental Congress, 1774–1789*. 34 vols. Washington: Government Printing Office, 1904–37.

Johnson, *Greene*

Johnson, William. *Life and Correspondence of Nathanael Greene, Major General of the Armies of the United States*. 2 vols. Charleston, S.C., 1822.

Johnston, *Harlem*

Johnston, Henry P. *The Battle of Harlem Heights, September 16, 1776*. New York and London, 1897.

Johnston, *NY 1776*

Johnston, Henry P. *The Campaign of 1776 around New York and Brooklyn (Long Island Historical Society Memoirs*, Vol. III). Brooklyn, 1878.

Kemble *Journal*

Kemble, Stephen. "Journal." In *Kemble Papers*, New-York Historical Society *Collections*. 2 vols. New York, 1884.

*Kemble Papers*

Kemble, Stephen. "Order Books." In *Kemble Papers*, New-York Historical Society, *Collections*. 2 vols. New York, 1884.

Ketchum, *Winter Soldiers*

Ketchum, Richard M. *The Winter Soldiers*. Garden City, N.Y.: Doubleday & Co., 1973.

Knollenberg, *GW*

Knollenberg, Bernhard. *Washington and the Revolution: A Reappraisal*. New York: Macmillan Co., 1941.

Knollenberg, *Ward*

Knollenberg, Bernhard, ed. *Correspondence of Governor Samuel Ward, May 1775– March 1776*. And *Genealogy of the Ward Family*, compiled by Clifford P. Monahon. Providence: Rhode Island Historical Society, 1952.

Koke, "Hudson"

Koke, Richard J. "The Struggle for the Hudson: The British Naval Expedition under Captain Hyde Parker and Captain James Wallace, July 12–August 18, 1776." *New-York Historical Society Quarterly* 40 (1956): 115–75.

Kurtz & Hutson, *Essays*

Kurtz, Stephen G., and James H. Hutson, eds. *Essays on the American Revolution*. Chapel Hill: University of North Carolina Press, 1973.

*Lee Papers*

Lee, Charles. *The Lee Papers*. New-York Historical Society, *Collections*. 4 vols. York: 1872–75.

Leiby, *Hackensack*

Leiby, Adrian C. *The Revolutionary War in the Hackensack Valley: The Jersey Dutch and the Neutral Ground, 1775–1783*. New Brunswick, N.J.: Rutgers University Press, 1962.

Lovejoy, *R.I. Politics*

Lovejoy, David S. *Rhode Island Politics and the American Revolution, 1760–1776*. Providence, R.I.: Brown University Press, 1958.

Lundin, *Cockpit*

Lundin, Leonard. *Cockpit of the Revolution: The War for Independence in New Jersey*. 1941. Reprint. New York: Octagon Books, 1972.

MacKenzie, *Diary*

MacKenzie, Frederick. *The Diary of Frederick MacKenzie*. 2 vols. Cambridge, Mass.: Harvard University Press, 1930.

Mackesy, *War*

Mackesy, Piers. *The War for America, 1775–1783*. Cambridge, Mass.: Harvard University Press, 1964.

Martyn, *Ward*

Martyn, Charles. *The Life of Artemas Ward: The First Commander-in-Chief of the American Revolution*. New York: Artemas Ward, 1921.

Mathews, *Americanisms*

Mathews, Mitford M., ed. *A Dictionary of Americanisms on Historical Principles*. 2 vols. Chicago: University of Chicago Press, 1951.

MHS, *Coll.*

Massachusetts Historical Society, *Collections*.

MHS, *Proc.*

Massachusetts Historical Society, *Proceedings*.

Monahon, Clifford P. See Knollenberg, *Ward*.

Morgan, *Vindication*

Morgan, John. *A Vindication of His Public Character in the Station of Director-General*. Boston, 1777.

Morgan, *Captains*

Morgan, William James. *Captains to the Northward: The New England Captains in the Continental Navy*. Barre, Mass.: Barre Gazette, 1959.

Morgan, William James. See Clark, *Naval Docs.*

Murray, *Life*

Murray, John. *The Life of the Rev. John Murray*. 7th edition, with notes by L. S. Everett. Utica, N.Y., 1840.

N-YHS, *Coll.*

New-York Historical Society, *Collections*.

NY MSS

*Calendar of Historical Manuscripts Relating to the War of the Revolution in the Office of the Secretary of State, Albany, N.Y.* Albany, 1868.

Onderdonk, *Queens County* — Onderdonk, Henry, Jr. *Documents and Letters Intended to Illustrate the Revolutionary Incidents of Queens County.* New York, 1846.

Onderdonk, *Suffolk and Kings* — Onderdonk, Henry, Jr. *Revolutionary Incidents of Suffolk and Kings Counties.* New York, 1849.

PCC — Papers of the Continental Congress.

Peckham, *Toll* — Peckham, Howard H. *The Toll of Independence: Engagements & Battle Casualties of the American Revolution.* Chicago and London: University of Chicago Press, 1974.

*PMHB* — *Pennsylvania Magazine of History and Biography.*

*R.I. Biog. Cycl.* — *Biographical Cyclopedia of Representative Men of Rhode Island.* Providence, 1881.

*R.I. Hist.* — *Rhode Island History.*

RIHS, *Coll.* — *Collections* of the Rhode Island Historical Society (1827–1902). Rhode Island Historical Society, *Collections* (quarterly 1918–41).

RIHS, *Proc.* — Rhode Island Historical Society, *Proceedings.*

Roelker, *Franklin-Greene* — Roelker, William Greene, ed. *Benjamin Franklin and Catharine Ray Greene: Their Correspondence, 1755–1790.* Philadelphia: American Philosophical Society, 1949.

Rossman, *Mifflin* — Rossman, Kenneth K. *Thomas Mifflin and the Politics of the American Revolution.* Chapel Hill: University of North Carolina Press, 1952.

Sabine, *Loyalists* — Sabine, Lorenzo. *The American Loyalists, or Biographical Sketches of Adherents to the British Crown in the War of the Revolution.* Boston, 1847.

Serle, *Journal*

Serle, Ambrose. *The American Journal of Ambrose Serle, Secretary to Lord Howe, 1776–1778*. Edited by Edward H. Tatum, Jr. San Marino, Calif.: The Huntington Library, 1940.

Shipton, Clifford K. See Sibley, *Harvard Grads*.

Sibley, *Harvard Grads*.

Sibley, John L. *Biographical Sketches of Those Who Attended Harvard College*. Vols. 1–3, 1873–85. Vols. 4–17 by Clifford K. Shipton. Cambridge and Boston: Harvard University Press and Massachusetts Historical Society, 1933–75.

Smith, *Loyalists*

Smith, Paul H. *Loyalists and Redcoats*. Chapel Hill: University of North Carolina Press, 1964.

Staples, *R.I.*

Staples, William R. *Rhode Island in the Continental Congress, with the Journal of the Convention that Adopted the Constitution, 1765–1790*. Edited by Reuben A. Guild. Providence, 1870.

Stiles, *Diary*

Stiles, Ezra. *The Literary Diary of Ezra Stiles*. Edited by Franklin Bowditch Dexter. 3 vols. New York: Charles Scribner's Sons, 1901.

Syrette, *Hamilton*

Hamilton, Alexander. *The Papers of Alexander Hamilton*. Edited by Harold C. Syrette. New York: Columbia University Press, 1961–.

Thayer, *Greene*

Thayer, Theodore. *Nathanael Greene: Strategist of the American Revolution*. New York: Twayne Publishers, 1960.

Tilghman, *Memoir*

Tilghman, Tench. *Memoir of Lieut. Col. Tench Tilghman, Secretary and Aid to Washington*. 1876. Reprint. New York: Arno Press, 1971.

Valentine, *Lord Stirling*

Valentine, Alan. *Lord Stirling*. New York: Oxford University Press, 1969.

Van Doren, *Secret*

Van Doren, Carl. *Secret History of the American Revolution*. Garden City, N.Y.: Garden City Publishing Co., 1941.

Wade and Lively, *Glorious Cause*

Wade, Herbert T., and Lively, Robert T. *This Glorious Cause*. Princeton: Princeton University Press, 1958.

Ward, *Delaware*

Ward, Christopher L. *The Delaware Continentals, 1776–1783*. Wilmington: Historical Society of Delaware, 1941.

Ward, *War*

Ward, Christopher L. *The War of the Revolution*. 2 vols. Edited by John Richard Alden. New York: Macmillan Co., 1952.

Whittemore, *Sullivan*

Whittemore, Charles P. *A General of the Revolution: John Sullivan of New Hampshire*. New York and London: Columbia University Press, 1961.

Willcox, *Clinton*

Willcox, William B. *Portrait of a General: Sir Henry Clinton in the War of Independence*. New York: Alfred A. Knopf, 1964.

# A GLOSSARY OF MILITARY TERMS

ABATIS
: A barrier of felled trees, with limbs pointing toward the enemy; usually temporary.

ARTILLERY PARK
: An encampment for artillery.

ARTILLERY TRAIN
: An army's collection of cannon and the materiel for firing them.

BARBETTE
: A platform or mound of earth for artillery, usually separated from a main fortification.

BASTION
: An outward projection of a fort enabling gunners to fire along the wall of the fort at an enemy.

BATTALION
: See Regiment.

BOMB, BOOMBE
: A powder-filled iron sphere that is fired from a mortar and fused to explode after falling.

BREASTWORK
: An improvised fortification, usually consisting of a trench and earthen barrier.

BRIGADE
: A formation of two or more regiments.

BROADSIDE
: The firing of all artillery on one side of a warship.

CANISTER
: A tin cylinder containing metal balls that scattered when fired from a cannon.

CARCASS
: An incendiary device fired from a cannon at wooden structures or ships.

CARTOUCHE
: Cartridge made of a paper cylinder, containing powder and lead ball.

CHANDELIER
: Wooden frame filled with fascines, for protection where earth could not be dug.

CHEVAL-DE-FRISE
: Used usually in the plural; a portable defense barrier bristling with long, iron-tipped wooden spikes. An underwater version consisted of a rock-filled wooden frame, on which sharpened timbers were set at an angle to rip the hull of a vessel.

COULOURMAN
: Soldier responsible for the more disagreeable cleaning and sanitation tasks.

DIVISION
: A unit of two or more brigades.

DRAGOON
: Once a mounted infantryman, by 1775 term was used interchangeably with cavalryman.

DURHAM BOAT
: A shallow-drafted boat developed to transport iron ore. Varying in length from forty to sixty feet

and around eight feet in width, it could carry a company of troops and was usually poled.

EMBRASURE An opening through which cannon were fired.

ENFILADE To sweep with gunfire along a line of works or troops from end to end.

FASCINE A firmly tied bundle of wooden sticks or small limbs.

FATIGUE Manual and menial duty performed by troops.

FIREBOAT A vessel filled with a variety of combustibles for burning enemy vessels.

FLECHE An outwork of a fort, shaped like an arrow, the point toward the enemy.

FRIGATE A two-decked warship built for swift sailing, mounting twenty to thirty-eight guns on the upper deck.

GLACIS A bank sloping away from a fortification.

GRENADE A hand-thrown metal device that exploded when the lighted fuse reached the powder inside.

GRENADIERS Once hurlers of grenades, by 1775 an elite corps.

GUN Although technically used to describe a cannon, the term was also regularly used in the colonies for a musket or rifle.

INVALIDS Disabled soldiers who were assigned to limited duties.

JÄGER German light infantry chosen for their marksmanship with the German rifle (not the German-American long-barreled rifle).

LIGHT INFANTRY Lightly equipped, highly mobile troops.

MARQUEE A canvas tent designed especially for officers; also, a cover for another tent.

MATROSS Assistant to an artillery gunner.

MORTAR A short-barreled cannon used for lobbing shells, bombs, etc., over an obstacle.

MUSQUETEER Soldier armed with a musket.

ORDNANCE Military equipment and supplies.

OUTWORK A defensive work outside a fort.

PALISADE Timbers set in the ground, close together and sharpened at the top.

PAROLE A prisoner's oath on being freed that he will not bear arms until exchanged.

PETTY AUGER An open, flat-bottomed boat, generally two-masted, carrying some thirty tons.

PICKET, PICQUET An outguard to warn of an enemy approach.

PIKE   Wooden spear of varying length, with a steel point.

PIONEERS   Men responsible for digging trenches, repairing roads, preparing fortifications, etc.

PLATFORM   A wooden bed upon which a cannon was placed.

PRIVATEER   A privately owned armed vessel commissioned to take enemy merchantmen as prizes.

REGIMENT   During this period, regiment and battalion were used interchangeably. Usually composed of eight companies and at full strength numbering from 520 to 780.

REVETMENT   A wall to retain an earthen rampart or side of a ditch.

ROW GALLEY   A low, flat vessel with one deck, varying in length up to 130 feet; manned by oarsmen and carrying several small cannon.

SCHOONER   A small fore-and-aft-rigged vessel with two masts.

SHIP   A large vessel with three masts, each composed of a lower mast, top mast, and top gallant mast.

SLOOP   Small, one-masted vessel.

SUBALTERN   Commissioned officer below the rank of lieutenant.

SUTLER   A provisioner for an army camp who operates for profit.

TRANSPORT   A vessel for carrying troops.

| 1742 | 27 July (OS) | Born at Potowomut in Warwick, R.I. |
| 1753 | 7 Mar. | Death of his mother, Mary Motte Greene. |
| 1754 | Nov. | His father remarries. |
| 1765 | 14 Apr. | Admitted as freeman in Warwick. |
| 1768 | | Takes over management of family's interest in Coventry forge. |
| 1770 | Summer | Moves to house in Coventry near forge and mills. |
| 1770 | 16 Nov. | Death of his father. |
| 1772 | 17 Feb. | HMS *Gaspee* captures the Greenes' sloop *Fortune*. |
| 1772 | 22 July | Greenes bring suit against Lieut. Dudingston of *Gaspee*. |
| 1774 | 20 July | Marries Catharine Littlefield of Block Island. |
| 1774 | Aug. | Formation of Military Independent Company at East Greenwich. |
| 1774 | 25 Oct. | Formation of Kentish Guards. |
| 1775 | 8 May | Commissioned brigadier general of R.I. Army of Observation. |
| 1775 | Late May | Arrives in Roxbury (outside Boston) with first R.I. troops. |
| 1775 | 22 June | Commissioned brigadier general in Continental army. |
| 1775 | 22 July | Takes command of Prospect Hill in siege of Boston. |
| 1776 | Feb. | Birth of his first child, George Washington Greene. |
| 1776 | 20 Mar. | Takes command in city of Boston after British evacuation. |
| 1776 | 1–17 Apr. | His brigade en route from Boston to New York. |
| 1776 | 29 Apr. | Takes command on Long Island. |
| 1776 | 9 Aug. | Commissioned major general in Continental army. |
| 1776 | 15 Aug.–5 Sept. | Seriously ill; does not participate in battle of Long Island. |

| | | |
|---|---|---|
| 1776 | 16 Sept. | Sees his first battle action at Harlem Heights. |
| 1776 | 19 Sept. | To Ft. Constitution (Ft. Lee) to take command of forces in New Jersey. |
| 1776 | 16 Nov. | Fall of Ft. Washington. |
| 1776 | 20 Nov. | Evacuation of Ft. Lee. |
| 1776 | 26 Dec. | Battle of Trenton. |
| 1777 | 2–3 Jan. | Battle of Princeton. |

# THE PAPERS OF
# General Nathanael Greene

# Nathanael Greene, Jacob Greene, Nathanael Greene, Jr., and Eber Sweet *v*. Jonathan Slocum[1]

Kent, ss [East Greenwich, R.I., 23 Dec. 1766]

To the Honbl Inferior Court of Comon Pleas to be held at East Greenwich in and for the County of Kent on the third Monday of January AD 1767.

Nathaniel Greene, Jacob Greene, Nathaniel Greene, Jur and Eber Sweet all of Warwick in the County of Kent, Forge masters in company,[2] complain of Jonathan Slocum of Warwick in the County of Kent, yeoman alias Blacksmith, in the Custody of the Sheriff in an action of the Case that he the deft [defendant] Render and Pay to the Plts [plaintiffs] the Sum of Four Pounds Eight Shillings and three Pence one Farthing lawfull money.[3] Which to them he oweth and unjustly Detaineth, for that at the Times and for the Causes Set forth in the annexed accompt the Deft Became Justly indebted to the Plts in the aforsd [aforesaid] Sum on Book accompt and Being So indebted Promised and upon himself assumed to Pay said sum to the Plts when he should be afterwards thereunto Requested, yet the Deft altho often Requested said Sum to the Plts is Still unpaid and the Same to them to Pay the Deft hath at Times Refused and Still Denyeth which is to the Damage of the Plts Nine Pounds lawfull money as by Writ Dated the Twenty third Day of December in the Seventh year of his Present Majesties Reign AD 1766 and thereon they [Swear?] by

A. CAMPBELL their atto [attorney]

## Statement

Dr [debtor] Jonathan Slokum to Nath'el Greene & Comp

1764

| | | | | | | | |
|---|---|---|---|---|---|---|---|
| 6 mo 27 | To/ 2 hundred of Nail rods | £ 26 | 0 | 0 | Lawfull £1 | 2s | 3/4d |
| 1765 | | | | | | | |
| 5 mo 24 | To 1 hundred of Nail Rods | 56 | – | – | – 2 | 8s | 0 |
| | To 42 lb. of Nail Rods | 21 | – | – | – 18s | 0 | |

| | £103 | 4 | 8s | 3/4d |
|---|---|---|---|---|

Supra

By 3 loads of Charcoal Quantity 264 Bushels

Measured at our Works at 6s per Bushel £79 4s 0 £3 7s 8 3/4d

Errors Excepted per Nathanael Greene & Comp.

D (Kent County Court Records, Rhode Island State Records Center).

1. Of many similar documents bearing the name of Nathanael Greene (often misspelled), this is the first in which the name of NG, Jr., appears, and the accompanying bill is the earliest known document in his hand. It was written when he was twenty-three years old, in the legible but unnatural style of a scribe or clerk. He had practiced his penmanship, which resulted later in a natural, free-flowing style that makes his wartime letters easy to read. (See illustration, p. 223.)

2. From their Quaker father Jabez (1673–1741), Nathanael Greene, Sr., (1707–70) and his brothers had inherited extensive property on both sides of Hunts River in the towns of Warwick and North Kingstown (see map, p. 5). Included were dwellings, barns, wharf, warehouse, store, dam, sluiceways, forge, anchorworks, and sawmill. NG, Sr., enlarged his inheritance by buying his brothers' share of the Potowomut forge and mills. Except for his Quaker preaching, he devoted his time to his business and his extensive property. In 1763 he was the second highest taxpayer in Warwick (Tax Records of Warwick, R-Ar). In 1741 he and two brothers started a new complex of forge, anchorworks, and mills on the Pawtuxet River in Coventry, of which Nathanael Greene and Co. now owned one-fourth. NG, Jr., had just joined his older brother Jacob as a member of the company; later his younger brothers also became partners (for their identification see note, bond, 27 Aug. 1772, below). Although NG, Jr., and Jacob had been anchorsmiths, this was one of the few documents to designate them either as forgemasters or anchorsmiths. In some fifty surviving legal documents, they and their brothers are usually listed as "merchants in company." In the late 1760s the company engaged in coastwise trade in a small vessel. By Newport standards they were small merchants, concentrating on the sale of anchors that they made but also handling a variety of products not of their own manufacture. When NG became quartermaster general of the Continental army, his experience as a merchant served him well.

3. Most transactions were in terms of English coins, although the Spanish-milled dollar was used when available. "Lawful money," redeemable in specie, was worth approximately six shillings to an ounce of silver or to a Spanish dollar. Thus, the pound of twenty shillings was worth about $3.30. Old tenor currency, which was still circulating, had depreciated to 1/25th of its value; or $1.00 in old tenor was worth four cents. Its circulation was stopped by law in 1771. (Field, *R.I.*, 3:200, 218–19) The farthing was worth 1/4 of a pence.

## Nathanael Greene et al. to Stephen Hopkins & Co.[1]

Gentleman                    Warwick [R.I.] October 10th, 1768

Pursuant to our appointment We have met and after deliberately considering the delivering up our Lease agreeable to your Request we find no disposition to do it. If you have any farther propositions that might compromise this matter Whereby you would be Willing to purchase the premises and We hold our lease as Something of that Tennor Was mention'd by the late Govenor Hopkins We on consideration of them Will give you an answer.[2]

NATHANAEL GREENE JUN
STEPHEN POTTER[3]
THOS POTTER
RICHARD SARLE, JUN
CHARLES HOLDEN JUN
CALEB POTTER

STEPH. HOPKINS ESQ. & CO.

ADS (RPJCB).

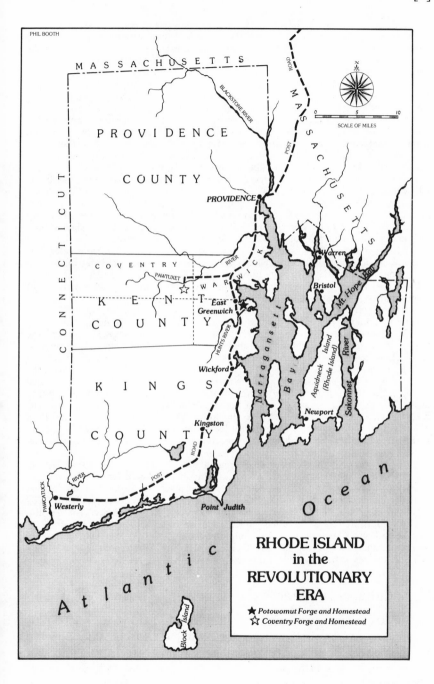

PHIL BOOTH

MASSACHUSETTS

PROVIDENCE

COUNTY

CONNECTICUT

BLACKSTONE RIVER

POST ROAD

MASSACHUSETTS

PROVIDENCE

COVENTRY

PAWTUXET

RIVER

WARWICK

Warren

Bristol

Mt. Hope Bay

KENT

COUNTY

East
Greenwich

HUNTS RIVER

Narragansett Bay

Aquidneck
Island
(Rhode Island)

Sakonnet River

Wickford

KINGS

Newport

Kingston

COUNTY

POST ROAD

PAWCATUCK

RIVER

Westerly

Point Judith

Atlantic Ocean

Block Island

N

SCALE OF MILES
0   5   10

**RHODE ISLAND
in the
REVOLUTIONARY
ERA**

★ *Potowomut Forge and Homestead*
☆ *Coventry Forge and Homestead*

1. Stephen Hopkins (1707–85), who gave his name to the firm, was Rhode Island's most prominent leader from 1750 to 1778. He served several terms as governor and chief justice, was a delegate to both Continental Congresses, and was a signer of the Declaration of Independence. With politics as his main interest, he "dabbled in commerce," David S. Lovejoy has written, "built, owned, and fitted out vessels for trading, and joined the Brown brothers in smelting iron at Hope Furnace." (Lovejoy, *R.I. Politics*, p. 10) He was also interested in science and was a trustee and chancellor of Rhode Island College (later Brown University) for many years. His forte, however, was politics. He headed a faction centering in Providence that was bitterly opposed by Samuel Ward and his supporters, who found their main strength in Newport and Kings County. NG's family favored the Ward faction, partly because of their close relation to Samuel Ward's family. (See note 1, NG to Samuel Ward, Jr., 24 Sept. 1770, below, on the Wards.) But NG undoubtedly maintained friendly relations with Hopkins, since a word from Hopkins would have blocked his appointment as head of the Rhode Island Army of Observation in 1775. See note, NG's commission, 8 May 1775, below.

2. A notation on the back reads: "Letter from the Potters to the Furnace Owners about their Silver lease of Jer. Burlinggames land." It is not recorded whether the group made a deal with Hopkins or found any silver on their leasehold. A few days earlier, NG had joined with his cousin Griffin Greene and John Pettingal [Pettingell] to purchase seven acres of land in the adjoining township of Cranston from Peter Burlingame, Jr., at the unheard price of 1,000 Spanish-milled dollars. The land was near an iron mine, but they may also have hoped to find silver. The deed specified (as deeds seldom did) that they were to have "all the ores Clay Mineral appurtenances and Commodities." (Cranston R.I. Records of Deeds, vol. D-2, p. 65) The purchase did not assure their fortunes, for one year later Burlingame was suing NG for £309 (Writ of Execution to Sheriff of Kent County, Rhode Island State Records Center).

3. Whether the group had other mutual interests is not known. NG was the youngest and the least prominent. Stephen, Thomas, and Caleb Potter were brothers, all of whom had served in the Assembly, Stephen representing Coventry, Thomas and Caleb, the town of Cranston. (See numerous index references in Bartlett, *Records*, vols. 6–9; Jeremiah Potter, *A Genealogy of the Potter Family* [Phenix, R.I., 1881.]) Richard Sarle, Jr., (often printed as Searle) represented Cranston in the Assembly many times after 1761; in 1785 he was elected to the upper house (index references, Bartlett, *Records*, vols. 6 and 7). Charles Holden, Jr., from Warwick, was five years older than NG and later represented that town with NG's brother in the Assembly. During the latter part of the revolutionary war, he was commissary general of purchases for the state of Rhode Island (ibid.).

The most influential member was Stephen Potter. Fifteen years older than NG, he had been a lieutenant colonel in the French and Indian War, had then served numerous terms in the Assembly, and was elected associate justice of Rhode Island's highest court ten times between 1764 and 1790. He seems to have been associated with NG's familiy in business. Judge Potter was a noted critic of formal religion. He told the Rev. John Murray, the Universalist minister who spent an evening with him in 1773, that he had never been pleased with pulpit exhibitions because they were so replete with contradictions (Murray, *Life* [1827 ed.], p. 242). In his numerous contacts with NG over the years, he may have influenced the young man's religious views.

# Nathanael Greene & Co. to Nicholas Brown & Co.

Respected Friends                    Warwick [R.I.] 11 mo [Nov.] 26th 1768

We received your favour yesterday dated October 20th. Observe the contents. The propositions made are no ways satisfactory. We have thought proper to make some further proposals Which if agreeable we will Make some further Tryal for we have already Tryed some of your Mettle and find it Works very slow and What is Still more discourageing is it dont make Warrantable Iron. The proposals we have to offer are for you to Let us have pig Iron at Twenty five dollars per tun delivered at our Forge in Coventry, and take for pay anchors at 6d Lawful money per pound and bar Iron at Eighty dollars per Tun and take an Equal Quantity of Tuns of Each, you to Receive your Iron at the Forge and the anchors at Newport both the Iron and anchors to be made of your Mettle. If these terms Suits let us know as soon as possible. We are your friends[1]

NATHANAEL GREENE & COMY

ALS (RPJCB).
1. The Greenes purchased pig iron from Hope Furnace, which the Brown brothers had built during 1765–66 up the Pawtuxet River from the Coventry forge. They sometimes paid the Browns with finished anchors, which the Browns, in their role as merchants, then sold. On the Browns' extensive iron business see Hedges, *Browns*, pp. 123–54.

## To the Rhode Island General Assembly

[Coventry, R.I., before 27 October 1769]
To the Honourable the General assembly To be Holdon at Little Rest in the County of Kings County and Colony of Rhode Island.

Your petitioners humbly Shue that Whereas Nathanael Greene & Company John Greene & Company Griffin Greene and Christopher Greene, Have been at a very great Expence in Erecting and building Dams Forges anchor Works and Saw Mills upon the South branch of Patuxet River,[1] Further more in prepareing Suitable Stock and providing a proper Number of Hands to procecute the business in all its branches And as the Emolument ariseing from those works are the principle Sources of Support for them and their dependants Who are upwards of one Hundred in Number, But as the act of Goverment now Stands relative to dams a Cross Patuxet River[2] they are Lyable to be Wholely obstructed in their business from the twenty first day of April untill the first day of June if any Evil disposed Freeholder sees cause to Enter Complaint against their dams, that they are not Fishways made proper and Convenient for the fish to pass repass agreeable to the Law made and provided in that Case, Which embarrassment should it Take place it would render it almost impossible for them to pursue their business for the following reasons which would be a publick loss as Well as private injury and first, The season of the year the Law requires the dams to be open is the best part of the year to procecute the business to the most advantage, for its free from almost Every obstruction and Hindrance That the other parts of the year are Subject too, for in the Winter the frost greatly distresses the business and in the Summer its Commonly too Hot for the Constitution of the Workmen to Endure it and in the Fall theres often a Want of water; Secondly the people who are of that occupation are Wholely ignorant of Every means to get a Support but by their Trade Therefore when the Works were Stopt they would be reduceed to the Necessity of Looking Employ else where and When they Had got disperseed it Would be attended with much difficulty and Expence to get them together again; Thirdly Your petitioners are fully Sensible that all such Kind of Works go to decay nearly as fast when out of use as when at Work, Which would be a great burden for to Have such Costly Works stopt considering the first Expence of Erection and then their Continual decay; Fourthly the Nature of Such business requires a very Costly Stock to be prepar'd and Kept up Continually for the advantage of the business Which Stock will be altogether useless as Long as the works are Stopt, and Consequently the interest of the money Lost; Fifthly and Lastly opening Such Large holes in the dams as the Stream is Exceeding rapid will naturally carry of[f] Large Quantities of Gravil the repairs of Which will be very difficult and Expensive.

Therefore as there is not nor has not for many years been but a very Small and Contemptible number of Fish come up to the foot of those dams and those works being of great Utillity to the publick much more so than the fish can possibly be, Your petitioners humbly prayeth that those dams afore Enumerated Standing on the South branch of Patuxet River may be Establish'd by act of Goverment and Totally Exemted from preparing and providing fishways as the North branch of the same river is now Establish'd for the relief of Works under much the Same Circumstances, Which will be a confirmation of a benefit once Granted them, and your petitioners as in duty bound will Ever pray &so[3]

| STEPHEN POTTER[4] | FRANCIS BRAYTON |
| JOHN GREENE | FRANCIS BRAYTON JUNIOR |
| BENJA GREENE | DANIEL BRAYTON |
| ABRAHAM CHACE | BENJAMIN BRAYTON |
| NATHANAEL GREENE, JUN | THOMAS BRAYTON |
| JOHN PETTINGELL | GIDEON BRAYTON |
| DANIEL GARDNER | JONATHAN BRAYTON |
| THOMAS KNOX | JONATHAN ROBERTS |
| GRIFFIN GREENE | STEPH ARNOLD |

ADS (R-Ar). The petition is unmistakably in NG's hand; the style strongly suggests that he was also the author. He was a natural choice, being older than his cousins Griffin and Benjamin (signers) and more literate than his uncle John Greene, the elder partner of the Coventry works.

1. The Coventry forge and mills were six miles inland (as the crow flies) from their old mills on Hunts River. (See above, note 2, *Greene* v. *Slocum*, 23 Dec. 1766.) In 1768 it

was decided that NG, Jr., should represent the family's interest in the Pawtuxet mills, while his father and brothers would manage those at Potowomut. NG rode horseback daily between the two until he moved into a new house near the Coventry mills in the summer of 1770. See Clarke, *Greenes*, pp. 87–88, 125–29, and Greene, *Greene*, 1: 37–38.

2. An act of Feb. 1767 made illegal any obstructions in the Pawtuxet and Pawcatuck rivers which prevented the passage of fish in the spring (*Acts and Resolves*, 1765–69, pp. 72–73), but it had not been previously enforced.

3. The petition was persuasive. In Feb. 1770 the Assembly granted the "prayer of the petitioners" (Bartlett, *Records*, 7: 7–8).

4. Stephen Potter may have signed only because he represented Coventry in the Assembly, but all the rest of the signers were employed at the forge.

# A Memorial to the Corporation of Rhode Island College[1]

[Before 16 Nov. 1769]

To the Honorable members of the Corporation of the College convened at Newport the 16 day of Novemb 1769. Your memorialist[s] beg Leave to represent that they concieve That the County of Kent is the most proper place for Erecting said College Edifice for the following reasons.

First. It is situated nearly in the Centre of the Colony Which will more effectually accomodate each respective County than any other place that can be fixt upon. Therefore if the Corporation should ever Petition for the aid and assistance of Goverment its more probable they will unite in forwarding and promoteing Such grants.

Secondly. The local subscriptions of Kent uniteed with the several General subscriptions are sufficient to build and Compleat said College and those temporary subscriptions will be found altogether insufficient for Keeping up and perpetuateing the Institutional Expences. It is therefore necessary to place it where the Goverment will be most likely to take it under their consideration and immediate protection that being as we think very Justly urgeed by certain Gentlemen before the General assembly to be the most probable means of Enlargeing the donations from abroad. Which advantagies considered together that will result to the institution by its being Fixt at Kent We trust will be thought by the corporation a matter of more Consequence than large sums raised by Local subscriptions.

Thirdly. As Institutions of this kind have been found by Experience not to prosper in popular Towns, We think the Town of Providence too large now in its present condition and as its a place well Calculated for trade its altogether reasonable from Thence to Conclude that the growth and Enlargement of it in a very few years will render it Quite unsuitable for Seminaries of Learning to be placed in.[2] Therefore as the Town of East Greenwich is Well situated as to pleasantness Surrounded with a Large Country abounding with Every necessary supply to render the Scholars Comfortable, the town being Large enough to accomodate the Students effectually and Situated upon the post road so that an easy Correspondence might be [had?] with any part of the Continent, There being likewise a post office in the Town and Every other advantage as to Communication With other Goverments that Providence can urge.

Furthermore as it Hath been Strongly argued this Institution is founded upon the most Catholick plan therefore they[3] say they have singular advantagies over Kent as to the accomodation of the different Religious denominations. In Answer to that We can say in behalf of Kent We have a Freinds and Baptists meeting Houses nearly Situated to the place where the College is proposed to be set, also a meeting House of the Seperates within three Miles of East Greenwich upon a Good road free from ferries and its Highly probable if the College is fixt at Kent there will be a Church and Prysbyterian meeting House built soon.[4]

WM GREENE[5]
NATH[ANA]EL GREENE JUN
PRESERVED PEARCE
CHARLES HOLDEN JUN
} Committee

ADS (Brown University Archives: RPB).

1. Rhode Island College (later Brown University) had been located in the town of Warren since its incorporation by the Baptists in 1764. The need for funds had induced the trustees to relocate it in the community that offered the most money (Bronson, *Brown University*, pp. 43–45).

2. The population of Providence was probably under 4,000. In the census of 1774, it was 4,321, compared with 1,663 for East Greenwich and 979 for Warren. Newport was the easy winner with over 9,000. (Bartlett, *Records*, 7: 299)

3. "They" refers to the Providence promoters.

4. The East Greenwich memorialists did not know that, by the time their memorial was received, the trustees had already voted to move the school to Providence on the promise of $9,000 from a group of its citizens, unless Newport topped the offer by 1 Jan. This Newport did (see below, petition of 7 Feb. 1770).

5. William Greene (1731–1809), a distant kinsman of NG, was the son of an earlier governor of the same name. He lived near the "compact part of East Greenwich," just across the line in Warwick, which he represented in the General Assembly. He was later chief justice and served as governor from 1778 to 1786. (*DAB*) His wife was Catharine Ray, the sister of Samuel Ward's wife and a friend of Benjamin Franklin. Her niece, Catharine Littlefield, who married NG in 1774, lived with her from the age of ten.

Preserved Pearce, a friend of NG, was a tavern keeper in East Greenwich and was currently sitting in the Assembly, a post to which he was reelected many times. He later served as justice in the Court of Common Pleas of Kent County. (See index references in Bartlett, *Records*, vols. 7 and 8; see also his MS account books, RHi.)

*Nathanael Greene birthplace at Potowomut in Warwick, Rhode Island, built in 1684 by his great-grandfather. Oil painting after a mid-nineteenth-century photograph, taken before change was made in the facade. House now owned by collateral descendants.*

## A Memorial to the Trustees and Fellows of Rhode Island College

[Before Feb. 7, 1770]

To the Honble, the Board of Trustees and Fellows of Rhode Island College, Present at Warren, this Seventh Day of February A.D. 1770.[1]

We the Subscribers, being appointed a Committee, by a Large Number of the Inhabitants of the County of Kent, who were lately concerned in a Local Subscription, relative to Erecting the College Edifice, to wait upon this Honble Board and make Such Representations as comport with the real Sentiments of our said Constituents, Do beg Liberty humbly to Revive our Claim to the College by Continueing Said Subscription. For that whereas it Yet Remaineth a matter of uncertainty in what County the College Edifice will be erected, and as the Present Contest Subsisteth between the Respectable Counties of Newport and Providence and each of those Counties by a laudable Design of Promoting the future Interest and Prosperity of the Institution, we humbly conceive they will both, upon Mature Deliberation, Resign their Claims and concede that it shall be Placed in Some other Part of the Colony.[2] The Reasons which induced us to form this Conclusion are many, Some of which, with the greatest Defference, we shall take the Freedom to offer. We are fully convinced that no Seat of Literature in America has ever arrived to any considerable Degree of Eminence and Utility but what hath recieved large Donations from Great Britain. That Institution of Science therefore, which fails of that Source must remain in Infancy and obscurity. But, if the very Creators of such an Institution cease to Patronise and protect it, Surely Strangers will have no Powerfull Motive left to encourage or assist it; Consequently, it must be placed in Such a Part of that Colony which gave it Being, as best to Commode the whole. Otherwise, the greater Part being dissapointed, will abandon it to its own Impotence. But were a College to be erected in Newport or Providence, it must fail of Countenance from the Colony, both being Scituated so far from its Center.

It is likewise well known that Newport and Providence have ever been the Capital Sources of Party in this Colony, And Consequently the Institution must Annually be Subject to the Attacks of one party or the other if Placed in either, and So liable to Continual Vicisitude, if not Demolition it Self; To avoid which the Wisdom and Prudence of Newport and Providence will both be exerted. Should these contending Parties mutually Resign it to another Place, it will be Sufficiently removed from any domestic Obstructions of this Sort And both being Sincere Friends to the Institution, they have it in their Power, as both would be happily agreed in the Same thing by their concurrent Influence to Cause it to enjoy the favorable Smiles of this Colony, and therefore of Great Britain, If by any Means Great Britain could be excited to Shelter and defend it. By this Method it will Undoubtedly arrive to Such a Degree of Superior Grandeur as to Command Veneration and esteem from all its Neighours, A Consideration of the Last Importence! It is also a general Maxim (and a very true one) that Such is the fluctuating Disposition of Youth, that a Considerable Degree of Retirement is very Requisite in Order to acquire any Great Proficiency in literary Pursuits. The Subjects of Science are so numerous, the Prospects so Extensive and the Researches so deep, that a Young Mind, entangled by the more captivating Allurements of Life will never Soar to those Sublime Heights as to answer the noble Ends of a College Education. But is there

Sufficient Retirement in Newport or Providence? With the Greatest Modesty, it may be Asserted that every Populous Town affords all those Opportunities for Avocation and Amusement that a luxuriant Imagination can aspire after. Moreover, as the Enlargement of usefull Knowledge and Promotion of Religion are the Principal Ends for which all Seats of Learning ought to be established, So that Place in a Colony, which is best Scituated for these Purposes, is most eligible to be fixed upon. But that Convenient Place which is nearest the Center of the Colony is best adapted herefor; from whence its Salutary Influences may equally be extended to every Part.

Money after all must be had, and we doubt not (Should we be Indulged with an Opportunity of dispersing our Subscriptions through the whole Colony) but we Could procure a Sum almost equal (if not Superior) to any that has been already Presented, For the Encouragements we have Received from every County in this Colony (Bristol only excepted) are very promising. Our own Subscribers are reanimated with a desire to Promote the Good of the Institution, even to such a Degree that many of them would largely add to their Subscriptions. Many there are likewise in the Same County that have not yet Subscribed who express their Warmest Desires to become Subscribers Should Kent ever have another opportunity to Exert its Generocity.

Upon the whole, Srs, The Encouragement and Assurance we had Afforded us by Some of the Principal Gentlemen in Providence, joined by many in Newport, were originally the moveing Cause that excited us to propagate a Local Subscription. Had we been in the least apprised that either Newport or Providence would ever lay a Claim we Should have emediately desisted from such an undertaking And for the Same Reason we make not the least Pretention while the Contest Remains between them, but Should they now relinquish their Claims we cordially hope and fully expect that the Same Benevolence that first befriended us will again be exerted and by that Means; that you Gentlemen will grant us Indulgence. In the mean Time Reserving to Ourselves the Advantage of all further necessary Suggestions[3]

J.M. VARNUM[4]
NATH[ANA]EL GREENE JUN
CHARLES HOLDEN JUN
ADAM MAXWELL[5]

DS (Brown University Archives: RPB).
1. The trustees met on 7 Feb. to debate Newport's offer, which topped that of Providence. (See note 4, previous document.)
2. This was sheer bravado. Neither city had any such idea. NG and friends were gambling on a deadlock, at which point they would be standing ready in the wings.
3. Although Newport's bid was somewhat higher, the trustees stuck with Provi-

dence. This was attributed to the greater number of Baptists in the city, the support of Pres. Manning, and, not least, the zeal of the Providence promoters. The removal of the college from Warren is well told in Bronson, *Brown University*, pp. 43–50, and Hedges, *Browns*, pp. 194–98.

4. James Mitchell Varnum (1748–89), then studying law, was barely twenty-one when he signed this petition. After being expelled from Harvard, he had attended the College of Rhode Island in Warren and was a member of the first class to graduate in 1769. He and NG had become friends the previous year, and for the next half dozen years, their lives would be intimately associated. After Varnum was admitted to the bar, he represented NG and brothers in numerous suits over the next several years; he was also their lawyer in their celebrated suit against Lieut. Dudingston of the *Gaspee* (see below, *Greene* v. *Dudingston*, 22 July 1772). Varnum married Martha Child the day after signing this petition and settled in a house in East Greenwich, which is still standing and open to the public. In 1772 NG purchased the adjoining house and lot from him but apparently found it too far from the Coventry forge (East Greenwich, Real Estate Mortgage Book II-B, pp. 72–75).

Varnum was a very able lawyer, with an inquiring, well-stocked mind, which attracted the self-educated NG. NG was influenced by Varnum's religious ideas, which Ezra Stiles called "deistical" (Stiles, *Diary*, 1:421). Shortly after moving to East Greenwich, the young lawyer had published an article in the Providence *Gazette*, saying among other things, "It would require much Time and Paper to point out the many Evils which have befallen Mankind, in different Periods of the World by the Usurpation of the Clergy" (Peck MSS, 3: 24, RHi). NG became a friend and admirer of John Murray, the founder of Universalism in America, through meeting him at Varnum's. (For relations between the two men in the Kentish Guards, see below, NG to Varnum, 31 Oct. 1774.) After serving as a colonel under NG, Varnum became a brigadier general in the Continental army, resigning his commission in 1779 to return to the law. From 1780 to 1787 he served off and on in the Continental Congress while holding a commission as a general in the R.I. militia. The highlight of his legal career came as defense attorney in the celebrated case of *Trevett* v. *Weeden* in 1786. In 1787 he became a director of the Ohio Company and moved to Marietta, Ohio, where he also sat briefly as a federal judge in Northwest Territory. He died there at the age of forty-one in 1788. (*DAB*; more complete is an article by Clifford K. Shipton in Sibley's *Harvard Grads.*, 17: 266–79. In his correspondence NG reveals that he found Varnum a vain and difficult man at times. Their friendship was strained after NG became a brigadier general.

5. Adam Maxwell was a Scottish-born schoolmaster who had settled in East Greenwich and for a time ten years earlier had tutored NG. Maxwell's strict Presbyterianism did not accord with NG's liberal religious views. (See below, note, Varnum to Murray, 24 May 1775.) By 1775 Maxwell was running a school in Newport. It was he who delivered to NG the incriminating letter that led to the conviction of Dr. Benjamin Church as a British spy (see below, Henry Ward to NG, 26 Sept. 1775). When the British captured Newport, Maxwell's Tory neighbors and the British troops made his life difficult because of the Dr. Church episode, although he withstood it for two years before moving his family back to East Greenwich. He honored his former pupil by naming a son Nathanael Greene. (Little is known about Maxwell except through his few letters to NG; for example, letters of 1 Sept. and 24 Oct. 1779.)

## To [Samuel Ward, Jr.][1]

Dear Sir                                        Coventry [R.I.] September 24, 1770[2]

I was much pleas'd Last Evening at the receipt of two of your Letters, but Inconceiveably more so in Examining the Content, Which represented to me an Author possest of a fertile invention under the regulation of a Judgment that indicated and promis'd many advantages to Society if Virtue continued to be the Rule of your Conduct.

Altho I express my Sentiments freely, yet think not they flow from the Corrupt fountain of Flattery or Insincerity, for that of all things I most abhor. For I verily believe its our incumbent duty to give Merit its due praise and its also the duty of those that receives it not to Suffer their minds to be fild with Vanity and Ostentation upon which consideration I was induc'd to Speak my Oppinion being under no apprehension but that it would be properly receiv'd and prudently applied. Altho I much admir'd your production Nevertheless I have somewhat against thee.[3] That is for being so unmercifully severe upon poor Self. Oh poor Self is there no one appears to defend thy Cause? If there is not yet shalt thou be Conquerer. For as when a man undertakes to Quarrel with his Victuals is Convinc'd by Experience of his imprudence by the Injury he finds he has sustain'd so Shall they be convinc'd who form a Resolution to Contend with Self properly considered. Therefore I must beg leave to dissent from you with respect to the Exercise of our Selfish principles for I do not consider them in that criminal point of Light that they appear to you in, and I apprehend if you'll only suffer yourself a moments recollection and consider what is the Spring of all Action youl find they stand Bottom'd upon Self. But what renders many of our Actions Criminal is the unlawful Gratification of our passions and Sensual appeti[t]es to the great Injury and detriment of the more noble purposes of Self, and that Injury We sustain in Consequence of our preferring a present Scheme of pleasures to a future state of Happiness. This false Estimate Springs from our consulting our passions and appetites and not our Reason Which would inform us better.

Its apprehended by some that all Religious acts are devoid of Self but I am so far from thinking them so that I consider them the most Selfish acts in Nature for as Religion is Calculated as a medium for us to obtain Salvation by, the preservation of our Souls being a Subject of the highest Concern, therefore there is no one Subject that we are so deeply Interested in as the discharge of all our Religious duties. For what can a man be Religious for but to recommend himself to the Favor of His God by which he expects (if he Succeeds) Everlasting Happiness? Thus we shall find by Examination that all our Civil moral and Religious obligations are discharged upon the Same principles. For if a man takes upon him the Sacred Carector of a Minister of the Gosple by which he is Expos'd to many perils dangers and distresses moreover he is Obliged to Walk Blameless with respect to the Laws of his Country, it is Expected also that his Conduct should be so uniform as to Convince us from practical observations that he possesses every Human Virtue. Further more he must punctually Keep Inviolate the Moral and Divine Laws and all these things he is Strictly confind too the observance off. Now is not such a Restricted

Life incompatible with the present Gratification of our Sensual appetites? It must be allowd; it is. From hence many have taken Occation to say that such acts do not Spring from that common Selfish principle but if you'l Search from the Effects too the Cause youl find their Origen to be at the Same Fountain; it is only their Views are more Extended. For no person would deprive themselves of the present Enjoyment of things unless they Had a prospect of a future advantage to result from that Restraint they Lay upon themselves.

Therefore those persons who acts in that Ministerial Capacity in the propagation of Theology must be Concious before they undertake such an arduous task, that it is a Service requir'd of them by their Creator and therefore their duty and Interest to Comply for a Want of Compliance might very Justly Subject them to the Just Indignation of an offended Deity by which [Offence] they may Loos the Salvation of their Souls, and as the Preservation of our Souls is of the Highest concern to our Selves, from that consideration there is a Freedom Effected to Subject our Selves to all those Temporary Inconveniencies in order to promote and Secure to our Selves a permanent Happiness. Methinks he that neglects the Nobler purposes of Life, by the pursuit of Transitory Pleasures (If there is a Volition in the mind) is not so Selfish as he Ought to be or he has but an incompleat Idea of the Consequence of our Selves to prefer our present pleasures to a future Happiness, when there is such a disproportion in the degrees of Quantity and Continuance. Thus you see how I extend the Idea of Self so as to Unite in one all the propertyes of the Body and the Faculties of the Mind and their various operations which union Constitute but one proper Self. Self thus uniformly and Connectively Considered we shall find to be the Original Cause and Spring of all action or motion. For all Religious Services and duties, Self is promis'd a future reward and that future reward being of such a Nature our present prospect of pleasure is Entirely Enveloped therein and made Subservient to that Contemplative prospect of Felicity. For if we were not Confident that its absolutely necessary to Subject [and restrain] our Sensual appeties within certain Limitations in order to Establish our Future Happiness, What cause should we have for doing of it? When we by that restraint are Subjected to many uneasy Sensations Now as all our passions and appetites are put in motion, by representing or proposing Certain Object and Subjects to the View of our Mind Which Naturally Creates a desire of Gratifying ourselves in the Enjoyment of them, What is there to hinder us from a free indulgence therein? There is nothing untill there is something Newly proposed that will have a more powerful influence and opperation upon us than the present prospect of pleasure has. Does not the mind here bring the two prospects in Contrast and by its power of Comparing and Considering with itself which measure will most Effectually conduce to its happiness, form a resolution from that considerative View which to pursue? I am apt to believe it does and if that Conclusion be just it Necessarily follows that all our Thoughts and actions flow from a Selfish principle, only the Enjoyment is propos'd to be Experienced at different Periods and enjoyed under different forms and Carrectors. For the mind is ever attentive to its own Felicity When our desires are agreeable to Rectified Nature and the Lessor Considerations is Obliged to give place to the greater, but what makes us to Mistake our true happiness is the powerful operation of our passions and prejudices which makes the Lessor appear to be the Greater and by that False representation we are decoyed. From what I have said it appears that all our Religious dispositions and Moral Conduct is Fundamentally Establisht upon a Self exalting Principle or a Natural Desire to promote our own happiness.

Therefore I think it may be Safely concluded that if there is any disenterrested actions they are of a Religious Nature. But as there dont appear to be any under a religious Carrector, Consequently there are none at all. For if Great and Exalted Spirits undertake the pursuit of Hazardous actions for the good of others at the same time they have in View the Gratification of their passion for glory, and again if Worthy minds in the domestick way of Life deny them Selves many advantages to Satisfy a Generous Benvolence which they bear to their friends who are Surrounded with distress and Calamity do they not propose a greater happiness to result from the Contemplation of relieveing our friends in distress than the Enjoyment of the Benefits bestowed could have afforded us? Thus you see there are no Actions either practical or Speculative but that Self is the primary mover and first Principles, and now agreeable to my Selfish principles being no Longer able to please my self with writeing, and far from thinking the reading will please you I am determind to Quit the Subject, But not without first asking your pardon for Intruding upon your Patience, and shall proceed to your Second Epistle upon a Rural retreat.

I entirely agree with you in Sentiment respecting the happiness Enjoyed in a Country Life, but I do not apprehend my self so well Quallified to Relish them as you are, being always accustom'd thereto for our Natures seems to require a Variety of Objects and Subjects to amuse our Selves with and as you Spend part of your time in the City and part in Country you thereby are Enabled from Comparison to determine the precise difference. But the Idea that I have formd of the difference Subsisting between a Court and Country Life, is as the Succession of fair Weather after a Storm, for a Clear Sky and a Serener air Seems to diffuse a General Joy into all the annimal and

Vegable World Whereas a Storm is big with Horror and seems to portend immediate destruction and tho the Laws of nature say this Succession is Necessary yet they Cloath her face with a Certain Gloominess which every annimal is a Common sufferer in. Thus I compare a Country Life to a Clear Sky and a Serene air for there and there only its to be enjoyed and which alone can Quallify our minds properly for Speculation, for here Nature seems to move Gently on, undisturbed with Noise and tumult, and here we may Contemplate the beauty and order of the Creation untill we arrive to that pitch of Knowledge and understanding (in our Enquiry) that the god of Nature hath Quallified us to Soar too. Thus if we are amind to turn Our attention to the Annimal World the Country affords a Great Variety of Objects Which Objects if we are dispos'd to observe their progression and attend to the Laws of Nature we shall find the Living Creatures observes the Laws prescribed them after their manner producing their own Species; or if we are amind to attend to the plants of the Earth and observe their Succession from age to age from Small seeds they spring up and proceed from Stature to Stature after their kinds till they arrive at the perfections assign them. Is not this practical and Contemplative view of things matter of Solid joy when Experienced with a placid temper of Mind? But to return to the Storm and the City and Enquire after their Similarity. A Storm is a State of Confusion so is a City; a Storm often Changes the Face of things, so are the face of things Often Changed in Cities by the tumults and uproars which they are Subject to from the Contention of Opposite Interests; a Storm is Necessary to promote Vegetable production in the Country, a City is Necessary to receive and Consume them when produced. Thus you see a storm and a City are both Necessary to promote the Country both Necessary to promote the Country Interest.

I am now a going to Greenwich which obliges me to Lay down my pen and I dare say you are not Sorry for it, but I do not intend to take my Leave of you till I have asked Pardon for one of my usual Blunders, that is for not Sending my Compliments to your father, Family, and in particular to Nancy[4] and Kitty[5] in my Last Letter, all which please to do at the receipt of this Letter in a duplicate ratio to atone for the former Neglect, and now being about to depart I must bid you farewell in an affectionate manner, and am with the greatest respect your Sincere [friend] and Well Wisher

[*signature removed*]

NB I have not time to Correct the Errors in this Long Epistle and therefore must Intreat you not to Expose it to any bodies View but your own Whose good Nature I dare say will Excuse them

AL[S] (RHi). Eighteen of the letters NG wrote Samuel Ward, Jr., between 1770 and 1774 have survived. None of young Ward's letters to NG have been found. When the correspondence began, Sammy Ward, as NG called him, was not quite fourteen; NG was twenty-eight. To anyone familiar only with NG's military career, some of the letters might seem pompous and immature. They appear less so when one remembers that he was a self-educated young man who had read a variety of books (mainly between tasks), sometimes reading more than he could digest, bursting to share his self-discovered riches, but having no one with whom he could discuss them.

In Sammy Ward he found an eager and understanding listener who was impressed by the intellect and learning of his older friend and who was flattered by the attention. Some of the letters sound like school exercises. This essentially is what they were. They gave NG an opportunity for improving his composition, for organizing his thinking, for enlarging his vocabulary. They were preparation for a leaner style of writing which he developed during the war. Quite often the letters sound like a teacher's admonition to an apt pupil; the difference in their ages must have tempted NG to assume such a role, consciously or unconsciously. Too often they sound like preaching, although young Sammy probably took this in his stride, inured as he was to his father's preaching (see his father's letters in Knollenberg, *Ward*). The "Sammy letters" however, also tell us a great deal about NG's life, and occasionally they display a welcome sense of humor. The letters were published in *R.I. Hist.*, vols. 15–17 (1956–58), edited by Clifford P. Monahon and Clarkson A. Collins III.

1. Samuel Ward, Jr., (1756–1832) was of a distinguished Rhode Island family. His grandfather, Richard Ward, was governor of the colony; his uncle, Henry Ward (1732–97), was for thirty-seven years secretary of both the colony and the state; and his father was one of the leading political figures of Rhode Island. (See biographical note below.)

When this letter was written, Samuel, Jr., was attending Rhode Island College in Warren (soon to move to Providence). After graduation in 1771 he worked in his father's store until the outbreak of war. He served under NG as a captain in the siege of Boston, distinguished himself in Arnold's ill-fated march to Quebec, and was held captive by the British for a year. He returned to the army to serve throughout the war, retiring as a colonel at the age of twenty-six. After the war he was a none-too-successful merchant in New York, returning to Rhode Island in 1804 to spend most of the remainder of his life on a farm. His sons John and Samuel III were leading bankers in New York; the latter was the father of Julia Ward Howe. (Both Samuel, Sr., and Samuel, Jr., are listed in the *DAB*; see also "Biographical Introduction" in Knollenberg, *Ward*, pp. 3–36.)

Samuel Ward, Sr., (1725–76) was a successful Newport merchant who turned to politics, being elected governor several times in the 1760s and heading a faction that challenged the redoubtable Stephen Hopkins. (On the rivalry of the factions see above, note 1, NG et al. to Stephen Hopkins & Co., 10 Oct. 1768.) He married Anna Ray of Block Island and settled on a farm in Westerly (in the southwest corner of Rhode Island) where he also ran a successful store. One of Anna's sisters, Catharine, married the governor-to-be, William Greene; another sister, Phebe, married John Littlefield and became the mother of Catharine Littlefield—NG's future wife. An ardent patriot, Samuel, Sr., served in both Continental Congresses alongside his old political rival, Stephen Hopkins. By this time he had become both a friend and advocate of NG and carried on an intimate and important correspondence with him—cut short by Ward's death from smallpox in March 1776 while serving in Congress.

2. This is the first letter written from NG's Coventry house to survive. Located above the Pawtuxet River near the family forge, the house had been completed only a short time before. (See above, petition, before 27 Oct. 1769.) The house still stands, now in the village of Anthony within the township of Coventry, and is maintained and

shown to the public by the Gen. Nathanael Greene Homestead Association (see illustration, p. 67).

3. The one book NG's father approved of his reading was the Bible, and his letters often reflect his familiarity with it. This is a paraphrase of Rev. 2:4, King James Version.

4. Anna Ward (1750–98), called Nancy by family and friends, was one of Sammy's six sisters. NG apparently was in love with Nancy, but his feelings were not reciprocated (see NG to Sammy 29 Aug. 1772). In 1776 she married Ethan Clarke. Their daughter, Anna Maria Clarke, married NG's son, Nathanael Ray Greene. Thus, Nancy Ward became the grandmother of NG's grandson and biographer—George Washington Greene. (See Monahan, "Ward Family" in Knollenberg, Ward, pp. 215–17.)

5. Catharine (Kitty) Ward (1752–82), another sister, married NG's brother Christopher in 1773. Upon her death Christopher married her sister, Deborah (1758–1835). Ibid.

## To Samuel Ward, Jr.

Dear Friend                                    Coventry [R.I.] March the 5, 1771

Think not from my long silence that my friendship for you is in the least abateed. I have too happily experienceed the sweets resulting therefrom to be so much my own enimy as to drop such an advantageous acquaintance. Altho you have much reason to complain of my long, long, long silence yet I can assure you that its not for want of Affection nor regard but imputeable entirely to another Cause, Namely the death of my Honnoured Father[1] whose dissolution turnd all our affairs into quite different Channels that made it requisite for me to give the closest application and attention in the Settlement of matters, but haveing almost accomplisht my work I am determin to make such a Recess from business as to enjoy the Social happiness resulting from a friendly intercourse both personal and Epistolary. From which consideration I have ventureed to send this letter to answer yours of January the first[2] and to redeem my promise made you at Greenwich, if it is not past the equity of redemption. I hope my neglect is not unpardonable but am sensible that I must be indebted to your goodness to pass it bye. Altho I have not seen you nor wrote to you for some time past yet I am confident there's not a friend of yours that hath thought more times on you than I have done since our last meeting; many hath been the pleasing moments I have spent in contemplating the excellence of friendship and how happy I was in my acquaintance. Language would fail me if I were to attempt to point out to you the fine feeling of the Human mind when exerciseed upon that Excellent subject of Friendship. A principal fruit of friendship is the ease and discharge of the fulness and Swellings of the Heart which pasions of all kind do cause and enduce. I dare not attempt to write to you, who are at the feet of Gamaliel,[3] upon any particular subject, being Conscious of my own ignorance. I confine myself to such Homely fare as I have been accustom'd to. I have nothing more to recommend myself to you than a sincere regard for

your person and interest which I hope to manifest upon All Occa-
tions. Being Just about to depart from Home on a voyge to Newport
am under a necessity to conclude which I shall do with a promise to
write to you Longer next time. Friends are generally in good health in
our Neighbourhood. Present my respects to Mr and Misis Manning,[4]
to friend Tommy Arnold and Mr Foster, also to Mr David Howel and
Brother. I conclude with much regard your Sincere friend

NATH GREENE, JU

ALS (RHi).

1. The Providence *Gazette* for 24 Nov. 1770 put his father's death on 16 Nov. The
entire account, in which his name was misspelled and his residence incorrectly noted,
follows: "Friday se'nnight [week] died at East-Greenwich Mr. Nathaniel Green, of
that Place, a public Teacher among Friends." NG undoubtedly did not know that
Sammy Ward's mother had died three weeks after NG's father (Knollenberg, *Ward*,
p. 20). The six brothers continued to operate their family business as Nathanael Greene
and Company until they made a division of the property in 1779. At this time Jacob was
the only married brother. The four younger brothers stayed on in their father's house at
Potowomut.

2. Letter not found.

3. Gamaliel was the teacher of St. Paul.

4. The Rev. James Manning (1738–91), a graduate of Princeton, was a founder and
first president of Rhode Island College, a post he held for twenty-five years along with
that of minister of the First Baptist Church of Providence (*DAB*; also above, memorial
of NG et al., before 7 Feb. 1770).

Thomas Arnold (1751–1826), a graduate of Rhode Island College, tutored Sammy
Ward in science and later became a distinguished member of the bar and justice of the
R.I. Supreme Court. He was one of NG's closest friends, the only guest outside the
family who was invited to NG's wedding in July 1774. His older brother, Welcome
Arnold, was also a friend.

Theodore Foster (1752–1828) was in the class of 1770 at Rhode Island College and
had just begun the practice of law in Providence. He was later a long-time clerk of
Providence, a member of the Assembly, and United States senator. (*DAB*) For a
proposed history of Rhode Island, Foster made transcripts of NG's letters to Jacob after
Jacob's death (see below, source note, NG to Jacob, 28 June 1775).

David Howell (1747–1824) was a Princeton graduate who, with Pres. Manning,
constituted the entire faculty of Rhode Island College at this time. He was later a
member of the Continental Congress and attorney general of Rhode Island. (*DAB*)
Howell was impressed with NG as a self-educated man. Once, upon spending the
night at NG's, he was surprised on arising to find his host up before dawn reading a
book (Greene, *Greene*, 1:38–39).

## To Nicholas Brown & Co. (?)[1]

[From Coventry, 27 March 1771. Will try to get floor boards for them,
but they are scarce and so are teams to cart them. ALS (RPJCB), 1 p.]

1. Although the Greenes owned a sawmill, this is the only reference to
lumber that has been found.

# Petition

[Coventry, R.I., 2 May 1771]

Rhode Island ss To the Honble the General Assembly to sit at Newport with and for the Colony of Rhode Island on the first Wednesday in May Annoque Domini 1771.

Subscribers being a Committee chosen by the Town of Coventry to enquire into the Damage said Town hath sustaind by means of the late Flood[1] and likewise to Petition this Honble Assembly for Assistance concerning the same, beg Liberty humbly to shew that by the uncommon and Extraordinary Flood aforesaid, the entire Loss of four large Bridges extending across the Southerly Branch of Patuxet River besides a considerable number of Lesser ones[2] has happen'd unto Said Town of Coventry Adding to this the deal Injury done to the Roads (which are rough and naturally very Stony and Rugged) as also the Indigence of many of the Inhabitants, as incident to a large tract of uncultivated stubbon Land (a very Considerable Part of which disdains the approach of Plow or Hoe) In Consequence whereof the People find themselves invironed into many difficulties too great to be overcome by them, without the kind interposition of this Respectable House. They therefore by us apply to your Honnours submiting their unhappy Situation to your wise consideration not doubting but they shall obtain relief for the which they are the more emboldned to ask when they Consider that the Good of any Community ultimately depends on the prosperity of each Constituent part, and that the offices and Duties of Society are Reciprocal between the whole and its Branches, and that from a due Sense of this Maxim in Policy the Legislative Body of this Colony has granted relief to others, who have heretofore laboured under somewhat similar (tho not altogether so distressing) Circumstances as Ours, We therefore on their Behalf most humbly pray that your Honors would Grant them such a Sum towards rebuilding said Bridges as you shall think Adequate to their Necessaties and your Petitioners as in duty bound will ever pray &c[3]

|                        |                     |
| ---------------------- | ------------------- |
| STEPHEN POTTER         | CALEB VAUGHAN       |
| THOS MATTESON          | DANIEL GARDNER      |
| NATHANAEL GREENE JUN    | JOHN JOHNSON JUR    |
| THOMAS STAFFORD        | JAMES WATERMAN      |
| NATHANAEL GREENE[4]    | MATTHEW REMINGTON   |
| ICHABOD BOWEN          | ISRAEL BOWEN        |
| THOMAS BRAYTON         |                     |

ADS (R-Ar). Although NG was not chairman of the committee, the petition was written by him, probably because he had acquired something of a reputation for writing forceful and sometimes persuasive memorials. His petitions were more literary than most; it was not every member of the committee who could describe stubborn land "which disdains the approach of Plow or Hoe."

1. The flood occurred in March 1771.

2. The four bridges with estimates of repairing each are listed on a separate sheet: "Greens Bridge by the Forge, £45; Braytons Bridge, £45; Maple Root Bridge, £30; Johnsons Bridge, £30; Several Lesser Bridges Estimated together, £50."

3. At the May session, the legislature approved a lottery for the replacement of a bridge in Warwick and appropriated $200 (about £60) to replace Pawtuxet Bridge, but they did not act on the Coventry petition. Three of the signers to this petition submitted a second petition at the Oct. session (see below, petition, before 30 Oct. 1771).

4. This is the first document in which the "other" Nathanael Greene of Coventry (also a junior) has spelled his name in full. See discussion of the various "Nathl" Greenes in the introduction.

## To Samuel Ward, Jr.

[From East Greenwich, R.I., 21 May 1771. Acknowledges receipt of Ward's letter and sends compliments to his sisters. ALS (RHi), 1 p.]

## To Samuel Ward, Jr.[1]

Dear Friend                                Coventry [R.I.] September 26 1771

I Fear my Promise to Write to you is so Deeply Mortgaged that its almost past the Equity of Redemption. But as you cannot Plead the Statute of Limitations, I determin to avail my Self of the present Opportunity to Redeem it, and that you maynt be too great a Sufferer by my long, long, long, silence. If quantity will serve in lieu of Quallity I determin to Write sufficient for three or four common Letters. It is very Fortunate for you to be able to Enumerate a long Train of Noble Ancestors, but to equal the best and excell the most is to have no Occation for any. It is a laudable Emulation to endeavour to surpass all our Progenitors in Knowledge, and to exceed them in worthy Actions. Should we not my Friend think him a poor Husbandman who haveing received a large Patrimony spends his Days in slothfulness without enlargeing his Fortune or rendering his Estate more considerable by Improvements. So he that enters into Life with all the advantageis of a Noble Birth, Adornd with a Liberal Education and Improvd by the most Pious Example, cannot be excus'd short of an improvement propotionable to the Opportunity given. To pursue Virtue where theres no Opposition is the Merit of a common Man, But to Practice it in spight of all Opposition is the Carrector of a truly great and Noble Soul. My Friend let the Practice of Virtue be your Aim for on that depends your Future Importance [and] usefullness in Life. Virtuous Manners I call such acquired Habits of Thought and Correspondent Actions as lead to a steady Prosecution of the generall Welfare of Society: Virtuous Principles I call such as tend to confirm these Habits by Superinduceing the Idea of Duty. Virtuous Manners are a permanent Foundation for civil Liberty, because they lead the Passions and Desires them selves to coincide with the appointments of Publick Law. The infant Mind is Pregnant with a Variety of Passions, But I apprehend it is in the Power of those who are entrusted with the Education of Youth in a considerable Degree to determin the Bent of the Noble Passions and to fix them on Salutary Objects, or let them loose to such as are pernicious or destructive. Here then lies the Foundation of civil Liberty; in forming the Habits of the Youthful Mind, in forwarding every Passion that may tend to the promotion of the Happiness of the Community, in fixing in our selves right Ideas of Benevolence, Humanity Integrity and Truth, For what purpose to study and Letters if they do not render us Beneficient and Humane?

What shall I say to you upon Benevolence? The Example of God teacheth the Lesson truly. He sendeth his Rain and maketh his Sun to shine upon the Just and Unjust but he doth not Rain Wealth nor shine Honnor and Vertues upon Men equally. Common Benefits are to be communicated with all, but peculiar benefits with choice. For Divinity maketh the Love of our selves the Pattern [of] the Love of our Neighbour but the Portraiture. Therefore regard is to be had to the Merit of the Objects the worth of the Occation in the display of Our Bounty it is our Duty to seek the good of All Men but never to be in Bondage to their farces or fancies for that is but faulletly or softness which maketh an honest mind Prisoner, for tho Riches are for Spending they should be spent in Honnor and Good Actions. Learn my Friend to distinguish betwixt true and false Modesty. What I call false Modesty is not to have Resolution to deny an unreasonable request or Power too oppose a corrupt Custom. The one often proves destructive to our Interest the [other] to our Manners. But never be too precipitate in an [action?] for Consideration would often prevent what the best Sk[ill in?] the World cannot Recover. Our Weakness, our Want of Resolution, of Sagacity, of Knowledge and Abillity, seems in some sort to put it out of our Power to form a Medium of Conduct to Govern our selves by through the different Occurrencies in Life. Its much safer to follow Truth alone, than to have all the World for Company in the Road of Error; Therefore when Sinners Entice consent thou not, for to remove a present inconveniency and consequence entail upon our selves a lasting disadvantage cannot be a prudent Measure; study to Please where you can do it with Honnor and Conscience and not injure your interest. Envy, Malice and Detraction seems to be ruling Vices of this age so that you need not Expect without the aid of Omnipotence to prevent Falsehoods, nor stop the mouth of Invention: You must therefore gard against report, which is but another Name for Forgery. A Fiction may be Cloathed with probabillity, and the disguise of Truth become a pasport for a Mischievous Lye. The Grossest story, when artificially Cookt by cunning Envy, may appear likely, and gain belief. A seeming Reason, is, till it be discovered as powerful as a real one. But Truth tho it may be Disguisd and Veild for a season; Yet like the Sun in the Firmament, whose Glory is often Eclipst by the interception of his Rays; He does by the Efflux of his own light, dispel the Mist, and leave his Native Beauty unblemisht, so shall Truth rise upon Falsehood.

I hope youl now take off the Mortgage of my Promise. It begins to grow late and I weary, for I have stole these Moments to Write when I should have been a Sleep, For being, (as the Proverb goes) like a Waterford Merchant very full of Business and nothing to do, I could not find Time to Write in the Day. Commend me to your Sisters, my Respects to your Father. I was not a little Charmd with the agreeable manner in which he Treated his Children. Such Paternal care as was display'd in every Action its to be hoped is repaid by perfect Obedience and Fil[ial] Respect. I saw your Sister Hannah a few Days [ago] and she informs me that she enjoys her Health [as] well as she hath done of Late.[2] I am going to Write to Mr [Thomas] Arnold to give him an invitation to come and spend a Week or Fortnight with me. Should be exceeding glad of your Company to make a Little Society. I make no doubt of finding you amusement in Fishing Fowling and Studying. I can Write no more for my Eyes begins to want props already. Write to me soon for I wont send you another Letter till you answer this for I intend to be as particular as the Ladies are in their Visits. I am your sincere Friend.

NATHANAEL GREENE JR

P S Despise the Disrespect of those, who through Ignorance of your Worth, give you ill Usage and learn to overcome Affliction by the Hopes of getting out of Them; this is a way to be too hard for ill Fortune it self.

ALS (RHi).
1. The letter was addressed: "For Mr. Samuel Ward Jun. To the Care of Miss H. Ward in Westerly." Samuel Ward, Sr., still maintained his farm at Westerly on Long Island Sound, near the Connecticut border.
2. Hannah (1749–74) was the oldest of Samuel and Anna Ward's daughters. In Sept. 1774, while her father was attending the first Continental Congress in Philadelphia, she died, after several years of ill health, at the age of twenty-five (Knollenberg, *Ward*, p. 29).

## Petition to the Rhode Island General Assembly

[Before 30 Oct. 1771] Colony Rhode Island
To the Honble General Assembly siting at South Kingstown within and for said Colony on the last Wednesday of October A D 1771

We being a Committee specially appointed by the Town of Coventry to Address this Honble House for relief and assistance in repairing the Bridges and publick ways so much injured by the late remarkable Flood, Beg liberty to shew that notwithstanding the discouragement they met with in their former application[1], they are yet further encouraged to make a second application from a full conviction that our difficulties are insurmountable unless we receive Benefit from the helping Hand of this Assembly. We cannot persuade ourselves that your Honors are actuated by partial motives or unequal principles. We therefore are confident when you shall strictly examin our request you'l find it Reasonable and that when you survey our motives you'l see they are founded in Necessity. Consequently you'l relieve them For its very hard that one of the poorest Towns in the Colony should pay a considerable sum annually towards defraying the Governments expences, and we receive no Benefit from the same Government when our Necessity entitles us thereto by los[s]es sustain'd That would be in effect to destroy the primary and most Essential Laws of Human Society. We therefore earnestly entreat you to take our unhappy situation under consideration and make us such a Grant as your Wisdom and prudence shall dictate to be our due to have Granted and your duty to Grant from the Nature of social connexion and your Petitioners as in duty bound will ever pray &c.[2]

NATHANAEL GREENE
STEPHEN POTTER
ICHABOD BOWEN[3]

ADS (R-Ar).

1. See petition of 2 May 1771 above.

2. The Assembly, as noted on the back of the petition, voted $25 "toward Rebuilding the Bridge called Braytons Bridge and that the same be paid to Mr. Nathaniel Greene Jun." The House of Magistrates upped the amount to $50 but went back to $25 when the Assembly would not concur. NG was especially interested in Braytons Bridge because it was near the forge.

3. Ichabod Bowen (1727–1816) represented Coventry in the Assembly (misprinted as Borden in Bartlett, *Records*, 7: 26).

## To Samuel Ward, Jr.

Dear Oratour                           Coventry [R.I., April? 1772][1]

I receivd your Letter of Feby 6th.[2] As you said nothing of your Jorney I take it for Granted you got Home safe. I should Wrote you an answer long since but have been engageed in the pursuit of a Searover[3] who took into his Custody a quantity of Our Rum and carried it round to *Boston* (contrary to the Express words of the Statute) for Tryal and condemnation. The illegallity of his measure together with the Loss sustaind createed such a Spirit of Resentment That I have devoted almost the whole of my Time in devising and carrying into execution measures for the recovery of my Property and punnishing the offender. So much for an excuse.

I observe in your Letter the Strongest inclination for obtaining a large fund of useful Knowledge to be drawn from reading History. If we act only for ourselves, to neglect the Study of history is not prudent. If we are entrusted with the cares of others it is not just. Ignorance when it is voluntary is criminal, and he may be properly chargeed with evil who refuses to learn how he might prevent it.

There is no part of History so generally useful as that which relates to the progress of the human mind, the gradual improvement of Reason, the successive advances of science, the Vicissitudes of Learning and ignorance, which are the light and darkness of thinking Beings, the extinction and begining of Arts and all the revolutions of the intellectual world. Accounts of Battles and invasions seems to be the peculiar Business of Military Men; and the useful and elegant Arts should be the Study of those who are to Govern the state and form the manners of Mankind.

I cannot help cautioning you against a practice which by habit may be so strongly confermd as to prove prejudicial to your interest and Reputation. I mean that of being so confind to your Books as to neglect the converse of mankind. The faculty of interchangeing our thoughts with one another has always been represented by moral writers as one of the noblest priviledges of Reason, and it is that which more particularly sets Mankind above the Brute Creation.

If we consider the whole scope of the creation that lies within our view, as in the natural and corporeal part, we shall perceive throughout a certain correspondence of parts, a similitude of operations and unity of design. So in the moral and intellectual World we shall observe in Spirits and minds of men a principle of Attraction whereby theyre drawn together into communities, friendships and the various species of Society. This corresponding social appetite in human Souls is the great spring and source of moral Actions. It inclines us to an intercourse with our Species and produces that sympathy in our Natures whereby we feel the pains and joys of our fellow creatures. The benefit of conversation, if there was nothing else in it, would be no inconsiderable improvement, for discourse creates a light within us and dispels the gloom and confusion of the Mind. It raises Fancy, reinforces reason, and gives the production of the mind a Better coulour.

Think not, my dear friend, because I caution you against evil I think you already vicious. Before Habits are establisht, Friendship confermd, and life planned into method, The infant mind is susceptible to every impression, whether good or evil, exhibited to its view. The care of education is a work of the highest moment as all the advantages or miscariages of a mans life are in a great measure dependant on it. It is the duty of Parents in particular and Friends in general to infuse into the untainted youth early notions of Justice and honour that so all possible advantages of good parts may not take an evil turn nor be perverted to base and unworthy purposes.

The mind is to be made obedient to discipline and pliant to reason while it is yet tender and easy to be bowed, but if we suffer ill principles to get ground on infancy, vice to debauch or passion to pervert reason in that unguarded age; when we have once made an ill Child, it is a foolish expectation to promise ourselves he will prove a good man. Shall we wonder afterwards to taste the waters bitter when we ourselves have first poisond the fountain?

Study to be wise and learn to be prudent. Learning is not Virtue but the means to bring us an acquaintance with it. Integrity without knowledge is weak and useless, and Knowledge without integrity is dangerous and Dreadful. Let these be your motives to action through Life, the relief of the distressed, the detection of frauds, the defeat of oppression, and diffusion of happiness. Then shall you appear before God and men like Apples of Gold in pictures of Silver.[4]

Men of great talents by nature and polisht by Art, if to these accomplishments be added that of a general Acquaintance with mankind, are the most dangerous persons to be connected with unless they steadily persevere in the practice of Virtue. For they know the secret avenues to the human Heart and, haveing the power to make the worse appear the better reason, we are often betrayd before we conceive ourselves in any danger.

I love you with brotherly Love and wish your welfare. My best respects to your whole Family.

NG JR

It is not Customary for me to write so bad a hand but make no doubt if you take pains youl find out the Contents. Now for Popes part. The Colonel[5] is well very well but much out of humour, the reason I have not room to explain. The Squire and his Lady are both tolerably well together with thier Children.[6] They are all in Health at Potowomut except Perry who has been unwell all Winter with what the Vulgar call the Spleen. Jacob has lately been Sick but is restord to Health. We had a Letter from Christopher Dated 26 December in good Health and high Spirits in Maryland.

ALS (RHi).
    1. The approximate date is established by the capture of the rum, which occurred on 17 Feb. 1772, and on the activities in the weeks that followed that event.
    2. Letter not found.
    3. This is the only account we have by NG of an incident that marked a turning

point in his life and led indirectly to Rhode Island's most celebrated defiance of British rule in the prerevolutionary period—the burning of HMS *Gaspee*. The "Searover" (i.e., pirate) who took the Greenes' rum was Lieut. William Dudingston, commander of the *Gaspee*, who had been sent by Adml. Montagu into Rhode Island waters to put a stop to smuggling—a practice long popular with most colonists, but especially Rhode Islanders. The Sugar Act of 1733 had levied a prohibitory duty on sugar, rum, and molasses, but since the British lacked the means of enforcing the act, they winked at constant infractions over the years. The habit of smuggling thus became ingrained among a generation of saltwater colonials; smuggling, in fact, was considered by many as their God-given right.

When England tightened the revenue laws after 1764, she reduced the sugar duty to a fraction of what it had been in order that the duty might be collected, but by this time Americans looked upon even the most honest customs collector as a virtual pirate. Since most were venal officeholders bent on feathering their own nests, there seemed even greater virtue in defying them. "From 1768 to 1772," writes a student of the navigation acts, "almost open warfare existed between the agents of the Commissioners [whom he calls racketeers] and the trading fraternity of New England and some of the other major ports" (Dickerson, *Navigation Acts*, p. 210).

In Newport, where vessels had to be unloaded under the nose of the collector, merchants commonly bribed or intimidated the officials, knowing they had the support of the elected governor and Assembly. They were not beyond using force when necessary. In 1769 a Newport mob unmasted HMS *Liberty* and burned her. Two years later Collector Charles Dudley was severely beaten in Newport, supposedly by drunken sailors, none of them, Gov. Wanton assured the ministry, being from Rhode Island. As David Lovejoy has written, the government was powerless to prevent such offenses and "deliberately negligent in discovering the offenders and bringing them to justice" (Lovejoy, *R.I. Politics*, p. 47).

Against this background Adml. Montagu chose for the R.I. mission Lieut. Dudingston, who had a reputation for toughness, if not downright meanness. Three years earlier, for example, he had been sued for beating a Pennsylvania fisherman while a mate held the man. Even Dudingston's supporters did not think him civil. The conservative chief justices of the *Gaspee* commission (friends of the Admiralty) admitted there was "too much reason to believe, that in some instances Lieutenant Dudingston, from an intemperate, if not a reprehensible zeal to aid the revenue service, exceeded the bounds of his duty" (Bartlett, *Records*, 7: 180). Justice Horsmanden of N.Y. thought Dudingston "might probably have treated the boatmen with severity, roughness and scurrillous language" (ibid., p. 184).

On 17 Feb. the Greenes' small sloop, the *Fortune*, lay at anchor in Narragansett Bay off North Kingstown with twelve hogsheads of rum, some Jamaica spirits, and brown sugar aboard. In command of the sloop was NG's twenty-three-year-old cousin, Rufus Greene, of East Greenwich. Dudingston, who had just sailed into Narragansett Bay, never explained why he sought out such small fry in that obscure place; perhaps it was because the chances for finding contraband were best in small ports where there was no collector. In any case, as cousin Rufus recalled in a later deposition, Dudingston sent an officer named Dundas aboard the *Fortune*; Dundas ordered Rufus to "unlay the hatches" and go into the cabin. When asked by what authority, Dundas replied, "If you do not go into the cabin, I'll let you know," then drew his sword, and pushed him into the cabin. When Capt. Greene went forward to stop the anchor from being weighed, Dundas "clenched upon this deponent again, thrust him into the cabin, jammed the companion leaf upon his head, knocked him down upon a chest in said cabin, and confined him there for a considerable time." After marking the hatches with the king's "R," Dundas "towed said sloop to said schooner (it being calm), with three boats." Capt. Greene was taken aboard the *Gaspee*, where Dudingston first ordered him confined in the gangway and later put ashore. (The deposition was given before Justice Hopkins Cooke, who testified that the deponent "is of a respectable family, sober life, and ought to be credited." [Bartlett, *Records*, 7: 145–46]).

Dudingston then took the sloop in tow to Newport, where he was faced with a dilemma. If he kept watch over the sloop, as he pointed out to Montagu, the relatively small amount of rum would merely serve as "a bait, [which] the inhabitants of this government would willingly put in my way, if that could fix the schooner" [i.e., keep the *Gaspee* fixed in port]. His alternative was to send the sloop to the Boston Admiralty Court, which could dispose of cargo and vessel, but this violated one of the king's statutes (as NG notes in his letter), which required such cases to be tried in the Admiralty Court of Rhode Island. "I was not, at the time," he continued to Montagu, "ignorant of the statute to the contrary; but never doubted, if the sloop got safe, I should be supported by them [the board of commissioners] as I informed the board." The board did not support him, but even if they had, Dudingston had made himself liable to a suit by NG and his brothers, which was not long in coming. (His letter to Montagu of 22 May 1772 is in Bartlett, *Records*, 7: 64–66.)

In the meantime news of the *Fortune*'s fate spread rapidly. On 24 Feb. the *Newport Mercury* commented on a report that the "piratical schooner belongs to King George the Third" by saying "we should think it a little below His Br-t-n-c Majesty, to keep men-of-war employed in robbing some of his poorest subjects" (Bartlett, *Records*, 7: 92). As Dudingston reported to Montagu in March, "every invention of infamous lies calculated to inflaim the Country is put in the News Papers." There was talk, he said, "of fitting and arming a Vessel to prevent my carrying any seizure to Boston." He dared not "send a boat on shore with safety," nor could he go ashore because "two or three writs are now ready to be served on me on that account" (Dudingston to Montagu, 24 Mar. 1772, RIHS, *Proc*. [1890–91]:80).

The principal writ that awaited him was as defendant in *Greene* v. *Dudingston* (see below, 22 July 1775). He told Montagu that he had thought of turning to the legislature for relief but that "Mr. [Jacob] Greene is one of the house, the owner of the rum. I could expect no quarter from people of that stamp." (Bartlett, *Records*, 7:66. It is assumed that he spoke of Jacob since the suit was brought by "Jacob Greene & Co," and since Jacob was in the legislature. Rufus Greene said the cargo belonged to "Nathaniel Greene & Co," [ibid., p. 145], but since the family business had no formal or legal title, the names of the two older sons were used interchangeably.) Dudingston told Montagu in the same letter that he had asked the commissioners to condemn the sloop "as it was the intention of the people here, to have the sloop sold in the manner they have been used to, and which always falls into the old owners' hands, without opposition" (ibid., p. 66). The commissioners apparently took no such action, however, since the suit did not mention the sloop itself. Dudingston managed to avoid having the writ served on him for three months by staying on board the *Gaspee*; only after the vessel was burned and he was confined in bed with injuries was the sheriff able to arrest him. (See below, *Greene* v. *Dudingston*, 22 July 1772.)

As stated at the beginning of this note, Dudingston's actions on 17 Feb. 1772 marked a turning point in NG's life. As a Rhode Islander, he had enjoyed many rights prior to this time which he took for granted—more political rights, perhaps, than freemen of any other colony. He had also enjoyed considerable economic freedom. Neither as an anchorsmith nor as a forgemaster had he been greatly affected by the restrictive Iron Act; nor as a small merchant had he felt the pinch of the navigation acts. We do not know whether he had been involved in the stamp act controversy, but his surviving letters show no concern with imperial relations until the *Gaspee* incident. A year earlier, on 5 Mar. 1771, for example, thousands of New Englanders put aside their work to commemorate the first anniversary of the Boston Massacre, but in a letter that NG wrote to Sammy Ward on that memorable day, he made no mention of the widely hailed ceremonies being held in Providence.

He was concerned after 17 Feb. 1772, however, with American rights. His references to England or the ministry after that time were usually a villification. The following Jan., for example, he feared that the "Priviledges and Liberties of the People will be trampled to Death by the Prerogatives of the Crown" and added that the Assembly appeared to have "sunk down into a tame submission and intire acquiescence to Ministerial Mandates." (See below, NG to Samuel Ward, Jr., 25 Jan. 1773. See also his letter of 10 July 1774.) As will be seen below in the letters he wrote after entering the army, his references to the British government are always in the same vein. Unlike those veterans of the French and Indian War who had grown fond of British soldiers with whom they had served, NG's feelings were not softened by memories of comradeship with the British. Until the Revolution, in fact, the English were virtual strangers to him.

When NG and his brothers first learned of their loss, they had no way of knowing they would eventually be recompensed. Their apparent economic loss was severe, sufficient to bring about a swift change in their attitude, but without doubt they were equally incensed over the treatment accorded cousin Rufus. Soon their misfortune became a cause célèbre throughout the Narragansett Bay region. In the following two months, Dudingston found no contraband on some two hundred other vessels, which, in Gov. Wanton's words, he "searched and rummaged with the greatest severity," (Bartlett, *Records*, 7: 91), but the resentment that built up against him and exploded in the burning of the *Gaspee* found its inception in his capture of the Greenes' sloop. As other Rhode Islanders made the Greenes' cause their own, so NG and his brothers began to see the cause of other Rhode Islanders—even other Americans— as their own. (On the burning of the *Gaspee* see note at *Greene* v. *Dudingston*, 22 July 1772, below.)

4. Paraphrase of "A word fitly spoken is like apples of gold in pictures of silver." (Prov. 25, King James Version)

5. The "Colonel" refers to NG. See note 8, NG to Sammy, 25 Jan. 1773, below.

6. The "Squire and his Lady" are William and "Aunt" Catharine Greene.

## From Nicholas Brown & Co.

[Providence, 12 May 1772. Disallows bill for mending a faulty anchor. Balance on note due can be paid for with another anchor. Cy (RPJCB) 1 p.]

## To Catharine or Mary Ward[1]

[From Coventry, R.I., 4 July 1772. A long, rambling letter depicting a dreamlike reverie that is somewhat belabored with truisms. In reference to his fantasy, he wrote: "The power that fiction hath over the mind affords an endless Variety of amusements, always at hand to employ a vacant hour." Nancy, of whom he was especially fond, was pictured in "the Bay of troubled Waters, where the Wind and Sea had contary directions, She had lost the Anchor of constancy and Hope, Sometimes moveing Involuntarily with the motions of the Tide and then drawn back again with the gentle Gales of Gratitude and Generosity." Presumably the image described her ambivalent feelings toward him.[2] ALS (RHi) 4 pp.]

1. Mary Ward (1754–1832) was Samuel Ward's fourth daughter, who took over the management of his house when her mother died although she was at the time only sixteen. Four years later, while her father was attending Congress in Philadelphia, she managed the farm at Westerly (see her father's letters to her in Knollenberg, *Ward*, pp. 60–62, 106–8, and 163). She never married.

2. The letter is printed in full in *R.I. Hist.* 15 (1956): 50–52.

## To Samuel Ward, Jr.

Dear Friend                    Aunt Greens [Warwick, R.I.] July 20, 1772[1]

I expect you to Greenwich today and I am bound for Coventry

and shant be Down till tomorrow Night. I charge you by all the Gentle ties of Friendship to let me see you before you return. I have some things to mention to you which I should not be willing to write. I flatter myself I have interest enough in your friendship to ensure me this interview. If I have not I have been greatly deceivd. You may have friends that you regard more than me, but none that Loves you better than your honest Friend Nat. I never presumed to have any accomplishments to entitle me to Peoples regard but Gentleness of Manners, Humanity of Soul and a Benificeint temper. If these quallities are worth your regard you shall share as largely of their influance as anyone with whom my Heart is bound by the Bonds of Friendship or the ties of Gratitude. Come to Coventry if you can. You know my Heart will bound to meet you. The greatest and most noble function of the human Heart is to confer Happiness and felicity on as many of your Species as you can. If this be true come and see me.

[*signature removed*]

To be deliverd if present but not to be sent.[2]

AL[S] (RHi).
    1. NG had come to East Greenwich to attend the opening of court on Monday, 20 July. The case of *Greene* v. *Dudingston* was slated to be heard on Wednesday, 22 July, so he went back home to Coventry with plans to return to East Greenwich, as he told Sammy, "tomorrow Night." He was staying, as he had done before, with Sammy's Aunt Catharine and Uncle William Greene who lived at the edge of East Greenwich. Catharine Littlefield, NG's future wife, who lived with her Aunt Catharine, was a pretty girl of sixteen. NG apparently paid no special attention to her, but she could hardly help being impressed at this time by her aunt's occasional houseguest, because he was at the center of a court case that was of concern to the entire county—if not the entire colony. The burning of the *Gaspee* and the wounding of Lieut. Dudingston, which had occurred six weeks earlier, was still the prime subject of conversation.
    2. Written on the address sheet.

## Greene v. Dudingston[1]

[22 July 1772]

Be it Remembered That William Dudingston now residing in Cranston in the County of Providence Gentleman alias Manner [mariner], was attached to answer the Complaint of Jacob Greene of Warwick, Nathaniel Greene of Coventry, William Greene, Elihu Greene, Christopher Greene, and Perry Greene of Warwick aforsaid, all in the County of Kent, Merchants in Company; Whereupon the said Jacob Greene, Nathaniel Greene, William Greene, Elihu Greene, Christopher Greene and Perry Greene Complain of the said William Dudingston in the Custody of the Sheriff in an Action of the Case upon Trover. For that whereas the Plaintiffs on the Seventeenth Day of February last past, were Possessed of Twelve Hogsheads of West

India Rum containing about Fourteen Hundred Gallons; Forty Gallons of Jamaica Spirits and One Hogshead of Brown Sugar, all of the Vallue of Two Hundred and Ninety Five Pounds Lawful Money (as their own proper Estate) and being so possessed they afterwards Vizt on the same Day and Year at Warwick aforesaid casually lost the said Rum, Jamaica Spirit and Sugar out of their hands and Possession, which Rum, Jamaica Spirits and Sugar aforesaid, on the same Seventeenth Day of February, last past, at said Warwick came to the hands and Possession of the Defendant by Finding, who knowing the said Rum, Jamaica Spirits and Sugar, to be the Goods and Chattels of the Plaintiffs and of Right to belong and appertain to them the Plaintiffs, and intending craftily and Subtilly to Deceive and Defraud, the Plaintiffs in this Behalf, hath not delivered the said Rum, Jamaica Spirits, and Sugar to the Plaintiffs altho' the Defendant was by the Plaintiffs often thereto requested, but the Defend't afterwards, Viz, on the Nineteenth Day of February last past, at said Warwick, Converted and Disposed of the said Rum, Jamaica Spirits and Sugar to the Proper Use and Benefit of him the Defendant, which is to the Damage of the Plantiffs Six Hundred Pounds Lawful Money &c. And be it further remembered That here cometh the said William Dudingston and saith, he is not Guilty in manner and form as the Plaintiffs have Declared against him, and of this puts himself upon the Country; And the Plantiffs in like manner; Let therefore a Jury come before the Justices here, to Try the Issue aforsaid;[2] And afterwards (to wit) on Wednesday the Third Day of the Term Nathan Spencer, Jonathan Tibbits, Peleg Salsbury, Arnold Stafford, John Levalley, Thomas Bix (the 4th) Elisha Potter, Elisha Greene, David Hopkins, Job Vaughan, Benjamin Nichols, and Thomas Arnold are duly Impaneled and Sworn the better to Try the Facts aforsaid; Who upon Oath return the following Verdict (to wit), "We find for the plaintiffs Two Hundred and Ninety five Pounds Lawful Money and Cost." Which Verdict is accepted by the Court; And afterwards (to wit) on Wednesday aforesaid; Here come as well the said Jacob Greene, Nathaniel Greene, William Green, Elihu Greene, Christopher Greene and Perry Greene, by James Mitchel Varnum their Attorney, as the said William Dudingston by James Brenton his Attorney and the said Jacob Greene, Nathaniel Greene, William Greene, Elihu Greene, Christopher Greene and Perry Greene Demand Judgment of and upon the Premises aforesaid; Which being by the Justices, Here Seen and fully understood; It is therefore Considered that the said Jacob Greene, Nathaniel Greene, William Greene, Elihu Greene, Christopher Greene and Perry Greene Recover and Have of the said William Dudingston as well the aforesaid Sum of Two Hundred and Ninety Five Pounds Lawful Money, for the Damages they have Sustained by the Means of the Conversion aforesaid; as one Pound Eighteen Shillings and Two Pence, like Money, for their Cost, in and about the Prossecution of this Suit Expended.

The Defend't Appealed, and Bond is given as the Law requires.[3]

D (Book 4 of Kent County Court of Common Pleas, pp. 720–21; in Supreme Court Vault, Providence.)

1. For the background of this suit, see note 3, NG to Samuel Ward, Jr., Apr. (?) 1772, above. As stated at the end of that note, Dudingston managed for three months to avoid having a writ served on him as a defendant in the suit, which had been initiated in early Mar. 1772 by James M. Varnum, attorney for NG and his brothers. His immunity ended on 9 June when, late in the afternoon of that day, the *Gaspee* went aground in Narragansett Bay off Namquit Point, just seven miles south of Providence. Word of the schooner's plight spread rapidly along the western shore of the Bay.

During the evening a mob gathered in Providence with the objective of doing some violence to Dudingston or the *Gaspee*—or both—before high tide freed the craft. Among the group were respectable merchants who had viewed Dudingston as a constant threat to them from the time he had seized the Greenes' sloop in Feb. (the only vessel Dudingston had actually taken). They also resented his insults and the manner in which he had "rummaged" their ships for contraband (see Gov. Wanton's letter to Earl of Hillsborough, 16 June 1772, Bartlett, *Records*, 7: 91). They assembled eight longboats and near midnight rowed silently to the *Gaspee*, coming up under her guns. When Dudingston ran on deck at the alarm, an overanxious member in the lead boat put a musket ball through his arm and into his groin. He surrendered the ship, and after his wounds were dressed, his captors removed him and the crew, then set fire to the *Gaspee*. Dudingston was placed in a house in Pawtuxet, where a Providence surgeon was brought to care for him.

As NG made clear in a letter to Samuel Ward, Jr., the following Jan. (see below, 25 Jan. 1773), he was not involved in the incident, but it seems quite likely that his cousin Rufus Greene, captain of the captured sloop *Fortune*, was one of the mob. The only one who was identified by the *Gaspee*'s crew was a man "named Greene," who was named by one Peter May as the man he had previously seen in "the cabin of the Gaspee the day after they had seized a sloop [the Greenes'], of which he appeared to be the owner." Greene, he said, was "a tall, slender man; wearing his own hair, of a brown color." (Bartlett, *Records*, 7: 152) The description pointed directly at cousin Rufus, but Chief Justice Hopkins and his associates on the superior court stated, in feigned innocence, that "the family of Greene being very numerous in this colony, and the said Peter [May] not giving the Christian name, or describing him in such a manner as he could be found out, it is impossible for us to know, at present, the person referred to" (Bartlett, *Records* , 7: 176).

Whether other relatives of NG were involved is not known, but the Greenes' loss was much on the minds of the men who went on board the *Gaspee* that night. Peter May testified that he heard several people on deck ask Dudingston whether "he would make amends for the rum which he had seized out of the sloop" (Bartlett, *Records*, 7: 152); and Dudingston wrote Montagu that after he was taken off the *Gaspee* and put into a longboat, one of the leaders said, "If I did not consent to pay the value of the rum, I must not expect to have any thing belonging to me, saved." Dudingston told them "whatever reparation the law would give, I was ready and willing." (Letter to Montagu, 12 June 1772, Bartlett, *Records*, 7: 86–87)

Three days after Dudingston was wounded, still confined to his bed, doubting—or so he said to Montagu—that he would survive his wounds, he was visited by the sheriff of Kent County, who came to arrest him as defendant in the Greenes' suit. According to a letter of 24 July in the Providence *Gazette* (22 Aug. 1772), Dudingston had been wounded by "the Narragansett Indians in a riot." He was arrested in Pawtuxet because, the paper said, "he could not fly from the sherriff" as he had done before. Thus was Dudingston brought to trial in East Greenwich on 22 July 1772. (On the commission appointed to bring to trial those responsible for burning the *Gaspee*, see below, NG to Samuel Ward, Jr., 25 Jan. 1773, note 7.)

2. The lawyers' arguments before the jury are summarized in the appeal heard by the superior court of judicature in its session of Apr. 1773. Brenton, Dudingston's lawyer, maintained the seizure was "made at sea, agreeable to the Acts of Parliament." Varnum based the Greenes' case primarily on the fact that Narragansett Bay was not on the high seas but well within the colony's boundaries, and that, according to the "Statute of the Eighth of George the Third, his present most gracious Majesty, Chapter twenty second," the case could not be tried in Boston. Varnum also questioned the authenticity of Dudingston's commission and the admissibility of the Boston decree, but the jury hardly needed those additional charges. (The appeal is found in Book 1, Kent County Superior Court Records, 1751–89, pp. 398–99; Supreme Court Vault, Providence.)

3. When the appeal came up at the October session of the Kent County Superior Court, Dudingston, as the court put it, was "three times solemnly called, but cometh not" (ibid., p. 394). Dudingston was in England attending his courtmartial (at which he was exonerated for loss of the *Gaspee*), and Attorney Brenton, according to a later petition, was absent because "the Weather for that and the Succeeding Days Proved So exceeding Tempestuous, and Dangerous, that Your Petitioner's Attorney could not, by any Possibility cross the Ferrys [from Newport] to attend in Season his Tryal." In this petition, submitted to the December session of the Assembly, Brenton asked for, and was granted, the right to bring up the appeal at the next session. (Vol. 15 of Petitions, R-Ar). At the April session of the superior court (cited above), Dudingston lost his appeal by the findings of another jury, and was assessed an amount slightly over £300. The court ordered that he be made "safely secure in Our Goal in Newport" until the sum was paid, which was done by Collector Charles Dudley on 21 May "as Bail to William Duddingston." Whether Dudingston had to repay the amount is not recorded. (A MS copy of the order to W. Chaloner, sheriff of Newport County, is in RHi.)

The trials are carefully covered in Samuel W. Bryant, "Rhode Island Justice—1772 Vintage," *R.I. Hist.* 26 (1967): 65–71. The court records that Bryant cites as then in the Kent County Courthouse have since been moved to the Supreme Court Vault in Providence.

## Petition to the Rhode Island General Assembly

Colony Rhode Island ss.                                    [Before 20 Aug. 1772]

To the Honble the General Assembly of said Colony sitting at Newport within and for the Colony aforesaid the Third Monday in August A D 1772.

John Greene and Company, Griffin Greene all of Coventry and Nathanael Greene and Company[1] humbly shew That on the Night of the Seventeenth Instant the Buildings of the forge in said Coventry and to them belonging were intirely consumed by Fire.[2] The Loss is so great that they cannot repair it without Assistance; Especially some of your Petitioners are considerably indebted, have increasing Famalies to maintain, and by this Misfortune are deprived of their principle Dependence. Altho your Petitioners are the immediate Sufferers by this unhappy Accident, yet many other People must consequentially share in the Calamity; For a considerable part of the Country adjacent was employed by means of said forge. The Colony in general, they humbly conceive, may be remotely affected thereby, for one material and expensive Article for Shipping has been furnished by said Works, And the Anchor Works which still remain will be, in a great Measure, useless should not the forge be repaired. They come therefore to your Honors, in humble Confidence that the same benevolent Disposition which has ever distinguished the General Assembly of the Colony of Rhode Island, for Humanity and Compassion towards the distressed, will on this occasion incite you to afford Relief. They pray your Honors to grant them a Lottery[3] to raise the sum of Twenty Five hundred Dollars under the Direction of William Greene, Christopher Greene and Charles Holden with the usual prerequisites of giving Bond for the faithful Discharge of said Trust, and as in Duty bound, will ever pray.[4]

JOHN GREENE & CO
GRIFFIN GREENE
NATHANAEL GREENE & CO

DS (R-Ar).
  1. This represented NG and his brothers.
  2. For NG's brief reaction to the fire, see his letter below to Samuel Ward, Jr., 29 Aug.
  3. After lotteries were legalized in Rhode Island in 1744 (Bartlett, *Records*, 5: 100), the legislature was regularly asked to approve them for a variety of public or quasi-public ventures, from the building or rebuilding of bridges, churches, and ships down to the relief of an imprisoned debtor. If an individual's loss affected the community, the legislature was generally compliant. In the absence of insurance, a lottery was a way of spreading a loss over many individuals. To ensure fairness in its operation the legislature required a bond (see document below, 27 Aug.).
  4. On 20 Aug. both houses noted their approval on the back of the petition. The lottery was not altogether successful. In May 1774 cousin Griffin Greene reported that although part of the money had been raised, "the greatness of the plan, hath proved an insurmoutable obstacle to its further progress." NG and brothers, he said, were willing to relinquish their interest, but he, being a "great sufferer," stood in need of a further lottery. His petition was granted (Bartlett, *Records*, 7: 243).

## To William Greene

Coventry [R.I.] August 23, 1772

News of our misfortune in the destruction of the forge doubtless will reach you before this. We have made application to the General Assembly for a lottery, which have obtained a grant of. You, Mr. Christopher Greene, and Charles Holden, are appointed directors. I must entreat you to accept of that trust, lest it should defeat the whole scheme. I am confident the satisfaction of assisting the unfortunate will give you as much pleasure as will balance the trouble and difficulty you'll experience upon the occasion. I urge it more on my uncle and Griffin's account than our own; and had it not been for them we had not adopted this method to recover part of our loss, but the injury was too great for them to recover themselves without the aid and assistance of their friends. The loss is much greater in its consequences to us than it would be in its own nature, for uncle's[1] loss is our loss, for this unhappy affair will put it out of his power to pay us our demands for some time, if ever he gets able. . . . I have had a most severe turn of the phthisic or asthma. I have not slept six hours in four nights, being obliged to sit up the two last nights. I hope you and your family enjoy a better state of health. If ever I felt the benefit of philosophy it has been upon this occasion, for I felt as calm and as contented as old Socrates when condemned unjustly by the Athenians.

Reprinted from Greene, *Greene*, 1: 64–65.
1. The reference is to his father's brother, John (1709–1802).

# Bond

[Warwick, R.I., 27 Aug. 1772]

Know All men by these presence that we Nathaniel Greene of Coventry and Jacob Greene, William Greene Junr:[1] Elihu Greene, Christopher Greene and Perry Greene of Warwick All in the County of Kent in the Colony of Rhode Island &c in Company Merchants are Holden and firmly do stand bound and obliged unto William Greene of Warwick Esqr in the full and just sum of Fifteen Hundred pounds lawful money to be paid unto the said William Greene his Executors Administrators or Assigns The which payment well and Truly to be made we bind ourselves and each of us and our and each of our heirs executors and Administrators jointly and severally firmly by these presents sealed with our seals Dated this Twenty seventh Day of August In the Twelfth year of his present Majesties Reign George the third King over Great Britain &c A D 1772.

The Condition of the above Obligation is such that whereas the General Assembly at their sessions began and held at Newport on the third monday of August A D 1772 did Grant the above said persons and others a lottery in order to contribute seven Hundred and fifty pounds lawful Money Toward rebuilding their Iron works which were consumed by fire on the Night of the seventeenth Instant whereby the said William Greene together with Christopher Greene and Charles Holden is appointed a Director or Maniger of said lottery, Now Know Ye that if the abovesaid persons their Heirs executors or Administrators shall strickly Adhere to and forever Keep harmless and Indemnify the said William Greene his heirs executors and Administrators from all and all manner of dammage that shall or may arise in and about said lottery in either of the Classes to be Compleated in said lottery then the above Obligation to be Void and of

None Effect, otherways to stand and remain in full force and Virtue.
Signed Sealed Delivered In the presence of

C. GREENE

WILLIAM GREENE

BENJ'N GREENE

ELIHU GREENE

NATHANAEL GREENE JR

CHRISTOPHER GREENE

JACOB GREENE[2]

PERRY GREENE

DS (RHi).

1. As will be seen in the signatures, the designation of junior should be at NG, not William.

2. Jacob Greene (1740–1809) was married in 1761 to his cousin Margaret Greene, the sister of Griffin, who was an especially close friend and partner of NG. Jacob was associated all of his life with the family business and took a more active part in public affairs than any of the other brothers (his public role is noted in the introduction). He was also more closely associated with NG than any of the brothers, as is seen in numerous letters printed below.

William (1743–1826) was the only brother not to marry. He too was associated all of his life with the family business. Although he inherited holdings in the Susquehannah Company from his father, it is not known whether he ever visited the land.

Elihue (1746–1827) took over NG's role in managing the Coventry forge when NG went off to war. In 1776 he married Jane Flagg of Boston, the granddaughter of Benjamin Franklin's sister, Jane Mecom. He and Christopher were very close as their sloop, the *Two Brothers*, attested.

Christopher (1748–1830) inherited the homestead at Potowomut where his father and grandfather had lived. In 1774 he married Catharine Ward, daughter of Gov. Samuel Ward; after her death in 1782 he married her younger sister, Deborah. He continued to manage the forge and mills at Potowomut until he was an old man. During the battle of Rhode Island in 1778, he served in the R.I. militia.

Perry was born in 1749, but his death is not recorded. From the age of four, he was raised by a stepmother. NG thought him a wild young man and a ne'er-do-well (see below, NG to Christopher Greene, 29 Jan. 1776), although Perry was said to be his favorite. Perry's son, Albert C. Greene, was a celebrated lawyer, serving nineteen years as attorney general of Rhode Island.

## To Samuel Ward, Jr.

Spell Hall [Coventry, R.I.]

Dear friend                                           Sunday August 29, 1772

Time is precious and I am drove to the Necessity to neglect the Duties of Friendship or discharge them on this Day of the Week. Therefore I hope youl excuse me, and Especially when I inform you it is very Early in the morning. Day stands tiptoe and the rays of the Sun begins to guild the tops of the Highest Hills and Tallest trees.

Your Letter reacht me the Morning after the Destruction of the Forge.[2] I sat upon the remains of one of the old Shafts and read it. I was surrounded with Gloomy Faices, piles of Timber still in Flames,

Heaps of Bricks dasht to pieces, Baskets of Coal reducd to ashes. Everything seemd to appear in Ruins and Confusion. I read over your Letter once or twice before I could satisfy myself whether the surprise I felt was the Effects of the loss or from the contents of the Letter. But upon a more Strict enquiry and closer attention I found it to originate from your Letter. If you was surprisd ⟨at mine⟩ I was still more so at yours. A persons remorse for doing wrong is generally in propotion to the consequence and oppinion we have of the person to whom the injury is done, and the agitation that a mind feels from reflection gives it a keen attention, and prepares it in the most Effectual manner for receiving the deepest impression. Tho I was not Conscious of writing anything in my Letter that had the least Shadow of reproach, Yet I could not help feeling mortified that I had wrote with so much obscurity and Ambiguity as to leave your mind in doubt. I indeavour'd to recollect what I wrote. But the confusion without and the tumult within prevented my remembering one Sentence, and your Letter must have remained a secret to me to this Day had not brother Kitt explain'd the Mistery. I ask't him if he saw my Letter. He told [me] he did and read it, and told me you mistook the meaning.[3] What, my Dear friend, could give your mind such a twist. Did you ever discover in me a coldness? Did I not always ⟨meet⟩ you with a Chearful and a friendly Face? Did I ever give you any Reason to suspect me to be a Hypocrite? How then could you think I could suffer such ungenerous thoughts to harbour in my Boosom and not acquaint you with them by pointing out the Time, place and manner how it is, was done. I am not of a suspicious make. It is no difficult matter for one whom I profess an Esteem for to practice such an imposition upon me: for I am a stranger to distrust where I engage in friendship, for that Chills Benevolence and quenches the Virtuous Flame. I had much rather sometimes be impos'd upon by those who are base enough to betray such a confidence than always Live in perpetual Jealousy. If my Heart is capable of Love or my Soul of Friendship, I feel it for you.

There is not one amongst all my friends whose sincerity I have less Reason to call in question than that of yours. I must be guilty of ingratitude to reproach you, and a Stranger to generous feelings to harbour mistrust where I have had so many Instances of candour and ingenuity. Indeed, my Dear friend, [I] have not doubted, I will not doubt, I cannot doubt, I know your Soul was much above such low art as [the Hea]vens is higher than the Earth. If ever such a thought ⟨hovered⟩ in the immagination it was a Stranger to the ⟨Climate⟩. I have never found my mind tainted with its Baneful influence, nor the Ardor of friendship damped by suspicions of Infidelity. I know there has been a contest in my Boosom between the Exorbitant passions, and the superior faculties of the Soul. My Breast has been like a Theater of Strife and a field of Battle where Reason and Passion contends with Various successes of power and Victory. I am at Variance with my Self and am continually distracted and torn with Civil feuds of my own disturbed immagination.[4] If ever anything so ungenerous stole into the Mind it must have been in one of those unhappy moments, and Vanisht at the approach of cool reflection like a mist before the Sun; for upon the Strictest examination I cannot find any such Sentiments rooted in the Heart or lurking in or about the Soul. I esteem you too much and Value your friendship too high to trifle with you in that sort. ⟨Not all⟩ the Cruelty of Tyrants, the sublety and Craft of secret Enemies, or the malice of Devils, shall ever disunite our Minds if you continue to merit my future regard as you have done heretofore. I feel the Celestial flame to warm my Heart and Cheer my Soul. To Love without a Reason is as absurd as it is ridiculous to resent without a Cause. Your Notions are exactly agreeable to mine. Plainness and Sympathy of Manners, stript of all the paint and ornament of policy, is what I ever admird. It wins the Affections by the force of its persuasion and Charms the understanding by the reasonableness of its precepts.

If you would know any mans affections towards you consult his Behavior; that is the best Evidence of a Virtuous Mind. Though a persons professions be ever so Voluminous and his Zeal ever so noisy, yet he is not entitld to our Esteem, but only Civility; for professions is but the Shadow of friendship, and saying is not proving . If a Person would be considered in the Character of a Friend, let it appear by generous and friendly Offices; for that is the only testimony upon which we may safely ground our Esteem. If [a man] professes friendship one Day and proves himself an [enemy] the next, why should I give Credit to one who so Effectually contradicts himself. Why should we trust any mans professions before he has prov'd them to be sincere by Noble and generous Actions. It is not always the consequences of a Benefit bestowed or the importance of a favor done that determines our Value of one, or commands our Gratitude for the other. The Value of a favor is not measured when Sentiments of Kindness are perceivd, then a matter frivilous in itself becomes important because it serves to bring to Light the Charector and intention of the benefactor. Numerous are the Instances of this kind which I have experien[c]d from you in the course of our Connexion, and tho they escap'd your Notice from the overflowing of Kindness yet they made a deep impression upon my mind, and have endeard your person to me for Ever, so that nothing "but insult and wrong, shall ever Efface its delightful form."

As the mind is not at Liberty to Love or admire without a Cause, so it never ought to take Offence without a Reason. Insult and intentional wrong are the only injuries that can justly excite our resentment and his that tamely submits to them when offerd wants penetration to discover the imposition or lacks Courage to punnish the offender. Heaven forbid that I should ever have Reason to resent any part of your conduct. Though I Love you as a second self, yet would I sooner sacrifice all the Social Joys and endearing ties than consent to submit to insult and imposition.

How could you think I wanted you to lessen your Esteem for your patron.[5] By what means could I expect to bind you to me that you was not bound to him. If you could so soon forget such numerous kind offices as he rendered you in leading you through all the difficult paths of Science, I say if you could so soon forget Such obligations, and it was possible for me to rival him in your Affections, Must not that have convincd me I had no better fate to expect from a temper so fickle and a Mind so ungrateful. I am not that persons Enemy. Nay I Love and Esteem him and will always be his friend unless I have greater Reason to alter my Sentiments than I ever have had. What part of his conduct can I complain of. It is true we generally hold a Rival in a disagreeable point of Light because we apprehend they use every argument in thier Power to supplant us. Who has been the aggressor in the present Case, his Connexions more prior to mine, and if they were particular, he has had much Reason to complain of me than I of him. I am not Jealous of your regard for him. I will not harbour such a mischeveous and Vile Miscreant. It is one of the worst of plagues and often productive of the greatest Evils that attends Mankind. We may be upon our guard against all other Calamities. But here the enemy is within us, and admited at all times to the innermost recesses of the Soul where he acts the part of a false and treacherous friend, betrays under the pretence of Serving of us, [and] Administers pison in Cups of seeming Nectar [and] Ambrosia. I thank God I am not of a Jealous Make. I would not be tormented with such an evil, not for the Mines of Peru.

I have seriously considered of the connexions between me and your Sister,[6] the way it began and the manner it has been carried on, and if I was to consult my pride instead of my Reason, perhaps I might think I had a sufficient Cause to Lay a foundation for resentment. It is the oppinion of many that a rejection is sufficient for resentment, and I believe it is somewhat Natural to man to take ⟨offence⟩ at being repulseed, and it too commonly happens when People are disappointed of those objects which they most admire, that their Love and Esteem is turned into hate and Envy. Tho I think for my part these principles are bad, The Reasons that are offerd in support of them are that the Person that rejects an offer must do it from feeling a certain superiority in themselves, and where a person think himself their equal, that piques his pride and consequently excites his resentment. This might be just if every person was under an Obligation from anothers signifying their regarde to make an equal return, whether they meritd our Esteem or not. It is true we cannot help haveing some regard for an object that has a Veneration for us. Yet we are under no obligation from their esteem to injure our own happiness to promote theirs. The Choice of Companions for Life are to[o] Delicate for Reason to regulate all the opperations of the mind. Fancy will have her Voice. Therefore as our Choice or refuse [refusal?] are greatly dependant upon the internal Operations of the Mind, I can see no Reason why a Person should resent a Young Ladies refusing to enter into a Connexion with him when she is conscious it will win her own happiness and not promote his. This way of thinking comes from the prejudices of Education. Our Minds as well as Bodies are easily distorted and put out of their Natural frame. Absurdity is to be Learned and good Natural faculties may be improvd into foolish Opinions. For my own part I think a Virtuous mind and an amiable form is to be admird whether we meet with an equal return or not. Yet I think it impossible to feel for any Length of time all the endearing ties where our affections are not mutual, as where they are. But if I was to determin this point from the opperations of my own mind I should give it against the general principles.

It is your advice to stop our Correspondence.[7] What can I say to it? If you was to see her last Letter perhaps youd be of a different oppinion. To stop the Correspondence is to loos her for Ever; to continue it is to overwhelm myself with agreeable Distress and pleasant pains. Cease to expect, says Reason, and no longer flatter thy hopes with things imposible.

Kitt was charmd with his Visit at Westerly.[8] Poets tell us that Midas changed everything which he touched into Gold; and that Medusa's head, everyone who saw it, into stone. Your family seems to have an equal influence to change hard substances into the most soft and penetrable matter. They inspire the mind with a secret Charm and gently instill into the Boosom the Tender passions of Love and Affection. Heaven has Blest your Family with every Virtue and good Quallity necessary for your own happiness. I wish you may ever possess a becoming Zeal for the Glory of God which will be best manifested by diffusing happiness amongst his Creatures.

Poor Hannah that excellent Girl. Her state of probation is a test for the tryal of ⟨an⟩ Angles Virtue and patience. My Soul weeps for her. To be afflicted with the afflicted is an instance of humanity and the demand of good nature and good breeding. There is a Gloomy pleasure in being dejected and inconsolable. Melancholy studies how to improve itself and sorrow finds great relief in being still more sorrowful. My Sister, how hard does it seem to us short Sighted mortals that so much Virtue and innocence does not Entitle you to an exemption from pain and disquiet, the proper rewards of Vice and folly. O Sammy, She is a Christian without gloominess. She is Chearful, but free from Levity. She is a pattern well worth our immation [i.e., imitation].

I hope you profit by her Example. I expect one Day or other to see you a good and great Man, Diffusing Joy through the Hearts of your friends and showering Blessings on the Children of misfortune. I am sorry to hear you are got very uneasy about what manner of Business you shall enter into for Life. Be not too precipitate. You have Youth on your side. Reign in your ambition. Remember the race was not [to] the swift, nor the Battle to the Strong. Wait with patience but neglect no promising prospect. Trust not your happiness in the hands of Fortune. She often defeats us in the midst of our most sanguine expectation. Perhaps it is necessary that the most guiltless Lives Should ⟨be chequerd with⟩ Evils and Disappointments les[t] an ⟨intemperate⟩ flux of delights tempt us to stay in a World which is by no means worthy of immortallity.

Nancy writes me your Daddy is tormented with them confounded Noyses,[9] and that party Rage and implacable envy had had a large share on the determination of his cause. I am sorry to hear that the age is so depravd and the times so Corrupt that Justice and Equity cant Breath in the Land. But with regard to the peoples spight against your Daddy, I dare say heel despise the disrespect of those who, through ignorance of his worth, give him such ill usage. Hees a philosopher at Heart and will learn to overcome affliction by the hopes of geting out of it; that is, a way be to[o] hard for ill fortune itself. I wish him and all his Family all possible happiness here and never ending Joy in the paradise of God.

I shall be very glad to see your face in Coventry where I shall be confind in rebuilding the Works for some months. I am not very well in Health. I have had a fit of the phthisick,[10] lasted me four Nights during which time I did not ⟨sleep. Six hours⟩. ⟨This produced an⟩ inflamation in one ⟨of my⟩ Eyes but I am better.

N G

ALS (RHi). Original damaged; portions in angle brackets have been supplied from a late nineteenth-century transcript made before the original had deteriorated (MWA).

1. Spell Hall was his house in Coventry.
2. Letter not found. On the fire at the forge, see above, petition to Assembly, before 20 Aug.
3. NG's controversial letter has not been found.
4. No external events have come to light that would explain his disturbed mind.

From the tenor of the letter, it might well be that the "Exorbitant passions" that were contesting with the "superior faculties of the Soul" were his intense feelings toward a fifteen-year-old boy which were considered unnatural for a man of thirty.

5. Undoubtedly refers to Thomas Arnold who had tutored Sammy. (See note 3, NG to Sammy, 5 Mar. 1771, above.)

6. Nancy (Anna) Ward.

7. No letters between NG and Nancy have survived.

8. Brother Christopher was probably courting Sammy's sister Catharine, whom he married the following year.

9. The reference is to Joseph and Sanford Noyes, who had a long-standing feud with Samuel Ward over land (Monahon and Collins, "Letters to Ward," *R.I. Hist.* 15 [1956]: 51n).

10. A difficulty in breathing, which he sometimes refers to as asthma.

## To Samuel Ward, Jr.

Spell Hall [Coventry, R.I., after Aug. 29, 1772?]

If Coventry ever was tollerable, it has now become insupportable. Nature was very spareing of her gifts in the first formation of the Globe unless they be conceald in the Bowels of the Earth, which possibly may be the Case, for the Face of Nature seems to ware such a Ghastly Countenance, as if her Bowels was tortur'd with the most Excruciating pains, and Labourd to be deliverd of some Valuable Treasure. If ever this should happen I hope to be a Sharer, for I am sure I have sufferd enough to entitle me to a right. The Trees looks as surly, the Bushes as Sour, and the Shrubs as Cross, If I happen to put my head out of Doors at any time, as if I had been thier sworn Enimy, what particular spight they can have against me, I cant immaging. If they knew my pacifick disposition, I am sure they could not apprehend any injury. I am determind to Court thier favour and to effect a reconciliation if possible for I like to Live in good fellowship, and more especially with things that appear so pregnant with mischief. This is agreeable to the Hottentot plan, who Worship the Devil rather than the Deity, for one, they say, is good and will do them no harm, the other must be prevented by kind and Courtly usage. I have but one respectful Tree on my plantation, that is a Certain reverend old Oak which has a peculiar Modesty at all Times, and seems to be sensible of its condition, for when at any time he happens to be robb'd of his bushy Perriwig or Brawny Branches, how disconsolate and ashameed I have seen it appear. I Love this old oak for its Modesty and Diffidence. He has not half the Effrontery and Confidence of some of our little upstart pragmatical Shrubs that will stand and make mouths at one as they pass along, by the half hour together, and yet The old Tree is of more Value than a thousand of them. Here stop and rest a moment for I dare say you are Heartily tird, and I am sure I am Heartily Sick of such disagreeable Ideas.

Man for all his noble Nature and Dignifyed Reason is as Variable in his notions and feelings as any Creature perhaps in the Creation, hees perpetually falling out with himself and sustains three or four opposite Charactors every Day he lives, nay very often he acts over these Charactors ten Times in a Day, and is Chearful and Angry, pleased and despairing, all in the space of half an hour. In one of these fits I fell foul of poor Coventry, and have sufficiently gratified my Ill Nature and now feeling a little better humourd, I propose a new subject and that Shall be Friendship, if you please.

The excellence [essence?] of friendship is faithfulness. The Affections of the human Soul is not Copious enough to enter into a Close connexion with many Persons. Our Sentiments are so Various, Our Interest so Opposite and our Vieus, ends and designs so different that we can scarcly go hand and Glove for one Day. I should be glad to Live in good fellowship with all mankind. But here I think myself at Liberty either to interest myself or not, just as my particular Circumstance may require. But it is not so in friendship, for there seems to be but one Soul occupying Two Bodies, and we are so deeply Interested in Each others Happiness that one cannot be afflicted without the others feeling a Sensible pain, and where ever we are reduced to the Necessity of opposing our friends happiness from some prior Connexions or particular Circumstances, it damps the ardor of our friendship and Chills the Noble passion for Benevolence. But! O how must that Mind feel that finds his Boosoom friend and Brother in Soul reduced to the disagreeable Necessity of disappointing him in a matter that his happiness ultimately depends upon. Think then how I felt the other Day when you exprest the difficulty you found in dischargeing your Duty, and maintaining an equal balance between your friends. I think you have too Noble a Soul to basely prostitute that confindence reposd in the most refined Delicasies of friendship, and therefore have no doubt but that youl faithfully discharge your Duty with honour and trust according as you stand related to the objects. I have never yet Vouchsaft to solicit one Person (that I remember) to Interest themselves in my favour in my addresses to your Sister [Nancy], and altho I should esteem such a connexion the greatest Blessing that could attend me here, I should sooner suffer my Heart to burst than adopt such an expedient. But was I disposd, or should I ever be, to increase my Interest by a third person, you would be one of the first to whom I should apply myself. The Choice of our friends is one of the most interesting points in Life, and nothing requires more deliberation and circumspection than that of choosing a boosom friend. If we are forward [i.e., on the verge] of contracting an Intimacy Let our Judgment first examin with whom. There are fatal consequences attending a Rash connexion as well as ⟨real⟩ advantages in a well grounded Union. Tis not he ⟨who⟩

makes the highest professions or greatest promises that is to be the soonest trusted, for let us consider betimes, before we are ensnared or Seduced, that there are more Companions in the World than good ones.

I hope if you are convinc'd of my Love and regard for you, it hath been rather from my actions than from my professions. If youl please to reflect back and examin my conduct through every stage since our Connexion first commenceed, youl find I have been rather Backward than forward of contracting too great an Intimacy before we both had time and opportunity to examin each others Dispositions and Tempers which is absolutely necessary to lay a lasting foundation for friendship. I thought I discoverd some very valuable quallities in you, Altho you was very young, that first created in me a desire to Contract an acquaintance. As I was the Eldest I thought it my business to make the first Overtures which accordingly I did. And finding from acquaintance you answerd my expectations I gradually increas'd the freedom, untill time and intimacy formd a reall Affection and fix't a Settled habit of friendship Which I hope may continue through all the Vicissitudes of imperfect Life, and that we may be supporters to each other in our prosperities, safeguards in our difficulties, councillors in our Doubts, and comforters in adversities and that youl regard me as I do you. Then I shall be happy in your friendship, and it would hurt me very much if I did not think you did. It is late and am sleepy, therefore Ill conclude with wishing you a good Night and many happy Days. ⟨

N. GREENE JR

P S I have wrote to Nancy offering to stop the Correspondence [if] she thinks it most for her happiness. But I cant help ⟨wishing⟩ a continuance, and yet I dont if we must part for Ever.[1]

ALS (RHi). Portions in angle brackets from a nineteenth-century transcript (MWA).
1. Notes 6 and 7, NG to Sammy, 29 Aug., above, refer to the same subject.

## To [Samuel Ward, Jr.]

Dear Friend          Spell Hall [Coventry, R.I.] October 9th 1772
A person must have an uncommon Genius to write a panegyrick upon a Barren Letter. He must possess a surprising penetration to discover Beauties where they dont exist. Was I not acquainted with you I should immagin from the Language of your Letters, that you was a French Courtier Educated at Paris in the Art of Compliment. Surely you cannot mean to Flatter my Vanity and its Obvious my

Letters are undeserving your praise. I hope you are too Generous to impose upon your friend, was I weak enough to to give you an Opportunity. Where then is the defect, in point of Judgment or Sincerity? I have no reason to think its the former and very little the latter. I know its common for us to be partial to our Friends. We often over rate their Actions; that which is but an indifferent act in another, appears glorious and important in them. We may be prejudiced as well for as against a thing; and this prejudice is often so secret and subtle in its opperations that the Mind receives an insensible bias without perceiving its Influence. Perhaps my Dear friend this might be the case with you when you wrote your two last Letters,[1] for they seemd to Breath an uncommon Spirit of Friendship, altho the Language appear'd to border upon Flattery. I wish it was in my Power to write you anything that might please and improve you. I hope one Day to see you shine like a Star of the first Magnitude, all glorious both Evening and morning.

I lament the want of a liberal Education; I feel the mist [of] Ignorance to surround me, for my own part I was Educated a Quaker, and amongst the most Supersticious sort, and that of its self is a sufficient Obstacle to cramp the best of Geniuses; much more mine.[2] This constrained manner of Educating their Youth, has prov'd a fine Nursery of Ignorance and Supersticon, instead of piety; and has laid a foundation for Form instead of Worship. It was not the original intention of the Friends to prevent the propagation of useful Literature in the Church, but only to prohibit their Youth from reading such Books as tended to make them Fools by industry; and in the midst of an appearing profusion of Knowledge to want common Sense. They consider'd Youth as the great Opportunity of Life, which Settles and fixes most men either in a good or bad course; and that the imprissions then made were commonly the most durable, especially those which are bad. Youth is most certainly a time of Innocence when we have horror for Vice; which we never commit at first without doing Violence to our Nature. How our Souls Startles when we attempt to perpetrate a Crime prohibited by Laws both Human and Divine. I can well remember when I first began to make excursions into the Field of Eniquity. O: what conflicts have I felt in my Boosom between Virtue and Vice. If I were to Judge from the opperations of my own Mind with regard to the Innocence of Youth, I should think that the first and most Natural thoughts of Men were to be honest and Just.

These were the Sentiments of the first founders of our Society, and as that was an Age wherein Priest Craft prevaild, the most useful Branches of Literature was much neglected. For it was the Interest of the Order to Cultivate the Youthful Minds to be subservient to their After purposes. This they could not do without locking up all the

Avenues and passages to Wisdom so that their Scholars had neither the Reason of Philosophers or the Affibillity of Gentlemen. It was no difficult matter to Educate their Youth in this sort seeing they had the entire direction of the Seminaries of Learning. Therefore their pupils came out of the Universaties, with a Starchness of behaviour, Sourness of looks, and full of Starved conceits, which made them haughty and imperious in their conduct. This false zeal and ill breeding, under the Affectation of Learning, was what first disgusted our Society with Literature. For when they contrasted the Learned with the Laity, they observd an easiness of Address, softness of Speech and a freedom of thought in one; and nothing but Pedantry and Magisterial Grimace in the other: and as they found the Learned neither wiser nor better Men, than the Laity. The friends concluded that a Liberal Education was rather prejudicial than Beneficial to Society. Not rightly discovering where the Evil lay, they argued from the abuse to the disuse of the thing.

These were the reasons why the Quakers cry'd down Literate [i.e., literature]; it was not the most useful parts thereof, but only Vain Philosophy; and such Metaphisical distinctions as rather confounded than improvd the understanding. They lookt upon plainness and Symplicity as inseperable marks of Truth, and that Religion good Sense and humanity was a far better Ornament to a man; than such a Stock of Philosophy, that only perplext and confounded him in a maze of improvisd Nonsense and Absurdity, which only Servd to fortify and make him impregnable against Common Sense. These were the Sentiments of our fore Fathers with regard to Human learning, it was their intention only to lop off the dead Branches of Literature, as being altogether superfluous and useless. But Supersticion and Ignorance increas'd in to the decay of Learning; and in the Country Churches they soon confounded the useful with the useless Branches of Literature, prohibiting the reading of all Books except the Holy Scriptures, Barckleys Apology, Fox Journal[3] and a few others of the same tennor and date.

This my Dear friend was the foundation of my Education; and I believe youl agree with me, it requires an uncommon Natural Genius or a very free conversation, to get the better of such a constrained and corrupt Education: Nature with held the former from me and Fortune the latter, so that I remain without the Verge of Science, like Moses of old I can behold the Beauties of Canaan but Jordan prevents my entrance. My Father was a Man of Industry and brought up his Children to Business. Early very early when I should have been in the pursuit of Knowledge, I was diging into the Bowels of the Earth after wealth,[4] so that had Nature given me a Genius fit to cultivate an Acquaintance with the polite Arts, I have not had opportunity for such an Acquisition. Besides there was no one to inspire me with Noble and generous Sentiments equally fit for Dominion or subjection. My Father was a man [of] great Piety, had an excellent understanding; and was govern'd in his conduct by Humanity and kind Benevolence. But his mind was over shadow'd with prejudices against Literary Accomplishments. Notwithstanding all these Obstructions I have Read a few Books, but they have rather amus'd than improvd me. After this explanation I hope youl [be] less liberal of your praise for praise unmerited is nothing but Ridicule in disguise. You are not indebted to me for any part of that manly dignity which you display. Your indebted to Nature for your Genius to your Father for an opportunity to Cultivate that Genius, to Mr. Maning for Inspireing you with Noble and Elevated Sentiments to Mr [Thomas] Arnold for holding A Lamp to direct your Steps through the Difficult paths of Science. If I deserve your praise it is for the steadiness of my Friendship for there is no one that Loves you with a more Cordial Affection.

I should be sorry that Mr Varnum through blindness or prejudice should give his Enemies an opportunity to reproach him justly. I should think my self happy if I could open or let in any new rays of understanding that might discover his folly; for I love and esteem the man. But I should be sorry to disoblige him where I cannot serve him. Who ever goes about to reform the World undertakes an Office Obnoxious to malice and often beset with great difficulties. It speaks a confidence of our own Capacity, that prompts us to set up for the School Master of mankind and it infers a charge of Corruption or Ignorance in the Object out of which we mean to lead or whip them. Every man has a good conceit of him self and his own merit. He thinks him self under valued by instruction and is provoked by correction. The confession of our weakness and that of anothers better sense is generally both contained in that of takeing Advice, which is seldom taken for that reason. How my Dear Friend could you think me a suitable Person to correct the errors in a man of such exalted Talents as Mr Varnum posseses?

I have lately had a Visit from the once Celebrated Susa Harris. She enjoys but a poor state of Health. She appears like a Gaudy flour nipt by the pinching Frost. I fancy she is not long for this World. Tho she flies swiftly on the Wings of wild desire after "Matrimony"

How Rich how Valued once avails the[e] not
To whom related or by whom begot
A heap of Dust alone remains of thee
Tis all thou art and all the proud shall be.[5]

There has been a Famous Preacher[6] at Greenwich; he is a Gentleman of Elevated Faculties, a fine Speaker, and appears by his Language to be a Lover of Mankind. I refer you to the Boys for further particulars for they wont wait a moment longer. Distribute my Love where due. Amen.

NG

I wrote this after the Boys set out upon the Road. I trust to your generosity for incorrectness.

ALS (RHi).
1. Letters not found.
2. Among contemporary documents, this letter tells us most of what we know about NG's education. He was tutored by Adam Maxwell (see above, note 5, memorial, 7 Feb. 1770), but for how long we do not know. Maxwell taught him a little Latin and tutored him in geometry. NG's brother Christopher remembered his studying in a small room above the kitchen (Greene, *Greene*, 1: 13), and from his later familiarity with geometric problems, we can assume he was a diligent scholar of Euclid. The family members also tell of his reading books while operating the grist mill. One thing is certain: he read a great many books of which his Quaker father did not approve, and he read them wherever and whenever an opportunity presented itself. He also sought out men who had had a college education, such as Sammy Ward, Thomas Arnold, James M. Varnum, and Pres. James Manning and Prof. David Howell of Rhode Island College (see index references). His letters to Sammy Ward, as discussed in source note at NG to Sammy, 24 Sept. 1770, above, were a part of his education.
3. Robert Barclay, a Scot, wrote an English version of his *An Apology for the True Christian Divinity as . . . Preached by the People Called, in Scorn, Quakers* in 1678. The *Journal* of George Fox, the founder of the Society of Friends, was published in 1694, shortly after his death.
4. He could be referring to digging coal or bog iron ore, both of which his father used in the forge.
5. The quatrain is from Pope's "Elegy to the Memory of an Unfortunate Lady." The last three lines are quoted correctly; the first should read "How lov'd, how honored once, avails thee not."
6. The Rev. John Murray, the founder of Universalism in America (see note, Varnum to Murray, 24 May 1775, below).

## To [Thomas] Aldridge [Aldrich]?[1]

Friend Aldrige                    Coventry [R.I.] January 12, 1773

The town of Coventry has ordered me to make the best defence against your suit brought against Wood that I can, and to spare no pains nor expence. I wrote to the Town meeting, as I told you I would, since which I have been to Newport and never heard their resolution till today. I therefore take the earliest opportunity to acquaint you of their intentions lest you should blame me of holding the matter in suspence to your prejudice. They say the interest is the towns in Justice if you recover it. How that matter is, will appear from the complexion of things in the prosecution of the suit. You go fourth to battle armd with solemn instruments, executed by the hands of Lawful Authority. We shall appear clad in honesty and innocence. How far that will stand us in stead in the day of tryal, remains to be provd. The Race is not [to] the swift nor the battle to the strong. Happily there may be some way found out for our escape, altho we seem to be hemd in with a circle of pompous and parading instruments. As for my own part I feel no inclination to sacrifice the interest of the town nor do injustice to you. I therefore shall make an honest defence such as the Case will justify, and therein I hope to walk blameless between you and the town, observing a just medium between the extremes, that one may not tax me with neglect nor the other with injustice. People has taken a great freedom with your reputation in this affair, but truth dont always run with the vulgar cry. Yet the sound very seldom continues long without strong suspicions to support it. Your deed being in the hands of the Grantor gives great room for suspecting the validity. But men that are honest to each other dont always guard in the transactions of their private concerns against the view of the Publick Eye.

N. GREENE

ALS (RHi).
1. This letter is shrouded in mystery. It may have been to Thomas Aldrich, who built the East Greenwich Courthouse in partnership with the future governor, William Greene, but the Coventry town records make no mention of the case. Although G. W. Greene says that NG owned "Jacob's Law Dictionary" and "four beautiful quartos of Blackstone from the Oxford Press" (Greene, *Greene*, 1:25, 56), this letter is the only evidence that he ever represented a "client." James M. Varnum continued to represent him and his brothers in court.

## To [Samuel Ward, Jr.]

Dr Friend          Sunday Morning Coventry [R.I.] January 25, 1773
    I Receivd your Kind Letter by your Aunt Greene[1] and your agreeable Essay by Brother Kitt and am sorry I am obligd to make an apology for not Answering them sooner; I intend Writeing you by your Aunt but she was gone before I knew it. Kitt went a Week sooner than I expected. I thought I would not miss an Opportunity so favourable as that of writeing by your Father. I spent the Evening with him, Mr Merchant[2] and sundry other Gentlemen, at your Uncle [William] Greens, and intended to have Wrote in the Morning, and returnd to Greenwich for that purpose; But he past my Lodgings just as I got up, By which means I have been deprivd of any opportunity till the present. One Truth I can assure, it was not for want of Affection. I love and Esteem you as I ever did. So remote and hidden are the motives of our actions even amongst the most Intimate Friends, that its necessary for us to possess the most Charitable Disposition towards them and their conduct through Life, otherwise we shall often injure them by Evil suspicions and groundless jealosies. We ought to Keep our Eye Single in viewing [each] others Actions and

weigh them in the Scales of Friendship with that Allowance that Human Nature in its imperfect state requires. Friendship being a strong and Habitual Inclination in Two Persons to promote each others Happiness, We are Naturally led to discharge all the important Duties with mutual Goodwill, and when any Accidents or Occurrences happens that begets mistrust they will Loos their very Name in the Channel of Friendship, as small Brooks do theirs when they fall into Larger Rivers. But there are many Professors of Friendship who appear Like a well Drawn Picture to resemble its Original but wants that warmth and Vital Heat that Constitutes the finer feelings of the Soul. It is somewhat unhappy where we have made Choice of such a Friend, and no less difficult to maintain a good understanding, for they Judge by events, and not by Intentions. But I hope you and I act upon different Principles towards each Other, and that our Profession and Sincerity go hand in hand. I thank you for your Invitation to Ward Hall, But I should be guilty of imprudence, and unjust to my self to accept it at this Time.[3] It would give me a particular Pleasure to see you Here, and I can say with Pope "come to Coventry and Enjoy over a Generous Bowl, the feast of Reason and the flow of Soul." The Sound of the Hamer is once more heard in our Land,[4] the Forge is now compleat, Long and tedious has been the Business, and has been rendered much more so for want of good and faithful Hands; altho we had some that deservd that Charactor yet we had many that were like Old ⟨Coats⟩ Dog that Shund Chores and watcht meals. I am glad to hear your good Oppinion increases upon a further Acquaintance with Kitt. I wish he may prove the Happy Link to Unite the two Families by the ties of Interest as well as Social regard.[5] Kitt informs that Hannah thinks me guilty of unkindness and wanting in Friendship; I am sorry She should indulge a thought so unjust and Injurious to my Intentions. I am sure if I know my Own Soul, Thers not a Friend on Earth thats more Affectionate towards her than I am, and I am, and I believe neither distance of Time or Place will ever alter my regards. Remember me to Her with that Cordial Affection that my Soul feels from a review of our past Intercourse.

Kitt Sail'd last Sunday for Virgina, his last Charge after being under Sail was to be Frugal, Industrious, and to get Money if Possible. Brother Will inculcates that Doctrine as much as if it was his Creed. Welcome and Patience[6] are just upon the Brink of Matrimony. I hope to see you at Greenwich when that Event happens. I was yesterday at Providence and saw Mr Harris and heard of Mr [Thomas] Arnold both of which are Well. Judge [Stephen] Hopkins inform'd me that the new Fangled Court at Newport was adjournd to May, and that One of the Gaspees People had sworn against me as being concernd in the Destruction of Her.[7] This absurd Practice of offering Large rewards, will have pernicious Effects and be sensibly felt by many. The Temptation to Perjury is so Powerful that the People cannot easily resist it Tho the Law has Ordaind that Oaths shall be administered with great Solemnity and accompanied with every Circumstance that tends to Inspire the Mind with Religious Reverence or Superstitious Awe. Yet these Impressions are not strong enough to bind ⟨People⟩ of Abandond Principles to a Strict Observance of Truth. The Institution of this Court when taken in the obvious View of all its consequences is Justly Alarming to every Virtuous Mind and Lover of Liberty in America. There appears such a universal declension of Publick and Private Virtue throughout the Nation, that I fear the ⟨Priviledges⟩ and Liberties of the People will be trampled to Death by the Prerogatives of the Crown; Our General Assembly seems to have lost all that Spirit of Independence and Publick Virtue that has ever distinguisht them since their first being Incorporated, and sunk down into ⟨a tame submission and intire acquiescence to Ministerial Mandates.⟩

What will be the Issue of this Affair God only Know. I expect Our General Assembly will be Stigmatisd as a Pusillanimous Crew and betrayers of the Peoples Liberties not only those within our own Jurisdiction but even all America, for if this Court and mode of Tryal is establisht into a Precedent it will naturally Affect all the other Colonies. If this Fellow should continue his Accusation against me, I shall be call'd to the Bar as a Criminal. Would it not make you Laugh to see the Colonel stand in that Attitude;[8] But I am Happy in haveing Witnesses to Establish my Innocence. Kitt Greene and Cousin Griff Spent that Evening at my House and Mrs Utter an Old Lady Sat up with me till near Twelve OClock. Kitt and Griff staid till 10 O Clock, Mrs Utter saw me go to Bed, and my People saw me get up, and Griff Saw me about Sunrise. We went to Providence together that Morning and as I Live 13 Miles from Providence and 12 from where the Schooner was Burnt it will be Obvious at first Blush his Accusation is false.[9] I should be tempted to let the Sunshine through him if I could come at Him. I am going to Boston to morrow. Wish you was here to go with me. All Friends are well and so am I. Mr Varnum is here a Bed, by whom I write. He and his Wife is comeing to see you. I hear Nancy has had the Long Fever and remains very Low. Wish She may be restord to Health soon. Hannah I hear is Better and Caty has got very Fat; tell Her I will Answer Her Letter at my return from Boston. Remember me to all the Family. I shall always be proud to be reckoned amongst the number of your Friends and am with Esteem yours

[*signature torn*]

PS I hope you can Read it but I doubt it.

AL[S] (RHi). Letter damaged; portions in angle brackets supplied from a nineteenth-century transcript (MWA).

1. Letter not found. The aunt was Catharine Ray Greene.

2. Henry Marchant is identified in note, NG to unidentified person, 20 May 1777, below.

3. He probably refers to breaking off with Sammy's sister, Nancy. See notes 6 and 7, NG to Sammy, 29 Aug. 1772, above.

4. Pope's couplet (from *Imitation of Horace*, Satire I, Book II) reads:
There St. John mingles with my friendly bowl
The feast of reason and the flow of soul.
"The Sound of the Hammer" was a paraphrase of the Song of Solomon's "voice of the turtle," commonly used with respect to construction after a winter lull.

5. Brother Kitt (Christopher) was married to Catharine Ward the following December.

6. Welcome Arnold (1745–98) was an older brother of NG's friend Thomas. Their Quaker father, a farmer and lime manufacturer, sent Thomas to Rhode Island College, but Welcome was self-educated. After establishing himself as an extremely successful merchant in Providence, he entered politics, serving a number of times as speaker of the Assembly. On 11 Feb. 1773 he married Patience Greene, niece of William and Catharine Ray Greene, who like NG's future wife, lived with her aunt and uncle. In NG's last years, he turned to Welcome for financial help. For his life see Franklin S. Coyle, "Welcome Arnold (1745–98), Providence Merchant: The Founder of an Enterprise" (Ph.D. diss., Brown University, 1972).

7. The "new Fangled Court" was the *Gaspee* commission (on the burning of the *Gaspee* see note 1, *Greene* v. *Dudingston*, 20 July 1772, above). When the news of the 9 June incident reached London, the king issued a proclamation offering £1000 for the arrest and conviction of the two leaders and £500 for any others involved. At the same time, a royal commission was named to bring the culprits to justice. It was composed of Gov. Joseph Wanton of R.I., the chief justices of New York, New Jersey, and Massachusetts—Daniel Horsmanden, Frederick Smythe, and Peter Oliver—and the judge of the Admiralty Court at Boston, Robert Auchmuty. After frustrating months of finding no witness who would testify against the leaders, the commission wrote an innocuous final report. (Bartlett, *Records*, 7: 178–82) A recent historian of Rhode Island has written: "The commissioners were all remarkably complacent in the face of Providence people who professed complete ignorance of the event. Prudently the board of inquiry balanced the lassitude of its investigation with almost total apathy in probing the conduct of naval officers in Narragansett Bay." (Sydney V. James, *Colonial Rhode Island*, New York: Charles Scribner's Sons, 1975), p. 314.

Between sessions of the commission, the word went around that perpetrators of the crime would be sent to England for trial. Although it was not the intention of the ministry, the mere appointment of a royal commission gave credence to the rumor. The Virginia House of Burgesses responded to this threat by voting to establish a standing Committee of Correspondence and invited the other colonies to do the same. By midsummer 1773 all of the New England colonies and South Carolina had joined Virginia in establishing such committees. They were the forerunners of the first Continental Congress.

8. NG is obviously referring to himself as the "Colonel." It was a private joke between NG and Sammy, the implications of which are unknown.

9. In telling NG that a witness had implicated him, Judge Hopkins was confused. As seen in note 1, *Greene* v. *Dudingston*, 20 July 1772, above, the witness had identified a "Mr. Greene" who was on the sloop when captured; this would have been NG's cousin Rufus. Because NG and Jacob would have been prime suspects (considering their losses), NG was extremely careful to see that he had witnesses to his being at home on the night the *Gaspee* was burned. Jacob must also have made certain that his noninvolvement was witnessed.

## To Thomas Allen

[From Westerly, R.I.,[1] 20 Feb. 1773. Has arranged with master of a vessel to pick up rum and "to pay the Naval Officer his Perquisit."[2] ALS (MWA) 1 p.]

1. NG was visiting the Ward family; see his letter to Samuel Ward, Jr., 2 Mar., below.
2. Whether this was Lieut. Dudingston's successor is unknown. The "Perquisit" sounds suspiciously like a bribe, which Rhode Islanders had regularly given to customs agents, if not to naval officers. See Lovejoy, *R.I. Politics*, pp. 154–59.

## To Mary Ward[1]

Aunt Greene's [Warwick, R.I., Feb. or Mar. 1773][2]

Here I am Strokeing my head and adjusting my Band, with as much formallity and importance as Doctor Babcock[3] introducies a subject of Science. Matrimony between Miss Patia and Mr Arnold flourishes like a "green Bay Tree."[4] You come within one of haveing a Visit from them, but they turnd their Course to Block Island, and was gone a whole Week almost. They had a Yankee frolick there, Silk and flannel joind, hand in hand, to carry on the Dance. I should laught heartily to have seen Flannel salute Silk; his rough coat sliding across Silks soft Skin, would have made her Grin as bad as your Sanford. I have not got our Ticket yet but expected it soon.[5] I intend to turn Beau with my part of the Money, and make a Shining Figure amongst the Greenwich Bucks. I fear I shant be able to equal Doctor Joslin[6] in powder, for he only Shook his Head yesterday in the Barbers Shop and he made such a dust that I mistook Mrs Hubbard for Mina Brown. What do you intend to do with your part of the increase? Caps, Lawns, Laces, Furbaloes &c &c will swallow it all up, I warrant it. We are so much politer in Greenwich in common than you at Westerly. I fear youl outshine me with equal expence. There is another advantage you have over me; you are sure to be repaid by the *poor Country* Gentry who endeavours to ape you in the Fashions, whereby you sell a large quantity of Goods every new mode thats introduceed.[7] Thus you follow the maxims of the Wise and prudent, pray upon other *Peoples follies* and turn their *pride to your* own advantage.

Miss Suca will be with you this Evening. But I hope your fears are abated; if they are not, youl agree you may abate a great part of them when I tell you She has been twice to Coventry and once to Block Island. Ile warrant her, as Doctor Swift says, she has by this got a set of Durty Ideas. She is a chearful agreeable old Soul. Make things agreeable to her in your usual way and I presume she will be much pleasd. Farewell amen

N GREENE JR

ALS (RHi).
1. The letter is not addressed, but a modern notation on the last page and a reference to a [lottery] ticket identifies the recipient as Mary "Polly" Ward.
2. The date is established by Welcome Arnold's marriage of 11 Feb. and his week's honeymoon on Block Island (see note 4).
3. Joshua Babcock (1707–83), a friend and neighbor of the Wards, was a Yale graduate who studied medicine in England and returned to practice in Westerly. By reputation he was a man of great learning, reading the Scriptures in the original Hebrew and Greek (R.I. Biog. Cycl.).
4. On Welcome Arnold and his wife, the former Patience Greene, see above, NG to Samuel Ward, Jr., 25 Jan.
5. A lottery ticket, the winnings from which he guesses later in the letter she will spend on "Furbaloes &c &c."
6. Dr. Joseph Joslyn emigrated from Scotland to East Greenwich in 1770 (Monahon and Collins, "Letters to Ward," R.I. Hist. 16 [1957]: 119n). He was NG's friend as well as his physician. In 1776 he was surgeon of Col. Joseph Stanton's R.I. militia regiment (Bartlett, Records, 8: 84).
7. Samuel Ward, Sr., had a store in Westerly, probably near his farm (Knollenberg, Ward, p. 5).

## To Samuel Ward, Jr.

Friend Sammy          East Greenwich [R.I.] March 2, 1773
I embrace this opportunity by Mr Leonard Duson to write you, not because I have anything to write, but to fulfill my Promise. Mr [Thomas] Arnold and I arrivd at Littlerest [Kingston] about 6 o'Clock the Evening after we left your House. We Lodgd that Night at Nathan Gardners, by Virtue of the Invitation of John Hazzard,[1] and set out next morning for Home, which was Sunday, and I believe will be rememberd by the Name of the Cold Sunday for half a Century. We Dind at Lodowick Updikes where Tom Arnolds delicate feelings was put out of Tune by Miss Lydia Gardners appearing in her Night Cap.[2] Her Person and appearance was so different from his expectations that he could not help forming some of Swifts durty Ideas. We got that Night as far as Potowomut the land of my Nativity, where we receivd a Hearty welcome from their desire to Learn my success in the New London Expedition.[3] We spent Monday at East Greenwich at Mr. Nat Greens[4] where we was Joind by Mr Hitchcock and Tuesday the cry was every man to his Tent, O Israel. I could not prevail on Mr Arnold to go to Coventry then, but obtain'd a promise of a Weeks Visit very soon. I wish Fortune for once would shew us she can be Kind and favor us with your agreeable Company at the Time. I flatter myself we Should form a very Happy Society. No news of Kitt or Perry.[5] I Long to see their Faces. Your Friends are all well in these parts, and if I thought it would not feast your Vanity, I would inform you you are much enquired after. Make my Compliments agreeable to all the Family, particularly Miss Hannah who I wish to

see to make Acknowledgment for favours done me that I were Ignorant of till very lately. Yours

NATH GREENE J

This Letter is in the Scotch Stile of particulars.

ALS (RHi).
1. John Hazard (1746–1813) had married Sarah Gardiner, daughter of Nathan Gardiner (1712–92), a prominent man in Kings County (Monahon and Collins, "Letters to Ward," *R.I. Hist.* 16 [1957]: 86n).
2. Ludowick Updike (1725–1804), although trained as a lawyer, was occupied with the management of his large estate in North Kingstown, where he was noted for his hospitality.
His imposing dwelling, known as Smith's Castle or Cocumscussoc, had been built almost a century before. It was famous even in NG's day as one of the places where Roger Williams had preached. The house today is one of Rhode Island's noteworthy attractions for visitors. Lydia Gardiner was Updike's sister-in-law. (*R.I. Biog. Cycl.*)
3. NG and brothers did business with a New London, Conn., merchant—Thomas Allen. See above, NG to Allen, 20 Feb. 1773.
4. Nathanael, the son of Richard Greene, was a merchant in East Greenwich and a distant relative with whom NG has often been confused.
5. Brother Kitt had sailed for Virginia on a commercial trip in Jan., as noted in NG to Sammy, 25 Jan., above. Brother Perry is not mentioned there.

## To Thomas [Arnold][1]

Sir Thomas                    Coventry [R.I.] March 12, 1773
I receivd a Letter this instant from Sam Ward who informs me he intends to be at Coventry next Week where he desires to see you, to give him and myself a peculiar satisfaction. I give you an Invitation for that purpose in the Language of Pope "Come to Coventry and enjoy over a generous Bowl, the feast of Reason and the flow of Soul."[2] I will endeavour to make everything as agreeable to you as possible, and hope to give you no cause to repent of your excursion. Altho Nature appears with a Sour aspect in our Land, I dont despair of rendering it tollerable by generous and Hospitable entertainment. Bring Hitchbiddy with you. I am in great Haste as youl see by my writing. Farewell

NATH GREENE

ALS (Original in possession of David Coblentz, Raphine, Va., 1973).
1. The letter is undoubtedly to his good friend Thomas Arnold.
2. See note 4, NG to Sammy, 25 Jan., above.

## To Samuel Ward, Jr.

Greenwich [R.I.]
Friend Sam          Sunday Evening 11 oClock [30 May 1773][1]
I receivd your Letter[2] inclosd in a Line to your Sisters. You see its

late when I begin and youl excuse me for being short. Kitt saild for Maryland Wednesday last. Joy go with him, and Guardian Angels protect and secure him from the innumerable Evils incidental to Human Nature. Ring the Bells backward. Cry fire, the Church is in danger. There has been a play acted in Providence known by the Name of the unhappy Orphan.[3] Joseph Rusel [Russell] acted Monemia; Mr [Thomas] Halsey, Polid[ore]; Mr Harris, Castalis; Mr Bloget,[4] Thamont. I have forgot the under Charactors, but it is said they performd inimitably well, and to the satisfaction of all the spectators. They had Hackers Hall with regular Scenes formd for that prupose, all tastely and in good order. You say there's nothing new under the Sun. This is new, for its the first attempt ever made in this Colony by its Inhabitants. Various are the Sentiments with regard to its Consequences, but the Priests and Levites of every Order cries out against it as subversion of Morallity, and dangerous to the Church. I was in Mr [Thomas] Arnolds Office a few Days ago. He has a pretty Law Library, and promises himself a fine run of Business. I wish his success may equal his expectation. Thank you for your Compliment upon my Millitary Dignity, and thank you again for the [ridicule of?] its author.[5] He is vain above measure, and emty beyound Conception. I was almost Offended with Mr Varnum for such a freedom before the supreme Court of the Colony.[6] General Meeting News and all other Neighbourly Occurences refer you to the Girls for particulars. Not another word.

N. GREENE JR

ALS (RHi).
1. The date is established by a theatrical notice in the Providence *Gazette*, Saturday, 29 May.
2. Letter not found.
3. The performance was in defiance of an act of 1762 that prohibited "stage plays, interludes, and other theatrical entertainments" (Bartlett, *Records*, 6: 325). According to the *Gazette* (note 1) two plays were given: "Otway's Tragedy of the Orphan, or unhappy Marriage, with Miss in her Teens."
4. William Blodget became NG's aide during the war.
5. The reference to "Military Dignity" is lost in obscurity.
6. This probably refers to James M. Varnum's defense of NG and brothers in the Apr. session of the highest court, at which Lieut. Dudingston appealed the decision that had gone against him the previous summer (see *Greene* v. *Dudingston*, 20 July 1772, above).

## To Samuel Ward, Jr.

Dear Sir                              Coventry [R.I.] 21 July, 1773
    Whats your amusement, whats your employment, whats the Object in view? Happiness I warrant. The anxious mind of man is ever in busy quest of those Objects that promise much Felicity in the Acquisition. The prospect however engageing at first often terminates

in empty disappointment, and sometimes in bitter regret. We all with eagerness grasp at the substance, ⟨but⟩ too many embrace the shadow. How happy he whose most Elevated expectation are answer'd in Fruition. Gratification upon ⟨barter⟩ is like a fleeting Vapour, but when heithened by the Smiles of Virtue how sublime. Every enjoyment is ennobled by Esteem, how the Approbation of our friends warms our Heart, and instead of enduring Chagrin and Inquietude, assists the gentler calls of Nature to a kind repose, and then when kind Zephyrs fan us awake, the ⟨Graces⟩ dance anew. I have been reading Butlers anallogy between Natural and revaled Religion,[1] and find that its not every one that draws a fine picture of Moral Excellence, that ⟨feels⟩ the Benefit of Virtue, but he who bends his Mind to the ⟨practice⟩ of her sacred rules. I have not fulfilld my promise to ⟨Hannah⟩. Tell her Pride and the Worlds dread Laugh baffles all my ⟨resolution⟩. I should be glad to see her, to give scope to the exercise of Gratitude ⟨friendship⟩ and Benevolence. Permit me to mingle my Joy with the ⟨rest⟩ of her friends and relations for the partial recovery of her ⟨Health⟩. I saw Mr [Thomas] Arnold yesterday and heard of the welfare of Mr [Tom] ⟨Harris⟩. Perry saild about two weeks past. I heard of Kitt a few Days ⟨ago⟩ in health but ⟨perplext⟩ with bad Markets. All friends ⟨are well⟩ except Elihu[e]. John Pettingill[2] is ⟨failed and keeps concealed⟩. Griffin pursued him through Coneticut as Death did Tristram Shandy[3] through France. Many are likely to be great Sufferers by him, and amongst the rest poor me. Make my Compliments agreeable to your Family. I hope to see some or all of you at Commencement. Let Coventry share with the rest of your friends part of the Time you spend this way. Charles hurries me.[4] Blame him for bad writing and a bad Letter, for I knew not of his going till a few minutes ago. In haste am your sincere friend.

NATH GREENE

ALS (RHi). Original damaged; portions in angle brackets supplied from late nineteenth-century transcript (MWA).

1. Joseph Butler's *Analogy of Religion, Natural and Revealed, to the Constitution and Course of Nature* (1736) was written to combat Deism in England.

2. John Pettingell had been a partner with NG and cousin Griffin in buying a potential iron mine (see note 2, NG et al. to Stephen Hopkins & Co., 10 Oct. 1768, above). He had apparently gone bankrupt, owing the Greenes money (see *NG & Co.* v. *Pettingell*, 20 Dec. 1773, Kent County Court Records, Rhode Island State Records Center).

3. Sterne's *Tristram Shandy* was one of NG's favorite books which he often quoted. His brothers remembered all their lives his comical portrayal of Dr. Slop.

4. Charles, Sammy's oldest brother, was born in 1747 but his death is not recorded. In 1775 NG helped him obtain a commission as an ensign in the Continental army. From his father's letters to the family, he appears to have been an irresponsible person (Knollenberg, *Ward*, index references; Heitman, *Register*).

# Warrant

Coventry, R.I. 3 Aug. 1773
Colony Rhodisland ss Georg the third by the Grace of God of Great
Brittan France and Ireland King, King Defender of the Faith &c

To the Sheriff of our County of Providence his Deputy or Either of the
Cunstabls in said County Greeting

Where as it appearith unto us by the Information and Complaint of
Nathanial Greene Juner of Coventry in Said County Gentleman made
upon oath before our Trusty and Well Beloved Stephen Potter Esquier
one of the Justices of our Superior Court of Judicature Court of Assize
and General Goal Delivery within and throughout our Said Colony of
Rhodisland that he the said Nathanial on the Night of the thirtyth day
of July Last past was Lawfully Possessed in his Stable in Said Coventry
under Lock and key, of Certain bay Colourd Stallen horse Known by
the name of the Britan and of the Vallue of one Hundred and Twenty
Pounds Lawful money and that Some Evelminded Person or persons,
on the same Night in a forceable manner broke said Lock Entered said
Stable and feloniously took Stole and carrid away said horse against
our peace and the Laws of our Said Colony and that the said Nathanial
hath Just Cause to Suspect Richard Atwell of Situate in our County of
Providence blacksmith to have Committed the Crime aforesaid or
Conserned therein

Wee Command you the aforesaid officers to Apprehend the Said
Richard Atwell and him Safely Secure So that You Have him forth-
with Before our beloved Stephen Hopkins Esqr our Cheaf Justis of
our Colony aforesaid at Providence there to be Examind and Delt
with acording to Law. Witness Stephen Potter Esqr at Coventry the
third Day of August in the Thirteenth year of Geor Reign Annoque
Domni 1773[1]

STEPHEN POTTER

D (Kent County Court Records: R.I. State Records Center).
    1. The only criminal complaint lodged by NG which has come to light is this
warrant concerning the theft of his favorite horse, Britain. Among several supporting
witnesses was one Joseph Holley, who testified that Richard Atwell and John Pettingell,
his host for the night, sent Holley to "Nat Green's Stable and see if the Britain was
there." Then Atwell, who had put on "Pettingell's Night Gown" that he might not be
known, "drawed the Staple with a Piece of Iron, opened the Door . . . went into the
Stable took out the Horse, rid him away and say'd he was his." (Deposition taken by
Stephen Potter and attached to the warrant.)
    Although a nightgowned figure astride a galloping stallion should have been
easily traced, it is not recorded that either Atwell or Britain was ever found.

## To Samuel Ward, Jr.

Potowomut [Warwick, R.I.] Sunday 5 o'Clock P M [1773?]¹
I have been to Meeting today.² Our silence was interrupted by a
vain conceited Minister. His Sermon made me think of a certain Diet
cald Whistle Belly Vengeance: he that eats most has the worst share.
He began with asking us what could be said that had not been said.
Much more, thinks I, than you ever thought off or ever will. Poor
man. He had a little morsel to comfort himself, and he couldnt be
content to Eat it alone, but feeling the Springs of Benevolence rise in
his Mind, he thought it his Duty to make a distribution amongst the
whole Congregation. The Assembly was so large and the matter so
light that it evaporated off like Smook and left us neither the fuller
nor better pleasd than when he began.

Debby [Ward] deliverd the Doctor your letter. I was at Mr Caseys³
this morning and he cald me out to speak with me and began with a
great deal of emotion and said he had receivd a Letter of a surprising
Nature from you, and gave it me to read. I took it and began with
an audible Voice. The Doctor soon hush't me saying the people
would hear. I did that to see whether he intended to be openly angry.
If he had, I intended to Justified the truth of your Observations
as openly. When I had read it he askt me what I thought on't. As to
the ⟨intent⟩, says I, you must be convinc'd its good, for whoever
wanted ⟨to⟩ mend a fault in an Enimy, it would be as absurd as for the
Devil to fright us for doing wickedly. As to the subject, I mu[st?] confess you have given to[o] much reason for his remarks. I m[y]self
have ⟨been⟩ in doubt whether I ought to impeach your understanding
or Integrity, for truth and Justice of Observation always ought to
regulate our Praise, and where there appear'd neither the one or the
other in his Observations, what could I think but that he had a mind
to sell wind for a round Sum of ready Money. I told him a flatterer or
Sycophant that blows up the Mind of a Person into a Tympany was
like a Physician that administers Poison and then demands a large fee
for it. He began to Justify himself with regard to his integrity. I told
him it might be easily done but then it must be at the expence of his
understanding; and I should have the better Oppinion of him to give
up the latter to save the former. Hees going to write you a Letter. If he
appears very Serious I advise you to turn the subject into ridicule for
many Persons has yealded to the force of Ridicule in a point which
they could never [have] been argued out off. The Doctor will take
his Wig off, and what will there appear; why a bare Pole. You have
seen the lecture upon Heads, I suppose, and remember my remark
upon his Wig. Should you get into a paper war I shall pity you, for his
Letters will be so barren and your Subject so dry that it wont give
scope to your Genius or entertainment to your Mind.

Dont fail of being a good Boy. Improve in knowledge and increase in Virtue. You ought, after all has been done for you, to be a very good Lad. I am in hopes of seeing you a Star of the first magnitude. It would please me to see you shine like the Sun in the Firmament, but then I and all my friends [must?] lye buried in the Efflux of your Light untill you was pleasd to disappear. So I thought He make a Star of ⟨you⟩ and shall rejoice to see you shine with great Light. Mr Varnum is calling for me. I cant write [or?] think anymore.

My best respects to your Dady. Tell Polly [Mary Ward] I have not got our Ticket but expect it soon. I wrote a letter to Caty [Catharine Ward], and whether I left it at Coventry or lost it out of my pocket I cant tell. I fear I shant have opportunity to Write again, being oblig'd to go to Bristol tomorrow in company with Jacob and Mr Varnum. My Love to all the Family. I have been in the Dumps for two or three days past. I have sat brooding over mischief and hatching Evils. I began a wrangle with myself this morning and turnd Melancholy and all her train out of Doors. I had as good write natural as study to be Dull. Its my own Ink and paper and you'l have no postage to pay, therefore youl be unreasonable if you find fault because you ant oblige[d] to Read [it.] Debby kept me very chearful and Merry all the way Home. I warrant you'l have a fine History from ⟨her⟩. To her I refer you for Greenwich Particulars. I have no more to say. Amen.

N G

I wrote this Letter and intended to have sent it by ⟨way⟩ of Newport, but haveing no opportunity to forward it till you arrivd and part of it being upon the subject you enquird about, and I feeling Lazy, I thought I would let it go, and it would save me the trouble of writing anew ⟨upon⟩ the Doctor.

ALS (RHi). Letter damaged including signature. Portions in angle brackets are from nineteenth-century transcript (MWA).

1. He was visiting his old home in Warwick, where his four younger brothers continued to live. The date is pure conjecture. It is before December 1773 because Caty Ward was married to brother Christopher by that time.

2. Friends Meeting, which he attended infrequently after his father's death.

3. Probably Silas Casey, a prominent East Greenwich merchant, who owned a farm in North Kingstown near the Potowomut homestead. As plaintiff in several hundred lawsuits in Kent County, he was the personification of the litigious Yankee. His son Wanton was the youngest founding member of the Kentish Guards; his grandson Silas was a major general in the Civil War. (See Kent County Court Records, Rhode Island State Records Center; Bartlett, *Records*, 7: 454, 493; see also account of his grandson in *R.I. Biog. Cycl.* and *DAB*.)

## To Samuel Ward, Jr.

Friend Sammy          Potowomut [Warwick, R.I.] 17 January 1774
I have just returnd from Mr Benj Gardners weding.[1] We kept it up three or four days. I am almost perswadeed to think myself a person of some consequence as there was only a few choice Spirits there, and they selected out of a great number claiming equal right from a Relationship and connexion. The Bride was dressed in a Cadeed Lutestring Gown deprieg'd flownced and furbelow'd in high taste, her head was dressed with a Laceed Fly, Long Lappets. The rest of her dress was of a pice [piece] which [I] leave your immagination to frame. As I am no great connissur in female furniture am at a loss for names to convey my Ideas. The Bride looked Rich but not neat, Amiable, but not hansome. So much for weding. There has been snow storm upon snow storm. All the face of the Earth is coverd with Virgin Snow. Altho its deep and difficult to get abroad yet I cant confine myself long from[2] Potowomut where we appear as the People of old did that went into the ark Male and Female.

Captain Sweet is arrivd and altho he has made us a bad Voyage yet its very agreeable to receive the remains of a Shatterd fortune. As to the health of the Family here, Polly will give you an Account. Our Court is coming on, a flood of Lawyers is poreing in upon us from all quarters, Mr [Thomas] Arnold amongst the rest.[3] If this collection of triffles is or can be of any service to you, you are wellcome to it. Polly is waiting. I cant write any more. Make my Compliments agreeable to all friends. In haste your assured friend

N GREENE JR

ALS (RHi).
1. Benjamin Gardiner, whose father was one of the wealthiest of the south county planters, married Elizabeth Wickes of East Greenwich. (Monahon and Collins, "Letters to Ward," *R.I. Hist.* 17 [1958]: 15n)
2. He undoubtedly meant that he could not confine himself long *at* Potowomut (where he was staying with brother Christopher) but needed to get back to Coventry.
3. The Kent County Court of Common Pleas met in Jan. in East Greenwich.

## To Samuel Ward, Jr.

Dear Sir          Potowomut [Warwick, R.I.] March 7, 1774[1]
Your Daddy has made us an agreeable Visit. I could not prevail on him to go to Coventry, the most I could obtain was a promise next time he came to Greenwich. He informs me of your disagreeable situation. You have my good wishes for your speedy recovery. I wish you had acquainted a physician with your complaint a little earlier. It might have been cured with less pain and difficulty. I had a very agreeable Visit at Coventry from Sister `Greene,[2] Nancy and Tom

Arnold. They favord me with their company several days. I receivd a letter from Tom and Jo Harris Yesterday full of I know not what, but Bachelors and old Maids were the principal subjects. The warm season is coming on. I suppose like other Animals the blood begins to warm in their Vains and raises thoughts of Matrimony. Brother Bill has got home and is not a little mortified at the ill success of his endeavours. I have been promiseing myself the pleasure of your company in Coventry ever since I saw you. Many happy moments has fancy painted out in immagination, but your dady has disturbd the agreeable reflection by the information he gave of your situation. Make us a Visit to Greenwich as soon as ever your able to Ride. Give us a line to notify us before your Arrival, as a herald. My heart is large but you hold a large share in it, and it is so vain and Covetious as to wish and expect an equal return, and nothing could mortify it more than a conviction to the contrary. If I am out in my reckoning I charge you not to undeceive me. Your Daddy is waiting with as much impatience as he dares when Dinner is detaind, and he very hungry. My Compliments to good Naturd Poll, to friendly Hannah and Chattering Debby and all the rest of the Family. I wish you all well and happy and am with great esteem your sincere friend

N GREENE

ALS (RHi).
    1. He is writing from his old home, where by then Christopher and wife were living.
    2. Sister Greene, who came with Nancy (Anna) Ward, was Sammy's sister Catharine, since Dec. the wife of NG's brother Christopher. NG often referred to his sisters-in-law as sisters.

## To Samuel Ward, Jr.

Friend Samuel                    Coventry [R.I.] July 10, 1774
    Please to deliver the inclosd Cards to your Sisters. On the 20th this Instant I expect to be married to Miss Kitty Littlefield[1] at your Uncle Greens. As a Relative of hers and a friend of mine, your company is desird upon the occasion. The company will be small consisting only of a few Choice spirits. As she is not married at her fathers house she declind giveing any an invitation but a few of her nearest relations and most intimate friends. There will be my brothers and their Wives, Mr Varnum and his Wife, Polly Green, Phebe Shuffield, and Betsy Greene, Christopher Greene[2] and Griffin Greene and their Wives, and who from Block Island I dont know, and Mr Thomas Arnold. These are all excepting your family. Your uncle Hubbard and aunt,[3] and your aunt Green was up here Yesterday.

Both your Aunts seems to be in a declining way, tho I think they are rather better than they have been sometime past.

Your Daddy is appointed one to attend the Congress,[4] for which I rejoice, as the mean motives of Interest, or Partial distinction of Ministers of State will have no influence upon his Virtuous Soul; like Cato of old, heel stand or fall with the Liberties of his Country. Heaven bless their consultations with his seasoning grace, and crown their resolutions with success and triumph. The Ministry seems to be determind to embrace thier cursed hands in American Blood, and that once Wise and Virtuous Parliment, but now Wicked and weak Assembly, lends an assisting hand to accomplish thier hellish schemes. The Solders in Boston are insolent above measure.[5] Soon very soon expect to hear the thirsty Earth drinking in the warm Blood of American Sons. O how my eyes flashes with indignation and my boosom burns with holy resentment. Should any of that Pest of men, those Scourgers of Society, fall a sacrifice, how would the Earth heave in her very bowels to disgorge such Pisonous matter as runs from thier Veins. O Boston Boston, would to heaven that the good Angel that destroyed the Army of Senacherib might now interpose and rid you of your oppressors. How is the design of government subverted. That which was instituted for the increase of the happiness of individuals and for the preservation of society in general should be made an instrument to rob us of one and destroy the other. How happy has been our situation when cloath'd with the white robes of Peace and every one enjoyed the fruits of his Labours. But these are days that serves but to embiter our present reflections by contrasting our former happy condition with our present distressed situation. Wheres that Principle that Philosphers tells us is implanted in the human Soul, that Smiles with approbation upon noble and generous Actions? Those wretches must be lost to every sense of Shame and principle of Virtue, or else from the smiles of one and the harrowings of the other we might receive better treatment from them. I am just going to meeting, therefore must conclude. They were all well at Potowomut. Make my Complements agreeable to all the family. My regards in particular to your Sister Hannah and believe me to be your sincere friend

NATH GREENE

ALS (RHi).
1. NG's romance had blossomed suddenly. Friends thought he might never marry. One said that "Nat and Miss Nancy [Ward]" had got "in such a way of leaning Backward that I have given them over Intirely." The same friend suggested that brother William "go Right off and See Polly Greene, Caty Littlefield, or some Agreeable Girl" (Arnold to Christopher Greene, 15 Mar. 1774, RHi). Instead, it was Nat who went "Right off" to see Caty—whom he had watched grow to maturity at Aunt Greene's. Except on the occasion of the wedding, he called her Caty, not Kitty.

Catharine Littlefield (1755–1814) was born on Block Island, the daughter of John and Phebe Littlefield. At age ten, a few years after her mother's death, she went to live with her mother's sister, Catharine Ray Greene, wife of the future governor. Aunt Catharine was an attractive, vivacious woman and a charming hostess. Caty's book learning may not have been extensive, but she was an apt pupil of her aunt's charming ways, which, combined with her natural good looks and animation, made her a favorite with NG's associates such as Washington, Hamilton, and Lafayette. A number of men fell in love with her, and she was not beyond encouraging them.

Like other wives of generals, she joined her husband when practicable. Although she had four children during the war years (two more were born later), they never prevented her from joining him. Until he went south in Oct. 1780, she was with or near him for half the time, once for an entire year. At such times she left her children with members of the family, to the consternation of friends and relatives. After NG's death in 1786, she proved herself a capable manager of plantations in Savannah and on Cumberland Island, Ga. In 1796 she married Phineas Miller, the children's tutor and a friend who had helped in the management of her affairs. Miller, whom her children greatly loved, died six years later; Catharine died in 1814 on Cumberland Island. An irony noted by her children was that she who disliked sea voyages ended her days as they had begun—on an island.

2. Polly (Mary) Greene was the daughter of Richard Greene of Potowomut Neck and the sister of another Nathanael Greene, with whom NG stayed on a trip back from New London (see above, NG to Sammy Ward, 2 March 1773); Phebe Sheffield from Jamestown, R.I., later married a cousin of NG, Charles Greene, who lived in East Greenwich; Betsy was the sister of Christopher Greene, a third cousin who won fame in the revolutionary war. Clarke, *Greenes*, pp. 129, 217, and 235, gives a great deal of information on the relatives but must be used with care.

3. Aunt Judith, the sister of Catharine Ray Greene (Knollenberg, *Ward*, p. 4).

4. On 13 June the Rhode Island Assembly had appointed Samuel Ward, Sr., and Stephen Hopkins as delegates to the first Continental Congress, which had been called to meet at Philadelphia in September (Bartlett, *Records*, 7: 246).

5. After the closing of the port of Boston and the arrival of General Gage with four thousand British troops, tension had risen steadily in the city, heightened by the diligent Boston Committee of Correspondence. Insolent soldiers undoubtedly there were, but they were on the defensive against a populace that took out long-standing frustrations on the hapless troops. No merchant could sell to them, no carpenter or bricklayer was allowed to erect barracks, and the unruly crowds burned their straw, destroyed their lumber, and called them names. It is likely that NG's remarks were based on propaganda, not on first hand observation.

# A Wedding Invitation

[Before 20 July 1774]

Nathanael Greene ⎱ Presents their compliments to Miss Polly Greene
Kitty Littlefield  ⎰
and desires the favor of her company at William Greene's Esq[1] the 20th this Instant at 10 oclock A. M.

AL (document in possession of descendants of William Greene, Warwick, R.I., 1975).

1. After the wedding, Catharine moved into NG's Coventry house, which they would share less than a year before he went off to war.

Home of Nathanael Greene, 1770–1776, in the village of Anthony, Coventry, Rhode Island. Shown to the public by General Nathanael Greene Homestead Association.

## Subscription

[East Greenwich, R.I., 29 Aug. 1774]

We the Subscribers[1] Inhabitants of the Town of East Greenwich in the Colony of Rhode Island, taking into the most serious Consideration the present alarming Situation of Our Brethren in the Town of Boston and Charlestown in the Province of the Massachusetts Bay, occasioned by the Late Cruel, malignant and more than savage Acts of the British Parliment, And Whereas a Tame Submission To the first Approaches of Lawless Power will undoubtedly involve this Extensive Continent in one Scene of Misery and servitude Than which a glorious Death in Defence of Our Unquestionable Rights is far more eligible; Convinced Likewise that the only True Glory and unfadeing Grandure of the British Monarch Consists in governing his Extensive

Empire with equal and impartial Laws, founded in Reson and rendered sacred by the Wisdom of Ages; And that every Attempt to
impair that noble Constitution, which hath ever been the Envy and
Terror of Europe Constitutes the Blackest Species of Treason: From
the most unfeigned Loyalty to our Sovorign From the most settled
Abhorrance to the Deep Laid Schemes of his Prime Minister, whom
we Esteem the most Determind Foe To Royalty, and from an ardent
Love to our Country Which Nothing but Death Can abate We do
therefore promise and engage To pay by the first Day of October Next
the respective Sums, to Our Names annexed, to Messrs James Mt
[Mitchell] Vernum [Varnum], P Peirce, A Mumford, Wm Peirce, to be
Laid out and Expended in Such Articles of Provision for our said
distressed Brethren as the Majority of us shall agree to be sent to the
Committee of Ways and Means of imploying the Poor of Boston by
the First Conveyance.[2]

August 29 A D 1774

D (RHi).
   1. The list of subscribers contains some eighty names, including NG's. Other
Coventry residents joined with East Greenwich because Coventry did not have a
separate subscription list. (Arnold, *RI*, 2: 341, lists fourteen of the twenty-nine Rhode
Island towns as sending donations.)
   2. East Greenwich donations ranged from a few pence to a pound. NG gave £2 8s.,
which was topped only by his friend James M. Varnum, chairman of the committee,
who gave £6. It was 8 Nov. before the committee collected the pledges, with which
they bought forty-four sheep and four oxen. It took Preserved Pearce another five days
to drive the stock to Boston. (See MS Report of East Greenwich "Comity," RHi.) Those
who saw Boston's streets filled with flocks and herds thought that Boston must never
have eaten so well.

## Agreement on the Formation of a Military
## Independent Company[1]

[August? 1774]

Deeply impressed with a Sense of the shameful Neglect of military Excercise and being willing and desirous to repair and revive that
decayed and necessary Spirit of regular Dicipline at this alarming
Crisis, We the Subscribers do unanimously join to establish and
constitute a military independent Company; That on every Tuesday
and Saturday in the afternoon for the future, or as long as Occasion
require, or it shall be judg'd necessary or expedient, a Meeting be
held at the House of William Arnold in East Greenwich for the
Purpose aforesaid.

| | |
|---|---|
| ARCHIBALD CRARY | JOSEPH WHITMARSH |
| WM GREENE | ABIAL BROWN |
| DANIEL GREENE | WANTON CASEY |
| JNO DEXTER JR | HOPKINS COOKE |

| | |
|---|---|
| CHARLES HOLDEN JUN | CHRIS GREENE |
| JOB PEIRCE | GRIFFIN GREENE |
| JOHN GLASIER | JOHN COOKE |
| RICHARD FRY | JOB RICE |
| THOMAS HOLDEN | JOHN GORDOM [GORDEN] |
| STEPN MUMFORD | JOHN GREENE, SON OF RICHARD |
| CHARLES GREENE | REUBEN WIGHTMAN |
| ADAM COMSTOCK | WILLIAM WATERMAN |
| JOB HAWKINS | JOHN FRY |
| GIDEON MUMFORD | OLIVER GARDNER |
| RICHARD MATHEWSON | CLARK BROWN |
| NATHL GREENE [SON OF RICHARD] | BENJ'D SPENCER |
| JAMES SEARLE | STEPHEN GREENE |
| WM ARNOLD | CHRISTOPHER GREENE |
| AUGUSTUS MUMFORD | ISAAC TRIPP JUN |
| JOHN REYNOLDS | DUTEE JERAULD JNR |
| GIDEON FREEBORN | PELEG OLIN |
| JOSEPH JOSLYN | PARDON ALLEN |
| SYLVESTER GREENE | JOHN SHAW JUNER |
| ANDREW BOYD | SAMUEL HOMES |
| SAMUEL BROWN | ABRAHAM GREEN |
| NATHANAEL GREENE COV[ENTRY] | THOMS ARNOLD |
| EZER WALL | JOSEPH GREENE[2] |

DS (Kentish Guard Papers: RHi).

1. The Military Independent Company of East Greenwich was the immediate predecessor of the Kentish Guards.

After the French and Indian War, the Rhode Island militia had steadily deteriorated. As the new Congress met in Philadelphia to discuss matters of a most solemn import, many Rhode Islanders suddenly realized, as did other colonials, that, if a shooting war should lie ahead, they were sadly unprepared for it. The military company of East Greenwich was an informal group that did not ask for government sanction. Out of their own personal funds, they hired two veterans of the British army to teach them basic military drills and to provide martial music for the same (see two following documents). In keeping with Rhode Island civil tradition, the company was completely democratic, with a moderator instead of a commanding officer. Within two months the members had decided to seek official status and petitioned formally for incorporation under the new name of the Kentish Guards. (See below, petition of Kentish Guards, 25 Oct.)

2. One conspicuous absentee among the signers was James M. Varnum, who subsequently pushed for the incorporation of the group under the name of the Kentish Guards, of which he was elected the captain.

Equally conspicuous among the signers were NG, Christopher Greene (his third cousin), and other members of the pacifist Society of Friends. Judge Johnson, NG's biographer, related a story that has often been repeated: NG and his cousin Griffin had been expelled from the East Greenwich Society of Friends for having attended a military parade in Connecticut in Sept. 1773. (Johnson, *Greene*, 1: 18–19) They were, in fact, suspended (not expelled), but it was not for attending a military parade. The charge against them, as stated in the minutes of the Monthly Meeting on 5 July 1773, was for having been at "a Place in Coneticut of *Publick Resort* where they had No Proper Business" (italics added). (Friends Minutes, vol. 1751–1806: 5, RHi) Judge Johnson quoted the same minutes, but he interpreted the "Publick Resort" as a "grand parade," where, he wrote, NG saw an assemblage of men "in all the pomp and circumstance of glorious war." (Johnson, *Greene*, 1: 18)

A "public resort" at the time, in fact, was a place of pleasure (*OED*, citation of 1773); it was a name that some gave to alehouses, while nineteenth-century dictionaries defined a resort simply as "A disorderly house or other place of questionable repute." (Mathews, *Americanisms*, 2: 1387) Even if NG had attended a military parade in 1773, the society would have been unlikely to take any action against him, much less such a drastic measure as suspending him. The following year, for example, the Greenwich Meeting was most reluctant to punish far more serious infringements of the peaceful commitment: NG's third cousin Christopher had joined the military company in Sept. 1774 and had been made a lieutenant of the Guards in Oct. Yet it was Feb. 1775 before a committee of the Greenwich Meeting remonstrated with him, and it was Apr. before charges were brought against his "under taiking in the Millitary Way,"—and then only because the committee reported that "he still continues in it." And after all this, he was not expelled but put "from under their Care until he makes satisfaction for his out Going" (Friends Minutes, vol. 1751–1806: 59, RHi).

NG remained a member of the Greenwich Meeting for two years after being named brigadier general, and then it was he who severed his connection with the Meeting (see below, note, NG to Jacob, 4 June 1777).

## Articles of Agreement between William Johnson and the Military Company

[East] Greenwich [R.I.] Oct the [1st-5th] 1774

I the Subscriber Do by these Presents firmly Bind my Self To the Military Company in Greenwich To teach them the Manual Exercise and Evolutions Maunuvres With Every other movement as taught in the English Army and Likewise Do Engage to teach two Lads to Beat the Drum So as they Shall be able to Beat the English Duty as it is Done in the Service. On Consideration of their paying me the Sum of       to be paid att the fulfiling of this Bond or if I want Half ont Before the Company is Dismissd They Shall Let me have it: in Witness Whereof I have hereunto Sett my Name.

NB Tis to be Understood the Company are to Board Me and find a horse to fetch and Carry me Between Here and Where I am Engaged at Present.

We the Subscribers Do promise for Value Re'd to pay to Will'm Johnson or Order the Sum of       Dollars att the Expiration or fulfiling given To the Company of Greenwich.

We the Subscribers for Value Re'd Do promise to pay Will'm Johnson or order the Sum of       Dollars att fulfiling of his Bond to us Subscribers in Witness Whereof We have hereunto Respectively Subscribed our Names This[1] [*document ends here*]

DDf (Kentish Guards Papers: RHi).
1. This contract was drawn up some time after Johnson had been hired, for he submitted a bill on 29 Sept. for "three Pounds lawful Money in part of the sum promised me, for teaching said Company the regular military Discipline." (Kentish Guards Papers, RHi) Beyond the fact that he had been in the British army, nothing is

known of him. He may be the deserter whom biographers Johnson and Greene refer to as having been brought from Boston by NG at the same time he brought back a musket concealed in a load of hay (Johnson, *Greene*, 1: 22, and Greene, *Greene*, 1: 51–52). He stayed on with the Kentish Guards at least into Dec.

## Articles of Agreement between William Williams and the Military Company

[East Greenwich, R.I., 6 Oct. 1774] Articles of Agreement made and concluded on this sixth day of October in the Fourteenth Year of the Rign of King Geo. the Third Annoque Dom. 1774; by and between William W[illia]ms now residing in Pro.[vidence] in the Co[unty of] Pro.[vidence] Herald Painter[1] of the one part and the military Company in East Greenwich in the County of Kent of the other part Witnesseth, That the said William in Consideration of the Covenants herein after expressed by the said Co to be done and performed doth engage to attend on said Company in East Greenwich every tuesday, wednesday and thirsday in each succeeding Week, commencing the seventh day of October instant, to fife for said Company while under arms and instruct at all Times, when exempt from the fifing for them and teach (to the best of his Ability) two lads which shall be nominated by said Co. to play on the Fife.

In Consideration whereof the said Company do engage to transport the said Wm from Providence to Greenwich and from thence back to said Providence again during the Time of performing said Service at their Expence and to bord the said William while at East Greenwich, and at the Expiration of the said two Months to pay unto the said William the sum of two Pounds and eight Shillings lawful Money.

signed, sealed and delivered In Presence of
PETTER GODEPURSE
ADJUTANT

D (Kentish Guards Papers: RHi).
1. Heraldic painting was obviously not a full-time occupation in the small city of Providence, although such specialists also painted signs and decorated household commercial objects. The Kentish Guards continued to hire him to fife and teach fifing.

## Petition to the Rhode Island General Assembly

Colony of Rhode Island ss. [East Greenwich, R.I., 25 Oct. 1774] To the Honble the General Assembly to be holden at Providence in sd Colony the last Wednesday in Oct. 1774

Inhabitants of the Town of East Greenwich and The Subscribers [of] Warwick and Coventry humbly represent unto this Honble Assembly, that for the better Encouragement of milatary Knowledge and Discipline in the County of Kent, especially at a time when lawless Sway appears to bid Defiance to the essential and unalianable Rights of Nature, they are anxious to be formed into a Company, with such others as shall be joined to them, subject to the Exemtions and Restrictions your Honors shall direct, and pray for an Act of Incorporation accordingly.[1]

| | |
|---|---|
| J VARNUM[2] | ARCHIBALD CRARY |
| RICHARD FRY | STEPHEN GREENE |
| CHRIS. GREENE, son of Phillip | GRIFFIN GREENE |
| HOPKINS COOKE | CLARK BROWN |
| STEPHEN MUMFORD | JOHN GLASIER |
| NATHANAEL GREENE [son of Richard] | JNO. COOKE |
| | JOHN FRY |
| RICHARD MATHEWSON | ABIAL BROWN |
| AUGUSTUS MUMFORD | SYLVESTER GREENE |
| GID[EO]N MUMFORD | WILLIAM ARNOLD |
| CHARLES GREENE | GIDEON FREEBORN |
| JOHN GREENE, son of Richard | WANTON CASEY |
| JOS. WHITMARSH | SAM[U]EL BROWN |
| BENJ'N SPENCER | JOB PEIRCE |
| JAMES SEARLE | WILLIAM GREENE |
| JOSEPH JOSLIN | JOHN REYNOLDS |
| ANDREW BOYD | OLLIVAR GARDNER |
| EZER WALL | DANIEL GREENE |
| JNO S DEXTER | CHRISTOPHER GREENE Potwt |
| NATHANAEL GREENE Cov[en]try | [Potowomut] |

DS (R-Ar). This document, in the hand of James M. Varnum, is in vol. 15 of Petitions, pages 117A and 117B. It is followed by the manuscript copy of the act in response to it, which is printed below.

1. The Military Independent Company (also calling themselves "Cadets") met in East Greenwich on 21 Oct. and named a committee of James M. Varnum, Hopkins Cooke, and "Nathl Greene son of Richard" (not our NG) to "Draw a Charter For the incorporation of sd Company and to Lay the Same before the Next Meeting," to be held four days later. In the interim the group had decided on a new name, and the minutes of the 25 Oct. meeting begin "At a Meeting of the Military Company of Kentish Guards." That night the group approved and signed the petition and elected officers (see list of officers at the end of the formal act printed below; minutes of the two meetings are in Kentish Guards Papers, RHi).

2. A comparison between the list of petitioners and the members of the earlier company printed above (Aug. 1774) will reveal that some names have disappeared and others have been added, but it is essentially the same group. The last signer was NG's brother, Christopher.

# Act Establishing Kentish Guards[1]

[Providence, R.I., 29 Oct. 1774]

Whereas the preservation of this Colony in Time of War depends under God upon the milatary Skill and Discipline of it's Inhabitants; and whereas a Number of the Inhabitants of The Towns of East Greenwich, Warwick and Coventry (Viz) James Mitchel Varnum, Richard Fry, Christopher Greene (son of Phillip), Hopkins Cooke, Nathaniel Greene (of Coventry), Daniel Greene, Griffin Greene, Joseph Joslyn, Jos Whitmarsh, Augustus Mumford, John Cooke, Richard Matteson, Jno Dexter, John Fry, Gideon Mumford, Nathl Greene (son of Richard), Wm Arnold, Archibald Crary, John Glasier, Stephen Mumford, Christopher Greene, Andrew Boyd, Ezer Wall, Abiel Brown, Oliver Gardner, Clarke Brown, John Greene (son of Richard), Benjamin Spencer, Stephen Greene, Charles Greene, James Searle, Gideon Freeborn, Sylvester Greene, Wanton Casey, Job Pearce, William Greene (son of Richard), John Reynolds, and Samuel Brown have Petitioned this Assembly for an Act of Incorporation, forming them and such others as shall be joined unto them (not exceeding one Hundred Rank and file) into a Company by the name of "Kentish Guards." Wherefore this Assembly, to encourage a Design so laudable have ordained, constituted and Granted and by these Presents do ordain, constitute and appoint that the said Petitioners, and such others as shall be joined to them (not exceeding the Number of one Hundred Rank and file) be, and they are hereby declared to be an independent Company by the Name of "Kentish Guards," and by that name shall have perpetual Succession and shall have and enjoy all the Rights, Powers and Priveleges in this Grant hereafter mentioned.

Imprimis. It is Granted unto said Company that they or the Major part of them, shall and may once every Year (Viz) on the last Wednesday in April, meet and Assemble themselves together in some convenient Place by them appointed, then and there to choose their officers (Viz) Capt., two Lieutenants and one Ensign, and all other officers necessary for the training, disciplining and well ordering said Company. At wch meeting no Officer shall be choosen but by the greater Number of Votes then Present: the Captain, Lieutenants and Ensign to be approved by the Governor and Council for the time being and shall be commissionated and engaged in the same manner as other military Officers in this Colony are.

Secondly. That the said Company shall have Liberty to meet and exercise themselves upon such other Days and as often as they shall think necessary and not to be subject to the Orders or Directions of the Colonel or other Field officers of the Regiment in whose District they live, in such Meetings and exercising: and that they be obliged to meet for exercising at least four times each Year upon the Penalty of paying to and for the Use of the Company (Viz) the Captain for each Days neglect, three Pounds Lawful Money, the Lieutenants and Ensign each Twenty shillings Lawful money. The Clerk and other subaltern Officers, each Twelve shillings Lawful Money, and each Private Soldier Six Shillings Lawful Money, to be collected by Warrant of Distress direct to the Clerk from the Capt. or other Superior officer.

Thirdly. That said Company or the greater Number of them make all such Laws, Rules and Orders among themselves as they shall deem expedient for the well ordering and disciplining said Company, and to lay any Penalty or fine for the breach of such Rules not exceeding Twelve shillings Lawful Money for one Offence, to be collected as beforesaid.

Fourthly. That all those who shall be duly inlisted in the said Company, so long as they shall continue therein, shall be exemted from bearing Arms or doing other milatary Duty (watching and waiting only excepted) in the several Companies or Train Bands in whose District they respectively live, excepting such as shall be Officers in any of the said Companies or Train Bands.

Fifthly. That if any Officer or Officers of said Company shall be disapproved by the Governor and Council or shall remove out of said County of Kent or shall be taken away by Death, that then and in such Cases the Capt. of said Company or superior Officer for the Time being shall call a Meeting for the election of another or others in his or their stead thus removed.

Sixthly, And for the farther Encouragement of said Company, It is Granted that the Capt of said Company shall be of the rank of Colonel, that the first Lieutenant be of the Rank of Lieutenant Colonel, that the second Lieutenant be of the rank of Major, and that the Ensign be of the Rank of Captain; and that the said officers shall be of the Court martial and Council of War in the Regiment in whose district they live: and that upon all general Reviews and general musters the said Company shall rank the first independent Company for the County of Kent; And that in Time of Alarm the said Company shall be under the immediate Direction of the Commander in Chief of the Colony.

Oct. 29th 1774                    To the House of Magsts [Magistrates]
Voted that the beforegoing pass as an Act of this Assembly and that the Secretary be directed to make a fair Copy thereof, annex the Colony Seal thereto, and transmit the same to the Company and whereas the said Company have signified to this Assembly their Request that James Mitchel Varnum be their Captain, Richard Fry first Lieutenant, Christopher Greene (son of Philip) Second Lieutenant

and Hopkins Cook, Ensign, wch Request of the said Company is granted accordingly.

D (R-Ar). This MS draft of the act is in vol. 15 of Petitions, pp. 117C, 117D, and 117E, immediately following the above petition.

1. The act as drawn here is changed only slightly from James M. Varnum's draft that was approved by the members on 25 Oct. (See note 2, petition, above. The Varnum draft is owned by NjMoW). The final printed version, pp. 101–4 of the *Acts and Resolves* (1773–75), differs only in minor details from this version, which was engrossed and passed by both houses of the legislature on 29 Oct. At the same session, the legislature chartered the Newport Light Infantry, Providence Grenadier Company, and Pawtuxet Rangers. At the December session, it chartered the Scituate Hunters, Providence Train of Artillery, Providence Fusiliers, and North Providence Rangers (Bartlett, *Records*, 7: 260–64).

# To Colonel James M. Varnum

Dear Sir     [Coventry, R.I.] Monday 2 oClock pm [Oct. 31 1774][1]

As I am ambitious of maintaining a place in your esteem, and cannot hope to do it if I discover in my actions a little mind and a mean spirit, I think in justice to my self I ought to acquaint you with the particulars of the subject upon which we conversed today.[2] I was informd the Gentlemen of East Greenwich said that I was a blemish to the company. I confess it is the first stroke of mortification that I ever felt from being considered either in private or publick Life a blemish to those with whom I assosiateed. Hithertoo I have always had the happiness to find myself respected in society in general, and my friendship courted by as respectable charactors as any in the Government. Pleasd with these thoughts, and anxious to promote the good of my country and ambitious of increaseing the consequence of East Greenwich, I have exerted myself to form a military company there, but little did I think that the Gentlemen considerd me in the light of an obtrudr. My heart is too susceptible of pride, and my sentiments too delicate to wish a connexion where I am considerd in an inferior point of light. I have always made it my study to promote the interest of Greenwich and to cultivate the good Oppinion of its Inhabitants, that the severity of the speech and the Union of sentiment, coming from Persons so unexpected, might wound the pride of my heart deeper than the force of the observation merited. God knows when I first entered this company I had not in contemplation any kind of office, but was fully determind not to accept any, but Griff[3] and others had been endeavouring to obtain my consent for some weeks past. I never expected that being a member of that company would give me any more consequence in Life, either as a private soldier or commissiond Officer. I thought the cause of Liberty was in danger and as it was attackt by a military force it was necessary to cultivate a military spirit amongst this People, that should tyranny endeavor to make any farther advances we might be prepard to check it in its first sallies. I considerd with my self that if we never should be wanted in that charactor it would form a pretty little society in our meetings where we might relax ourselves a few hours from the various occupations of Life and return to our business again with more Activity and spirit. I did not want to add any new consequence to my self from the distinction of that company. If I had been Ambitious of promotion in a publick charactor you your self can witness for me I have had it in my Power, but I always preferd the pleasures of private society to those of publick distinction.

If I concieve right of the force of the Objection of the Gentlemen of the town it was not as an officer but as a soldier, for that my halting was a blemish to the rest. I confess it is my misfortune to limp a little[4] but I did not concieve it to be so great: but we are not apt to discover our own defects. I feel the less mortified at it as its natural and not a stain or defection that resulted from my Actions. I have pleasd my self with the thoughts of servering under you, but as it is the general Oppinion that I am unfit for such an undertaking I shall desist. I feel not the less inclination to promote the good of the Company because I am not to be one of its members. I will do every thing thats in my power to procure the Charter.[5] I will be at my proportion of the expence untill the company is formd and compleatly equipt. Let me intreat you Sir if you have any regard for me not to forsake the company at this critical season, for I fear the consequences. If you mean to obblige me by it, I assure you it will not. I would not have the company break and disband for fifty Dollars. It would be a disgrace upon the county and upon the town in particular. I feel more mortification than resentment, but I think it would manifested a more generous temper to have given me their Oppinions in private than to make proclamation of it in publick as a capital objection, for nobody loves to be the subject of ridicule however true the cause. I purpose to attend tomorrow if my business will permit, and as Mrs Greene is waiting will add no more only that I am with great truth Your sincere friend

NATHANAEL GREENE

ALS (Original in possession of Albert E. Lownes, Providence, R.I., 1972).

1. The date is established by the election of officers as related in note 2.

2. The subject was the election of officers which had taken place on the previous Tuesday, 25 Oct. At that meeting Varnum had been elected captain; Richard Fry, first lieutenant; Christopher Greene (son of Phillip Greene), second lieutenant; and Hopkins Cooke, ensign. NG, who had been a prime mover in forming the guards, expected to be elected a lieutenant. He was shocked and deeply hurt by the rejection.

3. Cousin Griffin Greene.

4. His limp was barely noticeable, never seriously hampering his physical activities.

Some biographers have attributed it to his working the huge bellows at the forge by foot, but he explains it here as "natural" and not resulting from his "Actions."

It is the only known reference in his writing to a subject about which he was extremely sensitive.

5. He thought better of resigning and became, in fact, one of the most faithful attendants of meetings. In saying that he would help to procure the charter, he apparently did not know that the Assembly had voted to incorporate the guards before adjourning the previous Saturday, 29 Oct.

## Proposed Resolution of Kentish Guards[1]

Monday Evening East Greenwich [R.I.]
17 April 1775

Whereas by the malitious Contrivance of some evil minded Person or Persons a Report hath been industriously propagated, that the Independent Company of "Kentish Guards" have either made or are about to make Application to the General Assembly requesting an Allowance for the Loss of Time and the various Expences they have been at in cultivating the military Art, furnishing themselves with Guns, Clothing &c; From a just Indignation at so undeserved a Falsehood, said Company are induced to Resolve, that they possess Principles and Sentiments too inseperably connected with the good of this Colony, the Liberties of America and the Rights of Mankind, ever to have harboured a Thot so derogatory to their Honor; and farther signed by order of the Company.

That if an Allowance was offered them they would refuse it [with?] just Resentment.[2]

D (Kentish Guards Papers: RHi).

1. It is not known to whom this indignant resolution was directed. The Guards may have intended to have it printed in the Providence *Gazette*. In any case, it was lost in the clamor and confusion that accompanied the news of Lexington and Concord two days later.

2. Not all members present were in favor of this final proposition (written in the margin of the original); when a vote was taken, the tally keeper made twenty-three notches under the heading of "not" and thirteen under "In," although it is not clear whether it was the minority or the majority who favored accepting the allowance.

The records of the Guards between their petition of 25 Oct. 1774 and this resolution are sparse, consisting mostly of a few weekly roll calls and a few letters and scattered bills. The company was far from idle during those months, however. Membership grew from the thirty-eight original signers to a high of sixty-four members in January. Attendance was kept reasonably high by the imposition of fines for nonattendance. NG was among the most faithful attendants; some attended rarely and eventually dropped out. The forty or so who remained looked more and more like a military outfit. William Johnson continued to drill them, three days a week at first, and William Williams continued to fife and to teach the fife and drum.

Members, moreover, soon after organizing began to equip themselves with guns (the term they used in this resolution for muskets, although some modern writers mistakenly believe the term was used only for cannon). They also set about to contrive uniforms. No painting or description of their first uniform has survived, but from MS account books of East Greenwich merchants (RHi), it is clear that they were colorful. Gideon Mumford's accounts during the winter are filled with a variety of items to

"William Johnson Master of Miletry," as well as to individual members. These articles include yards and yards of "Red Brod Cloth," "Red Gimp," "Red Tammy," "Blew Dusset," and "Blew Tammy." There were innumerable "Silver Baskite Jacket buttons" of two sizes, "taild Wigs" and powder for wigs, knee garters and buckles. Merchant Silas Casey sold to the Guards among other items, "3 yds Nonesopritty" at two shillings per yard. The wife of Dr. Joseph Joslyn, a member, made shirts and stocks for some of the men. The company bought several quires of paper, ink, lead, and cartridge paper.

How thoroughly trained in the martial arts they were by Apr. 1775 is not known. What is known is that they furnished two generals to the Continental army (Varnum and NG) and at least three colonels, including Col. Christopher Greene, the hero of Red Bank. Lieutenant colonels, majors, captains, and lieutenants also came from their ranks. It is doubtful if any similar colonial group did as well. It is possible that it was not entirely the result of coincidence. They could and did boast of one thing: whatever training Gen. Nathanael Greene carried with him to the siege of Boston he had received as a member of the Kentish Guards. Two days after this meeting, the group headed for Boston to aid the Massachusetts militia, only to be turned around at Pawtucket by word that the British had withdrawn into Boston after their disastrous march from Concord. Pvt. Nathanael Greene could hardly have dreamed as he returned to Coventry that in two weeks he would be Brig. Gen. Greene, in command of Rhode Island's Army of Observation. (Sources for the above account are manuscripts in RHi. In addition to the papers of the Kentish Guards, the account books of Gideon Mumford, Silas Casey, and Preserved Pearce—who kept tabs of the drinks he served them—are useful. Most of the papers of the Guards have only recently come to light, having been buried in the voluminous papers of Richard Ward Greene and Albert C. Greene—prominent nineteenth-century Rhode Island attorneys and collateral descendants of NG.)

# Appointment as Brigadier General
## of the Rhode Island Army

By the Honorable the General Assembly of the English Colony of Rhode Island and Providence Plantations in New England in America.

To Nathaniel Greene Esquire Greeting[1] Whereas for the Preservation of the Rights and Liberties of His Majesty's loyal and faithful Subjects in this Colony and America, the aforesaid General Assembly have ordered Fifteen Hundred Men to be inlisted and embodied into an Army of Observation, and to be formed into One Brigade under the Command of a Brigadier General and have appointed you the said Nathaniel Greene Brigadier General of the said Army of Observation; You are therefore hereby in His Majesty's Name George the Third by the Grace of God King of Great Britain etc. authorised, empowered and commissioned to have, take and exercise the Office of Brigadier General of the said Army of Observation, and to command, guide and conduct the same or any Part thereof. And in Case of an Invasion or Assault of a Common Enemy to disturb this or any other of His Majesty's Colonies in America, you ⟨are to alarm and gather⟩ together the Army under your Command or any Part thereof as you shall deem sufficient, and therewith to the utmost of your Skill and Ability you are to resist, expel, kill and destroy them in Order to preserve the Interest of His Majesty and His good Subjects in these Parts. You are also to follow such Instructions, Directions and Orders as shall from Time to Time be given forth either by the General Assembly or your superior Officers. And for your so doing this Commission shall be your sufficient Warrant.[2]

By Virtue of an Act of the said General Assembly I Henry Ward Esq., Secretary of the said Colony have hereunto set my Hand and the Publick Seal of the said Colony this Eighth Day of May A.D 1775, and in the Fifteenth Year of His said Majesty's Reign.

HENRY WARD

DS (Governor's Office, Providence, R.I.). Portion in angle brackets from Greene, *Greene*, 1: 81–82.

1. Rhode Island reacted to the news of Lexington and Concord by calling a special session of the legislature at Providence on 22 Apr. After setting aside 11 May as a day of "fasting, prayer and humiliation," the Assembly took up consideration of some less passive measures. One of these, which was approved, was the formation of an army of observation, following a preamble in which they justified their action: "At this very dangerous crisis of American affairs; at a time when we are surrounded with fleets and armies, which threaten our immediate destruction; at time when the fears and anxieties of the people, throw them into the utmost distress, and totally prevent them from attending to the common occupations of life; to prevent the mischievous consequences that must necessarily attend such a disordered state, and to restore peace to the minds of the good people of this colony, it appears absolutely necessary to this Assembly, that a number of men be raised and embodied, properly armed and disciplined, to continue in this colony, as an army of observation, to repel any insult or violence that may be offered to the inhabitants" (Bartlett, *Records*, 7: 309–10). Although Gov. Joseph Wanton and Deputy Gov. Darius Sessions had shown themselves among the strongest adherents of Rhode Island's rights, especially during the trying period that followed destruction of the *Gaspee*, they joined with two members of the council in opposing an army "to repel any insult or violence that may be offered to the inhabitants"; and although nothing was said in the Assembly's version of the act about sending troops to Boston, Wanton and Sessions, knowing this was in the legislators' minds, said further that they were against marching "them out of this colony, to join and co-operate with the forces of the neighboring colonies." Their reasons, stated simply, were that "such a measure will be attended with the most fatal consequences to our charter privileges; involve the country in all the horrors of a civil war; and, as we conceive, is an open violation of the oath of allegiance which we have severally taken, upon our admission into the respective offices we now hold in the colony." (Bartlett, *Records*, 7: 311)

The legislature was not moved by the formal protest. They refused to give the oath of office to Gov. Wanton (who had just been reelected); then, because he had not taken the oath, they voted to replace him with Deputy Gov. Nicholas Cooke, who *was* willing to approve the army. The next session was due to meet in Newport on 3 May, but fearing Wanton's "Tory" friends, the Assembly changed the location to Providence. One of their first acts was to specify an army of fifteen hundred men, each to receive a bounty of $4, embodied in one brigade of three regiments. (The number was reduced in the June session by over one hundred men who were assigned to the new Rhode Island two-ship navy (Bartlett, *Records*, 7: 346–47). One regiment was to be raised in Newport and Bristol counties under Col. Thomas Church; one in Providence County under Col. Daniel Hitchcock; and one in Kent and Kings counties under NG's friend, the captain of the Kentish Guards, James M. Varnum.

On the choice of Private Nathanael Greene to head up this army in preference to dozens of militia officers, ranking from ensigns through majors and colonels to Gen. Simeon Potter (many of them veterans of the French and Indian War), see discussion in the introduction.

2. The wording would indicate that Sec'y Ward used the form for commissioning subordinate officers, for NG is directed to take orders from his "superior Officers," although the Assembly had made the post of brigadier general subordinate to no other officer. The act approving the appointment was omitted in the manuscript and printed *Acts and Resolves* but was noted in the MS House Journal for 8 May 1775 (R-Ar). The misspelled first name is typical of most documents concerning him, including his two commissions in the Continental army.

## To General John Thomas[1]

Sir                                                    Roxbury [Mass.] 23d May 1775[2]

Upon a full View of the Situation at Jamaica Plains, we have concluded to incamp upon the forfeited Lands of the Arch-Traitor Barnard.[3] The Reasons which induce us hereto are: In the Front is a Pond, In the Rear and upon the left Flank an Hill gradually descending on every Side, capable of being defended to the greatest Advantage, and form a most excellent post for observation; is likewise tolerably contiguous to both Camps. We hope for your Approbation in this Choice; which, if we obtain Our Quartermasters' will proceed upon the Necessary Steps for incamping &c. I am Sir, in due Respect, your Friend and hb Servant

N GREENE

ALS (NHi).

1. John Thomas (1724–76) was in command of the Massachusetts militia in the Roxbury-Dorchester sector from 20 Apr. 1775 until the British evacuation in Mar. 1776. Although nominally under Gen. Artemas Ward, whose headquarters were in Cambridge, he was virtually independent during the two months that NG served under him (*DAB*; French, *First Year*, p. 48). If the Rhode Island Assembly gave NG instructions on his role in the siege of Boston, they have not survived. The placement of Rhode Island troops in Roxbury was probably settled informally by NG and Gen. Ward.

2. Since his appointment on 8 May, NG had wasted no time in overseeing the recruiting, equipping, and training of the new army. The officers named by the legislature to serve in the three regiments had set about immediately to recruit. Although many of them had had some training, at least in such newly chartered companies as the Kentish Guards, most of the rank and file recruits were untrained boys in their teens or older men without skills. Some were riff-raff. Not all members of the newly chartered companies volunteered for army service, and even if all had joined, their total number was far below fifteen hundred. In their May session, the legislature adopted formal rules and orders for the green army consisting of fifty-three articles. Based on the English army's Articles of War and resembling the articles adopted a month later by the Continental Congress, they were harsh rules for men who, except for those who had served on board ship, had known little discipline.

Before recruiting was complete, NG was forced to go to Roxbury to choose a camp site because, as Gen. Thomas wrote, "Troop from Rhode Island govnt are comeing in Every Day in Small Parteys." (John Thomas to his wife, 24 May 1775, MHi). NG decided on the site the same day he wrote Gen. Thomas, returning after a few days to Rhode Island to encourage recruiting and acquire supplies; in this last objective, he was greatly aided by his brother Jacob. He went back to Roxbury on 2 June, but it was almost two more weeks before Varnum's regiment arrived in Roxbury.

3. Gov. Francis Bernard had been recalled to England in 1769. The next owner, William Pepperrell, lost the property because of loyalist sympathies. It consisted of some sixty acres, including a spacious mansion house set among exotic plantings. The

Rhode Islanders who encamped around the house turned the hothouse into a powder magazine. (Francis S. Drake, *The Town of Roxbury* [1878], p. 429) Officers of the Third R.I. Regiment used the house for their headquarters (William T. Miller to his wife, 29 May 1775, reprinted in *N. Eng. Hist. and Gen. Reg.* 11 [1857]: 136–38). NG and his staff occupied the nearby Loring-Greenough House at Jamaica Plains (Justin Winsor, *Memorial History of Boston, 1630–1880*, 4 vols. [Boston: 1880–81], 3: 116).

## Colonel James M. Varnum to the Rev. John Murray[1]

Dear Sir,                                                                        [? R.I.] May 24, 1775.
Amidst that concurrence of events which the great Creator in infinite wisdom directs, for the accomplishment of his own purposes, a British armament hath set hostile foot upon American ground. What the design of the Almighty may be, we cannot at present absolutely determine. One thing we know, *our cause is just*, and also that the Parent of the universe can do no wrong. An army hath been raised in this Colony, which is now stationed upon Jamaica Plains, in Roxbury, and that this army may do honour to themselves, and the cause in which they are embarked, it is requisite, propriety of manners, regularity of conduct, and a due reliance upon the Almighty controller of events, should be cultivated and enforced. The most probable human means we can devise to effect an object so ardently to be desired, consist in a decent, sincere, and devout attendance, at opportune seasons, upon divine worship. We have, therefore, selected you, as a Chaplain, to our Brigade, well convinced that your extensive benevolence, and abilities, will justify our choice. We cannot, without doing violence to the opinion we have formed of your character, doubt of your ready compliance with our united request. The support you will receive shall *exactly correspond with your feelings, and your wishes*. We are, dear sir, &c. &c. &c. Signed in behalf of the Brigade.

J. N. [M.] VARNUM.

Reprinted from Murray. *Life*, pp. 213–14. Varnum undoubtedly wrote this letter at Greene's direction. See last sentence.
1. The Rev. John Murray (1741–1815), founder of Universalism in America, had come from England in 1770 and first preached in Newport in 1772. In the fall of 1772, he was at East Greenwich where he preached in the courthouse to a large audience. Varnum invited him to dinner at his house along with NG (Murray, *Life*, p. 188). Ezra Stiles was horrified to hear from NG's former tutor, Adam Maxwell, that Murray offered to administer the Lord's Supper as the guests were having a glass of after-dinner wine; he was equally horrified at Murray's denying Eternal Punishment (Stiles, *Diary*, 1: 421).
    Murray was in Rhode Island "visiting friends" when the Army of Observation was formed; he was in Gloucester at the home of Winthrop Sargent when a "respectable messenger" delivered this letter of Varnum's (Murray, *Life*, p. 213). On his appointment as chaplain of NG's continental brigade, see Washington's orders for 17 Sept. 1775 (Fitzpatrick, *GW*, 3: 497). For NG's continuing admiration and defense of his radical friend after he left the army and was being persecuted for his beliefs, see below, NG to whom it may concern, 27 May 1777.

## To Joseph Clarke[1]

Sir                    East Greenwich [R.I.] 29 May 1775[2]
The Commisary[3] will wait on you in his way to Camp, for a sum of money to furnish the Troops with fresh provisions. There is no mode of supply agreed on by Government.[4] The Committee I conceive has power to regulate all those matters, but as they wont be together till he goes out of the Colony, youl please to take the advice of the Committeemen in Providence rellative to his drawing cash out of the Treasury. My reasons for it are it will save one and half per Cent Commissions, and frugallity is necessary in these times of difficulty. My brother gives his consent for the Commisary to draw from the Treasury for the purposes aforesaid.[5] If the Committee in Providence approves, youl please to furnish him with one hundred pounds Lawful. The Committee will meet in Providence on Wednesday next, when theyl take no doubt such further measures as may be necessary. I am sir yours to serve.

NATH GREENE

ALS (MiU-C).
1. Joseph Clarke (1718?–92) was general treasurer of the colony and later of the state from 1761 to his death.
2. On his return to R.I. see below, note 2, NG to Jacob Greene [6–10] June.
3. The commissary was Peter Phillips (1731–1807), a member of the R.I. legislature during much of the revolutionary period, and later chief justice of the Court of Common Pleas. (R.I. Biog. Cycl.)
4. There was, indeed, "no mode of supply agreed on" at this time. An act of 3 May 1775 ordered the printing of £20,000 in currency to pay for supplies, but it gave overlapping authority to the commissary and the Committee of Safety in disbursing the funds. (R.I. Acts and Resolves, 1773–1775, May session, p. 11)
5. Jacob was chairman of the Committee of Safety of Kent County and a member of the five-man Rhode Island committee.

## To Catharine Greene[1]

My Dear Wife                Providence [R.I.] June 2, 1775
I am this moment going to set of for Camp, haveing been detaind by the Committee of Safety till now. I have recommended you to the care of my brethren; direct your conduct by their advice, unless they should so far forget their affection for me as to request anything unworthy of you to comply with. In that case, maintain your own independance untill my return, which, if Providence allows, I will see Justice done you; but I have no reason to think but ⟨that you'll be very kindly and affectionately treated⟩ in my absence. I have not so much in my mind that wounds my peace, as the seperation from you. My bosom is knited to yours by all the gentle feelings that inspire the softest sentiments of conjugal Love. It had been happy for me if I

could have lived a private life in peace and plenty, enjoying all the happiness that results from a well-tempered society, founded on mutual esteem. The social feelings that accompanies such an intercourse is a faint emblem of the divine saints Inhabiting Eternity. But the injury done my Country, and the Chains of Slavery forgeing for posterity, calls me fourth to defend our common rights, and repel the bold invaders of the Sons of freedom. The cause is the cause of God and man. Slavery shuts up every avenue that leads to knowledge, and leaves the soul ignorant of its own importance; it is rendered incapable of promoting human happiness, piety or virtue; and he that betrays that trust, being once acquainted with the pleasure and advantages of Knowledge and freedom, is guilty of a spiritual suicide. I am determined to defend my rights and maintain my freedom, or sell my life in the attempt; and I hope the righteous God that rules the World will bless the Armies of America, and receive the spirits of those whose lot it is to fall in ⟨action into the paradise of God, into whose protection⟩ I commend you and myself; and am, with truest regard, your loving husband

N GREENE

ALS (MiU-C). Original damaged; portions in angle brackets are reprinted from Greene, *Greene*, 1: 83–84.
    1. His bride of less than a year stayed on in the Coventry house. NG had no time to see her when he returned to R.I. briefly. This is the first of his letters to Catharine that has survived.

## To Colonel James M. Varnum

Sir                               Providence [R.I.] June 2, 1775
    This moment accounts arrivd from Portsmouth New Hampshire that the Pirates has began to make Captures of four Vessels. I saw Mr Beene last night and he says that Mr Murray will undertake as Chaplin to the Brigade.[1] Mr John Jenks[2] and John Brown[3] desires that you would with the Companies that March with you attend divine service at your arrival at Providence in their new Meeting-house.[4] If the time and other circumstances will allow it, be kind enough to gratify them, as it will be a pleasing gratification. The Kentish guards I fear will be broke up, if you carry into execution your intended punnishment.[5] I would recommend moderation. The times are so critical, and Union so necessary, that private resentment had better wait a fitter opportunity for satisfaction.

N. GREENE

ALS (RHi).
    1. See Varnum to Rev. John Murray, 24 May, above.
    2. John Jenks (1730–91) was a Providence merchant and prominent patriot; he

served on the Committee of Correspondence and the Committee of Safety and was later active in erecting a powder mill to supply the army (William Browne, *Genealogy of the Jenks Family in America* [Concord, N.H.: 1952], pp. 61–62).

3. John Brown (1730–1803) was a member of Rhode Island's well-known family of merchants, manufacturers, and philanthropists. He was an outspoken critic of England's colonial policies from the Stamp Act onward. After the battles of Lexington and Concord, one of his ships was captured by the British and he was made prisoner for a time. His elegant house, built after the Revolution, is now owned by the R.I. Historical Society. See Hedges, *Browns*, for an excellent account of the family.

4. He refers to the Baptist meeting house, a handsome example of colonial architecture, designed by John Brown's brother Joseph. The building still stands.

5. The nature of Varnum's difficulties with the Kentish Guards is not known. Varnum had been captain of the company but should have relinquished the post when he was made a colonel of one of the three R.I. regiments in the Army of Observation.

## General Greene's Orders[1]

Rhode Island Camp [Roxbury, Mass.] June 4th 1775

The Strength of the Brigade to be given in to Parade at Five oClock and attend Prayers at Six. The officers are Desir'd to Treat the Troops that behave well with all the gentleness and Humanity that they Can wish or Expect, but Punish the Refractory and Seditious with Exemplary Punishment. The officers are Desired to Supress as much as Posable all Debauchery and Vulgar Language Inconsistent with the Character of Soldiers.[2] The Soldiers are desired to be told that all their Complaints Comeing up in proper Channells Shall be Duely attended too and their grievances Redressed. The Commizary is Directed to Supply the Troops agreeable to the Massachusetts mode of Supply, But if the People are Desirous to have Part of their Supply in milch the Capts are Requested to make out a List of their names and Present them to the Commissary who is Required to make Provisions for their supply a Pint of milk for Each man and Deduct the value thereof out of their Dayly Supply of Meat. The State of the Magazine to be made out as Soon as Posable.

Hitchcock Orderly Book no. 1 (RHi). This is the earliest of NG's orders to survive. Three MS orderly books at RHi, which were kept by unnamed company commanders, are designated as Hitchcock no. 1, no. 2, or no. 3. While captains were not chosen primarily for excellence in spelling and grammar, few carried phonetic spelling to the extent that these three did. Most of their orders that follow are abstracted, but verbatim examples are found at NG's orders of 2 and 14 Aug. and 19 Sept., below. From the spelling it is apparent they copied the orders as they were read aloud and did not see the written copy kept by the adjutant.

1. Orderly books followed the command structure: headquarters orders (originating with Washington or a commander in an area far removed from him); division orders (originating with a major general or other general officer in command of several brigades); brigade orders (originating with a brigadier general or senior colonel); and regimental orders (originating with a colonel in command of several companies). Each level repeated the orders of those above it.

NG's orders are less significant documents than those originating with Washington, whose orders reflect the gradual shaping of the Continental army in the first year of the war. NG's brigade orders often merely reinforce Washington's; other times they reflect the uniqueness of NG's brigade or of his thinking. When he was put in command of the Southern Army in Oct. 1780, his orders took on a new significance.

Several points about orderly books are worth stressing: (1) they did not record events, (2) the orders copied in them were not necessarily carried out, and (3) they omitted orders directed to an individual officer or general orders given in the course of an action.

2. Swearing was commonplace among the rank and file. A Connecticut man wrote from Roxbury 15 June 1775 that the "moral state of the Camp it is bad . . . my ears are filled with the most shocking oaths and imprications; and the tremendous name of the great God is taken at the most trifling occasions. The principle part of the Troops that are here belong to this and Rhode Island Governments; ours are not so bad as theirs but we are far from having any thing to boast of" (James Cogswell to Levi Hart, MHS, *Proc.* 59 [1925]: 115). NG and his fellow generals believed the patriot cause might be unfavorably judged by such swearing; to stop such behavior may have seemed like turning back the tide, but they continued the effort. In the articles of war that Congress adopted a few weeks later for the Continental army (similar to Rhode Island Articles 1 and 2), it was "earnestly recommended" that officers and soldiers "diligently . . . attend Divine Service." Any man behaving "indecently or irreverently at any place of Divine Worship" (Article II) or "guilty of profane cursing or swearing any where" (Article III) would be punished, the soldier more severely than the officer. (*JCC*, 2: 112; the R.I. Articles are in Bartlett, *Records*, 7: 341.)

# To Jacob Greene

Rhode Island Camp [Roxbury, Mass.] June 2 [6–10] 1775[1]

I arrived in camp on Saturday last and found it in great commotion. A few days longer in the state of excitement in which I found our troops would have proved fatal to our campaign.[2] The want of government, and of a certainty of supplies, had thrown every thing into disorder. Several companies had clubbed their muskets in order to march home. I have made several regulations for introducing order, and composing their murmurs; but it is very difficult to limit people who had had so much latitude without throwing them into disorder. The commissaries had been beaten off at my arrival and were about returning home the next day. I believe there never was a person more welcome who was so little deserving as myself. I wish you would forward Colonel Varnum's regiment; he will be a welcome guest in camp. I expect much from his and his troops example.

Excerpt reprinted from Johnson, *Greene*, 1: 31–32.

1. Johnson dated this 2 June, but NG did not return from Providence until Saturday, 3 June. The phrase "Saturday last" would indicate he had been in camp no more than a week, while the "several regulations" he had made would imply a few days' lapse.

2. Only the most compelling need for supplies could have induced NG to leave the two regiments of raw recruits in Roxbury (under Col. Hitchcock and Col. Church) and return to Rhode Island for meetings with the Committee of Safety, although an additional motive may have been to encourage recruiting of the third regiment under Col. James M. Varnum.

The Providence regiment was under the command of Col. Daniel Hitchcock (1739–77), who was born in Springfield, Mass., and educated at Yale University. Having established a successful law practice in his native state, he moved to Providence in the early 1770s, where he soon proved himself one of the colony's ablest lawyers. A strong advocate of American rights, Hitchcock, like NG, joined an independent military company in 1774—the Providence Train of Artillery—and was soon elected a lieutenant colonel. In May 1775 the Assembly appointed him a colonel in the Army of Observation. As a regimental commander, he served directly under NG until Aug. 1776, proving himself one of NG's ablest officers and winning the respect and affection of the men under him as well as his fellow officers. (On his rivalry with Col. James M. Varnum, who was nine years younger, see Hitchcock's letter to Washington, printed in a note, NG to Washington, 12 Aug. 1776, below.) Hitchcock fought with distinction at the battles of Trenton and Princeton; he died a week after Princeton from a fever and exhaustion. A biographical sketch can be found in Henry P. Johnston, *Yale and Her Honor Role in the American Revolution, 1775–1783* (New York, 1884), pp. 226–28.

The other regiment in Roxbury, which had been recruited from Bristol and Newport counties, was commanded by Col. Thomas Church (1727–97). Church, a devoted patriot, had served several terms in the Rhode Island Assembly and would later serve in the upper house of the new state, but NG considered him a poor disciplinarian. Consequently, when Rhode Island's three regiments were reduced to two in the fall of 1775 and the men reassigned to the new regiments, it was Col. Church who lost his command. Returning to Rhode Island, he carried out various military tasks for the state during the remainder of the war. See index references in Bartlett, *Records*, vol. 7, and John A. Church, *The Descendants of Richard Church of Plymouth Massachusetts* (Rutland, Vt.: Tuttle Co., 1913), a book that should be used with care.

## To [the Rhode Island Committee of Safety][1]

Roxbury [Mass.]

Gentleman [Gentlemen]                    Sunday [18 June 1775][2]

I have examined the Magazine and find that we have but Eleven Casks of Powder and four hundred weight of ball. Our stocks are far too small for our critical situation. Our forces are now engaged with the Regulars on Charles Town side. The action began yesterday, continued all last night and Charlestown is burnt down, and they are now closely engaged today. The number of the slain and wounded on either side is not known, but very considerable. Doctor [Joseph] Warren is missing, supposd to be dead as he was in the action, but I hope its not true. There has gone a detachment from our Roxbury Troops of one hundred men, commanded by Major [Christopher] Greene. They were detached before my arrival at Camp. I rode all last night and got into Camp about Day break. We are hourly in expectation of an attack. Youl please therefore to forward us about two Tons of Powder and as many ball as you can conveniently spare.[3] The action is warm and prosecuted with great spirit on both sides. Forward Colonel Varnums Regiment as fast as possible. I had like to have forgot flints. We have not enough for the Troops; dont forget them. If theres any thing particular from the Congress please to acquaint me with the contents. I am Gentlemen your most obedient humble servant

NATH GREENE

ALS (MH).
1. The addressee is identified by a reference in the following letter to Deputy Gov. Cooke.
2. The date is established by the Battle of Bunker Hill the previous day.
3. What action the Committee of Safety took is not known. Since it is unlikely that it had any ammunition in its possession, each county committee would have to requisition the supplies from the towns to which the Assembly had apportioned more than a ton of powder and two tons of lead in Apr. (*R.I. Acts and Resolves, 1773–1775,* Apr. 1775, pp. 165–66) So desperate was the need that the Assembly now ordered an inventory taken of the powder and lead in the hands of each individual in the colony (Bartlett, *Records,* 7: 356).

# To Deputy Governor Nicholas Cooke of Rhode Island[1]

Roxbury [Mass.]
May it please your honnor                                    18 of June 1775
Your favor of this day I receivd.[2] I thank your honnor for the seasonable supply as we have but a very small quantity for action. I sent an express of a few hours past for Powder, Ball and flints to the Committee of safety. Youl be kind enough to let them know what you have ordered forward, and advise them to forward the Ball and flints I wrote for. With regard to the Militia we have no occation for them. We have here as many of the Province militia as we know what to do with. The action began yesterday at Bunkers Hill. About day break General [Israel] Putnam had taken post there and flung up an entrenchment with a detachment of about three hundred.[3] The Regulars land[ed] about two thousand and attempted three times to force their entrenchment, but was severely repulsed, and it was thought would have gone off, but some of the Provincials imprudently called out to their officer that their powder was gone. The Regulars heard it, turnd about, charg'd their Bayonets and forced the entrenchment. A smart action ensued, our People fought with amazing resolution but from the difference in number, and the want of Powder they were after a great struggle forced to give way. They took a few field pieces. The action continued all last night and today, with some small intermission. General Ward wrote this afternoon that we had lost about forty men killed and a hundred wounded. It is supposd Doctor [Joseph] Warren is among the number of the slain, and he says they have killed more than three times that number of the Regulars.[4] Whether that is to be depended upon I cant say, but from what I can learn from other hands I think it is true. They set the Town of Charles Town on fire yesterday in the afternoon, and it continued burning all last night. Today several houses has been burnt. They have got almost all their force over on that side, and strongly entrenched on Bunkers Hill. Our people has entrencht on a Hill opposite them called Prospect Hill. They are constantly fireing Cannon shot at us which from the scarcity of Powder in general our People dont think proper

to Answer. But they are in high spirits. There went a detachment
from Roxbury last night of a thousand men, one hundred of which
was drawn out of our Brigade. Commanded by Major [Christopher]
Greene. I heard from him a little while since, unhurt and very well. I
rode all last night to get down to Camp. I found the Troops in good
order. They [the Regulars] flung a few Boombs amongst them yesterday. Their disagreeable face and noise put them into a little disorder. But they express a strong desire to fight. Had we powder in
plenty they should have an opportunity to distinguish themselves
tonight. The forgoing is as true a state of the Matters and things now
transacting in about Boston as I am able through hurry and confusion
to give you. I am your honnors most obedient humble servant

NATHANAEL GREENE

ALS (MH).
    1. Nicholas Cooke (1717–82), after a career as a shipmaster, became a successful
merchant and distiller in Providence. When Gov. Joseph Wanton was refused the oath
of office in May 1775 for failing to approve the Army of Observation, Deputy Gov.
Cooke was persuaded to become acting governor over his protests of "advanced age"
(he was fifty-nine). Cooke developed into an energetic and resourceful chief executive,
and in Nov. 1775 the Assembly appointed him as governor in his own right, a post to
which he was subsequently elected each year until he refused reelection in 1778.
Cooke's career has been slighted by historians, despite the availability of voluminous
correspondence. The *DAB*, for example, omitted him. A brief sketch is found in *R.I.
Biog. Cycl*.
    2. Apparently a shipment of powder.
    3. Although the battle was fought on what is now Breed's Hill, NG was not alone
in calling it Bunkers Hill. According to Frothingham (*Boston*, p. 119), the name Breed's
Hill had not yet been given to the several pastures that were the scene of battle on the
hill below Bunker Hill. Historians disagree as to whether there were three attacks on
the American lines as related by NG. Frothingham, *Boston*, a classic work, is still
valuable on the most serious defeat the British were to suffer until 1781. An accurate,
readable account is Richard M. Ketchum, *The Battle for Bunker Hill* (Garden City, N.Y.:
Doubleday, 1962).
    Israel Putnam (1718–90), a veteran of the French and Indian War, was a general of
the Connecticut militia. "Old Put," as his men affectionately called him, had a somewhat ambiguous role at Bunker Hill (Frothingham, *Boston*, pp. 168–69). Congress
appointed him one of four major generals a few days later (*DAB*). At the battle of Long
Island, he replaced NG who was ill.
    4. Dr. Joseph Warren (1741–75), a year older than NG, was president of the
Massachusetts Provincial Congress as well as a general of the state militia. His death
was widely lamented throughout the colonies. A modern biography is John Cary,
*Joseph Warren: Physician, Politician, Patriot* (Urbana: University of Illinois Press, 1961).

## To General Thomas (?)

[From Rhode Island Camp, Jamaica Plains, Mass., 21 June 1775.
Request for a pass to permit Capt. Thayer[1] and Lieut. Black to go to
British lines in order to capture a sentry. ALS (RHi) 1 p.]

1. Capt. Simeon Thayer of Providence is remembered for the *Journal* that he kept on the march to Quebec with Benedict Arnold. It is printed in RIHS, *Coll.* 6 (1867): 1–45.

## Commission

[Formal printed commission to "Nathaniel Green Esquire" as eighth brigadier general "in the army of the United Colonies, raised for the defence of American liberty, and for repelling every hostile invasion thereof," signed by John Hancock, president of Congress and attested by Charles Thomson, secretary. (22 June 1775)[1] DS (MiU-C)]

1. On 16 June, Congress decided there should be eight brigadier generals in the Continental army, each to be paid $125 per month. On 22 June they named, in order from one to eight, Seth Pomeroy, Richard Montgomery, David Wooster, William Heath, Joseph Spencer, John Thomas, John Sullivan, and Nathanael Greene. (*JCC*, 2: 93, 103) All but Montgomery were from New England. NG's appointment was almost automatic, since Congress was not about to slight Rhode Island by taking away a general; NG, in turn, had already begun to win the admiration of both Rhode Island delegates— Samuel Ward and Stephen Hopkins—as well as most of the patriot leaders in the colony. See note 3, NG to Jacob Greene, 28 June, below.

## To Deputy Governor Nicholas Cooke of Rhode Island

Rhode Island Camp Jamacai Plains [Mass.] June 22, 1775

I receivd your favor the 19th of this instant rellative to the Powder.[1] You may depend upon my doing every thing to preserve our stock. I fully agree with you that our stock of powder is small, and that occonemy is absolutely necessary, as my fate, your fate and all the Continent depends upon that Article to make a proper defence. I should think my self criminal to the last degree to neglect so cappital a matter. You may depend upon my doing everything for the service of the Government and the Good of the cause so far as my small abillities enables me. I lament the want of knowledge in Generalship. But as we have all been cultivateing the arts of Peace, its no wonder that we are deficient in the Art of War. I am confident the opposition will be crowned with success finally, but when or how lies in the womb of futurity. My confidence dont arise from our dicipline and military knowledge, but from the Justice of the cause and virtue of America.

It is agreed on all hands that the Enemy lost killed and wounded a thousand men. Major Pitkern [Pitcairn], Major Sheriff and many other officers fell in the action. We have lost about Eighty men and had about one hundred wounded.[2] The Troops are now in good order and seem to be spirited, but action alone can determin their Courage and fortitude. I hope to be preservd with a becoming forti- tude and the Troops from womanish fears in time of action. Tho our enemies has gain'd ground upon us, it is at too dear a rate for them to rejoice much at their success. As Marshal Saxe[3] said once upon obtaining a victory being complemented on the Occasion, said a few such Victories would ruin him, so a few such Victories would ruin them. An express arrivd from the Provincial Congress, New York, that there had cruised a ship off about Sandy Hook to acquaint the Fleet expected in there that they must bear up for Boston. These orders were deliver'd a few days past and three thousand Troops are hourly expected. We are fortifying at Roxbury. I am in hopes in a few Days to compleat so many posts, that we shall be able with half our men to make a better defence than we could at my arival with the whole. They are strongly fortifying on Prospect Hill, on the other side the Bay opposite to the Regulars who are encamped on Bunkers Hill. They turnd out of Boston a large number of Poor People yesterday and told them they were determind to travel through and search every part of America. I immagin theyl have Liberty to do it from the prince of the power of the air, but it must be after a seperation of their wretched Souls from their miserable Bodies. I am with great defference your honnors most obedient humble servant

NATHANAEL GREENE

ALS (MH).
1. Letter not found.
2. The figures for American losses are much too low, but those on British losses are remarkably accurate. Ward lists 226 British killed, 828 wounded—92 of the total being officers. (Ward, *War*, 1:96). Maj. John Pitcairn was respected by the patriots despite his having led British troops at Concord. Ezra Stiles called him "a good man in a bad cause." (Stiles, *Diary*, 1:604)
3. Maurice, Comte de Saxe, was marshall general of France until just before his death in 1750. His *Memoirs Concerning the Art of War*, translated into English in 1759, were widely read. Henry Knox put them first on the list of military works he prepared for John Adams in 1775 (Callahan, *Knox*, p. 35). The book was very likely among those that tradition tells us NG purchased from his young friend, Henry Knox, at his Boston bookstore the previous year.

## To Deputy Governor Nicholas Cooke of Rhode Island

Rhode Island Camp Jamaica Plains [Mass.]

Sir                                                              June 28, 1775

Agreeable to the request you made in your last,[1] I have inclosd the strength of the Regular forces and the Provincial Army lying round Boston.[2] It is the exactest state that I am able to collect from the irregular returns made by the Province Massachusetts and Conecticut Forces.

I dont suggest any new regulation for the Army at present. Should any thing occur to my mind I shall take the earliest opportunity to acquaint you with it. I observe there has been application from this Province for an Augmentation of the Troops. I have only one thing to observe if you wish them to be of service to their Country—be careful in the appointment of the Officers not only the Field Officers but the Captains and Subbalterns—for there are many inconveniences that arise from the bad conduct of Officers that you cannot conceive off unless you had occular demonstration of the evil. A ship arrivd last night with Troops, it has been observd to Day that a ship or two are missing out of the Harbour, it is suspected that they are coming to Rhode Island. But I dont apprehend any attention ought to be paid to the suggestion. I heard a letter read Dated the first of May from Holland, in which is said the Dutch are affronted with the English and have orderd the English Frigates away from the Texel.[3] The French refuses to prohibit the exportation of Ammunition to America in any other way than that of laying a small fine. The Spannish Monarch refuses to lay any restraint upon his Merchants. If these accounts are true which no doubt they are, we may expect soon to have a great plenty of Powder. May God prosper so desirable event. There can no offensive Opperation go forward untill we are better supply'd with Ammunition. But should they sally I hope they'l meet with a very warm reception by the small Arms. The Troops seems to be very quiet at present. And General Gage it is said has sent [out?] a Flag of truce to Day to Putnams Camp the purpose not yet known. This is a condesension in his Excellency; its manifest he dont look upon us in the light of Rebbels but as a common Enemy. I am with great defference Your most Obedient humble servant

NATHANAEL GREENE

ALS (MH). Enclosure missing, but see note 2 for contents.
    1. Letter not found.
    2. Cooke reported to Gov. Trumbull of Connecticut that NG had listed 1,390 effective Rhode Island men at "Jamaica Plains and Roxbury." (Cooke to Trumbull, 1 July 1775, RIHS, *Coll*. 6 [1867]: 108) The figures were probably exaggerated. Even by 21 July the Rhode Island regiments reported to Washington only 1,041 rank and file fit for duty and 215 commissioned and noncommissioned officers, putting them 240 short of authorized strength. (Force, *Archives* [4] 2: 1629–30) The same day that NG wrote Cooke, the R.I. legislature voted that the Army of Observation be under the "command and direction of the commander in chief of the combined American army," but only "during the operations of the present campaign" (Bartlett, *Records*, 7: 355).
    3. Texel—one of the Dutch Frisian Islands.

## To Catharine Greene

My Dear          Rhode Island Camp [Roxbury, Mass.] June 28, 1775
    My thoughts tho greatly employed from the constant round of business on my hands, often steals away to visit your peaceful habitation. The fears and anxieties that must accompany you on my account in my present situation often makes me wish to fly to your arms to

hush those distresses into silence. The Enemy has made several feints to deceive us: their intentions are unknown. Altho they are narrowly watched I make no doubt they'l meet with a deserved fate for their oppression and crueltys and I make no doubt that I shall be safely conducted through the showers of Tory hail. But what ever be my fate let my Reputation stand fair for the inspection of all enquiring friends. I am in health and have been ever since I arrivd at Camp. I rode all Night after I left you, and arrivd here next Day morning when I found Charles Town all burnt to ashes and the Troops engaged on the other side of Cambridge Bay. My compliments to all enquiring friends Nancy Varnum, Betsy Flagg &c, &c. Adieu

N GREENE

ALS (RHi).

## To Jacob Greene

Dear Sir          Rhode Island Camp [Roxbury, Mass.] June 28, 1775
    The Hurry I have been in and the Numberless Employments I am called to have left me no opportunity to write you. I regret it the less as I am confident you have heard every Day from the Camp and almost every Particular Transaction here and many that never were transacted here or anywhere else.
    The Particulars of the late Battles have been differently repre-sented. Sometimes they have lost a Hundred sometimes over Thou-sand and now it goes Fifteen Hundred. I believe from the best accounts I can collect they have suffered near as many as the last Accounts. Many officers fell in the Action. The Welch fuzileers, the finest Regiment in [the] English Establishment, was ruined. There is but one Captain and Eleven Privates left in the Regiment. It is said if some Regiments on our Side had done their Duty as well as others did the Regulars must have sufferd a Total Defeat and they never could have got possession of the Intrenchments. But upon the whole I think we have had little Reason to complain. There is but about Fifty killed on our side in Question. Thirty taken prisoners and about forty wounded. I wish [we] could Sell them another Hill at the same Price we did Bunkers Hill.[1]
    The Regulars are now encamped on Bunkers Hill and our People[2] on Prospect and Winter Hills both strongly intrenched, and our People are in good Spirits. But Regularity and Discipline are much wanting. Our People are raw, irregular, and undisciplined yet bad as they are they are under much better Goverment than any Troops round about Boston.[3] There are some officers in each Regiment that exert themselves to bring the camp into Regulat[ions]. There are

some captains and many Subaltern officers that neglect their Duty, some through Fear of offending their Soldiers, some through Laziness and some through Obstinacy. That makes the Task of the Field officers very Laborious. I have warned them of their Negligence many Times. I determine to break every one of them for the future that lays himself liable.

My task is hard and fatigue great. I go to bed late and rise Early. The numerous Applications you cannot conceive of unless you were present to behold the Round of Business. But hard as it is if I can discharge my Duty to my own Honor and to my country['s] satisfaction, I shall go through the Toil with Chearfulness. My own officers and Soldiers are generally well Satisfied, nay I have not heard one complaint.

The General officers of the Neighbouring Camps treat me with the greatest Respect much more than my Station or Consequence entitle me to. Were I to estimate my Value from the attention paid to my Sentiments and opinions, I should have great Reason to think myself some considerable Personage. But fatal Experience teaches me every day that Mankind are apt to pay the Defference due to the Station and not the Merit of the Person. Therefore when I find myself surrounded by their flattering Address, I consider them as due to my office and not to Me. I shall study to deserve well but cannot but lament the great Defects I find in myself to discharge with Honor and Justice the important Trust committed to my care. You know I never made much Parade nor was ambitious of raising Peoples Expectation higher than I had any Reason to expect my conduct would be answerable to. The world in General are too good Judges not to learn the true Merits of men after being furnished with an opportunity to inspect it. I hope God will preserve me in the Bounds of Moderation and enable me to support myself with proper Dignity, neither rash nor timorous but between them, that my conduct may appear to be regulated by a manly Firmness not of Frenzy.

My Love to All Friends in General. To the Brotherhood in Particular. In hast I remain with great Regard your loving Brother

NATHANIEL GREENE

You'l please to come into some Agreement with the committee of Safety about furnishing the Commissary with Money. He drew £200 lately.

Tr (Foster Transcripts, RHi); Theodore Foster (1752–1828), lawyer, Providence town clerk, and later United States senator (*R.I. Biog. Cycl.*), collected transcripts of many revolutionary papers for a proposed history of Rhode Island. He left ten transcripts of NG letters, possibly made by a nephew who married a daughter of Jacob. Where comparison can be made with originals the transcripts are accurate.

1. See note 2, NG to Cooke, 22 June 1775, above.
2. "Our people" here refers to all American troops. Two sentences later he uses it to designate the Rhode Island troops.
3. In confiding his innermost thoughts to brother Jacob, he was not being unduly boastful; Rhode Island troops *were* considered by more than one observer to rank above other New England troops in discipline and order. From Congress, Samuel Ward reported of the Rhode Island troops that "every Gentleman who has been at [camp] speaks of them with great Encomiums" (to his son, Samuel, Jr., 29 July 1775, RHi). Early in July the Rev. William Emerson thought most of the shelters in camps around Boston reflected the individual styles of a great variety of occupants; but, he added, "Some are your proper tents and marquees, looking like the regular camp of the enemy. In these are the Rhode Islanders, who are furnished with tent-equipage, and everything in the most exact English style" (Frothingham, *Boston*, p. 222). NG was not exaggerating when further on he related the respect in which he was held by his fellow general officers.

## To Deputy Governor Nicholas Cooke of Rhode Island

Rhode Island Camp Jamacai Plains [Mass.]

Honnored sir                                                      July 4, 1775

I have nothing special to acquaint you only that his Excellency General Washington has arrivd and is universally admird.[1] The excellent Charactor he bears, and the promising Genius he possesses gives great spirit to the Troops, and I make no doubt his conduct will manifest the Wisdom and prudence of the Continental Choice. I sent a detachment today of two hundred men commanded by a Colonel, Lieutenant Colonel and Major with a Letter of Address to welcome his excellency to Camp. The detachment met with a very gracious recieption and his Excellency returnd me a very polite answer and Invitation to visit him at his Quarters. A few minutes after the Detachment was drawn out I receivd a Letter directed to his Excellency under cover of one to me[2] from Mr [Henry] Ward, Secretary, who acquaints me that the General Assembly has appointed him to the Command of our Troops, all which is perfectly agreeable and I shall conduct myself accordingly, and hope by his wise direction, accompanyed with my best endeavors and that of all my officers to promote the service of the Colony agreeable to their wishes. I expect the General next Day after tomorrow to Visit our Camp.

There is continual Complaints made to me about the Provisions falling Short, some Barrels not haveing much more than one half and two thirds the quantity they ought to Contain. I wish your honnor would desire the Committee through out the Colony to examin all the Provisions sent to Camp, for I am very positive they must have been greatly imposed upon. The field Officers are continually complaining to me of the imposition, and requesting me to have a stop put to it as soon as possible. Many People in Camp suspects the fidelity of the Committee to suffer such repeated impositions, and still no check put to them. Such unfavorable sentiments propagated abroad must do great injury to their Characters and perhaps render it very difficult for them to settle their Accounts with the Colony and do justice to themselves and those they are concernd with. A quantity of Bread arrivd from Providence last Week and today the much greater part was mouldy and unfit for use. The first parcel I pickt out what was good and condemn'd the rest. This today appears all Bad upon Examination, except a few single Buiskets.[3]

Such Bread being brought here begets Jealosyes amongst the People, that they are going to be imposd upon, and little grieveances are sufficient reasons to grownd their Complaints and murmurs upon especially as they find themselves strongly supported by their friends and Relations that comes to visit the Troops in their quarters. There was a quantity of Beef condemnd last Week as being horse meat. When it first took rise, I thought it merely Chimerical, but Captain Jery Olney, Capt Kitt Olney and many others came and informd me that the People had let in a conceit that it was horse flesh, that they had gone without Victuals all Day, and they desird me to enquire into the matter. I accord[ing]ly did, got a Jury of Butchers to examin it, and they condemned it as unfit for use, a considerable part being horse flesh. Captain John Collins of Newport happend to be at Camp at the same time, and he said he had seen a Bundance of horse Beef, and he said he was confident this was of that kind.

You must, worthy sir, be sensible that the task is difficult and trouble great to form people into any regular Government that comes out with minds possest of notions of Liberty that is nothing short of Licentiousness. I am willing to spend and be spent in so Righteous a Cause, but unless I am supported by the helping hand of Government, my indeavors will be defeated, and your expectations blasted. God knows I am far from complaining out of Prejudice to any mortal, but necessity on the one hand and justice on the other calls on me to represent the matter to you that the evil may be put a stop too as early as possible. Many officers blames me for being so silent upon the Occasion and thinks I dont do Justice to the Colony, but as I am fully sensible that many acts upon such narrow principles of policy, influenceed by party and Prejudice, I have carefully studyed to avoid their Captious advice. But from mature deliberation I have thought it prudent to make you acquainted with the state of the matter that you may take such steps to remove the complaints as the subject requires. If the Troops are comfortably subsisted, if they dont do their duty, they can be punnisht with great justice, but if they are not well fed and properly clad, they excuse all their misconduct from one or the other Reasons. Everything with respect to the Enemy remains much in the same situation as in my last. I am your most Obed

N GREENE

ALS (MWA).
1. The rather pretentious designation for the new commander of the continental forces—His Excellency—was undoubtedly one that someone in Washington's retinue passed along to the general officers. It was certainly not his companion on the trip from Philadelphia, Maj. Gen. Charles Lee, who wrote Dr. Benjamin Rush, "I cannot conceive who the Devil first devis'd the bauble of Excellency for their Commander in Chief, or the more ridiculous of His Honour for me—Upon my Soul They make me spew—" (Lee to Rush, 19 Sept. 1775, *Lee Papers*, 1: 207). For the rest of his life, NG seldom failed to use the honorific in speaking of Washington or to address him as "your Excellency" in letters.
2. Letter not found.
3. See below, NG to Cooke, 12 Sept. 1775, concerning Charles Bowler, the baker for the Rhode Island regiments.

## From Deputy Governor Nicholas Cooke of Rhode Island

Sir                                    Providence [R.I.] July the 8, 1775

Yours of the 28 of June covering the return of our men came duly to hand but as I had nothing meterial to rite I have not answered it before. I observed the caution you gave in respect to the choice of officers and think it was a very Just one. I am not a little sensible of the difficulties arising in the camp from the ungovernable disposition of some of the officers as well as the Privets, and spoke of it publickly in the Assembly when upon the choice of officers. I am in hopes now Generll Washington is arived and the troops of all the provinces seem to be put more immedietly under him that matter will be in some measure Remedied. I allso Remarked what you observed Respecting the Dutch and French and Spanyards Respecting their trade with us in Regard to powder. I am in hopes by the blessing of God that some way will be opened to provide a Sufficiancy of that article for this season. I am in hopes from the intilligence I Receivd from Briggadier Sullivan of New Hampshire one of the continental Congress [that?] in one year more we shal have the means within ourselves to supply that article for the futer.[1] He informd me that Docter Franklin and Docter Rush of Philadelphia had set up a salt peter manufactery in which they had made a small Experiment which turnd out far beyond their Expectation and it was Expected that if their works turnd out as well as it seemed to promise at present they would be able to make a sufficiancy of salt peter in one year to make a sufficiant stock of Powder to last all America in a War of seven years duration.[2]

I have allso Received yours of the 4th of July informing of the arivels of the Generals Washington and Lee and am very glad to hear that they were Received with such a general satisfaction throughout the whole camp, and pray God that there may be a Spirit of Harmony and unannemity Prevail throughout the camp which I look upon under God will be a great means of disapointing our Enemies in their wicked scheams to inslave us. I am very sorry to hear that you have so much Reason to complain of the provisions sent to the camp and am allso Very sensable that if bad provisions are sent there it will make a generall oneasiness immedietly and for that Reason I went immedietly upon the information Mr Phillips[3] gave me when he was hear to the comite of safty in this town and charged them to be very cairfall of what provisions they sent to the camp and not to send any but what they were certain would bear Examming. I have allso now sent a letter to Each committeman throughout the colony upon the Subject a coppy of which I have inclosed you and am in hopes we shall have no occasion of any further complaints of that nature for the futer.[4] We have nothing new to Rite to you from this Quarter Except the men of war seems determined to break up the trade as much as Possable Especially of this town. There is three men of war and a tender now in our bay atacking and plundering Every thing they can lite of, Except some Vessels that belong to Newport whom they suffer to pass without molestation and I am sorry I have so much Reason to tell you that there is such a strong party at Newport that countenances and Joyns with them and gives them all the intilligence and supplies in their power. In short I think there is great Reason to fear they will soon be the strongest party in that town if some method is not taken to prevent it. I am Sr with great truth yr most Humble Servant

NICHOLS COOKE

ADS (RHi). For enclosure of 7 July, see note 4, below.

1. John Sullivan (1740–95), a vain and often contentious lawyer, was appointed a brigadier general while serving as a delegate from New Hampshire to the Continental Congress. He was en route to a command in Boston, where, after 22 July, he served with NG under Gen. Charles Lee in the sector between Cambridge and Charlestown. (See *DAB* and Whittemore, *Sullivan*.) His war career, which was often to prove a tempestuous one, would touch NG's at various times. In spite of disagreements between them, their relations were shaped by mutual respect and affection.

2. In the fall of 1774, Dr. Benjamin Rush of Philadelphia had manufactured saltpeter (potassium nitrate) from tobacco stalks. An account of his experiments was printed in the *Pennsylvania Magazine* for June 1775. Sullivan undoubtedly heard the article discussed in Philadelphia. (Hawke, *Rush*, p. 127) Neither Rush's nor Franklin's biographers refer to Franklin's collaboration. Cooke's optimistic second-hand account was far too rosy. Rush was far from alone in his amateur attempts to manufacture the badly needed product.

3. Peter Phillips, commissary of the Rhode Island army.

4. Cooke's letter of 7 July 1775 to the R.I. Committee of Safety reads: "Representations having been made to me, that some of the provisions supplied the Rhode Island army, encamped at Jamaica Plains, have fallen extremely short in weight, and other parts have been greatly damaged, by which means the Colony not only suffers loss, but discontent and uneasiness prevails among the soldiery, which may be productive of very bad consequences. I therefore think it necessary, and do require you, that you re-pack and weigh all kinds of salt provisions, by you purchased for the use of the said army, that you mark the weight of each cask, and the two initial letters of your name upon each barrel; and that you are very careful with respect to the flour and bread, and all other provisions purchased for the use of the said army" (RIHS, *Coll.* 6 [1867]: 112).

## To Deputy Governor Nicholas Cooke of Rhode Island

Honnored Sir     Rhode Island Camp [Roxbury, Mass.] July 9, 1775
A General Council of War was held to Day at Cambrige, at the close of which his Excellency General Washington, directed me to acquaint you, that he thinks it necessary that the recruits be forwarded as soon as possible, and What Tents are made or can be got made be forwarded as soon as may be. The Captains or one of the Subbalterns come forward with the recruits of each Company.[1]

I am informd by his Excellency that the expense is to be a Continental expence, this you may be assurd off. And as every Government will receive pay for the number of Troops they send I hope the People will enlist chearfully.

Our Troops here are in great want of cloathing and I wish the Commisary might be furnish't by the Committee of safety with a quantity of course Linnens for shirts, and some thing for Coats and Breeches. They also want Hats shoes and Stockings. But every thing that is sent, ought to be at a moderate price as a large Advance gives great uneasyness in the camp not only among the men but among the Officers, for they stand by the People belonging to their respective companies and condemn every appearance of extravagance. There is some People is louzy, and there is no possibillity of getting them clean without a shift of Cloaths which many want and cannot get without they are furnisht by the Committee. I am your honnors most obedient humble servant

NATHANAEL GREENE

ALS (MH).
1. On 28 June the R.I. Assembly authorized two additional companies for each of the three regiments "encamped near Boston." Each company was to consist of sixty men, but the company was to "be sent forward, under the care of one commissioned officer" as soon as twenty men enlisted. (Bartlett, *Records*, 7: 354)

## To Samuel Ward, Senior[1]

Sir                              Roxbury [Mass.] July 14th 1775
I receivd your favor of the 18 and 19th of June and kindly thank you for the favorable sentiments you express for me.[2] But I consider myself more indebted for your good oppinion to your prejudices in my favor than to any real merit that I possess. However I hope not to betray a good cause by an unworthy conduct. As the Government has honnord me with the command of their Troops I shall be guilty of ingratitude not to attempt to deserve it. How far I have and shall succeed I leave to the voice of the impartial Publick at the close of the

Campaign. This you may be assur'd of that my best endeavors shall not be wanting to promote so Righteous a cause. I can only lament that my abillities to plan are not proportionable to my wishes to execute.

His Excellency General Washington has arrivd amongst us, universally admird. Joy was visable on every countenance and it seemd as if the spirit of conquest breathed through the whole army. I hope we shall be taught to copy his example and to prefer the Love of Liberty in this time of publick danger to all the soft pleasures of domestic Life and support ourselves with manly fortitude amidst all the dangers and hardships that attend a state of war. And I doubt not under the Generals wise direction we shall establish such excellent order and stricktness of Dicipline as to invite Victory to attend him where ever he goes.

We are Soldiers who devote ourselves to arms not for the invasion of other Countries but for the defence of our own; not for the gratification of our own private Interest, but for the Publick security. Nevertheless they that assumes this Character and possesses a happy Genius accompanyed with a prudent conduct and fortunes smiles on their endeavors, they have an Opportunity of traveling the shortest Road to the greatest heights of Ambition, and may the deserving obtain what their merit entitles them to.

I am informd by his Excellency that the Idea of Colony Troops is to be abolisht, and that the whole army is to [be] formd into Brigades and the Generals to be appointed by the Congress. If I am continued I shall chearfully serve, if not I shall patiently submit. I wish that good and able men may be the objects of the Continental Choice rather than subjects of particular Interests.

I shall say nothing about the state of things round about Boston, as you will have a more regular and authentic account from his Excellency General Washington than I can give you. Your Son Sammy behaves himself exceding well and is in good health, but the Regiment to which he belongs is not with the Brigade, being orderd some few Days past over to Cambrige. Brother Christopher and his Lady is down here and are gone to Cambrige today. Nancy is at Potowomut and is much better in health than she has been. Charles is in the Army and belongs to the Train of Artillery and has conducted himself very prudently since he joind the Army.[3]

I am informd that some of the Conecticut Generals are disgusted at the appointments of the General officers by the Congress.[4] I should be extreme sorry for any sizms that may creep in through the Posts of honnor from real or immaginary degradation.

Our Troops are Generally healthy and under pretty good dicipline for the time. Without doubt youl have a particular state of all the

Forces. General Lee gives them high encomiums, and I flatter myself they comparitively deserve it.[5]

I have not time to write any farther being called of to attend Business, haveing this opportunity of writing by Mr Morgan, a Gentleman belonging to Philadelphia. Tho it was short I could not deny myself the pleasure of acknowledging your favor. I must trust to your generosity to excuse the incorrectness of this letter as I have not time to correct and copy it. My best Respects to Governor [Stephen] Hopkins and all the Gentlemen of my acquaintance belonging to the Congress, and believe [me] to be your most obedient humble servant

NATHANAEL GREENE

PS I shall write you every opportunity

ALS (MiU-C).
1. Ward was in Philadelphia as a delegate to the second Continental Congress.
2. Letter not found. Until Ward's death in Mar. 1776, seven long letters from NG to him have been found; none of Ward's many letters to NG have appeared. Judging from the correspondence that has survived this is a severe loss, especially during the winter of 1775 when Ward was chairman of the Congressional Committee of the Whole and at a time when he was NG's "most considerable Correspondent," as NG wrote Ward's daughter. "Whole Sheets," he continued, "nay sometimes three or four are sent in one Letter" (NG to Catharine Ward Greene, 13 Jan. 1776, below). If NG's letters between Oct. 1775 and Feb. 1776 are read in conjunction with Ward's letters to his children (Knollenberg, *Ward*, pp. 101–94), there is some evidence that Ward's thinking was at times influenced by NG. If Ward's letters to NG reappeared, they would undoubtedly reveal Ward's influence on NG.
3. Brother Christopher's "Lady" was Ward's daughter, Catharine. "Nancy" was his daughter Anna, and Charles was his oldest son. Charles had joined the army as a private, to the chagrin of his father and the criticism of John Adams, who, like NG, later worked to get Charles a commission. See below, 13 Jan. 1776, NG to Catharine Ward Greene.
4. Gens. David Wooster and Joseph Spencer.
5. Charles Lee (1731–82) was appointed major general in the Continental army in June 1775 in recognition of his professional military background. At the end of July, Greene moved to Prospect Hill, between Cambridge and Charlestown, and, along with Sullivan, was placed under Lee. Lee valued both men, and when in Jan. it seemed as if he would be placed in charge of the Canadian expedition, he asked that either Greene or Sullivan accompany him. Whatever assessment one accepts of his character, the expertise of this witty, eccentric Englishman-turned-patriot was badly needed by the raw Continental army. For a scholarly study of his career see Alden, *Lee*; for an evaluation of Lee as a radical leader, see John Shy, "Charles Lee: The Soldier as Radical," in Billias, *Washington's Generals*, pp. 22–53, and his "American Revolution: The Military Conflict Considered as a Revolutionary War," in Kurtz and Hutson, *Essays*, pp. 121–56.
    Lee later became critical of Greene, but when he was nearing the end of his life in disgrace and solitude, Greene's loyalty and kindness lightened his days. NG had never gotten over the wonder that this English officer of "quality" had taken him under his wing.

## To Deputy Governor Nicholas Cooke of Rhode Island

Rhode Island Camp, Jamaica Plains [Mass.],
Honored Sir                                                              July 17, 1775
I received your favor the 8th of this instant, from which I learn that the Tory party gains ground in Newport. May God defeat their wicked councils and scatter their collected force. It is very surprising that the once highly respected town of Newport for liberty, spirit and freedom, should be willing to bow down their necks with base submission to the galling yoke of tyranny.[1] They have stood as high on the list of fame as any people on the continent, but how great must be their fall from universal respect to universal contempt. With shame and confusion they will soon be obliged to crawl into the secret corners of the earth to hide themselves from the face of the sons of freedom, whose hearts must burn and faces glow with just indignation at such base miscreants that dare attempt the subjugation of the common rights of mankind. Yesterday, a manifesto from the Continental Congress was published at Cambridge, setting forth the accumulated grievances of all the Continent in general, the Massachusetts Bay in particular, and pronouncing this to be a just and necessary war.[2] It was read with great solemnity, and followed by three cheers that made the heavens and earth ring with the approbation of the camp. The following is an account taken from one John Roulstone, a man esteemed for integrity, that came out of Boston last Thursday.[3] 1500 men killed and wounded and missing, at the engagement on Bunker's Hill; and he further adds that there were so many that were mortally wounded, he got it from their hospital returns. There are 5550 inhabitants now in Boston. This account was taken some few days past by General Gage. Beef is sold for 1s. 4 per lb., and other fresh meat in proportion. A calf was sold there last week for 20 dollars. James Leod, Master Leech and one Hunt, the Crier, are prisoners in Boston.[4] A press gang impressed one hundred of the inhabitants into the town of Boston last week, but the greater part of them were soon released. The refugees, &c., are taken but little notice of by either party, that will not enter into actual service. A party has entered, their number unknown; they do duty nights to conceal their number; by that they are small. They have considerable stores of salt provisions, consisting principally of pork. Eight ships arrived last week in Boston. They had about 1600 troops on board. Roulstone thinks they have about 9000 troops in Boston now. They keep about half at Bunker Hill and half in town. From information given them from our lines on the Cambridge side, by persons in women's clothes, they have altered the plan of their lines at Bunker Hill. By this, you [see] there are some traitors amongst us. But the troops in Boston are

greatly intimidated. The inhabitants are tolerably civily treated if they say nothing to the soldiers. They [the soldiers] are exceedingly abusive and insulting. By a gentleman from New York I learnt last evening that there had three parcels of powder arrived there, the quantity unknown. There is, also, fifty quarter casks of powder arrived at Cape Cod. This gentleman says that great pains are taking to raise a body of Canadians to bring into the field against us.

I hope your honor will pardon me for not writing you so often as is my duty. The hurry and confusion that I am constantly kept in, leaves me but little time. I shall endeavor to double my diligence for the future. I must trust to your generosity to excuse all incorrectness, as I have not time to write fair copies or amend clerical errors. I wish your honor constant health that you may be able to go through the fatigue of your employment with spirit and resolution. I am with great esteem your honor's most obedient humble servant,

NATH. GREENE.

Reprinted from RIHS, *Coll*. 6 (1867): 114–16.
1. Newport, chiefly because of its vulnerability to British warships, was the center of loyalist sympathies in Rhode Island. During the May 1775 session of the Assembly, which had been moved to the safety of Providence, Gov. Joseph Wanton and four Newport deputies refused to approve the Army of Observation. As a result Wanton was not permitted to take the oath of office again. Although he had once been a stout defender of Rhode Island rights, by this time he was a confirmed Tory, and he stayed on in Newport until his death in 1780 as one of the more important of the king's friends. Loyalists were a minority in Rhode Island's largest city, but the more numerous neutrals and patriots often feared to express their sentiments. NG did not fully appreciate the hazards of espousing the patriot cause under the guns of HMS *Rose*, commanded by the redoubtable Capt. James Wallace. See Lovejoy, *R.I. Politics*, pp. 180–84; and Joel A. Cohen, "Rhode Island Loyalism and the American Revolution," *R.I. Hist.* 27 (1968): 97–112.
2. The *Declaration of the Causes and Necessities of Taking Up Arms*, passed by the Continental Congress, 6 July 1775.
3. An unsigned letter printed in Force, *Archives*, (4) 2: 1671, and dated 16 July 1775 calls him Mr. Rolston, a goldsmith, who got out of Boston in a fishing schooner.
4. Another unsigned letter of 12 July (Force, *Archives* [4] 2: 1650–51) says that Leech was jailed because of incriminating letters removed from the body of Dr. Joseph Warren. Hunt, the town crier, was jailed for saying that he wished the Americans might kill all the British.

## General Greene's Orders[1]

[Prospect Hill, Mass., 30 July 1775. To prevent continued transgressions of orders through pleas of ignorance, general orders are to be read twice to each company; captains are to take copies for their own conduct and for the information of their companies. If the troops are ignorant of orders, officers will be answerable. Hitchcock Orderly Book no. 1 (RHi) 1 p.]

1. This is NG's first order from his new command post on Prospect Hill. By Washington's orders of 22 July 1775, the army was organized into three grand divisions, each under a major general: Gen. Ward was to command the right wing, with responsibility for protecting Roxbury and the southern dependencies; Gen. Lee was given command of the left wing, covering the area from Cambridge to Charlestown Neck; and Gen. Putnam was assigned the center wing, which covered the area from Roxbury to Cambridge and included the reserves. (Fitzpatrick, *GW*, 3: 354–57) This deployment gave Washington a sound geographical coverage of the British positions for the first time.

Sullivan's and NG's brigades made up the left wing under Lee. Sullivan's brigade was stationed at Winter Hill, NG's at Prospect Hill (also called Mt. Pisgah). This was a high hill that commanded a fine view of Bunker Hill and, beyond Back Bay, the city of Boston. Along the bottom of its southern slope ran the Cambridge-Charlestown Road. To NG's original R.I. regiments, which had just been moved from Sewall's farm in Roxbury, Washington added the Massachusetts regiments of Whitcomb, Gardner, Brewer, and Little which had been stationed at Prospect Hill since June (they are identified at the end of this note).

The fortification of Prospect Hill was begun on 18 June, the day after Bunker Hill, and had never stopped. On 10 July, Washington reported to Congress that entrenchments had been thrown up on both Prospect and Winter hills, "the Enemy's Camp in full view, at the distance of little more than a mile" (Fitzpatrick, *GW*, 3: 321). At one time some four thousand were working on the hill. By the time NG took command, forts had been completed on two eminences, connected by a rampart and fosse (Frothingham, *Boston*, pp. 210–11, 411). In front of the main fort was the parade ground, and nearby was NG's dwelling, where his wife visited soon after (Col. William T. Miller to his wife, 29 July 1775, *N. Eng. Hist. and Gen. Reg.* 11 [1857]: 138).

A few days after the R.I. regiments had moved to Prospect Hill, Gov. Cooke wrote the R.I. delegation in Congress that, from reports of various people who had visited the R.I. camp, the entrenchments were so "strong that it seems almost impossible they should be forced" (to Hopkins and Ward, AAS, *Proc.* 36 [1926]: 258). Gen. Gage had no intention of testing their effectiveness, but since Prospect Hill was within artillery range of Bunker Hill, he ordered sporadic bombardment of NG's fortified positions to keep the Americans guessing.

So effective had been the existing bulwarks of trees and stone walls at Bunker Hill, it is little wonder that the colonials should construct more substantial defenses that would be even more costly for the British to overcome. Throughout the siege of Boston, the American commanders, with the consistent exception of Charles Lee and the occasional exception of Washington, geared their thinking primarily to defensive fighting from behind entrenchments. Lee thought that the colonials were better fighters than they realized, that only in their own minds were they "no match for the Regulars, but when cover'd by a wall or breast work. This notion is still further strengthen'd by the endless works We are throwing up—" (Lee to Benjamin Rush, 19 Sept. 1775, *Lee Papers*, 1: 206). It was a common observation that Americans were more fearful of being shot in the legs than in the head. For the next year, the spade would be the constant companion of most of Washington's soldiers.

Asa Whitcomb was made colonel of a Mass. militia regiment in June 1775 and later commanded the Sixth Continental Regiment (Heitman, *Register*).

Col. Thomas Gardner, who was at Lexington Alarm in Apr. 1775, died 3 July from wounds received at Bunker Hill (Heitman, *Register*). The Mass. Provincial Congress named Col. William Bond to replace him, although the regiment continued to be called "Gardner's Regiment" for some time, a practice that was not unusual with regiments whose commanders had died.

Jonathan Brewer, a colonel of the Mass. militia since May 1775, was also wounded at Bunker Hill. In the spring Brewer had offered to take five hundred volunteers on a march to Quebec by way of the Kennebec and Chaudiere rivers, the route later followed by Benedict Arnold (Ward, *War*, 1: 163–64). He later commanded the Mass. Regiment of Artificers (Heitman, *Register*).

Moses Little (1724–1815), a surveyor who had been born in New Hampshire and became a landowner in Newbury, Mass., had fought in the French and Indian War and commanded a regiment from Essex County at the Lexington Alarm. He remained in NG's brigade throughout the siege of Boston and the defense of New York in the summer of 1776. At the end of 1777, illness forced him to resign his commission. (Heitman, *Register*; George T. Little, *Descendents of George Little* [Auburn, Me., 1882])

## General Greene's Orders

[Prospect Hill, Mass.] August 2, 1775

The Rodislant Magazine to be Examined Imediately. Make an Imediate Retorn by Rigament of the number of Catrages Each parcen has with their Naims and Numbers.[1] The flag is for the futer is to be Strock at 8 in the Eavaning and then to be histed morning. It is to be a Signal for Dismising for the Alarm post threw out the hole Brigade. The adgitant to attend for orders at the Brigade mager tent. There attendance will be Notified by the Beat of Drum, their [three] Rols and Nine flams.[2] The Call on Comand for the time being of Each Rigment are Required more Eariley in the morning in Brining their forces under Comand to their Several alarm posts. Our Situation Being the Utmost Viglant at prasant to us, Supears [Surprise] will be Disagreeable to the Last Degree.

Hitchcock Orderly Book no. 1 (RHi). On the phonetic spelling in this order, see source note, NG's orders of 4 June 1775, above.

1. On 3 Aug., Washington had ordered all brigades to take inventory. He called a council of general officers to report a distressing discovery: according to the inventory, the entire stock of powder amounted to only ninety barrels. The council's first reaction was the dubious proposal of attacking the magazine at Halifax, Nova Scotia. A more practical suggestion was to make an effort to get powder from "the neighbouring Provinces of New Hampshire, Rhode Island and Connecticut," (Varick transcripts, Washington Papers: DLC) Washington emphasized the greatest secrecy, and the secret seems to have been kept from the enemy.

2. A modern dictionary defines a flam as "a drumbeat of two strokes of which the first is a very quick grace note."

## To Commissary Joseph Trumbull[1]

[From Prospect Hill, Mass., 2 Aug. 1775. Lumber left on the hill by General Putnam not to be used by riflemen[2] because it is intended for barracks. ALS (Ct). 1 p.]

1. Joseph Trumbull (1737–78), son of Gov. Jonathan Trumbull of Connecticut and brother of painter John, served ably as commissary general of the Continental army from the summer of 1775 to 1777, when ill health forced him to retire (*DAB*).

2. Col. William Thompson's eight Pennsylvania rifle regiments had just arrived in Cambridge, the first troops from outside New England to join Washington's army. They were assigned to Prospect Hill although not directly under NG. Congress had also authorized two rifle regiments each from Virginia and Maryland. A few days later, Capt. Daniel Morgan arrived from Virginia with his company of riflemen, having covered some six hundred miles in twenty-one days. In 1781 Morgan would serve with

NG in Carolina, having by then proved himself "with the possible exception of Benedict Arnold . . . the outstanding combat officer in the Continental army" (Higginbotham, *War*, p. 102).

Equipped with the long-barreled rifles developed by the Pennsylvania Germans, the frontiersmen in their long white hunting shirts impressed Americans along their route and on Prospect Hill with exhibitions of their marksmanship. They also impressed the British with their ability to pick off sentries at great distances. (Washington reported only two days after this letter that three British captains were "taken off by the Rifle Men" (Fitzpatrick, *GW*, 3: 394). Both the colonials and the British regulars, however, tended to exaggerate the distances at which their rifles were accurate (see discussion in Higginbotham, *War*, p. 120n).

The Pennsylvania contingent on Prospect Hill was not an unmixed blessing. They tended in the first few months to be boisterous and unruly. Gen. Charles Lee said with some exaggeration "their Privates are in general damn'd riff raff—dirty, mutinous, and disaffected." (*Lee Papers*, 1: 212) Lee's opinion was partially formed from his and NG's experience with one group (see below, note, NG to Washington, 10 Sept. 1775).

## General Greene's Orders

[Prospect Hill, Mass., 5 Aug. 1775. Colonels are desired to examine guard reports and appoint regimental courtsmartial. Hitchcock Orderly Book no. 1 (RHi) 1 p.]

## General Greene's Orders

[Prospect Hill, Mass., 8 Aug. 1775. Carpenters not to leave their work except on an alarm. Master carpenter to employ as many men as needed. Hitchcock Orderly Book no. 1 (RHi) 1 p.]

## To Deputy Governor Nicholas Cooke of Rhode Island

Sir                                   Prospect Hill [Mass.] August 9, 1775
    I have been deeply engaged since I removed to this place that I have not had Opportunity [to write you]. I must beg your pardon for my long silence altho it has resulted from necessity. I have nothing special to communicate from the army. Things continue much in the same situation they have been for a fortnight back saveing a few skirmishes that are daily kept up between our Rifflemen and the Regulars. This partisan War cannot amount to any considerable effect. By a Letter from Belcher Noyes out of Boston we learn that the Regular Army has it in contemplation to Plunder the Town of Boston and go off, for he says that money is scarce, Provisions bad, and fewal scarce, and that theres no harmony among the Troops.[1] The Inhabitants are now permited to come out of Town by giveing in their Names to the Town Major, who procures them Certificates and passes. Many of the People that comes out are real Objects of pity, their suffering has been exceeding severe, especially among the poorer sort. Great Violence is done to the cause of humanity in that Town. It

has been very sickly there among the Inhabitants and Troops too; Thirty a Week are buried among the Troops. They have lost since the 19th of April 2500 kild in action and what has dyed with sickness.

Our Troops are now very sickly with the Dysentery. There was about a Week of exceeding hot Weather, thought brought on this distemper, but they are now geting better, and from the change of air and the healthy situation we posted in, I hope we shall recover a perfect state of health very soon.

His Excellency General Washington complains bitterly about the supernumery officers that draws pay. There is most certainly a large number in this province, that has Commisions and very few men.[2] I Perceive that this practice in this Government has given rise to some disagreeable sentiments with regard to the virtue and Justice of their proceedings. His Excellency thinks that where a Government has created more officers than are necessary for the Government of the Troops they send, that the supernumerary Officers must be paid by the Colony's that appoint them. To remove any unfavorable impressions that might arise among the Southern Colonies, and to retrench every unnecessary expence as well as to render the Regiments more perfect and compleat, I would propose to the General Assembly to recall all those Officers that the Field Officers of each Regiment shall not recommend to be continued in service, for I am very confident from my own observation, and it is dayly confirm[ed] by all the Field officers of the different Regiments, that if such a measure was to take place, that the Troops would be better Govern'd, better provided for, and the Battallion render'd infinitely more compleat. There are a number of Vacancies that the supernumery Officers will fill up to form Eight Companies to each Regiment. This measure perhaps may millitate with some particular Interests, but as we are engaged in an expensive War the event of which is uncertain, Every principle of good policy calls for frugallity and good Occonemy. Therefore as this measure will promote so many desirable purposes I wish it may take place. I have proposed this plan to General Washington and it met his highest Approbation and he exprest a hearty desire for its success for the honnor of the Colony and the good of the service. He has exprest a great deal of satisfaction at the conduct of Government and their Troops,[3] and I wish for the benefit of the Colony that there may nothing take place either in the Cabinet or Field that may injure the just claims of our Colony for their equal propotions of what ever the Continental Congress thinks proper from an Estimate of the whole expence to refund us. I make no doubt but that there will be a strickt examination into the different claims of each Colony and every charge that is not well founded will be rejected. This ought to make us careful how we involve the Colony in any unnecessary expence. I am well in health, and in great haste conclude with great esteem your most Obedient humble servant.

NATHANAEL GREENE

ALS (MH).
1. Belcher Noyes (1709–85), a Harvard graduate, was a physician who, though sympathetic with the patriot party, generally avoided politics. He was caught in Boston at the outbreak of hostilities and remained in the city until he escaped in November 1775. (Sibley, *Harvard Grads.*, 8: 235–39).
2. By "this province" he refers to Massachusetts, where according to law a general was also a colonel of a regiment (Hatch, *Administration*, p. 13).
3. He refers to the Rhode Island government.

## To Joseph Trumbull

Sir                    Prospect Hill [Mass.] August 9th 1775
The bearer Mr Griffin Greene informs me that there is no person appointed to bake for the four Regiments of the Massachusets Troops that falls within my Brigade.[1] I shall esteem it a favor if youl confer that small branch of business upon Mr Greene. He is a young Gentleman whose fidelity and honesty may be depended upon. I shall think myself happy in an opportunity to manifest my grateful sense of the Obligation you'l Lay me under in granting my request. For this and all former Civilities I acknowledge myself your debtor and am with the greatest regard your most Obedient humble servant

NATHANAEL GREENE

ALS (Ct).
1. Griffin Greene (1749–1804), a first cousin and long-time favorite of NG, was a partner in the Coventry forge and mills. A member, like NG, of the Society of Friends, he was also one of the cofounders of the Military Company of East Greenwich and the Kentish Guards. As a result of the above letter, Griffin was made baker to the Massachusetts regiments in NG's brigade (see NG to Peter Phillips, 6 May 1776 below). In 1777 he was paymaster in Col. Christopher Greene's regiment (he had married Christopher's sister, Sarah); he then served for a while as a deputy quartermaster under NG. Their joint ventures in several of Griffin's shaky enterprises, as well as the posts that Griffin held under his cousin, aroused criticism, but aside from favoritism (as common then as in later periods of America), it is doubtful that either behaved unethically.
As an investor in the Ohio Company, Griffin emigrated to the frontier settlement of Marietta, Ohio, in 1788, where he was soon commissioned a justice of the court of Quarter Sessions. In 1790 he helped found the settlement of Belpre, and was acclaimed for regularly traveling the five miles to Marietta by canoe to hold court during five years of Indian uprisings. At his death in 1804, he was serving as postmaster of Marietta. (A good short biographical manuscript is in RHi; Griffin saved many of NG's letters, which, thanks to his descendants, found their way into the library of Marietta College.)

## General Greene's Orders

[Prospect Hill, Mass., 11 Aug. 1775. Officers and noncommissioned officers to instruct the men, especially sentries, in camp duties. Henceforth, if sentries are ignorant they will be punished severely. Those found pillaging will be dealt with harshly. No unnecessary drum beating at night.

A local farmer has complained of soldiers gathering and roasting his corn near the guardhouse. "Eney parson [as keeper of the orderly book has it] Detected with Corn or pertators to be sent prisoner to the main gard hoose." A subaltern to be responsible for flags of truce and to conduct the blindfolded enemy to Prospect Hill in the event of a conference or meeting. Hitchcock Orderly Book no. 1 (RHi) 2 pp.]

## General Greene's Orders

[Prospect Hill, Mass.] August 14, 1775
The Camp Coloman[1] of Each Ridgment to Clean the Spears three times a week against there Several alarm posts. The Corl [colonels] are Requested to see it Don. There appears to be a Grate negtlect of the people Reparing to the Neserys [necessaries] agreeable to General orders but to Void there Exerments about the fields pernishously? and Dont fill the Vaults that are Dug as Directed by his Exclently. As the healths of the Camps is greatly Dangred by these Neglects it is Recomended to the ofisers of the Several Ridgments to pay due attention to futer transgresion and Let the Transgresor be ponished with the Utmost Severity.[2] Generals Lee Gard to be furnished with Camp Cittels and to Draw provisions by them selves. The Cort marshal for Coln mansfield is agorned tomorow at 9 Clock as appointed in General orders. The Cort and the partis are to attend at the time and place appinted. Coln Gridly[3] to Draw out a fetege party and to widen and Depen the Ditches Round these Linds at Lest 2 feet and from glaised [glacis] 16 or 18 inshes higt.

Hitchcock Orderly Book no. 1 (RHi). On the phonetic spelling in this order see source note at NG's orders of 4 June 1775 above.

1. The camp colourman (as it was normally spelled) was generally assigned the most disagreeable tasks, including digging and filling latrines. Although the name may have originally derived from those who carried the colors, and later from those who marked out a camp with colours, no such meaning was attached to it in Washington's army.

2. Few commanding officers, including those with medical backgrounds, were more concerned with the health of their men than NG; see below, NG to Washington, 11 Aug. 1776.

3. Richard Gridley (1710–96), chief engineer of the provincial forces, had studied military engineering under a British officer; he supervised the erection of the British batteries surrounding Louisbourg in 1745 (DAB).

## General Greene's Orders

[Prospect Hill, Mass., 18 Aug. 1775. Adjutant to make a report of all men fit for duty or whether sick or absent. Hitchcock Orderly Book no. 1 (RHi) 1 p.]

## General Greene's Orders

[Prospect Hill, Mass., 18 Aug. 1775. To prevent any chance enemy wounding of the guards, they should be paraded under shelter of Plowed Hill.[1] Hitchcock Orderly Book no. 1 (RHi) 1 p.]

1. Plowed Hill completed the line of fortifications from Prospect Hill and Winter Hill to the Mystic River. British troops on Charlestown Neck would come within range of the guns on Plowed Hill.

## General Greene's Orders

[Prospect Hill, Mass., 19 Aug. 1775. Officers to list persons who retail liquor without having permission as sutlers along with the places where they sell, so that they may be brought to "Due punishment."[1] Hitchcock Orderly Book no. 1 (RHi) 1 p.]

1. The misuse of alcohol, greatly aggravated by greedy sutlers, was a severe problem among all the troops near Boston. Many soldiers spent their meager pay on liquor, and courtsmartial abound with cases of drunkenness interfering with the safety of troops or the outcome of an engagement. NG took the lead in attempting to stop the abuses. Before Washington's arrival in Cambridge, NG had requested the Massachusetts Provincial Congress to stop the abuses; and although his letter has not been found, it must have been persuasive, for the "committee appointed to consider the subject of a letter from General Green" made, on 8 July 1775, a tough recommendation that the Provincial Congress promptly passed.

The preamble acknowledged the troubles arising from "divers evil-minded persons selling spirituous liquors" whom the officers were powerless to stop; the resolution went on to authorize a courtmartial for persons selling inside the camps without a license and without an officer's permission, even providing for a courtmartial of licensed civilians selling to troops outside the jurisdiction of the camp. (*Journals of Each Provincial Congress of Massachusetts, 1774–1775* [Boston, 1838], p. 475.) For an application of this last part of the resolution, see NG's orders for 2 Sept. 1775.

## General Greene's Orders

[Prospect Hill, Mass., 20 Aug. 1775. All men to attend grand parade until dismissed. Hitchcock Orderly Book no. 1 (RHi) 1 p.]

## General Greene's Orders

[Prospect Hill, Mass., 21 Aug. 1775. A confusing order directing Brigade Maj. Daniel Box to arrest unnamed officers and men who

sent to Col. Brewer a derogatory letter that subverts the discipline
and regular operation of the army. Capt. Hastings[1] of Col. Whitcomb's
regiment is identified as the person who brought the matter to NG's
attention. Hitchcock Orderly Book no. 1 (RHi) 1 p.]

1. Benjamin Hastings, a captain in the Lexington Alarm of Apr. 1775, served in
Whitcomb's regiment until the end of 1775 (Heitman, *Register*). The charge was based
on misinformation; see NG's orders, 24 Aug. below.

## General Greene's Orders

[Prospect Hill, Mass., 24 Aug. 1775. Since Capt. Black's[1] arrest was
based on misinformation and not from disobedience, he is released.
Hitchcock Orderly Book no. 2 (RHi) 1 p.]

1. John Black was a captain in Brewer's regiment. See order of 21 Aug., above.

## General Greene's Orders

[Prospect Hill, Mass.] August 25th 1775
That the Quartermaster Make a List of vigatabls For the Diferent
Companeys and Return them to the Commoserey general [w]ho will
Deliver them the Money To purches them according to thair allow-
ence, Which is to be Distrebuted To the Diferent Capt[s].[1]

Hitchcock Orderly Book no. 2 (RHi). On the phonetic spelling see source
note at NG's orders of 4 June 1775 above.
1. For the exorbitant prices charged for vegetables see below, NG's orders for 19
Sept.

## To Commissary General Joseph Trumbull

[From Prospect Hill, Mass., 25 Aug. 1775. Trumbull's deputies complain that provisions are not adequate to supply the men according to
Washington's instructions, bringing complaints from them. Keeping
accounts of provisions owed the men is as much work as "dealing out
the Provisions," NG hopes for reform in the "mode of supplies." ALS
(Ct) 1 p.]

## General Greene's Orders

[Prospect Hill, Mass., 26 Aug. 1775. A fatigue party of five hundred
privates and officers and a covering party to parade with arms.[1]
Hitchcock Orderly Book no. 2 (RHi) 1 p.]

1. The work party of five hundred was joined by the same number from Sullivan's brigade to undertake the fortification of nearby Plowed Hill, the weakest link in the defensive ring around Boston. (See map, p. 129.) They set to work on the night of 26 Aug., continuing all the following day in the face of a heavy British bombardment from Bunker Hill. Although the fortification was a formidable one, there was concern among the general officers that the British might risk an attack. (Frothingham, *Boston*, p. 234) See also NG's orders of 27 and 29 Aug. and NG to Catharine 27 Aug., below.

## General Greene's Orders

[Prospect Hill, Mass., 27 Aug. 1775. Due more to neglect than to ignorance, the sentries and officers of the guard are failing to do their duties. Those so failing will be put under arrest. Field officer of the day to inspect the guard around sundown and report its state impartially. Captains of the guard to patrol constantly to prevent sleeping on posts. "As silence is essentially necessary to get the earliest intelligence of the Enemies Motions, no singing or Music is to be allowed in any of the Guards." There is to be frequent inspection of guards, with officers remaining at their posts. The grand rounds requested to go at different times and routes than customary, to detect true state of guards.[1] NG Orderly Book (MWA) 2 pp.]

1. The failure of guards and sentries to carry out their duties was a constant source of annoyance to NG (see his orders of 11 Aug. above), but the occasion for this strong remonstrance was the fortification of Plowed Hill and the corresponding British bombardment.

## To Catharine Greene

My Sweet Angel                    Prospect Hill [Mass.] August 27, 1775
     The anxiety that you must feel at the unhappy fate of Mr Mumford.[1] The tender sympathy for the distress of his poor Lady. The fears and apprehensions for my safety, under your present debillitated state, must be a weight too great for you to support. We are all in the hands of the great Jehovah, to him let us look for protection. I trust that our controversy is a Righteous one, and altho many of our friends and rellatives may suffer an untimely fate, yet we must consider the evil Justified by the Righteousness of the dispute. Let us then put our confidence in God and recommend our souls to his care. Stifle your own grief my sweet creature and offer a small tribute of consolation to the afflicted Widow. I could wish from my Soul that you was removed from this scene of horror,[2] altogether inconsistent with the finer feelings of a delicate mind. I would come and see you, but prudence forbids my Absence. I sent Colonel Varnum to communicate to you the wretched Loss his [Mumford's] poor Lady has met with. My heart melts with pity, but dumb silence must speak my grief until I am in a situation to give scope to the natural sentiment of

the human heart. I hope his good sense and knowledge of the human heart will point out the most prudent method. Adieu my love

N GREENE

ALS (MiU-C).

1. Augustus Mumford, first clerk of the Kentish Guards and adjutant of Varnum's regiment, was helping to fortify Plowed Hill in the face of a furious British cannonade when, according to a fellow Rhode Islander, he was "kild with a cannon bawl from Bunker Hill" (Philip Peirce, MS Acct. Book and Diary, 1774–75, RHi). Mumford, whose brothers were prominent in Rhode Island politics, was the first Rhode Island soldier killed in the Revolution. His grisly death (his head was blown off) brought home the terrible reality of war to his comrades as three months of impersonal siege had completely failed to do. That his commander shared in the shock is evident in this disturbed letter.

2. Catharine Greene was four months pregnant with her first child.

## General Greene's Orders

[Prospect Hill, Mass., 29 Aug. 1775. Col. Brewer's regiment to march immediately to Plowed Hill if sentry at the Citadel sees British movement from Bunker Hill.[1] Hitchcock Orderly Book no. 2 (RHi) 1 p.]

1. The occasion for this order is found in his orders of 26 and 27 of Aug. above.

## General Greene's Orders

[Prospect Hill, Mass., 30 Aug. 1775. A surgeon to attend reliefs on Plowed Hill. Hitchcock Orderly Book no. 2 (RHi) 1 p.]

## General Greene's Orders

[Prospect Hill, Mass., 1 Sept. 1775. Rain-damaged cartridges to be collected and "manufactured anew." Hitchcock Orderly Book no. 2 (RHi) 1 p.]

## General Greene's Orders

[Prospect Hill, Mass., 2 Sept. 1775. Maj. Box orders fatigue party of three hundred to Plowed Hill; carpenters to select timber. Col. William Bond complained that two men who keep sutlers stores outside the jurisdiction of the brigade have sold liquor without a license, by means of which the "Throops are much Debauched the Soldiers rendered undutiful." Maj. Box ordered to arrest and imprison the sutlers and take possession of their stores.[1] Hitchcock Orderly Book no. 1 (RHi) 1 p.]

1. For the resolution of the Massachusetts Provincial Congress covering the court-martial of such violators see note, NG's orders for 19 Aug., above.

## General Greene's Orders

[Prospect Hill, Mass., 4 Sept. 1775. All cider in the regiments to be accounted for. Hitchcock Orderly Book no. 1 (RHi) 1 p.]

## To General Charles Lee

[From Prospect Hill, Mass., 5 Sept. 1775. Asks permission for a fourteen-year old soldier, who is ill, to go home with his father, along with another ill soldier; both to return when well.[1] Reprinted from Lee, *Papers*, 1: 204.]

1. A five-weeks leave of absence was approved for both soldiers (ibid., p. 205).

## General Greene's Orders

[Prospect Hill, Mass., 6 Sept. 1775. Assigned 250 men to work on Plowed Hill. Courtmartial to try men who are in guardhouse, Col. Whitcomb serving as president. Hitchcock Orderly Book no. 1 (RHi) 1 p.]

## General Greene's Orders

[Prospect Hill, Mass., 8 Sept. 1775. Men to be clean for inspection by field officer tomorrow at 6:00 A.M. Hitchcock Orderly Book no. 1 (RHi) 1 p.]

## To Joseph Trumbull[1]

Sir                                        Prospect Hill [Mass.] Sept 8, 1775
    There has arrivd between one and two hundred head of horn Cattle from the Colony of Rhode Island and near a thousand Sheep. They are sent here by orders of the General Assembly of our Colony. They were taken of[f] several Islands in our Goverment, and are come for the use of the Camp. The Cattle were taken of[f] the Island[s] by his Excellencies direction to Governor Cook.[2] You will please to order them confirmed as soon as possible as they will be upon expence here. Let the whole Brigade on Prospect Hill be victualld out of them. I hope youl give such direction in this matter as may be most beneficial to the Colony and the Continent. As the Cattle were taken of[f] the Island by his Excellencies order and advice and his promise that this would be confirmd here, our Colony

will expect that the loss upon the Cattle will be a Continental loss, and as you are a Continental officer it will be expected that you make provision accordingly that the loss may be as small as possible. The Prospect Hill Brigad will consume a great part of the sheep and best beef seasonably and the other ought to be put out to Pasture at the Colony expence as they are now unfit for killing. In great haste I am your most obedient humble servant

NATHANAEL GREENE

ALS (Photostat at MiU-C. The original, once owned by the First Light Infantry Regiment of Rhode Island, is lost.)
1. NG mistakenly addressed the letter to Jonathan Trumbull, the governor of Connecticut instead of to his son Joseph, the commissary general.
2. Washington had asked Deputy Gov. Cooke of Rhode Island on 14 Aug. to have the stock removed from the islands, as much to deprive the British as to supply the Americans (Fitzpatrick, GW, 3: 422). Two weeks later Cooke reported that three hundred men had been engaged in the removal (except from Aquidneck Island—the site of Newport). The General Assembly, he told Washington, wanted the island stock to be used to feed the army rather than any stock "which is secure in the country." (RIHS, Coll. [1867] 6: 119) A list of owners and number of animals taken, is in Bartlett, Records, 7: 379–81.

## From George Washington to the Council of War[1]

Gentn                                    Cambridge [Mass.] Septr 8th 1775

As I mean to call upon you in a day or two for your opinions upon a point of a very Interesting nature to the well being of the Continent in general, and this Colony in particular, I think it proper, indeed an incumbant duty upon me, previous to this meeting, to intimate the end and design of it, that you may have time to consider the matter with that deliberation and attention which the Importance of it requires.

It is to know whether, in your Judgment, we cannot make a successful attack upon the Troops in Boston by means of Boats, co-operated by an attempt upon their Lines at Roxbury. The success of such an Enterprize depends, I well know, upon the all wise disposer of Events, and is not within the reach of human wisdom to foretell the Issue, but if the prospect is fair, the undertaking is Justifiable under the following, among other reasons which might be assigned.

The Season is now fast approaching when warm and comfortable Barracks must be erected for the Security of the Troops against the inclemency of the Winter. Large and costly provision must be made in the article of Wood for the Supply of the army, and after all that can be done in this way, it is but too probable that Fences, Woods, orchards, and even Houses themselves will fall Sacrifice to the want of Fuel before the end of the Winter. A very considerable difficulty, if not expence, must accrue on account of Cloathing for the Men now ingaged in the Service, and if they do not inlist again, this difficulty will be Increased to an almost insurmountable degree. Blankets, I am inform'd, are now much wanted, and not to be got. How then shall we be able to keep Soldiers to their duty, already impatient to get home, when they come to feel the severity of Winter without proper covering? If this army should not Incline to engage for a longer term than the first of Jany what then is to be the consequence but that you must either be obliged to levy new Troops and thereby have two Setts (or partly so) in pay at the same time, or by disbanding one sett before you get the other, expose the Country to desolation and the Cause perhaps to irretrievable Ruin. These things are not unknown to the Enemy, perhaps it is the very ground they are building on, if they are not waiting a reinforcement; and if they are waiting for succours, ought it not to give a Spur to the attempt? Our Powder (not much of which will be consumed in such an enterprize) without any certainty of Supply is daily wasting. And to sum up the whole, in spite of every saving that can be made, the expence of supporting this army will so far exceed any Idea that was form'd in Congress of it, that I do not know what will be the consequences.

These among many other Reasons which might be assigned, induce me to wish a speedy finish of the dispute, but to avoid these evils we are not to loose sight of the difficulties, the hazard, and the loss that may accompany the attempt, nor what will be the probable consequences of a failure.

That every circumstance for and against this measure may be duely weighed, that there may be time for doing of it, and nothing of this Importance resolved on but after mature deliberation, I give this previous notice of the Intention of calling you together on Monday next at Nine oclock, at which time you are requested to attend at head Quarters. It is unnecessary I am perswaded, to recommend Secrecy, as the Success of the Enterprize (if undertaken) must depend in a great measure upon the suddenness of the Stroke. I am with the greatest esteem Gentn yr most obedt and Hble Servt[2]

GO: WASHINGTON

ALS (MHi)

1. The council (as named in the list of addressees) consisted of Maj. Gens. Artemas Ward, Charles Lee, and Israel Putnam; and Brig. Gens. John Thomas, Joseph Spencer, William Heath, John Sullivan, Nathanael Greene, and Horatio Gates.

2. Although the council discussed Washington's query at great length at a meeting on 11 Sept., the minutes are brief: "After duly weighing the above proposition, considering the State of the Enemy's lines and the expectation of soon receiving some important advices from England, it was unanimously agreed that it was not expedient to make the attempt at present at least." The "advice" from England was the expected downfall of the North ministry. See Freeman, GW, 3: 538–41.

## Agreement

[Cambridge, Mass., 9 Sept. 1775. Agreement between NG and Nathanael Ruggles and John Gardner to butcher cattle and sheep sent from Rhode Island. ADS (RHi) 1 p.]

## General Greene's Orders

[Prospect Hill, Mass., 10 Sept. 1775. If gun taken from private in Hitchcock's regiment is not returned, possessor will be punished. Hitchcock Orderly Book no. 1 (RHi) 1 p.]

## To Catharine Greene

My Dear                                    Prospect Hill [Mass.] Sept. 10th 1775
    I embrace this opportunity to write by Mrs Greene[1] who has paid us a friendly Visit to Camp. She has spent a few Days with us, I hope agreeable. To be sure the pleasure of meeting her best friend must quallify the situation. Tho naturally disagreeable, her visit has been shortened by her Husbands going abroad. He is engagd in a Canada Expedition, a long and tedious Voyage. I am sorry that so good an Officer is going from the Hill. His Regiment will feel a severe loss. Captain [Samuel] Ward [Jr.] is also embark't in the same Expedition. I did everything that lay in my power to dissuade him from the undertaking, but the heat and Zeal of Youth ambitious of distinguishing himself overcame all the cool Reasons that I could offer. It will be a very pretty tour if his strength and resolution enables him to endure the fatigue; that will be great. I had the pleasure to hear of your safe Arrival, and recovery of your health. I expected a line at the return of Johnson from you, but was disappointed. I hope you was better employed. Things here remain much in the same situation as when you was here. A few Days past a Ship arrivd from England, since which there has been no firing on our side. They are meditating an attack or have receivd orders to discontinue their firing; which, I am not certain. However, we shall watch their motions with great attention. Mr. [John] Murray gave us a Sermon today.[2] This is the first Sermon I have heard since your first arrival at Jamaica Plains.[3] Perhaps you stood between me and the Gospel, but I fear if the true reasons should be enquired after you would escape the Charge. I am now going to dine with his Excellency General Washington and Mr Murray with me. I wish you could fly to Cambrige and partake of a friendly repast and return to the peaceful shades of Coventry again. My Compliments to all friends, to Nancy Varnum, Betsey Flagg, to

sister Nancy, the latter of whom tell her I receivd her Letter. I shall answer it soon. My respects to Mrs Hathaway and all my old friends in the neighbourhood, particularly Daniel Gardner. Adieu my Dear

N GREENE

ALS (NjP).
1. Wife of Col. Christopher Greene, the former Anna Lippitt.
2. John Murray, the Universalist chaplain; see Varnum to Murray, 24 May 1775, above.
3. This is the only reference to Catharine's having visited him before he moved to Prospect Hill.

## To George Washington

8 oClock Prospect Hill [Mass.] Sept 10, 1775

This moment reported me from the Whitehouse Guard that a deserter had made his escape into Bunker Hill. Two Centries fir'd at him but he made his escape, I believe unhurt. As it is uncertain who it is or what he is I have thought proper to alter the Parole and Counter-sign for these Guards which if your Excellency Approves youl please to signify it at the return of the Sergeant. If this deserter has carried in the Countersign they may easily convey it over to Roxbury. It would [be] a pretty Advantage for a partisan frolick. The Rifflers seems very sulky and I am informd threatens to rescue their mates tonight, but little is to be feard from them as the Regiment are all ready at a moments warning to turn out, and the Guards very Strong.[1] I am with due defference your Excellencys most Obedient humble servant

N GREENE

Parole Coventry
Countersign Germany

ALS (MHi).
1. A reference to Capt. James Ross's company of Pennsylvania riflemen, who, upon hearing that one of their members was confined in the guardhouse for a mis-demeanor, set off to free him. Washington, Lee, and NG pursued and caught the mutineers, and another Pennsylvania company helped subdue them. At a courtmartial the next day, thirty-three members were fined twenty shillings each (to go to the hospital fund), and the ringleader, John Seamon, was ordered to be confined six days (Fitzpatrick, GW, 3: 490–91; see also Freeman, GW, 3: 525–26, and Martyn, Ward, p. 179).

This was the most serious though not the first case of insubordination among the "shirtmen." The rowdier ones frequently defied superiors, and most of them refused to work on the entrenchments—the lot of the New Englanders whom the riflemen called "musqueteers." The minority who misbehaved were an embarrassment to most of the officers. Col. Hand, commander of the Lancaster Regiment, was especially ashamed of their undisciplined behavior.

Edward Hand (1744–1802) was a native of Ireland, who had studied medicine at Trinity College in Dublin and joined the Eighteenth Royal Irish Regiment as surgeon's mate. He was sent to America in 1767, where he settled upon leaving the service. (DAB) In the summer of 1776, he proved to be one of NG's most valuable officers on

Long Island. On 23 Sept. 1775 he wrote an old friend in Lancaster, Jasper Yeates, about the mutinous incident and the general lack of discipline among other Pennsylvania companies. "The respect and indulgence our people met on their arrival here are much, and deservedly, lessened. They now take a proportion of every duty and fatigue [as per Washington's orders]. The expedition with which the York Company was raised does not attone for their misconduct. I would not wish to publish this intelligence as it would undoubtedly give uneasiness to the gentlemen of that town, whose Zeal and activity deserve a better return." Col. Hand implied that Capt. [Matthew] Smith had virtually been sent along with Arnold to Canada as a punishment. "Had C. Smith's company been better behaved they might probably have saved themselves a disagreeable jaunt." At the same time, he said that the York company was so bad that "Genl [Arnold] refused peremptorily to take the York Company. Shameful disgrace!" (The letter, Hand to Yeates, of 23 Sept. 1775, is in Edward Hand Coll., Force transcripts, DLC.)

## General Greene's Orders

[Prospect Hill, Mass., 12 Sept. 1775. Relief party to go to Jamaica Plains. No more apple trees to be cut down.[1] Hitchcock Orderly Book no. 1 (RHi) 1 p.]

1. This is the first of several orders concerned with troops stealing wood. Wood was as vital to the success of the besieging colonials as food and clothing. It had been used in some form for huts and barracks, for fortifications and gun emplacements, and most importantly as fuel for cooking. The quartermaster department could never meet the demand. Since the area occupied by the army was cleared farmland, every farmer's wood lot, rail fence, and fruit and shade trees were endangered. With the chill of autumn coming on and the cold of winter not far behind, the army would soon have disbanded had there been no wood to steal. On the desperate need for firewood in midwinter see below, note 6, NG to Samuel Ward, Sr., 31 Dec. 1775.

## To Deputy Governor Nicholas Cooke of Rhode Island

Dear Sir                                          Prospect Hill [Mass.] Sept 12th 1775
    I had the honnor of your favor of the 9th of this instant.[1] I am very sorry that Mr Bowlers son has conducted himself in such a manner as to forfeit the good oppinion of the Gentlemen and Soldiery of the Army. Had he paid the least attention to the business he was sent upon he might have reapt the advantage from his Appointment that his father expected, for whom I should have been glad he might have been continued in employment. The young Gentleman is guilty of ingratitude as well as condesintion. His bread was so bad that the whole Army was in an uproar about it several times and applications made to me continually by officers of every rank for his dismission. But the respect I pay to Governmental appointment and the regard I had for his father made me more tender towards the young Gentleman than I ought to have been to done Justice to the Troops. I cannot conceive why Mr Bowler should think me capable of such an ungenerous Act towards him. Let him examine my conduct in private or

Publick life and see if he can find an instance of such low artifice to circumvent any Gentlemen to accomplish my wishes. I detest the thought and despise the man that can seriously think me capable of such an unworthy act. But I am sure Mr Bowler cannot seriously entertain such a sentiment.[2] After his Excellency had appointed the Comisary General or rather the Congress I applyed to him for the continuation of all officers, Commisaries and Bakers and Mr Bowlers son was appointed by the Commisary General to bake for the Rhode Island Troops and continued sometime in actual employment. For the care and convenience of the Army his Excellency issued in General orders that every man might have a pound of flour or bread. This was donn to put a stop to the imposition practiced throughout the army in the Article of bread, for it was not only Mr Bowler but many others that neglected their duty by reason of whose negligence the Troops were ill fed and their health much endangered. But besides this consideration it was a considerable saving in the article of expence, for the baking amounted to considerable. Whereas they are allowed nothing now for baking but turn out a pound of flour for every pound of Bread. I am a total stranger to the business and its emoluments and declare upon the honnor of a Gentleman and the faith of a Christian that I did nothing directly or indirectly to supercede Mr Bowler in his employment. It was out of my power, Mr Commisary Philips power and out of the power of the Commisary General to prevent the Regiments from drawing their flour and geting whom they pleasd to bake it into Bread after Issuing the above mentiond General Order. I did not know how nor when Mr Bowler was dismist. I find my time sufficiently engrossed without troubling my head about pecuniary matters amongst my friends.[3]

The Cattle sent here by John Northup and others I had disposd on before the arrival of Daniel Mowry Ersqr appointed by the Committee for the sale of the Cattle.[4] However he had the opportunity to make a better sale if a better offer presented. I had sold it for 20s and 6 for the Beef and Sheep.

Things here remain much in the same situation as they have been for sometime past. For several Days past firing has ceast totally. It is said by several Deserters out of Boston that the last Ship arrivd brings accounts that the difference is soon to be settled, but unless the ministry is overset the dispute never will be settled. If we can preserve our freedom and continue our connexion I should be very glad of it, but I had rather continue in the field seven years than submit to their tyrannical measures. John Northam [Northup] Ersqr was very angry because General Washington would not take the Cattle at the prices he paid the owners for them. Methinks the General Assembly did not conduct that matter with their wonted

Wisdom and saving oeconemy. I am sir with the greatest esteem your most obedient humble servant

NATH GREENE

ALS (NHi).

1. Letter not found.

2. Metcalf Bowler (1726–89), a Newport merchant, was a delegate to the Stamp Act Congress, speaker of the R.I. Assembly from 1767 to 1776, and chief justice in 1776 and 1777. It was not known until 1930 that he also served as a spy for the British during their three-year occupation of Newport. In letters signed "Rusticus" or "SH," he informed the British commander of patriots' activities. If his own activities were to be discovered, he once warned Gen. Clinton, "nothing short of my Life—would pay the Forfeit." Jane Clark of Clements Library identified the letters as Bowler's. The letters with her annotations are in RIHS, *Coll.* 23 (1930): 101–17.

In June 1775 Bowler's son Charles was appointed by the R.I. Assembly to be "baker to the army of observation," undoubtedly at the behest of his father (Bartlett, *Records*, 7: 356–57).

3. NG had recommended his cousin Griffin as baker to the Mass. regiments (NG to Jos. Trumbull, 9 Aug., above). It can be assumed that he received the appointment from the letter NG wrote to Peter Phillips, 6 May 1776, below.

4. John Northup sat in the R.I. Assembly and was a member of the Committee of Safety from Kings County in 1775 and 1776. There are indications that he may have sold provisions to the R.I. troops as a personal venture. (Bartlett, *Records*, 7: 357)

Daniel Mowry represented Smithfield in the Assembly from 1766 to 1776. He was an active patriot during the Revolution and in 1780 was elected delegate to the Continental Congress.

## General Greene's Orders

[Prospect Hill, Mass., 15 Sept. 1775. A lost pocketbook has been found, but more than $40 is missing. If finder returns money, he will get $5 reward; if not, the entire regiment will be examined under oath to determine the guilty.[1] Hitchcock Orderly Book no. 1 (RHi) 1 p.]

1. Although in this instance NG intervened, lost and found objects were often merely noted in orderly books. By carrying such "advertisements," as they were called, orderly books served as rudimentary camp newspapers. So besieged were the adjutants with notices that their use eventually had to be greatly restricted.

## Discharge

[Prospect Hill, Mass., 15 Sept. 1775. Discharge of Ens. James Brown, signed by NG. DS (MiU-C) 1 p.]

## General Greene's Orders

[Prospect Hill, Mass.] Sept 19th 1775

The Cols. of Diferent Regements are Requested to Eaven thair Companys that Each Company Have an Eaquell Number in them. The Porseedings of the garason Cort martialls of which Colo Varnum was Presedent Is aproved of By the general. The porseedings of the garason Cort martial of Which Lt. Colo Cornell was presedent is allso a Proved of By the General and the Centence of Both Cort Martials are orderd to take Place accordingly at 6 OClok this Evning.

A Grate Imposisstion has Been imposed on the Solders by Reason the inhabetence asking Exorbetent prices for the provisions and Roots And all kinds of produce.[1] Mr Asa Minor of Colo Varnums Regt is appointed Clark to the maquet [market] and is Desired to appoint a place for that purpis in the frunt of Col Brewers Regement. No ma[r]keting what Ever is to Be allowed in any oather part of the Camp but at that place So appointed by the Clark. He is allso to Regulate the Prises of all porduce Brought into Camp and no Parson to Exseed the prices on penelty of having thair Porduce Saized and taken From them for the Benefit of the armey.

Hitchcock Orderly Book no. 2 (RHi). As noted at NG's orders of 4 June 1775, above, Hitchcock's company commander, not NG, was responsible for the phonetic spelling.

1. Soldiers supplemented their monotonous fare with fresh produce that they purchased with money provided them by the commissary general (see order of 25 Aug., above).

NG's complaint of exorbitant prices is the opening note in a refrain that was to mount in intensity throughout the war. High prices were due in part to the shortage of supplies that accompanies any war, often intensified by human greed in profiteering. But high prices also resulted from monetary inflation, which rose roughly proportional to the amounts of paper money issued. (The two types of inflation are clearly distinguished by a graph in Bezanson, *Prices*, p. 61.) Attempts to control prices during the war were unsuccessful. In 1776 Rhode Island passed an act "to prevent monopolies and oppression, by excessive and unreasonable prices for many of the necessaries and conveniences of life"—an act that was as rigid in its provisions as it was lax in its enforcement. (Bartlett, *Records*, 8:85) When NG issued the above order, he still had hopes that prices could be controlled, but his own experience and that of Rhode Island the following year made him a foe of price controls. (See NG to unknown person, 20 May 1777, below.)

## General Greene's Orders

[Prospect Hill, Mass., 21 Sept. 1775. Court of inquiry to investigate the wounding of a soldier by gunshot. A work detail to repair the pillory and to guard same.[1] Hitchcock Orderly Book no. 2 (RHi) 1 p.]

1. The pillory consisted of vertical planking shoulder high, with holes for neck and wrists. Although men were sentenced to a period in the pillory for so-called minor offenses, it was a painful and humiliating punishment.

## General Greene's Orders

[Prospect Hill, Mass., 23 Sept. 1775. Three hundred men to work on redoubts between Prospect and Plowed hills. Hitchcock Orderly Book no. 2 (RHi) 1 p.]

## To Deputy Governor Nicholas Cooke of Rhode Island

Dear Sir                    Prospect Hill [Mass.] Sept 23, 1775
    I receivd your favor the 16th[1] of this instant rellative to Mr
Northups conduct, which in my Oppinion was something unaccountable unless we allow he made a sacrafice of the publick interest for his
own private advantage. Mr Mowrey has acquainted you before this of
the sales of the Cattle and Sheep. It was low but it was the best
disposition that could be made. Had they not been hurried down
here in the manner they were, they might have been sold at a higher
rate. I take it extreme hard of Mr Bowler that his suspicions of my
integrity towards his Son still lurks about him.[2] I have always taken
as much pains to serve Mr Bowler as any Person. He has always
commanded my interest and influence as far as my honnor and
Conscience approvd. If he is still dissatisfied let him come to Camp
and enquire as Critically as he pleases. I have no objection. I am
conscious of haveing discharg'd my duty to his son.
    I am sorry to hear of the divisions in the house of Assembly.[3] I
am informd it was proposed to recall the Troops. Should such a
measure as that take place we are an undone people. I hope the little
paltry consideration of private interest obtaind through the different
channels of Committee business will not frees up the spirit of Patriotism in their once warm boosoms. I hear the Committee of safety are
greatly disgusted at the mode of supplying and paying the Continental Army. I love my own Government and am strongly attacht to
interest honnor peace and happiness. But in the present situation of
things we ought [to] divest ourselves of private motives in our
publick conduct where they millitate with the publick good. We have
to consider whether the modes Established are calculated to promote
the General interest better than the former; if they are than they are
warrantable, because it is the whole and not a part that the Congress
have to consider. The southern Gentlemen has infinitely more reason
to Complain than we. They must pay a considerable part of the
expence and are scarcely connected with the Army and from their
situation entirely deprivd of any Emolument from it. I hope the little
Colony of Rhode Island so highly favord with the blessings of freedom
so nobly distinguisht for their patriotism wont be the first to oppose
the measures of the Continental Congress, the united council and
strength of America. We are but as the drop of a bucket, and unless
we adhere to the rest of the Colonies we shall be swallowed up by the
tyrants now gapeing with their mouths open ready to devour us.
God preserve Unity amongst you and bless your Councils with Wisdom and prudence to direct the ship through the Rocks and Shoals
into the Port of Freedom, and bless us with peace and plenty once

more, is the prayer of him who is your sincere friend and humble servant

NATH GREENE

ALS (CSmH).
1. Letter not found.
2. On Northup, Mowry, and Bowler, see NG to Cooke, 12 Sept., above.
3. Cooke's answer of 26 Sept., below, denies any such division; certainly NG's informant greatly exaggerated it. His response, though unjustified by the facts, does reveal him as a far more ardent friend of unity among the colonies than most members of the R.I. Assembly. When he says in the final sentence, "God preserve Unity amongst *you* and bless *your* Councils with Wisdom and prudence" [italics added], he is speaking, perhaps unconsciously, from the eminence of the continentalist and no longer as a man who had spent almost his entire life within the provincial boundaries of the smallest American colony. For an even more forthright expression of the sentiment, see his letter to Samuel Ward, Sr., 16 Oct. 1775, below.

## To General John Sullivan

[From Prospect Hill, Mass., 23 Sept. 1775. Formal reply to Sullivan's criticism that his brigade furnished more men for fatigue party than Greene's. NG cannot say how it happened, but he intends to "furnish upon equal terms."[1] AL (NhHi) 1 p.]

1. Varnum wrote Sullivan the following day to say that he hoped Sullivan did not accuse *him* "of Neglect of Duty." (Hammond, *Sullivan Papers*, 1: 92) Sullivan took offense easily at what he considered slights. NG's formal note, written in the third person, showed that he too could take offense easily. Despite their sensitivity, they became good friends.

## General Greene's Orders

[Prospect Hill, Mass., 25 Sept. 1775. Courtmartial and court of inquiry to try prisoners and inquire into complaint against acting adjutant. Plowed Hill to be relieved by 250 men; 300 men to finish works between Prospect and Plowed hills. Officers of guards to give written report to relieving officers. Hitchcock Orderly Book no. 2 (RHi) 1 p.]

## To Jacob Greene[?][1]

Dear Sir                    Prospect Hill [Mass.] Sept 25, 1775
    Inclosed you have the Paper signed by Mr. Phillips. It will serve you for a memorandum of the Agreement and doubt not you may profit by it.[2] If [divine] Providence should dispose of All here, You'l do justice to my Family I doubt not when I am no more.[3] If there is no News favorable for America in three weeks you may expect to hear something terrible. Be silent on this Head as it may be a Disadvantage to the Attempt. Hundreds will perish and I amongst the Rest perhaps.

My Hand so cold this morning I can scarcely hold my Pen. I am with great Respect your Friend and Brother

N GREENE

Tr (Theodore Foster Transcripts, RHi). Enclosure missing.
1. Although addressee is not given, it is almost certainly Jacob, because the Foster transcripts were taken from documents in possession of Jacob's descendants.
2. Jacob's agreement with Commissary Phillips has not come to light.
3. Since the general officers had ruled out an attack on Boston and Gage gave no indication of breaking out of the siege, the foreboding sense of doom may have arisen from a mild depression.

## From Deputy Governor Nicholas Cooke of Rhode Island[1]

Sir                              Providence [R.I.] Septemb. 26th 1775
    I am favoured with yours of the 23d instant, and cannot help expressing my Surprize at your mentioning Divisions in the Assembly, and a Proposal made to recall the Troops in such a Manner as to shew that you give Credit to the Reports; which I assure you so far as I can learn are entirely void of any Foundation in Truth. There hath not been the least Division in the General Assembly from any Motive of Departure from the common Cause. On the contrary, the Firmness of the General Assembly is perfectly to be depended upon. Nor was any Motion ever made for withdrawing our Troops. If these Reports have been propagated in the Army I must desire you to take Pains to set the Matter in a true Light, otherwise they may prove injurious to the common Interest.[2]
    I have recommended to General Washington the paying the earliest Attention to the reinlisting the Troops, and have assured him that this Colony will heartily concur in every prudent Measure for that Purpose.[3] I am greatly apprehensive that almost insuperable Difficulties will arise in accomplishing that essential Service; and earnestly desire you to use your Influence that it may be entered upon as soon as possible. I am with great Regard, Sir Your most obedient and most humble Servant.

NICHS COOKE

Df (MH).
1. This is one of two letters that have survived out of several dozen that Cooke wrote to NG between June 1775 and Aug. 1776.
2. See note, NG to Cooke, 23 Sept. 1775, above.
3. Most troops had enlisted through 31 Dec., but some had signed up only until the first week in December.

## From Secretary Henry Ward of Rhode Island

Sir:                                    Providence [R.I.], September 26, 1775

This letter waits upon you by Mr. Maxwell, who goes down to Cambridge upon a matter into which I think the strictest inquiry ought to be made.[1] It is, in short, this: In July last, a woman, with whom Mr. Wainwood[2] had an acquaintance in Boston, came to his house and wanted him to assist her in procuring an opportunity of seeing Mr. Dudley or Captain Wallace;[3] and by all her behaviour showed that she had some secret of consequence. He artfully drew from her that she had been sent from Cambridge with a letter to be delivered to either of the persons named, to be forwarded to Boston. It immediately occurred to him that the letter was probably sent from some traitor in our army. Upon which, he started every difficulty in the way of her seeing Dudley or Wallace, that he could think of, and finally prevailed upon her to intrust him with the delivery of the letter. He kept the affair to himself some time, being at a loss what step he should take in it; and at length imparted the secret to Mr. Maxwell, who, upon opening the letter, found it written in characters which he did not understand. Here it rested until very lately, when Mr. Wainwood received a letter from the woman, discovering great uneasiness about the letter she had intrusted him with, which naturally induced a suspicion that the writer of it still continued his correspondence in Boston, and had received information that the letter had never been transmitted. Mr. Wainwood and Mr. Maxwell, who are both of them friends to the cause of America, rightly judging that the continuance of such a correspondence might be attended with the most pernicious consequences to the interest of America, thought proper to come to Providence and consult me upon it, having prudently kept the matter entirely to themselves. By my advice, they proceeded to Cambridge, to lay it, with all the circumstances, before you.

I think it best to introduce Mr. Maxwell[4] to General Washington, and for you and the General, with not more than one trusty person besides, to consider as to the most prudent measures to discover the traitor. Perhaps the first step should be take up the woman, who is now at Cambridge, in so private a way as to create no suspicion; and it is probable that rewards and punishments, properly placed before her, will induce her to give up the author; in which case he, with all his papers, ought to be instantly secured. If the woman should be obstinate, some clew may be found from her connections, that will probably lead to a discovery. But I beg pardon for undertaking to give my advice in this case, when you, upon the spot, possessed of all the circumstances, will be so much better able to judge of the measures proper to be pursued. As Mr. Wainwood is well known to many of the inhabitants of Boston, I have advised him to go no farther than Dedham, where he may be sent for as soon as it shall be thought proper for him to appear. I will only add, that if they are happily the means of discovering a treacherous correspondence, carried on by any person of note and trust in our publick affairs, they will do a most essential service to their Country, and deserve an adequate reward. I am, with great truth and esteem, Sir, your most obedient and very humble servant,

HENRY WARD

Reprinted from Force, *Archives* (4) 3: 809.

1. Sec'y Ward could not suspect when he wrote this letter, nor could NG when he read it, that it would reveal one of the most respected patriots in the army as a spy. See below, NG to Ward, 30 Sept.

2. Godfrey Wainwood was a baker in Newport.

3. Charles Dudley was the British collector in Newport; Capt. James Wallace was commander of HMS *Rose*.

4. Master Adam Maxwell was the same schoolteacher who had previously lived in East Greenwich and had tutored NG—a connection that undoubtedly led him to Greene's rather than to Washington's headquarters.

## General Greene's Orders

[Prospect Hill, Mass., 28 Sept. 1775. Before cold weather, troops should be comfortably lodged in barracks. Col. Miller to oversee party digging cellars.[1] Hitchcock Orderly Book no. 1 (RHi) 1 p.]

1. The weather, lack of lumber, and shortage of carpenters conspired to delay the building of the barracks. The last one on Prospect Hill was not completed until January.

## To Deputy Governor Nicholas Cooke of Rhode Island

Dear Sir                    Prospect Hill [Mass.] Sept 30, 1775

Your favor of the 26th of this instant came safe to hand. I am glad to hear there is no foundation in the report of the division of the Assembly. I felt great uneasiness at the report as I was fully sensible that a division must be productive of the worst consequences and would strengthen and encourage our Enemy and weaken and discourage our People. The Salvation of the Colonies will depend upon the Union and harmony subsisting among them and in them. The legislative body of the Colony of the Rhode Island has been active and uniform in their conduct. If any divisions takes place amongst them now it must appear they are not so well affected as heretofore. I have waited upon his Excellency General Washington upon the subject of reenlisting the Troops. He is waiting for a return from the Continental Congress to direct his motions. As soon as he gets a return I expect we shall have orders for recruitting. I expect great difficulty in recruitting as a Winter Campaign must be very tedious. However, I hope if the Legislature and the principal Characters of each Province lends a helping hand we shall succeed according to our wishes.

There is nothing new here except a rumour of an engagement between our forces and the Kings forces at St Johns and that our forces had taken St Johns with the loss of five hundred men; two hundred Provincials, two hundred Canadians, and one hundred Indians. How far this report is to be credited I am not able to say. The Troops are healthy and in good spirits here. His Excellency General Washington has a very good Oppinion of our Colony and their forces, and so has all the Western Gentlemen.[1] I wish that nothing may be done in a Legislative or Military way that may forfeit the Good Oppinion conceiv'd of us. However the interest as well as the Reputation of the Colony must be attended too. Great prudence is necessary in the conducting of the publick administration as expences of every sort are multiplying amazingly. I am sir with great esteem your sincere friend and very humble servant

NATHANAEL GREENE

ALS (NjP).
    1. New Englanders were often called "Easterners" by the residents of New York, New Jersey, and Pennsylvania; they, in turn, were often called "Westerners" by New Englanders who might also at times refer to Jerseyites and Pennsylvanians as "Southerners."

## To Secretary Henry Ward of Rhode Island

Sir                       Prospect Hill [Mass.] Sept 30, 1775
    Yours of the 26th of this instant covering a Letter from Governor Cook to me and one to his Excellency General Washington came safe to hand by Mr Maxwell. The subject of Mr Maxwells and Mr Waynwoods business has been stricktly examind into. The Author is found. You cannot guess who it is. It is no less a man than the famous Doctor Church.[1] He is now under arrest, but whether the Letter was wrote with a good or ill intention remains to be prov'd from the Contents of the Letter. There is no person here that can decipher it. I have sent Mr Gouch express for Mr Silas Downer[2] who I am informd is very expert at deciphering. Youl be so good as to provide him a horse and furnish him with money and send him to Camp as soon as possible. Must intreat you not disclose the subjects of Mr Downers business to any Person until you hear farther from me except to Govenor Cook. If the Letter contains nothing criminal it will be a pity to ruin his publick Character, but let the contents be what it will, he deserves punnishment for his imprudence, to carry on such a Correspondence without

the commander in chiefs being made acquainted with it. There is a report prevails here that there has been a Battle between our forces and the Kings Troops at St Johns and that the Canadians and Indians have joind our people. It is said we lost five hundred: two hundred Provincials, two hundred Canadians and one hundred Indians. But as this report comes indirectly from the Camp at St Johns, it is not credited much here. Several Ships arrivd a few Days past supposd to be from England, since which not a Gun has been fird. They are taking down the Houses at the South end of Boston and Erecting a strong Battery with two fraises one towards Dorchester Neck and one towards Cambrige Bay. There is no news from the Congress. His Excellency is waiting with great impatience for a return from the Congress to direct him with regard to reinlisting the Troops. He has sent several expresses but no return is made him. The Troops are generally healthy and in good spirits. We are building Barracks as fast as possible to lodge them in. We have taken a Vessel from Canada and one from the West Indies with provisions for the Troops in Boston, one Loaded with Cattle, the other with Turtle—the latter is a glorious prize. In haste I conclude your friend and humble servant

NATHANAEL GREENE

ALS (RHi).
    1. NG had lost no time in delivering the enciphered letter to Washington, who soon elicited from the young woman the identity of her lover and writer of the letter as Dr. Benjamin Church—outspoken patriot, member of the Massachusetts Provincial Congress, and head of the Military Hospital. The revelation was a shock that jolted civilian and military alike in Massachusetts. The best account of Church's spying, trial, and imprisonment is in Allen French, *General Gage's Informers* (Ann Arbor: University of Michigan Press, 1932). See also note, NG to Catharine, 26 Oct.
    2. Silas Downer (1729–85) was a Harvard graduate who, before practicing law in Providence, had earned his living as the finest scrivener in the city and, according to NG's letter, was apparently known also as something of a cryptographer. He was better known in Providence for his writings in the local paper on imperial relations, but he was best known for his stirring "Liberty Tree" speech delivered on 25 July 1768 (and soon printed), in which he denied the authority of Parliament over the colonies. Whether John Gooch reached Downer is not known; in any case Washington got two independent decipherments from a Rev. Mr. West and Col. Elisha Porter, aided by Elbridge Gerry (Freeman, *G.W.* 3: 548). Downer's writings and the details of his life have been rescued from undeserved obscurity by Carl Bridenbaugh in his *Silas Downer: Forgotten Patriot* (Providence: The Rhode Island Bicentennial Foundation, 1974). On the disposition of Dr. Church's case, see below, NG to Catharine, 26 Oct.

# From Nicholas Brown

[Providence R.I., 30 Sept. 1775. Asks for payment of lottery tickets (possibly for Baptist meetinghouse fund) and reports lottery for Coventry meetinghouse has fallen through. ACy (RPJCB) 1 p.]

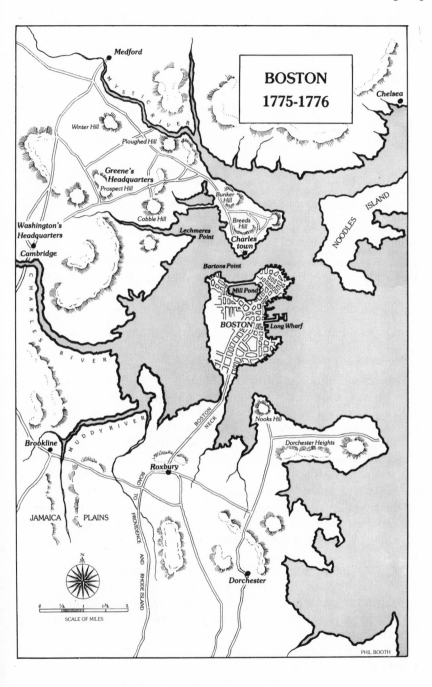

BOSTON
1775-1776

Medford

Chelsea

MYSTIC RIVER

Winter Hill

Ploughed Hill

Greene's
Headquarters
Prospect Hill

Bunker
Hill

NOODLES ISLAND

Washington's
Headquarters

Cambridge

Cobble Hill

Lechmeres
Point

Breeds
Hill
Charles
town

Bartons Point

Mill Pond

CHARLES RIVER

BOSTON

Long Wharf

BOSTON NECK

Nooks Hill

Brookline

MUDDY RIVER

Dorchester Heights

ROAD TO PROVIDENCE AND RHODE ISLAND

Roxbury

JAMAICA PLAINS

N

Dorchester

0      ½      1      1½      2

SCALE OF MILES

PHIL BOOTH

## George Washington to General Artemas Ward and Other General Officers

[Cambridge, Mass., 5 Oct. 1775. He lists four questions posed by Congress in a letter of 26 Sept., adding five of his own. The questions are found in the document below. Closes circular letter with "Your close attention to the foregoing points against Monday 10 O'Clock at which time I shall expect to see you at this place will much oblige Sir."[1] (Varick transcripts, Washington Papers: DLC) 2 pp.]

1. There was no need for Washington to report what his general officers already knew—that Gen. Gage had been recalled to England and replaced by Gen. William Howe, as Washington had informed Schuyler on 4 Oct. (Fitzpatrick, *GW*, 4: 5) Since Gage himself had not received the news until 26 Sept., Washington's intelligence was remarkably up-to-date. (On Gage's recall see Alden, *Gage*, pp. 272–86.) The change in command did not represent any shift in British policy, as Howe was to demonstrate in the next few months.

## General Greene's Opinion on Washington's Queries of October 5[1]

[6–7 October 1775]

Q. 1. What number of Men are sufficient for a Winters Campaign?

A. Twenty five Regiments, amounting in the whole to thirteen thousand one hundred and thirty Men including Battalion Officers, to be posted, nine Regiments on the right Division, nine on the left and seven in the centre, to act offensive and defensively, thirty eight Regiments to be distributed as before mentioned.[2]

Q. 2. Can the pay of the Privates be Reduced?

A. No. Because a sudden reduction would impede the filling the Regiments to such a degree, as would possibly weaken the Lines, at the expiration of the old establishment. The people have not as yet felt the necessity of entering the service for the support of themselves and families; they will consequently refuse inlisting for a time, with the view of reducing the Congress to the necessity of raising the wages.

Q. 3. What Rations should be allowed the Men?

A. As the Rations do not enter into the nature of the establishment, but are variable at the pleasure of the Commander in Chief, I do not think it eligible to make any alteration at this time of the present Provision.

Q. 4. What regulations are further necessary for the Government of the forces?

A. As to appointments, a Provost Martial is wanted. As to Martial

Laws, Treason against the United Colonies, committed in the Army, should be clearly designated, and the punishment expressed.[3]

Q. 5. What is the most eligible method of Clothing a new rais'd Army? ⟨What method would you recommend, as most eligible, to Clothe the new raised Army with a degree of decency and regularity? Would you advise it to be done by the Continent? In that case, would you lower the men's wages, and make no deduction for clothing, or let it stand and make stoppages? And how much per month?⟩

A. The Clothing should be procured by the Continent, and delivered to the Men at prime cost and charges, to be paid for by Monthly deductions, each deduction amounting to twelve Shillings lawful Money.[4]

Q. 6. How are the Men to be paid? ⟨As there appears to be great irregularity in the manner of paying the men, and much discontent has prevailed on that account, in what manner, and at what fixed periods would you advise it to be done under a new establishment?⟩

A. I esteem Monthly payments the best calculated to quiet the minds of the Soldiery, who must frequently contribute to the support of their families. To this purpose, Regimental Abstracts should be made, signed by the Colonel or Commanding Officer of the Regiment, who should apply to his Excellency for a warrant to the pay Masr. Genl. The Colo should deliver the Money to the Capt of Companies, who will be accountable to the Colonel, who will be answerable to the Pay Masr. Genl.[5]

Q. 7. What sized Regiments upon the new Establishment? ⟨that is, how many men to a company, how many companies to a Regiment, and how Officered?⟩

A. The Regiment should consist of five hundred and twenty six including Officers: one Colonel, one Lt Colo, one Major, Eight Companies to each Regiment, one Captain, one Lieut. and one Ensign, three Serjeants, three Corporals, one drum and one fife, Staff officers, one Chaplain, one Adjutant being a Subaltern, one Quarter Master being a Subaltern, one Surgeon and one Mate.

Q. 8. Can the best Officers be retained without impeding the inlistments? ⟨Is there any method by which the best of the present officers in this Army can be chosen without impeding the Inlistment of the men by such choice and preference under any complete establishment, even if all the privates in the Army were engaged again, many of the present Officers must be discharged, as there is an over proportion; of course we ought to retain the best?⟩

A. It is a matter of great delicacy and to accomplish it with propriety, I feel the want of Military knowledge. However, I beg liberty to propose that the Officers now in the service, receive inlisting orders first to engage all that are fit and willing now in service. Then every one who shall have leave of absence by furlough, as well as the rest, be directed to engage for the establishment as many effective men as possible, each Government or Colony having a certain number of Regiments assigned to it, and when the whole number shall be raised, his Excellency will retain such Officers as he shall think best qualified, after receiving recommendations for the Field Officers from the Brigr Generals, and of the Commissioned Officers, from the Colonels or Commanding Officers of Regts and also from the Brigr Generals.[6]

Q. 9. For how long a time should the men be engaged?

A. For one Year, unless sooner discharged by the Continental Congress, because every contract should be fixed and certain in all its parts, and Men esteem confinement (of which the service partakes) without any fixed period to its duration, a boundless gulph, where the fruitful Imagination creates ten thousand nameless horrors. They will therefore startle at visionary Ills, supposing their inlistments be during the pleasure of the Congress, not considering that the importance of the contest should banish every private consideration which may rise in competition with the public good.

Tr (Varick transcripts, Washington Papers: DLC). For use of angle brackets, see last paragraph in note 1, below.

1. In his letter of 5 Oct. (abstracted above), Washington listed four queries from Congress and five of his own to be considered by his general officers before meeting with him on 8 Oct. This meeting, in turn, was in preparation for a conference to be held with a congressional committee the following week. (See note, NG to Samuel Ward, Sr., 16 Oct. 1775, below.) Why NG submitted his opinions in writing is not known. Perhaps he had not expected to attend the meeting at the time he received the circular letter. A contemporary summary of the council's opinions is found in the Washington Papers (DLC).

NG's written opinions, as noted, differ somewhat from the collective opinions found in the 8 Oct. proceedings. At that meeting Washington added a tenth question: "Whether it will be advisable to inlist any Negroes in the new Army? Or whether there be a distinction between such as are slaves, and those who are free?" The council agreed unanimously to reject all slaves and, by a "great majority," to reject Negroes altogether. Whether NG voted with the majority or the minority on the last question has not been determined. From his Quaker background and his approval in 1778 of forming a Negro regiment in Rhode Island (first recommended by his friend, James M. Varnum, and commanded by his kinsman Christopher Greene), one would expect him to have voted with the minority that favored enlisting free Negroes.

NG copied the four congressional questions verbatim as a preface to his answers, but he only summarized Washington's questions. Where his summaries are overly brief or where portions of questions are omitted, Washington's full questions are supplied in angle brackets, the wording being taken from the proceedings of the 8 Oct. meeting.

2. Since the thirty-eight regiments are not "before mentioned," it is apparent that in revising the answer he omitted the early reference. The council did not specify, as he did, the number of men or regiments to be posted. The total number of men unanimously recommended to be enlisted, however, was approximately the same as NG's thirty-eight regiments—i.e., about twenty thousand. The difference was in the size of the regiments. In his answer to Query 7, NG recommended 528 men to a regiment; the

council voted for 728 men. The council's recommendation, which Congress later accepted (*JCC*, 3: 322), greatly reduced the number of regimental officers and did away with one man holding two commissions—a move strongly urged by NG earlier.

3. NG undoubtedly had in mind Dr. Benjamin Church, who was later turned over to the Mass. Provincial Congress for trial because a courtmartial was not authorized to try a case of treason. (See below, NG to Catharine Greene, 26 Oct. 1775.) The council side-stepped the query because some members were not prepared to "give their sentiments."

4. The council went further in the selection of uniforms by agreeing that "each Genl officer clothe a person according to his own fancy and judgment and then the best dress to be selected as a model." They voted for deductions of ten shillings per month.

5. The council divided evenly on this question. Greene, Sullivan, Heath, Lee, and Washington (in that order) voted for payments every month; Gates, Spencer, Thomas, Putnam, and Ward for every three months, feeling perhaps that the saving in paper work more than compensated for the dissatisfaction of the troops. The new army continued to be paid monthly.

6. Several members, believing it a question of a "very difficult and delicate nature," requested further time. It is typical of NG that he seldom hesitated to express his opinion to the commander in chief, and he rarely asked for more time to do so.

## General Greene's Orders

[Prospect Hill, Mass., 9 Oct. 1775. Officers to "have a strict" watch to prevent waste of ammunition, as has happened in the past. Hitchcock Orderly Book no. 3 (RHi) 1 p.]

## General Greene's Orders

Head Quarters [Cambridge, Mass.] Octr 10, 1775
The officers of the Rhode Island Regts are requested to furnish Capt Martindale with a party for a Sea expedition.[1] If a sufficient number cannot be got out of the 3 Regts, the Colos and officers of the other Regts in Genl Greens Brigade are desired to supply the remainder.

Hitchcock Orderly Book no. 3 (RHi).
1. Sion Martindale, a seaman of long experience, was captain in the Third R.I. Regiment. Knowing of Washington's interest in fitting out a privateer and manning it with Continental soldiers with sailing experience, Martindale offered to refit and take command of a Plymouth vessel with which he was familiar. Among Washington's instructions of 8 Oct. to Martindale was one (no. 6) that stated "For your own Encouragement & that of the other Officers & Men to Activity & Courage in their Service over & above your Pay in the continental Army you shall be intitled to one Third Part of the Cargo of every Vessel by you taken & sent into Port . . ." (Printed in Clark, *Naval Docs.*, 2: 354). There was no problem in getting volunteers from NG's brigade. When Martindale took an unusually long time at refitting the vessel, Washington sent Capt. Ephraim Bowen of Rhode Island to help him. Joseph Reed said that the army could not possibly supply as many guns as Martindale requested unless he "means to go without Powder" (ibid., p. 537). On the 16 of Nov., Washington's Muster Master General, Stephen Moylan, asked "Shall we ever hear of Capn Martindale's departure?" (ibid., p. 1042). Finally at the end of Nov., after suppressing a mutiny, Martindale set sail from Plymouth and was scarcely out of port when HMS *Fowey* captured the *Washington* and took her crew as prisoners to England—the first American ship captured in the Revolution. Moylan summarized the short history of the *Washing-*

*ton* by saying "she was fitted out at an enormous expense, did nothing, and struck without firing a gun" (ibid., 3: 572). (The story of the *Washington* is fully and interestingly told in Clark, *GW's Navy*.)

In May 1776 Martindale was returned from England to Halifax prison, from which he and Lieut. Moses Turner escaped. (See below, NG to Hancock, 8 Sept. 1776, on NG's request for back pay for the men who had just shown up in his camp.)

## General Greene's Orders

[Prospect Hill, Mass., 14 Oct. 1775. Masons in R.I. regiments and carpenters not already in work party to work on barracks. Hitchcock Orderly Book no. 3 (RHi) 1 p.]

## To Samuel Ward, Sr.

Dear Sir                                    Prospect Hill [Mass.] Octo 16, 1775

Your favor of the 24 of Sept and the 2d of Octo came safe to hand.[1] It gives me great pleasure to hear that the Troops from Rhode Island stand as high in the publick esteem as the Troops of the Neighbouring Colonies. I have spard no pains Night or Day to teach them their duty. How far I have succeeded I leave to his Excellency to say. Colo Varnum and Col Hitchcock are good Disciplinarians but Colo Church knows nothing about it, nor never will. Major Sherburne is the only Field Officer in that Regiment that understands the out Lines of his duty.[2] To him the Regiment are indebted for all their knowledge, which is far short of the other two Regiments.

The Complaints of The Committee of safety of our Colony against Mr Trumbull are not well founded.[3] He has always offerd either Mr Phillips or the Committee to furnish their full Propotion for our Troops. But they must turn it into the Stores through the Contractor he had Appointed for the whole Army, and he to account for whatever was turnd in at the same Rate as the other Colonies were allowed, this I told them and desird they would undertake it. But the loss of the Commission for paying the Soldiers their Wages was the principal grievance notwithstanding they complaind against Mr Trumbull, Who I have not seen since the receipt of your first Letter. He has been gone to Conecticut ever since and is Expected back every Day. As soon as he arrives I purpose to lay the matter before him and doubt not of accomodating it to the Colony satisfaction.

With regard to paying the Troops part of their Wages and the Committee part, it will be productive of a multitude of Inconveniences. The Colonels can retain part of their Wages, for their families at home. The People [i.e., the Troops] may give Orders to those that supplies their families to receive it. This will give less dissatisfaction and Answer every salutary purpose. A man from each Town or

County may under take to supply the families of those that are engaged in the Army. The Colonels are the best Judges of the prudence and good Oeconomy of his Soldiers. Those that behaves well and makes a prudent use of their money dont want any Agent for they'l receive Monthly payments and such parts as they can spare for the support of their families can be easily conveyed home. As the Troops are considerd Continental and not Colonial, there must be some sytematical plan for the payment without any reference to particular Colonies, otherwise they will be partly Continental and partly Colonial. His Excellency has a great desire to Bannish every Idea of Local Attachments. It is next to impossible to unhinge the prejudices that People have for places and things they have had a long Connexion with. But the fewer of those Local Attachments discovers themselves in our plan for establishing the Army the more satisfactory it must be to the Southern Gentry. For my own part I feel the cause and not the place. I would as soon go to Virginia as stay here.[4] I can assure the Gentlemen to the southward that there could not be anything more abhorrent proposd than a Union of these Colonies for the purpose of conquering the Southern Colonies.

The pay and provision of the Troops cannot be lowered at present; they do not feel themselves under a necessity to enter the service for the support of themselves and families, and therefore would refuse to reinlist again. That might produce a recess at the termination of their present Enlistments which might be dangerous to the Liberties of America. At some future period when the people are Obligd to resort to the Army for employment such a measure may be prudent and practical, but by no means at present. We are in the infancy of the dispute and it is too early to Alarm the Peoples fears. Should they grow jealous of the Justice of the Continental Congresses intention it might greatly injure the service. The Officers pay are too low, but its a matter of some doubt if they were to be raisd equal to their desert whether it would not rather Prejudice than Benfit the service. However if they were to be raisd about one Eight part I think it would Answer very good purposes. I am in hopes great part of the Troops will engage in the service again. There is no objection made to entering into the Continental pay and service. The Troops in General will as chearfully enter into the Continents service as the Colonies to serve till a fixt period.

The Committee from the Congress arrivd last Evening[5] and I had the honnor to be introduced to that very great Man Mr. Franklin whom I viewd with silent Admiration during the whole Evening. "Attention watched his Lips and Conviction closd his periods." Colonel Harris[on] is a very facetious good humourd sensible spirited Gentleman. He appears to be calculated for Military employment. Mr

Lynch was much fatigued and said but little, but appeard sensible in his enquiries and observations. You may depend upon our paying the Gentlemen every mark of Respect and Attention during their stay.

I had the pleasure to hear from your Son Sammy the 26th of Sept. He was at Fort Weston just going to set off on their Jorney All in health and good spirits.[6] I had the same Apprehensions with regard to Sammy health and strength to endure the fatigues of such a Campaign as you. I advisd him to decline it. But the heat of Youth and the thirst for Glory surmounted every Obstacle and renderd Reasoning Vain and persuasion fruitless. Colonel Christopher Greene is gone with him; his going made me the more readily consent to your Sons going. I gave the Colonel a particular charge to lend him a helping hand in every case of difficulty and the Col promised his aid and assistance should not be wanting. By several Letters from Quebeck things wear a promising appearance. If the Expedition suceeds, and we get Possession of Canada, We shall effectually shut the back Door against them. And I make no doubt of keeping them from entering the Country at the front Door.

We have several Cutters cruising about Boston Bay and more fixing out dayly. I have man'd one with the Rhode Islanders entirely, Commanded by Capt Martindale. There has several Captures been taken, One Transport from England loaded with flour, she had 2,000 Barrels on Board.

The Troops in Boston are very still in Boston and have been for some time, they have not fird a shot for above a week past. They are taking down a number of houses at the south end of Boston near the Hay Market and diging a Deep Ditch across the neck from one Water to the other. They are also framing three large Block Houses for Barracks ⟨to keep Bunkers Hill in this Winter. They are calculated to hold a thousand Men who are to be regularly relieved once a Week.⟩

We are building Barracks for our Troops and are in hopes to get them all under cover in a fortnight or three weeks at most. If we can get Cloathing they will be comfortablly provided for. You may depend upon my influence to obtain Charles a Commision upon the New establishment [*the remainder of this letter is missing*]

AL (MiU-C). Incomplete; portions in angle brackets taken from G. W. Greene transcripts (CSmH).

1. Letters not found.

2. Henry Sherburne (1747–1824), who retired from the Continental army as a colonel in 1781, served as general treasurer of Rhode Island, 1792–1808 (*R.I. Biog. Cycl.*).

3. Joseph Trumbull, the commissary general.

4. For a similar expression of NG's growing continentalism, or nationalism, see his letter to Deputy Gov. Cooke above, 23 Sept. 1775.

5. Congress had appointed Benjamin Franklin, Benjamin Harrison, and Thomas Lynch as a committee to confer with Washington and New England civil authorities on

"the most effectual method of continuing, supporting, and regulating a continental army" (30 Sept. 1775, *JCC*, 3: 266). Benjamin Harrison (1726?–91), a leading Virginia revolutionary leader, would as governor of his state, 1781–84, carry on an extended correspondence with NG during the southern campaign. Thomas Lynch (1727–76), one of the strongest South Carolina advocates of American rights, was not well. He suffered a stroke a few months later from which he never recovered. His son Thomas is remembered as a signer of the Declaration of Independence. (*DAB*) The proceedings of the four-day conference, and the minutes of the committee's further meeting with Washington, are printed in Force, *Archives* (4) 3: 1156–63.

6. En route to Quebec with Gen. Arnold.

## General Greene's Orders

[Prospect Hill, Mass., 17 Oct. 1775. Regimental commanders to return names of officers who wish to continue in service of the United Colonies. Off-duty field officers to attend general quarters to give their opinions on some questions. Hitchcock Orderly Book no. 3 (RHi) 1 p.]

## General Officers' Response to Washington's Query on Attacking Boston

At a Council of War held at Head Quarters
[Cambridge, Mass.] October 18th 1775
Present: His Excellency General Washington

| M. Generals | Ward | B.Generals | Thomas |
|---|---|---|---|
| | Lee | | Heath |
| | Putnam | | Sullivan |
| | | | Greene |
| | | | Gates |

The General acquainted the Members of the Council that he had called them together in consequence of an intimation from the Congress, that an attack upon Boston if practicable, was much desired. That he therefore desired their opinion on this subject.[1]

Genl Gates — That under the present circumstances it is improper to attempt it.

Genl Greene — That it is not practicable, under all circumstances, but if 10,000 men could be landed at Boston thinks it is.[2]

Genl Sullivan — That at this time it is improper, the Winter gives a more favourable opportunity.

Genl Heath — Impracticable at present.

Genl Thomas — Of the same opinion.

Genl Putnam — Disapproves of it, at present.

Genl Lee — Is not sufficiently acquainted with the men to judge, therefore thinks it too great a Risque.

Genl Ward — Against it.

Genl Washington

Tr (Varick transcripts, Washington Papers: DLC).
    1. When Washington had asked the general officers on 11 Sept. for their opinion on attacking Boston, the individual views were not recorded, but they agreed unanimously that it was "not expedient to make the attempt." See note, Washington to Council of War, 8 Sept. 1775, above.
    2. Since Washington was extremely impatient of the stalemated siege, NG's answer was probably closer to his own thinking than the other opinions expressed at the meeting. NG was considerably bolder here than he was two weeks later when he wrote to Deputy Gov. Cooke, "How far that [i.e., an attack on Boston] might be prudent I dont pretend to say. But the best of Veterans are required to Storm a Town" (NG to Cooke, 5 Nov. 1775, below).

## General Greene's Orders

[Prospect Hill, Mass., 20 Oct. 1775. Officers to prevent "as much as possible their People Burning rails"[1] and to report amount of fuel needed for each regiment. Hitchcock Orderly Book no. 3 (RHi) 1 p.]

    1. With the continued depletion of the supply of wood, stealing of wood by the troops was treated with increasing leniency.

## To Samuel Ward, Sr.

Dear sir                      Prospect Hill [Mass.] October 23th 1775
    I wrote you last Week giveing you an account of the State of the Army and the situation of the Enemy Since which nothing new has happend in the Army. An Express arrivd from Casco Bay last Evening that brings an account that the Enemy had been firing a Day or two upon Falmouth.[1] What has been the consequence we have not yet learnt; the Enimy had orders to burn Falmouth and Portsmouth unless the Inhabitants would deliver up their Arms and give Hostages for their future good behavior. The Enimys conduct fulfills the Scripture "Whose tender Mercies are Cruelties." Will not this brutal conduct rouse a spirit of Indignation throughout America? Such a shocking scene as was Exhibited at Bristol you cannot conceive off.[2] The People of Newport are all moveing into the Country. The Night after Wallace returned from Bristol the confusion in Newport was near equal to what it was there. The Inhabitants Carted out there Goods and furniture and stord them in Barns and out Houses all about the Island. They must sustain very great losses from the confusion and disorder the Goods were moved in. Capt Esek Hopkins commands a party of about two hundred men stationd there by order of Governor Cook.[3] Capt Wallace has made the Inhabitants the following proposition; if they will supply his Vessels with fresh Provisions, Beer &c and remove the Troops off the Island he will spare the Town, but if they dont comply with these conditions he has positive orders to lay the Town in Ashes, which he is determind to execute. What will be

the Event God only knows. There is a Committee from Newport down here to see Governor Cook[4] to get an order for the Removeal of the Troops and Liberty to furnish the Ships with fresh Provisions. The Committee are Capt. John Jepson, Mr John Malbone and Sam Dyer Esqr. The matter was laid before the Continental Committee who advisd to furnishing the Ships with fresh Provisions, but not to remove the Troops off the Islands, Which I suppose will take place accordingly.

But there appears a strange hobble in our Gait; here we are at Loggerheads, at other places only Sparring, and others again in perfect Tranquillity. Here we are cuting them off from geting fresh Provisions and removing the Stock from the Islands which amounts to an entire Depopulation, While at New York, Philadelphia and many other parts of America their Ships are supplied with every thing they Stand in Need of and live in the midst of peace and plenty. If we are to be considerd as one People and they as a common Enimy upon what principles are they so differently treated in different Governments. O! could the Continental Congress behold the distresses and wretched condition of the poor Inhabitants driven from the Seaport Towns, it must, it would kindle a blaze of Indignation against those Commisiond Pirates and Licensed Robbers that they would find no rest or Abiding Place in America. The fate of Kingdoms depends upon the just improvement of Critical minutes. Suffer not the noble Ardor to slaken for want of Action nor smother the generous flame for want of Vent. The tempers and Dispositions of men can be wrought up to a certain pitch, and then like all Transitory things sickens and dies away. This is the Time for a Wise Legislator to avail himself of the advantage the favorable Disposition of the People gives him to execute whatever sound Policy dictates. It is not in the Province of Mortals to reduce human Events in politicks to a certainty; it is our duty to provide the means to obtain our Ends and leave the Event to him who is the Alwise disposer and Govenor of the Universe.

The Goverment of Rhode Island from its situation must suffer amazingly. The Stock which lies exposd to the Enemies Ravages would be a plentifull supply for the Enemy in Boston.[5] An Object so considerable will not escape their Attention. Without doubt theyl make an attempt to avail themselves of the Advantages the situation of the Island[s] affords and must be successful unless some provision be made to frustrate their measures. As their defeat is a General benefit it is but just it should come within the line of a General Charge against the Continent. Fresh Provisions will be of infinite service to the Troops in Boston. If they dont provide some very fine Antiscorbuticks they must suffer amazingly by Scurvy. By two Capt of Vessels out of Boston Day before Yesterday we learn that its extreme Sickly. Eight or Ten are buryed in a Day. Cold Weather coming on the Scurvy lockt up in their Blood produced by feeding on Salt Provisions, must produce a prodigious mortality. Nothing can heithen their distress equal to cuting them off from Fresh Provisions. Therefore I think it an Object Worthy of Publick Attention to lend a helping hand to Rhode Island to secure the Stocks on the Islands. It must be grievous to the Inhabitants to be subject to such an expence themselves and also unjust seeing the whole Continent are to be equally Benefited from its Consequences.

The Committee has been closely engag'd in forming a Plan for Regulating the Army. I hope when the Army is reinlisted and the best of the Officers selected out, the Troops will be under better Regulation. Good order and subbordination will take place, which cannot fail of producing the Advantages expected from the Army. The Number agreed on may be larger than may Appear Necessary at first blush, but when you consider how Raw and undisciplind the Troops are in General, and what War like preparations are going on [in] England, and how necessary it is to have a good Army in the Spring and the favorable prospect we shall have of making ourselves masters of Boston this Winter, I doubt not you chearfully concur in the Establishment. The General Officers fixt upon 20,000; what number the Committee has determin'd upon I have not heard this Morning, but make no doubt they'l approve of the number agreed on by the Generals.[6] I wish we had a Large Stock of Powder that we might Annoy the Enimy where ever they make their Appearance. We could easily in my Oppinion drive them out of Boston if we had the means, but for want thereof we are Obligd to remain Idle spectators, for we cannot get at them and they are determind not to come to us. However I hope ere long fortune will favor us agreeable to our Wishes.

Mr Trumbull has not Yet returnd, that I've had no Opportunity to settle the matter you mentiond in your last. I have had no News from Colo Arnolds Detachment since I wrote You before. There is a Report in Boston that Quebeck is taken and that it was taken by the Canadians. If it proves true it will be much better than if Our People made themselves masters of it. They'l now be Obliged to enter the List.

I Just hinted in my last that People began heartily to wish a Declaration of Independence.[7] I would make it Treason against the state to make any further Remittances to great Britain. Stop all supplies to the Ships throughout America. We had as good begin in earnest first as last, for we have no alternative but to Fight it out or be slaves. We should Open our Ports to all that has a mind to come and Trade with us. But it will be necessary to keep a Check upon Commerce, lest it take the lead of the Military. The Merchants in general are a body of People whose God is Gain, and their whole plan of Policy is to bring Publick measures to square with their private Interest. We have not begun to Commision the Officers anew, but expect it to take place every Day.

The French never will agree to furnish us with Powder as long as there is the least probabillity of an Accomodation between us and Great Britain, for they can have but two Objects in view: A sepiration from Great Britain or subjugation to her; in either case Great Britain will receive as a Nation little or no Advantage from the Colonies, for slavery is ever unfriendly to Trade and thats the Strength and sinews of Great Britain. Therefore France as a real Enimy to Great Britain Acts upon a true plan of Policy in refusing to intermeddle until she is satisfied that there is no hopes of an accomodation between us and Great Britain. Then she can interpose with propriety by lending us a helping hand. She'll secure to herself an Exclusive right of our Trade—and thats an Object worthy Any National Consideration. Should France undertake to furnish us with Powder and other Articles we are in need of and the breach between Great Britain and the Colonies be healed, She will incur the displeasure of Britain without reaping any solid Advantage from her plan of Policy.

I have but little time to write and generally very much interrupted while I am writing. I must beg your friendly allowance for the defects And believe Me to be with great esteem Your sincere friend

NATH GREENE

ALS (MiU-C).

1. See NG to Cooke, 24 Oct. 1775, below.

2. On the night of 7 Oct., Capt. James Wallace bombarded Bristol, a small port just to the north of Newport. Although no one was killed, the guns of HMS *Rose* did damage many buildings. The people of Bristol finally gave him forty sheep to withdraw and he did so after plundering nearby farms. (Arnold, *R.I.*, 2: 358)

3. Esek Hopkins (1718–1802), brother of Stephen Hopkins, Rhode Island delegate to Congress, had been a sea captain and successful merchant (*DAB*). NG does not acknowledge here that two weeks earlier Hopkins had been made a brigadier general in charge of Rhode Island's naval and land forces. Within two months the Continental Congress (undoubtedly influenced by his brother) named him "commander in chief of the fleet." (*JCC*, 3: 443; the journal spelled his name Ezek.) Since it was a "Small Fleet," as his brother Stephen called it, Congress did not imply by the title that his status at sea was comparable to Washington's on land. Several ships, in fact, were added to the navy without coming under his command. (The point is covered in Allen, *Naval History*, 1: 29–31, 139.) He was commonly called Commodore Hopkins.

4. Cooke, the deputy governor of Rhode Island, was in Cambridge meeting with Washington and the three delegates from Congress to whom NG refers later as the "Continental Committee."

5. On the earlier removal of stock from the islands, see note, NG to Joseph Trumbull, 8 Sept. 1775, above.

6. The committee had voted unanimously four days earlier for an army of at least 20,372.

7. In previous letters, NG has regularly used the term "People" for the men in the army; he appears to use it here in the same way. There is no evidence that he had recently had any contact with people outside the army; there is, in fact, strong

evidence from his orders and letters that military problems almost totally absorbed him during the fall of 1775.

In Oct. of 1775 there were no widespread sentiments among the colonies for independence. Jeremy Belknap, then a chaplain in the army, noted in his journal for 19 and 22 Oct. that a "plan of independence was becoming a favorite point with the army, and that it was offensive to pray for the King" (MHS, *Proc.* 4 [1860]: 78–84). It is not surprising that such sentiments were especially strong among the military. To men who had fought at Bunker Hill or who had looked out at the British army for several months in anticipation of a daily attack, the siege of Boston more nearly resembled a war between sovereign powers than an insurrection. Col. Edward Hand of Thomson's Pennsylvania Battalion had noted a month after arriving at Prospect Hill in August: "I think I can plainly see that a spirit of Independence prevails among the New Englanders." He was referring to the soldiers—the only New Englanders he had met. (Hand to Jasper Yeates, Edward Hand Coll., Force transcripts, DLC) The word "Independence," of course, was susceptible of several meanings (as noted by Gov. Cooke in a note, NG to unknown person, 14 May 1776, below), but as Hand used the word, it seems to have concerned America's relation with England.

News of the king's unbending speech to Parliament would be needed to crystallize the thinking of NG and his colleagues, but in the meantime, the desperate need for powder was another factor that pushed them toward independence. The argument was indirect but logical: despite the combined efforts of Congress and the colonies to establish powder manufacturing, the product was still so scarce that Washington had decreed thirty-nine lashes for any man who so much as wasted a single cartridge. The one hope for powder was England's traditional enemy, France; and, as NG argues in the next paragraph, the French would not agree to furnish the colonies with powder (openly, that is) as long as there was the "least probability of an Accomodation" between the colonies and the mother country. And to powder could be added other vitally needed items such as guns, uniforms, shoes, tents, and blankets. Two months later Thomas Paine used precisely the same argument in his *Common Sense.*

## To Deputy Governor Nicholas Cooke of Rhode Island

Sir                                        Prospect Hill [Mass.] Octr 24th 1775

By an Express that arrived from Falmouth last Night, we learn the greatest part of the Town is in Ashes.[1] The Enemy fired about three thousand Shot into it; and a large Number of carcases and Bombs; which sat the Town on fire. The Enemy landed once or twice to set fire to the Stores; they lost eight or ten men in the attempt and had one taken Prisoner. The inhabitants got out a very considerable part of their furniture. No Person Killed, or wounded during the whole time of their firing. The Enemy produced orders from Admiral Graves to burn all the Towns from Boston to Hallifax. Capt Mowat informed the Committee at Falmouth, that there had arrived orders from England about ten Days since, to burn all the Sea port Towns upon the Continent, that would not lay down and Deliver up their Arms, and give Hostages for their future good Behavour.[2] He also acquainted them that he expected the City of Newyork was in ashes; by these accounts we may learn what we have to expect. I think New Port should be fortified in the best manner it can be. Doubtless the Enemy will make an attempt to get the Stock of the Island. Provission should be made to defeat them. Death and Desolations seems to mark their Foot Steps. Fight or be Slaves is the American Motto; the first is by farr the most Elligable. In haste I am with ⟨great respect and esteem, your most obedient humble servant,

NATHANIEL GREENE.⟩

G. W. Greene Tr (CSmH). Words in angle brackets supplied from Force, *Archives* (4) 3: 1168.
    1. The site of the later Portland, Maine.
    2. The account relayed by NG is essentially correct, although it is doubtful if any one could say how many shots were fired. Admiral Samuel Graves, stung by the criticism of British army officers as well as by the depredations of American privateers, had gotten Gen. Gage's support to dispatch two vessels under Capt. Henry Mowat to punish the port towns. Mowat set out in the *Canceaux* and the *Halifax* with one hundred soldiers aboard. Graves's resolve was reinforced by orders from Germain authorizing him to use his judgment in punishing the ports. Of the several hundred structures in Falmouth, most were destroyed and the remainder greatly damaged. No single British act was more conducive to hardening American opposition. The reactions in England and in America caused Graves to abort further such forays, although New Englanders had no way of knowing this at the time. (The best account of the incident is in French, *First Year*, pp. 537–44, and Appendices 43 and 44, pp. 765–66.) The destruction of Falmouth also focused attention of the congressional committee (Franklin, Harrison, and Lynch) on naval matters and helped to expedite the arming of privateers (Clark, *GW's Navy*, p. 23).

## General Greene's Orders

[Prospect Hill, Mass.] Octr 25th 1775.
Genl Green is Greatly displeas'd with a number of Evil dispos'd persons that are endeavouring to beget Jealously and discontent amongst the Troops by promoteing and propagating a Spirit of Reflection amongst the different Regts, as such a Conduct has a tendency to bring on the Great Confusion and disorder in the Brigade and to alienate the affection of one Colony from another and distroy that confidence and Union now happily subsisting amongst us.[1] The General intreats all the officers of whatever rank to suppress as much as possible such growing Evil As National, Colonials, Regimental or personal reflection, and requests the Field officers of the Several Regts to punish every person that is Guilty of such high misdmeanors with the utmost Severity.

Hitchcock Orderly Book no. 3 (RHi).
    1. There was rivalry enough between one New England colony and another, but here Greene may have had especially in mind "reflections" by some of the Pennsylvania riflemen. On 15 Dec., Washington wrote to Joseph Reed that the "extracts of letters from this camp, which so frequently appear in the Pennsylvania papers, are not only written without my knowledge, but without my approbation, as I have always thought they must have a disagreeable tendency." Washington was less sanguine than Greene in believing such evil could be suppressed: "there is no restraining men's tongues, or pens," he continued, "when charged with a little vanity, as in the accounts given of, or rather by, the riflemen." (Fitzpatrick, *GW*, 4: 165–66)

## To Catharine Greene

My Dear Wife                    Prospect Hill [Mass.] Octob 26, 1775

It is past nine oClock, the room still and the Company all gone. My attention is turnd towards you. Permit me to address you my Dear with Sentiments of warm affection. My Soul breaths a secret prayer for your happiness amidst these times of general Calamity. How fondly should I press you to my Boosom was you with me. Cruel seperation, but I console myself that you are happily provideed for and I in the way of my duty, offering my small services United with others who are endeavering to preserve an Oppressed People from cruel slavery, the worst of Misseries. May God speed our efforts and Crown us with success. I hope youl be well enough to come to Camp in January where youl meet with a hearty Welcome from me. It gives me great pleasure even to contemplate my future bliss. How happy in the tender embraces of each other. Permit the few intermediate Days between this and that delightful period to steal away in silently contemplating our future happiness. Dont murmur at your lot nor repine at your ill fortune. Few have less reason to complain. You are happily provided for. If not, let me know it and your wants shall be speedily provided for and supplied. You can make yourself merry amidst the Little circle of your friends in chit chat about the News of the Day, and the state of the Times, with Anxious Boosoms pet[it]ioning the Throne of Grace for your respective friends. Surely Providence will hear the prayer of the Innocent. It will come up before him like a sweet smelling savour, like frankensence from the Alter of Innocence. O! America what a black Cloud hangs over this once happy Land, but now Miserable and Afflicted People.

I attended the General Court of this Province today to Doctor Churches Examination rellative to his Treason.[1] With art and ingenuity surpassing whatever you saw he Veild the Villany of his conduct and by implication transformd Vice into Virtue. But notwithstanding all his art and address, and his faculty of makeing the worsd appear the better Reason, He could not establish his Innocence, either satisfactory to the Publick in General or the General Court in particular.

I wrote some time ago for two more shirts and some Books; please to forward them per the first safe of Opportunity. Colo Varnum is well and Col Hitchcock. The Col will visit Nancy with a smileing Countenance in about a fortnight. Commend me to all friends and believe me to be your very Affectionate Husband

NATH GREENE

ALS (Original in possession of David Coblentz, Raphine, Va., 1974).
1. For NG's role in the affair of Dr. Benjamin Church, see above, Ward to NG, 26 Sept. 1775, and NG to Ward, 30 Sept. Upon Church's arrest Washington called a

council of officers for 3 Oct. which NG attended. The council adjourned until the following day when Dr. Church could be present for questioning. At that meeting the officers agreed with Washington that Church had "carried on a criminal correspondence with the Enemy," but since the Articles of War provided only "very inadequate punishment" for a crime of such "enormity," they referred the matter to Congress for its "special direction." (Varick transcripts, Washington Papers: DLC; and Fitzpatrick, GW, 4: 10–11) Congress took no action except to have Church continue to be confined (JCC, 3: 334). The Massachusetts Provincial Congress subsequently found him guilty of treason. It was a sticky point, however, for since he was accused of helping the king's officers, he could hardly be accused of treason against the king. In the end he was imprisoned in Connecticut for some months, then exiled. In 1776 he sailed from Boston in a ship that was never heard from again.

For NG's recommendation on punishment for treason, see note 3, his opinions of 6–7 Oct. 1775. Congress did strengthen the penalty in Nov. 1775 (JCC, 3: 331); thus, in the words of a leading student of treason, "Congress, prodded by the army, took a long step toward independence by authorizing the death penalty for American soldiers who adhered to George III," Bradley Chapin, *The American Law of Treason: Revolutionary and Early National Origins* (Seattle: University of Washington Press, 1964), pp. 32–33.

## To Catharine Ward Greene[1]

Sister Greene          Prospect Hill [Mass.] Octo 29th. 177[5]

In June last You sent me a Letter which I had no Opportunity to Answer at that time. As I have receivd none since from you, I take it for granted you mean to have the old Ballance paid first. Therefore I have taken up my Pen to remit you the Ballance, with offers of a further trade if you can find your Account in it. I know your Anxiety to hear from your Brother gone upon the Canada Expedition.[2] His welfare and safety is often the subject of your Petition to the Throne of Grace. May God return him safe to the Boosom of his friends. I had the pleasure to hear from the Party about Sixteen Days past, all well and in high spirits. But the fatigue they endure is inexpressible. I hope as he was very hearty when he engagd in the Expedition his strength and resolution may hold out. I was very much afraid of his abillity to endure the fatigue and disswaded him from Attempting the Jorney, But the Zeal of Youth and thirst for Glory Rendered Reason empty and perswasion Idle. Colo [Christopher] Greenes going with the party made me more willingly consent to the Attempt. The Cols prudence, Moderation, and steadiness will be a fine guide, and an useful friend to your Brother during the Campaign. To his particular care I recommended him, with the strongest injunctions to lend him a helping hand in every case of difficulty. All things were prosperous and appearances favorable in the last accounts, and the party within about thirty or forty miles of the French Inhabitants. By this [time] I Hope the party is safely Landed in Canada. Charles I have not seen for some time but he was well and was going home on Furlough.[3] Whether hees gone or not have not heard. If he concludes to continue in service I purpose to get him if possible an Ensigncy, but whether I shall be able upon the new Establishment of the Army I am not Able to say. I have had two Letters from your father last Week. He was well. Remember me to all freinds and believe me to be your sincere frend

NATH GREENE

ALS (MWA).
1. Although not addressed the letter is unmistakably to Catharine Ward Greene, wife of his brother Christopher and daughter of Samuel Ward, Sr.
2. Samuel Ward, Jr., had volunteered to go with Arnold on the march to Quebec.
3. Charles Ward was Catharine's eldest brother, who had entered the army as a private. For John Adams's reaction to such a lowly post for Samuel Ward's son, see note 4, NG to Catharine Ward Greene, 13 Jan. 1776, below.

## General Greene's Orders

[Prospect Hill, Mass., 31 Oct. 1775. Several deep-sea lines used for marking out fortifications have disappeared. Anyone found possessing them will be punished. Hitchcock Orderly Book no. 3 (RHi) 1 p.]

## General Greene's Orders

[Prospect Hill, Mass., 1 Nov. 1775. Artificers to begin half hour before sunrise and work as long as they can see; to examine their guns and cartridges weekly. Regiments to "equal" the cartridges among the men. Sergeants and corporals should give each sentry a proper detail of his duty. Regiments to report guns out of order. A sentinel to be at the well at Col. Hitchcock's hut. Hitchcock Orderly Book no. 3 (RHi) 2 pp.]

## General Greene's Orders

[Prospect Hill, Mass., 1 Nov. 1775. Tools to be delivered each night to the artillery captain in the citadel, to be signed out each morning. Blacksmiths to report at armorer's shop. Hitchcock Orderly Book no. 3 (RHi) 1 p.]

## General Greene's Orders

[Prospect Hill, Mass.] Novr 5th 1775.
The Genl Court of this Colony haveing Engag'd to furnish the troops with wood as soon as possible the Genl strictly forbids any person Cutting Apple trees or Locusts for the future, and that there may be a present supply Each Regt is authorisd to form proper parties to Cut and transport Wood from the Grove between Colo Pattersons Regt and Leechmors [Lechmere] Point. Genl Greene Orders three men to

be sent to Cambridge to stand Centries over the Wood boated up the River by a party of this brigade, to take a tent with them, to suffer no wood to be taken for any Regts, only those in this Brigade. The Subaltern and the party that boats The Wood and the Centrie that stands over it to be regularly releaved once a Week and to be Continued till further orders.[1]

Hitchcock Orderly Book no. 3 (RHi).
1. On the desperate need for wood later in the year, see note 6, NG to Samuel Ward, 31 Dec., below.

## To Governor Nicholas Cooke of Rhode Island[1]

Dear Sir                    Prospect Hill [Mass.] Nov 5th 1775
By an Express from General Skuyler[2] we have the agreeable Intelligence of the reduction of Fort Chambler [Chambly] upon the River Sorel. There was Eighty Royal Fuziliers and about an hundred Women and Children made Prisoners of War. There was 124 Barrels Powder, two Mortars, a large quantity of Shot, 230 stand of arms, about 100 Flour, 60 or 80 Barrels of Beef and Pork, and a quantity of Butter taken in the Fort; no Lives lost in the Reduction.[3] St Johns is closely Blocked up and t'was expected would Capitulate in two Days after the Capitulation of Fort Chamble [Chambly]. There was one Major, two Capt, and three Subalterns made prisoners at this Fort which I had like to have forgot to mention. There is a party gone on to Invest Moreal [Montreal] where very little opposition was expected as the Peasantry of Canada are warm in our Cause. By Letters from Colo [Benedict] Arnold this Day Dated the 13th of last month we expect he is in Possession of Quebec for he expected to be there in Ten Days from the Date of his Letter. We are informd by a Gentleman who left Canada about Six Weeks ago that there was not 20 soldiers in Quebec and that Governor Charlton [Carleton] was at Moreal [Montreal]. The City of Quebeck quite defenseless, there being only two Guns mountd on Carridges in the City. Colo Arnold writes his party are in high spirits and have gone through incredible fatigue with out a murmur. In all probabillity Canada is wholely reduced by this, as Carltons party are small and the French noblesse Lukewarm, but on the other hand Our Army is large and strongly reinforc'd by Canadians, who are rising in the Cause of Liberty.

Our Sloops of War have taken a Vesel Bound for Boston with 120 Pipes of Maderia Wine, and Two other vessels of some considerable consequence. We are Just carrying into Execution the plan you and the other Gentlemen of the Committe establish'd for the Rule of our conduct in the New Establishment of the Army. The Local prejudices common to all Independent States I apprehend will create some difficulty, but I hope it may not be productive of any very dissagreeable consequences. We are compleating the Barracks.[4] Those that continues in service will have a fine Accomodation, and extraordinary good living, high Wages and New Clothes, powerful motives for the Soldeiry to engage anew seting a Side their Zeal for the Glorious Cause of Liberty. The Rhode Island Regiments are reduced to two, agreeable to your Advice.[5] If all three of the Regiments were to Engage they would not compleat two. But make no doubt but that Recrutts can be had to compleat these two Regiments. General Lee intends to set out in a Day or two for Newport if nothing happens to prevent his present Resolution. The Enemy in Boston are throweing up some works on Mount Whoredom[6] and on the Common, they are greatly Apprehensive of an Attack. How far that might be prudent I dont pretend to say. But the best of Veterans are required to Storm a Town. What success might attend an Irregular Attack without great superiority in numbers, requires no spirit of Phophesey to foretell. Our opperations here may appear something tardy. I am but a young Officer and therefore an incompetent Judge of Military Opperations. By old Experienced Officers its thought to be a great point gaind to keep the Enemy Hencoop't up within their Lines. Their situation must be very dispiriting, to have but a small Range, and cut off from all the refreshments of Life; and had we plenty of what we wish [i.e., powder], they would meet with Dayly and hourly insults, which would make their situation still more disagreeable, if not compel them to come and shew themselves in the open fields. God send us a speedy supply is the hearty wish of sir your most obedient humble servant

NATHANAEL GREENE

ALS (MH).
    1. Cooke, who had been deputy governor, had just been elected governor (see below, NG to Cooke, 29 Nov., note 1).
    2. Philip John Schuyler (1733–1804), a member of a prominent New York Dutch family, was one of four major generals appointed by Congress in 1775 (*DAB*). Schuyler had moved up Lake Champlain with a small army to drive the British from the Sorel River, but when illness forced him back to Ticonderoga, his second in command, Richard Montgomery, took over. Montgomery's capture of Ft. Chambly on 18 Oct. and the consequent capture on 2 Nov. of nearby Ft. St. Johns were two bright episodes in an otherwise dismal series of disasters in the 1775 invasion of Canada.
    3. NG's account differs somewhat from Montgomery's figures, which Schuyler forwarded to Congress (see enclosures in Schuyler to John Hancock, 20 Oct. 1775, printed in Force, *Archives* [4] 3: 1132–33).
    4. He was somewhat premature in his assessment; the barracks were still incomplete by early Jan.
    5. Church's regiment was absorbed into Varnum's and Hitchcock's.
    6. On Mt. Whoredom, see note 2, NG's orders no. 1, 20 Mar. 1776, below.

# General Greene's Orders

[Prospect Hill, Mass.] Novr 7th 1775.
There being an open and daring Violation of a Genl Order in fireing
at Geese as they pass over the Camp, Genl Greene gives positive
orders that any person that fires for the future be immediately put
under guard. Every officer that stands an Idle Spectator and sees
such a wanton Waste of powder and dont do his utmost to suppress
the Evil may expect to be reported.[1]

Hitchcock Orderly Book no. 3 (RHi).
  1. The chronic shortage of powder is reflected in many of Washington's orders and
communications. On 11 Nov. he wrote Congress, "Our Powder is wasting fast, not
withstanding the strictest care, oeconomy and attention is paid to it; the long season of
wet weather . . . renders the greater part of what has been served out to the men of no
use" (Fitzpatrick, GW, 4: 84). Had the men only known the powder would be ruined,
there might have been more wild geese to relieve the monotony of camp routine and
diet! On powder shortage see references at end of note 1, NG's orders, 12 Nov., below.

# General Greene's Orders

[Prospect Hill, Mass., 9 Nov. 1775. Unbroken bunches of cartridges
delivered today are to be collected and delivered back when needed.
Anyone firing his gun without orders to be immediately punished by
courtmartial. The general will order the first transgressor to be tied up
and whipped as an example. Officers to read this order immediately
to the companies.[1] Hitchcock Orderly Book no. 3 (RHi) 1 p.]

  1. On powder shortage see references at end of note 1, NG's orders, 12 Nov.,
below.

# General Greene's Orders

[Prospect Hill, Mass.] Novr 10th 1775
Genl Greene is inform'd that the Soldiers have got into a practice of
Stealing Cartidges from one another and those that go on Furlough or
are dischar'd cary them home. As this conduct is both dishonourable
and villanous, the Genl Hopes there are but few if any that are so lost
to honour and honesty as to commit so dirty a Crime. If any are
detected in the fact, they may expect to be punish'd without mercy.
The Officers of this brigade are once more desir'd to pay perticular
Attention to the persavation of the Cartridges. There has been such a
wanton waste for sum time past and still continues upon every alarm
that it is really disgraceful. It is impossable to Conceive upon what
principle this strange Itch for fireing originates, as it is rather a mark
of Cowardise that [than] Bravery to fire away amunition without any
intention. If the Soldiers are desireous of defending their rights and

Liberties the Genl desires they would not deprive themselves of the means to execute so laudable a purpose.[1] The Artillery on Prospect Hill to mount a Guard of 1 Subaltern, 4 Non Commissiond Officers, and 25 privates every day to mount at the same time the Main Guard does, and to be subject to the Command of the Capt of the gd to keep a Slow match constantly burning. Genl Greene is greatly displeasd with the Officers of the Artillery that they were so ill provided with wads today. The Genl gives positive orders that proper provisions be made immediately that the Artillery may be in readiness upon an alarm at the first notice.

Hitchcock Order Book no. 3 (RHi).
    1. On the shortage of powder see references at the end of note 1 to NG's orders, 12 Nov., below.

## General Greene's Orders

[Prospect Hill, Mass.] Novr 12th 1775
The Capts every day to Examine their arms and amunition of their Co and see that their arms are kept Clean, the locks in Good order, and the flints well fixt; to count the Cartridges and Flints of each individual, for every Cartridge that is lost to be charg'd 1 shilling L[awful] M[oney] and for every Flint missing 3 pence, a report to be made daily of the Regt to the Colo in what Condition they find the guns and amunition.[1] Any Capt or Subaltern that neglects to make a daily return to his Colo or Commanding Officer, the Colo to report him to the Genl of Brigade that he may report him to H Quarters. Upon an Alarm Colo Brewers Regt[2] to take post in the Citadle on the left, Colo Littles Regt to form on Parade in the long lines next to the Baracks, Colo Thompsons in the front of Colo Littles there to wait for orders, no officer to stir from his post nor to suffer his people to strangle [straggle] but to keep them silent and attentive. The Field Officer of the day to examine the Sally ports in these fortifications and if the Chevaux de frise are out of repair they are to put them in Order, and if any of the picketts are out of place to have them rectified. The fireing of the morning Gun to be discontinued. The Reveille to be beat at grey day light, at the beating of which the Troops to man the lines with as much expedition as possible. All the Centries on the lines to be posted on the parapet and to hail every person that approaches the lines on the out side as soon as it is dark and to suffer no one to come near the lines without giveing the Countersign. All the Soldiers for the future to repair to their Quarters at 9 oClock, and if any are catched abroad after that hour and cannot give a Satisfactory account of their Business, to be sent to the main Guard as none

but Drunkerds and Thieves will be out at a later hour unless upon some spetial Business. No Soldier to go out of camp without leave from his Capt or Commanding Officer.

Capt [Noel] Allen of Colo Churches Regu has had within these two days four guns stole out of his bell Tent. Genl Greene orders the Colo or Commanding Officer of each Regt to make a Strict Sarch for them thro the Brigade; Enquirey also to be made at all the Suttlers stores. Ten dollars reward to any person who will bring out the Thief. Any Soldier that is dischar[g]d or goes home on Furlough that offers to carry away his gun, Powder or Cartridges to be immediately sent prisoner to the M[ain] Guard. Every Soldier that is recommended for discharge, first to go and deliver up his gun and Bayonett if any he had; harness [the] number of Cartridges, flints, blanket, and Canteen before he comes for a discharge; and the Capt to observe the same line with those recommended for furloughs. No guns are to be permitted to be carried away from the army on any Condition. If any has guns here of their own private property and are fit for service they will be paid for them by the Continental Congress.

Hitchcock Orderly Book no. 3 (RHi).

1. NG's anxiety over his troops' readiness to withstand a British attack was shared by his fellow generals and the commander in chief. On 19 Nov., Washington warned Hancock that "we may expect the Enemy will take the Advantage of the first hard weather" and attack. "That this is their intention we have many reasons to suspect"— deserters reported that a train of artillery and an Irish regiment had arrived, that fresh ammunition and flints had been "served out," and that grenadiers and light infantry had orders to hold themselves in readiness. (Fitzpatrick, GW, 4: 100) Although Howe had shifted Gen. Clinton from his comfortable quarters in John Hancock's Boston mansion to take command of the troops at Charleston Neck, it did not presage an attack (Willcox, Clinton, pp. 59–60). The truth was that the British were also short of supplies—not powder, as were the Americans, but food and fuel. They were also short of the will to undertake a bloody offensive. Could they have known of the powder shortage in the American camp, Washington's fears would have been fully justified. For other orders concerning powder see those of NG for 7, 9, 10, 12 Nov., above, and 15 Nov., below.

2. In the interests of economy, as Washington put it, Col. Asa Whitcomb's regiment was merged the following day with Col. Jonathan Brewer's. Whitcomb had accepted an appointment as barracks master, but his men refused to serve without him. With Brewer's consent Whitcomb was then put in command and Brewer accepted the appointment as barracks master. In his orders of 16 Nov., Washington praised both men for their willingness to step down. (Fitzpatrick, GW, 4: 94)

## General Greene's Orders

[Prospect Hill, Mass.] Novr 15, 1775

Every Col. or Commanding Officer of a Regt to appoint 30 Men that are active, bold and Resolute to use the Spears in the defence of the lines Instead of Guns, to form in the Center of the Rear of the Regt to Stand ready to push the Enemy of[f] the breast work if they should Attempt to get over the Parapit into the lines. Let those be appointed that are the worst Equipt for arms and those that have none at all, provideing the size, strength and activity are Agreeable for the Purpose of their Appointment to be commanded by a Subaltern and Sarjt.

Hitchcock Orderly Book no. 3 (RHi).

## General Greene's Orders

[Prospect Hill, Mass., 17 Nov. 1775. Captain of the guard to see that guardhouse is swept daily. He is accountable for the number of watch coats belonging to the guard. He is to notify the general immediately if the enemy make any uncommon movement. Hitchcock Orderly Book no. 3 (RHi) 1 p.]

## From General Charles Lee

[17 Nov. 1775. Asks NG to choose an officer in compliance with a request that Washington made 17 Nov. through his aide, Robert Harrison,[1] to Lee. Harrison's letter asks that Lee send a "Judicious and sensible" officer to Col. Baldwin[2] at Chelsea to agree on signals: "First, if the Enemy should parade on the Bank or near the Water; 2d If they come down to their Boats, and 3d If they embark and seem to be crossing over."[3] (Lee's brief note to NG is written at the bottom of Harrison's letter; NG's autograph appointment of Jeremiah Olney, printed below, is on the back of Harrison's letter. The document is in MHi.)]

1. Robert H. Harrison (1745–90) was from Alexandria, Va., where he enlisted as a lieutenant in the Third Virginia Regiment in 1775. He had just become an aide-de-camp to Washington two weeks earlier (see Washington's orders for 6 Nov., Fitzpatrick, GW, 4: 68). He succeeded Joseph Reed as Washington's secretary the following May and served into 1781. According to Fitzpatrick (ibid., note 79) "he was probably closer to Washington and as much in the Commander in Chief's confidence as any other aide." After the war he became chief justice of the general court of Maryland. (Heitman, Register; DAR Lineage, 14: 356)
2. Loammi Baldwin had served as a major in the Mass. militia at Concord. At this time he was a lieutenant colonel in Col. Gerrish's Mass. regiment (Heitman, Register).
3. In a letter to Gen. Artemas Ward the same day, Washington thought "as it is more than possible that General Howe, when he gets the expected Reinforcements, will endeavour to relieve himself from the disgraceful confinement, in which the Ministerial Troops have been all this Summer; common prudence dictates the necessity of guarding our Camps, where ever they are most assailable." (Fitzpatrick, GW, 4: 96–97) Col. Baldwin's position in the town of Chelsea, which lay north of Boston harbor and east of Charlestown, permitted him to observe a British embarkation from Boston. NG's orders of 21 Nov., below, describe a series of signals to be used on Prospect Hill if either Col. Baldwin in Chelsea or NG's own sentinels spotted a British movement. Since Howe had no intention of "crossing over," none of the signals were put to use.

## Appointment of Captain Jeremiah Olney

[17 Nov. 1775?]

General Greene appoints Captain Jeremiah Olney to agree upon certain Signals with Colonel Baldwin as directed within.[1]

AD (MHi). NG's appointment was written on the back of Harrison's letter to Lee as noted in the calendared item above (Lee to NG).

1. Jeremiah Olney at this time was in Colonel Hitchcock's regiment. He succeeded Lt. Col. Israel Angell upon Hitchcock's death in Jan. 1777. At the war's end, he was made a colonel and commanded what was known as "Olney's Rhode Island Battalion." He served as collector of customs in Providence during the Federalist period. (Heitman, *Register*; as collector of customs his correspondence with the secretary of the treasury, Alexander Hamilton, is printed in Syrett, *Hamilton*, vols. 15–17)

## General Greene's Orders

[Prospect Hill, Mass.] Novr 21st 1775

The following Signals to be observed:[1] First Signal to be observed in Case the Enemy should parade on the bank or near the water; by day a square sheet hoisted on the pole or flagg staff Erected on Prospect or Powdor Hill by the party that makes the discovery; by night, the discharge of a Single Sky Rocket from Green Hill or the vicinity if First discovered by the Chelsea party; if by the other party a Rocket from Prospect Hill. Second Signal in Case the Enemy should come down to the Boats; By day another square Sheet in addition to the 1st affixed to the same Halyards about 6 feet space between. 3d Signal in case the Enemy should embark or seem to be Crossing over; by day a fire smoke near the Pole and the 2 Sheats moving up and down to show that the smoke is the 3d Signal least it should be taken to proceed from the barracks.

If the night or grey of the Evening or morning, the discharge of 3 Sky Rockets. The Capt of the main Guard is requested to post a Centinel on the Parapet for the purpose of makeing the Discovery of either of those Signals, who is immediately to acquaint the Capt of the guard when he discovers either of them and the Capt of the guard to acquaint the Genl. Particular care is to be taken that every Centinel releiving has his proper detail of duty. A Subaltern and 24 private that understands woodcutting to parade tomorrow morning at 8 oClock at the store to draw a weeks allowance and to repair to the Assistant Quarter Master Genl John George Fraser [Frazer] Esqr at Mistick to receive instructions.[2]

Hitchcock Orderly Book no. 3 (RHi).

1. On a possible British attack, see NG's orders of 10 Nov., above, and Charles Lee to NG, 17 Nov., above.

2. John G. Frazer of Mass. served as assistant quartermaster general from Sept. to

Dec. 1775, and as a major in the Sixth Continental Infantry until the end of 1776 (Heitman, *Register*).

## To Governor Nicholas Cooke of Rhode Island

Dear sir                    Camp on Prospect Hill [Mass.] Nov 29, 1775

I beg leave to congratulate you on your promotion to the chief seat of Government.[1] Your patriotism and Publick spirit justly entitles you to that Appointment. I hope Divine Providence may direct your Councels and prosper your Administration which I apprehend to be both Critical and perplexing. But Patience and perseverence surmounts almost all Obstacles in human Affairs. Your Love of Liberty and dread of Slavery will arm you with a becoming fortitude to stem the Tide of Adversity and go through the toil with pleasure. I wish your Administration may terminate as glorious as it begins. There never was a Govenor in the Colony before you whose fortune it was to concert and execute a Plan that was to prove its future glory or immediate Ruin since the Government was first establisht. May you be the happy Instrument in the hand of Providence to compleat our deliverance from our Tyrannical Oppressors.

This is a most alarming Crisis of American Affairs. Shoud the British Parliament join in the measures of the Ministry and the Troops belonging to the Colonies get sick of the service, We shall find from sad Experience that our Vanity led us to attempt what we had not Virtue to execute. I must confess I feel no small anxiety from the present disposition of the Troops. I greatly fear the conduct of the Soldiery will disgrace the New England Colonies. The present backwardness the Troops discover in engaging in the service[2] again will in all probabillity protract the War for Years, by encouraging the Ministry to hold out in hopes of our geting sick of the dispute and divided amongst ourselves. If they were to enter the service chearfully again it would damp the spirits of the Ministry and they would despair of success and would be oblig'd to propose Terms of Accomodation to our wishes. Where is that Enthusiastick Love of Liberty that has ever been the distinguish[ed] Characteristick of a New Englandman? I fear it is not a little abateed from the lukewarm indifference they discover in engageing again in the service. If the Aversion of the Troops should continue to the service, and no measures can be hit upon to fill up the Regemints, certain Ruin must be the consequence. If neither the Love of Liberty nor dread of Slavery will rouse them from the present stupid state they are in, and they obstinately persist in quiting the Service, they will deserve the curses of the present and future Generations to the lateest agees. These New England Colonies will be the most wretched of all Gods Creation and the Inhabitants considerd a set of the vileest Paltroons in the Universe. They'l be a laughing Stock and subject of derision for all Europe. After they had insulted the King and Ministry in bid[d]ing defiance to their Unconstitutional Laws, after they had engagd the whole Continent in support of their Opposition, and every thing prospering beyound their most sanguine expectations to basely desert the cause and at a time too when every thing round us promises success—What can equal such an infamous desertion.

We shall recieve the curses of all the Southern Govemments, New England will be held in detestation and Abhorrence in every part of the Globe. We that have boasted so loud of our private Virtue and publick spirit, not to have the very Vital principles of Liberty. We have been considerd a brave and spirited People, but without a great alteration we shall be as contemptable as we ever were honnorable. A People to sell their freedom for present Ease and a little paltry gain, how shameful. The Southern Governments begins to be alarmd at the backwardness the Troops manifest at engaging again in the service. Our Soldiers have Ten shillings Lawful Money and worth more than the Congress gives the Troops rais'd to the Southward and yet ours dont enlist one quarter so fast as theirs. Troops were never better fed nor paid than ours are; in a word the conditions are so liberal it may be said with great propriety we are brib'd into the preservation of our Liberties. Can New England men be so lost to their own happiness and that of posterity as to neglect this favorable Opportunity of establishing our freedom upon a permanent footing? We shall despise the Goodness of God, who smiles upon the Arms of America, if we neglect to compleat the glorious work so happily began. Can the People rest easy at Home when their Countries cause calls them to the Field? Is it possible for a Rhode Islander to betray such a want of Publick spirit; are there any that are of so delicate make that they fear the fatigues of a Campaign? Is the Brave Rhode Islanders grown so selfish as to wish to enjoy the blessings resulting from this Controversy without shareing in the toil? Call upon all such if any there be for the Love of God, for the Love of their Country, themselves and all posterity, to chearfully enter the service again and give the World a convinceing proof that the Rhode Islanders are deserving the Character they have obtaind for bravery and publick spiritedness.

If the Troops dont enlist the several Legislatures must furnish their propotion by draught. If they have not this power or dare not exercise it, the common People will have it in their power to enslave themselves and others. However I will not indulge a thought so de[rog]atory to free men as to think they would Obstruct any measures necessary for the preservation of the Rights and Liberties of

America. Should be glad of your Oppinion upon this subject whether it would be practicable if necessity requires it.

I am very sorry to hear the Merchants and Country[3] have got into a dispute about the price of merchandise. We ought to lay aside all party, prejudice, and private Interest and unite our whole strength to carry on the glorious work. They who stirs up these commotions are unfriendly to their Country and notwithstanding they may sanctify their conduct by some plausable Reasons, yet they are doing Violence to the Interest of America and sapping the foundation of her future freedom. I cannot Justify the Merchants for enhanceing the prices of their Goods at such Enormous Rates, neither can I think the Country Reasonable in expecting them at the former prices, seeing the risque of Importation has become four fold greater than usual, and the price of all foreign goods must be in propotion to the expence and risque of Importation.[4] This is a maxim in all Commerce. This dispute is infinitely more destructive to the interest of the Merchants than to the Country. It is but Reasonable that both should be sufferers as both are to be gainers by the issue. This is not a Time for those petty disputes, when all our Commerce is interdicted and all our Interest threatned to be confiscated [*remainder of letter missing*][5]

AL (MWA). One or more pages missing at the end.

1. Since May, when Gov. Joseph Wanton had been suspended for not approving the Army of Observation, Cooke had served as deputy governor. Convinced by this time of Wanton's loyalist sympathies, the legislature formally declared the office vacant on 7 Nov. and elected Cooke governor. (Arnold, *R.I.*, 2: 361)

2. Rhode Island troops, like most of the New England militia, had enlisted only until the end of the year. Many had indicated they did not intend to reinlist in the new army, an attitude that was clearly reflected in the failure of captains to fill their companies. See also note 2, NG to Samuel Ward, Sr., 10 Dec. 1775, below.

3. In this paragraph the word "country" has two meanings. In this instance NG refers to the noncommercial part of the population—farmers, craftsmen, laborers— who are economic adversaries of the merchants. In the following sentence, he speaks of "their Country" as the united colonies. Further references in the paragraph are to the noncommercial sector.

4. Maj. Israel Angell, then serving under NG, wrote to his brother two days later from Prospect Hill about protests in Rhode Island against the merchants: "Brother I am much allarmd At the News of the Conduct of the people in Providence And the towns Adjacent, to hear that they are likely to Rise in mobs on the account of Salt rising and Some other Small Articals. I begg of Every honost and well meant Person, both in town and country, to Exert them Selves to The utmost of their power to Surpress any riotous proceeding Among them Selves, Especily at this Time. For God Sake Let us unite all as one in America" (Israel Angell to his brother, Hope Angell, Military MSS, vol. 1, RHi).

5. This was probably written at white heat to relieve his feelings, but it was also written with design, for Cooke's influence was considerable, and NG wanted his sentiments driven home where they counted. Unfortunately, it is repetitious. Had NG been fortunate enough to have an aide to edit and shorten the letter, it would stand as an eloquent statement by a self-educated patriot.

## To Christopher[?] Greene[1]

[Prospect Hill, Mass., 30 November 1775][2]

I am sure all good and sensible Men will Lay aside those partial disputes and attend to the general Interest. I long to see a returning harmony, when with one Accord we shall join heart and Hand to compleat the great work so successfully began. God grant the issue may be as glorious and happy as the begining.

As many of the Friends and Relations of the Soldiery that comes to Camp from a mistaken kindness are perswadeing their Children and Relations to quit the service I wish some measure might be devised to put a stop to it.[3] Nothing will hinder the Troops from quiting the service so effectually as making it disgraceful for any to return home that are fit for service. I believe it might have a happy effect if the several Towns that has Soldiers here Was to strongly Recommend their stay in Letters directed to me or to the Colonel of the Regiment assureing them they would meet with a very cold Reception if they left the service of their Country when they were so much wanted.[4] If Neither Rewards nor punnishments, honnor nor disgrace will engage the Soldiery again they must taste the misery consequent to Slavery.

I supposd you have heard that Moreall [Montreal] is taken, I hope Quebeck will soon be ours. We had a fine Store Ship taken Yesterday, 2200 Stand of arms on Board, 2 Brass sixpounders, one 13 Inch Mortar and between thirty and forty tun of small arm Balls, with a prodigious quantity of Military stores of all kinds except Powder.[5] Several small prises have been taken within a Day or two. There is another store Ship more Valueable than this taken we hope will fall in our way. God grant it may, as it will soon unfold the Reason of our long silence. We have taken possession of Cobble Hill and compleated the Work and not a Gun fird at us. The Reason of their silence is unaccountable as they might cannonade us to great advantage. This night we are forming a Bomb Battery at Lechmere's Point, within three hundred Yards of the Ship. I expect they'l fire in the morning. The Army is generally healthy and in good spirits, but want to get Home. They are exceeding [*indecipherable*]. One Campaign more will Wean them from such Unsoldierly attachments as now has but too much Influence. I am my Dear sir with the greatest Respect your most obedient humble servant

NATHANAEL GREENE

ALS (MWA). One or more pages are missing at the beginning and end.

1. The letter is unaddressed. The recipient is surmised from the fact that the letter came down through Christopher's descendants.

2. The date is determined by the arrival of the *Nancy* in port on 29 Nov., which NG refers to as "yesterday."

3. From soldiers' journals and correspondence, it is evident that friends and family did a great deal of visiting in camp. Samuel Ward wrote Samuel, Jr., on 15 Aug. that one thing he had never thought of "which must create you many heavy Expences, that is your being so near as to have much Company from all the Colonies" (RHi). With Prospect Hill within a long day's journey of Providence and little danger from enemy fire, there was nothing to stop the home folks from going to camp. Later NG advised that each colony send its men to a distant sector in order to stop furloughs to home as well as visitors from home.

4. If any such letters were sent to NG, they have not appeared.

5. See note 5, NG to Jacob, in the letter following.

## To Jacob Greene[1]

Dear sir                    Camp on Prospect Hill [Mass.] Nov 30, 1775

By some Papers come to head Quarters I find Sloop Speedwell, Captain Cory master, is made a Capture on or rather taken and brought in to Cape pan [Ann]. She appears by the Papers to be the property of Peter Bonnamy.[2] I had an opportunity to write to the Captain last Night and gave him orders to come to me if he met with any difficulty. She was cleard out from Quebeck and bound to Grenada, had on board as appears by her papers four hundred Quintle[3] dry fish and thirty Barrels of Fish Oyl. As soon as I receive any accounts from Capt Cory shall forward the contents to you. I suppose you have heard of the Reduction of Moreall [Montreal]. I hope Quebeck will soon be ours. Thats the Key of America.[4] An Armd Sloop took a large Brigantine from England with 2000 stand of Arms on board between 30 and 40 tuns of small Arms Balls, two Brass Six pounders, one thirteen inch Mortar and a prodigious quantity of Booms [bombs], Carcases and shot and a great variety of military Stores sufficient to form almost a Compleat Labortory.[5] The Ministry seems by their preparations to intend our destruction. We have nothing to do but to get everything in readiness to give them a good Reception.

You that are in the Country must endeavor to make it disgraceful for any of the Soldery to return home from Camp. What think you of draughting the Militia if the Army cant be fild up by enlistments; this will be disagreeable if practicable, Start the question among you. See what will be said to it. New Hamshire has made a tender of 5000 Troops besides those they have in the Army to keep the Lines if they are wanted. They will engage for one two or three months or longer if Wanted. This looks like doing business; it's noble and Spirited. The enlistments goes on slow. The People will not attend to the necessity of the case; if neither the Love of Liberty nor dread of slavery, the promise of rewards or fear of punnishment, the prospect of honnor and the certainty of disgrace will engage them in the service of their Country, Theyl soon experience the Misery consequent to Slavery. I think every thing round us looks as if Divine Providence fought our Battles. May he shield this distressed Country from the [Evils?] intended it. In great haste believe me to be your Loving Brother

N GREENE

ALS (MWA).

1. The close of the letter identifies the recipient as a brother; the concern with the sloop *Speedwell* narrows the brother to Jacob.

2. In saying the sloop appeared "to be the property of Peter Bonnamy," NG was feigning ignorance, probably for fear the letter might go astray. He and Jacob were the principal owners, but since it was no secret, his ruse was unnecessary. The official records showed Jacob Green and Co. as owners (Maritime Records, R-Ar), and people in East Greenwich knew that NG was a partner. Washington, moreover, knew of his interest in the sloop, as is clear in the Harrison letter cited below. His fear of its becoming public knowledge was based not on any wrong-doing but on his over-sensitivity to what people might say. In truth, without an outside source of income, no general officer in the Revolution could have survived on his salary of $125 a month in steadily depreciating currency. Like most members of the Continental Congress, they had an interest in an enterprise that continued to be operated by family or partners. Thus did NG continue as a partner in the family business. As will be seen when he became quartermaster general, an apparent conflict of interest did become an issue.

The capture of the *Speedwell* is told in Clark, *GW's Navy*, in a fascinating chapter (pp. 46–57) entitled "The Fantastic Cruise of Broughton and Selman." Those two sea dogs persuaded Washington to put them in command of the *Hancock* and the *Franklin* in order to intercept powder brigs. In virtual acts of piracy, they took prizes from friend and foe alike, catching their victims in the Gut of Canso—the strait separating Cape Breton from the Nova Scotia mainland. Thus was the *Speedwell* taken on 13 Nov. 1775 and brought with a prize master into Cape Ann two weeks later.

In response to this letter, Jacob journeyed to Cape Ann via Prospect Hill to investigate the capture (see below, NG to Elihue Greene, after 11 Dec. 1775), but in the meantime, Washington had Harrison countermand the seizure, saying "it appears that the Vessel belongs to Genl Greene and he will dispose of her as he shall think proper." (Clark, *Naval Docs.*, 2: 1259)

3. A quintal was a hundred weight.

4. NG was passing along the conventional wisdom of those around him. From the time Col. Jonathan Brewer had offered to lead five hundred volunteers to Quebec in late May, most New Englanders were in general agreement on the need to win over Canada (the fourteenth colony), either by force or persuasion. This would add men and resources to New England and would prevent the British from coming down the Champlain-Hudson waterway, thus cutting New England off. Judging from British attempts to do just this (until Burgoyne's defeat), New Englanders were justified in their anxiety. Military historians have begun to question, however, whether a British occupation of the Champlain-Hudson waterway would have been such a disaster for the Americans. A complete cut-off would have required thousands of troops, would have been impractical, in fact; and Americans would still have had the ocean to unite New England with the middle and south Atlantic regions. After NG moved into the New York City and New Jersey areas in 1776 and 1777, he would no longer say that Canada or Quebec was the key to America.

5. The brigantine was the unarmed *Nancy*, which had been separated from her armed escort and captured by Capt. John Manley in the *Lee*, one of the small armed vessels in "Washington's Navy." NG's account of the captured stores was not exaggerated; he does not even mention 100,000 much-needed flints. The thirteen-inch mortar was famed as the *Congress*, so christened by Gen. Israel Putnam in a colorful ceremony. The much-heralded capture of the *Nancy* was a great boost to American morale. (French, *First Year*, p. 498) It was Capt. Manley in the *Lee* who had captured a British schooner loaded with much-needed firewood in early Nov. (Washington to Congress, 11 Nov., Fitzpatrick, *GW*, 4: 81).

## General Greene's Orders

[Prospect Hill, Mass., 7 Dec. 1775. A woodyard to be cleared for use of this hill. Regimental officers to report need of wood daily on a frugal basis. The quartermaster of each regiment to proportion to each company its share. Hitchcock Orderly Book no. 3 (RHi) 1 p.]

## To Samuel Ward, Sr.

Dear sir          Camp on Prospect Hill [Mass.] Decem 10, 1775
    As I receive no Answer to my last I continue to write on in hopes to teaze you into a compliance to Perform your promise which was to write me every Opportunity.[1] In my last I mention'd to you that the Troops enlisted very slow in general. I was in hopes then that ours would not have deserted the cause of their Country. But they seem to be so sick of this way of life, and so home sick that I fear the greater part and the best part of the Troops from our Colony will go home. Conectecut Troops are going home in Shoals this Day; five thousand of the Militia, three from this Province and two from Hamshire are called in to take their places. There is a great defection among them Troops, but from the spirit and resolution of the People of that Province I make no doubt they will furnish their proportion without any difficulty. New Hamshire behaves Nobly; their Troops engage chearfully. The Regiment raisd in the Colony of Rhode Island has hurt our Recruiting amazingly; they are fond of serving in the Army at Home, and each feels a desire to protect his own family.[2] I harrangued the Troops Yesterday. I hope it had some effect; they appear of a better disposition today. Some have Enlisted and others descovers a complying Temper. I leave nothing undone nor unsaid that I think will promote the Recruiting service. I fear the Colony of Rhode Island is upon the decline; there has been and now is some unhappy disputes subsisting between the Town and Country Interest, and some wretches for the sake of a present popularity are endeavoring to foment the dessention to build up their own Consequence, to the prejudice and Ruin of the Publick Interest. God grant they may meet with the disgrace they deserve. This Province [i.e., Massachusetts] begins to exert itself; the General Court has undertaken to provide for the Army Wood &c. Their Troops enlist now very fast; they are Zealous in the Country to engage in the service. I sent home some Recruiting Officers. They got scarcely a man and Report that there are none to be had there. No Publick Spirit prevails. I wish you and your Colleagues was at home a few Weeks to spirit up the People. Newport I believe from the best Intelligence I can get is determind to Observe a strict Neutrality this Winter, and join the strongest party in the Spring.

I feel for the honor of the Colony ⟨which I think in a fair way by the conduct⟩ of the People at Home and the Troops abroad to receive a wound. It [morti]fies me to Death, that our Colony and Troops should be a whit behind the Neighbouring Goverments in private Virtue or Publick spirit.

The Enimy remains much in the same situation as mentiond in my last. Our Arm'd Vessels are dayly makeing Captures. General How is sending all the useless mouths out of Boston. They have never fird a Gun at our People, that is a Cannon, since my last, notwithstanding they have been exposd every Day in compleating the Works on Cobble Hill, which by the bye is now very strong. I have been strengthing the Works on this Hill for fear if the Soldiery should not engage as chearfully as we expected we might be able to defend them with a less number of men.[3] But I am fully convinceed they will not come out unless drove out by Boombs and Carcasses which hope soon to effect. Believe me to be with great truth your sincere friend and humbl servant

N GREENE

ALS (MiU-C). Original damaged; portion in angle brackets taken from Force, *Archives* (4) 4: 231–32.

1. NG's last letter to Ward has not been found. His letter above of 23 Oct. to Ward does not mention troop enlistments.

2. On 1 Nov. the R.I. legislature approved raising a regiment of five hundred men for the "defence of the united colonies in general, and of this colony in particular" (Arnold, *R.I.*, 2: 359). With the British October raid on Bristol in mind, the legislature was more concerned with the defence of Rhode Island than of the united colonies. For background on R.I. troops leaving the Continental army, see NG to Cooke, 29 Nov., above.

3. Washington had decided rather belatedly on 25 Nov. to fortify Cobble Hill, since it lay some six hundred yards closer to Bunker Hill than Prospect Hill and would be more useful if it were decided later to bombard British positions. Washington joined NG's and Sullivan's brigades the night of 25 Nov. to help get the entrenching started, since, as he told Richard Henry Lee, it "could not be delayed, as the earth here is getting as hard as a rock." (Fitzpatrick, *GW*, 4: 116) To his "great surprize," the work progressed without their receiving a "single shott from Bunkers Hill," from a ship, or from the floating battery (ibid., p. 118).

## General Greene's Orders

[Prospect Hill, Mass., 11 Dec. 1775. All officers and men "acquainted with the Value and Goodness of Guns" to report their names tomorrow. Four men from each Rhode Island regiment to dig vaults. Reports from guardhouses to include receipts for watch coats. Hitchcock Orderly Book no. 3 (RHi) 1 p.]

## To Elihue Greene

Dear sir                    Prospect Hill [Mass., after 11 Dec. 1775][1]

I am informd from different hands that you manage the business at Coventry. Mrs Greens state requires your particular Attention.[2] I hope the regard you have for me and the Laws of humanity will induce you to treat her with that delicacy and care that her situation claims. As she is very young and not had a great deal of experience in Life, she may mistake her duty, the Paths of Prudence being very narrow while the Roads of Error are broad and hung with Alluring Ensigns to invite her astray. I must intreat you by the bonds of Brotherly Affection that you Councel her in all matters that respects her Interest or Reputation, and endeavor to direct her practice to her own honnor and your Interest. She is without Father, without Brother, with[out] Husband to apply to for aid and assistance. Let her find them in you with the Addition of a sincere friend. I am in hopes that the harmony of the family may contribute to her happiness. She must be very dull in contemplateing her approaching, painful tryal that she has to pass through. There is one thing which I wish you could Effect; that is a Reconciliation between Cousin Sally and Mrs Greene.[3] The dispute was whimsical in the begining and its Ridiculous to continue it. Endeavor to bring them together. A few conde[s]cending Notes on both sides will soon harmonies them again. I have wrote to them both about it advising a Reconciliation. But the first Overtures will be the most difficult to Obtain for the Human Heart is so proud, that its difficult to bring it to think of conde[s]cension. I have known People heartily wish a Reconciliation, but so loth to submit to the necessary forms to Open the Door that they chose rather to continue at Enmity.

Mrs Greene wrote me[4] She had sent to Cousin Sally to come and Visit her, but that She had not come. I do not wish no mean condecension on either side and if Sally is not willing to bury the dispute upon such terms as are Reasonable Let her Live by herself. She has and still may want the Assistance of her Friends amongst whom none has servd her and hers with more fidelity than myself. I have not Receivd a line from one Soul of you for months past. Was you abroad and I at home I should not Neglect you. But perhaps you are more Agreeably employ'd.

The Army begins to recruit very fast. I hope it will be full very soon. There is Rumours of a Spannish War. It is reported that some French Vessels are Arrivd with Powder at Bedford, but what quantity is not known. Jacob is gone to Cape Pan [Ann] to see about Sloop Speedwell.[5] I have heard nothing from him since his departure from here. No News from Quebeck sin[c]e my last to Mrs Greene. Let me hear from you soon and the state of the family Affairs. How your farming went on this summer. How the Iron business goes on. We hear of the Enemys Ravages on Conanicut. Wallace keeps his faith finely.[6] I hope theyl treat him as a Robber where ever they find him. As to his burning Newport theres not the least danger. They'l Reserve it as a place of Retreat, if fortune should drive them from hence, but before I would suffer him to be supplyd in the infamous way he now is, and as now conducts, I would burn the Town to Ashes and roast the Tories by the Fire. Adieu Dear sir

N GREENE

ALS (MWA).
1. The earliest possible date is established by the 10 Dec. British raid on Conanicut Island.
2. Catharine was pregnant with her first child.
3. Cousin Sally was apparently Sarah, the wife of cousin Griffin Greene and sister of Col. Christopher Greene.
4. Letter not found.
5. See NG to Jacob, 30 Nov. 1775, above.
6. Capt. James Wallace of HMS *Rose*. NG was right in prophesying the British would not burn Newport. Although they never imagined the war would last for another year, almost exactly one year after NG wrote the above letter, the British captured Newport, and it would be three years before they left.

## General Greene's Orders

[Prospect Hill, Mass., 18 Dec. 1775. A committee is appointed to appraise the value of the arms in this brigade, to be exempted from all other duty until task is completed. Hitchcock Orderly Book no. 3 (RHi) 1 p.]

## To Samuel Ward, Sr.

Dear Sir                    Prospect Hill [Mass.] December 18, 1775
     Yours of the 9th this Instant came to hand Saturday Night.[1] The Army is filling up slowly. I think the prospect is better than it has been. Recruits comes in out of the Country plentifully, and the Soldiers in the Army begins to be of a better disposition and to engage more chearfully. Your observation is exceeding Just; this is no time to disgust the Soldiery when their aid is so essential to the preservation of the Rights of Human Nature and the Liberties of America. His Excellency is a great and a good man.[2] I feel the highest degree of Respect for him. I wish him immortal honnor. I think myself happy in An Opportunity to serve under so good a General. My happiness will be still greater if fortune gives me an opportunity in some signal instance to contribute to his glory and my Countrys good.
     But his Excellency as you Observe has not had time to make

himself thoroughly Acquainted with the Genius of this People.[3] They are Naturally brave and spirited as the Peasantry of any Country, but you cannot expect Veterans of a Raw Militia from only a few months service. The common People are exceeding Avaricious; the Genius of the People is Commercial from the long intercourse of Trade. The Sentiment of honnor, the true Characteristicks of a Soldier, has not yet got the better of Interest. His Excellency has been taught to believe the People here a superior Race of Mortals, and finding them of the same temper and disposition, passion and prejudices, Virtues and Vices of the common People of other Governments they Sink in his Esteem. The Country round here has no bounds to their demands for Hay, Wood, and Teaming, which has given his Excellency a great deal of uneasyness, that they should take this Opportunity to extort from the necessity of the Army such Enormous prices. The General has often exprest to me his Apprehensions about the expences; they so far exceeded the expectations of the Congress that he was in fear whether they would not sink under the weight of the Charges. Oeconomy is essential in this dispute and that there be no Wanton Waste of publick Property, but if you starve the Cause, you'l protract the dispute. If the Congress wishes to put a finishing stroke to this dispute, they must exert their whole force at once, give every measure an Air of decision. I pray God we may not loos the critical moment. Human Affairs are ever like the Tide constantly upon the Ebb and flow. Our preperations in all parts of the United Colonies ought to be so great as to leave no Room to doubt of our Intentions to support the Cause or else Obtain our conditions. This will draw in the weak and wavering; this will give such a turn to the minds of People, as small shocks will not obstruct the general plan of Opperations. Your proclamation in answer to the King's of August past, is noble; its glorious.[4] Was it Unanimous or else only the Voice of a Small Majority.

The Papers Announces to you the much greater part of the Military Opperations here. Yesterday we took possession of Lechmere's Point. There was a thick Fog all the morning. The Troops broke ground within three Hundred Yards of the Ship. They continued their Work untill about One oClock when the fog cleard off. The Ship then began a severe fire upon them but did no other damage than wounding a man in the Thigh. We fir'd at Her from Cobble Hill. She went out of the Harbour this morning. Cambridge Bay is now all clear. From the best Accounts we can get out of Boston they are prodigiously distrest. It begins to grow very sickly. The Scurvy descovers itself. The Small Pox prevails. General Howe is Innoculateing all the Soldiery that have not had it. I think they cannot hold out the Winter through if we were to leave them unmolested, which God grant we may not. It is reported here that Quebeck is taken. General Montgomery and Colo Arnold will Acquire immortal honnors. O that we had but plenty of Powder, I should then hope to see something done for the Honnor of America. Our Barracks are almost Compleat. Blankets and cloathing will be much wanting notwithstanding your supply from the Congress. The Conecticut Troops are gone home; the Militia from this Province and New Hampshiere are come in to take their places. Upon this Occasion they have discoverd a Zeal that does them the highest honnor. New Hampshire behaves nobly. [Capt. James] Wallace at Newport bullies and destroys Just as he pleases; doubtless you have heard of his Ravages. General Lee is going to Newport tomorrow. The Island can and ought to be fortifyed and Conannicut too. I think the Point may be fortifyed so as to prevent any Ship from doing much damage; it certainly will command the Harbour. Colo Joseph Wanton['s] Negroes piloted Wallace crew about the Island and pointed out the Houses to burn.[5] He deserves to be taken up as much as any Tory upon the Continent. I cannot help differing with you in Oppinion about Great Britain sending twenty or Thirty thousand Troops here in the Spring. I allow them fifteen thousand provided the Peace of Europe is preserv'd. Two french Gentlemen are coming to Congress, their business to me unknown.[6] In haste I conclude your most Obedient humble servant

NATH GREENE

ALS (MiU-C).
1. Letter not found.
2. In his letter of 9 Dec., Ward had undoubtedly referred to some criticism voiced privately by Washington of New Englanders, a criticism that had then been circulated. It may well have been comments Washington had made in a letter of 29 Aug. to Richard Henry Lee, a Virginia delegate to Congress who was not as discreet or as good a friend as Washington then thought him to be. He had told Lee that the reason New England troops were not more fearful of a British attack was because of "an unaccountable kind of stupidity in the lower class of these people," and he went on to say that the same stupidity "prevails but too generally among the officers of the Massachusets *part* of the Army who are *nearly* of the same kidney with the *Privates*." (Fitzpatrick, *GW*, 3: 450; italics are Washington's) The letter to Lee could be countered, of course, by other private letters in which he complimented New England soldiers and officers.
3. Here NG is apparently talking about New Englanders in general; later in the paragraph, when he speaks of the "Country round here" charging the army enormous prices for produce, he is undoubtedly speaking of Massachusetts people.
4. On 23 Aug. the king had proclaimed that subjects in "divers parts" of America were in "open and avowed rebellion," and he ordered all his other subjects to help bring "the authors, perpetrators, and abetters of such traitorous designs" to punishment (Jensen, *English Docs.*, 9: 850–51). In response to the proclamation, Congress approved a lengthy declaration on 6 Dec. to "wipe off, in the name of the people of these United Colonies, the aspersions which it is calculated to throw upon our cause." If friends of American liberty should be punished, the document said, there would be retaliations upon those who aided the "system of ministerial oppression." The threat was softened somewhat by the assertion that the sole view of Congress was to prevent punishments, not multiply them. (*JCC*, 3: 409–12) Whether it was passed by a large majority was not recorded.

5. On 10 Dec. the British landed on Conanicut Island in Narragansett Bay, burned a dozen or so houses and barns, and carried off livestock. Col. Joseph Wanton, whose servants supposedly pointed out houses of outstanding patriots to Capt. James Wallace, was the son of the deposed Gov. Joseph Wanton. When Gen. Charles Lee marched to Newport two weeks later and demanded that the inhabitants take an oath to defend the patriot cause, Col. Wanton and two customs officials were the only ones imprisoned for refusing to take the oath. (Arnold, *R.I.*, 2: 364–65) Washington reported the raid briefly to Congress on 14 Dec. (Fitzpatrick, *GW*, 4: 162)

6. M. Pennet and M. De Pliarne, who were referred to Washington by Gov. Cooke of Rhode Island, and by Washington, in turn, to the Continental Congress, had come to sell French arms and ammunition to the united colonies. See Washington to president of Congress, 14 Dec. 1775, Fitzpatrick, *GW*, 4: 162–63; and *JCC*, 3: 466.

## To Jacob Greene

Prospect-Hill, [Mass.] December 20, 1775.

[Capt. James] Wallace, I hear, continues a thorn in your side; burning and destroying wherever he can get an opportunity.[1] It is to me a most astonishing thing that the Committee of Newport are desirous of nourishing such a serpent in the bosom of the country. If his depredations were to cease in all parts of the country, there might be some small reason for listening to his propositions. But, for him to obtain his supplies, and grant an indemnity only to the town of Newport, is sacrificing the rest of the Province to the benefit of that town only; for he will be continually committing piracies upon all the islands and shores that he can get footing upon. I think Wallace's conduct has been such, from the insults and abuses he has offered to Government, that it is highly dishonourable to have any further intercourse or commerce with him. Besides, these separate treaties weaken the chain of connection and injure the general interests of the Continent. We must expect to make partial sacrifices for the publick good. I love the Colony of Rhode-Island, and have ever had a very great affection for the town of Newport; but I am not so attached to either as to be willing to injure the common cause for their particular benefit.

It is a very great unhappiness that such a division of sentiment in political matters prevails in the Colony; it distracts her councils and weakens her exertions. The Committee in the town of Newport, you say, seem inclined to counteract the prevailing sentiment in the Government. It is astonishing that ancient prejudices and selfish motives should prevail, at a time when every thing that is dear and valuable is at stake. I hear some of the inhabitants of Newport are very jealous of the views of the town of Providence; fearing that the latter has in view the destruction of Newport, for their own private advantage. I cannot harbour a thought so derogatory to the patriotism of the people of Newport, as to suppose that such a fear can have any real existence. Can the inhabitants of Newport suppose that the Legislature of the Colony acts upon such absurd principles as to make a sacrifice of one town for the benefit of another?

George the Third's last speech has shut the door of hope for reconciliation between the Colonies and Great Britain.[2] There are great preparations going on in England, to prosecute the war in the spring. We have no reason to doubt the King's intentions. We must submit unconditionally, or defend ourselves. The calamities of war are very distressing, but slavery is dreadful. I have no reason to doubt the success of the Colonies, when I consider their union, strength, and resources. But we must expect to feel the common calamities which attend even a successful war. We are now driven to the necessity of making a declaration of independence.[3] We can no longer preserve our freedom and continue the connection with her. With safety we can appeal to Heaven for the necessity, propriety, and rectitude of such a measure.

I flatter myself the King's speech will induce the Congress to raise one large Continental army proportionable to the extent of our undertaking; to be under one command, and by him directed to the security and preservation of the several united Governments. This will unite and cement the whole strength of the several Colonies. If this method is not adopted, some Governments, from their natural situation, will be subject to fourfold the expense of others, for their own particular security. As we have one common interest in the opposition, and it is merely accidental and uncertain where the enemy may exert their greatest force, I think the Continent ought to provide for the security of every Colony.

Letters were received this day from General Montgomery, near Quebeck. He says he expects to be master of the place in a very little time. He has powder and all kinds of military stores to facilitate the reduction. He and his troops are in good health, and he speaks very highly of Colonel Arnold and his party. Many officers, and a large number of the privates, belong to our Government [i.e., Rhode Island].[4]

The regiments fill up very slowly here. It is really discouraging. I fear the advantages proposed from so large an armament as our establishment was to consist of, will be defeated by the length of time it takes to fill the army. However, I still hope for better things, and pray God my expectations may not be defeated. If the Congress had given a large bounty, and engaged the soldiery during [i.e., for the duration of] the war, the Continent would be much securer, and the measures cheaper in the end. The wisest may sometimes err. To profit rightly by past evils is the only right use that can be made of former misfortunes. God grant that our future measures may be so taken as to render our success equal to our wishes.

Excerpt reprinted from Force, *Archives* (4) 4: 367–68.

1. For his attacks on Bristol and Conanicut Island, see NG to Samuel Ward, Sr., 23 Oct. and 18 Dec., above. The first letter discusses the approval that the special Congressional Committee gave Newport to furnish Wallace with supplies.

2. On 26 Oct., George III opened Parliament with a speech declaring that, despite the forbearance of Parliament and his own conciliatory efforts toward his American subjects, the "rebellious war now levied is become more general, and is manifestly carried on for the purpose of establishing an independent empire." To put a speedy end to such disorders, he continued, he had increased the land and naval forces and was pleased to announce that he had received "the most friendly offers of foreign assistance." (The speech is printed in Commager and Morris, *Spirit of '76*, 1: 253–54.)

3. It was two weeks before he spoke as forcefully to anyone outside the family. In his letter to Samuel Ward, Sr., of 4 Jan. 1776, he repeated the "necessity, propriety, and rectitude of such a measure." A scholar of the period, Allen French, has said of NG's use of "Declaration of Independence": "This is perhaps the first use of a term now so common and so famous" (French, *First Year*, p. 594).

4. Less than two weeks later, the Canadian invasion ended in disaster, with Montgomery dead, Arnold wounded, and two-thirds of their troops killed, wounded, or captured. Among the captured were NG's kinsman Col. Christopher Greene and his young friend Samuel Ward, Jr.

## To Christopher Greene [?][1]

[Prospect Hill, Mass., ca. 20 Dec. 1775]

My Dear sir God knows whether Ever I shall see you again; if any thing happens to me, let my family share an Equal regard, with a double propotion of Attention. The War begins to grow very Serious. The Tyrant's last Speech closses all hopes of an Accomodation. There is no Alternative but Freedom or Slavery, the latter is too horrible to think on, the former too dessireable to lose. Great Preparations are makeing in Great Britain and also in America. The Plains of America will be staind with Human Blood the next Campaign. The Moments are swiftly Roleing on that is to open this Tragic Scene. The King is as Obstinate as the Devil and as Cruel as a Turk. His boundless Ambition has plunged too [two] happy Countries into an endless train of Misery.[2] We must console our Selves with the hopes of better Days, when the Clouds of sorrow shall be dispersed, and Peace and plenty return and comfort this Afflicted Land.

I suppose the Generallity of People with you are trembleing at the thoughts of another Campaign. Never distrust Divine Providence. He will protect his Children. Small afflictions often preserve us from greater Evils.

Mrs Greene writes me that Father Littlefield has a mind to move off Block Island and that he has some mind to hire or purchase the Stafford Farm as there is not much Wood on it and as business is very dull. Interest money going on I think it would be well worth while to Sell it, providing he will give anything near the Value. I did not write for Mrs Greene to Camp before she got well. The Bed I want providing it can be spard. Whether she comes or not, I want it to Lodge a friend in when they pay me a Visit. I would have Mrs. Greene consult her own [remainder missing]

ALS (MWA). One or more pages missing at beginning and end.
  1. Christopher is the most likely recipient since the collection at MWA came down through his descendants. Of the five brothers, Christopher and Jacob have been the most concerned with Catharine Greene's welfare.
  2. See NG to Jacob, same date, above.

## General Greene's Orders

[Prospect Hill, Mass., 21 Dec. 1775. Watch-coat receipts to be noted by captains of each guard and the number to be reported. Sentries to be relieved every two hours and frequently examined by the patrol for proper execution of duty. All unusual movements of the enemy by land or water to be reported to the general at once by the captain of the guard. (Detailed instructions given for the placement of sentries both day and night.) When weather is very cold or stormy the sentries are to be relieved every hour. Captain Warner[1] to oversee the armorers' and blacksmiths' shops in the brigade. Hitchcock Orderly Book no. 3 (RHi) 2 pp.]

  1. Nathaniel Warner of Col. Little's regiment (Heitman, *Register*).

## General Greene's Orders

[Prospect Hill, Mass., 24 Dec. 1775. A detail to go to Cambridge lumberyard to lay out material for the brigade. Another to provide storage space for material necessary to complete the barracks. Quartermasters to collect all tools without handles and deliver them to the brigade major. Hitchcock Orderly Book no. 3 (RHi) 1 p.]

## General Greene's Orders

[Prospect Hill, Mass., 25 Dec. 1775.[1] Lists of carpenters and masons working on the hill to be made out, none to be allowed wages as artificers but those on the lists.[2] Such groups to report at 7:00 A.M. each day for roll call and to march to their employment. They are to work until an hour after sun down, with an hour off for breakfast and one for dinner. Those neglecting to observe these regulations to be removed from lists and put in guardhouse. The brigade major to appoint drummers for the regiments to insure parties are alerted for work calls. Hitchcock Orderly Book no. 3 (RHi) 2 pp.]

1. Christmas was not celebrated in New England as it was in the southern colonies. New Englanders worked as usual, unless the day fell on Sunday.
2. The artificers, though privates, received additional pay for their skills. On 2 Dec., Congress had passed a resolution approving the "terms on which the artificers of different sorts have been employed in the Army; and [agreed] that the General go on upon the present Agreement, as being the best that can probably be made" (*JCC*, 3: 400), but there is no document in Washington's printed papers concerning the arrangement.

## To Samuel Ward, Sr.

Dear Sir          Camp on Prospect Hill [Mass.] December 31, 1775

Yours of the 9th came to hand before that of the 7th, the former was a little unintelligible untill I receivd the latter.[1] You intreat the General officers to recommend to the Congress the giveing a bounty. I wish we dare do it. But his Excellency General Washington has often assurd us that the Congress would not give a Bounty, and before they would give a bounty they would give up the dispute. The Cement between the Southern and Northern Colonies is not very strong if Forty thousand Lawful will induce the Congress to give us up. Altho I dont immagin that the necessity of allowing a bounty would have broken the Union yet it was a sufficient Intimation that the bare mention was disagreeable.[2] Can you think we should hesitate a moment to recommend a Bounty if we thought ourselves ⟨at liberty. We should then⟩ have an opportunity of picking the best men, filling the army soon, keeping up a proper decipline and preserveing good order and Government in the Camp, while we are now Obligd to relax the very Sinews of Military Government and give a latitude of indulgence to the Soldiery incompatible wi[th] the security of the Camp or Country. What Reason have you to think A proposition of that sort if it came Recommended by the General Officers would be acceded too by the Congress? Most of the Generals belong to the Northern Governments; if the Congress refuse to hear their Delegates I apprehend they would the Generals also. The Congress cannot suppose that the Generals are better acquainted with the temper and Genius of this People than the Delegates are from these Colonies, and why they should refuse to hear you and not us I cannot immagin. A good politician will ever have an Eye to Oeconemy, but to form an extensive plan and not provide the means for its execution betrays a defect in Council or a want of Resolution to procecute. There is nothing that will encourage our Enimies both External and Internal like the difficulties we meet in raising a new Army; if we had given a good bounty and raisd the Troops speedy it would have struck the Ministry with Asstonishment to see that four Colonies could raise such a prodigious large Army in so short a time. They could not expect to conquer a people so United, firm and resolutely determind to defend their Rights and Privileges, but from the difficulties we meet, the confusion and disorder we are in, the large number of Soldiery that are going home, Our Enimies will draw a conclusion we are like a Rope of Sand and that we shall soon break to pieces. God grant it may not be the case.

You misunderstood me Dear sir or I wrote what I did not mean; it was not the lower Class of People that I meant to complain of but the merchants and wealthy Planters who I think does not exert themselves as they ought. This is no time for geting Riches but to secure what we have got. Every shadow of Oppression and Extortion ought to disappear, but instead of that we find many Articles of Merchandise multiplied four fold their original Value, and most Cent per Cent [i.e., doubled]. The Farmers are Extortionate where ever their situation furnishs them with an Opportunity. These are the People that I complain mostly of; they are wounding the cause. When People are in distress its natural for them to try everything and everywhere to get relief, and to find oppression instead of relief from these two orders of men, will go near to driving the poorer sort to desperation. It will be good policy in the United Colonies to render the poorer Sort of People as easy and happy under their present circumstances as possible, for they are Creatures of a Day, and present gain and gratification, tho small, has more Weight with them than much greater advantagies at a distance. A good Politician must and will consider the temper of the times and the prejudices of the People he has to deal with when he takes his measures to execute any great design. The current Sentiment in the New England Colonies greatly favors the Opposition but if the distresses of the People are multiplied their Oppinions may change. Theyl naturally look back upon their former happy Situation and contrast that with their present wretched condition, and conclude that the source of all their Misery Originates in the dispute with Great Britain.

If all the Maritime Towns throughout the United Colonies had a body of Troops in Continental pay it would in a great measure remedy this Evil. Provision must be made for those that are thrown out of employ by the decay of Trade; if they are not engag'd for us necessity will drive them to engage against us, for they cannot live upon the air. What signifies our being freight[en]ed at the Expence; if we succeed we gain all, but if we are conquerd we loos all; not only our present possessions but all our future Labours will be Appropriated to the Support of a Haughty, Proud, Insolent, set of Puppies whose greatest merit with the Crown will be to render the People as compleatly misserable as possible.

I agree with you that the Congress should embody Seventy

thousand men. All the Troops raisd in the different Colonies to be under Continental pay and where there are any stationd for the Security of any particular Province to be considerd as a detachment from the Grand Army and all in every Province to be subject to the commander in chief and at his disposal and direction. A body of Troops in each Colony would support the spirited, confirm the weak and wavering, and awe our Opposers into submission, for there are no Arguments, however well supported by Reason, that carries such conviction with them as those that are enforced from the Muzzle of a Gun or the Point of a Bayonet.

If the Southern and Northern Troops were exchang'd it would be serviceable to the cause; it would in a great measure cure the itch for going home on Furlough and save the Continent a needless expence of paying a large body of Troops that are Absent from Camp.

You complain and say the New England Colonies are treated ill; why are they treated so. You think there ought to have been a bounty given. The Congress always had it in their power to give a bounty if they pleasd. Why were not the New England Delegates sent to establish the plan, for the constitution of the New Army, why were strangers sent at so critical a period.[3] History dont afford so dangerous a Manaeuvre as that of disbanding an old Army and forming a new one within pine [point] Blank shot of the Enimy the whole time. This task was rendered very diffcult by the reduction of Eleven Regiments and the discharge of such a number of Officers who has done everything to Obstruct and retard the filling the new Army in hopes to ruin the Establishment and bring themselves into place again.

From whence Or[i]genates that groundless Jealosy of the New England Colonies. I believe there is nothing more remote from their thoughts; for my own part I abhor the thought and cannot help thinking it highly injurious to the New England People who ever have been distinguisht for their Justice and Moderation. I mentiond this subject to Mr Lynch and Col Harrison who assurd me there was no such Sentiment prevaild in Congress nor amongst the Southern Inhabitants that was of any consequence.[4] I am sorry to find they were mistaken. It grieves me to find such Jealousies [i.e., suspicions] prevail. If they are nourisht they will sooner or later sap the foundation of the Union and dissolve the Connexson. God in mercy avert so dreadful an Evil. How unhappy for the Interest of America that such Colonial prejudices prevail and personal Motives influences her councils. The Interest of one Colony is no way incompattible with that of another. We have all one common Interest and one common wish; to be free from parliamentary Jurisdiction and Taxation. The different Climates and produce of the Colonies will ever preserve a harmony amongst them by a circuitous Trade and commerce. Each Colony will have the benefit of its own staples whether they are Independent or connected with Great Britain.

Govenor Franklin and the Assembly goes on with a high hand.[5] His impudence and the Congress silence astonishes all this part of the World, to suffer such presumption to go unpunnisht betrays a want of spirit to resent or a power to punnish. The dignity of the Congress ought to be held sacred, or else the Authority will soon be brought into contempt. His conduct is calculated to breed a mutiny in the state, such buding mischiefs cannot be to[o] early Nipt. Diseases that might have been easily remedied if seasonably attended too, has often been renderd incurable by being too long neglected. I wish this may not be the case.

This is the last day of the old enlisted Soldiers service; nothing but confusion and disorder Reigns. We are obligd to retain their Guns whether private or publick property. They are prized [priced] and the Owners paid, but as Guns last Spring run very high, the Committee that values them sets them much lower than the price they were purchast At. This is lookt upon to be both Tyrannical and unjust. I am very sorry that necessity forces his Excellency to adopt any Measures disagreeable to the Populace. But the Army cannot be provided for any other way and those we retain are very indifferent, generally without Bayonets and of different Sizd Bores. Twenty Thousand Troops with such Arms as we are provided with are not equal in an Engagement to fifteen thousand with as good Arms as the Kings Troops. I wish our Troops were better furnisht. The Enimy has a great Advantage over us.

We have sufferd prodigiously for want of Wood. Many Regiments has been Obligd to Eat their Provision Raw for want of firing to Cook, and notwithstanding we have burnt up all the fences and cut down all the Trees for a mile round the Camp, our suffering has been inconceiveable.[6] The Barracks has been greatly delayd for want of Stuff. Many of the Troops are yet in their Tents and will be for some time especially the Officers. The fatigues of the Campaign, the suffering for want of Wood and Cloathing, has made abundance of the Soldiers heartily sick of service. The Conecticut Troops went off in spite of all that could be done to prevent it; but they met with such an unfavorable Reception at Home that many are returning to Camp again already. The People upon the Roads exprest so much abhorrence at their conduct for quiting the Army that it was with difficulty they got Provisions. I wish all the Troops now going Home may meet with the same contempt. I expect the Army notwithstanding all the Obstacles we meet will be full in about Six Weeks. Some Ships came in Yesterday and it is said brought Troops in but what grounds there is for the report am not Able to say.

We never have been so weak as we shall be tomorrow when we dismiss the old Troops; we growing weaker and the Enimy geting stronger renders our situation disagreeable. However if they Attack any of our Posts I hope theyl meet with a severe repulse. They can scarcly make a movement on this side Cambridge Bay but that we on this Hill shall have a slap at them.

General Lee has Just returnd from Rhode Island. He has taken the Tories in hand and swore them by a very Solemn Oath that they would not for the future grant Any supplies to the Enimy directly nor indirectly, nor give them any kind of Intelligence nor suffer it to be done by others without giveing Information.[7] [Col.] Joseph Wanton and Doctor Hunter were the Principals. He gives a very good Account of the Spirit and Resolution of the People, but thinks the Colony at too great an Expence for its present defence. The Minute men are a very heavy charge. General Lee got intimately acquainted with your brother and is prodigiously pleasd with him.[8] I beg leave to congratulate you on the recovery of your health which may God in his Providence long preserve that you may enjoy happiness your self and continue a blessing to your Country. Make my Compliments agreeable to your Colleagues, Col Harrison, Mr Lynch and Doctor Franklin. and believe me to be your most Obedient Humble Servant

NATH GREENE

N B I hope youl pardon me for trespassing upon your Time and patience by such a lengthy Letter; ile engage for the future to be more modest.

ALS (MiU-C). Portion in angle brackets from G. W. Greene transcripts (CSmH).

1. Neither letter has been found.

2. Washington had told the civil authorities in New England that Congress had declared against a bounty, thinking that the soldiers' pay even without a bounty was "greater than ever Soldiers had" (Washington to Gov. Cooke, Fitzpatrick, GW, 4: 145–47). This sentiment was especially strong among southern delegates because the pay was considerably higher than that of southern militiamen, and the sentiment was reinforced by southern resentment of the fact that New Englanders were getting most of the Continental army funds. This is developed in Hatch, Administration, pp. 71–73. The attitude toward soldiers' pay is discussed at some length by John Adams in a letter to Joseph Hawley, 25 Nov. 1775 (Adams, Works, 9: 366–68). The reluctance to vote bounties, however, was not confined to the South. Many northern delegates hesitated to urge establishing bounties for long-term enlistments because such enlistments smacked too much of a standing army. Washington had been won over only slowly to the need for bounties. By Feb. 1776 he was strongly urging Congress to authorize bounties of "20, 30 or more Dollars" because it would save money and provide better troops. (Washington to the President of Congress, 9 Feb. 1776, Fitzpatrick, GW, 4: 317)

3. The delegates sent to Cambridge by Congress are discussed above, NG to Ward, 16 Oct. 1775, note 5.

4. Thomas Lynch of South Carolina and Benjamin Harrison of Virginia were two of the delegates referred to above in note 3. Their assurance that there existed no such

jealousy—i.e., suspicion—of New England may have been an understatement for the purpose of smoothing ruffled feathers, but it was probably closer to the truth than the exaggerated differences apparently noted in Ward's lost letters to Greene or in several of John Adams's letters.

5. William Franklin (1731–1813), son of Benjamin Franklin, was the last royal governor of New Jersey. As a loyalist he broke with his father and in 1776 was imprisoned for aiding the enemy. (*DAB*)

6. In a letter to the Massachusetts Provincial Congress, 2 Nov. 1775, Washington said the army had only a four-hour supply of wood and it needed at least ten thousand cords to see it through the winter. Although he and his general officers had threatened dire punishment upon those who stole firewood, the need had become so critical that Washington now admitted it was out of his power to prevent such theft. He warned the legislature that "from Fences to Forrest Trees, and from Forrest Trees to fruit Trees, is a Natural advance to houses, which must next follow." (Fitzpatrick, *GW*, 4: 60–61)

7. NG's summary phrase "without giveing information" was worded in the original oath as "I pledge myself, if I should, by any accident, get the knowledge of such treason, to inform immediately the Committee of Safety." The oath is printed in full in Arnold, *R.I.*, 2: 365–66.

8. Henry Ward, secretary of the colony of Rhode Island.

## To George Washington

[From Prospect Hill, Mass., December 1775. Encloses a letter from Col. James Varnum to GW dealing with recommendations for promotion in Varnum's regiment, including that of Christopher Greene, NG's kinsman, from major to lieutenant colonel. (Maj. Greene was with Gen. Benedict Arnold nearing Quebec; Varnum, of course, could not know that he would soon be a prisoner of the British and would remain so for a year.) In his covering letter, NG agrees with Varnum's recommendation and hopes GW will approve. Cy (Washington Papers: DLC) 1 p.]

## General Greene's Orders

[Prospect Hill, Mass., 1 Jan. 1776. The Sixth, Ninth, Eleventh, Twelfth, and Twenty-fifth regiments to report exact number enlisted for a month and those for a year. Barracks in the long lines to be divided between regiments of Varnum and Hitchcock. Mitchell Orderly Book (NHi) 1 p.]

## General Greene's Orders

[Prospect Hill, Mass., 3 Jan. 1776. The colonels to furnish troops with arms and accouterments as soon as possible. The small number of troops makes any negligence very dangerous.[1] Mitchell Orderly Book (NHi) 1 p.]

1. Two days earlier NG could have mustered no more than seven hundred men on Prospect Hill, "notwithstanding the returns of the new Enlisted Troops amounted to

Nineteen hundred and upwards" (see below, NG to Ward, 4 Jan. 1776). Many of the troops had no weapons.

## To Samuel Ward, Sr.

Dear sir          Camp on Prospect Hill [Mass.] Jany 4th 1775 [1776]
     Your kind favor of the 23 Ult is now before me,[1] In which I am extremely happy to find your Vieus so affectionately extended to the combined Interest of the United Colonies. Your apprehensions that George the Third is determind at all Hazards to carry his plan of Despotism into Execution is fully confirmd by his late Gracious Speech to both Houses of Parliament which I have seen.[2] In that you will find he breaths revenge and threatens us with destruction. Indeed it is no more than common sense must have foreseen long since had we not been blinded by a too fond attachment to the Parent State. We have consulted our wishes rather than our Reason in the indulgence of a Idea of accomodation. Heaven hath decreed that Tottering Empire Britain to irretrievable ruin and thanks to God since Providence hath so determind America must raise an Empire of Permanent Duration, supported upon the Grand Pillars of Truth, Freedom and Religion, encouraged by the smiles of Justice and defended by her own Patriotick Sons.
     No Doubt but a large Army must be raised in Addition to the Forces upon the present Establishment. You are acquainted with my Sentiments upon that head Already. How they must be divided and where stationed is a matter at present problematical. However one thing is certain. The Grand Body must be superior in Number to any Force the Enimy can send, as they will without a scruple make one Grand Effort to defeat the main Force, thereby expecting the other Bodies like Streams from a Fountain will be lost. Then they may detach to the Various parts you mention, whether they succeed or not in the first Attempt. From hence it follows that all the forces in America should be under one Commander raised and appointed by the same Authority, subjected to the same Regulations and ready to be detacht where ever Occasion may require. In this Idea is also comprehended the Necessity of a Regiment of Light Horse well acquiped. Your observation with regard to the Canadians hath often struck me that their Attachment to the one party or the Other will greatly depend upon the Superiority of Force. To prevent which in some measure and fix them to the common Interest, let us raise one or more Regiments of Canadians to serve in New England. Send enough Troops there to compensate them in Addition to the number you have proposed.
     With Regard to the scanty measure dealt out to the Army upon

the New Establishment, we are not altogether different in Sentiment. Yet I am convinceed the Regiments will fill to their Compleat Establishment. I believe they are more upon an Average than half full. Undoubtedly the detaining of Arms being private property is Repugnent to many Principles of Civil and Natural Law, and hath disgusted many; But the Great Laws of Necessity must Justify the Expedient Till we can be otherwise furnished.[3] The Pay of the Soldiery is certainly Generous and the Officers likewise, all except the Field Officers whose pay is much below that of any other, considering their Rank and Experience, which forms an Oppinion derogatory to their Merit.

My Dear Sir I am now to open my Mind a little more freely. It hath been said Canada in the last War was Conquerd in Germany. Who knows but that Britain may be in the present Controversy. I take it for Granted that France and Spain have made Overtures to the Congress of assistance, in Case of necessity. Let us embrace them as Brothers. We want not their Land Forces in America; their Navy we do, their Commerce will be equally Beneficial to them and us; they will doubtless defray the expence of their Fleet as they will be employed in the protection of their own Trade. Their Military Stores we want amazingly. Those will be Articles of Commerce. The Elector of Hannover hath orderd his Germain Troops to relieve the Garrisons of Gibrhaltor and Port Mahon. France will in Consequence attack and subdue Hannover with little trouble. This may bring on a very Serious War in Germany and turn Great Britains Attention that way, which may prevent Immence Expence and Innumerable Calamities which would otherwise happen in America. Permit me then to Recommend from the Sincerity of my Heart, ready at all times to bleed in my Countrys Cause, a Declaration of Independance and call upon the World and the Great God who Governs it to Witness the Necessity, propriety and Rectitude thereof; Open a free but not an exclusive Trade with France and Spain.[4]

New York affords an Instance unfriendly to the Rights of Mankind. The Forces there are numerous and very Potent; should the Enimy get Footing there the Difficulty of dislodging them would be unconceiveable. Witness Boston. That they intend it, is evident from the Situation of the place and Govenor Tryons continueing on board the Dutches of Gordon. Immediate attention therefore should be paid to the Fortification and defence of that City. New York is a post of so Vast Importance to the Enimy as it communicates in a manner with the River St Lawrence that the keeping it from them should be esteemed as almost inseperably connected with the General success of our Arms. Lord Dunmore affords another Instance of what mischief their geting any foothold may prove to the Grand Cause. If the Provincial Congress of that Province opposes the fortifying the place, you may be Assurd they intend to deliver it up to the Enimy as soon as they get Strong enough to take possession there. These is but one of two measures to be adopted. Burn or Garrison the City. The Whig Interest is upon the decline; if the Tide of Sentiment gets against us in that Province it will give a fatal Stab to the strength and Union of the Colonies.[5]

My worthy Friend the Interest of Mankind hangs upon that truly Worthy Body of which your are a Member. You stand the Representative not of America only but of the Whole World, the Friends of Liberty and the supporters of the Rights of Human Nature. How will Posterity, Millions yet unborn, bless the memory of those brave Patriots who are now hastening the consumation of Freedom, Truth and Religion. But want of Decision renders Wisdom in Council insignificant as want of Powder hath prevented us here from destroying the mercenary Troops now in Boston.

Frugallity, a most amiable Domestick Virtue, becomes a Vice of the most Enormous kind when opposd to the common Good. The Tyrant by his last speech hath convinced us that to be free or not depends upon ourselves; nothing therefore but the most Vigirious Exertions on our part can Shelter us from the Evils intended us. How can we then startle at the Idea of Expence when our whole Property, our dearest Connexion, our Liberty, nay Life itself is at Stake? Let us therefore Act like Men, Inspird with a Resolution that nothing but the Frowns of Heaven shall Conquer us. It is no time for Deliberation, the hour is swiftly rolling on when the Plains of America will be deluged with Human Blood; Resolves, Declarations and all the Parade of Heroism in Words will never obtain a Victory. Arms and Ammunition are as necessary as Men and must be had at the Expence of everything short of Britains Claims. An Army unequiped will ever feel the want of Spirit and Courage but properly furnished fighting in the best of Causes will bid defiance to the United force of Men and Devils. When a finishing Period will be put to the present dispute God only knows. We have just experienced the Inconveniency of disbanding an Army within Cannon Shot of the Enimy and forming a new one in its stead, an Instance never before known; had the Enimy been fully acquainted with our situation I cannot pretend to say what might have been the consequences. A large Body of Troops Probably will be wanted for a considerable Time. It will be infinitely safer and not more expensive in the End for the Continent to give a large Bounty to any Number of Troops that may be orderd in addition to the present Establishment that will Engage during the War, than to Enlist them from year to year without a Bounty, and should the present Regiments incline to engage for the same Term, Let them receive the same Encouragement.[6] There is not the least prospect of our ever being able to disband and form a new Army again without the Enimies Availing themselves of the Advantage.

I have taken the Liberty to shew your last Letter to General Lee whose knowledge of Europe and America, Genius and Learning enables him to give you the Advice you want. He has wrote you fully upon the subject. It is mere Arrogance in me to say anything upon the matter after he took up the Pen, but I hope the goodness of my intentions may excuse my Presumption. I this Day man'd the Lines upon this Hill and feel a degree of pleasure that I have not felt for several Days; our situation has been critical. We have no part of the Militia here on this Hill and the Night after the old Troops went of[f] I could not have mustered seven hundred Men, notwthstanding the returns of the new Enlisted Troops amounted to Nineteen hundred and upwards. I am now strong enough to defend myself against all the Force in Boston. A deserter came out this afternoon but brings nothing new. Recruiting in Conecticut goes on exceeding well and in this Province too. I hope ours will do better by and by. God bless you and preserve [you]. Adieu

NATHANAEL GREENE

ALS (MiU-C).

1. Letter not found.

2. See note 2, NG to Jacob Greene, 20 Dec. 1775, above. Ward's response to NG's letter is lost, but upon reading the speech, he wrote his daughter that George III was a savage who had always meant to "make himself an absolute despot i. e. Tyrant" and that "every Idea of Peace" was now over. (Ward to an unnamed daughter, 8 Jan. 1776, RHi)

3. The scarcity of arms had led Washington in a general order of 20 Nov. to demand that the departing troops should sell the army any guns that were fit for service (Fitzpatrick, *GW*, 4: 102–3). In reviewing the Connecticut troops on 7 Dec. for the purpose of selecting the best guns, he warned Sullivan not to divulge his reasons for fear that "some of the best Arms will be Secreted" (ibid., 4: 152–53). His fears were well justified; despite every precaution, he later told the Massachusetts legislature that the regiments had "by stealth borne them away" (ibid., 4: 235–36). Only the patriotic or those who were lacking in stealth were thus forced to sell their arms; and it is small wonder that they were resentful, especially since they were paid in depreciating currency or even in promissory notes.

4. Since NG's 23 Oct. 1775 letter to Ward proposing a declaration of independence, the idea was slow to win acceptance, even among congressional radicals. It was to receive a tremendous boost a few days later with the publication of Thomas Paine's *Common Sense*. NG's emphasis here on the need to justify to the world the "Necessity, propriety and Rectitude" of independence is an early expression of a sentiment that was eventually to be embodied in the preamble of the declaration of 4 July.

5. NG's views on New York City reflected to a large extent the thinking of Washington and Gen. Charles Lee. In a letter to Washington on 5 Jan., Lee offered to collect a body of Connecticut volunteers for the purpose of fortifying New York and dealing with the Long Island loyalists ("these Serpents"), a suggestion that Washington was quick to adopt. For Washington's views on New York's strategic value and his recommendations for safeguarding it, see his letters of 7 and 8 Jan. to Gov. Trumbull, John Adams, the Committee of Safety of New York, and his instructions to Lee (Fitzpatrick, *GW*, 4: 217–23; Lee's letter is quoted in a note on p. 221). The burning of New York as an alternative to fortification may have been NG's own idea. It was one

he later urged on Washington just before the capture of the city by the British (see below, NG to Washington, 5 Sept. 1776).

    6. Bounties are discussed in note 2, NG to Ward, 31 Dec. 1775, above.

## General Greene's Orders

[Prospect Hill, Mass., 6 Jan. 1776. Working party to gather up boards in camp; another party of twenty-three men "Accustomed to Cut Wood" to go to Woburn where quarters will be provided.[1] Clerk of the market to furnish each of the following with half a cord of wood weekly: barracks room of twenty men; a captain and his subaltern; a major; a lieutenant colonel. And "five feet to the Col," (i.e., ⅝ of a cord).[2] Entrenching tools about camp to be collected, and henceforth the clerk to take receipt for all those issued. In the future wood is to be carted from the wood yard to selected places on Prospect Hill. Mitchell Orderly Book (NHi) 2 pp.]

    1. As the winter progressed and the hills near Prospect Hill were denuded, wood-cutting parties had to go farther and farther afield. Woburn was almost ten miles from the camp.

    2. New England militia officers may have traditionally shared the cold with their men on principle, but the practice was obviously not extended to the Continental army. It could be argued that twenty men supplied some body heat to raise the temperature of their barnlike room, but an officer in quarters one-third the size must have been considerably more comfortable. Colonels' comfort level must have been even higher, especially since they tended to be somewhat heavier than captains and majors.

## General Greene's Orders

[Prospect Hill, Mass.] 10 January 1776
This Post being Considerably strengthned By the Number of Recruits that have Come in Since the Order was Issued to stop the Granting of Furloughs. That Order is Counter Orderd And the Colonels are at Liberty to Grant Furloughs Again, but as the Lines are but thinly Mannd Still the Genl desires the Colonels to Grant as few as possible, and None only but where there appears a Pressing Necessity.

    The General is informd Gaming with Cards prevails in this Brigade. That practice is strictly forbid by the Continental Congress.[1] And as it brings on a Habit of Drinking; and the Habit of Drinking [in turn], Disputes and Quarrels, disorder and Confusion which disturbs the Peace and Tranquility of the Camp, and often proves fatal to Individuals, the General desires the Officers of all Ranks to exert themselves to suppress such a growing Evil, and as there is Great Danger of having the Barracks sett on fire in one of those disorderly Hours, the Officers of each Company are requested to visit their Troops in Quarters every evening att Tatoo beating and see that they retird to bed and the fires are secured.

The Tatoo to beat att Eight O Clock, it is to be performd by the drum Major and all the Drummers and Fifers of that Regt that gives a Capt to the Main Guard that Day. The Troop in the morning at Nine O Clock and the Retreat att Sundown is to be performd in the same Manner.

They are to begin at the Main Guard, beat thro the lines to the Genls Quarters, and return back and finish where they began. They are to be escorted by a Serjeant and a File of Men from the Main Guard.

They are to be answered by four Drummers and Fifers of each Regt in their Respective Quarters. The Tattoo is the signal given to the Soldiers to retire to their Barracks or Quarters, to put out their fires and candles and go to bed. All Sutlers are att the same time to shutt their doors and sell no mor Liquor that night upon penalty of severe punishment.

General Lee having prevaild on Brigade Major Box to continue longer in the service, he is to be obey'd accordingly.[2]

A Subaltern Officer and twenty Privates to parade to Morrow Morning at 8 0 Clock to cutt Wood. They are to march to Winter Hill and receive Instructions from Capt Francis.

The Guard to parade to morrow at Ten O Clock, the Adjutants are requested to be very punctual in bringing their men on the parade exactly att the time appointed.

Colo Littles and Colo Thomsons Adjutants are requested to be more punctual for the future in bringing on their men on the parade as any future neglect will not be overlook'd.

Each Regt to turn out a party to strike all their tents and Marquees that are evaquated.

Mitchell Orderly Book (NHi).
1. NG had no moral objection to cardplaying, as is seen in his earlier defiance of the Quaker prohibition against it (see his letter below of 29 Jan. to Christopher). A congressional resolution on cardplaying has not been found, but there may have been a committee report on it. Although NG's orders do not mention gambling, that aspect of cardplaying was part of the objection that Washington and his general officers had to the pastime. Although not the only way that a man could lose his meager pay through gambling, it was the most popular.
2. On what grounds NG's old friend Daniel Box had threatened to quit is not known. He did continue with NG for the remainder of the year, although no longer directly under him after NG was made major general.

## To Catharine Ward Greene[1]

Madam               Prospect Hill [Mass.] January 13th 1776

Yours of the first of this instant came safe to hand. I thank you for the information you give me rellative to the welfare of my family and freinds. I am sorry you have so poor oppinion of my Family regard as to think the pleasure I should Receive not be equal to those which I should give in the Exchange of Camp for family occurrences. When your Dearest Connexion are remote from us you are anxious to know every little Incident that happens to them from Day to Day. Things triffleing in their own Nature become important when connected with certain Objects. If you was to write to some Persons here giving them History of the family at Potowomut and at Coventry perhaps it might not offord them pleasure or amusement. But when you write to me who is so nearly connected and so deeply interested in the Subject of your Letter, the contents becomes Valuable. Doubtless you have felt the Anxiety for absent Friends, and the happiness of hearing from them. If you have felt the pains of the one and the pleasures of the other You can form some Judgement how Valueable such information is. There is but few things transacted here, but that is announceed to you in the Papers before it wold reach you in a Letter. Therefore I think the Ballance of Trade is in your favor instead of mine, Unless you Value the Letters more for the Writers sake than the contents. If that is the case perhaps our commerce may be equal, for I confess I have often felt a pleasure in hearing an account of a matter by Letter that I had heard it confirm'd by common Report before; this happiness I apprehend could not arise from the subject but the Object. But not to be tedious upon the subject, I think enough has been said to convince you that our Correspondence may be equal and will be acceptable to me. But if you meant, by pointing out the inequallity of our Correspondance as a polite refusal, Good manners will oblige me to cease urgeing you any farther upon the subject.

I am very glad to hear you are so happy. I wish it may continue to the End of your Days. I never thought you had much Reason to be otherwise. But we are but ill Judges of one anothers pleasures or pains. The source of Misery often springs where others thinks nothing but happiness flows. Truth honnor and Religion are the only foundation to build human happiness upon. They never fail to yield a mind solid satisfaction, for concious Virtue gives pleasure to the Soul. Clouds of sorrow often overshadow us, but they are soon dispersed, if we dont mistake the means to effect it. But our Pride and Vanity often leads us astray untill we get so entangled as it becomes equally dishonnorable to retreat as to go forward. This is a most shocking situation but often happens in real Life. I know of no way to avoid such Evils but by carefully examining things and not taking them upon trust. Many fashionable Vicees we indulge ourselves in not because they afford any pleasure but because they are marks of dignity and greatness. If mankind was to follow Nature more and fashion less in the choice of their Pleasures there would be fewer sighs and more chearful Countenances than Appears upon the Stage at this Day.

It is generally agreed that George the Tyrants last Graceless Speech made to that Stupid Ignorant wicked, Pensiond, Perjur'd Parliament [shuts?] the Door of hope for a Reconciliation between us and great Britain. The Calamities of a War are shocking, but the consequences of Slavery are dreadful. May God in Mercy preserve us from so great an Evil.

By a Vessel just arrivd from England at Portsmouth New Hampshire we have the English Prints to the 4th of November. Great preparations are going on. But the Duke of Graften, the Earl of Rutland and General Conway are turnd about. They are, of the leading Men in England and are allowed to be fully Acquainted with all the secrets of the Cabinet. This change of sentiment or sides in three [not] inconsiderable Personages is a matter of great speculation. It is our business to be prepard for the worst; if any thing agreeable turns up it will not be the less acceptable.

The most considerable Correspondent that I have is your Daddy. Whole Sheets, nay sometimes three or four are sent in one Letter. Doubtless you hear from him as to his Health. I hear he is paying his addresses to a very Rich Widow worth Ten thousand Pounds Sterling. How does it relish with you? Mother in Law[2] has an ill sound, but a fathers happiness doubtless will quallify the Evil. Letters from Quebeck says Colo Arnolds party are all well, in high Spirits and Join'd by General Montgomery, Richly furnisht with Powder, a Battery ready to open upon Quebeck, which they expect soon to be masters of. It will give you unspeakable delight to see your Brother return in February with Honnor.[3] Charels is appointed an Ensign in the new Establishment.[4] The Army fills up slow. The Enemy continues quiet in Boston. They are greatly distressed, reduced to the necessity of Eating Cats and Dogs. We burnt some of of the Houses near the Enemies Lines a few Nights past. They were prodigiously freighted by their manner of fireing. A large Artillery is expected in a few Days. One thing more and then, Who raw for America.[5] My Complements to all friends. God bless you all with Health and happiness is the prayer of yours

N GREENE

ALS (MWA).
1. Several references identify her as brother Christopher's wife. In a letter of 5 Feb. to her father, Samuel Ward, she speaks of a letter from "my Brother nat," (Ward Papers, RHi). Her letter to NG of "first of this instant" not found.
2. He meant stepmother. Samuel Ward did not remarry; he died of smallpox while attending Congress two months later.
3. He had not learned of the 31 Dec. disaster at Quebec. Her brother Sammy was captured and was to remain a prisoner until exchanged in Aug. 1776.
4. He had worked to get a commission for brother Charles, who had enlisted as a

private, possibly to embarrass his father. John Adams, who had also interceded to get the commission, thought it unfair and demeaning for the son of the chairman of the Congressional Committee of the Whole to serve as a private "when Multitudes of others in Commissions have no such Pretentions" (Adams to James Warren, reprinted in Knollenberg, *Ward*, pp. 114–15).

5. "Who raw for America" was one of NG's rare puns. The "large Artillery" mentioned in the previous sentence refers to the guns that Col. Henry Knox was bringing from Ft. Ticonderoga. Word had preceded Knox by some days, for he did not reach Cambridge until 18 Jan., according to Gen. Heath, and it was another week before the guns arrived from Framingham (Heath, *Memoirs*, pp. 46). See below, end of note 2, NG to Jacob, 8 Feb.

## To General Charles Lee

Dear General            Prospect Hill, [Mass.] January 21st 1776

We are all in Mourning for the loss of the Brave General Montgomery, whose unhappy Fate is an irreparable loss to America. We are all in the dark as to the number kil'd, wounded and taken prisoners in that unfortunate attack notwithstanding General Woosters open Letter, a copy of which I suppose you have seen. General Schuyler is going to make an attack upon a Body of Tories in Tryon County and you upon Queens County.[1] God grant you may be both successful. Three Regiments are ordered to be rais'd immediately for the Reinforcement of the Troops at Quebeck: one Regiment in this Province, one in New Hampshire, and one in Connecticut. I hear you are raising 1500 Troops for your Expedition. I hope you'll give that many headed Monster the Tory Faction a fatal wound—it is expected from your strength, spirit and Resolution. The Papers will annouce to you Capt. Wallace's depredations in the Colony of Rhode Island and the severe Repulse he met with from the Troops there.[2] We have had several Deserters out [from Boston] within a few days; they all agree that the scurvy prevails amongst the troops, but disagree very much as to the Mortallity of it. It has been very dull in this division since your departure. I wish you a safe and speedy return. Mr. Eustace lodges at Hobgoblin Hall, he says by your Order.[3] Should be glad to know your pleasure in the matter. He is young and fond of diversion and many ill Councellors about him. Perhaps his conduct may not be so prudent as you could wish. He has been but little at my lodgings, notwithstanding I am dayly calling upon him. I rejoice to hear my friend Bird escaped—so inglorious an Exit as he had like to have made by the Eggs. I hope this will prove an useful Lesson to him, and learn him to implicitly obey the Orders of his General for the future. Please to present my compliments to him and Mr. Palfrey.[4] All things quiet in Camp and no new movements of the Enemy, since your departure. I am with great Respect your most obedient and very humble Servant.

NATH.GREENE.

P. S. Please to favor me with a line from you.

Reprinted from *Lee Papers*, 1: 246–47.

1. For Lee's mission in New York see note 5, NG to Samuel Ward, 4 Jan. 1776, above.

2. The loyalty oath Lee had forced upon the Newport loyalists three weeks earlier (see note 7, NG to Ward, 31 Dec. 1775, above) was short-lived. Although Wallace was repulsed by R.I. militia at Prudence Island on 13 Jan., he maintained control of Narragansett Bay, and the citizens of Newport were soon petitioning again for permission to furnish his ships in return for the safety of their city.

3. Maj. John Eustace had served as Lee's aide (Heitman, *Register*). Hobgoblin Hall was Lee's designation of the elegant Royal Tyler House in Medford, his headquarters during his command in the Boston siege. Washington had objected to the location for Lee "on Acct. of the distance from his line of Command" and had told him that "he should not Sleep there" (Washington to Sullivan, 19 Feb. 1776, Fitzpatrick, *GW*, 4: 340).

4. William Palfrey of Massachusetts and Francis O. Byrd of Virginia had also served as aides to Lee (Heitman, *Register*).

## To Jacob Greene

Prospect Hill [Mass.] January 22d, 1776.

I am glad the certificate had some effect upon the tyranny of East Greenwich.[1] An exertion of arbitrary power not paralleled in history. The policy of that town has ever been narrow and confined, and generally as dishonorable as unjust.[2] Nature has formed it for a place of trade and commerce, but the genius of the people and their measures counteract its natural advantages. I am told the old inhabitants treat those who come in there for shelter with great incivility; and some few that have attempted to open a small trade with the country, have been prohibited in the most peremptory manner, unless they would agree to sell at certain stated prices, which rendered it impossible for them to support their business; and they have been driven off by it to Providence and other places. I wish to God their sentiments were more liberal. They would find great advantages in it. I am glad you did not adopt the advice of those who were for opposing the committee. You observe very justly—The populace borrow almost all their opinions. A few designing men can sometimes set the rabble foul of the best characters, and ruin their reputations for a time. It is unsafe to oppose the current of public prejudices, but one may seem to join with the throng and swim on with the tide of public sentiment for a time, until you can slip out unobserved, without injury to yourself or your country. For, when the first heat and zeal of the populace has had a little time to cool, many things may be done with safety that would have been deemed criminal even to propose but a little before. In human affairs we have only to watch the temper of the times, and the disposition of the people, and take our measures from them. This is all the politician can do. He cannot drive mankind into measures that are even necessary to promote their own interest and happiness.[3]

Excerpt reprinted from Johnson, *Greene*, 1: 51–52.

1. The certificate was undoubtedly one issued by the Assembly authorizing Jacob and William Greene to import four thousand bushels of salt into Kent County via East Greenwich. The salt was to be allocated to each town and sold at six shillings per bushel, thus undercutting the local merchants. In June the colony reimbursed Jacob for the loss of the sloop *Maryland* and its cargo of salt. (Bartlett, *Records*, 7: 441, 553)

2. NG, who was born and raised two miles from East Greenwich, had not always held it in such low esteem. He had been a leading booster of the community as the best location for R.I. College (see petitions above of 16 Nov. 1769 and 7 Feb. 1770, the former of which he wrote). His animus toward the commercial community was a recent one that grew out of both the profiteering by the merchants and their criticism of Jacob.

The price of salt brought down the wrath of many Rhode Islanders upon the merchants. See note 4, NG to Cooke, 29 Nov. 1775, above.

3. His observations on the limitations imposed on politicians by the times and "disposition of the people" exhibit an awareness of the political process not seen in earlier correspondence. He still had far to go, however, to reach the degree with which Washington accepted the legislative process—the patience, the accommodating spirit when necessary, and the ability to hide anger or censorious feelings behind placating words which Washington exhibited.

# General Greene's Orders

[Prospect Hill, Mass., 26 Jan. 1776. Assigns guard and alarm post duty to regiments (except Whitcomb's, which is leaving); warns sergeants and corporals that if they do not instruct sentries in duties, they will be "turned into the Ranks." Hitchcock Orderly Book no. 3 (RHi) 2 pp.]

# General Greene's Orders

[Prospect Hill, Mass., 27 Jan. 1776. A party to cut wood for one week in Woburn. Mitchell Orderly Book (NHi) 1 p.]

# To Elihue Greene[1]

Prospect Hill [Mass.] January 28, 1776

It is sometime since you favord me with a line. In your last you mention your haveing provided A Stack for this Year but knew not how to get another for the next.[2] I had before I left Coventry two trackts of Land in view, one lying joining to ours belonging to one Mr Waterman, Son to Ezra Deans present Lady. It contains about 250 Acres. Mr Sweet can tell you more fully about it. The other piece of Land belongs to Ebenezer Greene. It is very finely Wooded. Daniel Gardner can acquaint you about the price and situation. If you intend to prosecute the Iron Business you must make a new purchase of Wood Land, as little Coal is to be got besides what you make yourselves.

I am told by Griffin that you had taken the Refinery Wooden

Bellows to pieces to clean them and could not make them blow any since. I immagin the posts that holds down the Blocks wants to be settled down a little; if the post dont keep the blocks down close when the Bellows opens the Blocks rise and all the Wind flees out under them. Ichabod Prentice understands cleaning Bellows the best of any body at home now. If the blast is not exceeding good youl loos twenty or thirty per Cent in working the Stack, for the blast is the Life of the business, especially with a poor Workman which I am sure you are now tormented with, for Ged and Leonard are the Lazyest, carelessest fellows I ever had any concerne with. You must watch from Day to Day or else they'l neglect their business. All they care for is to get something for the present support. They think nothing [but?] about pay day. Have a care upon that head for if they can get largely in debt, they will not Work. I can assure you the Iron business is very difficult to carry on to Advantage. You may make Iron the year Round and sink money all the time. If you should Want Hull and Holly to work in the Forge I apprehend I could get them of[f] [from the army] for a trifle and I dont doubt theyl agree to come home. They are much better Workmen than Ged and Leonard. However, if you can make out without them I have no inclination they should leave the service. The others will be good for nothing here. They [are] so devilishly Hide bound with Quakerism that they are good for nothing at home or abroad.[3]

I hear from different quarters that notwithstanding the Gloominess of the times and the miserable prospect we have for family support, that little Cupid is tempting you to put on the Golden shakels. I am told the Young Lady is very hansome and cleaver. God grant you much happiness.[4]

I kindly thank you for your tenderness and care of Mrs Greene; I feel the warmest sense of gratitude for your goodness, and shall not fail to manifest it at some future period if Providence preserves my life to the end of this unhappy dispute. Doctor Joslen [Joslyn] informs me that Mrs Greene is exceeding well for the time considering, as the Old Women says. Should be glad to see Mrs Greene here if it was convenient and her state of health permits.[5] However I hope sheel consult her own pleasure.

I am now unwell with jaundice and have been for a Week past, but am in hopes to be about again in a few Days. Poor old M Letson was with me toDay. He wants you to advance him Seven Dollars, and to engage for another season. You may safely trust him, he haveing always provd himself an honest fellow. You need not fear his enlisting, for I believe you may depend upon it he wont. All things continue quiet here but I hope to have a Racket ere long. Remember me to all friends and believe me to be with Affection your Loving brother

N GREENE

John Gooch sends his Compliments; no, Love, I mean.
Your two Letters of the 12th and 16th[6] came to hand Just as I had
sealed this Letter.

ALS (MWA).
1. This previously unpublished letter to brother Elihue in Coventry is unique in
displaying NG's mastery of the various operations involved in a moderate-sized iron
forge. He is revealed as both a skilled craftsman and an able entrepreneur. No such
letters have survived to reveal comparable talents in the commercial sphere of the
family business.
2. A stack of hardwood, covered with earth to slow its burning, was converted to
charcoal. When he speaks below of losing "twenty or thirty per Cent in working the
Stack," he uses the word "stack" to describe a refining process.
3. For other harsh comments on his former religion, see below, NG to Jacob, 4 June
1777.
4. Elihue was courting Jane (Jenny) Flagg, granddaughter of Jane Mecom, Benjamin
Franklin's sister. She and her grandmother had come to stay with Catharine Ray
Greene in East Greenwich during the siege of Boston. She and Elihue were married at
the end of 1776 (see NG to Elihue, 6 Sept. 1776). Jenny died in 1782 at the age of twenty-
four (Clarke, *Greenes*, p. 211).
5. Catharine was expecting her first child, George Washington Greene, at any time.
As far as is known, neither the day nor place of his birth has ever been recorded. He was
probably born in Rhode Island before Catharine set out for Cambridge on 20 Feb. (see
note, NG to Jacob, 8 Feb., below).
6. Letters not found.

## To Christopher Greene[1]

Dear sir                    Prospect Hill [Mass.] January 29th 1776
     Yours of the 21st of this instant was this moment handed me by
Mr Whitmarsh. I am glad to hear of your health and happiness amidst
these times of general distress. The peaceful and once pleasant shores
where happiness dwelt Crownd with plenty are now become the
savage haunts of cruel Pirates that thirst for human Blood. The Calm
sea and smoth surface that use[d] to delight the Eye and chear the
spirits both morning and Evening is now guarded with Watchful
Attention against a Ravageing Enimy. How great the change. How
mournful the Prospects. You are doubtless greatly distress'd in Rhode
Island but there is no lack for Provisions. Turn your thoughts to the
poor Inhabitants of Boston still in Town, pent up amidst an insulting
and outrageous Soldiery, drove to despair from a long Siege and close
confinement. To behold the miserable wretches that are thrust out
of Boston must melt the Heart of a Nero, and soften him into pity.
Had you such spectacles as are spread for Miles upon the Roads
from Marblehead, Cape pan [Cape Ann], and Salem, you could not
help foregeting your own misseries to commiserate theirs. They have
neither food to Eat nor Raiment to cover them from the Weather. I wish
one decisive stroke could be struck to put a period to the sufferings of
the People, but alass, this is but the begining of sorrow. Chearfully

would I risque my Life for the salvation of my Country. I have bid adieu to the pleasures of domestick Life, a plan for which I was many years preparing, for a few Months enjoyment. No Sir, I shall never forget my family connexion. My Heart is too deeply interested in their happiness. God grant the brotherly regard that ever has been our spring of felicity may not suffer by these temporary seperations; let not our different employments create any difference in our family affection, nor suffer the Pomp and pageantry of the World to swell our Vanity into a Criminal negligence of family obligation. The Slippery Path of Life is difficult to tread with Publick Approbation and self satisfaction. But conscious Virtue is a never failing source of human happiness amidst the frowns of a Jaring [jeering] World.

I receivd a Letter toDay from your Daddy Ward containing Sixteen pages; one happy piece of intelligence in it: that is, that your brother Capt Ward is well tho a Prisoner.[2] The Prisoners are all treated with great humanity and Politeness. Colo [Christopher] Greene and all the party has done themselves immortal honnor. God grant they may in his own good time be all happily restord to their friends and families again. Your Daddy writes me he is in good health but greatly hurryed with business. He is one of the leading Men of the Congress. He belongs to the standing Committee that prepares all the business before the House resolves upon it. I saw Mr Adams a few days past.[3] He gives him a glorious Charactor. Heaven preserve his Life to reap the fruits of his Labour in peace and plenty surrounded with the Acclamations of a greatful people, sensible of the importance of his services.

I am extream sorry that Mr Gooch[4] and Nancy Varnum affronted Mother at my House with Cards. Surely Mrs Greene could not be present.[5] She must have known better. It was insult that I would not have sufferd the best friend I had in the World to have offerd to her. Altho I think Cards in themselves as innocent as any other pieces of Paper yet its criminal to play before her because they knew how Conscious the friends [Quakers] are in these matters. In the choice of all our pleasures regard should be had to time and place, private and publick Prejudices. Since the Resolution of Congress I have never had a Card in my hand to play, nor sufferd one in my House that I remember. I Love and Esteem the old Lady and should be very sorry that this disagreeable circumstance should be constered [construed?] into an intentiononal affront, for I dare presume it proceeded intirely from Ignorance and not out of any disrespect to her. People that have been Accustomed to these things all their Days dont feel upon the Occasion like you and me who have stole the pleasures in secret Corners.

What your Aunt Greene can mean by her conduct I cannot

immagin. I am sure it does her no honnor to endeavor to Ruin the Reputation of her Niece.[6] It is unworthy of every other Action of her Life—how she can Justify it upon Religious or friendly principles I cannot immagin—to persecute that poor Girl and indeavor to ruin her in the Oppinion of her father and family and at a time too when her Husband is absent, and she left without freind or protector if Fortune should tra[n]splant him from time to Eternity. Nob[od]y will undertake to deny Aunt Greene the merit of giveing them Girls all the education they ever had. They must have ever felt a weight of Gratitude in return, but her unnatural conduct has almost canceled the Obligation. I declare I cant help feeling a deep resentment for the Abuse and if God spares my Life and gives me an opportunity to see her I shall unfold my mind with that freedom which injurd freindship demands. Doubtless Mrs Greene has been faulty in many instances. It cannot be expected a Girl of her age and advantagees should be a pattern of perfection, but would it not have been more generous for her Aunt to have endeavourd to reclaimd her if She saw her in an Error rather than expose her faults. I really think Mrs Greene suffers her Resentment to betray her into a conduct that sullies the Glory of all other worthy Actions.

I have no prospect of coming home, not even for a few Days. The General wont suffer me to be out of Camp. I have been unwell for a week past with the Jaundice, and feel much out of order. Now I am almost continually Sick at my Stomach, accompanied with a Bilious fever every afternoon. I hope to Shake it of[f] in a few Days As a more active scene will render my presence necessary in a few Days. I am extreme sorry to hear that Brother Perry still continues lost to shame or his own happiness. O miserable Youth, how useful might you be, an ornament to yourself, a Blessing to your Country.[7] Remember me to all my freinds and Believe me to be Affectionately yours

N GREENE

ALS (MWA).

1. Address page is missing, but from the context, there is no doubt that it was to brother Christopher at Potowomut.

2. "Daddy Ward" is Samuel Ward, Sr., the father of Christopher's wife, Catharine; "brother Capt Ward" is Samuel, Jr.

3. John Adams had attended two meetings of the Council of War in Cambridge on 16 and 18 Jan. at which NG was present. (Varick transcripts, Washington Papers: DLC)

4. John Gooch, a friend who was then a captain in Varnum's regiment, later served under NG as assistant deputy quartermaster general. He won fame in the army by crossing the Hudson in a small boat and running through British fire to get messages to and from Ft. Washington (see below, NG to Knox, 17 Nov. 1776).

5. "Mother" was NG's stepmother, the widow of Nathanael Greene, Sr. "Mrs Greene" refers to NG's wife, Catharine.

6. Aunt Greene is Catharine Ray Greene of East Greenwich. The niece whose

reputation was at stake was NG's wife, Catharine, who was brought up in her aunt's home. The cause of their clash is not known.

7. Other references in NG's correspondence to brother Perry's misspent youth indicate that he was the black sheep of the family.

## General Greene's Orders

[Prospect Hill, Mass., 30 Jan. 1776. The chevaux-de-frise[1] are to be kept clear so they can be shut easily. Officers to bring troops to alarm post before reveille is finished. Mitchell Orderly Book (NHi) 1 p.]

1. The reference here is to the contrivances used to close the openings in the fortifications on Prospect Hill, not to the underwater variety used later in the year in the Hudson River.

## General Greene's Orders

[Prospect Hill, Mass., 31 Jan. 1776. Men to cut wood at Medford. Mitchell Orderly Book (NHi) 1 p.]

## General Greene's Orders

[Prospect Hill, Mass., 2 Feb. 1776. Concerns cleaning of barracks, repair of "slaw bunks" (sleeping bunks), and retrieval of pots and entrenching tools lying about camp. Mitchell Orderly Book (NHi) 1 p.]

## From Nicholas Brown[1]

Sir                                    Providence [R.I.] Feby 2nd 1776
    Having the Cause of our Bleeding Country much at Hart and being Confirm'd that we cannot Any way better Serve it than by distressing our Unnatural Enemis by every means in Our Power to prevent there geting the necessary supplys &c, We have with the Bearer Capt Zachariah Allin [Allen] and others Determened to fit the Arm'd Sloop Washington a very fast Saeler and is the same lately Dismissd from this Colonys servs [services]. Shes to Crews in and about Boston Bay and will be ready by Capt Allins return who tho' a man of Interest a Stranger in that Govermt. He now waits on the Council Bord of the Massachusetts for a commissn for Capt Gid Crafferd [Crawford] Comdr sd [said] Vessel. We have now to Desire of you to Assist Capt Allin if needed in standg with him in [giving] Bond. Our Govemt have the matter of makg a Law for this purpose under Consideration and have Appotd a Committee whose report cannot be made before the last of this month.[2] We hence thought best to pursue our Intentions before [ not completed ]

ADf (RPJCB); incomplete.

1. The draft is in the hand of Nicholas Brown (1729–81), the oldest of four brothers who built a modest family business into a commercial and industrial empire. (Hedges, *Browns*)

Brown's concern for his "Bleeding Country" did not arise entirely from patriotism. Robert Morris said of Nicholas and John that he understood they had "sacrificed every other pursuit" to the spirit of privateering (ibid., p. 279).

2. The legislature authorized privateers in the session beginning 18 Mar. 1776 (Bartlett, *Records*, 7: 481–83).

The *Washington* may never have engaged in privateering. In Apr., Capt. Gideon Crawford was bound for France in Brown's *Happy Return* with a cargo of "Sperma coeti white oyl" to be exchanged for military supplies (Outward and Inward Entries, R-Ar). Capt. Allen was on board the *Sally* when it was captured by *HMS Fowey* while en route to Hispaniola, 12 Apr. (Clark, *Naval Docs.*, 4: 1254).

## To Governor Nicholas Cooke of Rhode Island

Sir                          Prospect Hill, [Mass.] February 6, 1776

Your favor the 28th of January is now before me.[1] I thank you for particular statement of the Government you give. I am exceeding Sorry for the unhappy difference Subsisting between Providence and Newport.[2] The Jealousies excited amongst the Inhabitants of the latter, from the Military Operations, leaves but little hope of a cordial good understanding. However, I hope the Inhabitants of Providence will be very circumspect in all their action that relates to the Interest of Newport, to leave them no just room for complaint. You must expect Newport will Say hard things; they are delicately Situated; Property is dear as Life. To leave their homes, and feed upon the cold hand of charity is mortifying to those who have always lived Independent. But let them do or say what they will, I hope the People of Providence will preserve their moderation, and not Suffer themselves to be betrayed into any indiscretion. Application was made from Newport to Congress to obtain a Supply for Wallace; they referred it back to your Assembly.[3] So far as I am able to collect the Sentiments of the Congress, they are for granting a supply. It has always been my opinion that they ought not to be Supplied anywhere, but if any are Supplied, Newport may as well be as others, as it is a defenceless place at present. I hope General West will conduct the matter with prudence as he is a Providence man.[4] Their Jealousies take in not only the Town of Providence but the County. The Regiments here fill up very Slow as well as with you. I am afraid without a Bounty the Regiments will not complete their Establishment. We are getting in 10 Regiments of Militia; if Providence[5] favors us with an Opportunity we hope to Strike Some Capital Stroke. As Mr. Allen by whom this will be handed you is waiting, I have only time to add that I am with great truth Your most Obedient humble Servant,

N. GREENE

Reprinted from RIHS, *Proc.* (1873–74): 51. The original was among the Cooke-Greene letters stolen in 1898.

1. Letter not found. Most of Cooke's letters are lost, while this letter to Cooke is the only survivor of those that NG wrote him between Nov. 1775 and July 1776.

2. On the rivalry between the two cities, see NG to Jacob, 20 Dec. 1775, above. No other colonial city suffered such irreparable losses as Newport. Providence, scarcely a competitor before the war, was the chief beneficiary.

3. Congress, which received the memorial on 6 Jan. 1776, washed its hands of the problem by forwarding the memorial to the R.I. Assembly the next day (*JCC*, 4: 36).

4. In the middle of Jan., William West was named general of a new brigade that was to stop the trafficking with the enemy. While West assiduously carried out the Assembly's orders, that body buckled in the face of protests from Newport and ordered his troops off Aquidneck Island. In a remarkable display of irresolution, the Assembly released the "Tories" he had arrested while praising his actions (Bartlett, *Records*, 7: 467). The Assembly's failure to back him, plus a squabble between two colonels in his brigade, led him to resign in Feb.—ending one of the shortest generalships in the history of the American military.

5. The reference here is to "divine" Providence, not the city.

# To Jacob Greene

Prospect Hill [Mass.] February 8th 1776

I have got the jaundice, and have been confined twelve or fourteen days.[1] I am as yellow as saffron, my appetite all gone, and my flesh too. I am so weak that I can scarcely walk across the room. But I am in hopes I am getting something better. I am grievously mortified at my confinement, as this is a critical, and to appearance, will be an important period of the American war. Cambridge Bay is frozen over; if the weather continues a few days longer as cold as it has been some days past, it will open a passage into Boston. Sick or well, I intend to be there, if I am able to sit on horseback.

There is nothing new in camp, only preparations making for the attack. Whether it will take place or not, God only knows. Heaven grant us success if it should be made. That will depend upon the bravery of the troops; how they will act, time and the experiment only can determine.[2] If I am called from time to eternity, I hope you will see justice done to my family. I commit them to you and the rest of my brothers.

Excerpt reprinted from Johnson, *Greene*, 1: 52.

1. He had apparently recovered by 15 Feb. when he next wrote Jacob (see below). The news of his recovery was late in reaching home, for on 20 Feb., according to her Aunt Catharine, NG's wife "sat of[f]" for Cambridge because "the Genl. has been Very Poorly and Sent for Spoues" (Roelker, *Franklin-Greene*, p. 68).

2. On 16 Jan., a week before NG fell ill, Washington had laid before his general officers the "indispensable necessity" to attack the British before they received spring reinforcements, which would rule out an American offensive and might even permit the British to attack. Congress had been indecisive in its instructions on attacking Boston. A resolution of 22 Dec. authorized an attack "if General Washington and his council of war should be of opinion, that a successful attack may be made" (*JCC*, 3: 444). Washington could not know of Howe's long-nurtured plan to evacuate the city as soon as ships were available, but even had he known, he would still have favored

striking such a blow—at the very least to raise American morale and silence those who criticised his army's inactivity, and possibly even to end the war. NG and his fellow officers agreed unanimously on the plan, provided (1) that thirteen regiments of two-month militiamen could be brought in by 1 Feb., and (2) that sufficient arms could be obtained. (Council of War meeting of 16 Jan. is in the Varick transcripts, Washington Papers: DLC.)

The general officers were painfully aware of the continued shortage of powder, that unless large supplies were received it would be impossible to use the "noble train of Artillery" that Col. Henry Knox had labored so ingeniously to bring from Ticonderoga. The Continentals would be fortunate to have enough powder for small arms. It was hoped the bay would remain frozen over so the attack could be made over the ice rather than by boat or across the narrow Boston neck.

Although NG chafed that his illness might prevent him from participating in the attack, at the time he wrote this letter, the preparations were far from complete. (See below, NG to Jacob, 15 Feb.)

## General Greene's Orders

[Prospect Hill, Mass., 14 Feb. 1776. A neglect of reading orders to the men permits pleas of ignorance. Commanders to see they are read daily. Captains to read rules and regulations of army to companies at least once a month to "save men from punishment." Mitchell Orderly Book (NHi) 1 p.]

## To Jacob Greene

Prospect Hill [Mass.] February 15th 1776

Your apprehensions about attacking Boston are very well founded in many respects. The troops are raw and undisciplined, and consequently unfit for an attack sword in hand. But out of an army of 20,000 men, it will be hard if we cannot find 8,000 who will fight manfully. There must be some cowards among them, as well as among us. But, however, an attack upon a town garrisoned with 8,000 regular troops, is a serious object, and ought to be well considered before attempted. I always thought an attack with 20,000 men might succeed.[1] I still think so; and were the Bay to be frozen over, I should be glad to see the attempt made;[2] not but that it would be horrible if it succeeded, and still more horrible if it failed. But the advantage that America would derive from making ourselves masters of that garrison at this time, would be inconceivable. It would damp the spirits of Great Britain, and give ours a new spring. In a word, it would put a finishing stroke to the war; it would heal all the divisions among ourselves; silence the Tories, and work a general reformation throughout the continent. But I have little hopes now of such a happy event, as the weather is greatly moderated, and the scarcity of powder puts it out of our power to attempt anything by cannonading or bombardment.[3]

Excerpt reprinted from Johnson, *Greene*, 1: 52–53.

1. The figure of 20,000 was somewhat rhetorical. Even with 3,500 militia yet to come, American strength was less than 18,000. The figure of 8,000 "who will fight manfully" was closer to the truth, although undoubtedly too low. His estimate of 8,000 *British* troops was very accurate (see note 3, below).

2. He implies the bay is not frozen over. Although Washington had found it so two days earlier, the moderated weather NG speaks of at the end of this letter must have broken up the ice in places.

3. NG's pessimism on the probable outcome of an attack was shared by his fellow generals but was in sharp contrast to Washington's enthusiastic proposal for an all-out assault which he laid before the council the following day (NG was too sick to attend). This was just one month after the 16 Jan. meeting in which the council, including NG, had approved an attack (see note 2, NG to Jacob, 8 Feb., above). Despite the shortage of powder that prevented the use of artillery for bombardment and was barely adequate for the limited number of small arms available, Washington felt that with the ice soon to be gone, it was then or never. (Washington to Hancock, 18 Feb., Fitzpatrick, *GW* 4: 335–37)

The council was unanimous in rejecting his proposal—at least until powder for a bombardment was available. They believed, moreover, that he seriously underestimated British strength when he reported only five thousand effective troops in Boston. (The council minutes are in Varick Transcripts, Washington Papers: DLC.) They were right, for two British military historians have estimated Howe's forces at nearer nine thousand men (Fortescue, *British Army*, 3: 179; Mackesy, *War*, p. 80).

Washington bowed reluctantly to the collective rejection of his plan, but he was later convinced that it could have succeeded. On 26 Feb. he wrote sarcastically to Joseph Reed, "behold! though we had been waiting all the year for this favourable event, the enterprise was thought too dangerous!" (Fitzpatrick, *GW*, 4: 348)

Although NG was not in attendance to cast a vote, he was no less a target for Washington's sarcasm than those who did attend, for his views were not unknown. Remembering, as Washington must have, that NG was the only general who backed his plan for attacking the city in Oct. (NG et al. to Washington, above, 18 Oct. 1775), the commander in chief may have been especially disappointed in Greene's lack of support this time; if so, he gave no evidence of it nor did he hold it against him. Most modern historians believe the council acted wisely in restraining Washington. For example, see Ward, *War*, 1: 126. Excellent accounts of the last few months of the British occupation are found in French, *First Year*, pp. 648–79, and Freeman, *GW*, 4: chapters 1–3.

# General Greene's Orders

[Prospect Hill, Mass., 18 Feb. 1776. Concerns the immediate return of entrenching tools. Those who fail to comply to be treated as "defrauders of the Continental stores." Mitchell Orderly Book (NHi) 1 p.]

# Plan for Attacking Boston

[Prospect Hill, Mass., 18–25 February 1776][1]

To His Excellency General Washington, Commander in Chief of the Army of The United Colonies.[2]

In Obedience to Your Excellency's Orders we have considered the Matters referred to Us, and beg leave to recommend the following

Signals to be given from Roxbury in Case of any movement of The Enemy to Distress our People at Dorchester Hill.[3]

Signals in Case the Enemy begin to Embarque, a Flagg on Roxbury meeting House; If they Actually Land at Dorchester Two Flaggs, One over the Other. In case the Number of the Enemy Exceed Two Thousand men; a Flagg at the East and another at the West End of that Meeting House; in Case a reinforcement in Addittion to the Two Thousand are seen Embarqing, a Flagg on the East, a Flagg on the West, and a Flagg in the Middle of that Meeting House.

In case the Enemy begin to Retreat, Three Flaggs one above the Other.

In case the Enemy Carry the Works The Flaggs are to be Struck.

We further beg leave to recommend to Yr Excellency That should it appear from the Signals at Roxbury or in any other way, that an Attack may be made upon Boston, with good probability of Success, We Recommend that four Thousand Men Embark at the Mouth of Cambridge River, Two Thousand of Them to be Furnish'd from Cambridge and Two Thousand from Prospect and Winter Hill, One Thousand from each of those Hills. The Two Thousand from Cambridge to be Commanded By Brigadier Genl Sullivan and The Other Two Thousand By Brigr Genl Greene, The Whole to be Commanded By Major General Putnam.

Signal for the Embarkation, A Pendant Hoisted on Prospect Hill.

The First Division under Brigadier G. Sullivan to Land at the Powder House.

The Second Division under Brigadier G. Greene to Land at Barton's Point, or rather to the South of it.

Those who Land at the Powder House to Gain possession of Beacon Hill and Mount Whoredom.

Those who Land at Barton's Point, to Gain possession of Copps Hill, and after securing that Post, proceed to Join the other Division and Force the Enemys Works and Gates at the Neck, by which Means the Troops from Roxbury may be let in to Assist in the Reduction of The Town.

The Two Divisions to Consist of Eight Regiments of Five Hundred men each, The men to be Chosen, the Arms well Examined and the Officers to be the best, the most resolute and experienced.

The Three Floating Batteries here to go in Front of The Other Boats, and keep up a Heavy Fire on that part of The Town, where the Landings are to be made.[4]

ISRAEL PUTNAM
JNO SULLIVAN
NATHANAEL GREENE
HORATIO GATES

DS (Washington Papers, DLC).

1. The document is undated; it must have been drawn up only a few days after a definite plan was adopted for fortifying Dorchester Heights (see note below).

2. When the Council of War voted down Washington's plan for attacking Boston (see above, NG to Jacob, 15 Feb.), he alleviated his disappointment by throwing himself into a plan for fortifying Dorchester Heights, "with a view," he wrote Hancock, a few days later, "of drawing the Enemy out" (Fitzpatrick, *GW*, 4: 349).

Dorchester Heights was a peninsula just south of Boston jutting into Boston Harbor, with a lower eminence on the north side (Nooks Hill) which would permit artillery to cover Boston Neck (see map, p. 129). It had been left unfortified by Howe for reasons of his own—perhaps because it would thin his lines too much. With Knox's artillery available and powder from New York promised soon, the time for the Americans to act was at hand. According to William Gordon, who was no special advocate of Gen. Artemas Ward, it was Ward who first suggested the Dorchester alternative to Washington (Gordon, *History*, 2: 189). Intelligence of Howe's preparations for evacuating Boston which reached Washington by the middle of Feb. in no way deterred Washington or his generals from pushing the plan. It was the ardent hope of every officer that Howe would take the bait.

Large numbers of troops were set to work making wooden chandeliers, filled with fascines, to serve as defensive bulwarks, since the frozen ground made it impossible to throw up earthen works in one night. The men, like the officers, were aroused at the prospect of action after months of boring inactivity. Soon the rumors went among them that Dorchester was to be fortified and that it might bring Howe out to fight. The biographer of Ward cites journal entries of several soldiers during the last week in Feb. which showed the impending move was known by the troops (Martyn, *Ward*, p. 196).

3. "To Distress our People"—i.e., attack the hill as Washington hoped.

4. The three floating batteries were each to mount a twelve-pounder to bombard the shore. Some forty-odd boats were ready to ferry the four thousand troops across from Cambridge. (Freeman, *GW*, 4: 28–29) In addition to the "best, the most resolute and experienced" officers recommended by the generals, Washington recommended the "best and most approved Soldiers" (Washington's orders, 6 March, Fitzpatrick, *GW*, 4: 369–70).

## To George Washington

[From Prospect Hill, Mass., 21 Feb. 1776. Concerns appointment of two chaplains to serve four regiments.[1] ALS (Washington Papers: DLC) 1 p.]

1. At Washington's suggestion Congress had increased chaplains' meager pay as well as their duties by assigning two regiments to each man (*JCC*, 4: 61).

## General Greene's Orders

[Prospect Hill, Mass., 27 Feb. 1776. Concerns morning muster and picket duty of regiments. Carpenters to divide officers' room at main guard from soldiers. Chimneys to be repaired. No rum to be given to persons under guard (prisoners). Colonels to list guns to be repaired. Mitchell Orderly Book (NHi) 1 p.]

## General Greene's After Orders

[Prospect Hill, Mass.] 28 February 1776

All the Advanced Centries next to the Enemy from the White House Guard and Cobble Hill to be planted two together with Orders upon any uncommon discovery of the Motion of the Enemy or Noise by Day or Night in their Quarters, one of the Centries that makes the Discovery is immediately to report it to the Commanding Officer of the Guard. The Officer[s] commanding at those Posts are requested to be very Vigilant, as a surprize will be very disgraceful to the Officer, and perhaps ruinous to the Party. They who Command at such Out Posts cannot be too careful as they are answerable to God and their Country for the Party committed to their Charge. The Commanding Officer at Cobble Hill is to maintain that Post at all Events and he may rest assured he will be supported, and as the Post is exceeding strong nothing but negligence can endanger it or the Party station'd there. As there is nothing more disgraceful and dangerous than Noisy and Disorderly Guards, the Commanding Officers of the several Guards are desired to exert themselves to keep the Men silent and attentive to their Duty, it being necessary not only for the Security of the Post but their own Preservation. The Men are to be caution'd against leaving the Guard without permission and if any quit their Post without license or behave disorderly on the Guard or treat the Officers disrepectfully to be put under Confinement and fed upon nothing but Bread and Water. The General hopes and trusts there are but few in his Brigade if any that are of so loose and disorderly a Make, so Obstinate and self willed in their dispositions as to render severity necessary. None but the most Ignorant and Clownish will be Guilty of such unsoldierlike Behaviour, but if there should any prove Refractory, he is determin'd to treat them accordingly and at the same time he means to punish all Offenders that disgrace themselves and the Corps to which they belong. He assures those that behave themselves well that he will make it his Study to reward them according to their Merit.

Reprinted from "Henshaw Orderly Book," AAS, *Proc*. 57 (1947): 96–97.

## To George Washington

[From Prospect Hill, Mass., 2 Mar. 1776. A formal return listing 346 spears fit for service on Prospect and Cobble hills and 20 in need of repair.[1] DS (Washington Papers: DLC) 1 p.]

1. There were still more men than firearms, despite the improvement in the past fortnight. On 3 Mar., Washington's ordrs, which stated it not unlikely that "a contest

may soon be brought on, betwen the ministerial Troops, and this Army," asked that the brigadiers place firearms in the hands of those "fitest for duty" and that spears be used "to suply the defect of arms." Since spears were normally used only defensively at fortifications, it appears that Washington was still not ruling out an attack by the British.(Fitzpatrick, *GW*, 4: 363–65) The possibility appeared closer when the following day he ordered the barracks at "Prospecthill, or any other part of the Camp" to be prepared to receive a hundred wounded men and that hand barrows and other means of moving the wounded be provided (ibid., p. 369).

# To George Washington

[From Prospect Hill, Mass., 11 Mar. 1776. Maj. Nathaniel Cudworth, who left Bond's regiment because of its poor discipline, is recommended for appointment to Whitcomb's regiment. ALS (Washington Papers: DLC) 1 p.]

# General Greene's Orders

[Prospect Hill, Mass., 12 Mar. 1776. Orders concern stopping of all building, reports of certain marked guns, assignments to posts on Prospect and Cobble hills and Lechmere Point, and exercising of troops: "From the present situation of the Enemy there is a probability of our moving from hence in a few days, the Genl hopes the Officers will spare no pains to make the troops make a good appearance for their own credit as well as for the benefit of the service."[1] Mitchell Orderly Book (NHi) 2pp.]

1. Although Howe wasted no time in completing his preparations for leaving Boston, neither did he hasten his departure unduly. With his garrison intact, he surmised he was in no danger of an attack from Washington. He knew that he held a trump card in occupying Boston: he could burn the city on leaving. He tacitly agreed not to do so if Washington withheld his artillery fire; Washington honored the tacit understanding.

On 13 Mar., Washington called together the council of general officers, which NG attended, to consider the next steps to be taken in a war that had suddenly changed its course completely. The proceedings bear printing in full:

His Excellency the Commander in Chief inform'd the Council, that from the present appearance of the Ministerial Fleet and Army, the intelligence he had received from sundry Persons who had escaped from Boston, and from frequent Observations, he had reason to believe that the Troops were about to evacuate the Town; that in all probability they were destined for New York, and would attempt to possess themselves of that City, by which means they would command the Navigation of Hudson's River, open a communication with Canada, and cut off all intercourse between the Southern and Northern Colonies.

His Excellency then demanded the opinion of Council whether under the present circumstances (i.e. before the Town is wholly evacuated) it would be advisable to march any part of the Continental Army (now before Boston) to New York.

The Council were of opinion, that it will be proper that five Regiments with the Rifle Battalion should be detached immediately to New York. The Rifle Battalion to march tomorrow, and the others to follow as speedily as possible; that His Excellency be advised to write to the Governor of Connecticut, to desire he would immediately send two thousand of the Militia of his Government to New York, and that one thousand be requested from the Convention or Committee of safety of New Jersey, in order to reinforce the Troops already stationed there, until the detachments from this Army shall arrive.

His Excellency likewise demanded the opinion of Council whether, if the Ministerial Troops should totally abandon the Town of Boston, it would be necessary to continue any part of the Continental army for its defence.

Resolved, that if the Ministerial troops should totally abandon the Town of Boston, it will be unnecessary to imploy any part of this Army for the defence and security of the same, as the Militia of the Province will be adequate thereto.

The opinion of Council was also demanded by His Excellency, whether, if the Ministerial Troops should continue in the harbour of Boston, it would be advisable to fortify Newk's [Nook's] Hill in Dorchester.

Resolved, that if the Ministerial Troops should continue in this Harbour tomorrow, it would be advisable to fortify Newk's Hill the next Night at all events. (Varick Transcripts, Washington Papers: DLC)

Nook's Hill had been left unfortified on 4 Mar. and succeeding days because it was more crucial to fortify the upper hill. Since artillery on Nook's Hill could sweep the city of Boston itself, Howe ordered his artillery to stop American attempts to fortify it until just before his evacuation.

## General Greene's Orders

Boston 20th March 1776[1]

A Subaltern and twenty Men to parade imediately and assist Major Frazer, Deputy Quarter Master General in storing the Provisions. All the Officers of the different Guards to be at Head Quarters at the British Coffee House at Six oClock this Evening with the number of Guards and where station'd and also whose orders they have received upon an Alarm. At the beating the Tattoo All Officers, Non Commissioned Officers and Soldiers to retire to their Quarters and not stir out again till the beating the Revillie. All Officers of whatever Rank are desird to exert themselves in preventing the Troops from plundering or abusing any of the Inhabitants. Any Officer or Soldier detected in those kinds of offences will be punished to the Extent of the Law. A Fatigue party of 25 men that have had the small Pox, from each Colo[s] Whitcomb, Phiney [Phinney] and Hutchinson's Regts to cleanse the Barracks under the Inspection of the selectmen, or the Person they appoint for that Purpose. The Guards to be releiv'd at 8 of Clock in the morning. Upon an Alarm Colo[s] Phiney and Colo Hutchinson's Regt to man Fort Hill.[2] Four Companys of Colo Whitcombs on B[e]acon Hill and Mount Whoredom, Two Companys upon Corps [Copps] Hill, and two Company's to be a Reserve to form in King Street below the Town House, there to wait for orders. Colo Whitcomb to appoint the Capts to their several Posts. A fatigue to work upon Fort Hill tomorrow of 130 men from Phineys, Hutchinsons and Whitcombs Regts. Colo Phiney Field Officer of the day. Colo Hutchinson Officer of the day tomorrow. The Capt to examine dayly the Arms and Ammunition of the Troops that are brought upon the Grand parade to mount Guard, King Street is the Grand parade. The Adjt to apply tomorrow morng 7 OClock to the Brigade Major.

Israel Hutchinson Orderly Book (MHi).

1. The last of Howe's troops embarked Sunday morning, 17 Mar., but the ships did not leave the outer harbor. Within a few hours, Generals Ward and Putnam entered the city, and the following day Washington and his retinue entered, not in a triumphal march, but in a quiet trip of inspection. They found the streets quiet (partially because of a number of cases of smallpox); the depredation to property was less than expected (Washington reported to Hancock that the paintings in Hancock's house still hung on the walls intact), and they saw a great deal of British equipment—including spiked cannon that could be repaired.

On 20 Mar., Washington placed Greene in command of the city, although the orders for the day did not name him: "Whitcombs, Phinneys, and Hutchinsons Regiments are to march into Boston this day, and remain there until further orders, they are to guard the Town, and public Stores there, and do all such fatigue, and other duties, as the General commanding there, thinks proper to order. Every possible precaution will be taken to destroy the Infection of the small-pox. The Troops now in Boston are to march out, and join their respective Regiments" (Fitzpatrick, GW, 4: 411). The rifle regiments from Prospect Hill were already on the way to New York; the rest of NG's regiments on Prospect Hill were placed temporarily under Sullivan.

Washington left no record as to why he put Greene in command. Heath was on his way to New York and Ward had notified Washington of his desire to resign his commission, although ten days later Greene was on his way to New York also and Ward was in command of all Massachusetts defenses.

2. Boston peninsula was dominated by several high hills, long since cut down to size. Fort Hill stood south of Long Wharf along the southeastern shore, facing the harbor. Washington ordered its fortification as a precaution against Howe's returning (see note 2, NG Orders, 23 Mar., below).

Running across the city was a high ridge with three separate summits, making up Boston's famed Trimountain (from which Tremont Street took its name). Beacon Hill, in the center, originally stood almost 140 feet above sea level; Mt. Whoredom was a lower peak just to the west (near modern Louisberg Square); Mt. Pemberton was at the east end of the ridge. Copps Hill stood in the north end. Mt. Whoredom, formally named Mt. Vernon, acquired its popular name from the ladies who frequented every seaport; by 1775 the name had found its way into maps and military orders. See Walter Muir Whitehill, *Boston: A Topographical History* (Cambridge: Harvard University Press, 1959), pp. 6–8.

## General Greene's Orders

[Boston] 20th March 1776

Colo Learned is directed to Man Six Whale Boats every night while the Enemy remain in the Harbour, whose Duty it is to Row about and make discoveries of any movement of the Enemy, that the Garrison may be apprizd thereof. The Garrison already stationd in this Town is to remain here, as there is not Men sufficient in the Army that have had the small Pox to relieve them. The commandg Officers of the different Corps are directed to send such a number of Men for so much Baggage as they may necessarily want while here. It is the Genl[s] express orders that no Officer or Soldier attempt to take up or be aiding or assisting in taking up any Persons which may be suspected of being Enemical to the Country, and that no Insult or abuse be offerd to them. The Capt. and Subaltern Officers to examine the men to mount Guard, and see that their Arms and Ammunition are in good order, and that their men are drest as decent as their

Apparel will admit, their Face and Hands washed clean, and their Hair comb'd; Any Adjt that brings any men upon the Great Parade that are not prepared as above may expect the Censure due to their Neglience. The Capt. of the Guard to keep two Patroling Parties commanded by Subaltern Officers every Night patroling the Streets in every part of Boston, and take up all stragglers after Taptoo beating that cant give a good Acct of themselves, or have not the Countersign. Any Persons discoverd in plundering, to be sent prisoners to the Main Guard. The Officers of the different Guards to report all Occurrences happening while they are on Guard; tis expected that the Officers keep good orders on Guard and prevent any of the Soldiery from insulting or abusing any of the Inhabitants or Passengers that come in to Town upon Business. The Officers will be answerable for all the misconduct of their Guards. All General orders to be read once at least to the men, and all standing orders Three times; All Guards under Fifty men, not more than One man to be absent at a time, and not more than Two from any Guard under a hundred, and none without leave from the Commandg Officer of the Guard. The Provision to be carried to the Guards by their Mess Mates.

Israel Hutchinson Orderly Book (MHi).

## General Greene's Orders

[Boston] 23d March 1776[1]

The Guards to be left standing another day, and all that are off duty in Colo Phineys [Phinney's], Colo Whitcombs and Colo Hutchinsons Regt. except enough for Cooking to go upon fatigue tomorrow upon Fort Hill. The Genl flatters himself that both Officers and soldiers will chearfully submit to the necessary duty requird for Guardg and fortifying the Town. The situation of the Enemy below and the defenceless state of the Town render it absolutely necessary for the Troops to do double duty for a time, untill the Town is put in a better situation. The Genl has great Reason to suspect the Enemy may be meditating an Attack by surprise.[2] He therefore wishes the Guards may be Vigilant on their Posts, with their Arms and Ammunition in good order. The Captains are enjoind to examine the Arms and Ammunition of their Companies dayly. Every soldier to fasten his Accoutrements to his Gun every Night that they may be prepard at a moments warning upon an Alarm.

Israel Hutchinson Orderly Book (MHi).

1. As heavy as his duties undoubtedly were, NG took time to enjoy some moments of social life. On 22 Mar. he and Catharine dined with others at the home of John Rowe, a merchant who had stayed on through the siege, and the following day they had

dinner with "Mr and Mrs Inman." On 28 Mar., Rowe reported, the general court made "a handsome entertainment at Cpt. Marston's . . . for Genl Washington and the other generalls of the United Colonies." (*Diary of John Rowe* in Mass. Hist. Soc. *Proc.* 2d ser, 10[1895]: 97–98) Although this is the first mention of Catharine after she left Rhode Island on 20 Feb. to visit her ailing husband, it is presumed that she spent the four weeks at Prospect Hill, where she had stayed before, until she came into Boston with NG.

2. The American army was puzzled at the British fleet's lingering on in Nantasket Roads. Howe was preparing for the voyage to Halifax, but Washington was increasingly anxious that he might turn around and attack as soon as the militia had gone home and some of the American troops were well on their way to New York. Washington's orders of 24 Mar. warned of such a possibility: "The Enemy still continuing in the harbour, without any apparent cause for it, after Winds and Weather have favoured their sailing, leaves abundant reason to suspect, that they may have some design of aiming a blow at us before they depart." He warned the general officers to be on the alert and for Sullivan and Putnam to confer without delay. His order ended: "Genl. Green will dispose of the Regiments in Boston, to the best advantage." (Fitzpatrick, *GW*, 4: 423) Civilian and soldier alike heaved a sigh of relief when on 27 Mar. the fleet finally stood out to open sea—bound for Halifax.

## General Greene's Orders

[Boston, 23 Mar. 1776. All boats except Charleston Ferry to be collected, four of them to ply from Dorchester to Noddles Island nightly to take up boats coming in or out of Boston after dark. Israel Hutchinson Orderly Book (MHi) 1 p.]

## To Joseph Nightingale[1]

Dear sir                                         Boston March 24, 1776

The unhappy situation the Government of Rhode Island is in for want of a proper Person to command their Troops, makes me most heartily wish you would take upon you that command.[2] There never was a time when a demand was greater nor a People that had a juster claim to the services of a Citizen than the Colony has to yours. There appears by experience no Person so fit as your self to take the Command. The Colony is in the utmost distress; ruin and confusion prevails. The very intention of raising the Troops seems to be defeated, and from the disorder that prevails nothing but disgrace is to be expected. Rhode Island has as good Troops as are on the Continent; there are many excellent under Officers. For Gods sake dont let the whole be defeated and dishonnord for want of a commander. You have it in your power now to distinguish yourself to your own honnor and to your Countrys glory. Let not your private Interest defeat the Publick expectation. The Eyes of the People are upon you. Make a noble Sacrafice of your private Interest to the publick good, and give the World a convinceing proof that you are more social than selfish, and that the happiness of your Country is a greater object with you than the increase of Wealth. I am in haste and have only time to add that I most heartily wish you to accept the appointment. My compliments to Mrs Nightingale and the rest of my friends. Believe me to be with great truth your sincere friend and very humble servant.

NATHANAEL GREENE

ALS (RHi).
1. Col. Joseph Nightingale (1748–97) had been an active patriot before the war, having been in charge of removing the military stores from Ft. George to Providence in 1774 (Arnold, *R.I.*, 2: 343). He was a partner in the merchant firm of Clarke and Nightingale, which furnished the Continental army with supplies. They prospered so well in the revolutionary period that both partners built imposing mansions in Providence; Nightingale's still stands on Benefit Street between Power and Williams. His son, John Corlis Nightingale, married NG's daughter, Martha Washington Greene in 1795. For vital records on Joseph and John Nightingale, see William Waterman Chapin, "Genealogy of Nightingale Family" (Typescript, 1912), in RHi.
2. General William West had resigned in Feb. as commander of the Rhode Island Brigade for reasons explained above in note 4, NG to Cooke, 6 Feb. It is not known whether Nightingale was interested in or was considered for the post. Henry Babcock, who was appointed by the legislature to command the brigade, was dismissed after two months because it "incontestibly appeard" to the Assembly that he was "at times deprived of the perfect use of his reason" (Bartlett, *Records*, 7: 537). Cooke kept the office vacant in hopes that the brigade would be "put upon the Continental establishment" and that Congress would appoint a commander in chief of the brigade. With the British navy in control of Newport waters and much of Narragansett Bay, they posed a constant threat to all of Rhode Island. It no longer seemed fitting to Rhode Islanders that the Militia should be responsible for containing them. (Bartlett, *Records*, 7: 545) Washington approved Cooke's previous request in a letter to Hancock, 30 Apr. (Fitzpatrick, *GW*, 4: 539–40), and on 11 May 1776 Congress voted to take the Rhode Island brigade into the Continental army pay (*JCC*, 4: 347).

## To the Officers and Soldiers of the Boston Garrison

Boston Mar. 25th 1776

All Officers and Soldiers in this Garrison are hereby enjoined to afford any Assistance and Protection Joshua Bently may demand at any Time and at all Times whenever he demands it for the apprehending and securing such Person or Persons as he shall point out and the protecting the said Joshua Bently against any personal Insults or Abuses that the said Joshua Bently may [be] subject to by pointing out and apprehending Persons suspected to be acting as Spies upon the Continental Army.[1] Given under my Hand the Day and Year above.

NATHANAEL GREENE

DS (RHi).
1. Bently has not been identified, but it seems likely he had been in Boston during the occupation and had served as an informer to the Continental army. If Bently identified any spies, there is no record of the fact.

## To Colonel Moses Little

Dear sir                                                    Boston March 26, 1776

Your favor was handed me by Mr Coleman, in answer to which I can only say that I have ever thought myself happy in the command to which I was appointed. I still should think myself so. How his Excellency will dispose of me or you at present I am totally ignorant. I shall solicit to command my own Brigade, but that I shall obtain my request remains yet undetermind. I have no objection to your being absent for a few Days. You know the situation of the Enemy and the General orders rellative to marching.[1] All which you must attend too, and if you go give the necessary orders to the Lieut Colo how to conduct if anything should happen in your Absence. It will be unsafe to be long Absent. Beleive me to be with great esteem your sincere friend and humble Servant

NATHANAEL GREENE

ALS (MeHi).
1. Little's regiment, which had been in NG's brigade since the previous summer, was presently at Prospect Hill and would join NG again on the march to New York (see NG orders, 1 Apr., below).

## General Greene's Orders

[Boston] 27 March 1776

The Quarter Masters, to morrow Morning to make Return of the Victualing List of each of the Regts to which they belong to the Deputy Quarter Master Genl. that they may receive an order to draw Beer for the Troops. The Genl. once more warns the Soldiers against plundering, and at the same time acknowledges he feels a singular pleasure in reflecting that there never has been more than One or Two complaints and those only suspected. If any should be base enough to commit any Acts of Plunder and attempt to conceal the Effects, their messmates not discovering the same to the Commandg Officer of the Regt will be consider'd as accessary to the Crime, and should it be afterwards discover'd they will be punishd accordingly. If there should be a Fire in Town not a Man is to stir from his Guard or Quarters unless order'd by the Genl. at the Request of the select Men, or the Inhabitants. The Genl. strictly prohibits any of the Soldiery from Insulting any of the Inhabitants with the Odious Epithets of Tory, or any other Indecent language, it being ungenerous, unmanly and unsoldier like and cannot fail (if indulg'd) of disgracing both Officers and Soldiers.

Israel Hutchinson Orderly Book (MHi).

## General Greene's Orders

[Prospect Hill, Mass.] 31 March 1776

The Colos of the Ninth 11th and 12 Regts to have their Baggage ready to load Early to morrow morning and to wait His Excellencys Orders as to the time of Marching.[1] The Quarter Master Sergt of Each Regt and Corporal and Eight men to Collect all the tools, Pots and Kettles that are to be left behind into one Room in Each Regts Barracks. No Tables, Chairs, or Useless Luggage is to Go on board the Waggons that may Impede their march.

Mitchell Orderly Book (NHi).
1. Once Washington was convinced that Howe had left for good, he immediately ordered the regiments to New York. His order of Friday, 29 Mar., reads "Varnum's, Hitchcock's, Little's, Read's, and Bailey's Regiments to march on Monday morning [1 Apr.] at Sun-rise: Brigadier Genl. Green will take Command of this Brigade" (Fitzpatrick, *GW*, 4: 442).

Washington left Gen. Artemas Ward in command of Boston, but there were many who, though respecting Ward, wished he had chosen NG. As late as 22 Apr., William Cooper wrote John Adams that little or nothing had been done to repair the damage or improve the defenses of Boston. "The Court blame him for Inactivity, and He them," said Cooper. "There is a Report here that Ward has desir'd to resign—I wish from my Heart He would do it—He is a good Man, a thoro N. England man, & dispos'ed to do us ev'ry Service in his Power—But He certainly wants Decision & Activity—It is of absolute Necessity that some General Officer of the best Qualities be sent to this Department immediatly—Pray let [Nathanael] Green[e] or some other be plac'd here." Cited in Clark, *Naval Docs.*, 4: 1191–93.

## General Greene's Orders

[Prospect Hill, Mass.] 1 April 1776

The Ninth, 11th and 12th Regts to march Immediately for Providence.[1] The Colo or Commanding officer of Each Regt to appoint a Subaltern, A Serjt and 20 Men to load and Guard the Baggage Which is to Be left Behind. The troops are to take three days Provisions With them, Their Knapsacks and Blankets and Nothing Else as they are to march With all Possible Expedition. As there Cannot be Waggons Procurd for All five of the Regts under Marching Orders, Colo Hitchcocks Baggage is to be left until more Can be Procurd. Colo Varnum is to lead this Division.[2] Special Care is to be taken that No officer Or Soldier Leave the Regt to Which they Belong, or that Any of the Soldiers offer any Abuse to the Inhabitants on the Road. The Guard at Genl Lees to Join their Respective Regt Immediately.

Mitchell Orderly Book (NHi).
1. NG's original plan was not to "march immediately for Providence." The speed-up resulted from a report that Gov. Cooke of Rhode Island had sent by express to Washington the previous evening. Twenty-seven ships, said Cooke, were reported as being sighted near Newport, "undoubtedly having the ministerial [Howe's] troops on

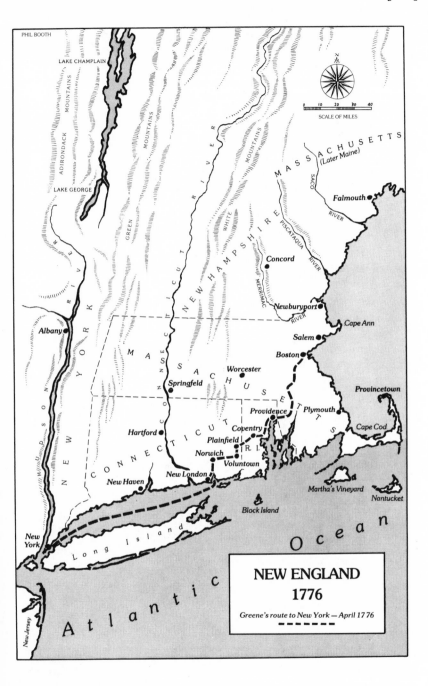

PHIL BOOTH

LAKE CHAMPLAIN

ADIRONDACK MOUNTAINS

MOUNTAINS

LAKE GEORGE

GREEN MOUNTAINS

NEW YORK

HUDSON RIVER

CONNECTICUT RIVER

WHITE MOUNTAINS

NEW HAMPSHIRE

MOUNTAINS

MERRIMAC

MASSACHUSETTS
(Later Maine)

SACO RIVER

Falmouth ●

Concord ●

Newburyport ●

Cape Ann

Salem ●

Boston ●

PISCATAQUA RIVER

MERRIMAC RIVER

Albany ●

M A S S A C H U S E T T S

Worcester ●

Springfield ●

Hartford ●

CONNECTICUT

New Haven ●

Providence ●

Coventry ●

Plainfield ●

R. I.

Norwich ●

Voluntown ●

New London ●

Plymouth ●

Provincetown

Cape Cod

Martha's Vineyard

Nantucket

Block Island

New York

Long Island

New Jersey

A t l a n t i c    O c e a n

N

0  10  20  30  40
SCALE OF MILES

**NEW ENGLAND
1776**

*Greene's route to New York — April 1776*

- - - - - - -

board." (Bartlett, *Records*, 7:506) Since Washington could not be certain that some of Howe's ships had not doubled back, he ordered NG to "hasten his march" and asked Sullivan to stand by to go also if necessary. Washington himself planned to join Greene immediately if the report were true (Washington to Sullivan, Fitzpatrick, *GW*, 4: 457–58); otherwise he would be more leisurely in arriving in Providence.

After NG's brigade had left, Washington received the embarrassing admission from Cooke that the persons who "sighted" the ships had been "deceived by the weather, which was very thick and foggy" (Bartlett, *Records*, 7: 507).

NG would not be called on again to defend his native ground until the American offensive against the British at Newport in the summer of 1778.

2. Varnum's *regiment* was to be the first to go.

## General Greene's Orders

Providence [R.I.] 4th April 1776

Colo Hitchcocks and Colo Littles Regts to turn out to morrow Morning to Escort His Excellency into town to parade at Eight O Clock. Both officers and men to be drest in uniform And None to turn out Except those who are drest [in] uniform; And those of the Non Commissioned Officers and Soldiers that turn out, to be Washd both face and hands Clean, their Beards shavd of[f], their hair combd and powderd, and their arms Cleand. The Genl hopes that both officers and Soldiers will Exert themselves for the honour of the Regt and the Brigade to Which they Belong. He wishes to Pay the Honour to the Commander in Chief in as decent And Respectable a manner as Possible.[1]

Mitchell Orderly Book (NHi).
1. NG was virtually eclipsed by the presence of Washington. Theodore Foster, Providence town clerk and member of the Assembly, recorded the event in his diary with only a bare reference to Greene: Little's and Hitchcock's regiments, he wrote, went to meet Washington on 5 Apr. and marched back into town, followed by two local military groups, Hitchcock's men in a uniform with the "uper Garment a Brown Frock Fringed" and Little's in "Blew faced with Buff Coulour." Behind the troops rode Gov. Cooke "at whose right Hand rode Genl Washington, then followed a Number of Gentlemen on Horseback," one of whom, presumably, was NG. "There was a Great concourse of People many having come a Number of Miles to have a Sight of his Excellency. The Houses through the Street were full of Women, the Eminenes [eminences] without covered with Men." (Foster Diary, RHi, 5 Apr. 1776) The *Providence Gazette* the next day (6 Apr. 1776) was completely blind to NG's presence: "Yesterday his excellency General Washington, Adjutant General Gates and several other officers, arrived here from Cambridge" read the opening of a short notice.

## General Greene's Orders

Norwich [Conn.] 8th April 1776[1]

Colo Baileys and Colo Reeds Regts to Parade to morrow morning by Sunrise and March for New London an hour after. As Soon as the Regts arive, they are to draw out of Mr Thomas Mumfords Store Six days Provision and have it Cookd as soon as Possible. The troops to hold themselves in Readiness to Imbark at A moments Warning, the

Quarter Master of Each Regt to Go forward and take up Quarters for the Regiments.

Mitchell Orderly Book (NHi).
1. Norwich was at the head of navigation on the Thames River, fourteen miles north of New London, from which place the brigade planned to take ship for New York.

## General Greene's Orders

[New London, Conn., 9 Apr. 1776. Orders to unnamed commanding officer of the transports that are to take troops to New York.[1] Mitchell Orderly Book (NHi). 1 p.]

1. See below, NG to Commander of the *Gale*, 10 Apr., where the orders are more fully spelled out.

## General Greene's Orders

New London [Conn.] 10th April 1776
Two Hundred men are wanted to Go on Board the fleet for a few days under the Command of Admiral [Esek] Hopkins.[1] All those Acquainted With Sea Service that have a mind to Join the Admiral as Volunteer have Liberty to the amount Above mentioned. They will be sent for in a few Days to Join their Respective Regts. The Genl Wishes to see upon this Occasion that Spirit and Resolution that has hitherto Distinguishd the New England Troops in the Land and Sea Service. The Names of those that turn out Volunteers to be Given in the Companies and Regts to Which they belong that a Proper Return may be made to the Admiral.

Mitchell Orderly Book (NHi).
1. Commodore (not Admiral) Hopkins had put into New London two days earlier with considerable damage to his ship, the *Alfred*, incurred when capturing two British ships in Long Island Sound and engaging HMS *Glasgow* in combat. Because of sickness among the crew, Washington "readily consented" to let him have the men to help repair the vessel. (Washington to John Hancock, 22 Apr., Fitzpatrick, *GW*, 4: 500–504) On 25 Apr., Washington asked Hopkins to send the men to New York as soon as possible because their Corps "are much weakened by their Absence." (Ibid., p. 521)

## To Commanding Officer of the Sloop *Gale*

New London [Conn.] April 10, 1776
To the Commanding officer on board Sloop Gale navigated by Wm Warner: you are requested to proceed on your Voyage to New York as fast as possible, Wind and Weather permiting, to keep in the Sound in company with the Fleet if possible.[1] You are to keep Conecticut Shore on board as near as the Pilots shall think safe. The men to

have their arms and ammunition in readiness to defend yourself if you should be attackt by any of the Kings Tenders; if any other Vessel should be attackt you are to lend all the assistance in your power, either by fireing with small arms or boarding, as occasion may require. But if you should be chased by a man of War you are to avoid her if possible and if there is no other way to avoid her you must Run the Vessel on Shore. If you should have the misfortune to be seperated from the Fleet, and meet with one of the Tenders, you must avoid her if you can, but if you cannot you must board her, which you may effect with a certainty of success from your superior numbers.[2] You are to Stop at Turtle Bay Just beyond Hell Gate and wait for further orders. By no means to suffer the Troops to straggle when you Land them.

NATHANAEL GREENE

ALS (MWA).
    1. The "Wind and Weather" did not permit. The night the troops embarked, a storm moved into Long Island Sound. We have no record of what must have been a rough trip, but Washington reported to Hancock from New York four days later that some of Greene's transports had still not arrived and that he feared the "severe Storm" has "done some Injury" to them (15 Apr., Fitzpatrick, *GW*, 4: 479–81). The transports were scattered and some had put back into New London. On 12 Apr. the *Intelligencer and Universal Gazette* of New London reported that almost all of the troops had sailed, but on 19 Apr. it reported there were still some companies in the brigades of Spencer and NG in port. NG's ship apparently put into New York on 17 Apr.
    2. Before the storm removed the threat of British ships, there seems to have been no plan to have Commodore Esek Hopkins convoy the troop transports. See above, NG orders of 10 Apr. on his supplying men to Hopkins.

## To George Washington

[After 20 Apr. 1776. At the bottom of Col. William Bond's recommendations to Washington for appointments in his regiment, NG approves same as most "judicious." Cy (Washington Papers: DLC). 1 p.]

## General Greene's Orders

[New York][1] 29 April 1776

The Quarter Masters of the 9th, 11th, and 12th Regts to apply to the Quarter Master General for Tents and Camp Utensils this Evening to be in readiness to Encamp agreeable to General Orders to Morrow Morning. At 4 o Clock this Afternoon Col Varnum, Hitchcock and Little are desir'd to attend at the General's Quarters to go over to Long Island and view the Encampment mark'd out. A Sergt and 20 Men to parade at Whites Hall to Morrow Morning at 7 o Clock to be under the direction of Engineer Smith.

Henshaw Orderly Book (MWA).

1. NG arrived in New York on 17 Apr. according to General Heath's memoirs, although a week passed before all his storm-battered transports came through Hell Gate to East River (see note, NG to commander of the *Gale*, 10 Apr. above). The following week Washington created five brigades under Heath, Spencer, Sullivan, Greene, and Lord Stirling. NG's brigade was made up of his veteran regiments of Varnum, Little, and Hitchcock, plus two temporary regiments under Anthony Wayne and William Irvine. NG was first assigned to Manhattan Island, but he was soon given the command of Long Island in the place of Sullivan, now on his way to Canada. On 29 Apr., Col. Edward Hand's regiment of Pennsylvania riflemen was added to Greene's brigade. The regimental and brigade assignments are found in Washington's orders of 24, 27, 29, and 30 Apr. (Fitzpatrick, *GW*, 4: 512–13, 526, 536, and 537). Sullivan, en route to Canada, wrote Washington 8 June, "I should . . . Rejoice to See General Green here with his Brigade, if he can be Spared from New York," but Washington chose to keep Greene on Long Island (Hammond, *Sullivan Papers*, 1: 226–29).

## General Greene's Orders

[Long Island,[1] N.Y.] 2 May 1776
The 9th, 11th and 12th Regiments to Pitch their Tents to Day, but as there is Straw only for one Regiment, the 12th Regt only to go into Tents to Night, the 9th and 11th to Remain in their Quarters. To-morrow Straw will be provided for the other two Regiments. Every Capt and Subaltern to Encamp with their Compys and by No means to Lodge out of Camp, except for a Night or so. Officers of all Ranks are requested to exert themselves to keep good Order in Camp, preserve the Inhabitants from Insults and their Property from Waiste, no trees or fencing stuff taken for fuel on any pretence whatever. Every Soldier discover'd Violating this Order to Be punish'd immediately on the Spot. The Quarter Master to attend particularly to the Articles of Wood and Straw and see that the Troops are properly supplied.

No Soldiers to Be out of Camp after Tattoo Beating. The Roll to Be Called twice a day.

Henshaw Orderly Book (MWA).

1. The camp was behind (i.e., west of) the line of fortifications that Genl. Charles Lee had laid out earlier in the year along Brooklyn Heights and that Lord Stirling had begun to construct. Lee's line of fortification was designed not to defend Long Island, which was impossible to fortify, but to back up the coastal defences that were to prevent British ships from entering the East River. (See map, p. 231.) The mile-long line closed off the base of a broad peninsula that was formed by Wallabout Bay on the north and Gowanus Bay on the south and that constitutes the part of present-day Brooklyn across the East River from New York's Lower East Side. It was hoped that any British land forces that came ashore on Long Island could be stopped from driving westward to the edge of New York harbor. The line of forts, in other words, faced eastward. For a description of the forts and bibliographical references, see NG's orders for 1 June, below.

## General Greene's Orders

[Long Island, N.Y., 3 May 1776. Soldiers or noncommissioned officers who take property without an order to be punished severely. Straw to be divided equally among regiments. Mitchell Orderly Book (NHi). 1 p.]

## General Greene's Orders

[Long Island, N.Y.] 5 May 1776

A Fatigue party to Morrow Morning of two hundred Men to Morrow Properly Officered.

No Non Commission'd Officer or Soldier to Pass [over] the Ferry to New York without permission from some of the Field Officers.[1] Any of the troops attempting to pass over without Permission will be Confin'd and Try'd for disobedience of Orders. Any of the Fatigue Parties that leaves the Works without Liberty shall do constant Duty for a whole Week. As the Security of New York greatly depends upon this Pass when these Works are Constructing, the General hopes the Troops will carefully forward the same as fast as Possible.

The Inhabitants having enterd A Complaint that their Meadow Grounds are injur'd by the Troops going upon them to gather Greens, they are for the future Strictly prohibited Going on Any of the Inhabitants Ground unless in the proper Passes to and from the Encampment and the forts without Orders from some Commission'd Officer. The General desires the Troops not to sully their Reputation by any undue Liberty in Speech or Conduct, but behave themselves towards the Inhabitants with that decency and respect that becomes the Character of Troops fighting for the preservation of the Rights and Liberties of America.

The General would have the Troops consider We came here to protect the Inhabitants and their Property from the Ravages of the Enemy but if instead of support and Protection, they meet with nothing but Insult And Outrage, we shall be considered as lawless Banditts and treated as Oppressors and Enemies.

Henshaw Orderly Book (MWA).

1. New York City was a magnet for the men encamped near the hamlet of Brooklyn. Larger than Boston, it was considered far more "sinful" by Bostonians. In one section, called "the holy ground," Col. Loammi Baldwin told his wife that the "whores (by information) continue their employ which is become very lucrative." (Cited by Freeman, GW, 4: 85)

## To Peter Philips[1]

[From Long Island, N.Y., 6 May 1776. Asks for account from Prospect Hill. Mr. Greene[2] tells him profit of sutlers and baking business small compared with profit at Cambridge. Supposes Philips's profits there were $8,000 to $10,000. If enemy does not arrive within a fortnight, the city will be impregnable. Provisions "above as dear agin" as in Cambridge. ALS (NN) 2 pp.]

1. Philips was commissary of Rhode Island troops at Boston.
2. Cousin Griffin, who had apparently come with NG from Boston as a supplier of bread.

## General Greene's Orders

[Long Island, N.Y., 10 May 1776. Duty to be assigned according to size of regiments. Sentries to guard stores and ferries. Ninth, Eleventh, and Twelfth regiments to draw twenty cartridges per man, rest to be left in laboratory with each man's name on his share.[1] Tents to be drawn for main guard. Orderly sergeant from each regiment to attend general's quarters daily. Commanders to report number of guns needed to give each man one. Henshaw Orderly Book (MWA) 1 p.]

1. The three divisions used muskets; Col. Hand's regiment was excepted because they used rifles.

## General Greene's Orders

[Long Island, N.Y., 12 May 1776. Three hundred spears to be brought from quartermaster and a grindstone to sharpen them. Col. Hitchcock to send out-of-order arms to King's Works shop. Any one whose gun is damaged by negligence shall pay cost of repair. Mitchell Orderly Book (NHi) 1 p.]

## To [                    ]

[Long Island, N.Y.] May 14th 1776
By a letter from Governor Cook, covering a late act past last session in your government, you have declared yourselves independent. Tis nobly done. God prosper you, and crown your endeavours with success.[1]

Excerpt reprinted from Johnson, *Greene*, 1: 55.
1. A great deal of confusion has surrounded the act of 4 May by which the people of Rhode Island, as NG told them, "have declared yourselves independent." Later

historians of the state have referred to the act in the same terms. Samuel Greene Arnold wrote in his *History of Rhode Island* in 1860 that the act was "in effect, a Declaration of Independence. It closes the colonial period of our history, for it established Rhode Island as an independent State two months before the general Declaration of the United Colonies." (Arnold, *R.I.*, 2: 373). The act, said William R. Staples ten years later, "severed the connection between Rhode Island and the British Crown, and the English Colony of Rhode Island became henceforth a sovereign State." (Staples, *R.I.*, p. 67)

The act, however, did not make Rhode Island an independent or sovereign state. Blaming George III for failing to live up to the compact signed by his "illustrious ancestors," it renounced allegiance to him. The name and authority of the king were no longer to appear on any public papers; instead, "in the room thereof," was to be substituted "the Governor and Company of the English Colony of Rhode Island and Providence Plantations." (Bartlett, *Records*, 7: 522–23) Gov. Cooke realized that, in still calling itself an "English Colony," Rhode Island had not declared its independence of England. This is evident in a letter he wrote to Stephen Hopkins three days later. He enclosed the act "discharging the Inhabitants of the Colony from Allegiance to the British King," but his letter was chiefly concerned with the instructions that Hopkins and Ellery had requested for voting on the subject of independency of the United Colonies. The committee appointed to draw up instructions to Hopkins and Ellery, he said, had thought "Dependency is a word of so equivocal a Meaning, and hath been used for such ill Purposes, and Independency, with many honest and ignorant people carrying the Idea of eternal Warfare, the Committee thought it best to avoid making Use of either of them." The upper house, he continued, argued that, since some towns would vote against independence, giving the "Appearance of Dissension," it would be better at this time not to go on record. Moreover, it was felt that the Continental Congress, with the act of Rhode Island before it renouncing allegiance to the king, "could not possibly entertain a Doubt of the Sense of the General Assembly." (Cooke to Hopkins, 7 May 1776, AAS, *Proc.* 36 [1926] 3: 323–25)

## General Greene's Orders

[Long Island, N.Y., 16 May 1776. Regiments of Varnum, Hitchcock, and Little to be reviewed next three days. Those without arms not to borrow from other regiments. No one to mount picket guard without shoes. Henshaw Orderly Book (MWA) 1 p.]

## General Greene's Orders

[Long Island, N.Y.] 16 May 1776

Tomorrow Being Appointed by the Continental Congress to Be observed as A Day of Fasting and Prayer.[1] And His Excellency Genl Washington having Orderd all duties discontinued Except the Necessary Guards till the Next day after to Morrow. There is No Fateague Party to Be turnd out tomorrow and the Reviewing Colo Varnums Regt is put of till Next day. The Other Regts to follow on in order as in the Morning Orders. The Genl Desires all the troops in the 9th, 11th And 12th Regts Except those on Duty to Be Brougt to Attend the Duties of the day in a decent and Cleanly Manner.

Mitchell Orderly Book (NHi).

1. On 16 Mar., Congress had passed William Livingston's resolution recommending that Friday, 17 May, be observed by the colonies as "a day of humiliation, fasting and prayer." The resolution went on to implore God's assistance "to frustrate the cruel purposes of our unnatural enemies; and by inclining their hearts to justice and benevolence, prevent the further effusion of kindred blood. But if, continuing deaf to the voice of reason and humanity, and inflexibly bent on desolation and war, they constrain us to repel their hostile invasions by open resistance, that it may please the Lord of Hosts, the God of Armies, to animate our officers and soldiers with invincible fortitude, to guard and protect them in the day of battle, and to crown the continental arms, by sea and land, with victory and success." (*JCC*, 4: 208–9)

## General Greene's Orders

[Long Island, N.Y.] 18 May 1776

Complaints Having Been made by the Inhabitants Near the Mill Pond that Some of the Soldiers Come there to swim In Open View of the Women and that they Come out of the Water and Run up Naked to the Houses with a Design to Insult and Wound the Modesty of female Decency. Tis with Concern that the General finds Himself under the Disagreeable Necessity of Expressing His disapprobation of such a Beastly Conduct. Who Ever Has Been so Void of Shame as to act such an Infamous part, Let them ⟨veil⟩ their past disgrace by their future good Behaviour, for depend upon it any New Instance of such Scandelous Conduct Will Be Punish'd With the Utmost Severity. This is Not Meant to Prohibit the troops from Going into the Water to Bathe, but Going in in Proper Places. Where is the Modesty, Virtue and Sobriety of the New England People for which they have been so Remarkable? Is a Good Character of a Soldier of No Value When it is Esteemed so Great a Blessing as a Citizen? What a miserable Change from a sober, Virtuous and Decent People into a Loose, Disorderly and Shameless sett of [*incomplete*]. Is there No Ambition Left Alive but that of Appearing the Most abandon? Have the troops No Regard for the Reputation of the Company or Regts to Which they Belong or for the Colony from Which they came? Have the troops Come Abroad for No Other Purpose than to Render themselves both obnoxious And Rediculous? ⟨Our Enemies have sought to Fix a Stigma upon the New England People as being Rude and Barbarous in their manners and unprincipled in their Conduct. For Heavens Sake dont let your Behaviour serve as an Example to confirm their Observations.[1] The Genl flatters himself notwithstanding the Complaints that have been made, the offenders are but few, but he is determin'd those few shall not have it in their power to bring Disgrase upon the whole Brigade.

The taking the Peoples Oysters out of the Beds where they have planted them is also complain'd of. The Troops are forbid to touch any for the future under such curcumstances. Is not the Crime of Indecency a sufficient Vice, but Robbery must be added to it to qualify it?

All the Armourers in the 9th 11th and 12th Regements to Parade at the Generals Quarters toMorrow Morning at 8 oClock. ⟩

Mitchell Orderly Book (NHi). Portions in angle brackets have been supplied from Henshaw Orderly Book (MWA).

1. If NG seems in this wordy order to have overreacted to a minor and amusing impropriety, it was undoubtedly because of a sensitivity to the criticism levelled at all troops by the numerous loyalist sympathizers on Long Island. There is, in fact, a hint of mockery in his indignant phrases.

## General Greene and Lord Stirling[1] to George Washington

[From New York, 18 May 1776. At request of GW, they recommend one of two lieutenants to fill post of captain in Col. (Samuel) Wyllys's regiment. ALS (Washington Papers: DLC) 1 p.]

1. William Alexander (1726–83), known to his associates as Lord Stirling from an unsubstantiated title he used, had carried on Charles Lee's planned fortifications on Long Island with great vigor. When promoted to brigadier in March, NG had objected to the advancement at the expense of a worthy New Englander, but they eventually became the best of friends; and in the spring of 1777, NG made Stirling's home in Basking Ridge, N.J., his headquarters. Stirling's nephew, William S. Livingston, the son of the New Jersey governor, became NG's aide in Aug. 1776. At the battle of Long Island in Aug. (which illness prevented NG from participating in), Stirling's intrepid leadership in a hopeless engagement became legendary. Although captured in the battle, he was soon exchanged. For a modern biography, see Valentine, *Lord Stirling*.

## To George Washington

Dear Sir                                    Long Island [N.Y.] May 21th 1776

From the last accounts from Great Britain it appears absolutely necessary that there should be an augmentation of the American forces in consequence of which I suppose there will be several promotions. As I have no desire of quiting the service, I hope the Congress will take no measures that will lay me under the disagreeable necessity of doing it.[1] I have ever found my self exceeding happy under your Excellencys command. I wish my abillitie to deserve was equal to my inclination to merit; how far I have succeeded in my endeavors I submit to your Excellencys better Judgment. I hope I shall never be more fond of promotion than studious to merit it. Modesty will forever forbid me to apply to that House for any favors. I consider my self immediately under your Excellencys protection and look up to you for Justice. Every man feels him self wounded where he finds him self neglected, and that in propotion as he is conscious of endeavoring to merit attention. I shall be satisfied with any measures that the Congress shall take that has not a direct tendency to degrade me in the Publick estimation. ⟨A measure⟩ of that sort would sink me in my own esteem and render me spiritless and uneasy in my situation and consequently unfit for the service. I wish for nothing more than Justice either upon a principle of merit or Rank and will at all times rest satisfied when your Excellency tells me I ought to be. I feel my self strongly attacht to the cause, to the Continental Congress, and to your Excellencys person, and I should consider it a great misfortune to be deprivd of an opportunity of takeing an active part in the support of the one and in the promotion of the other.

But should any thing take place contrary to my wishes, which might furnish me with a sufficient Reason for quiting the service yet I will not do it until the danger and difficulties appears less than at present. Believe me to be with the highest respect your Excellencys most Obedient humble servant

N GREENE

ALS (Washington Papers: DLC). Portion in angle brackets from Force, *Archives* (4) 6: 536.

1. One measure that Congress might take to cause him to quit would be the negative action of overlooking him when advancing brigadier generals to major generals. Congress did not overlook him; along with Heath, Spencer, and Sullivan he was elected a major general two and a half months later (*JCC*, 5: 641). It is almost certain that Washington would have made the recommendation without this importuning letter. It is also likely that John Adams strongly supported his advancement.

## From Captain James Wilkinson[1]

La Chine May 24th 12 oClock at Night 1776
My Dear Sir                    About 12 miles from Montreal
We are now in a sweet Situation; a part of the Garrison at Detroit in Conjunction with Indians and Canadians to the amount of one Thousand men have made themselves masters of Colonel Beattes [Bedel] Regiment who were station'd about nine Miles from this place among the Cedars, and have cut off our Freind Major Sherburne with 140 Men, who were detach'd to releive the Regiment which defended itself in a little fort. The Major with that Courage which marked his Character, pushed his way after an ingagement of four hours into the Fort, and was afterwards Obliged to yeild for want of Amunition and provision, since which time General Arnold with a handfull of Men have been Throwing up a Breast work here in Order to stop the Enemies progress, and had indeed meditated a plan of Attacking them, but Alass so astonishingly are matters Conducted in this Quarter that Notwithstanding the Generals most pressing solicitations, and the length of time since he took possession of this post, we cannot now muster more than 450 men, whilst the proximity and movements of the Enemy assure us that we shall be attacked within Six hours. Their Drums were heard this Evening at our Camp and a man of mine was Shot thro the Thigh within half a mile of it by an

Indian who took off a prisoner; but the Morning dawns, that morn big with the Fate of a few, a handfull of brave Fellows. I shall do my part but remember if I fall I am sacraficed. May God bless you eaqual to your Merits. Vale

JAMES WILKINSON

ALS (CSmH).
1. James Wilkinson (1757–1825), whose long, adventurous life is associated with almost endless intrigue and machinations, was only nineteen when he served briefly under NG at the siege of Boston. In Sept. 1775 he accompanied Arnold to Quebec. (*DAB*) From the tone of the letter, it would seem to be one of several he sent NG during the Canadian venture. NG maintained an acquaintance with Wilkinson throughout the war, chiefly because Wilkinson married the sister of Clement Biddle, one of NG's closest friends and associates after 1776, but their relationship was never close. A contemporary copy of the letter is found in the Papers of the Continental Congress (DNA), forwarded to Congress by NG or Washington for the intelligence it contained on the Canadian sector.

## General Greene's Orders

[Long Island, N.Y., 25 May 1776. Committee of officers to determine for commissary and quartermasters which provisions are acceptable. Men who are out after retreat or any sentry who allows them back in to be punished. Officers permitting negligence of duty by guards to be reported. Field officer of the day to instruct officers on their guard detail. Only general officers to be admitted by day to forts where there are cannon and ammunition except by leave of commander of the guard; at night, to be admitted, general officers must have permission of the commanding officer. Henshaw Orderly Book (MWA) 2 pp.]

## To John Adams[1]

Brookline [Brooklyn] Long Island [N.Y.]
Sir                                                 May 26 [24], 1776[2]
The peculiar situation of American affairs renders it necessary to adopt every measure that will engage people in the service. The danger and hardships that those are subject to who engage in the service more than those who do not, is obvious to every body which has the least acquaintance with service. Tis that which makes it so difficult to recruit. The large force that is coming against America will make it necessary to augment our forces. If I am to form a Judgment of the success of Recruiting from what is past, the time is too short to raise the Troops and be in readiness to meet the Enemy and as every argument has been made use of upon the present plan of recruiting to

engage people in the service there must be some new motives added to quicken the motions of the recruiting parties.

From the approaching danger, recruiting will grow more and more difficult. If the Congress was to fix a certain support upon every Officer and Soldier that got maim'd in the service or upon the families of those that were kild it would have as happy an influence towards engageing people in the service and inspire those engagd with as much courage as any measure that can be fixt upon.[3] I think it is nothing more than common Justice, neither; it puts those in and out of [the] Army upon a more equal footing than at present. I have not time to add anything more. Major Frazier now waiting for this. The desperate game you have got to play and the uncertainty of War may render every measure that will increase the Force and strength of the American Army worthy consideration. When I have more leisure I will presume so much upon your good nature as to write you upon some other matters. Believe me to be with great respect yours

NATHANAEL GREENE

ALS (MHi).

1. NG had met Adams, probably for the first time, at a council of war meeting held at Washington's headquarters in Cambridge the previous Jan. They became better acquainted at another meeting, and in the months that followed, their relationship developed into friendship. (See above, NG to brother Christopher, 29 Jan.) This is the first of some twenty letters between the two men before July 1777, when their friendship broke off after Adams reprimanded NG for writing an impolitic letter to Congress. (See Adams to NG, 7 July 1777, below.)

One of the most influential members of Congress, Adams was glad to learn about the army by corresponding directly with the generals under Washington's command, seldom going through the chain of command to initiate such an exchange. NG, for his part, was glad to have the ear of so important a member; he may well have hoped also (as in this letter) that Adams would help further his ambition to become a major general, since it followed by only five days his letter to Washington on the subject (see above, 21 May).

2. He misdated the letter; see NG to Adams, 2 June, below.

3. NG seemed more concerned with the needs of the disabled and the families of those who died in service than most of his fellow generals. Washington, for example, is not known to have initiated any congressional action on pensions, although he did not oppose them. Adams was sympathetic to Greene's suggestions but had little confidence that he could influence Congress (see below, NG's letter of 2 June). Nevertheless, partly at Adams's urging, Congress passed a resolution on 26 Aug. which provided half pay to anyone "so disabled . . . as to render him incapable afterwards of getting a livelihood," provided he obtained a certificate of disability signed by his commanding officer and attending surgeon. If the disabled men were capable of performing guard or garrison duty, they could be organized into a "corps of invalids." (JCC, 5: 702–5) Congress, however, did nothing at that time for the families of soldiers who were killed or died in service.

Washington wrote Hancock on 29 Aug. that the solutions were "founded much in Justice, and I should hope may be productive of many salutary consequences" (Fitzpatrick, GW, 5: 496).

## General Greene's Orders

[Camp Brooklyn, N.Y., 29 May 1776. Common passengers may use ferry until 10:00 P.M.; no soldier may do so after retreat without permission. Any one snapping his lock without orders to be confined for two days on bread and water.[1] Countersign to be "discovered" only to those with right to know it; to be given to the guard softly. The general wishes duty to be carried out as if the "Enemy was Encamped in the Neighbourhood" since bad habits are "difficult to get over." Henshaw Orderly Book (MWA) 2 pp.]

1. Snapping the lock of a musket wore out flint and steel, both of which were still in short supply.

## From Lieutenant John Holiday[1]

Sir                                    Far Rockway [N.Y.] May 29th 1776
    I send you three Prisoners whose testimony, and the circum-stances against them gives me the strongest Reason to Believe the[y] came for a supply of provision, or some other Necessarys for the Enemy.
    Last Sunday we saw them come with a sloop from the west and go toward the East end of the Island. I sent a sergeant and twelve men after them, to take them, if the[y] came in any of the inlets. About fourteen miles to the eastard the[y] came in sight of the sloop where she was ancored, and the[y] got Boats and went in to where the sloop Lay and took these prisoners and seven firlocks, which the prisoners say belongs to men that Left them Sunday evening which I suppose to be after Loading for the sloop. I am Sir your Huml Servt
                                                        JNO HOLIDAY

Cy (Washington Papers: DLC).
    1. John Holiday served as lieutenant in Col. Edward Hand's Pennsylvania Rifle Regiment, which was assigned to guard the southern coastline of Long Island. (Heit-man, *Register*, spells the name Holliday.)

## To Colonel Henry Knox[1]

Dear sir                         Camp on Long Island [N.Y.] May 29, 1776
    I am oblig'd to defer going up to Kings Bridge[2] till another day, being under an obligation to go to New Uttrich [Utrecht] this morning and to wait on the Committee of this town this afternoon about some business. Colo Chambers reported last Night that two Ships was seen off in the offing comeing in.[3] I will indeavor to see you this afternoon and fix upon some other time for Reconnoitering the ground up and about Kings Bridge. My Compliments and Mrs Greens to your Lady.[4]

Beleive me to be with the highest esteem your most obedt humble servant

N GREENE

ALS (MHi).

1. Henry Knox (1750–1806) was the portly young colonel who had brought the cannon from Fort Ticonderoga (see above, NG to Catharine W. Greene, 13 Jan. 1776, and end of note 2, NG to Jacob, 8 Feb.). Like NG a self-made man, before the war he had operated a Boston bookstore, where he had familiarized himself with military works. In 1772 he joined the famed Boston Grenadier Corps and shortly thereafter married Lucy Flucker—in defiance of her father, the royal secretary of the colony and later a leading loyalist. At the outbreak of war, he joined the army, where he soon attracted Washington's attention. In Nov. 1775 he was made colonel and chief of artillery (most of which was still in far-off Ticonderoga).

Knox's "jubilant personality" (as his biographer puts it) won the affection of Washington and his general officers. Knox and NG gradually became close friends. The trip to inspect Kingsbridge (note 2 below) was the first of several such reconnaissances they shared in the next year. At the low point in NG's life—the fall of Ft. Washington—it was to Knox that he spilled out his heart (see below, his letter of 17 Nov. 1776). In Dec. 1776 Knox was made brigadier general, and in Nov. 1781, major general. He was secretary of war under both the Confederation government and the Constitution. After NG's death in 1786, he was a devoted friend to Catharine, helping her to obtain restitution from Congress for NG's wartime losses. The quote describing his personality is from Callahan, *Knox*, (p. 34).

2. Kings Bridge (sometimes Kingsbridge) connected the northern tip of Manhattan Island with the mainland across the Spuyten Duyvel. There had been rumors the loyalists planned to blow up the bridge, and Knox was ordered to check the defenses.

3. Col. James Chambers served in the Pennsylvania Rifle Regiment that was guarding the coastline.

4. This is the first record of Catharine's trip to New York. Presumably she was staying in New York City at the time, as was Lucy Knox, who had just come down from Connecticut with her infant son (Callahan, *Knox*, pp. 63–64). There was no love lost between the two women.

## General Greene's Orders

[Long Island, N.Y.] June 1st 1776

A sergeant and 20 men to parade immediately to clear out Mr. Livingston's Dock filled up by the Picket pealings. No pealings[1] to be thrown into the dock for the future.

Six o'clock this evening the troops to be all under arms to man the works.

Five Companys of Col. Varnum's Regiment upon the right in fort Box. The other three upon the right of fort Green.

Col. Hitchcock's regiment to man fort Putnam and the redoubt upon the left of it. 5 Companies in the first and 3 in the Last.

Five Companies of Col. Little's regiment in Fort Green and 3 in the oblong square.

The independent Company to be reserved in the rear of fort Green.[2]

Colonel Moses Little Orderly Book. Reprinted from Johnston, *NY 1776*, part 2, p. 15.

1. The bark peeled from the trees that were sharpened and used in an abatis or palisade.

2. See map, p. 231, for the location and plan of the five forts. From right to left (south to north) they were Fts. Box and Greene, Oblong Redoubt, Ft. Putnam, and Redoubt on the left. Ft. Box was named after NG's brigade major, Daniel Box. He was a former British soldier, a veteran of the French war, who had helped to train the regiments in NG's brigade during the early months of the war. After serving under NG in Boston, he helped to lay out the fortifications on Long Island and at Ft. Lee (see NG to Pickering, 24 Aug. 1779, below, on his career). Ft. Greene, apparently named by Colonel Little, was the largest of the group. As noted in NG orders above, it accommodated eight companies. Ft. Putnam was named after Col. Rufus Putnam (1738–1824), a kinsman of Gen. Israel Putnam and the man responsible for the entire line of fortification. Putnam had won fame by fortifying Dorchester Heights, a move that hastened the British evacuation of Boston. He was later a brigadier general and surveyor general during Washington's presidency (*DAB*).

The five forts were interconnected by a strong line of entrenchment. On the effectiveness of the line of fortifications that were built under Greene's direction, see below, NG to Jacob, 30 Aug. 1776. The coastal forts that the line of fortification was designed to protect were Fts. Stirling and Defiance and Governor's Island. (See map, p. 231.) Together they constituted the first line of defense against British ships entering East River. General Lee had decided that the North (Hudson) River was too wide for shore installations to protect New York Island. The best he could recommend, work on which was going forward at the same time the Long Island defenses were progressing, were redoubts and street barricades that would cost the British dearly to overcome. An excellent description of the forts and the basis for the map is found in Johnston, *NY 1776*, part 1, pp. 67–84.

## To John Adams

Sir                                    Camp on Long Island [N.Y.] June 2d 1776

I have just receivd your favor of the 26th of May in answer to mine of the 24th.[1] You must not expect me to be a very exact correspondent; my circumstances will not always admit of it. When I have opportunity I will write you with freedom. If any information I can give you should be of service I shall be amply paid. I know your time is too precious to be spent in answering Letters; but a line from you at all times will be very acceptable, with such intelligence as you are at liberty to give.

By your Letter I have the happiness to find you agree with me in sentiment for the establishing a support for those that gets disabled in the army or militia; but I am sorry to find, at the same time, that you are very doubtful of its takeing effect. I could wish the Congress to think seriously of the matter, both with respect to the Justice and utillity of the measure. Is it not inhuman to suffer those that have fought nobly in the cause to be reduceed to the necessity of geting a support by common Charity? Does this not millitate with the free and independant principles which we are endeavoring to support? Is it not equitable that the State who receives the benefit should be at the

Camp on Long Island May 23 1776

Dear Sir

I am oblig'd to defer going up to Kings Bridge till another day – being under an Obligation to go to New Uttricht this morning and to wait on the Committee of that Town this Afternoon about some business – Colo Chambers reported last Night that there There was seen off in the offing some ingins I will endeavor to see you this Afternoon and fix upon some other time for Reconnoitering the ground up & about Kings Bridge My Compliments & Mrs Greens to your Lady Believe me to be with the highest esteem your most Obed't humble servant

N Greene

*From the original at Massachusetts Historical Society*

expence? The Community collectively considerd pays nothing more for the establishing a support than if they do not; for those that get disabled must be supported by the Continent in general or the Provinces in particular. If the Continent establishes no support, by the fate of War some Colonies might be grieviously burthened. I cannot see upon what principle any Colony can encourage the Inhabitants to engage in the army when the state that employs them refuses a support to the unfortunate. I think it would be right and just for every Government to furnish their equal propotion of the Troops or contribute to the support of those that are sent by other Colonies.

Can there be any thing more humiliateing than this consideration to those that are in the army, or to those that have a mind to come in it? If I meet with a misfortune I shall be reduced to the necessity of beging my bread. Is not this degradeing and distressing a part of the human species that deserves a better fate? On the other hand if there was a support establish't what confidence would it give to those engag'd, what encouragement to those that are not. Good policy points out the measure. Humanity calls for it, and Justice claims it at your Hands.

I apprehend the dispute to be but in its infancy; nothing should be neglected to encourage People to engage or to render those easy contented and happy that are engag'd. Good covering[2] is an Object of the first consideration. I know of nothing that is more discourageing than the want of it; it renders the Troops very uncomfortable and generally unhealthy. A few Troops well accomodateed, healthy and spirited will do more service to the state that employs them than a much larger number that are sickly, dispirited and discontented. This is the unhappy state of the army at this time, ariseing from the badness of the Tents. His Excellency has order'd every thing to be done to remedy the Evil that is in his power, but before the remedy can take place the health of the Troops will receive a severe wound.

From the nature of the dispute and the manner of furnishing the state with Troops too much care cannot be taken of those that engage; otherwise some particular Goverments more public spirited than others may be depopulated.

Good Officers is the very Soul of an Army; the activity and Zeal of the Troops entirely depends upon the degree of animation given them by their officers. I think it was Sir William Pitts maxim to pay well and hang well to have a good army.[3] The field officers in general and the Colos of Regiments in particular think themselves grieviously burthened upon the present establishment; few if any of that Rank that are worth retaining in service will continue if any dependance is to be made upon the discontent that appears. They say and I believe with too much truth that their pay and provision will not defray their expences. Another great grieveance they complain on is they are oblige to act as factors for the Regiment, Subject to many losses without any extraordinary allowance for their trouble, drawing from the Continental stores by wholesale and delivering out to the Troops by Retail.[4] This business has been attended with much perplexity and accompanyed with very great losses where the Colos have not been good accomptants [accountants?]. This is no part of the duty of a Col of a Regiment, and the mode in which the business has been conducted, too much of their time has been engrossed in that employment for the good of the service. There should be an agent for Each Regiment to provide the Troops with cloathing on the easiest terms, allowed to draw money for that purpose occasionally, to be stopt out of the pay abstract. Those agents could provide seasonably, fetch their goods from a distance and prevent those local impositions that arises upon every remove of the army.

The dispute begins to be reducd to a National principle, and the longer it continues the more that Idea will prevail. People engagd in the service in the early part of the dispute without any consideration of pay reward, few if any thought of its continuance; but its duration will reduce all that have not independant Fortunes to attend to their family concerns. And if the present pay of those in the service is insufficient for the support of them[selves] and their families they must consequently quit it.[5] The Novelty of the Army may engage others but you cannot immagin the injury the Army sustains by the loss of every good Officer. A young Officer without any experience in the Military Art or knowledge of mankind, unless he has a very uncommon Genius, must be totally unfit to command a Regiment.

I observe in the Resolves of Congress they have reservd to themselves the right of rewarding by promotion according to merit.[6] The reserve may be right but the exercise will be dangerous, often injurious and sometimes very unjust. [Of] two Persons of very unequal merit the inferior may get promoted over the superior if a single instance of bravery is a sufficient Reason for such promotion. There is no doubt but that its right and just to reward singular merit, but the publick applause accompanying every brave Action is a noble reward.

Where one officer is promoted over the head of another, if he has spirit enough to be fit for service, it lays him under the necessity of quiting it. It is a publick intimation that he is unfit for promotion and consequently undeserving his present appointment. For my own part I would never give any Legislative body an opportunity to humiliate me but once. I should think the Generals Recommendation is necessary to warrant a promotion out of the Regular channel. For Rank is of such importance in the Army and so delicate are ⟨the sentiments respecting it that very strong reasons ought to be given for going out of the proper channel, or else it will not be satisfactory to the army in general or to the party in particular.

The Emision of such large sums of money increases the price of things in proportion to the sums emited—the money has but a nominal value.⟩ The evil does not arise from a depreciation altogether but from there being larger sums Emited than is necessary for a circulating medium. If the Evil increases it will starve the army, for the pay of the Troops at the prices things are sold at will scarsely keep the Troops decently cloathed. Nothwithstanding what I write I will engage to keep the Troops under my command as easy and contented as any in the army.

I observe you dont think the game you are playing is so desperate as I immagin. You doubtless are much better acquainted with the resources that are to be had in case of any misfortune than I am, but I flatter my self I know the History, Strength, and state of the army almost as well as any in it, both with respect to the goodness of the Troops or the abillities of the officers. Dont be too confident the fate of War is very uncertain. Little incidents has given rise to great events. Suppose this army should be defeated, two or three of the leading ⟨Generals killed, our stores and magazines all lost, I would not be answerable for the consequences that such a stroke might produce in American politicks. You think the present army assisted by the militia is sufficient to oppose the force of Great Britain, formidable as it appears on paper. I can assure you⟩ its necessary to make great allowances in the calculation of our strength from the Establishment or else you'l be greatly deceivd. I am confident the force of America if properly exerted will prove superior to all her Enemies, but I would risque nothing to chance. It is easy to disband when it is impossible to raise Troops.

I approve your plan of encourageing our own Troops rather than seduceing theirs; let us fight and beat them fairly, and free our Country from oppression without departing from the principles of honnor, Truth or Justice. The conditions you propose are very honnorable, but I fear whether they are altogether equal to the emergency of the times, for mankind being much more influenced by present profit than remote advantagies, People will consider what benefit they are immediately to receive and take their Resolutions accordingly.

If the Force of Great Britain should prove near equal to what it has been represented, a large Augmentation will be necessary. If the present Offers should not be sufficient to induce People to engage in the Army, You will be oblige to Augment the bounty, and perhaps at a time when that order of People will have it in their power to make their own conditions or distress the state.[7]

As I have wrote a great deal and the Doctor waiting I shall add no more only my hearty wishes for your health and happiness. Believe me to be with great esteem your most obedient humble servant.

N GREENE

ALS (MHi). Portions in angle brackets are from G. W. Greene transcripts (CSmH).

1. Adams's letter not found. Since he was in Philadelphia, it seems unlikely he could have received and answered NG's letter of 24 May by 26 May. Which dates are wrong has not been determined. Adams's detailed answer to this letter of 2 June is printed below—22 June.

2. The reference is to shelter, not clothing.

3. The reference is obscure.

4. By a resolution of 17 June 1776, Congress forbade any officer to "suttle or sell to the soldiers" (*JCC*, 5: 449), but the practice of which NG speaks was dealing in items furnished by the army at a price to the men—including clothing. It is not clear whether the difference between wholesale and retail represented a profit to the colonel. From the complaints, one could presume there were no profits.

5. Adams was not the most sympathetic member of Congress to listen to complaints about officers' pay. He had reported in Congress in Feb. that people in New England were "averse to giving large pay to officers" because it "only gives them an opportunity of extravagance" (James Duane's "Notes of Debates," 22 Feb. 1776, printed in Burnett, *Letters*, 1: 360). Below, in his June 22 answer to this letter, he asked, "Is there not too much Extravagance and too little Economy among the officers?" In Aug., Henry Knox added his pleadings to NG's in a letter to Adams: "I wish you to consult Marshal Saxe on the matter of paying the troops. I am not speaking for myself, but I am speaking in the behalf of a great number of worthy men who wish to do the country every service in their power at a less price than the ruin of themselves and families." (Cited by Hatch, *Administration*, p. 78)

Inflation daily diminished the pay of both officers and men. On 24 Sept. Washington wrote Congress in much the same words as had NG and Knox—that the officer says he "cannot ruin himself and Family to serve his Country" (Fitzpatrick, *GW*, 4: 108). Other members of Congress were receiving letters similar to NG's and Knox's; on 7 Oct., Congress raised officers' pay to the following levels: colonels, $75 per month; lieutenant colonels, $60; majors, $50; captains, $40; lieutenants, $27; ensigns, $20; quartermasters, $27.50; and adjutants, $40 (*JCC*, 5: 853).

6. Although the resolution of 10 May (basing promotion on merit) applied to all officers, NG was probably thinking about himself and the possibility of being passed over. Since he was eighth among brigadier generals, any substantial enlargement of the Continental army would add more brigadiers and move him to the rank of major general—provided the old rules of seniority applied. See his letter to Washington of 21 May, above.

7. On 26 June, Congress voted a bounty of $10 to every noncommissioned officer and soldier who would enlist for three years (*JCC*, 5: 483).

## General Greene's Orders

[Long Island, N.Y.] 3 June 1776

One Captain, two Lieutenants, one Ensign, four Serjeants, four and Fifty Privates from each of Col Varnums, Hitchcocks and Littles Regiments all to have good Arms with Bayonets, every Man to be provided with Twenty Rounds of Cartridges, one spare flint, Two Days Provision Cook'd and half a Pint of Rum, the whole to be ready to March to Morrow Morning by 3 oClock. Every Man to take his Blanket and none to go but such as are decently Dressed.[1]

Henshaw Orderly Book (MWA).

1. The party was to round up the loyalists on Long Island. When Washington left for a two-week trip to Philadelphia on 21 May, he told his second in command, Gen. Israel Putnam, that the N.Y. Provincial Congress had a plan for "Siezing the principal Tories, and disaffected Person's . . . on Long Island, in this city, and the country round about." If Putnam should be called upon for military support on Long Island, Washington continued, "General Green will, tho' not in person perhaps, have a principal share in ordering the detachments from his Brigade on Long Island" (Fitzpatrick, *GW*, 5: 69–70).

The loyalists of New York, who were more numerous than in New England, had been the cause of spirited debate among patriots long before NG took command on Long Island. The previous winter the N.Y. Congress had informed Washington of Gov. Tryon's efforts to raise an army of loyalists. In Oct. 1775 Tryon had fled to a British warship in N.Y. harbor, from where two months later he tried unsuccessfully to get three thousand muskets from Howe in Boston (Smith, *Loyalists*, p. 41). At Cambridge in early Jan., Gen. Charles Lee had asked Washington's permission to raise a group of volunteers to secure N.Y. and to bring about the "expulsion or suppression of that dangerous banditti of Tories, who have appeared in Long Island." Lee went on to warn, "Not to crush these serpents, before their rattles are grown, would be ruinous" (*Lee Papers*, 1: 235). His request was refused largely because the Committee of Safety was not prepared for hostilities that might ensue (N.Y. Committee of Safety to Lee, 21 Jan. 1776, *Lee Papers*, 1: 242–44).

The strength of the N.Y. loyalists reinforced Howe's resolve to move his army to New York. Although Howe saw the loyalists' role there as political, not military, the N.Y. Provincial Congress had no way of knowing this. With Gov. Tryon in the harbor still communicating with various persons ashore, they had good reason to credit rumors of plots and conspiracies among the Long Islanders. Immediately upon taking command on the island, NG had been faced with the loyalist problem. County committees of safety had arbitrarily jailed some so-called "Tories," requesting that they be tried by courtmartial. Just before relinquishing the Long Island command, Gen. Sullivan, accompanied by NG, had visited the jail and had persuaded the patriots that the accused should have a civil trial (Sullivan to Adams, 4 May 1776, Hammond, *Sullivan Papers*, 1: 194–96).

For more on the arrest and detention of loyalists and their activities in New York and Long Island, see below, NG to N.Y. Provincial Congress, 6 June; Nathaniel Woodhull to NG, 6 June; Washington to NG, 20 [21] June; Morris, Jay, and Livingston to NG, 22 June; and Crary and Livingston to NG, 29 June. For a treatment of loyalists on Long Island by one of the first American historians to sympathize with loyalists, see Field, *Long Island*, pp. 1–121, a book written in 1869; see also Onderdonk's two volumes; *NY MSS*, 1; and Alexander C. Flick, *Loyalism in New York during the American Revolution*, (New York: Columbia University Press, 1901).

## To Commissary Joseph Trumbull

Dear Sir                    Camp on Long Island [N.Y.] June 4, 1776

My brothers has shipt to Mr Griffin Greene a quantity of molasses and New England Rum. If the army is in want of those Articles and you can take them off his hands, you would oblige my brethren very much.[1] The prices are high; but believe they can not be got upon more Reasonable terms. Your aid as far as is consistent with your agency will be gratefully Acknowledged by sir your humble servant

NATHL GREENE

ALS (Ct).

1. In a letter to brother Christopher, 7 June, below, NG reported that the offer was "not so large as Griffin expected." He identified his own role in the family venture by saying *"we'l* secure a liveing profit" (italics added). On NG's continued business relations with his brothers and cousin Griffin, see above, note 1, NG to Joseph Trumbull, 9 Aug. 1775.

## To the New York Provincial Congress

Gentlemen:                    Camp on Long-Island, [N.Y.] June 6, 1776.

I send you prisoner Mr. John Livingston and his barber, taken into custody by order of the Committee of Jamaica, as you will see by the papers accompanying this.[1] He was delivered by the Captain of the Minute Company to Lieutenant-Colonel Cornwell [Ezekiel Cornell], who commanded a detachment from this division of the army, by order of General Putnam, to Hempstead. The Captain requested that he might be delivered safely into the hands of the Congress; accordingly, I have sent him [Livingston] and his barber under the care of a number of officers. It is notorious that many of the inhabitants of Queens County are very unfriendly;[2] arms, I am informed by the officers of my brigade, are daily carrying by the camp down into that part of the Island; and the inhabitants here say they are the very people that are known to be unfriendly. I should be glad to know whether you approve or disapprove of such a practice. The officers tell me that not less than four or five hundred stand of arms have gone by the camp within a few days. I have given orders to stop all for the future, until I know your pleasure. Believe me to be, with the greatest respect, your most obedient, humble servant,

NATHANAEL GREENE

Reprinted from Force, *Archives* (4) 6: 1375, from the minutes of the N.Y. Provincial Congress (or Convention, as it was also called). The letter is preceded by this note: "Sundry Officers from General Greene's camp attending, with John Livingston, Jun., a prisoner in their custody, sent in a Letter from General Greene; which was read, and is in the words following, to wit:"

1. The committee in Jamaica charged that Livingston failed to produce furlough papers. When the Congress questioned him, they learned that he had deliberately not shown his papers. They decided that, since he had treated the committee with contempt, he should ask its pardon and pay all expenses. When he refused to apologize, he was ordered to be held in "close custody" until further orders. (Force, *Archives* (4) 6: 1376–77). See also the same day, Pres. Woodhull to NG, below.

2. Queens County, in the central part of Long Island, was far more populous than Kings County to the west—where NG's brigade was encamped.

## From President Nathaniel Woodhull[1]
## of the New York Provincial Congress

Sir                                    New York June 6, 1776

Your letter of this day, with the prisoners mentioned in it, have been safely delivered to this Congress. They direct me to return you their thanks for your vigilance on this occasion, and assure you that a continuance of the same attention will be exceedingly agreeable to them. They are alarmed at being informed that so great a number of arms have been carried into the country; and, as they passed in view of the camp, regret they were not detained, and the persons concerned in it apprehended. Should you be able to discover where the arms you allude to are deposited, or the persons who have been or may be concerned in that or the like business, they authorize and request you to take them and the arms found with them into custody, and send them under a proper guard to this Congress, and the names of the witnesses against them.[2] I am, very respectfully. By order.

Reprinted from Force, *Archives* (4) 6: 1376, from minutes of N.Y. Provincial Congress. The letter was drafted by "Mr. Jay and Mr. Morris" and ordered to be signed by "the President and transmitted to General Greene by the Officer who was the bearer of General Greene's Letter."

1. Nathaniel Woodhull (1722–76), had seen extensive service in the French and Indian War. He had been active in New York politics before the Revolution, serving in the Assembly during 1768–75, and in May of 1775 took a place in the new Provincial Congress. In Oct. 1775 he was appointed brigadier general of New York troops. After the British attack on Long Island, 27 Aug. 1776, he was cut off from support and was subsequently captured and wounded. He died from his wounds 20 Sept. and was to be remembered as a hero and martyr. (*DAB*)

2. There is no evidence that the arms were found.

## General Greene's Orders

[Camp on Long Island, N.Y., 7 June 1776. Until arms are repaired, pikes[1] to be placed as follows: Ft. Greene, 100; Ft. Box, 30; Oblong Redoubt, 20; Ft. Putnam, 50; "works on left," 20. Spears to be cleaned weekly. Ferry Guard to stop all arms coming to Long Island, report who has them and their destination to the general immediately. Sentries at the (Brooklyn?) church to stop arms going east of city and report names and abodes of persons stopped. Mitchell Orderly Book (NHi) 1 p.]

1. A long spear consisting of a wooden shaft and steel point.

## To Christopher Greene[1]

Dear sir                          Camp on Long Island [N.Y.] June 7, 1776

Your favor of the 25 of last month came safe to hand.[2] I thank you for the information of my family connections. Mrs Greene has arrivd safe here and tolerably healthy. I was very glad to hear of our little shaver.[3] I wish youd be so kind as to continue the information. Griffin arrivd a few days, past but the markets are much chang'd but

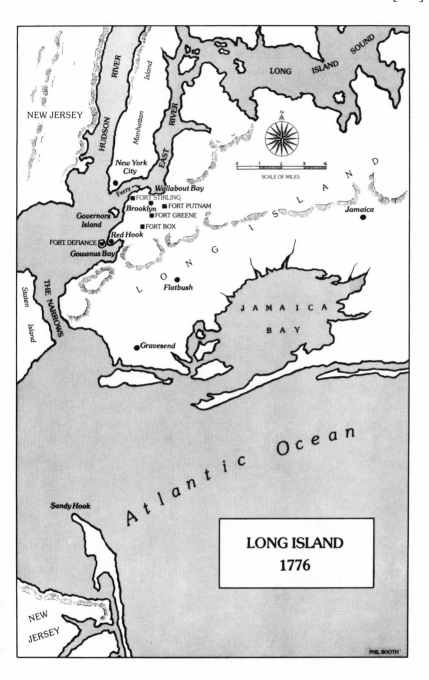

LONG ISLAND
1776

the Comisary General has made him an offer in consequence of a Letter I wrote him, that we'l secure a liveing profit, tho not so large as Griffin expected.[4] Molasses 5/4, N E Rum 6/3. Mrs Greene informs me your good Lady is fat and healthier than ever She new [knew?] her to be. A great blessing amidst the surrounding troubles. I should have wrote her, but I am continually engagd in the pursuit of one thing or another; and besides I have so many things crowding upon my mind at once that I find myself very unfit for Letter writeing. To collect and Arrange my thoughts is a difficult task where new objects are continually presenting themselves to view. I lament the loss of her poor Daddy, as well for the publick as the family sake.[5] Mr John Adams writes me he is greatly mist in Congress. He was the fast and undismayed friend of his Country. Mr Ellery may be a very good man but in no respect to be compard with the other.[6]

The unfortunate Campaign at Quebeck has removd all hopes of redeeming her brother. I have not heard from him only by a deserter that got out of Quebeck since he was made Prisoner. Another defeat has happend a little above Monttreal at a place cald the Cedars. Col Beattes [Timothy Bedel] Regt of New Hampshire militia was stationd at the Cedars in a small fort. They were Attackt by the Eighth Regt of the Kings Troops joind by about Seven or Eight hundred Indians. Major Sherburn with a detachment from Colo [John] Patersons Regiment of 150 men was orderd to throw themselves in the Fort. The Major[7] effected it after about four hours engagement but was Oblige[d] to submit at discretion a few Days after for want of Ammunition and Provision and are now all Prisoners. The face of things looks very unfavorable in that quarter. I fear matters have been very ill conducted in that department to say nothing worse.

We are now begining to be in expectation of the Enemy. The Congress begins to think it time to levy more Troops. Their policy is so narrow and Oeconomical that I fear they are makeing work for Repentance. They do not seem to have any Systematical plan. The Delegates of some Governments Clogs the necessary measures suggested by others; and thus the Chariot goes heavily on. That dam'd Idea of Reconciliation is continually damping and dividing the Assembly.[8] I wish the Devil would fetch it out of Congress and them that holds it up to view. Pitts maxim was to pay well and hang well if you intended to have a good Army. The present narrow policy will starve every man of merit and [in] the Army and discourage others from entering. However, I hear they are now going to order a large body of Troops into pay—20,000 here in addition to what we have got, 6,000 at Philadelphia, &c &c. This will be doing something. There has been a great creation of General officers. Whitcomb of Massachusetts Bay is made a Brigadier General, Mifflin and Mercer are made Brigd-General, General Gates a Major General.[9] How many more will be made I know not. I wish it was as easy to send men equal to the command as it is to appoint them.

The Fortifications in about this City are exceeding strong, and strengthning every Day. But the New England Colonies without the least fortification is easier defended than this Colony fortified in the strongest manner, owing to the different dispositions of the People. Tories here are as plenty as Whigs are with you. It is exceeding expensive liveing here; to live in Charactor equal to my Rank in the Army costs four or five Dollars a Day, and if one dont live up to their Rank they are dispisd by both Soldiers and Citizens. I should be greatly Oblige[d] to you to write me every Opportunity. I will answer you when Opportunity permits. My kind love to your better half and to all my brethren—to Sister Peggy[10] and all the domestick tribe. My Love and Duty to Mother Greene[11] if at Potowomut, in a word remember me to all friends of my old acquaintance. God bless the family with health and shield them from the approaching danger. Believe me to be with the highest respect affectionately yours

N GREENE

Let none read my Letter but the brothers &c.

ALS (MWA).
    1. The letter is unaddressed but references to Samuel Ward, Sr., as father of recipient's wife identifies brother Christopher.
    2. Letter not found.
    3. George Washington Greene, born early in 1776, was being cared for by Christopher and his wife while Catharine was in New York.
    4. See NG to Trumbull, above, 4 June.
    5. Samuel Ward had died of smallpox in Mar. while attending Congress in Philadelphia.
    6. William Ellery (1727–1820) was a graduate of Harvard College who belatedly entered the practice of law in Newport after a varied career. In May he replaced Ward in Congress, serving almost continuously until 1786. (DAB) Although an able man, he was not as influential as Ward. Relations between NG and Ellery were never close. A modern study is William M. Fowler, Jr., *William Ellery: Rhode Island Politico and Lord of Admiralty* (Metuchen, N.J.: Scarecrow Press, 1973).
    7. Henry Sherburne (1747–1824) was a major in the Third R.I. Regiment, serving under NG during the siege of Boston. Taken prisoner at the Cedars, he was soon released. In Jan. 1777 he was appointed colonel and put in command of one of the sixteen new regiments. From 1792 to 1808 he served as general treasurer of R.I. (*R.I. Biog. Cycl.*; Heitman, *Register*)
    8. He is still speaking of Congress. He could not know that on the day he wrote this letter, Richard Henry Lee rose on the floor of Congress to introduce his resolution calling for independence.
    9. Mifflin had been a general since mid-May, but Congress had named Whitcomb and Mercer as brigadiers only two days earlier (5 June, *JCC*, 5: 420).
    John Whitcomb had been a brigadier general in the Mass. militia at war's outbreak and later a colonel in the Continental army. He declined the promotion of 5 June. (Heitman, *Register*)
    Hugh Mercer (1725–77) was a Scottish doctor who had fought at Culloden for the

Young Pretender, Charles Stuart, before emigrating to Pennsylvania. After serving as a colonel in the French and Indian War, he returned to the practice of medicine in Virginia, where he became acquainted with Washington. In July, Mercer was appointed commander of the Flying Camp (see below, note 1, NG to Cooke, 22 July 1776). He was with NG in the autumn of 1776, fought under him at Trenton, and was killed at the battle of Princeton. (*DAB*)

Thomas Mifflin (1744–1800), an educated Philadelphia merchant, was read out of the Society of Friends for his support of the military. He had served in the Congress before becoming Washington's aide, and in Aug. 1775 he became quartermaster general—a post he held, except for a few months in the summer of 1776, until succeeded by NG in Mar. 1778. (*DAB*) Mifflin and NG were never friends. Mifflin thought NG had too great an influence on Washington, and NG criticized Mifflin's running of the quartermaster department. For a modern biography, see Rossman, *Mifflin.*

10. Brother Jacob's wife.
11. NG's stepmother.

## General Greene's Orders

[Camp on Long Island, N.Y., 13 June 1776. Colormen to keep streets clean, cover vaults daily, dig new ones weekly, and attend the hospital. Quartermasters to see that hospital is clean; colonels to appoint nurses for their sick. Since many soldiers have stolen and sold clothes to their fellow soldiers, anyone purchasing clothes from a soldier without leave of their officers will stand to lose the same. Mitchell Orderly Book (NHi) 1 p.]

## General Greene's Orders

[Long Island Camp, N.Y., 14 June 1776. A subaltern, sergeant, and twenty men to mount guard at Red Hook barbette battery every evening. Reprinted from Johnston, *NY 1776*, pt. 2, p. 17.]

## To President Nathaniel Woodhull of the New York Provincial Congress

[Camp on Long Island, N.Y., 14 June 1776]
I have a Brother here from Rhode Island (Mr Jacob Greene) that has an inclination to have the small Pox by Innoculation. He is much exposd often in the execution of the Publick business. He purposes to go upon the Hospital Island and there be Innoculated, and stay till he is properly cleansed.

If the Congress can grant him this Favour without injuring the Publick, shall esteem it a peculiar Kindness.

My Brother also wants to purchase a few small Cannon for a Privateer, he beg the Congress Permission for the same.[1] The Proprietors of the Cannon think it necessary to obtain your consent before they dispose of them, notwithstanding they are private Property.

You'll be kind enough to favour me with the Resolutions of the Congress upon the above Requests which will Oblige Your Most Obedient Humbl Servt

NATHANAEL GREENE

ALS (N). Damaged portions along the right margin of the original letter have been filled out from G. W. Greene transcript (CSmH).
1. Jacob Greene had just been reimbursed for the loss of the sloop *Maryland* and its cargo of salt (see note, NG to Jacob, 22 Jan., above). On 3 July, Jacob, for "self and Griffin Greene," along with five others from East Greenwich and Warwick, applied for letters of marque and reprisal as owners of the thirty-ton sloop *General Greene*. With a crew of thirty under Capt. John Garzia and equipped with four three-pounders, twelve swivel guns, and a quantity of "Muskets, Blunderbusses, Cutlasses, Pistols, Powder, Ball and other Military Stores," the sloop was ready to prey on British shipping (Maritime Papers, Letters of Marque, R-Ar). Although not a subscriber, NG was a part-owner of the privateer that bore his name. Jacob Greene and Co. were also owners of the sloop *Hope*, which on 26 Apr. was bound for St. Croix carrying flour, tobacco, and spermaceti candles (Outward and Inward Entries, R-Ar).

## From President Nathaniel Woodhull of the Provincial Congress of New York[1]

Sir: New-York, June 15, 1776.
    I am directed by the Congress to inform you that they would be very happy in giving your brother permission to be inoculated on Hospital Island,[2] but they cannot help considering that spot as improper for the purpose by reason of its exposed situation, and are, therefore, under the disagreeable necessity of declining a compliance with your request.
    The Congress have further directed me, sir, to inform you that they are equally unfortunate in being obliged to refuse their permission to purchase cannon in this Colony. The defence of this city and places in its vicinity, require such extensive works that, so far from parting with the guns now here, we are taking every method in our power to procure more. These reasons the Congress are confident will have full weight upon your mind, and therefore decline mentioning the propriety of reserving them for the sea-service of the Colony. I have the honour to be, &c. By order.

Reprinted from Force, *Archives* (4) 6: 1407; taken from the draft.
    1. A draft of this letter was read and approved by the New York Provincial Congress, the same to be sent out over the signature of the president. It was addressed to "General Green" at the "Camp on Nassau-Island."
    2. See NG to Woodhull, 14 June, above.

## General Greene's Orders

[Camp Long Island, N.Y., 17 June 1776. Courtmartial to settle ranks of captains in Little's regiment. Assigns regiments to alarm posts in the five forts. In the event of an attack, "Posts are to be Defended to the Last Extremity." Lines to be manned between daybreak and sunrise. Mitchell Orderly Book (NHi) 1 p.]

## General Greene's Orders

[Camp Long Island, N.Y., 18 June 1776. Picket discontinued, except guard at Red Hook. Three hundred men and officers to parade at 8 A.M. to receive orders from Engineer Smith.[1] Little's Orderly Book, reprinted from Johnston, *NY 1776*, pt. 2, pp. 17–18.]

1. According to Johnston this was Capt. William Smith, brought by Lee to Long Island in the spring to help with fortifications. Washington's orders for 19 June requested 150 of Greene's brigade to go to Governor's Island, "on the present emergency" to work till 6:00 P.M. unless "Wind and Tide make it necessary" to leave work sooner. (Fitzpatrick, *GW*, 5: 158)

## General Greene's Orders

[Long Island Camp, N.Y., 20 June 1776. Work party from Hitchcock's and Little's regiments to Governor's Island. Rest of men to "Abatee" between Ft. Putnam and redoubt on left. Pennsylvania regiment to furnish fatigue party for Cobble Hill.[1] General disapproves findings of courtmartial of 17 June and asks that court meet again to settle rank of captains in Twelfth (Little's) Regiment. Printed from Johnston, *NY 1776*, pt. 2, p. 18.]

1. Cobble Hill was between Ft. Greene and the harbor, about one-quarter of a mile back from the shore line (see map, p. 231). It was also known as Smith's Barbette, after the engineer, William Smith. The name Cobble Hill was apparently given by NG's men because it reminded them of Cobble Hill near Prospect Hill during the siege of Boston.

## From Esek Hopkins

Sir                                    Providence [R.I.] June 20th 1776
I receivd yours of the 24th May[1] and through a Continual hurry found no opportunity to answer it before. I am greatly oblig'd to you for the Intelligence you give me in it. I have nothing new to acquaint you with save that the Brig Andrew Doria has taken two Transports with two hundred Men on board, and I believe they are both Retaken by the Men of War in coming in here. We have lost twenty four Seamen by the bargain, and have in their Room four Scotch Officers and twenty six of the Ships Crews, with about One hundred broad Swords, and One hundred and sixty Small Arms which Captn Biddle took out.[2]
Captn Whipple had a small Engagement the day before yesterday

in which he lost one Man with the Cerberus of 28 Guns and 6 small ditto on the Quarter Deck and Forecastle.[3] There is three Frigates round Block Island which makes it difficult to get in or out as our Force is not Sufficient to Engage them.[4] Shall indeavour to make some other Rendezvous as soon as I can get the Vessels all out; at present think Boston the best I can find on this Coast.

I must request the favour of you to indulge three of your Soldiers with not Rating them as deserters: Vizt, James Dement, Andrew Ingersol and Edmund Paisons belonging (to Captn [Nathaniel] Warners Company in Coll Litles' Regiment) who went out in the Cabot, and two of them came back again in a Prize Ship sent in by the Cabot a few days ago and they tell me as soon as the Ship is discharg'd they will Return to the Regiment. They have behaved so well, should be sorry they should loose any Wages that may be due to them. Should be glad of your directions in that matter, whether I must send them back directly or Continue them on Service here. I am with Regard Sir Your most Obedt humbl Servt

E H

LB (RHi).
1. Letter not found.
2. Nicholas Biddle (1750–78) had served in the British navy and on board American merchantmen. In 1775 he was given command of the *Andrea Doria* and joined Commodore Esek Hopkins's fleet. (*DAB*) In 1778 he was in command of the *Randolph* when she was blown up during an engagement in the West Indies, with a loss of 301 men, the heaviest of the war (Peckham, *Toll*, p. 118).
3. Abraham Whipple (1733–1819), a veteran sea captain, was one of the ringleaders in the burning of HMS *Gaspee* in 1772. In June 1775 he was appointed commodore of Rhode Island's fledgling navy, consisting of two sloops. As master of the schooner *Providence* and a later frigate of the same name, his exploits against British shipping became legendary. Later in the war he was commander of a squadron that brought in British prizes valued at one million dollars. (*DAB*)
4. Block Island stands off the entrance to Narragansett Bay.

## From George Washington

[Friday afternoon, 20 (21) June 1776. Asks NG to have the attached warrant "executed with Precission and exactness by One Oclock the Ensuing Morning by a careful officer."[1] ADS (CSmH) 1p.]

1. Washington's note was written on the back of a 21 June warrant (signed by Philip Livingston, John Jay, and Gouverneur Morris) that ordered the arrest of David Mathews for "dangerous Designs and treasonable Conspiracies against the Rights and Liberties of the united Colonies of America." Mathews, the mayor of New York City, was suspected of involvement with Thomas Hickey in a plot to turn over the city to the British without a fight. Despite the lack of direct evidence against Mathews, he was imprisoned in Conn., although he escaped and returned to New York City when the British occupied it. After the war his estates were confiscated and he fled to Cape Breton, where he became a leading figure. (Sabine, *Loyalists*, p. 446; Van Doren, *Secret*, pp. 13–15; and Robert McCluer Calhoon, *The Loyalists in Revolutionary America, 1760–1781* (New York: Harcourt, Brace, and Jovanovich, Inc., 1965], pp. 372–73)

## To George Washington

[From Long Island, N.Y., 22 June 1776. In obedience to within warrant a detachment under Col. Varnum arrested David Mathews at
one o'clock this morning. Despite diligent search, no papers were
found in his house.[1] ALS (CSmH) 1p.]

1. NG wrote this note on the back of the warrant cited immediately above and
returned the document to Washington.

## General Greene's Orders

[Long Island Camp, N.Y., 22 June 1776. Lieut. Samuel Hughes of
Little's regiment to see that a well is dug in Ft. Greene. By 8:00 A.M.
110 men to be at St. Georges Ferry to go to Governor's Island; 40 to go
to Red Hook. Henshaw Orderly Book (MWA) 1 p.]

## From John Adams

Dear Sir                                   Philadelphia June 22, 1776
    Your favour of the second Instant has lain by me, I suppose these
Eighteen days,[1] but I fear I shall often have occasion to make Apolo-
gies for such omissions, which will never happen from want of
Respect, but I fear very often for want of Time.
    Your Reasoning, to prove the Equity, and the Policy of making
Provision for the Unfortunate Officer, or Soldier, is extremely just,
and cannot be answered, and I hope that when we get a little over the
Confusions arising from the Revolutions which are now taking Place
in the Colonies, and get an American Constitution formed, something
will be done. I should be much obliged to you for your thoughts upon
the subject. What Pensions shall be allowed or what other Provision
made? Whether it would be expedient to establish an Hospital &c. It
is a Matter of Importance, and the Plan should be well digested.
    I think with you that every Colony should furnish its Proportion
of Men, and I hope it will come to this. But at present, some Colonies
have such Bodies of Quakers, and Menonists, and Moravians, who
are principled against War, and others have such Bodies of Tories, or
Cowards, or unprincipled People who will not wage War, that it is as
yet impossible.
    The Dispute is, as you justly observe in all human probability,
but in its Infancy; we ought therefore to study to bring every Thing in
the military Department into the best order. Fighting is not the greatest Branch of the Science of War. Men must be furnished with good
and wholesome Provisions in sufficient Plenty. They must be well
paid. They must be well cloathed and well covered with Barracks and

Tents. They must be kept warm with suitable Fuel. In these Respects, we have not been able to do so well as we wished. But why the Regiments have not been furnished with proper Agents, I don't know. Congress, is ever ready to harken to the Advice of the General [i.e., Washington], and if he had recommended such officers, they would have been appointed. Collonells should neither be Agents, nor suttlers. Congress have lately voted that there shall be regimental Paymasters, who shall keep the Accounts of the Regiments; if any other Agent is necessary let me know it. Good officers are no doubt the soul of an Army, but our Difficulty is to get Men. Officers present themselves in supernumary abundance. As to pay there is no end to the Desire and Demand of it. Is there not too much Extravagance and too little Economy among the officers?

I am much at a Loss whether it would not be the best Policy to leave any Colony to raise their own Troops, to cloath them, to Pay them, to furnish them with Tents and indeed with every Thing but Provisions, fuel and Forage. The Project of abolishing Provincial Distinctions was introduced with a good intention, I believe, at first but I think it will do no good upon the whole. However, if Congress is to manage the whole, I am in hopes they will get into a better Train. They have established a War Office and a Board of War and ordinance [ordnance] by means of which I hope they will get their affairs into better order. They will be better informed of the state of the Army and of all its wants.[2]

That the Promotion of extraordinary Merit may give disgust to those officers is true, over whom the advancement is made, but I think it ought not. That this Power may be abused, or misapplied, is also true. That Interest, Favour, private Friendship, Prejudice may operate more or less in the purest assembly is true. But where will you lodge this Power? To place it in the General would be more dangerous to the public liberty, and not less liable to abuse from sinister and unworthy motives. Will it do, is it consistent with common Prudence to lay it down as an invariable Rule, that all officers in all cases shall rise in succession?

I am obliged to you for your Caution not to be too confident. The Fate of War is uncertain; so are all sublunary things. But, we must form our Conjectures of Effects from the knowledge we have of Causes, and in Circumstances like ours must not attempt to penetrate too far into futurity. There are as many Evils and more which arise in human life, from an excess of Diffidence as from an excess of confidence; proud as Mankind is, their is more superiority in this world yielded than assumed. I learned, long ago, from one of the greatest statesmen this world ever produced, Sully, neither to adventure upon rash Attempts from too much confidence, nor to despair of success in a great Design from the appearance of Difficulties. Without attempting to judge of the future which depends upon too many accidents, much less to subject it to our Precipitation in bold and difficult Enterprises, we should endeavour to subdue one obstacle at a Time, nor suffer ourselves to be depress'd by their Greatness and their Number. *We ought never to despair of what has been once accomplish'd.* How many Things have the Idea of impossible been annexed to that have become easy to those who knew how to take Advantage of Time, opportunity, lucky Moments, the Faults of others, different Dispositions, and an infinite Number of other circumstances.

I will inclose to you a Copy of the Resolution establishing a Board of War and ordinance, and as you may well imagine, we are all inexperienced in this Business. I should be extremely obliged to you for any Hints for the Improvement of the Plan, which may occur to you, and for any assistance or Advice you may give me as a private Correspondent in the execution of it. It is a great Mortification to me I confess, and I fear it will too often be a Misfortune to our Country, that I am called to the Discharge of Trust to which I feel myself so unequal, and in the Execution of which I can derive no assistance from my Education or former Course of Life. But my Country must command me, and wherever she shall order me, there I will go, without dismay. I am, dear sir, with the greatest esteem your humble servant

LB (MHi). Enclosure missing; see note 2, below.

1. See above, NG to Adams, 2 June, to which this letter is almost a point by point response.

2. Congress had appointed a committee in Jan. to determine whether a war office should be established. On 11 June they voted to establish the Board of War and Ordnance to consist of five members. Two days later John Adams, Roger Sherman, Benjamin Harrison, James Wilson, and Edward Rutledge were named as members and Richard Peters elected secretary. (*JCC*, 5: 434, 438) Adams enclosed the two resolutions in this letter; see last paragraph.

## From Gouverneur Morris, John Jay, and Philip Livingston

[22 June 1776. A warrant[1] directing NG to arrest George Brewerton and requesting a report of the success or failure of the execution of the warrant.[2] DS (Greensboro [N.C.] Historical Museum) 1 p.]

1. From members of the N.Y. Committee of Safety serving as a Committee on Conspiracies.

2. The warrant was addressed to Greene at "Nassau Island"—the name most often used for Long Island. George Brewerton was an alderman from New York City who was suspected of loyalist activities, including the possession of arms. After two unsuccessful attempts were made to arrest him, Brewerton voluntarily surrendered. When examined by the Committee on Conspiracies, he was found to be innocent of the

activities in question (*NY MSS*, 1: 340, 346, 352–53, 363–64). For the execution of this warrant, see below, NG to Jeremiah Olney, 22 June.

## To Captain Jeremiah Olney

[From Long Island, N.Y., 22 June 1776. Directs him to seize Brewerton and his papers as per attached warrant and bring them to NG.[1] ADS (Greensboro [N.C.] Historical Museum) 1 p.]

1. See warrant immediately above. At bottom of this document, a note is appended by NG to N.Y. Provincial Congress, dated 25 June, announcing that Brewerton has voluntarily surrendered and is being sent to the Congress under care of Capt. Bowen.

## To George Washington

[From Long Island, N.Y., 24 June 1776. Announces the arrival of eleven prisoners (including three women) and awaits GW's directions as to the disposition of same. Tr (G. W. Greene transcripts, CSmH) 1 p.]

## From George Washington

Sir                                    New York June 24th 1776
From your Brigade (and principally from the Riffle Regiment) detach as many men as will be sufficient to effect the purpose mentioned in the following Resolution of the Provincial Congress of New York.[1]

"In Provincial Congress New York June 24 1776. Whereas Information has been given to this Congress that Sundry Persons on Nassau Island disaffected and Inimical to the American Cause are in arms in opposition to the Civil authority of this Colony and with a view of aiding the enemies of America: Resolved unanimously that his Excellency General Washington be and he hereby is requested to take the most speedy and effectual measures to disarm and secure all such Persons. Order'd that one of the Secretaries wait upon his said Excellency with a certified copy of the aforegoing Resolution."

From the best Information I have been able to get, there are about Two hundred or Two hundred and Fifty of these Men in Woods and Swamps. A Mr Livingston who is just returned from Queens County can give you particular information into this matter. The necessity of Secrecy and caution are too obvious for me to give you any advice thereon. Wishing [you] success I am &c

G. WASHINGTON

Tr (G. W. Greene transcripts, CSmH).

1. For the results of this expedition, see below, Archibald Crary and William S. Livingston to NG, 25–26 June.

## From Colonel Archibald Crary and Major William S. Livingston[1]

Sir        Hempsted [N.Y.] Three OClock P. M. [ 25–26 June 1776][2]
Your Letter[3] I received about an Hour ago, immediately after our Return from the Scouting Parties. Colo Crary detach'd the men last Evening in two Parties; they were conducted thro' the Woods and Swamps by three of our Friends of this County and after a March of near Twenty Miles they return'd (having met with no Opposition and taken five Prisoners) about Noon. They discovered the Places of their Abode in the Woods and from the Fresh Footsteps that appear'd around them conjectur'd that they had been but a few Hours deserted. They left their Provisions and some Candles behind them. Since we have been here the Number of our Prisoners have increased and decreased hourly. The Committee of the County is now sitting and all such as appear before them who give surety and proper Assurances for their future Behaviour they discharge. We have had on the whole near one hundred. There is little hopes of our being able to proceed any farther in the Execution of your Orders. We have taken all that can be found and what few are still remaining are secreted in almost inaccessable Fastnesses thro' which we may wander for a Month and not find a Man.[4] Colo Crary will take every necessary Step this Evening, and wait here for further Orders. The Gentlemen who have been so faithful and constantly with us join Colo Crary and myself in Opinion that our Stay here can be now of no further Utility. The County has been well secur'd and will we hope act more consistant for the future. We shall wait with Impatience for your Orders and have the Honor to be your most Obedt humble Servts

ARCHIBALD CRARY

WM S LIVINGSTON

LS (Washington Papers: DLC).
    1. The letter was written by Livingston but signed also by Crary as the superior officer in the area. Archibald Crary had long been a military associate of NG. He was an original member of the Kentish Guards and an officer in the R.I. Army of Observation. After serving throughout 1776 as a lieutenant colonel in the Ninth Continental Infantry, he then saw extensive service in the R.I. militia until he resigned in May 1779, declaring he could no longer support his family on the depreciated pay. (Heitman, *Register*; Arnold, *R.I.*, 2: 439, 471–72)
    2. The first date is established by Washington's letter of June 24 above, which asked NG to order the men picked up. The last date is established by the fact that Washington read the letter to his council of war on 27 June.
    3. Letter not found.
    4. For list of prisoners taken, see below, 29 June.

# To George Washington

[Long Island, N.Y.] June 27, 1776

In Considering the Several matters which your Excellency has been pleased to referr to us, we do, with regard to Long Island and Staten Island, think it absolutely necessary for the Safety and defence of this Colony that all the Stock of Cattle and Sheep (Except such as may be requisite for the present Subsistence of the Inhabitants) be removed to a distance from the Sea Coast and that this be done immediately; as on the arrival of the Enemy it will be impossible to give attention to this matter, and Also that all the Horses be either removed or put under such regulations as that they may be removed on the first Approach of the Enemy.[1] And with regard to the disaffected Inhabitants who have lately been apprehended, we think that the method at present adopted by the County Committee of discharging them on their giving bonds as a Security for their good behaviour is very improper and ineffectual; and therefore recommend it to your Excellency to apply to the Congress of this province to take some more effectual method of Securing the good behaviour of those people, and in the mean time that your Excellency will order the officers in whose Custody they are to discharge no more of them untill the Sense of Congress be had thereon.

W HEATH[2]

JOS SPENCER[3]

NATHANAEL GREENE

STIRLING

DS (Washington Papers: DLC).

1. Washington had called a council of war earlier on 27 June to discuss several matters, including the removal of livestock. The proposals adopted were essentially the same as presented here in writing. Washington immediately sent the proposals to the N.Y. Congress, stressing the need to deprive the British of such supplies, "as will enable them to act with more Vigour and Spirit against us" (Fitzpatrick, *GW*, 5: 187). Removing livestock to prevent it from falling into British hands was no easy matter, and a satisfactory solution was never found. One difficulty centered on the phrase "Except such as may be requisite for the present Subsistence of the Inhabitants." The following day the council met with a committee from the N.Y. Provincial Congress and hammered out several proposals. They agreed that each family on Staten and Long islands would be allowed to keep two horses and one, two, or three cows—depending on whether it was a small, "midling," or large family. All the rest of the stock in Queens and Kings County "should be drove to the bushy Plains" (minutes of both meetings are in the Washington Papers: DLC). The joint decision was passed along to the Provincial Congress, which ordered the proposals carried out.

Benjamin Kissam, a devoted patriot, was well started on carrying out the orders in Queens County when he stopped to point out the obstacles in driving seven thousand cattle, seven thousand sheep, and one thousand horses to what he called the "Brushy Plains": the poor subsistence in the plains area, which was also almost "entirely destitute of water"; and the problem of herding the stock, which would require more men than could possibly be mustered. Real hardship would also ensue among the people. He reported that "some among the poorer sort, for aught I know, must be left to starve." Those who had been fattening a cow for butchering the following winter would be without food by that time. Since he found most people willing to "enter into obligations" to drive their stock in an emergency to any place that Congress might name, Kissam suggested that the N.Y. Congress and Washington might "fall on some method" for securing the stock if the British came. (Onderdonk, *Queens County*, pp. 76–77)

Washington was less tolerant than the N.Y. Congress toward farmers who evaded their orders. To Washington's consternation very little was done during the coming weeks. By late July the Congress informed him of the "Impracticability" of removing the stock. On 8 Aug. he told them he wished they "may not see Cause to regret, that they were not removed." (Fitzpatrick, *GW*, 5: 329, 400)

2. William Heath (1737–1814) was a Massachusetts farmer who had served in the general court in 1761 and during 1771–74. Upon the dissolution of that body by Gage in 1774, Heath became a member of the Mass. Provincial Congress. He was made brigadier general by his state in Feb. 1775. Commissioned in the Continental army along with NG, he was advanced to major general in Jan. 1777. A mediocre strategist, he served for most of the war in the Highlands of the Hudson. (*DAB*) His *Memoirs* are a standard source of revolutionary war history.

3. Joseph Spencer (1714–89), a veteran officer of the colonial wars and a long time Conn. public servant, was advanced to major general at the same time NG was. He served in the siege of Boston and in the New York campaign. In Dec. 1776 he was ordered to New England, where his actions in late 1777 came under question. Although a courtmartial exonerated him, he resigned in Jan. 1778. (*DAB*)

## List of Prisoners Sent by Colonel Archibald Crary

Hamstead [N.Y.] June 29th 1776.

Joseph Dorlant, }
John Hutchins, } from Jamaica Goal.

John Carman, Rec'd powder and absconded in the Woods.

Andrew Allen, Disaffected Parson, taken in the Woods.

Jacob Lamberson, found with his gun charged.

Benjn Pedet, In the Swamp in the fight & had Powder from Man of War.

Ezekiel Rainer, In the Woods hid.

Richd Smith, In the Swamp Battle & had powder from Asia.

Jeremiah Bedle, A Disaffected Parson.

Danl Smith, In the Swamp Battle.

Elija Rainer, Hid in the Swamp.

Joseph Bedle, Same Disaffected Person.

Nathan Smith, Recd Powder from the Asia, absconded in the woods & appeared to know much of the scheme.

Toundsend Weicks, A Dam'd Rascall & ye Greatest Tory.

Wm McCoon, }
Thos Fleet, } Declared they would sooner fight for the King than
John Fleet, } the Congress and totally Deny the Authority of
Peter Wheaber, } that Body.
Saml Tounsend, }

James Cogshall, Gun stealer or Informer from Newport.

Henry Dearling, Said Genl Washington was more Concern'd in the Conspiracy than any one.

Reprinted from *NY MSS*, 1: 372–73.

## To Colonel and Mrs. Henry Knox

Gen. Green and Lady present their Complimts to Col: Knox and his Lady and should be glad of their Company tomorrow at Dinner at 2 O'Clock

Long Island Thursday Evg [June, 1776] 8 O'Clock[1]

The writing is in the hand of Catharine Greene (MHi).
1. The invitation is undated, but it was probably early June. Catharine had arrived before 29 May. Dr. Samuel Kennedy of the Pennsylvania regiment wrote to his wife on 10 June: "On Saturday last General Green, his Lady, Col. Johnston, Capt. Frazer & his Lady . . . went to the Sea shore to observe the enemy's shipping by Telescope." (*PMHB* 8 [1884]: 113)

## General Greene's Orders

Camp Long Island [N.Y.] 1 July 1776
The Colo or Commanding Officer of the 9th: 11th: and 12th Regts are desired to Mark a line round each of the Forts and Fortifications for the Troops to begin a Fire upon the Enemy if they should attempt to storm the Works, and the Troops are to be made acquainted that they are by no means to begin a Fire sooner than at the Enemys Arrival at these Lines unless Order'd by the Commanding Officer at the Works.[1] This Line should be at about eighty yards from the Parapet. The Commanding Officer of the Guards at Fort Green and Fort Putnam to send a Patroling party every Hour round the Works for about a quarter of a Mile to detect the Enemy if they should attempt to get possession of the Works by surprize with a Partizan party. The Genl Thanks both Officers and Soldiers that turn'd out Voluntarily Yesterday to Work upon Cobble Hill. Such an Instance of Public Spirit is truly laudable and shall not go unrewarded if the Genl ever has it in his power to make a more suitable Acknowledgement. No Officer below the Rank of a Field Officer to lodge out of Camp from their Companies on any pretence What Ever, Sickness Excepted. The General recommends the strictest discipline and daily attention to the Arms and Ammunition that we may be prepard for Action at a Moments Warning.

The troops of this Brigade being very sickly, the General recommends a daily attention to the Cookery of the Provission and that Broiling and Frying Meat so destructive to Health be prohibited and that the Officers of each Company take it in turn daily to attend the

Messes for that Purpose. A Picquet of 100 Men to go to Red Hook to Night by Order of a private Message from the General.

Mitchell Orderly Book (NHi).

1. On 24 June, Gen. Howe finally arrived from Halifax aboard HMS *Greyhound*, followed in less than a week by no less than 120 ships. In preparing for a possible attack on Long Island at once, NG was not far off the mark. Howe had been dissuaded from attacking only at the last minute (according to a later account of Gov. Tryon) by the compelling argument of Gen. Robertson that "if you beat the rebels before the reinforcements arrive, you disgrace the ministry for sending them; if you are defeated, they will be of no use when they come." (This account is found in Willcox, *Clinton*, p. 99n.)

## To Whom It May Concern

[From Long Island Camp, N.Y., 1 July 1776. Since the trunks of one Evert Bancker Junr have been examined and nothing found but "Linnens and wearing Appearl," he should be permitted to pass.[1] DS (OC1WHi) 1 p.]

1. An example of the tightened security that followed the arrival of the British fleet. Some of the powder from HMS *Asia* that Crary and Livingston found in the possession of loyalists (see above, 29 June) had undoubtedly been slipped past the military guard NG had set up at the Brooklyn ferry.

## General Greene's Orders

[Long Island Camp, N.Y., 2 July 1776. Assigns picket duty at fortifications, including Ft. Stirling and Cobble Hill. Col. (Matthias) Ward's regiment of New Jersey militia[1] upon an alarm to form behind Ft. Greene. Patrols from Ft. Putnam hourly. Henshaw Orderly Book (MWA) 1 p.]

1. On the arrival of the British fleet, Washington had written an urgent letter to Gen. Livingston of the N.J. militia asking for reinforcements (Fitzpatrick, *GW*, 5: 198–99). Ward's regiment was sent the following day. In Washington's orders of 2 July, he noted that "Col. Cortland of the New-Jersey Brigade is to send over five-hundred of the Militia under his command to reinforce General Greene's Brigade; these troops are to be distinguished from the old Militia in future by being called New-Levies" (Fitzpatrick, *GW*, 5: 211). Two weeks later he ordered them back from Long Island to Manhattan Island (orders of 17 July, Fitzpatrick, *GW*, 5: 287).

## General Greene's Orders

[Long Island Camp, N.Y., 4 July 1776. Officers of guards responsible for everything in the forts, "more Particular for the Rum Lodged in the Works for the People in time of Action."[1] Damage to implements or liquors to be repaired out of the officer's "Private Purse" who

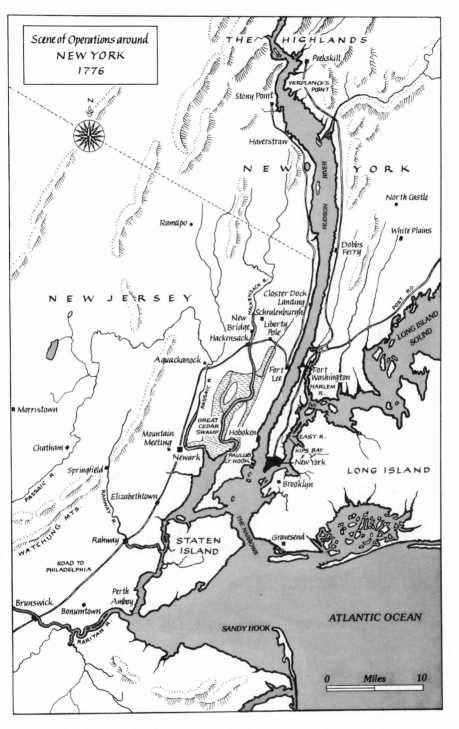

From The Winter Soldiers, copyright © 1973 by Richard M. Ketchum.
Reproduced by permission of Doubleday & Company, Inc.

allowed the damage. Daily inventories to be taken. Assigns picket guards and fatigue party. Mitchell Orderly Book (NHi) 1 p.]

1. Next to gunpowder, a supply of rum was considered of prime importance in a siege or battle. Although it had medicinal value, one must assume it was also used to keep the men's courage from ebbing.

## General Greene's Orders

[Long Island Camp, N.Y., 4 July 1776. Captains to have arms ready for action at all times. The general desires the officers will not "suffer the Pleasure and amusements of Life to Absent them from a Necessary attention" to their duties. Mitchell Orderly Book (NHi) 1 p.]

## To George Washington

Dear General                    Camp on Long Island [N.Y.] July 5, 1776
    I beg leave to recommend to your consideration the establishing a certain Guard at Red Hook. Tis undoubtedly a Post of vast importance. Detach'd Guards never defend a place equal to troops stationd at a particular Post. Both Officers and men contract an affection for a post after being there some time. They will be more industrious to have everything in readiness and obstinate in defence. The little baggage that each private has is of consequence to him, and will influence his conduct in time of action if it is at stake. The Officers also will have new motives. They knowing a post to be commited to their trust, and that the whole disgrace falls upon them if any misconduct happens will be much more likely to take every necessary precaution to avoid so great an Evil. But an officer that commands a detachment thinks little more than how to pass away his time during his tour of duty, it being uncertain whether he shall ever command there again.[1]
    I sent to General Scott this morning four Prisoners taken at the Narrows last Night. The following is a Copy of their Examination. They were taken seperate and agreed in their account in every thing except the number of men. The Captains account was the best and I beleive the rightest, and I apprehend not much from the truth.[2]
    The fleet saild from Hallifax the 10 of June and arrivd the 29th. The fleet consists of 120 sail of Topsail Vessels and that they have on board 10,000 Troops receivd at Hallifax besides some of the Scotch Brigade that have joind the fleet on the passage. The Troops from the West Indies Joind the Army at Hallifax and was there receivd with them.
    A list of the Generals: How, Pigot, Piercy, Grant, Jones.[3] A list of

the Ships of sail: Asia 64, Centurion 50, Chatham 50, Phoenix 40, Greyhound 30, Rose 20, Swan 16, Senegal 13.

Four days before the fleet sailed from Hallifax a packet arrivd from England that brought an account of Admiral Hows sailing with a fleet of one hundred and fifty Sail on board of which was 20,000 Troops. The fleet sail'd a few days before the Packet. They are expected in here every day.

General Carltons Regiment went from Hallifax to Quebeck. The Niger Ship that went from Hallifax in April to Canada met Burgoyne going up the River with 36 transports 6,000 troops on board.

General Carltons Son went into Quebeck painted like an Indian.

The People of Statten Island went on board the fleet as they lay at the Hook, several boat loads of them.

Our people are firing with the nine pounders at the Narrows but have not heard where they have done any execution. There was a smart fire heard at the West end of Statten Island about four this morning.

It is supposed to be an Attack upon Fort Smith in the South part of Statten Island. Nothing farther has happened since yesterday. Beleive me to be with the greatest respect your Excellencys most obedient humble servant.

N GREENE

ALS (Washington Papers: DLC).
1. Washington complied with the recommendation. See below, NG's orders for 8 July, where Varnum's regiment is ordered to Red Hook.
2. NG's information was remarkably accurate. For the list of ships that sailed from Halifax under Adm. Shuldham and ships listed in American waters, see Clark, *Naval Docs.*, 5: 445–46, 948–50. The total of 120 vessels in New York harbor and the 150 that had sailed from England under Adm. Richard Howe agrees with Ward, *War*, 1: 209.
3. Generals William Howe, Robert Pigot, Lord Hugh Percy, James Grant, and Daniel Jones.

## General Greene's Orders

[Long Island Camp, N.Y., 8 July 1776. Varnum's regiment to move to Red Hook to do duty.[1] Col. Forman's New Jersey regiment[2] to encamp where Hitchcock's regiment was and to take alarm posts at Ft. Box and the oblong redoubt lately manned by Varnum's regiment. The Jersey new levies to serve with guards from Eleventh and Twelfth Regiments that they might have "benefit of the knowledge of the standing Troops." Gen. Greene Orderly Book (Bergen County Historical Society) 2 pp.]

1. See above, NG to Washington, 5 July, suggesting a regiment at Red Hook.
2. Lt. Col. David Forman (1745–97) commanded a regiment of "new levies" that

had been raised by the legislature to serve until the first of December. Washington ordered the regiment to Greene's support as the size of Howe's fleet became known.

Forman was a tough disciplinarian with the unenviable reputation of treating loyalists and the disaffected "with extreme cruelty and inhumanity." (*DAB*)

## To [                                    ]

[From Camp on Long Island, N.Y., 8 July 1776. An introduction to the bearer, Dr. Senter,[1] who had gone to Canada as surgeon with Arnold. ALS (NHi) 1 p.]

1. Dr. Isaac Senter (1753–99), was studying medicine in Newport when the war started. He served under NG in Boston, then joined Arnold as a surgeon on the Canadian venture. His journal of the march to Quebec is a colorful source for the history of the ill-fated expedition (published by the Hist. Soc. of Pa. in 1846). Captured at Quebec, Senter was released just before this letter was written. After the war he returned to practice medicine in Newport, where NG and family were his patients briefly. He named his second son after NG. For a sketch of his life, see Edwin M. Stone's notes to the "Journal of Captain Simeon Thayer," in RIHS, *Coll.* 6 (1867): 65–70; and *R.I. Biog. Cycl.*

## General Greene's Orders

[Camp Long Island, N.Y., 9 July 1776. Adjutant of the day to transmit parole and countersign to guards at Red Hook, Cobble Hill, Ft. Box, Ft. Greene, Ft. Putnam, Ft. Stirling, and the Ferry Guard. Officer of the guards to see that they get their instructions and that those who are relieved collect the outsentries before marching off to be dismissed. Field officer of day is responsible for "marching off" of new guards, dismissal of old guards, and for making reports on them. Members of courtmartial from Col. Varnum's regiment to be replaced by men of same rank from Forman's regiment.[1] Henshaw Orderly Book (MWA) 2 pp.]

1. As noted in orders of 8 July, Varnum's regiment was transferred to Red Hook.

## General Greene's Orders

[Long Island Camp, N.Y., 10 July 1776. Commissary to issue provisions Tuesdays, Thursdays, and Saturdays. "It has Been Represented to the Genl that the putrid fever" among the troops is partly due to going into the water in heat of the day. In future they are to swim from 5 to 8 A.M. and 4 P.M. to sunset until Smith's Barbette[1] is finished. Mitchell Orderly Book (NHi) 1 p.]

1. Smith's Barbette was named for Capt. William Smith, the engineer that Gen. Charles Lee brought with him to Long Island. It was built on Cobble Hill (so named by

NG's troops) and mounted heavy artillery toward New York harbor. (Johnston, *NY 1776*, pt. 1, pp. 74–75)

## To George Washington

Camp on Long Island [N.Y.]

Dear Sir                    Saturday [10 July 1776] half past Eleven

Col Hand reports a large body of Regulars are drawn up at the Ferry on Statten Island, and boats ready to Imbark.[1] I am Sir your Excellencys obedient Servant

N GREENE

ALS (Washington Papers: DLC).
1. It was a feint. There would be no embarkation from Staten Island for more than a month.

## General Greene's Orders

[Long Island, N.Y.] 11 July 1776

The sick Being Numerous in the Hospital And But few Women Nurses to be Had, the Regimental Surgeon must Report the Number Necessary for the sick of the Regt and the Colonels are Requested to supply accordingly. A Daily Report to Be made to the Commanding Officers of Corps by the Surgeons of the Watchers wanting in the Hospital Which are to be supplyd Accordingly.[1]

The Serjt Commanding the Guard at Fort Sterling to be under Confinement for Not having His Guard Paraded at the Entry of the Grand Rounds.[2] The Commanding Officers of the several Posts are Required to Examine and Report the Best Method for Covering the Picquet Guard in the several Works. The Fatigue Party to be turnd out in time so as to Be to work on the Hill at 5 O Clock [A.M.]. No Excuse will Be taken for the future for any Neglect of this kind. The Adjutants will Be Answerable for their Men if they are Not brot to the Grand Parade Punctually at the time appointed.

Mitchell Orderly Book (NHi).
1. It was at NG's urging that Dr. John Morgan, the director general of hospitals, set up a hospital on Long Island. Dr. Morgan said later that Long Island was a "very improper place for establishing a Hospital, where the enemy were expected to land, especially when there was a General Hospital on the Island of New-York." (Morgan, *Vindication*, p. 112) If he had any such objections at the time, however, he did not voice them, perhaps because his relations with NG had been very friendly during the months they served together in the siege of Boston, where he had also treated NG for jaundice. Or perhaps, at the time, he was persuaded by NG's argument that a hospital located near the brigade could better serve a sick soldier than one to be reached only by an uncertain ferryboat trip.

At any rate he showed no reluctance in sending Dr. John Warren to Long Island on 12 June with instructions to "consult with Gen. Greene about proper houses for

forming a hospital." (Ibid., p. 116) A conscientious administrator, Morgan gave Warren detailed instructions on setting up and running the hospital, among which, for
example, was the hiring of nurses—not more than one for each ten patients, to be paid
fifty cents per week. He also asked Warren to keep a carpenter in order to "make
coffins" and to do other carpentry work (ibid., p. 117). Above all he made clear that the
general hospital on Long Island was to be part of the New York general hospital, and if
a man could not be adequately cared for on Long Island, he was to be sent to New
York. On Morgan's publishing the *Vindication*, see below, NG to Washington, 11 Aug.
1776. See the same letter on the establishment of regimental hospitals.
    2. In NG's orders of 12 July, below, the sergeant was exonerated.

## To George Washington

Dear Sir                    Camp on Long Island [N.Y.] July 11, 1776
    A report was sent in last Evening from the out Guards at the Nar-
rows that there was two Ships, one Briggantine and one Schooner,
standing in for the Hook last Night.
    I was mentioning some few days past that a putrid fever pre-
vailed in my Brigade and that I thought it partly oweing to their
feeding too freely on animal food. Vegetables would be much more
wholesome; and by your Excellencys Permission they may be provided for the Troops without any additional expence to the Continent. If the colonels of the Regiments were allowd to retrench in the
article of meat, and that they should draw its Value in money to be
apply'd by the Quarter Master of the Regiment to the procureing
necessary sauce, the Quarter master to draw the money weekly and
account to the Commanding officer of the Regiment how it is expended and for what. This method may be a little more troublesome
to the Commissary General and the Quarter Masters of the Regiment,
but if it will remedy so great an Evil as now prevails I think it worthy
your Excellencys attention. The Troops cannot complain that they are
scanted in their Allowance; leaveing them at Liberty to draw either
meat or money as the inclination of the Troops or commanding officer
may lead them, puts it out of their power to complain. People often
would adopt measures when left to their choice that they would think
a hardship to have imposd upon them.[1]
    Cleanliness contributes much to the health of the Troops. They
now do and have done so much fatigue that the allowance of soap
will not keep them clean. Their Cloathing gets exceeding dirty, and
they wear out twice as many cloathes on fatigue as doing other duty. I
should think it a piece of Justice due to the Troops for the extra-
ordin[ar]y fatigue to be allowd a double quantity of soap when they
are employ'd so much on fatigue. This is a grievance I have often
heard the officers complain on, that the fatigue wore out the Troops
cloathing faster than they could get them; and that they made them-

selves so dirty at Work that the allowance of soap would not clean them.

I have never mentiond anything of a farther allowance of soap to any Person except the other Evening at Head Quarters. I only beg leave to propose it to your Excellencys consideration and leave it for your better Judgment to determine the propriety and Utility of such an establishment.[2] Believe me to be with the greatest Respect your Excellencys most obedient humble servant.

NATH GREENE

ALS (Washington Papers: DLC).
1. Washington's order of 22 July permitted regiments to draw a quarter of their usual rations in money with which to buy vegetables (Fitzpatrick, *GW*, 5: 320). He warned troops who mistreated the farmers that, if they were to "drive off the Country people, and break up the Market," the healthy would be sick and the sick would perish "for want of Necessaries." (July 26 order, ibid., p. 340) When troops continued to destroy people's produce, on 6 Aug. he placed a guard at the market from sunrise until twelve noon with orders to put offenders in the guardhouse. He repeated the order to new troops a week later. (Ibid., pp. 376, 442) The harassment of the country people stopped, and it is assumed the men continued to get their fresh vegetables.
2. On receipt of this letter, Washington immediately issued a long order that pointed out to officers and men the "necessity of frequently changing their linnen, cleaning their persons" (orders of 11 July, Fitzpatrick, *GW*, 5: 263). Presumably by this time soap was available.

## General Greene's Orders

[Long Island Camp, N.Y., 12 July 1776. Ordering the confinement of a sergeant yesterday was due to the general's misunderstanding a report. Instead, he deserves praise for discharge of duty. Capt. Spur to enlarge armorer's shop by eight men. Gives orders for picket guards. Mitchell Orderly Book (NHi) 1 p.]

## To John Adams

Dear Sir                    Camp on Long Island [N.Y.] July 14, 1776
I receivd your Letter of the 22d of June. If it was necessary for you to Apologise for not writing sooner it is necessary also for me. But as the express conditions of my corresponding with you was to write when I had time and leave you to answer at your leisure, I think a Apology is unnecessary on either side. But I can Assure you, as you did me, that it is not for want of respect that your Letter has been unanswered so long.

I am glad to find you agree with me in the Justice and propriety of establishing some provision for the unfortunate.[1] I have not had time to fix upon any plan for that purpose, but I will write you more fully in my next. I have never mentiond the matter to but one or two particular friends for fear the establishment should not take place.

The Troops expectations being once raisd a disappointment must necessarily sour them. On the other hand if the Congress established a support for the unfortunate unsolicited, it must inspire the Army with love and gratitude towards the Congress for so generous an Act.

You query whether there is not a want of Oeconemy in the Army amongst the officers. I can Assure you there is not among those of my Acquaintance.[2] The expences of the Officers runs very high, unless they dress and live below the Gentleman. Few that have ever lived in Charactor will be willing to decend to that. As long as they continue in service they will support their Rank, and if their pay is not sufficent they will draw on their private fortunes at Home. The pay of the Soldiers will scarcely keep them decently cloathed. The Troops are kept so much upon fatigue that they wear out their cloathing as fast as the Officers can get it. The Wages given to common Soldiers is very high but every thing is so dear that the purchase of a few Articles takes their whole pay. This is a general complaint through the whole army.

I am not against rewarding merit or encourageing Activity, neither would I have promotions confind to a regular line of succession. But every man that has spirit enough to be fit for an officer, will have too much to continue in service after another of Inferior Rank is put over his Head. The power of rewarding Merit should be lodged with the Congress, but I should think the Generals recommendation is the best testimonial of a Persons deserving a reward that the Congress can have.

Many of the New England Cols have let in a Jealousy that the Southern Officers of that Rank in the Continental establishment are treated with more respect and attention by the Congress than they are. They say several of the Southern Cols have been promoted to the Rank of Brigadier General, but not one New England Colo.[3] Some of them appear not a little disgusted. I wish the officers in general were as studious to deserve promotion as they are anxious to obtain it.

You cannot more sincerely lament the want of knowledge to execute the business that falls in your department than I do that which falls in mine, and was I not kept in countenance by some of my superior officers I should be sincerely disposd to quit the command I hold in the Army. But I will endeavor to supply the want of Knowledge as much as possible by Watchfulness and Industry. In these respects I flatter my Self I have never been faulty. I have never been one moment out of the service since I engagd in it. My Interest has and will suffer greatly by my Absence, but I shall think that a small sacrifice if I can save my Country from Slavery.

You have heard long before this will reach you of the arrival of General and Admiral Howe. The Generals Troops are encamped on

*Part of Lord Howe's fleet on 12 July 1776, looking toward Long Island from Staten Island,*
*by Archibald Robertson*
*(Courtesy of Spencer Collection, New York Public Library)*

Statten Island. The Admiral arrived on Fryday last. A few hours before his arrival two Ships went up the North River amidst a most terrible fire from the different Batteries.[4] The Admiral sent up a flag today, but as the Letter was not properly addressed it was not receivd. The Admiral laments his not arriveing a few days sooner. I suppose he alludes to the declaration of Independance. It is said he has great powers to treat, as well as a strong army to execute.

I wrote you sometime past I thought you was playing a desperate game. I still think so. Here is Howes Army arrivd and the Reinforcement hourly expected. The whole force we have to oppose them dont amount to much above 9,000 if any. I could wish the Troops had been drawn together a little earlier that we might have had some opportunity of diciplining them. However, what falls to my lot I shall endeavor to execute to the best of my abillity. I am with the greatest respect your most obedient humble servant

NATH GREENE

ALS (MHi).
1. The subject of half pay for the disabled is discussed at length in NG to Adams, 26 May, above.
2. See NG to Adams, 2 June, above, on pay and promotion of officers.
3. Adams answers NG in letter of 4 Aug., below.
4. HMS *Eagle*, flagship of Adm. Richard Howe, dropped anchor at Staten Island on 12 July. Howe came with a carrot and a stick: the carrot was a peace proposal (which he genuinely hoped would be acceptable); the stick was 150 transports with 15,000 additional troops. Even if he had arrived before the Declaration of Independence was signed, it is doubtful if his mission would have been any more successful. (See Gruber, *Howe Bros.*, pp. 89–100.)

The two ships to which NG refers as going up North River (the Hudson) were the *Phoenix* of forty-four guns and the *Rose* of twenty guns, dispatched by Adm. Howe to test the shore batteries along the lower Hudson. To the embarrassment of Washington and his entire army, they ran the gauntlet without major damage and made their way thirty miles north to the Tappan Zee. Although some of the American artillerymen were sadly deficient—drunk, absent, or flustered by their baptism of fire—the truth was that the British fleet could sail up the Hudson anytime they chose.

The escapade, nonetheless, did little more for the British than to demonstrate the ineffectiveness of American shore batteries. The failure of the loyalists to supply the ships for the next month and the harassment by American row galleys and fire ships caused British Adm. Shuldham to call the venture a "fruitless expedition" and, he added, that at most they "very luckily made their escape." For an excellent modern account of the expedition up the Hudson, accompanied by good maps and illustrations, see Koke, "Hudson." The quote from Adm. Shuldham is on p. 170.

## General Greene's Orders

[Long Island Camp, N.Y., 16 July 1776. At mounting of the new guard, every prisoner to be released who is not charged with a signed complaint. Lieut. Col. Cornell[1] and Capt. Warner to oversee and complete works at Smith's Barbette. Fatigue party to work every cool day and to be industrious in completing works before an enemy attack. A guard to mount at Rapelljies Mill every night until sunrise. New guards to be instructed on duties. Henshaw Orderly Book (MWA) 2 pp.]

1. Ezekiel Cornell, an early Rhode Island patriot, was lieutenant colonel of Hitchcock's regiment. The following year he was made brigadier general of the R.I. Militia; in the last year of the war, he was inspector of the Continental army. (Heitman, *Register*; Bartlett, *Records*, 8: 348) He was known to his men, not altogether affectionately, as "Old Snarl." NG looked upon him as an effective disciplinarian and dependable subordinate.

## To George Washington

[From Camp on Long Island, N.Y., 16 July 1776. Col. Hand reports fleet lies much the same as yesterday. No deserters last night. Hopes to complete works at Cobble Hill in a few days. Could not finish sooner because so many on guard duty and had to consider health of troops. One ship and sloop under sail today. ALS (Washington Papers: DLC) 1 p.]

## To George Washington

Sir                                        Camp Long Island [N.Y.] July 18, 1776

I receivd a line from Col Webb[1] last evening directing me to enquire how many Ships had past the Narrows. Colo Hand reported one yesterday morning which I thought was reported in my morning report and if it is not reported there it was an omission of mine. I beg your Excellency to examin it. Colo Hand reported at four oClock in the afternoon that a Brigantine had gone down towards the Hook, and that the Ship that went through the Narrows in the morning had come too, off New Utrecht shore. At Seven in the Evening he reports that the Ship had gone down to the Hook, and that the Enemy were intrenching on the heights of Statten Island.[2]

The two last Reports I did not come to the knowledge off until within Night. I went over to the City at five and did not return until Eight. I thought it would be too late to get them to Head Quarters seasonably, therefore concluded to report them in the morning.

I have not receivd Colo Hands morning Report yet. I was down at Red Hook about sun rise and saw a Sloop streaching down towards the Narrows. Nothing extraordinary has happend the last twenty four hours. Our out Guards suspect that there are spies about the Camp. The Centris have fird half a dozen times A Night the three preceding Nights.

Col Hands morning report is this moment come in. He mentioned everything continues in the same situation as last Evening except the Sloop going through the Narrows that I observd from Red Hook.

I wrote to your Excellency yesterday morning[3] that I thought it would be an advisable measure to have Cobble Hill fixt upon to give notice by the fire of one, two or three Guns, that the Enemy had landed on this Island. Colo Carey wrote me an answer to that proposition and said your Excellency had no objection.[4] If it is to alarm the Camp on your side, it should be mentiond in general orders that the Guards may govern themselves accordingly.[5] We dont want it to Alarm this Camp. What I propos'd it for was to give your Excellency earlier intelligence than could be done by express; and the express to follow with the particulars. I submit it to your Excellencys further consideration. I am with all due respect your Excellencys most obedient humble servant

N GREENE

ALS (Washington Papers: DLC).
    1. Samuel Blachley Webb (1753–1807) of Conn. had recently been appointed an aide to Washington. He had become a lieutenant colonel at the age of twenty-three, due undoubtedly to the influence of his stepfather, Silas Deane. After leaving Washington's "family," he was captured in Dec. 1777 while leading a raid on Long Island. He was to remain a prisoner on parole for three years, during which time NG was one of several men in high position who sought to obtain his release. A warm friendship developed between the two men as revealed in their correspondence after 1779. (Worthington Chauncey Ford, "Biographical Sketch," in his *Correspondence and Journals of Samuel Blachley Webb* [New York, 1894], 3: 251–300)
    2. NG refers apparently to Sandy Hook, N.J., which stands at the entrance to New York's outer harbor. The Narrows is the strait to the north of Sandy Hook between Staten Island and Long Island; the New Utrecht shore is on the southern part of Long Island.
    3. Letter not found.
    4. Col. Richard Cary of Warwick County, Va., had been appointed an aide to Washington the same day as Webb. (Fitzpatrick, *GW*, 5: 165n; Freeman, *GW*, 4: 124n identifies him.)
    5. Washington's orders of 18 July specified "Two Guns fired from Cobble-Hill, on Long Island, are to be the Signal the enemy have landed on that Island" (Fitzpatrick, *GW*, 5: 299)

## General Greene's Orders

[Long Island Camp, N.Y., 19 July 1776. Work at Cobble Hill retarded for want of men who can lay turf.[1] Any that "Understand that Business" to be excused from other duties and given half pint of rum daily. Party to widen ditch at Ft. Stirling. Artillery guard to be mounted in Smith's Barbette on Cobble Hill. Patrols to advance silently, "Once in a few Rods to stop and Listen With Attention to Discover such as may Be Larking Round the Works as spies." Mitchell Orderly Book (NHi) 1 p.]

    1. Turf was laid over the raw earthworks to secure it against erosion.

## To George Washington

[From Camp on Long Island, N.Y., 19 July 1776. Col. Hand reports a British ship still at (Sandy) Hook. An armed sloop came up last night. Nothing extraordinary happened at camp since yesterday. Tr. (G. W. Greene Transcripts, CSmH) 1 p.]

## To George Washington

Sir                    Camp on Long Island [N.Y.] July 21, 1776, 2 oClock
    Colo Hands reports Seven large Ships are coming up from the Hook to the Narrows.
    A Negro belonging to one Strikser at Gravesend was taken prisoner as he says last Sunday at Coney Island. Yesterday he made his escape and was taken prisoner by the Riffle Guard. He reports Eight hundred Negroes collected on Staten Island, this day to be formd into a Regiment.[1] I am your Excellencys most obedient humble servant

N GREENE

ALS (Washington Papers: DLC).
1. Apparently there was no truth to his report.

## General Greene to Guards and Sentries
## in and about New York City

[From Camp on Long Island, N.Y., 21 July 1776. Permit for Capt. Abraham Whipple to pass through camps and fortifications.[1] Tr. (Transcription by C. W. Parsons in late nineteenth century is in RHi) 1 p.]

    1. Capt. Whipple was on his way back to his ship, the *Columbus*, after appearing before a congressional committee in Philadelphia on 11 July to answer charges against him by "divers of the inferior officers." The Marine Committee found that his wrongdoing amounted "to nothing more than a rough, indelicate mode of behaviour to his marine officers" and recommended that he "cultivate harmony with his officers." (Committee report is printed in Clark, *Naval Docs.*, 5: 1029.)

## To Governor Nicholas Cooke of Rhode Island

Dear Sir                    Camp on Long Island [N.Y.] July 22, 1776
    I may be chargeable with want of Respect for being silent so long, but I can assure you it is not for want of respect but time. General Hows army is encampt on Statten Island. Admiral How has arriv'd and has attempted to force a Letter upon General Washington without its being properly addressd. The Adjutant General of Hows army was in town upon that business a few days past but the General did not receive the Letter, therefore the contents remain a secret. The

forces are drawing together here on both sides. Seven Sail of large Ships got in yesterday, supposd to be part of [Admiral] Hows fleet. Our Troops comes in slowly, but I doubt not but that we shall have an army soon sufficient to act upon the offensive. The Enemy are entrenching upon Statten Island. They are apprehensive of some mischief. The flying Camp is expected to be all together this week. They are to be stationed in the Jerseys.[1]

General Lee has given General Clinton a cleaver snubing. It almost amounts to a total defeat. He lost only twelve men and twenty wounded. Clinton lost near two hundred.[2] Our people behaved with great spirit. Every thing still goes badly in the Northern Army. The Generals has come to one of the most mad resolutions I ever heard off; that is, to quit Crown Point.[3] There never could be a worse piece of policy. We loose all the advantages upon the Lake. We have now such a superiority there that the Enemy could not injure us this Summer. We lay all the back parts of New England open. Crown Point is a fine healthy spot and capable of being made exceeding strong. The post they purpose to take is strong but very unhealthy. General Sullivan has got mift at General Gates new appointment. He is coming home. General Scuyler dont act the General so much as he does the Commisary and Quartermaster or rather has not hither too. What he may do in future I am not able to say. The Southern and Northern People have got into a practice of reflecting upon one another. Animosity steals in and I greatly fear the consequences if not seasonably checkt. Something ought to be done to silence such foolish disputes. I have no Apprehensions upon my mind for any department but the Northern, and every thing there is strangely Perplext.

We are strongly fortified here. Every thing in readiness and the Troops in good spirits. I have not the most distant apprehensions for this army.

The Troops in my Brigade have been exceeding sickly. Those that were on board the fleet brought a putrid fever into the Camp at their return from the Ships that has raged to a prodigious degree, and swept off a large number, but its malignity begins to cease. The officers in general are well. Believe me to be with the greatest respect your Most obedient humble Servant.

NATH GREENE

ALS (MH).
1. In early June, Congress had authorized a Flying Camp (supposedly a highly mobile unit) of 6,000 militia from Pennsylvania, 3,400 from Maryland, and 600 from Delaware, to serve until Dec. 1776 (JCC, 4: 412–13). When substantial numbers arrived near Elizabethtown, N.J., in July Washington put them under Gen. Hugh Mercer of Virginia (Freeman, GW, 4: 147). After NG took command in N.J. in Sept., the Flying Camp came under him. By and large it was composed of poorly disciplined militiamen

who were anxious to get back home, and it began to disintegrate long before the enlistments expired.

2. The reference is to the battle of Charleston, S.C., on 28 June. Although Gen. Lee had gone to help secure Charleston, the battle was actually a naval engagement between Adm. Peter Parker's fleet and the fort on Sullivan's Island under Col. William Moultrie; neither Lee nor Clinton were participants (Willcox, *Clinton*, pp. 84–93). Peckham lists a third of the approximately two hundred British casualties as killed in action. (Peckham, *Toll*, pp. 18–19)

3. The decision to quit Crown Point was made jointly by Schuyler, Gates, Sullivan, and Arnold. (Ward, *War*, 1: 385) Had NG known of the pitiable condition of the half-starved, smallpox infested troops, he would not have called the decision "one of the most mad resolutions."

## To George Washington

[From Camp on Long Island, N.Y., 22 July 1776. Col. Hand reports troops that came yesterday appear to be dressed in "highland habits." ALS (Washington Papers: DLC) 1 p.]

## From Colonel James M. Varnum

[At Red Hook [N.Y.], 22 July 1776. Asks approval to discharge a captain whose wife is dying. The captain "cannot so far stifle the tender emotion of conjugal affection as to remain in absence." ALS (Washington Papers: DLC) 1 p.]

## General Greene's Orders

[In Camp Long Island, N.Y., 23 July 1776. Regimental commanders to send list of vacancies and proposals for filling them. Since the duty is "exceeding heavy," fatigue party to be reduced by one-half and the guard in Fts. Greene and Putnam by one third. Moses Little Orderly Book (NN) 1 p.]

## To George Washington

[From Camp on Long Island, N.Y., 23 July 1776. Encloses Varnum letter of 22 July above; says GW "can best determin the force of the Reasons offerd for a discharge." Col. Hand reports enemy continues as they were. ALS (Washington Papers: DLC) 1 p.]

## General Greene's Orders

[Camp on Long Island, N.Y., 24 July 1776. Party of forty men to cut fascines; four days' provisions to be provided. Passengers taking ferry to New York not to be stopped unless there is reason to suspect them. No one to come out without proper pass. Moses Little Orderly Book, reprinted from Johnston, *NY 1776*, pt. 2, pp. 23–24.]

## To George Washington

[From Camp on Long Island, N.Y., 24 July 1776. Col. Hand reports nothing changed since yesterday. ALS (Washington Papers: DLC) 1 p.]

## To George Washington

Sir                    Camp on Long Island [N.Y.] July 25, 1776

The Challenge I mentiond to your Excellency the other Evening I find is given and accepted and the parties have appointed tomorrow morning to fight. As I am made acquainted with the matter I beg your Excellencys direction in what manner I am to conduct myself.[1]

This moment Colo Hand was with me and acquaints me that I have mistaken his intentions respecting promotions. As he is coming to Head Quarters, I wish he may explain the matter to your Excellency, and the alteration be made on the return there, or send back to me and I'll make the necessary alterations here.

I apprehend it is necessary to have an order of Congress[2] for the removal of the Wheat along New Uttrecht, Graves End (&c) Shore, that if the Enemy should land there, they may not have it in their power to do us any injury for everything they destroy or carry off will be a matter of triumph. The Wheat is almost fit to thrash and can be speedily removd out of harms way.

I should be exceedingly glad if your Excellency would visit this post when at Liberty to see if there is any alteration or further regulations necessary. I am with due respect your Excellencys obedient servant

NATH GREENE

NB The Challenge mentiond in the fore part of my Letter was given by Lt Dunworth (discharg'd the other day) to Capt Talbut. I did not wish to know anything about it, but it was made known to me, and many of the officers knows that I doo know it. This Perplexes me a little Knowing Dueling to be against all Law both Civic and Military.[3]

ALS (Washington Papers: DLC).
    1. Washington's instructions, if any, have not survived. In a postscript below, NG names the principals.
    2. The N.Y. Provincial Congress.
    3. Capt. Silas Talbot, a Rhode Islander in Hitchcock's regiment, was a distinguished officer (see NG to Washington, below, 28 July). Article 11 of the Articles of War forbade dueling. Anyone associated with a duel, or anyone who "shall upbraid another for refusing a challenge," was to be courtmartialed, but no punishment was specified. The revised articles adopted in Sept. 1776 provided that any officer who challenged another was to be cashiered, but the punishment for a soldier was still to be determined by a courtmartial (Sect. 7, Arts. 2 and 3, JCC, 5: 793). Apparently the Dunworth-Talbot duel was not fought.

## To George Washington

Sir                    Camp on Long Island [N.Y.] July 25, 1776

I have just compleated a Brigade Return for the Vacancies in the different Regiments. My Brigade is so dispersed that it is difficult geting returns seasonably. I should have made this return yesterday but could not get Col Hands until last Evening.[1]

The out Guards reports nothing worthy your Excellencys notice this morning.

I am so confind writing passes etc that it is impossible for me to attend to the duties of the day, which in many instances prejudices the service. Such a confind situation leaves one no opportunity of viewing things for themselves. It is recommended by one of the greatest Generals of the Age not only to issue orders but to see to the execution; for the army being composd of men of Indolence, if the commander is not attentive to every Individual in the different departments, the Machine becomes dislocated and the progress of business retarded.

The science or art of War requires a freedom of thought and leisure to reflect upon the Various incidents that dayly occur, which cannot be had where the whole of ones time is engrossed in Clerical employments. The time devoted to this employment is not the only injury that I feel, but it confines my thoughts as well as engrosses my time. It is like a merchandise of small Wares.

I must beg leave to Recommend to your Excellencys consideration the appointing an officer to write and sign the necessary passes. The person I should wish to be appointed is Lt Blodget. If it was put in General orders that passes signed by him should be deemd Authentick as if signed by me, it would leave me at liberty to pursue the more important employments of my Station.[2]

I hope your Excellency wont think this application results from a lazy habit, or a desire to free myself from business; far from it. I am never more happy than when I am honnorably or usefully employ'd. If your Excellency thinks I can promote the service as much in this employment as any other, I shall chearfully execute the business without the least murmur. I am with all due respect your Excellencys most obedient humble servant

NATH GREENE

ALS (Washington Papers: DLC).
1. Col. Hand's rifle regiment was along the south shore of Long Island "scattered over 5 miles in length" according to Col. Little (Johnston, *NY 1776*, pt. 2, p. 42).
2. No one could more fully appreciate the burden of paper work than Washington. On the same day, he wrote John Hancock to ask for an additional aide as the "augmentation of my Command, the Increase of my Corrispondance, the Orders to give; the Instructions to draw, cut out more business than I am able to execute in time, with propriety" (Fitzpatrick, *GW*, 5: 337–38). Washington's orders of 26 July stated that

"General Greene being particularly engaged at present, passes signed by Lieut. Blodget, are to be allowed sufficient to enable persons to cross the ferries" (ibid., p. 340).

William Blodget of Hitchcock's regiment had been secretary of the R.I. Army of Observation; after the regiment was taken into the Continental army, he served as NG's personal secretary (Bartlett, *Records*, 7: 339). On NG's promotion to major general, he named Blodget as one of his two aides (see below, NG to Washington, 15 Aug.). Before the war "Fat Billy," as he was affectionately called, had been an actor in a Providence company (NG to Samuel Ward, Jr., 30 May 1773), and during the war his humor and histrionics lightened many a dull or anxious hour. In the latter part of the war, he served as chaplain on a navy vessel.

## Estimated Paper Requirements for the Military[1]

[Long Island Camp, N.Y., July 25, 1776]

For 5 morning Reports to be made by the Corporals of the state of each Company, one to each Officer in the Co and one to the Adjutant
8 Sheets per Day

Also a daily Report of the Sick to the Surgeon of the Regt by the Corporal, and of the absent men
1 sh per Day

The Adjutant must every day make a Report of the state of the Regiment to the Commanding Officer

The Sargeant of each Company to make a Provision Return every other day to the Qr. Master

The Adjutant to make three weekly Returns, one to H Qrs, one to Brigade Genl, and one to the Colo Regiment

The Surgeons to make 3 weekly Returns, One for H Qrs, one to Brigade Genl and one to Cols Regiment

He must moreover have paper to dispence medicines and send order for the reception of the men into the General Hospital

Daily Reports of Guards

Regimental Court Martials and orders on the Q. M. Gls store for necessaries for the men

Sheet paper per month to each Compy to make Abstracts and the like quantity to Register them

Paper for passes on necessary occasions

Reports of Arms and Ammunition necessary to be made by each Co at least twice a Week

Paper for necessary correspondance

A Ream per month to each Regiment thought sufficient

NATHANAEL GREENE    MOSES LITTLE

J M VARNUM      EDWD HAND

DAN HITCHCOCK

DS (Washington Papers: DLC).

1. In a general order the previous day, Washington had requested estimates on the

quantity of paper "absolutely necessary" for a regiment for a month (Fitzpatrick, *GW*, 5: 335–36). On 29 July he directed the quartermaster general to furnish each regiment twelve quires of paper (ibid., p. 353; a quire was twenty-four large, folded sheets).

The mass of paper that has survived from the period is evidence that fighting a war with paper is not a strictly modern phenomenon. The above estimate did not include the prodigious amount of paper needed for cartridges, which were made by placing powder and musket ball in a paper cylinder, the ends being tied or twisted together.

## General Greene's Orders

[Long Island, N.Y.] 26 July 1776

The Main Guard at Fort Green to Consist of 1 Subaltern, 1 Sergeant, 1 Corporal and 27 Privates to be Reinforc'd at Night with a Picquet of a Sergeant and ten Men. Colonel Little is desir'd to attend to the Posting the Centries. Centries to be Posted in Fort Box from the Main Guard by Day and Night as there will no Guard Mount there for the future untill further Order. A Corporal and six men to Mount Guard at Fort Putnam in the Morning to be reinforc'd with a Subaltern, Sergeant and 24 Privates as a Picquet at Night. Colonel Hitchcock is desir'd to attend to the posting the Centries. After the first Posting the Centries the Officers that Commanded the Old Picquet to acquaint the Officer that Commands the New Picquet the next Night where to post the Centries. This Mode to continue until further Orders.

The Artillery to Mount a Guard at Fort Stirling of 1 Gunner and 6 Matrosses. At Fort Putnam 1 Gunner and 3 Matrosses. At Fort Green 1 Gunner and 3 Matrosses. At Cobble Hill 1 Gunner and 3 Matrosses. Thee several Guards to Parade on the Grand Parade and to be Detach'd jregularly with the other Guards By the Brigade Major. The Guards to continue on Duty and at the Posts they are stationd until Regularly reliev'd the next Day.

The Guard at Fort Sterling [Stirling] to keep the Fort by Day and furnish the Centries. A Picquet to Mount there at Night to Consist of 1 Sergeant, 1 Corporal, and 12 Privates. The Ferry Guard to furnish the Centries for the Hospital. The Guard at Rapelljies Mill, at Cobble Hill and at the two Mill Dams to consist of the same Number as heretofore. Mr Champney, the Waggon Master Genl, is directed to deliver the proper Quantity of Wood for the use of the Regiments at the Encampments and to furnish the several Quarter Masters with Teams to Transport the Provisions for the Regt. This to be considered as a standing Order.

Henshaw Orderly Book (MWA).

## To George Washington

[From Camp Long Island, N.Y., 5:00 P.M., 26 July 1776. Col. Cham-

bers[1] sighted eight sail at great distance, possibly transports, standing for (Sandy) Hook. ALS (Washington Papers: DLC) 1 p.]

1. James Chambers was a lieutenant colonel in Hand's rifle regiment. As captain of
a Cumberland County, Pa., company, he was attached to NG's command in Aug. 1775.
He later headed a brigade in Gen. Anthony Wayne's division. (*PMHB* 35 [1911]: 339n)

## To George Washington

Camp on Long Island [N.Y.]
Dear Sir                                        Saturday morning [July 27, 1776]
   Colo Hand Reports five Ships one Brigg and five Schooners at
the Hook. One very large Vessel came up last Evening to the fleet.
One other Ship saild about one this morning, but the Col dont write
whether she went down or up.
   I have four Prisoners Inhabitants of Queens County that were
taken yesterday attempting to make their escape to the Enemy. I am
just going to examin them. If I discover any thing worthy your
Excellencys notice it shall be transmited you immediately.[1]
   I receivd information last Evening of there being thirty or forty
Tories on a little Island near the entrance of Jamacai Bay.[2] Three boats
full of men was seen off there day before yesterday but they did not
land nor speak with any Boats that the Guards could discover. I sent a
party of Sixty men to scour the Island this morning and to take all
they found there prisoners. I am with all due respect your Excellencys
very humble servant

NATH GREENE

ALS (Washington Papers: DLC).
   1. See below, his letter to Washington later the same day.
   2. Jamaica Bay is on the south shore of Long Island, some twenty miles east of
Long Island Camp.

## To George Washington

[Long Island, N.Y.]
Dear sir                                        Saturday 12 oClock [July 27, 1776]
   I have examind the prisoners and find them to be a poor parcel of
Ignorant, Cowardly fellows. Two are Taylors named John and James
Dunbar, and the other two are common labourers named Isaac Petit
and Will Smith. They candidly confess they set off with an intention
of going to Statten Island but not with any intention of Joining the
Enemy, but to get out of the way of fighting here. I believe the true
reasons of their attempting to make their escape were, there has been
a draught amongst the Militia to fill the New Levies and it was

rumord these were a part that were drawn. It was also reported they were to go into the Northern army and that almost all that went there dyed or were killed. The prospect was so shocking to them and to their Grand Mothers and Aunts, I believe they perswaded them to run away. Never did I see fellows more frighted. They wept like a parcel of Children and appear exceeding sorrowful.

One of them is in an exceeding ill state of health, very unfit for any fatigue. I beg your Excellencys direction how to dispose of them. They dont appear to be acquainted with one publick matter. They have been Toryish but I fancy not from principle, but from its being the prevailing Sentiment in the County.

Mrs Grant[1] desires to go on board the fleet tomorrow, and to carry the necessary provision for her passage, agreeable to the Order or Permit of Congress. Your Excellency will please to signify your pleasure in the matter. I have the honnor to be your obedient servant

NATH GREENE

ALS (Washington Papers: DLC).
1. Mrs. Penuel Grant's husband, in her words, "being bound by his allegiance and honour to apear to the royall standard by order of Governor Tryon . . . tocke the opertunity of forcing his Journy for the british Troupes" in New York City. She hoped to join him with her six small children. Washington was probably too harassed to deal with Mrs. Grant, because the following April she was again petitioning the N.Y. Congress for safe passage. Her request was rejected, but given British control of the area for the next seven years and Mrs. Grant's persistence, she undoubtedly succeeded. (Her petition is in NY MSS, 2: 92.)

## General Greene's Orders

[Long Island, N.Y.] 28 July 1776
The Success [of] the Campaign must in A Great Measure Depend upon the Health of the Troops. Nothing therefore should be Neglected that Contributes to that end. Good Policy as well as humanity Claims every Officers attention to this important Object. Upon this Depends our Honour as well as our success. The Good Officer is not Characterized for Discharging his Duty in one, but in every respect. It is a Mistaken Notion that the Manutia of Military Matters is only an imployment for little Minds. Such an Officer Betrays a want of Understanding and shews the person Ignorant of the Necessary Dependence and Connection of one thing upon another. For what signifies Knowledge without power to execute, he who studies only such Branches of military knowledge as relates to Dispositions and Neglects to preserve the Health of Troops Will find himself in a Disagreeable Situation.

Tis with Pain the General ⟨has⟩ of late Discovered to[o] much Inattention to the filling and Digging the Necessary Vaults for the Regiment, to the burying all Filth and Putrid matter brought into

Camp not Consumed. The General Directs in the Most positive manner that the Camp Coulerman of the Respective Regiments Dig new Vaults and fill up the old Ones every once in three Days and that there be some Fresh Earth thrown in upon the Face of the Vaults every Day and that all the Filth in and About the Camp be Daily ⟨buried⟩. The General requests the Officers of every Rank to pay Particular Attention to the execution of this Order and to the Mens repairing to their proper Vaults to ease themselves. Let no man go unpunished that Neglect it.

The General Also forbids in the most Positive Terms the Troops easing themselves in the Ditches of the Fortifications, a Practice that is Disgracefull to the last Degree. If these matters are not attended to, the stench Arising from such Places will soon Breed a Pestilence In the Camp. The sickley season now coming on and Putrid Fevers prevailing, the Genl recommends a Free use of Vegitables, and Desires the men may keep themselves and Cloaths Clean and Coock their Provisions Properly and little Injury is to be Dreaded from the Approaching season. But a Neglect in Attending to those matters at this Critical season may be attended with Dreadfull Consequences.

Many Complaints are made of the Troops stealing Watermellons In and About the Camp. Such Practices Continued will be punished in the most exemplary manner. The General Desires the Officers to bring every offendr to Justice. Altho the General is taking every ⟨measure⟩ In his Power to lessen the Duty of the Trôops, he nevertheless will Oblige the Troops to guard the Peoples property. If it Cannot be preserved any other way and as a few unprincipled Raskals may have it in their Power to Ruin the Reputation of a Whole Corps of Virtuous Men, the General Desires the virtuous part to Complain of every Offender that may be Detected in Invading People's Property In an unlawful manner, that a stop may be put to a Practice that Cannot fail, If Continued, rendring both Officers and men obnoxious to the Inhabitants.[1]

Moses Little Orderly Book (NN). Portions in angle brackets from Gen. Greene Orderly Book, Bergen County (N.J.) Historical Society.

1. With loyalists and neutralists far outnumbering patriots in the vicinity of Long Island Camp, NG was especially concerned with keeping on the good side of the inhabitants.

## To George Washington

Camp on Long Island [N.Y.] Sunday 12 o'clock [July 28, 1776]
Colonel Hands morning report contained nothing material. Lieutenant Colonel Chambers reports this moment that he saw at ten this

morning ten Sail of Vessels standing in for the Hook, but at too great a distance to discover what they were.

Mrs Grant applies again for Permission to go on board the fleet. Should be glad to know your Excellencys pleasure in the matter. She pleads great distress, but it can amount only to a family matter, make the best of it.[1]

The new levies that come in hanker after Milk and Vegetables. I should think it would benefit the service to allow all the Regiments to draw one third the Value of the Animal food in money to purchase milk &c and direct, in the most positive terms, the Quarter Masters here to provide it for the men.[2] I am with all due respect your Excellencys most Obedient humble Servant.

N GREENE

ALS (Washington Papers: DLC).
 1. See note, NG to GW, 27 July, above.
 2. See note, NG to GW, 11 July, above, which proposed this. Since Washington had authorized the regiments to purchase vegetables in his general orders of 22 July (Fitzpatrick, *GW*, 5: 320), NG must not have seen the orders.

## To George Washington

Sir                    Camp on Long Island [N.Y.] July 28, 1776

Col Hands reports that the Enemy continues as they were. They fird several Guns last Night different from any custom that has prevaild amongst them since the Arrival of the fleet. A considerable noise and movement of the Boats was heard after the Signal Guns, and the hurry and confusion they seemd to be in after the firing discoverd they were alarmd. Perhaps they have heard of the fire Ships.

Capt Talbut of Colo Hitchcocks Regiment begs the command of one of these Vessels.[1] He is a daring Spirit and I dont doubt will execute the command agreeable to your Excellencys wishes. As I am totally Ignorant of the matter I could give him no encouragement until your Excellencys pleasure was known. I have the honnor to be your Excellencys most obedient humble servant

N GREENE

ALS (Washington Papers: DLC).
 1. Shortly after HMS *Phoenix* and *Rose* made their way up the Hudson past the American batteries (NG to John Adams, 14 July, above), the Americans fitted out fireboats to destroy them (see Washington to Col. James Clinton, 17 July 1776, and to Gen. George Clinton, 26 July, Fitzpatrick, *GW*, 5: 294, 340; and Koke, "Hudson," pp. 153–64). It was undoubtedly as the commander of one of these fireboats that the daring Capt. Silas Talbot volunteered, but the command was given to his fellow Rhode Islander, Ens. John Thomas, who lost his life in the daring venture. Talbot volunteered for another such mission later in the year in which he was severely burned. In October 1777 Congress promoted him to major "in consideration of his Merit and Services in a

spirited Attempt to set Fire to a Man of War, supposed to be the *Asia* in the North River last year" and compensated him "433 ⅔ dollars" for his injuries (*JCC*, 9: 794, 796). Despite his injuries, Talbot went on to a remarkable career in the army and navy; he was twice injured, once captured, and once again rewarded for his bravery by Congress for commanding troops in the bold capture of the armed schooner *Pigot* in Rhode Island waters (*JCC*, 12: 1132; see also Heitman, *Register*). He ended his career as a captain in the U.S. navy (Morgan, *Captains*, pp. 179–81).

## To George Washington

[From Camp on Long Island, N.Y., 29 July 1776. Col. Hand reports nine ships, four brigs, and two sloops at [Sandy] Hook last evening. ALS (Washington Papers: DLC) 1 p.]

## To George Washington

[From Camp on Long Island, N.Y., 31 July 1776. Col. Hand reports two ships at (Sandy) Hook. ALS (Washington Papers: DLC) 1 p.]

## General Greene's Orders

[Long Island Camp, N.Y., 1 Aug. 1776. Slawbunks (sleeping bunks) in different regiments to be collected for the sick in Col. Forman's regiment. Party to cut wood for coal pit in armorers shop, to draw axes and be ready to march with weeks provision.[1] Henshaw Orderly Book (MWA) 1 p.]

1. Although Brooklyn Heights was covered with trees and brush, the wood was apparently unsatisfactory for charcoal, since the men were being sent some distance from camp.

## General Greene's Orders

[Long Island Camp, N.Y., 1 Aug. 1776. Courtmartial under Col. Little as president found Joseph Bennet not guilty of desertion. "Barna McMarren" of Col. Hitchcock's regiment was found guilty of "Getting asleep on his post and Insulting and Abusing the Capt of the Guards. (He) is Condemned to be whipped 39 lashes and Drumed out of the Regt, Camp and Army." The general (NG) orders that after punishment takes place, the provost guard be requested to send the "Guard out beyond Kings Bridge (Westchester) with the Prisoner that he may not have it in his Power to Desert to the Enemy." Gen. Greene Orderly Book, Bergen County (N.J.) Historical Society 2 pp.]

## To George Washington

Dear Sir                    Camp on Long Island [N.Y.] Augt 1, 1776
    Colo Hand Reports thirty Sail of Ships standing in for the Hook.
Perhaps this may be part of the foreign Troops.[1]
    I detacht for the Galleys between forty and fifty men yesterday.[2]
Two companies that have been with Col Foremans Regiment are
gone from this post to Join their Regiment under General Heard. The
Troops in general are exceeding Sickly, great numbers taken down
every day.[3] If the state of the army will admit of a Reinforcement at
this Post perhaps it may be prudent. If it does not, I will do the best I
can with what I have got. I am with all due respect your Excellencys
most obedient Servt

                                                            N GREENE

ALS (Washington Papers: DLC).
    1. See NG to GW, below, 2 August.
    2. Row galleys were being built in order to attack HMS *Phoenix* and *Rose* in the
Hudson (note 4, NG to John Adams, 14 July, above). Because a large proportion of
NG's R.I. troops had gotten their livelihood from the ocean, they often volunteered or
were chosen for maritime enterprises. (For example, see above, NG's orders for 10 Oct.
1775 and 10 April 1776.)
    3. Despite NG's efforts to maintain his troops' health through cleanliness and diet,
many fell victims to the same illnesses that infected a large part of Washington's army
(see above, orders of 28 July). Gen. Heath estimated the number of sick in the army at
ten thousand. "In almost every farm, stable, shed, and even under the fences and
bushes, were the sick to be seen," he wrote. (Heath, *Memoirs*, p. 61) Col. Parsons wrote
to Col. Little on 4 Aug., "My Doctor and Mate are sick. I have near two hundred men
sick in Camp; my neighbours are in very little better state." (Quotation is from Johnston, *NY 1776*, pt. 1, p. 125.)

## To George Washington

                                Camp on Long Island [N.Y.]
Dear Sir                                Augt 1, 1776 4 oClock P. M.
    The fleet reported coming in this morning consists of about forty
Sail, Tenders and all.[1] They are now off New Uttrecht Shore. Pilots
have gone down to bring them up. The dispute subsisting between
an officer in Col Littles Regt and Col Varnums I hope is in a fair way to
be accommodateed.[2] In todays orders a Regt of General Wadsworths[3]
Brigade is orderd on this Island. If they can have Tents it will be much
the best. I am with all due respect your Excellencys most obedient
Servt

                                                            N GREENE

ALS (Washington Papers: DLC).
    1. See NG to GW, below, 2 Aug.
    2. See NG to GW, above, 25 July.
    3. James Wadsworth was a brigadier general of the Conn. militia.

# To George Washington

Dear Sir                    Camp on Long Island [N.Y.] Augt 2, 1776
    Colo Hand reports nothing worthy your Excellencys notice this morning.
    I was at the Narrows last Evening and find the fleet that came in yesterday consisted of 36 Ships, 4 Briggs and five Sloops; one Ship and a Sloop still at the Hook. I could not learn with any degree of certainty who they are.[1] But I believe from their Uniforms they must be the Guards and artillery. If your Excellency has leisure, perhaps it may be worth while to pay a Visit to the Narrows to Reconnoiter and view the fleet.
    With respect to the Tents I wrote about Yesterday, I can easily dispense with them if there is barracks to be got for the Regt. I wrote to the Quarter Master General to send over his Barracks Master to take up Quarters for the Regiment this morning. Shall notify your Excellency the result of the Barracks Masters inquiry. I have the honnor to be your Excellencys obedient Servant

                                        NATHANAEL GREENE

ALS (Washington Papers: DLC).
    1. They were part of Adm. Peter Parker's fleet that had sailed from Charleston, S.C., following the disastrous attack on Sullivan's Island. (See above, 22 July, NG to Cooke, note 2.) Aboard were Generals Henry Clinton and Charles Cornwallis and some 2,500 troops. Parker himself did not arrive with the rest of his fleet until 14 Aug. (Lord Howe to Philip Stephens, Morgan, *Naval Docs.*, 6: 183).

# General Greene's Orders

[Long Island Camp, N.Y., 4 Aug. 1776. Col. Gay's regiment[1] to take Ft. Stirling and Cobble Hill for their alarm posts. Those who have spread the countersign outside the army will be severely punished. No one, including inhabitants, to pass within the camp after 10:00 P.M. except general or field officers, brigade major, and expresses. A private taken up after ten is to be confined in guardhouse until morning; a commissioned officer or an inhabitant who belongs within limits of the camp if taken up is to be escorted home by an officer of the guard. From dark until ten, the people to pass as usual, but no troops after tattoo. Two hundred men to work at Ft. Stirling tomorrow. All officers should acquaint themselves "with the Ground for Miles round the Camp that they may be able to Command a Detachment if it should be necessary." Moses Little Orderly Book (NN) 2 pp.]

    1. Washington had sent Col. Fisher Gay of Wadworth's Conn. militia to report to NG on Long Island, 2 Aug. (The order is not in Fitzpatrick, but is taken from Henshaw

Orderly Book [MWA].) On 12 Aug. he and his regiment were ordered back to N.Y. (Fitzpatrick, *GW*, 5: 422).

## From John Adams

Dear Sir                                        Philadelphia August 4, 1776

Your Favour of the 14 of July is before me. I am happy to find your Sentiment concerning the Rewards of the Army and the Promotion of officers, so nearly agreable to mine. I wish the general sense here was more nearly agreable to them. Time I hope will introduce a proper sense of Justice in those Cases where it may for want of Knowledge and Experience be wanting.

The New England Collonells, you observe, are jealous that Southern officers are treated with more attention than they, because Several of the Southern Collonells have been made Generals, but not one of them.[1] Thompson was somehow or other the first Coll upon the Establishment and so intituled to Promotion, by succession, and it was also supposed by ability and Merit.[2] This ought not therefore to give offence. Mercer, Lewis, Howe, More,[3] were veteran officers and stood in the Light of Putnam, Thomas, Fry, Whitcomb &c among the New England officers.[4] Added to this we have endeavoured to give Colonies General officers in some Proportion to their Troops, and Colonies have nice feelings about Rank as well as Collonells. So that I dont think our Colls have just Cause to complain of these Promotions. Lord Sterling was a Person so distinguished by Fortune, Family, and the Rank and Employment he had held in civil Life, added to his Experience in military Life that it was thought no great uneasiness would be occasioned by his advancement. Mifflin was a Gentleman of Family and Fortune in his Country, of the best Education and abilities, of great Knowledge of the World, and remarkable activity. Besides this, the Rank he had held as a member of the Legislature of this Province, and a Member of Congress, and his great Merit in the civil Department in Subduing the Quaker and Proprietaries Interests added to the Tory Interest of this Province to the American System of Union, and Specially his activity and success in infusing into this Province a martial spirit and ambition which it never felt before were thought sufficient Causes for his advancement. Besides all this my dear Sir, there is a political Motive. Military Characters in the Southern Colonies are few. They have never known much of War and it is not easy to make a People Warlike who have never been so. All the encouragement and every Incentive, therefore which can be given with Justice ought to be given in order to incite an Ambition among them for Military Honours.

But after all, my dear Sir, I wish I could have a few Hours free Conversation with you upon this important Subject. A General officer ought to be a Gentleman of Letters and General Knowledge, a Man of Address and Knowledge of the World.[5] He should carry with him Authority and Command. There are among the New England officers Gentlemen who are equal to all this. Parsons,[6] Hitchcock, Varnum and others younger than they, and in fairness to them too in command. But these are a great way down in the list of Collonells, and to promote them over the Heads of so many Veterans would throw all into Confusion. Reed, Nixon, and Prescott are the ablest Collonells.[7] They are allowed to be experienced officers, and brave Men. But I believe there is not one Member of Congress who knows the face of either of them, and what their accomplishments are I know not.

I really wish you would give me your advice freely upon these Subjects in confidence. It is not every Piece of wood that will do to make a Mercury, and Bravery alone is not a Sufficient Qualification for a General Officer. Name me a New England Coll of whose real Qualifications I can speak with Confidence, who is intituled to Promotion by succession and If I do not get him made a General Officer I will join the N. E. Collonells and outclamour the loudest of them in this Jealousy.

There is a real difficulty attending this Subject which I know not how to get over. Pray help me. I believe there would be no Difficulty in obtaining advancement for some of the N. E. Colls here. But by promoting them over the Heads of so many there would be a Difficulty in the Army.

LB (Adams Papers: MHi).

1. As chairman of the recently created Board of War, John Adams had done his homework on the general officers already named by Congress; he also knew a great deal about the regimental commanders of New England. Although he was often aroused by slights to New England, his argument here in answer to the complaining "New England Collonells" is a model of objectivity.

2. William Thompson (1736–81) was a southerner only to a New Englander. Born in Ireland, he had settled in Pennsylvania, where he enlisted in the French and Indian War. As commander of the famed Pennsylvania Rifle Battalion, he had been attached to NG's command at Prospect Hill the previous year. On 1 March 1776 he was made brigadier general; on 7 June he was captured while commanding a regiment on the St. Lawrence. (DAB)

3. The southerners Mercer, Lewis, Howe, and Moore not only qualified as veteran officers, they were also distinguished in their civilian roles. All but Mercer were made brigadier generals on 1 March 1776; Mercer's promotion dated from 5 June 1776.

Andrew Lewis (1720–81) was a Virginian of Scotch-Irish descent. A veteran of the French and Indian War, he won laurels in Lord Dunmore's war as commander of the victorious forces in the bloody Indian battle at Point Pleasant. He had served in the Va. legislature and revolutionary conventions. (DAB)

Robert Howe (1732–86) was a prominent planter in North Carolina. Educated in England, he became a leader of the patriot cause. He had served almost a decade as captain and colonel of the militia when he was placed in command of the N.C. Second Regiment. He commanded the troops who captured Norfolk, and when Charles Lee returned to N.Y. from Charleston, Howe was given command of the southern department. (DAB)

James Moore (1737–77) was also a North Carolinian. A captain in the French and Indian War, he sat almost ten years in the Provincial Assembly and was prominent in the Sons of Liberty. In Feb. 1776 he led the first N.C. regiment in the campaign that led to victory over the loyalist Highlanders at Moore's Creek Bridge, although he was not in the final engagement. He died the following Feb. en route with his troops to join Washington. (*DAB*)

4. Joseph Frye (1711/12–94) of Mass. saw extended service in the French and Indian War. As second in command of a regiment that was defeated at Ft. William Henry, he barely escaped with his life. Later he commanded Ft. Cumberland in Acadia. He was sixty-three when he was appointed major general of the Mass. militia and sixty-four when he received the same rank in the Continental army on 1 Mar. (*DAB*) Washington noted a few days later that "he keeps his room, and talks learnedly of emetics, cathartics, &c. For my own part, I see nothing but a declining life that matters him" (Fitzpatrick, *GW*, 4: 382). His infirmities caused him to resign a month later.

John Whitcomb, who had been a major general in the Mass. militia, declined his appointment as brigadier general in the Continental army (Heitman, *Register*).

5. A year and a half earlier, NG and his brothers would have been amused if not incredulous to have heard him considered a "Gentleman of Letters and General Knowledge, a Man of Address and Knowledge of the World." That Adams now implied this unconsciously was a tribute to NG's remarkable aptitude for learning as well as to his growing confidence. Adams's examples, below, of Parson, Hitchcock, and Varnum—lawyers all and graduates of Harvard, Yale, and R.I. College respectively— more nearly fitted the conventional pattern he had in mind.

6. Samuel H. Parsons (1737–89) was a Conn. lawyer and legislator, who as a colonel of militia helped capture Ticonderoga in 1775. He was made brigadier general in the Continental army in Aug. 1776 and fought in the battle of Long Island. He spent the rest of the war along the Hudson River or the Conn. shore. He was made major general in 1780. (*DAB*)

7. James Reed (1722–1807) of Mass. fought as a captain through much of the French and Indian War. At the Lexington alarm, he was a resident of N.H. and commanded a regiment of the colony's militia at Bunker Hill. As a colonel in the Continental army, Reed led troops to relieve Arnold in the spring of 1776, on which mission he was struck by an illness that blinded him. A few days later, Congress named him brigadier general, but he was unable to serve.

William Prescott (1726–95), a Mass. farmer who served in both King George's War and the French and Indian War, won fame as the hero of Bunker Hill. During 1776 he was a colonel in the Seventh Continental Regiment and took part in the evacuation of N.Y. in Sept. 1776. (*DAB*)

# To George Washington

Dear Sir                    Camp on Long Island $[$N.Y.$]$ Augt 4, $[$1776$]$

Col Hand Reports 21 Sail seen off last Evening, Eight arrivd at the Hook this morning and thirteen coming in.[1]

The Enemies Guard Boats pattrolled much higher up the Bay than usual last Night.

I apprehend a couple of Guard Boats are necessary to Pattrole from Red to Yellow Hook across the Bay leading to Rappelyeas Mills,[2] providing there are Boats to spare.

Inclosed is a return of the officers of Col Hands Riffle Regiment. As the return made me by Col Hand is not as intelligible as I could wish I shall send and get another as soon as may be. I must beg your Excellencys Pardon for suffering the return to escape my memory and neglecting makeing it agreeable to your orders some days past.

I shall send in a list of the Names in a few hours of the persons proper to be taken up on this Island.[3] I am with respect your Excellencys most obedient servant

NATH GREENE

ALS (Washington Papers: DLC).
1. These were mostly stragglers from two convoys, some separated, as Lord Howe reported, "in bad Weather by the Misconduct of the Masters" (Morgan, *Naval Docs.*, 6: 122). Although most of the four hundred British vessels arrived as part of four principal fleet operations, Col. Hand and Col. Chambers reported to NG some sixty stragglers during July and Aug.
2. This Dutch name was variously spelled; Thomas W. Field spelled it "Rapalye" (Field, *Long Island*, index entries, p. 543).
3. See second letter of 4 Aug. from NG to GW, below, for the list of "Tories."

## To George Washington

Camp on Long Island [N.Y.]

Dear Sir                              Sunday [Aug. 4, 1776] 11 oClock

Inclosd is a list of the principal Tories[1] in the different Towns given by one Mr Skinner, a young Gentleman bred to the practice of the Law and perfectly acquainted with all most all the political Charactors in the Province. Your Excellency will please to examin it, and if it meets your approbation signify the time youl have the execution take place by give [giving] your orders on the back of the List.[2] I have the honnor to be your obedient Servant

N GREENE

ALS (Washington Papers: DLC). See note 1 on enclosure.
1. List is printed below.
2. By "execution" NG refers to the arrest of the group. The original list, which is found in the Washington Papers (DLC), does not have Washington's orders on the back.

## Abraham Skinner's List of "Tories"

| | | | |
|---|---|---|---|
| Hugh Wallace | Jamaica | William Thorn | Great Neck |
| Alexr Wallace | | Justice Kissam | |
| Doctr Ardin | | Benjn Hewlet | |
| Mr Bethune | should be Secured | Richard Townsend | (North side) |
| Nathl Mills | | Justice Clowes | Hempstead |
| Joseph French | should be Secured | | should be Secured |
| Capt Benjamin Whitehead | | David Beaty | |
| Richard Betts | | Doctr Seabury | |
| John Troup | | Benjn Lester | |
| | | Samuel Langdon | |

—Van Brient (at the Mill)
Robt Ross Waddle
Thomas Willett Esqr, Sheriff
　Flushing
Edward Willett
David Colden
Judge Willett
Joseph Field
Charles Willett
Joseph Griswold at the Plains
Justice Isaac Smith

George Hewlet　Hempstead So
Stephen Hewlett
John Miller
James Coggeshall　should be
　　　　Secured
Richard Hewlett　Rockaway
Doctr Martin
Charles Hicks
Whitehead Cornell
Justice John Hewlett　East Woods

ABRM SKINNER[1]

ADS (Washington Papers: DLC). Enclosed in letter above, NG to Washington [4 Aug.].
　1. Young Skinner, having kinsmen among the "Tories," was undoubtedly in a position to know a great deal about the men listed. Among those enumerated were some of New York's most eminent loyalists, including Bishop Seabury and the son of Cadwalader Colden.

## General Greene's Orders

[Long Island, N.Y.] 7 August 1776
The Commanding Officers of the respective Fortifications are Requested to pay Particular Attention to the Provisions lodged at each Alarm Post for the support of the Troops in case of a seige and see that they are in Good Ordr and also that the Water Casks and Cisterns are filled and Whenever the Water Gets bad to have it pumped out and Fresh put in.

By a Deserter from Sir [Peter] Parkers fleet we learn the Hessians from England and Clintons Troops from South Carolina have arrivd and that the Enemy Are Meditating an Attack On this Island and the City of New York.[1]

The General Wishes to have The Troops furnished with every thing Necessary to Give a Proper reception. The Captains of every Company are Directed to examine the Arms of his Company immediately.

Moses Little Orderly Book (NN).
　1. On Clinton's troops see above, NG to Washington, 2 Aug. Although the principal body of Germans arrived on 12 Aug. (NG to Washington that day), the deserter was correct in reporting the arrival of some Hessian troops (see above, NG to Washington, 4 Aug.).

## To Colonel Moses Little

[Long Island, N.Y.] Wednesday morning
Dear Sir                                    6 oclock [7 Aug. 1776][1]
Mr Skinner has wrote for a few more men.[2] Please to pick out
about a dozzen; you and Major Angel to go to his assistance as soon
as possible, give them orders to take up Horses anywhere round the
Camp. Let them be equipt as soon as possible and march to Jamacai,
and take Mr Skinners further direction as he is the only person
acquainted with the People and Country. I am dear Sir your obed
Servant

N GREENE

I would attend to this business myself, but have taken a large Portion
of Physick.

ALS (MeHi).
    1. The letter is undated, but NG's order below of 8 Aug., taken from Col. Little's
Orderly Book, would seem to place this letter on Wednesday, 7 Aug.
    2. Abraham Skinner was the young lawyer who furnished NG with a list of
"Tories" (see above, second letter of 4 Aug., from NG to Washington).

## General Greene's Orders

[Long Island Camp, N.Y., 8 Aug. 1776. Twenty men to be decently
dressed to assist Lt. (Abraham) Skinner. Officers are to see that men
are not to offer "insolence or abuse to any person."[1] Moses Little
Orderly Book, reprinted from Johnston, *NY 1776*, pt. 2, pp. 25–26.]

    1. The men were to assist in rounding up loyalists. See above, NG to Col. Little,
[7 Aug.].

## General Greene's Orders

[Long Island, N.Y.] August 9, 1776[1]
A report from Col. Hand mentions a large number of regulars drawn
up at Staten Island Ferry, and boats to embark in. No officer or soldier
to stir from his quarters that we may be ready to march at a moment's
warning if necessary.

Moses Little Orderly Book, reprinted from Johnston, *NY 1776*, pt. 2, p. 26.
    1. It would appear that this order was written before Col. Varnum's report was
received on the evening of 8 Aug., although it may not have been posted until the
morning of 9 Aug.

# To George Washington

L Island [N.Y.] Wednesday [Thursday?] Evening
Dear Sir                                    [August 8, 1776] 9 oClock[1]
Col Varnum Reports from Red Hook about sunset and after as
many as one hundred Boats were seen coming from Statten Island to
the Ships full of Men. Three Ships went towards the Narrows previous to which about thirty Boats with Soldiers went on board them.
From the best observations made by Capt Foster and others there is a
general Imbarcation.[2]

I have inclosd a Report from the officer of one of Col Hands out
Guards sent by Express this Evening. Your Excellency will pay the
attention the intelligence deserves. I am your Excellencys most obedient Servant

NATH GREENE

ALS (Washington Papers: DLC). Enclosure missing.
1. NG designated the date as simply "Wednesday Evening," which would have
placed it on 7 Aug. His letter to Col. Little the next morning (see below) is headed
"Thursday Morning." It would appear from several other documents, however, that he
was mistaken on the day of the week in both letters. In his letter to Hancock on 9 Aug.,
Washington speaks of NG's report of "last night," and NG's next letter to GW, also
dated 9 Aug., refers to "my last Evenings Report." Other documents confirm the
probable date of this letter as Thursday, 8 Aug. The letter to Little would then be
redated as Friday morning, 9 Aug.
2. It is not recorded what General Howe had in mind by this operation. The actual
embarkation for the landing on Long Island did not occur for another two weeks. It
may have been a war of nerves; if so, it did have the effect of putting NG's troops on a
tense alert. On the other hand, it caused Washington to enlarge his forces.

# General Greene's Orders

[Camp Long Island, N.Y., 9 Aug. 1776. New courtmartial to try
prisoners now under guard. At an alarm in night, all troops to repair
to their alarm posts "instantly," but if in the day, regiments of Hitchcock, Little, Forman, and Gay are to parade near Ft. Greene. Troops
on guard not to load their guns without orders from their captain,
except outsentries, who may load and fire if a person refuses to "give
an Account of himself." Gen. Nathanael Greene Orderly Book (Bergen
County [N.J.] Historical Society) 1 p.]

# To Colonel Josiah Smith[1]

Sir                              Camp at Brookland [N.Y.] Augt 9, 1776
Inclosd is a Resolution of the Provincial Congress, ordering you
to Join my Brigade. Immediately on the Receipt of this youl march the
Troops under your command immediately to this Camp. You will
make all possible expedition. As the Enemy have Embarked part if

not all the Troops on Statten Island; and are makeing disposition as if they intended to land here, youl send out Scouts and parties to get intelligence. If the Enemy should make their Landing good on any part of the Island, and hear of your coming, they may send out a party to intercept your march. Keep good front, flank and Rear Guards to prevent being surprizd. I am Sir your most obedient humble Servant

NATHANAEL GREENE

ALS (DNDAR).
1. Col. Josiah Smith of South Haven, Long Island, commanded the Suffolk County regiment of militia. (Johnston, *NY 1776*, pt. 1, p. 110) Part of his regiment had been raised by a draft that the Provincial Congress approved 20 July 1776 (*NY MSS*, 1: 261).

## To Colonel Moses Little

[Long Island, N.Y.]
Dear Sir    Thursday [Friday?] Morning [9 Aug. 1776][1]
By Express from Col Hand and from Red Hook, and from on board the Sloop at Governers Island it is very evident there was General Imbarcation of the Troops last Evening from Statten Island. Doubtless theyl make a descent this morning. Youl please to order all the Troops fit for duty to be at their Alarm posts near an hour sooner than is common. Let their flints, arms and ammunition be examind and everything held in readiness to defend the Works or go upon a detachment. A few minutes past receivd an Express from Head Quarters. Youl acquaint the commanding officer of Col Hitchcock Regiment and Col Foremans Regiment of this, and desire them to observe the same orders, all the Artillery Officers. I am &c

N GREENE

ALS (MeHi). Document damaged; last half of transcript supplied by Maine Historical Society.
1. On dating this letter, see above, NG to Washington, Wednesday [Thursday] Evening [Aug. 8, 1776].

## Commission

[NG's commission as major general in the Continental army, signed by John Hancock as president of Congress and attested to by Charles Thomson, secretary, at Philadelphia, 9 Aug. 1776.[1] DS (R.I. Governor's Office) 1 p.]

1. The document is a printed form with name, rank, place, and date written in. The Congress of the new United States had not changed its printed form, since it refers to the army of the "United Colonies" some five weeks after they had ceased to be colonies.

## To George Washington

Dear General            Camp on Long Island [N.Y.] August 9, 1776
    Col Hand Reports the three Ships mentiond in my last Evenings Report gone down through the Narrows are at anchor in and a little below the Narrows. I was at Red Hook this morning about three oClock but nothing further had been discovered neither has there since that has come to my knowledge.
    General [Nathaniel] Heard gives furloughs to the Troops of Col Foremans Regiment.[1] I conceive it to be cappitally wrong and very injurious to me and Col Foreman both as neither can know what to depend upon if the Troops are Furloughed without our knowledge or consent. This is not the only Evil; for [if] the Troops are refusd the indulgence here they request and get it elsewhere, it will naturally lead them to form an oppinion that we are tyrannical.[2]
    I must beg your Excellency to put a stop to it immediately. I am with all due respect your Excellencys most Obedt Humble Servt

N GREENE

ALS (Washington Papers: DLC).
    1. Gen. Nathaniel Heard of the N.J. militia had shown himself a firm opponent of "Tories." In June 1776 the N.J. Convention, noting his "zeal and prudence," had sent him to take Gov. William Franklin into custody (Force, *Archives* [4] 6: 968). Washington had found an outlet for Heard's zeal in having him drive off stock and remove loyalists from Staten Island. (Fitzpatrick, *GW*, 5: 215, 227)
    2. Without mentioning Heard by name, in his orders of 11 Aug., Washington stated that because an action was expected hourly "No Furlough, or Discharges, are after this day to be granted to officers or soldiers without the knowledge and consent of the Commander in Chief" (ibid., p. 410).

## From John Hancock, President of the Continental Congress

Sir                            Philada Augt 10th 1776
    The Congress having yesterday been pleased to appoint you a Major General in the Army of the American States, I do myself the Pleasure to enclose your Commission. Confident of your Zeal and attachment to the Liberties of America, I am persuaded you will do every Thing to merit the Honour your Country has conferred on you. With the warmest Wishes for your Health and Prosperity, I have the Honour to be Sir your most obed. and very hble Servt

JH

To Major Genl Wm Heath
    Major Genl Joseph Spencer
    Major Genl John Sullivan
    Major Genl Nathaniel Green

N. B. They are to take Rank according to the order in which they stand.[1]

Cy (PCC: DNA).
1. The four brigadiers were advanced the same day (*JCC*, 5: 641). The order of the names is the same as before the promotions. NG ranked eighth among the major generals because Ward had resigned and Montgomery and Thomas had died.
Col. John Nixon of Mass. was promoted to brigadier general and given command of NG's old brigade, now composed of the regiments of "late" Nixon, Prescott, Varnum, Little, and Hand. Hitchcock's regiment was added to Gen. Mifflin's brigade. NG now headed a division, made up of Nixon's and Heard's brigades. (Washington's orders of 12 Aug., Fitzpatrick, *GW*, 5: 421–24). Since almost all orders directed to the troops originated either from Washington's headquarters or from brigade headquarters, orderly books after this date rarely contained NG orders—at least until he took command of the Southern Army in October 1780.

## To George Washington

Sir    Camp on Long Island [N.Y.] Augt 10, 1776
    Colo Hand reports three Ships at the Hook. A large Schooner saild from the watering place late yesterday in the afternoon. She seems to direct her course towards Amboy this morning. From the firing heard at Sea last Evening tis supposd the remainder of the Hessian fleet is at hand.[1] Everything at the watering place remains quiet.
    Nothing remarkable has happened in this Camp since yesterdays Report. I sent over Nine suspected Tories this morning to the City Hall under the care of Lt Randal. I Reported their names to Col Harrison. There is one Benjamin Hewlet that lives [on] the Northside [who] does not appear to be an object worth sending away. There appears several Insignificant Characters amongst these last. How extensive their influence may be I cant pretend to divine, but from their appearance they dont look like doing much mischief. Lt Skinner is as industrious as possible in apprehending the disaffected. By what he writes me, many have gone off. He says the Tories had an account amongst them that they were to be taken for several days before the attempts was made. I wonder where anything of this sort has been in contemplation by the Provincial Congress. It is surprising to me how it could be known. They expected it was an order from Congress. I am Dear Sir with the greatest respect your Excellencys most obedient Humble Servant

N GREENE

ALS (Washington Papers: DLC).
1. The firing at sea could have been from Adm. Hotham's fleet, which was nearing Sandy Hook with German mercenaries aboard. See below, NG to Washington, 12 Aug.

## To George Washington

Dear General          Camp on Long Island [N.Y.] Augt 11, 1776

There is no proper Establishment for the supplying the Regimental Hospital with proper Utensils for the Sick.[1] They suffer therefore for want of proper accomodation. There is repeated complaints upon this head. The Regimental Hospitals are and ever will be render'd useless nay grieveous unless there is some proper fund to provide the necessary Conveniencies. The General Hospital cannot receive all the sick and those that are in the Regimental Hospitals are in a suffering condition. If this Evil continues it must greatly injure the service as it will greatly dispirit the will to see the Sick suffer and prevent their engageing again upon any conditions whatever. Great humanity should be exercisd towards those indisposd. Kindness on one hand leaves a favorable and lasting impression; neglect and suffering on the other is never forgotten.

I am sensible there has formerly been great abuses in the Regimental Hospitals but I am in hopes in general Men of better principles are elected to those places and that the same Evils will not happen again. But the Continent had better suffer a little extraordinary expence than the sick should be left to suffer for want of those conveniencies that may be easily provided.

I would beg leave to propose that the Colonels of Regiments be allowed to draw Monies to provide the Regimental Hospitals with proper Utensils; an account of the disbursements Weekly or monthly to be rendered. This will prevent abuse and remedy the Evil.

Something is necessary to be done spedily as many sick are in a suffering condition.

NB       The General Hospital is well provided with everything and the Sick very comfortable. I wish it was extensive enough to receive the whole, but it is not. I am your Excellencys most obedt Servt

NATH GREENE

ALS (MiU-C). The address sheet bears the notation "This letter to Dr. Morgan Jan. 10 1779." Washington or NG sent the letter to Morgan so that he might use it in his hearing before Congress. See end of note 1, below.

1. When the general hospital was established on Long Island earlier in the summer to accommodate NG's brigade (see note, his orders of 11 July, above), there were no regimental hospitals. None had existed since Washington closed them during the siege of Boston because of the abuses to which NG refers in his second paragraph. Many of those abuses were due to incompetent and even dishonest regimental surgeons, but many were due to the failure of Congress to provide minimum funding. Bad as conditions may have been, the troops preferred them to a general hospital, undoubtedly because they were closer to "home" and were filled with friends or acquaintances from their regiments. Even an incompetent surgeon or surgeon's mate presented a familiar face to a sick, frightened soldier.

When the troops around New York pressed for reopening the regimental hospitals, Washington reluctantly responded by authorizing the barracks master of each regiment to "fix on some house convenient to the Regiment to be improved as a Hospital" (General Orders, 28 July 1776, Fitzpatrick, *GW*, 5: 345). In so doing he declared that "Notwithstanding the great abuses of Regimental Hospitals last Year, the General has out of Indulgence and kindness to the Troops, who seem to like them, permitted them to be again opened." If abuses should continue, he warned, he must "in justice to the public, break them up again." (Ibid., p. 366)

There was little that Washington could do to alleviate the shortcomings of the regimental hospitals. Whether he had the authority to allow the colonels to "draw Monies to provide the Regimental Hospital with proper Utensils," as requested here by NG, is uncertain. In any case there is no record that he either authorized them or sought authorization for them to do so. Nor does it appear that he took up the issue with Congress. It is clear from NG's strongly worded letter of 10 Oct. to John Hancock below that conditions in the hospitals continued to deteriorate.

NG's letter became the basis for a virtual diatribe by Dr. Morgan following his summary dismissal by Congress in January 1777. Morgan was so hurt by his unexplained termination that he struck out at several people who had supported him. He discussed the letter at some length in his *Vindication*, pp. 110–14. NG respected Morgan, and despite the published accusations, he supported Morgan in his hearing before Congress two years later. See NG's letter to Morgan, 10 Jan. 1779, below. See also NG to Hancock, 10 Oct. 1776, below. For a balanced account of Morgan's tenure as director general of hospitals and his eventual vindication, see Bell, *Morgan*, chapters 11–13.

# To George Washington

Dear General                    Camp at Brookland [N.Y.] Augt 12, 1776

Colo Hand reports this morning a twenty Gun Ship that came in last Evening fird as she past through the Narrows, and was answerd by the Admiral. Four Ships went through the Narrows yesterday. They are at Anchor along New Uttrech Shore. Twenty five Sail of ships are seen at a great distance at Sea coming in.[1]

If your Excellency think Col Varnum deserveing promotion and another Brigadier is to be appointed I wish he may be Appointed.[2] I am your Excellencys obedient Servant.

N GREENE

ALS (Washington Papers: DLC).

1. The ships were the vanguard of Commodore William Hotham's fleet that had left England on 6 May with well over eight thousand German mercenaries (most of them Hessians) and almost three thousand British troops. In a second letter to Washington later that day, NG reported "Sixty Sail of Ships are now standing in." (Letter not found; the quote is from Washington to Hancock, 12 Aug., Fitzpatrick, *GW*, 5: 419.) On 13 Aug., Washington put the total at ninety-six ships (ibid., p. 427). Adm. Richard Howe's contemporary account of "Eighty five Sail" was close to Washington's (Howe to Philip Stephens, Morgan, *Naval Docs.*, 6: 183).

2. Although Congress was responsible for promotions of officers, Washington and his highest-ranked general officers bore the brunt of complaints from those not promoted. Thus, when John Nixon of Mass. was advanced to brigadier general, along with five other colonels from states other than Rhode Island, Col. James M. Varnum was incensed to see men on the list who had less seniority than he. (The promotions are in *JCC*, 5: 641.) After speaking to NG, he went to see Washington in order to resign

his commission. "I remonstrated," Washington wrote Hancock, "against the Impropriety of the measure at this Time, and he has consented to stay 'till affairs wear a different aspect than what they do at present." (Fitzpatrick, *GW*, 5: 432) Varnum had placed both Washington and Greene in a most awkward position, of which Washington may not have been fully aware. What Varnum did not say was that Col. Daniel Hitchcock of Rhode Island had an equal claim for promotion. NG, of course, knew this, but was moved by Varnum's outburst.

Washington undoubtedly placated Varnum with some kind of promise of future promotion, rumor of which soon reached Hitchcock's ears. If NG had not taken desperately ill (see note 2, NG to Jacob, 30 Aug. 1776, below), Hitchcock would have written or gone to see him; instead he wrote directly to Washington. Since Washington was dependent upon NG for a solution, Hitchcock knew that the letter would end up on NG's desk—assuming he recovered from his illness. The letter, which is in the Washington Papers (DLC), follows:

May it please your Excellency                                    Long Island [N.Y.] Aug 19th 1776
It gives me Pain to trouble your Excellency at this Time, when Concerns the most important that ever filled the human Breast must lie with Weight upon your Mind; but when I see Promotions all around me, and am told that your Excellency has also assured Colo Varnum that he shall be promoted, your Excellency will not think it strange that it should sensibly touch me. Colo Varnum and myself are the only two Colonels that at the Beginning of the War came out from the Colony of Rhode Island. [He omits Col. Church who left the army at the end of 1775.] Both left the Bar there together and were then upon a Par. Ambition then must prompt us both to wish at least to rise alike, because in that Colony there will and must of course be a Stigma fixed indelibly on the Character of him who should be so unhappy as not to be promoted. It is true in the Settlement of Ranks he was made Seignior Colonel; tho while we lay at Roxbury by General Green's orders (for we came from the Colony without any Rank settled) we cast lots for Seigniority, which I then obtained. However your Excellency in your late orders has been pleased to assure Us that Seigniority shall not determine Promotions. What then should entitle him more than myself to Preferment I cant conceive? if I have not attended to the Cares of my Regiment, if I have not conducted my Regiment with as much Prudence, if I have not executed every Order and Command with as much Punctuality; or if my moral as well as military Conduct since I've entred the Service under your Excellency has not been as exemplary and as distinguished as Colo Varnum's, I wish not to be promoted with him. For the Determination of this, I will appeal to General Greene, who intimately knows us both. Did my State of Health permit I should have waited on your Excellency in Person; but as yet it does not, though, thank God, I am much better, and intend in a few Days to help drub those mercenary Sons of Tyranny.
I wish not [to] detract from the Character of any Officer, or to do any Act to prevent any from Promotion, I know tis the Pride and Ambition of every Military Person but I must with great Submission say that if I am so unhappy as to fall so far short of your Excellency's Esteem and Regard as not to be recommended to Congress equally with Colo Varnum, in Justice to my Character, which must suffer from whence I came, that moment that he shall receive Preferment and myself unnoticed, I shall beg Leave of your Excellency to resign my Commission and go Home, and at the End of the Campaign my whole Regiment, both Officers and Soldiers, will follow me. I dont mention this as hinting that I will ever be instrumental in it, because God forbid I should ever thus injure my Country, which constantly [engages] my whole Attention; but such has been and such is now the Ambition that runs through the Regiment because the Regiment which I command came from a Seignior County than that Colo Varnum commands, and they always thought they ought to have been the oldest Regiment, so that Im certain all the Persuasion that can be used will not then prevent their quitting the Service. With the greatest Esteem and Readiness to execute all Commands I am your Excellencys most obedt most Hble Servt

                                                                              DAN HITCHCOCK

Athough Hitchcock was popular with his regiment, he was undoubtedly bluffing when he said his "whole Regiment" would follow him home if Varnum were promoted. Washington's answer to Hitchcock has not been found. He may have talked to Hitchcock as he did to Varnum. He could have told him honestly that Varnum was not then being recommended for advancement. But Washington had not heard the last from Varnum. On 26 Aug., just after the British had landed twenty thousand men on Long Island and on the eve of the battle of Long Island, Washington found in his mailbag a letter Varnum had written the previous day. With NG still seriously ill, Varnum, like Hitchcock, had taken the opportunity of writing directly to the commander in chief. If Washington took time from the critical military situation that faced him to read Varnum's letter, he surely could not have contained his temper. The letter, which is in the Washington Papers (DLC), follows:

Sir                                          Red Hook [N.Y.] Aug't 25th 1776
    I am very sensible the important Concerns which engross your Excellency's Attention at this
Critical Period must render particular Applications very disagreeable. But the same Benevolence
and Philanthrophy which Characterize you the Father and the Friend of the Army in General, will
cause the Distresses of an Individual to find a Place in your compassionate Breast. Ever since I
waited upon your Excellency, the Expectation of a Battle hath continued me in my present
Command. New Difficulties arising I can derive no Satisfaction from that Quarter. A letter from Mr
Ellery, enclosed, convinces me that Promotions in the Army are not designed for those whose
Principles are disinterested enough to serve the Continent without. My Disgrace is unalterable fix'd
by conferring the detur digniori upon those of inferior Standing, without the least Competition of
superior Merit. Was Promotion in the Army a favor, my Tongue and my Pen should be silent. But it
is the Just Reward of Merit and Rank. I do not esteem myself obligated to the Public for the
Commission I hold, nor for the Greatness of the Pay annexed to it. They can challenge no farther
Services from me whose every Effort to deserve their good Opinion has been discountenanced. My
Continuance here can be of no possible Advantage. The Variety of Incidents that may happen in an
Engagement will possible demand my Submission to the Orders of a Brigadier General, whose
standing, till lately, hath been subordinate to mine. Disobedience, at a Critical Moment, may lose a
Victory which is courting our Embrace. My Pride is too great ever to bend to Reasons of Policy to
the wounding of my Honor. How cruel the Alternative to be obliged either to submit to my own
Infamy, or, by refusing, incur the Penalties of Death! However, I remember a Saying of Sertorius, A
just Man will receive Victory when it kindly offers, but will not seek or defend his own Life upon
dishonorable Terms. If my Conduct hath hitherto gained your Excellency's Approbation, and if my
Complaint is well founded, can you deny me, the only Consolation left, your Permission to retire
from a Service no longer eligible? My Philosophy is [at] an End. I can no longer command myself,
much less can I command others. Disappointment, Shame, Grief, Resentment, all harrow up my
Soul at once, and force me to adopt the Language of Young:
                    The Day too long for my Distress, and Night,
                    E'en in the Zenith [of] her dark domain,
                    Is Sunshine to the Color of my Fate.
The enclosed answer to Mr Ellery's Letter, with the other to Mr Hancock, I could wish to send to
Philadelphia as they are. But while acting under a Commission from the Congress, cannot. I am
your Excellency's most obedient humble Servant

                                                                        J M VARNUM

    NG could not have seen either letter until after he recovered. What advice he gave
Washington or what he said to Varnum and Hitchcock is not known, but he was in no
position to solve the dilemma. Varnum had been a friend for some years, had been
NG's attorney, and had commanded the Kentish Guards. Hitchcock, on the other
hand, had become one of NG's most dependable subordinates, and between the two
men a warm friendship had developed. Both men stayed on in the army (Varnum
became a brigadier general in the R.I. militia in Dec.), but their unyielding positions
blocked any Rhode Islander from being named a brigadier general in the Continental
army for the remainder of 1776. A week after the battle of Princeton, Hitchcock died of
exhaustion and illness, opening the way for Varnum to be advanced. On 21 Feb. 1777
he was one of ten colonels to be named brigadier general in the Continental army (JCC,
7: 141). He resigned his post in the R.I. militia and accepted the commission.
    The Varnum-Hitchcock problem was by no means unusual during the Revolution.
It was, in fact, fairly typical of the rivalry among commissioned officers, most of whom
suffered far more from bruised egos than from battle wounds. It was, perhaps, the
price to be paid for a hastily organized citizen army.

## General Greene's Orders

[Long Island Camp, N.Y.] 14 August 1776
A Captain and Twenty Men to Parade immediately to fetch over the
Flat Bottom'd Boats mention'd in Yesterdays Orders. A Serjeant and
eight Men to be Establish'd at Myfords Ferry as a Guard over the
Boats.[1] All the Troops that are off Duty to turn out and Exercise twice
a Day in the Morning and Afternoon. The General desires that the

most Essential Manoeuvres may be taught the Troops[2] as early as possible and that the Arms be daily examined.

Henshaw Orderly Book (MWA).
1. Washington's orders of 13 Aug. had read in part: "General Greene to send for ten of the flat bottomed Boats which are to be kept under Guard at Long Island: No Person to meddle with them, but by his special order." (Fitzpatrick, GW, 5: 425) The boats were to be used in ferrying newly arrived Conn. and N.J. troops to Long Island. Two weeks later the boats became part of the flotilla Gen. John Glover used to evacuate the troops from Long Island (Billias, Glover, pp. 100–101).
2. The newly arrived militia.

## To George Washington

Sir                                Long Island [N.Y.] Augt 15, 1776
It having appeard in orders that Colo Hitchcocks Regiment is to take Possession of the Post opposite to Fort Washington, I beg leave to acquaint you that their peculiar Attachment to the old Regiments that are here,[1] their thorough Knowledge of the ground, their Discipline, and the good Order in which they are respecting Arms, make me desirous of their remaining here, if it can possibly be dispensed with, and absolute Necessity does not require their removal. The most of the Troops that come over here are strangers to the Ground, undisciplined and badly furnish'd with arms. They will not be so apt to support each other in Time of Action as those who have long been acquainted, and who are not only attached to each other but to the Place. I have made this Application in Consequence of my own Observations; and to evince the Propriety of it send you inclosed the arrangement for your Inspection.[2]

Colo Hand, about eight oclock yesterday Evening, reported that the Hessians were landing on Staten Island to a considerable Number; that after their Landing they paraded upon the Beach, and marched up the Hill towards the Flag staff. I have received no report from him this morning, owing as I suppose to the Inclemency of the Weather. Should he not send one speedily, I shall dispatch an Express to inquire the Cause.

I have made Choice of Mr William Blodget and Major William Livingston for my Aid de Camps. Should it meet with your Approbation you will please to signify it [in] Orders.[3] I have the Pleasure to inform you that the Troops appear to be in exceeding good Spirits and make no doubt that if they should make their Attack here we shall be able to render a very good account of them.

I am carrying into Execution the late Resolve of Congress respecting the Removal of the Cattle, dismantling of the Mills, removing the Grain already thrashed, and having that which is still in Sheaf so stacked and disposed of that in Case of an Attack it may easily be destroyed.[4] The Militia of the County that was ordered here have not as yet made their Appearance notwithstanding the Promise I received from the Lieut Colo that they should be here last Night. Should they delay coming in any longer than this Day I am determined not to be trifled with and shall let them feel my Resentment by vigorous and spirited Exertions of Military Discipline and those Powers with which I am invested. A Part of the Militia from the East End of the Island under the Command of Colo Smith are arrived.

I am very sorry that I am under the necessity of acquainting you that I am confined to my Bed with a raging Fever.[5] The Critical Situation of Affairs makes me the more anxious but I hope thro the Assistance of Providence to be able to ride before the Presence of the Enemy may make it absolutely necessary. I am with respect your Most Obedt humbl Servt

NATHANAEL GREENE

LS (Washington Papers: DLC). Enclosure missing. Being confined to his bed, NG dictated the letter to his new aide, William S. Livingston.

1. Hitchcock wrote to Col. Little, with whom he had served for a year, "it gives me much Uneasiness that your Regiment is not going with mine" (letter of 15 Aug. 1776, MeHi).

2. Washington was not moved by NG's arguments. He repeated his order on 19 Aug. (Fitzpatrick, GW, 5: 462). When Howe's troops landed on Long Island, however, the regiment was rushed back, where it participated in the battle of 27 Aug. (Johnston, NY 1776, pt. 2, p. 75n).

3. Confirmed in Washington's orders of 16 Aug. (Fitzpatrick, GW, 5: 441).

4. In July the N.Y. Congress declared it was impractical to remove the more than 100,000 "Horned Cattle" and large numbers of sheep from Long Island (Force, Archives [5] 1: 1424). Instead, they resolved to have the militia guard the stock, prepared to drive it off if the British landed. When they received reports on Aug. 10, however, that the inhabitants of Kings County had "determined not to oppose the enemy," they authorized a committee to have NG destroy stock and grain and, if necessary, "to lay the whole County waste" (Force, Archives [5] 1: 1497). The measures he took must have driven many of the neutralists into the arms of the loyalists. NG's men did not destroy all the grain. When the British landed at Gravesend Bay, Baurmeister reported that "Barns, grain stacks, and the lighthouses built here and there were immediately set on fire" by the Americans (Baurmeister, Revolution, p. 35).

5. On his condition, which grew steadily worse, see note 2, NG to Jacob, 30 Aug., below. It is ironic that NG, the most concerned of Washington's general officers in the health of his troops, should have been the only one to have succumbed to the illness that struck so many of them. It would keep him out of the battle of Long Island, for which he had prepared since May. On that battle see note 3, the 30 Aug. letter to Jacob.

## General Greene's Orders

Long Island [N.Y.] 16 August 1776

Colonel Smith is to appoint an Adjutant Quarter Master, Sergeant Major and Q M Serjeant to his Regiment.[1] The General desires Colonel Smith will take care to have the Troops in his Regiment (not on Duty) Exercis'd Daily and Learn the Necessary Manoeuvres and

Evolutions. General Nixon and General Hurd [Heard] are to furnish a Fatigue Party from their respective Brigades to form the necessary Lines from Fort Box to Fort Putnam. The Gin Shops and other Houses where Liquors have been heretofore Retailed within or near the Lines (except the Houses at the Two Ferries) are strictly forbidden to sell any for the future to any Soldier in the Army and the Inhabitants of said Houses near the Lines are immediately to move out of them they are to be appropriated to the use of the Troops. If any Soldier of the Army shall be found disguis'd with Liquor as has been too much the practice heretofore the General is determin'd to have him punish'd with the utmost severity, as no Soldier in such situation can be either fit for defence or Attack. The General Orders that no Sutler in the Army shall sell to any Soldier more than one half pint of Spirit per Day. If the above Orders are not strictly Adher'd to he is determin'd that there shall be no more Retailed at all. The Colonels of the respective Regiments lately come in are immediately to make Returns to the General of the number of Men in their respective Regiments and where they are Quarter'd. Colonel Hitchcocks and Col Smiths Regiments are to do Duty in General Nixons Brigade.[2] Col Van Brunts and Col Gays Regiments to do Duty in General Heards Brigade. The Captains of the two Brigades are to be particularly careful that the Rolls of their respective Companies are called at least three Times a Day and that the Troops do not stroll from their Encampments or Quarters.

Henshaw Orderly Book (MWA).
  1. Col. Josiah Smith of New York militia had joined NG the previous week (see above, NG to Smith, 9 Aug.).
  2. Col. Hitchcock's regiment was sent instead to N.J. (see above, NG to Washington, 15 Aug.). Col. Rutgert Van Brunt commanded a regiment of N.Y. militia from Kings County (Onderdonk, *Suffolk and Kings*, p. 120). Col. Fisher Gay's regiment was part of the Conn. militia serving under Gen. Oliver Wolcott, who was due to arrive momentarily (Washington's orders of 12 Aug. 1776, Fitzpatrick, *GW*, 5: 421–24).

## George Washington from Major William Livingston

[At Long Island, N.Y., 16 Aug. 1776. NG requests him to report that Col. Hand saw Hessians landing again yesterday at east end of Staten Island. Appeared to be no immediate preparation for an attack. Three men from his regiment deserted, took six rifles. ALS (Washington Papers: DLC) 1 p.]

## George Washington from Major William Blodget

[At Long Island, N.Y., 5:00 P.M., 16 Aug. 1776. NG requests him to say that Col. Hand reports thirteen or fourteen vessels entered the

Narrows from the fleet. Officer of the ferry guard reported "some Red Coats" on board, but Hand says none have landed. The camps at "Flagg-staff and Ferry (on Staten Island) are pretty extensive." ALS (Washington Papers: DLC) 1 p.]

## Major William Livingston to George Washington

Sir                                     Long Island [N.Y.] Augt 17th 1776
    Colo Hand has this morning reported to the General that since yesterday Evening four Vessels of War, one of them the Solbay have sailed from the Fleet at the Narrows. Two Brigs a Sloop and Schooner came in from Sea and the Man of War that lay off the Hook these two Days past came in. The morning being very Thick he could discern nothing distinctly at the Hook but that late in the Evening of yesterday some of the Foreign Troops Landed at the Ferry Way on Staten Island.
    I am sorry to inform your Excellency that General Green had a very bad night of it and cannot be said to be any better this morning than he was yesterday. I have the Honor to be your most obedt Servt

WM LIVINGSTON

ALS (Washington Papers: DLC).

## To George Washington

Sir                                     Long Island [N.Y.] Augt 18, 1776
    I have thought proper to communicate to you certain Intelligence which I have received from my Brother respecting Captain Grimes whose Conduct (if I have been rightly informed) does not entitle him to that Place in your Esteem which he now holds, nor to that Confidence which you have thought proper to put in him.[1]
    His leaving the Galley at Rode Island in the time of the Attack, to take Convoy of the Prizes, the insults which he afterwards gave said Captain, who has ever been held in highest Esteem, whose Character stands fair and unimpeached, and who has given convincing Proofs of his Courage and Conduct, together with the Information that was given me of his refusing to make the Attack at the Time the Fire Ships went up the River, and the Reluctance that was shown this Morning to comply with the Orders given him by General Putnam, induces me to think that he is much more fond of Parade and show than he is desirous of signalizing himself in any Action that may be of Service to the Country.
    If the Report of his Refusal is founded in Fact, and General Putnam's Orders were not complied with, I think he ought imme-

diately to be put under an Arrest and instantly removed from his Command. I am Your very humbl Servt

NATHANAEL GREENE

LS (Washington Papers: DLC).
1. This is a puzzling letter. In the calmest of times, it would seem presumptuous for NG to advise Washington in this fashion about a matter that did not concern him; to do so when Howe's attack was expected momentarily would seem rash. His judgment may have been impaired by the "raging fever" that had laid him low for four days now. Although Blodget had reported earlier in the day that NG was "considerably better," he was still a very sick man—so sick, in fact, that within twenty-four hours Washington decided to hand over his command to Sullivan. It was two weeks before he was out of bed.
   It is ironic that he based the letter on inaccurate "Intelligence" from his brother—probably Christopher, who was in New York. The incidents centering about the row galley attack are described in note 4, NG to Adams, 14 July, above. Capt. John Grimes of the *Spitfire*, in fact, had acted courageously. (See correspondence in RIHS, *Coll.* 6 [1867]: 158–59.)

## Major William Blodget to George Washington

Sir                         Long Island [N.Y.] Aug 18, 1776
   Colonel Hands report mentions no Uncommon movements of the Enemy.
   The General desires me to acquaint your Excellency that he finds himself considerably better this morning than he was Yesterday, and is in hopes in a few days he'd be able to go abroad, tho still very weak. I am with Respect your Humble Servant

WM BLODGET

ALS (Washington Papers: DLC).

## To [Jacob Greene?][1]

[Manhattan Island, N.Y.] 30th of August 1776
   Providence took me out of the way. I have been very sick for near three weeks; for several days there was a hard struggle between nature and the disorder. I am now a little better, though scarcely able to sit up an hour at a time. I have no strength or appetite, and my disorder, from its operation, appears to threaten me with long con-finement.[2] Gracious God! to be confined at such a time.[3] And the misfortune is doubly great as there was no general officer who had made himself acquainted with the ground as perfectly as I had. I have not the vanity to think the event would have been otherwise had I been there, yet I think I could have given the commanding general a good deal of necessary information. Great events sometimes depend upon very little causes. I think from this manoeuvre the general proposes to retreat to Kingsbridge and there make the grand stand.[4] If this is the determination, two to one New York is laid in ashes.

Excerpt reprinted from Johnson, *Greene*, 1: 56.

1. Most of the familiar letters that Johnson printed from this period were addressed to NG's brother Jacob. It is a reasonably safe assumption that the recipient was Jacob.

2. NG's first reference to his illness was on 15 Aug. when he reported to Washington that he was confined to bed with a "raging Fever." On 20 Aug., Washington reluctantly turned over NG's command to Sullivan. At this point his recovery was uncertain. William Blodget, his aide, thought his condition "dangerous." Dr. John Morgan, who had visited him daily since diagnosing his illness as "a putrid and billious fever," considered "his life endangered" and prevailed upon him to leave Long Island.

Morgan had him moved to New York island to what he described as "the healthy, airey, safest and best accomodated habitations in the center, betwixt the two rivers, two miles distant from the city of New York." Blodget identified the place as "Doctr Rogers about 2 or 3 miles from Town, a very retired, pleasant situation." Morgan shifted his own headquarters to Long Island, and "Yet," as he later recalled, "I visited him, daily, once, twice or oftener, under a variety of difficulties, and watched over him with the strictest attention, and an affection little less than fraternal till his recovery was so far compleated, that he was out of all danger."

Morgan's account of NG's illness is found in his *Vindication*, pp. 107–8, and in a MS version of another "Vindication," dated 1 Feb. 1779 (item 63, PCC:DNA). Blodget's account is in a letter to Catharine Greene, misdated 28 Aug. 1776, but probably written on 26 Aug. (Greene Papers, RHi).

3. He is speaking of the battle of Long Island, the first time that British and American troops met face to face in formal battle. After several false alarms, Howe finally launched his amphibious attack on Long Island on the morning of 22 Aug. under the covering guns of Lord Howe's warships. By midday some fifteen thousand men had been ferried from Staten Island to the beaches at Gravesend Bay. Other landings the next three days brought Howe's total to twenty thousand men, including two regiments of Hessians. Col. Edward Hand, who had kept NG informed during the summer of every British move, could do nothing but fall back to the American lines at Brooklyn Heights, setting fire to grain and hay as he retreated. We have seen in the note above that Washington had replaced the ailing NG with Sullivan two days before the landings, and he now put in overall command Gen. Israel Putnam, a man completely unfamiliar with the ground. Washington went over the ground with Putnam on 25 Aug. and the following day sent reinforcements from Manhattan.

During the night of 26 Aug., the British moved across the plains from Gravesend toward the American positions. They were separated from the Americans by the heavily wooded Guana Heights, which lay to the east of Brooklyn Heights. But there was no lack of Long Island loyalists to show the British the four passes that traversed the Guana Heights. Howe assigned Gen. James Grant to attack the American right near the Narrows in order to draw off American strength from the center and left, where he planned to bring the main British forces to bear. Gen. Clinton, who saw that Putnam had assigned no force to guard the Jamaica Pass (the northernmost pass), persuaded Howe to concentrate British forces under Howe, Clinton, and Cornwallis along the Jamaica road in order to make a flanking movement through the pass to Sullivan's rear. As the Hessians fiercely attacked Sullivan's front, Howe's combined forces skillfully cut off Sullivan's rear. If even a single horseman had been stationed at Jamaica Pass, he could have warned Sullivan in time to save many of his men. As it was many were killed and many more captured—including Sullivan.

In the meantime Lord Stirling, whose Maryland and Delaware troops numbered less than a fourth of Gen. Grant's, put up a magnificent but hopeless defense. Stirling and many of his men were also captured. It was a severe defeat for American forces and a heavy blow to American morale. Some two hundred Americans were killed and almost nine hundred captured, while British casualties were under four hundred (Peckham, *Toll*, p. 22, and Ward, *War*, 1: 226–27). Defeat, moreover, would have turned into disaster except for a brilliantly executed retreat across East River to Manhattan.

NG would always believe, as he implies above, that the outcome would have been different had he been well. Modesty forbade him from saying, as John Adams wrote,

"Greene's sickness, I conjecture, has been the cause" of the enemy's "stealing a march on us" (*Works*, 9: 437). A month later Knox said that "had General Greene been fit for duty I flatter myself matters would have worn a very different appearance at present" (Am. Antiq. Soc., *Proc.* 56 [1946]: 217).

Just *how* different, of course, no one would ever know. NG could rightly say that no general officer had "made himself acquainted with the ground as perfectly." He could have said with equal assurance that no one knew the men and officers as he did. It was also undoubtedly true, as Christopher Ward has said (and as NG probably believed), that he was a "much abler general officer" than either Sullivan or Putnam, who was in overall command (Ward, *War*, 1: 213). It is hard to believe, moreover, that he would have spent the long, hot summer in pushing the weary troops to keep at the digging and embanking, at the practice drills in manning the forts and lines, if he had planned to meet Howe's attack far to the front of the fortifications as Putnam did.

With all such considerations in mind, however, no military historian has contended that the outcome would have been substantially different if NG had been there, although losses may have been much lighter. Even without American blunders or brilliant British tactics, Howe's superior forces made an American defeat all but inevitable. He had twenty thousand professional soldiers, supported by an overwhelming naval force, to throw against Washington's six thousand men—many of them green militiamen. Most historians would agree that defeat was rooted in Washington's initial mistake of trying to defend New York. They would disagree with Freeman that "New York had to be defended" (*GW*, 4: 369). The political necessity of "making a fight for the city," as William Willcox has written, "had put Washington into a military position that flouted common sense." (Willcox, *Clinton*, p. 102) Unlike Boston, water-girt New York was completely vulnerable to superior naval power, and no one questioned the overwhelming power of Lord Howe's fleet.

NG could have found great consolation, however, in the fact that his fortifications permitted the rest of the American army to escape. Howe's momentum was sufficient to have overrun the demoralized Americans who had fallen back behind their defense lines, but he stopped his troops to prepare for a siege against what appeared formidable fortifications. The Hessian adjutant general, Baurmeister, who described the fortifications in detail, thought them "strong enough to withstand an assault of fifty thousand men" (Baurmeister, *Revolution*, p. 39). Howe's preparations for a siege gave Washington and his officers a few days to make up their minds to evacuate the forts and the opportunity of slipping the men out under the cover of darkness to Gen. Glover's waiting boats on the East River.

The battle of Long Island is well covered by Ward (*War*, 1: 211–37) who included in his sources two nineteenth-century classics published by the Long Island Historical Society—Field, *Long Island*, and Johnston, *NY 1776*. Willcox (*Clinton*, p. 105) shows that the encirclement of Sullivan's brigades was Clinton's plan, which Howe only reluctantly accepted. The spectacular achievement of John Glover and his Marblehead regiment in getting the troops across East River is covered in Billias, *Glover*, pp. 96–104.

4. It is doubtful that Washington thought at this time of making a stand at Kings Bridge—at the north end of Manhattan. NG was probably projecting his own thinking, which he revealed to Washington in his letter of 5 Sept., below.

## Minutes of Corporation of Rhode Island College

Providence [R.I.] September 4th 1776

In consideration of the great Abilities, literary merit and the many eminent services performed by Major General Greene[1] to this State in particular, and the Continent in general

Voted that the Honorary Degree of Master in the Arts be conferred upon him.

D (Brown University Archives: RPB).
1. Because NG's promotion to major general had occurred only three weeks before, the minutes as first written had him as "Brigad Gen."

## To George Washington

Dear Sir                  New York Island Sept 5 1776

The critical situation in which the Army are in will, I hope, sufficiently Apologise for my troubling your Excellency with this Letter. The Sentiments are dictated I am sure by an honest mind, A mind who feels deeply Interested in the Salvation of his Country; and for the honnor and Reputation of the General under whom he serves.[1]

The object under consideration is whether a General and speedy retreat from this Island is necessary or not. To me it appears the only Eligible plan to oppose the Enemy successfully and secure ourselves from disgrace. I think we have no object on this side of Kings Bridge. Our Troops are now so scatterd that one part may be cut off before the others can come to their support. In this Situation suppose the Enemy should Run up the North River several Ships of force and a Number of Transports at the same time, and effect a Landing between the Town and middle division of the Army. Another party from Long Island should land right oppisite; these two parties form a line across the Island and Entrench themselves. The two Flanks of this Line could be easily supported by the Shipping; the Center fortified with the Redoubts would render it very difficult if not impossible, to cut our way through. At the time the Enemy are Executeing this movement or manouvre, they will be able to make sufficient diversions if not real lodgments, to render it impossible for the Center and uper Divisions of the Army to afford any assistance here. Should this Event take place, and by the by I dont think it very improbable, Your Excellency will be reduced to that situation which every prudent General would wish to avoid; that is of being obligeed to fight the Enemy to a disadvantage or Submit.[2]

It has been agreed that the City of New York would not be Tenable if the Enemy got possession of Long Island and Govenors Island; they are now in possession of both these places. Notwithstanding I think we might hold it for some time, but the annoyance must be so great as to render it an unfit place to Quarter Troops in. If we should hold it, we must hold it to a great disadvantage. The City and Island of New York are no objects for us; we are not to bring them in Competition with the General Interest of America. Part of the army already has met with a defeat; the Country is struck with a pannick; any Cappital loss at this time may ruin the cause.[3] Tis our business to study to avoid any considerable misfortune, and to take post where the Enemy will be obligd to fight us and not we them. The sacrafice of the Vast Property of New York and the Subburbs I hope has no influence upon your Excellencys measures. Remember the King of France when Charles the fifth, Emperor of Germany, invaded his Kingdom, he liad [laid?] whole Provinces waste; and by that policy he starvd and ruind Charles army, and defeated him without fighting a Battle.[4] Two thirds of the Property of the City of New York and the Subburbs belongs to the Tories. We have no very great Reason to run any considerable risque for its defence. If we attempt to hold the City and Island and should not be able finally, we shall be wasteing of time unnecessarily, and betray a defect of Judgment if no worse misfortune attend it.

I give it as my oppinion that a General and speedy Retreat is absolutely necessary and that the honnor and Interest of America requires it. I would burn the City and Subburbs and that for the following Reasons: If the Enemy gets possession of the City we never can Recover the Possession without a superior Naval force to theirs. It will deprive the Enemy of an opportunity of Barracking their whole Army together which, if they could do, would be a very great security. It will deprive them of a general Market; the price of things would prove a temptation to our people to supply them for the sake of the gain, in direct violation of the Laws of their Country. All these advantages would Result from the destruction of the City. And not one benefit can arise to us from its preservation that I can conceive off. If the City once gets into the Enemies hands, it will be at their mercy either to save or destroy it, after they have made what use of it they think proper.[5]

At the Retreat I would order the Army to take post, part at Kings Bridge and part along West Chester Shore where Barracks may be procurd for that part of the Army that are without Tents. I must confess I am too Ignorant of the Ground to form much Judgment about posting the Troops. Your Excellencys superior Judgment, formd from your own observation upon the ground, will enable you to make a much better Disposition than I can conceive off.

If my Zeal has led me to say more than I ought, I hope my good Intentions may atone for the offence. I shall only add that these Sentiments are not dictated from fear, nor from any Apprehensions of personal danger. But are the Result of a cool and deliberate survey of our situation, and the necessary measures to extricate us from our present difficulties. I have said nothing at all about the temper and dispositions of the Troops and their Apprehensions about being sold. This is a strong intimation that it will be difficult to get such Troops to behave with proper Spirit in time of action if we should be Attackt.

Should your Excellency agree with me, with respect to the two first points, that is, that a speedy and General Retreat is necessary; and also that the City and subburbs should be burnt, I would advise to call a General Council upon that Question and take every General Officers oppinion upon it. I am with due respect your Excellencys most obedient, humble Servant

N GREENE

ALS (Washington Papers: DLC).

1. Although Washington had consulted with some of his officers on defending N.Y. (i.e., the city as well as the rest of Manhattan Island), it is evident from the apologetic tone of NG's letter that his opinion had not been solicited. This was neither a slight nor an oversight, but because NG had barely recovered from his illness.

2. Washington was reluctant to admit the impossibility of defending Manhattan. On 2 Sept. he had told Hancock that he still had no doubt about his ability to defend it "if the men would do their duty" (Fitzpatrick, GW, 6: 6). Two days later he was still speaking in terms of "if" he had to abandon the place (ibid., p. 15). Washington's army, William Willcox has said, was "in what amounted to a bottle, with its neck the Harlem River; and the British had the power to cork it because they commanded the surrounding water." (Willcox, Clinton, p. 108)

The British tactic that NG conjectures is precisely the one that Howe's critics have blamed him for not using when his troops landed at Kips Bay virtually unopposed ten days later. (See NG to Cooke, below, 17 Sept.)

3. This sensible admonition must have returned to haunt NG after the loss of Fts. Washington and Lee.

4. He is referring to Charles V of the Holy Roman Empire and Francis I of France. NG's example of a scorched earth policy may not have been the best, since Francis was the loser in his four wars with Charles.

5. On 2 Sept., Washington had asked Congress to act in great secrecy if it should resolve on the destruction of New York City. Congress responded immediately that it "would have especial care taken, in case he should find it necessary to quit New York, that no damage be done to the said city by his troops on their leaving it." (JCC, 5: 733) NG had not seen a copy of the resolution when he wrote this. After Washington's army had evacuated Manhattan Island (except Mt. Washington), someone did start a fire that consumed a fourth of the city. "Had I been left to the dictates of my own judgment," Washington wrote his nephew Lund, "New York should have been laid in Ashes before I quitted it; to this end I applied to Congress, but was absolutely forbid." (Fitzpatrick, GW, 37: 532)

## To Elihue Greene

Dear Sir                                      New York Sept 6, 1776

I receivd a Letter[1] from you some time past, but I have been Sick ever since almost or else I should have answer'd it before this. With respect to your proposition about Matrimony I have no objections. Engage in Venuses War as soon as you please if you can promise yourself a crop of pleasure sufficient to ballance the expence and trouble. A happy choice makes a married life exceeding happy. I hope you have fixt upon a good Naturd, Sensible, Comely, prudent and industrious Girl.[2] She will be a comfort to you by Day and a pleasure to you at Night. I wish you abundance of happiness and am affectionately yours. I would write you more but Christopher is impatiently waiting.

N GREENE

ALS (MWA).
1. Letter not found.
2. On Elihue's bride-to-be, see note 4, NG to Elihue, 28 Jan. 1776, above.

## To John Hancock, President of the Continental Congress

Sir                              Camp at New York Sept 8, 1776

This will be handed you by Capt Sion Martindale and Lt Moses Turner that was taken in the Brigg Washington in Boston Bay last fall.[1] They were sent home Prisoners to England and ordered back to Hallifax, where they were confind in Gaol for some time. At last they found means to cut a passage out and made their escape and have got safe home. There is one Lt Child that was made prisoner with them and made his escape at the same time the others did. They apply to Congress for their Wages and Rations due during their Captivity. They also apply for an allowance for the losses they met with and for several advancements they made for the Brigg Washington and the crew during the time they were fiting for the Cruise. All which doubtless the Congress will take under consideration and grant what Justice and equity entitles them to. They all belong'd to the Rhode Island Regiments, and while they were under my Command they Discharged their duty as became good and faithful Officers. How they behavd after they enterd on board the Brigg Washington I am not able to say. They are men who have families and no means of support for them but by their Industry. I am with due Respect your obedient Servant

NATHANAEL GREENE

ALS (PCC: DNA).
1. The luckless Capt. Martindale and many of the men he recruited for the privateer *Washington* were from NG's Rhode Island regiments. For an account of the fitting out and capture of the *Washington* and the imprisonment of her crew, see above, NG's orders, 10 Oct. 1775.

## Petition of Nathanael Greene and Others to George Washington[1]

May it please your Excellency:                    September 11, 1776

The Situation of the Army under your Excellencys Command is, in our Opinion, so critical and dangerous that we apprehend a Board of General Officers should be immediately calld for the purpose of considering it.

We do not mean to condemn as unwise or imprudent any Measures which have heretofore been taken, but we conceive a Reconsideration of an important Question determined at the last Board of General officers to be absolutely necessary to satisfy our own apprehensions and the apprehensions of many excellent Field officers and others from the Dispositions now making by the Advice of that Board.

We know the Danger and bad Policy of giving way to Applications for the Reconsideration of common Propositions which may have been solemnly determined, but the present Case is of such Magnitude and is big with such Consequences to all America that a Breach of common Forms and even the Risque of establishing wrong precedents should in our opinions be now overuled.

What we have to offer to your Excellency in general Council proceeds not from Fear of personal Danger nor the Expectation of deriving to ourselves any Honor and Reputation from a Change of measures. It proceeds from a Love of our Country and a determined Resolution to urge the best and wisest measures: and finally to execute if possible even erronious ones which on cool dispassionate Reconsideration cannot be avoided.

NATHANAEL GREENE[2]

THOMAS MIFFLIN

JNO. NIXON

REZIN BEALL

SAML H. PARSONS

JAMES WADSWORTH

I think it a mark of Wisdom to reconsider opinions upon subjects of high Importance whenever so many respectable Gentlemen request it as have signed above me. I therefore heartily concur with them in the application above mentioned.

JOHN MORIN SCOTT

DS (Washington Papers: DLC).

1. This petition was circulated by NG only four days after a meeting of the general officers had voted to defend New York City with five thousand troops. That decision was made, as Freeman points out, "over the vigorous opposition" of NG (Freeman, GW, 4: 187–88).

Although a record of the meeting is missing, Washington summarized the results in a letter to Congress, 8 Sept. Because of the difficulties attending removal, he wrote, "a Course was taken between abandoning it totally and concentrating our whole strength for its defence." Some were swayed, he continued, because they suspected Congress wished the city to be maintained at every hazard. (Fitzpatrick, GW, 6: 30)

2. NG was the only major general to sign the petition. Sullivan was a prisoner (along with Brig. Gen. Stirling) and Putnam was on leave.

# Council of War[1]

Held at Gen. McDougal's Quarters [Sept. 12, 1776[2]]

The General read a letter signed by some general Officers proposing that there should be a Reconsideration of the Matter determined in Council last Week with Respect to the State and farther Disposition of the Troops.

The question was put whether the Determination of last Week should be reconsidered and the Opinion [was] as follows

| To reconsider | To adhere |
|---|---|
| Gen Beall | Gen Spencer |
| Gen Scott | Gen [George] Clinton |
| Gen Heard | Gen Heath |
| Gen [James] Wadsworth | |
| Gen Nixon | |
| Gen McDougal | |
| Gen Parsons | |
| Gen Mifflin | |
| Gen Green | |
| Gen Puttnam | |

It was considered what Number of Men are necessary to be left for the Defence of Mount Washington and its Dependencies; agreed that it be 8000.

D (Washington Papers: DLC); in the hand of Joseph Reed.

1. Reed's sketchy notes scarcely do justice to the important debate. It is apparent from the reversal of opinions among the general officers after the 7 Sept. meeting that NG was persuasive. His arguments are outlined in his 5 Sept. letter to Washington above. The petition, dated 11 Sept., is printed above.

The only reference to a debate was a paragraph that was later deleted—probably because it represented only the view of the three dissenters. The question they proposed was whether N.Y. should be evacuated "whenever it shall be found difficult or impracticable to maintain the city." Since the only purpose of the meeting was whether indeed that time had come, Washington must have had the question crossed off after it had been debated with "great Solemnity and Attention." McDougall later depicted the dissenters—Spencer, Clinton, and Heath—as "a fool, a knave, and an honest, obstinate man." (Freeman, GW, 4: 188n)

2. The list of those present given at the head of the document (in addition to Washington) does not square with the tally of opinions at the end. Gen. Heard is not listed as present, and Gen. Fellows's name does not appear among those voting.

Only by implication did the vote to reconsider the council's earlier decision constitute a decision to evacuate New York City. There was no doubt of the intent of the vote, however. Washington did not cast a vote, but he made clear to Congress two days later that he was now "fully convinced" the city could not be defended. Unfortunately, evacuating it was not as simple as casting a vote. Time was short, and Washington reported in the same letter, "We are now taking every Method in our Power to remove the Stores &ca. in which we find almost insuperable difficulties." (Fitzpatrick, GW, 6: 53–54) When the British landed at Kips Bay on 15 Sept., the evacuation of stores had barely begun and removal of troops had not even started. (See below NG to Cooke, 17 Sept.)

## To Governor Nicholas Cooke of Rhode Island

Sir  Camp at Harlam Heights [N.Y.] 17 Sept 1776

I suppose you have heard of the Retreat from Long Island and the Evacuation of New York.[1] The Retreats were both Judicious and necessary, our numbers being very insufficient to hold such an extent of ground. His Excellency had proposd to Evacuate the City and Subburbs of New York sometime before the Enemy made their last landing, and had the Quarter Master General been able to furnish the necessary Waggons to remove the stores and Baggage the Retreat would have been effected in good order, had the Enimy delay'd their landing twenty four hours longer. Almost all the old standing Regiment was drawn out of the City in order to oppose the Enimy at Hell Gate where they made an appearance of a very large body of Troops, and movements as if they intended a landing. We made a miserable disorderly Retreat from New York, owing to the disorderly conduct of the Militia who run at the appearance of the Enemies advance Guard. This was General Fellows Brigade. They struck a pannick into the Troops in the Rear, and Fellows and Parsons whole Brigade run away from about fifty men and left his Excellency on the Ground within Eighty Yards of the Enimy, so vext at the infamous conduct of the Troops that he sought Death rather than life. The Retreat was on the fourteenth of this instant from New York. Most of the Troops got off but we lost a prodigious deal of Baggage and stores. On the 15th we had a skirmish at Harlam Heiths.[2] A party of about a thousand came and attackt our advance post. They met with a very different kind of Reception from what they did the day before. The fire continued about an hour and the Enimy Retreated. Our people pursued them, and by the spirited conduct of General Putnam and Col Read [Reed], the Adjutant General, our people advanced upon the plain ground without cover and Attackt them and drove them back. His Excellency sent and orderd a timely retreat to our advance Post for he discoverd or concluded the Enimy would send a large reinforcement, as their main body lay near bye. I was sick when the Army retreated from Long Island, which by the bye was the best Effected Retreat I ever read or heard off, considering the difficulty of the Retreat. The Army now remains quiet but expect an Attack every Day. Col Varnum and Col Hitchcocks Regiments were in the last action and behaved nobly. But neither of the Cols was with them, both being absent; one sick, the other takeing care of the Sick. Time wont permit me to say much more as I am wanted to go into the Jerseys.[3]

I had the honnor of seeing and conversing with your Committee.[4] I think and so does his Excellency that the opperations of the Campaign will have no Effect upon you as it will be impossible for the Enimy to detach any part of the Army while our Army is able to make any stand. I would not Evacuate one foot of ground, as it will tend to encourage the Enimy and dispirit our People. I am sure the Government is safe and will remain so unless the Enimy can ruin this Army. This is their grand object and every nerve will be exerted to effect it. That they will not have opportunity and strength sufficient to molest you. I have not time to add one word more. I am with all due respect your most obedient humble servant

N. GREENE

ALS (R-Ar).
1. NG was not an eyewitness to these events. On 1 Sept., Washington gave him command of the "Centre Division," but until his complete recovery, Gen. Joseph Spencer replaced him (Fitzpatrick, GW, 6: 4). Washington ordered the five thousand troops out of New York City, but the evacuation had barely gotten started when Howe—after dallying for two weeks—finally decided to launch his attack.

In the meantime Washington had pulled half his army to the north end of Manhattan to Harlem Heights, where NG had taken up quarters. On Sunday, 15 Sept., Howe preceded his landings by an intensive bombardment from ships in the East River along Kips Bay—at what is now 34th Street. Panic spread among the untrained American militiamen in their makeshift breastworks, and they fled virtually without firing a shot as British troops landed. Panic spread to adjacent American troops, and when Washington arrived on the scene, half his army was in full flight northward. He tried desperately to rally the men, but to no avail. It was then that NG reported him so "vext" that he "sought Death rather than Life." (Freeman says, "Traditions of Washington's behavior on the field are numerous but, as usual, are improbable or unverifiable," GW, 4: 194n.)

If Howe had permitted Clinton to cut across the island to the Hudson River, he would have cut off several thousand Americans to the south, but by the time the rest of the British troops had landed, Putnam and Knox had extricated their men from the city and were well along on their twelve-mile march to Harlem Heights. The "baggage and stores" described by NG as abandoned included sixty-seven cannon—half of Washington's artillery. By nightfall most of the troops had reached Harlem Heights. Howe had again failed to crush Washington's army, but there was little joy in the Harlem camp. It had been an oppressive, humiliating day, wearying to body and spirit. (NG was incorrect in dating the retreat 14 Sept.)

2. Although the battle of Harlem Heights was not a major encounter, NG's account is extremely brief, omitting, for example, his part and ignoring the boost to troop morale. (He did say in a letter of 4 Oct., below, that the enemy attacked where "I had the Honor to Command.") It required remarkable restraint to treat his first experience in battle so cooly, almost cavalierly, as if he were a veteran of many battles.

Harlem Heights was a narrow, rocky highland that ran several miles along the Hudson at the north end of Manhattan Island. Howe completed his first day of the invasion by sending part of his troops south to occupy New York City and part toward the north to establish a line across the island only a mile south of Harlem Heights. To counter a possible British advance up the Heights, Washington placed Spencer's and Putnam's divisions near the center of the ridge and NG's division at the southern slopes facing the "Hollow Way" (a low area near present 125th Street). If the British pushed northward, NG's sector would be their first objective. His division included his old brigade—now Gen. Nixon's—and the brigades of Sargent and Beale.

Early Monday morning American scouts under Col. Thomas Knowlton engaged advance units of the British light infantry. To draw out more of the enemy, Washington ordered NG to send 150 volunteers from his old brigade toward the Hollow Way as a feint so that Knowlton's detachment could slip past the British troops on the Heights south of the Hollow Way, and cut them off from their base. With NG's approval Nixon chose Col. Archibald Crary of Rhode Island to lead the volunteers, most of them from Rhode Island and Massachusetts. British troops took the bait; they moved down the hill toward Crary's volunteers, but before Knowlton's men could get behind them, a shot from the American troops warned the British, so that the Americans could only make a flanking attack. Knowlton and Col. Leitch were both fatally wounded, but their men fought on. The rest of Nixon's brigade were sent to reinforce Col. Crary.

The skirmish took on the proportions of a fierce battle. Troops who had run in panic the day before fought like veterans. They pushed the British up Morningside Heights to a buckwheat field, and for the first time American troops saw the backs of the "lobster backs." Both sides brought up reinforcements until there were some two thousand men fighting on each side. Putnam, Greene, Reed, and others rode back and forth among their troops, in order, as Reed put it, to "animate the Troops," although he admitted it might be considered "rash and imprudent for Officers of our Rank to go into such an action." (Johnston, Harlem, p. 138) Again the British retreated, and the Americans, in their elation at having overcome their defeatism, would have followed if Washington had not wisely ordered them back. Their spirits were high. John Gooch, an old friend of NG's, said the victory was "Glorious" and that "New England men have gained the first Lawrells." (N. E. Hist. and Gen. Reg. 30 [1876]: 335) Washington told Congress that the battle had "greatly inspirited the whole of our Troops." (Fitzpatrick, GW, 6: 69)

In addition to excellent accounts in Ward (War) and Freeman (GW), an extremely readable and scholarly account of the action on 15 and 16 Sept. is Bruce Bliven, Jr., Battle for Manhattan (New York: Henry Holt and Co., 1955). He has related the action to the streets and landmarks of modern Manhattan. For the battle of Harlem Heights, all authorities have relied heavily on a classic work—Johnston's Harlem.

3. He had been ordered to Ft. Constitution (later Ft. Lee) on the west side of the Hudson opposite Ft. Washington. Nixon's brigade was ordered on 19 Sept. to report to NG (Fitzpatrick, GW, 6: 73).

4. On hearing of the evacuation of Long Island, the R.I. Assembly sent a committee of three under Joshua Babcock, general of the militia, to confer with Washington and NG on the defence of Rhode Island. They arrived two days before Howe's landing on Manhattan and stayed only twenty-four hours. (Cooke to Washington, 6 Sept., Bartlett, Records, 7: 619, and Babcock to Cooke, 21 Sept., R-Ar)

# To George Washington

Dear Sir          Camp Fort Constitution[1] [N.J.] Sept 23, 1776

The Enemy are landed at Powley's Hook[2] They came up this afternoon and began a Cannonade on the Battery and after Cannonadeing for half an hour or a little more they landed a party from the Ships. General Mercer had ordered off from the Hook all the troops except a small Guard who had orders to Evacuate the place from the first approach of the Enimy. General Mercer mentions no Troops but those Landed from the Ships, but Colo Bull and many others that were along the River upon the Heights saw twenty Boats go over from York to Powleys Hook. This movement must have happen'd since General Mercer wrote. I purpose to Visit Bergen tonight as General Mercer thinks of going to his Post at Amboy tomorrow. I purpose to detain him˚ one day longer. I am with due respect your Excellencys obedient servant

N GREENE

ALS (Washington Papers: DLC).
1. The name was soon changed to Ft. Lee (see below, NG to Hancock; 20 Oct. 1776). Although gun platforms had been constructed at Burdett's landing during July and Aug., the main fortification of Ft. Constitution was just taking shape. It stood across the Hudson from Ft. Washington, some three hundred feet above the river, atop the palisades that bordered the west bank. Barracks were planned several hundred yards southwest of the fort (see NG's orders, 8 Oct., below). On the Bluff Point promontory that stood to the north of the fort were several breastworks and guns protected by abatis. (A good description of Ft. Constitution [Lee] with map is found in Hall, "Ft. Lee," pp. 169–70 and 241.)
2. Paulus (or Powles) Hook was the New Jersey terminus of the ferry from New York City, an island at high tide but connected with the New Jersey mainland by a long causeway across a swamp. It was eleven miles south of Ft. Constitution and guarded the lower Hudson River. In a letter to Washington on the following day, NG gave more details on the British takeover (letter not found, but reported by Tench Tilghman, Washington's aide, to William Duer, 25 Sept., and printed in Force, *Archives* [5], 2: 523). "General Greene," wrote Tilghman, "informs that General Mercer, seeing the enemy were determined to possess themselves by a stronger force of ships and men than we could oppose, removed all the stores and useful cannon, so that nothing fell into the enemy's hands but the guns that had been rendered unfit for further service." Baurmeister reported two twelve-pounders abandoned by the Americans. (Baurmeister, *Revolution*, p. 54) No better example could be found of the impotence of coastal artillery in the face of strong British naval forces.

# To Jacob Greene [?][1]

[Fort Constitution, N.J.] September 28th 1776
I apprehend the several retreats that have lately taken place begin to make you think all is lost. Don't be frightened; our cause is not yet in a desperate state. The policy of Congress has been the most absurd and ridiculous imaginable, pouring in militia men who come and go every month. A military force established upon such principles defeats itself. People coming from home with all the tender feelings of domestic life are not sufficiently fortified with natural courage to stand the shocking scenes of war. To march over dead men, to hear without concern the groans of the wounded, I say few men can stand such scenes unless steeled by habit or fortified by military pride.[2]

There must be a good army established; men engaged for the war, a proper corps of officers, and then, after a proper time to discipline the men, everything is to be expected.[3]

The congress goes upon a penurious plan. The present pay of the officers will not support them, and it is generally determined by the best officers to quit the service, unless a more adequate provision is made for their support. The present establishment is not thought reputable.[4]

The congress has never furnished the number of men voted by near one half, certainly by above a third. Had we had numbers we need not have retreated from Long Island or New York. But the extent of ground to guard rendered the retreat necessary; otherwise the army would have been ruined by detachments. The enemy never could have driven us from Long Island and New York if our rear had been secured. We must have an army to meet the enemy everywhere; to act offensively as well as defensively. Our soldiers are as good as ever were, and were the officers half as good as the men they would beat any army on the globe of equal numbers.

Excerpt reprinted from Johnson, *Greene*, 1: 58–59.

1. Johnson called this an excerpt from a "private letter." Most such letters that he printed from this period were to brother Jacob.

2. Since their gallant action on Bunker Hill more than a year before, few militiamen had covered themselves with glory. His objections to the militia had intensified after the retreat from Long Island, when he saw thousands of them melt away.

3. NG did not know that Congress had finally overcome its opposition to a standing army when, on 16 Sept., it approved eighty-eight battalions to be "inlisted as soon as possible, to serve during the present war." Privates were to receive a twenty-dollar bounty and the promise of free land at the end of the war—from one hundred acres for a private or noncommissioned officer to five hundred acres for a colonel. The selection of officers below the rank of general was left to the states. (*JCC*, 5: 762–63) NG comments on the resolves in another letter to Jacob on 3 Oct., below.

4. For earlier comments on the pay of officers, see his correspondence with John Adams, especially letters of 2 June and 22 June, above.

## General Greene's Orders

Fort Constitution [N.J.] Sept. 30th 1776

Major Box is appointed and requested in conjunction with the Engineers of this Department and Col. Bull[1] to oversee and forward the fortifications at Fort Constitution. Lt. Col. Cornell is appointed Dep. Assistant Adj. Genl. for this Division. The Quarter Master General is directed to provide tools of all kinds necessary for a Blacksmith's and Armorer's shop, large enough to do the business of this part of the army. Many transgressions of general orders happen for want of their being read and explained to the men.[2] The General directs that all orders issued be read to the men in Regiments or Companies, and that every Captain provide himself with an orderly book that the men may be fully informed of their duty. The adjutants of regiments are to report any neglect.

Col. Moses Little Orderly Book, reprinted from Johnston, *NY 1776*, pt. 2, pp. 141–42.

1. Thomas Bull was lieutenant colonel of the Pennsylvania battalion of the Flying Camp. He was taken prisoner at the fall of Ft. Washington, 16 Nov. 1776 (Heitman, *Register*).

2. John Adlum was a private stationed at Ft. Lee when NG arrived from Harlem

Heights. "There was," he wrote later, "immediately a great change with respect to the discipline of the troops which before that was very lax. . . . The first thing done after General Greene arrived was to review our brigade, when he observed our officers were generally so deficient in their movements that he ordered them to be drilled first in the manual exercise, and also to be taught how to take their places in the regiment which they were obliged to submit to for about three hours after breakfast. In the afternoon they were exercised with their companies and sometimes by regiments." (John Adlum, *Memoirs of the Life of John Adlum in the Revolutionary War*, ed. Howard H. Peckham [Chicago: The Caxton Club, 1968], pp. 23–24)

# General Greene's Orders

[Ft. Constitution (Lee), N.J.] October 2d 1776

The Brigadiers or officers commanding Brigades[1] are requested to send the Brigade Majors or some other proper officers to fetch the new regulations of the army, and distribute them among the Regiments of their Brigades and the Commanding officers of each regiment or corps are directed to have them read, to have the rules and regulations read first to the whole regiment drawn up for that purpose and then order the Captains to read them again to each of their companies the day after they have been read to the regiments, to be continued the first Monday in every month.[2] Lt. Mills of Col. Hitchcock's Regiment is requested to collect a party of carpenters from either of the Brigades, regiments or corps in this Division of the army, that are willing to enter the work for the same pay, that was allowed last campaign.

Col. Moses Little Orderly Book, reprinted from Johnston, *NY 1776*, pt. 2, p. 142.

1. NG's return of troops on 29 Sept. from the "English Neighbourhood," (the area around Ft. Constitution) lists the brigades of Clinton, Ewing, and Nixon (the latter still on "York Island") and the regiments of Col. [Theunis] Dey and P. B. Bradley (Force, *Archives* [5] 2: 607).

2. Washington had urged a revision of the Articles of War for some time, especially in respect to harsher punishment for such offenses as plundering, desertion, and dealing with the enemy. John Adams, who guided the revised regulations through committee and Congress as a whole, virtually lifted the English Articles of War intact. One exception was the number of lashes a man might be given; although the limit was raised from 39 to 100, it still fell far short of the 1,000 that a British courtmartial could order. (The articles, as passed 20 Sept., are printed in *JCC*, 5: 788–807.) For Adams's role, see ibid., pp. 670–671n; for Washington's views on the need for harsher punishment see, for example, Fitzpatrick, *GW*, 6: 91, 114–15.

# To Jacob Greene[?][1]

[Ft. Constitution, N.J.] 3d of October 1776

The Congress have ordered eighty-eight regiments to be raised for the war. This looks well. For God's sake let us have good officers from Rhode Island, if you wish to preserve its reputation. We want nothing but good officers to constitute as good an army as ever marched into the field. Our men are infinitely better than the officers. I do not speak of Rhode Island officers, for they are generally good, and behaved exceedingly well in the late action. They did themselves a great deal of honour. I shall send a list to the governor of such as deserve a preference. I think you may officer your regiment as well as any on the continent if you will consult nothing but the *merit* of the man. . . .

This fall will be the last of the harvest. After this season, all the navigation of Great Britain will go armed sufficiently to manage the small cruizers of America. If your privateers should take any vessels bound to America or Great Britain, let the prize master assume the character, and personate the original captain; if he should have the misfortune to fall in with an enemy's vessel, let him answer, "bound to and come from the port mentioned in the ship's papers." If the captain or prize master does this with sufficient effrontery, nothing but personal knowledge can detect him.[2] It would be a good method to engage the crews of the prizes by giving them an opportunity to enter on board the privateer, and to share in all the prizes made after they entered on board. This may enable the captain of the privateer to continue his cruize, and bring in a number of prizes, when he would otherwise be obliged to return home for want of men. And as to the fidelity and attachment of the sailors, you may depend upon it, they will be as faithful after becoming interested, as the generality of our own seamen.

This fall is the golden harvest. I think the fishing ships at the eastward may be objects of attention this fall. In the spring, the East India ships may be intercepted on the coast of Africa. Were I at liberty, I think I could make a fortune for my family. But it is necessary for some to be in the field, to secure the property of others in their stores.

Excerpt reprinted from Johnson, *Greene*, 1: 59–60.
1. Johnson identifies the addressee only as "a gentleman who was interested in several privateers and who had suffered by repeated recaptures." He also calls it a "private" letter, a term he uses for letters to a friend or family. Jacob would fit both categories.
2. Although it was not uncommon for merchantmen and privateers to hide their identity with false papers, NG's suggestion that a captain of a privateer assume the identity of the captain of an enemy merchantman was certainly an extraordinary one. It went counter to congressional instructions issued on 3 April 1776 to the captains of privateers, requesting them to bring prizes into a convenient port and to bring or send masters of the vessels to a maritime court "as soon after the capture as may be" (*JCC*, 4: 253–54).
NG's first biographer, Judge Johnson, called it a *ruse de guerre* that exhibited "a mind fertile in resources" (Johnson, *Greene*, 1: 59). One of Johnson's severest critics, a son of "Lighthorse Harry" Lee, excoriated Johnson for his approval of Greene's promoting "public war by private rapacity, [which] can only be *palliated* upon the dangerous principle of justifying the means by the end." In defense of NG, Lee weighed this extraordinary suggestion against NG's "great virtues." (H. Lee, *Campaign*

*of 1781 in the Carolinas with Remarks Historical and Critical on Johnson's Life of Greene* [Philadelphia, 1824], pp. 13–16)

## General Greene's Orders

[Ft. Constitution (Ft. Lee), 4 Oct. 1776. A guard to relieve over Hackensack River. Moses Little Orderly Book, Johnston, *NY 1776*, pt. 2, p. 142.]

## To William Ellery [?]¹

[Ft. Constitution (Lee), N.J.] 4 Oct. 1776
The Panic that struck Gen. Fellows's and communicated itself to Gen. Parson's Brigade, disgraced the last Retreat.² The 2 Brigades run away from about 40 or fifty Men, and left Gen. Washington standing alone within an hundred yards of the Enemy. This disagreeable Circumstance made the last Retreat very disgraceful. The Enemy next day at Harlem Heights, flushed with the Successes of the day before, approached and attacked our Lines, where I had the Honor to Command. The Action or rather Skirmish lasted about two hours; our people beat the Enemy off the Ground. Col. Varnum and Col. Hitchcocks Regts behaved exceedingly spirited and all the officers that were with the Regiments. The Colonels were both absent. Had all the Colonies good Officers, there is no danger of the Troops; never was Troops that would stand in the Field longer than the American Soldiery. If the officers were as good as the Men, and had only a few months to form the Troops by Discipline, America might bid Defiance to the whole World. Gen. Putnam and the Adjt General [Joseph Reed] were in the Action and behaved nobly.

Excerpt reprinted from Stiles, *Diary,* 2: 76.
1. Stiles does not give the addressee, but the excerpt follows a long letter of 11 Oct. from William Ellery in which he refers to the subject of NG's letter, although he does not mention enclosing the letter.
2. On Howe's landing on Manhattan and the battle of Harlem Heights, see notes, NG to Cooke, 17 Sept., above.

## From Governor Nicholas Cooke of Rhode Island

Sir                                                    Providence [R.I.] October 5th 1776
I am favoured with yours of the 17th ulto which came to Hand when I was in the Hospital under Inoculation. By the Blessing of God Mrs Cooke myself and the rest of my Family who entered being Ten in Number went through the Distemper and have come out very well. I have the Pleasure to inform you that Mrs Greene, your Lady, was yesterday at my House in good Health.

I have written this Day to General Washington upon the Requisition of Congress to this State to raise Two Battalions during the War, and inclose you a Copy of the Paragraph upon that Subject.[1] I am by the Advice of the Committee to request your Attention to this Matter and that you will give every Assistance and Information relating to it in your Power. I am Sir Your most obedt and most hble Servt

NICHO COOKE

P. S. At the Request of the Secretary I send you the inclosed which are from a young Lad a Volunteer who was taken by Capt. Biddle; we shall be glad if youll serve him.

FC (R-Ar). Enclosure missing; see note 1, below.
1. On the new Continental army, see note 3, NG to Jacob Greene [?], 28 Sept., above. The portion of Cooke's letter to Washington which he enclosed for NG's attention is taken from Bartlett, *Records*, 8: 31:

> I last night received the resolutions of Congress, for enlisting eighty-eight battalions in the Continental service, during the war; copies of which, without doubt, have been transmitted to Your Excellency. By them, a requisition is made for two battalions from this state; at the same, we are informed by Mr. President Hancock, that the troops now in service, belonging to the several states, who shall enlist for the war, will be considered as part of their quota in the American army.
> There are two battalions in Continental pay, which were originally raised by this state, viz.: Col. Varnum's, Col. Hitchcock's, Col. Lippitt's, who are now in the army, under your immediate command, and Col. Richmond's which is under orders for New London.
> I write by this opportunity, to the three former, to make report to me of the officers in their several battalions who will engage to serve during the war; and by the advice of the committee, I request Your Excellency to transmit to me, to be laid before the General Assembly, at their session on the 28th instant, the names of such of them as you shall think merit promotion.

(Col. Christopher Lippitt [1744–1824] took command of Col. Babcock's R.I. militia when Babcock was removed because of illness [see note 2, NG to Joseph Nightingale, 24 March 1776, above]. The regiment was taken into the Continental army in the summer of 1776 and in Sept. was sent to join Washington at Harlem Heights. [*R.I. Biog. Cycl.*] Col. William Richmond's battalion was en route to join Washington when, with his permission, it was sent instead to New London, Conn., as a preliminary to an invasion of Long Island—an invasion that was soon canceled. [Cooke to Washington, 5 Sept. 1776, Bartlett, *Records*, 7: 30–31])

## General Greene's Orders

[Ft. Constitution (Lee), N.J., 6 Oct. 1776. Party of four hundred to finish fortifications. Four regiments to form brigade under Gen. Roberdeau[1] "until his Excellency's pleasure be further known." The deputy adjutant general to appoint a grand parade. Col. Moses Little Orderly Book, Johnston, *NY 1776*, pt. 2, p. 142.]

1. Daniel Roberdeau (1727–95) was a brigadier general in the Pa. militia. Born on the island of St. Christopher of French ancestry, he became a successful Philadelphia merchant and prominent patriot. As a member of Congress from 1777 to 1779, he signed the Articles of Confederation (*PMHB* 9 [1885]: 278n).

## General Greene's Orders

[Ft. Constitution (Lee), N.J.] October 7th 1776

A guard of 50 men to relieve the guard at Hoebuck's Ferry[1] immediately, to take 4 days provisions. The commanding officers of Regiments in the English neighborhood are to take care that none of the rails are burnt in their Regiments for fire wood.[2] Regiments are to be furnished with firewood daily, apply to Quarter Master General for teams. A subaltern and 30 men to go immediately for the stock brought from Bergen.

Col. Moses Little Orderly Book, reprinted from Johnston, *NY 1776*, pt. 2, pp. 142–43.

1. Hoboken Ferry, a mile north of Paulus Hook and some ten miles below Ft. Constitution.

2. Peter Bourdet, whose farm lay near Ft. Constitution, made formal complaint that he had "125 acres in good fence and not one left" (damage claims cited by Leiby, *Hackensack*, p. 52).

## To the Convention of New York at Fish Kill

Gentlemen          Fort Constitution (Lee) [N.J.] Octob 17 [7], 1776[1]

William Bradford Adjutant of Col. Hitchcocks Regiment, after the Enemy landed on Long Island, took a Horse belonging to one Jacob Wicoff, a person that had Joined the British forces, the Adjutant run a very great risque in fetching the Horse off; and he must inevitably have fallen into the Enemies hands if the Adjutant had not made the attempt. But as property belonging to Tories is not nor ought not to be the reward of those that takes it into possession only under certain limitations, I think it my duty to acquaint you that I have the Horse in my possession and shall be delivered to your order, either to the Adjutant as a reward for his bravery or to be sold for the benefit of the State, as you may think proper. If the Horse is to be sold, I should be glad of an opportunity to purchase him as I am in want of a Horse, mine being worn out in the Service. I am gentlemen with great respect your Obedient Servant.[2]

NATHANAEL GREENE

Tr (GWG transcript: CSmH).

1. The transcriber erred; 7 Oct. is correct (see note 2).

2. The letter was read at a meeting of the N.Y. Committee of Safety on 10 Oct., where it was referred to a committee composed of "Mr. Roosevelt, Mr. Van Cortlandt, and Mr. Adgate" (Force, *Archives* (5) 3: 236). The committee reported back on 12 Oct. (ibid, p. 242) and approved an answer on 16 Oct. See N.Y. Committee of Safety to NG, 16 Oct., below.

## General Greene's Orders

[Ft. Constitution (Lee), N.J.] October 8th 1776
Application for leave of absence from camp for a short time on the occasional business of the regiment is to be made to the Brigadier General or the commanding officers of Brigade. Brigadiers are desired not to grant liberty of absence unless on real business. The houses upon the water side, near the ferry are to be cleared of the present inhabitants for the use of the guards and ferrymen.[1] A captain and 40 men well acquainted with rowing to be drawn for the management of the ferryboats. This party to be excused from other duty and to be continued in that employ. All the Axes in the different regiments are to be delivered to the Quarter Master General Col. Biddle,[2] and he is to deliver an equal proportion to the Regiments retaining enough for the Public works. Captain [Jeremiah] Olney of Col. Hitchcock's Regiment and Captain Warner of Col. Little's are appointed to assist in overseeing the fortifications and are to be excused from all other duty. Commanding officers of Regiments are requested to fix upon proper places for Barracks, none to be nearer the fort than 50 rods.[3] The General desires commanding officers to divide the regiments into messes of 8 men. The men must build timber huts, as boards are not to be had. Boards are to be had only for the roof. The huts are to be 12 feet long by 9 wide, to have stone chimneys and to be ranged in proper streets. The guard at the Bridge to be relieved immediately. The Captain of the Artillery is directed to examine the state of the amunition in the magazine and report to the Deputy Assistant Quarter Master. The General directs that none of the troops go out of drum call, without liberty from the Commanding officer of the regiment. The rolls of companies are to be called 4 times a day. Men not to be found when the regiments are called to parade may expect to be severely punished and the officers if negligent of their duty are to be arrested. Adjutant Colman is appointed to do the duty of Brigade Major for General Nixon's Brigade while Major Box is employed on the Fortifications.

Col. Moses Little Orderly Book, reprinted from Johnston, *NY 1776*, pt. 2, p. 143.
    1. Burdett's Ferry was just beneath the Ft. Constitution bluff. (See NG to Washington, 23 Sept., above.) By what authority the inhabitants were dispossessed is not known, other than the dubious justification of "military necessity."
    2. Clement Biddle (1740–1814), a prosperous Philadelphia merchant, was appointed quartermaster general of the Pa. militia in July 1776. It was the beginning of a close association between Biddle and NG that lasted throughout the war. Biddle was with him at Trenton, Brandywine, and Germantown. In Nov. 1776 NG made him an aide-de-camp, and in July 1777 appointed him commissary general of forage, a post he held for three years. Upon NG's strong recommendation, Pennsylvania appointed Biddle quartermaster general of the state militia in 1781. (*DAB*) The two were associated

in several investment enterprises. Catharine Greene occasionally stayed with the Biddles when visiting NG.

3. Before NG's order was issued, some of the soldiers had already started constructing huts. Lieut. Joseph Hodgkins of Col. Little's regiment had moved from Harlem to Ft. Constitution the same day NG had been reassigned (20 Sept.), and by 30 Sept. he wrote his wife that he hoped the regiment would stay there the "Rest of the Campan as I have Ben at the Truble of Building a Log House with a ston Chimny I got it fit to live in 3 days ago Before which time I had not Lodged on any thing But the ground since we Left Long-island" (Wade and Lively, *Glorious Cause*, p. 223). A month later NG reported many were in huts and that tents were being sent to Washington's army as huts were finished (NG to Washington, 5 Nov., below). In 1909 Edward Hall found "regular rows of heaps of stones" some 50 rods (825 feet) southwest of the main fort (Hall, "Ft. Lee," p. 188).

# To John Hancock, President of the Continental Congress

Sir          Camp at Fort Constitution, [N.J.] Octr 10th 1776

The Sick of the Army who are under the Care of the Regimental Surgeons are in a most wretched Situation, the Surgeons being without the least article of Medicine to assist Nature in her efforts for the Recovery of Health.[1] There is no Circumstance that strikes a greater damp upon the spirits of the Men who are yet well, than the miserable Condition the Sick are in. They exhibit a Spectacle shocking to human feelings, and as the knowledge of their distress spreds thro the Country will prove an unsurmountable obstacle to the Recruiting the new Army.

Good Policy as well as humanity in my humble opinion demands the immediate attention of Congress upon this Subject; that the Evil may be sought out and the Grievance redressed. The Sick in the Army are too numerous to be all accomodated on the Contracted Plan of the General Hospital. The Director General[2] says he has no authority by his Commission to supply the Demand of the Regimental Sick, and the General Hospital being too small to accomodate much more than one half, the remainder lies without any means of relief than the value of the Rations allowed to every Soldier. Many hundred are now in this Condition and die daily for want of proper assistance, by which means the Army is robbed of many valuable Men at a time when a reinforcement is so exceedingly necessary. Both Officers and Men join in one general Complaint and are greatly disgusted at the Evil which has prevailed so long. Some Measures should be taken to Qualify the Director General, or to empower the Commander in Chief to qualify him, to furnish the Regiment Surgeons under the direction of the Cols of the Regiments with such Supplies as the State of the Sick may demand.

Great Complaints have been made that the Regimental Surgeons abuse their Trust and embezzle the Public stores committed to their Care. This among others is a reason urged why the Regimental sick suffer as they do. The Surgeons, it has been said, cannot be trusted with the necessary Stores. Whether this Complaint be well or Ill founded I am not a Judge of; perhaps in some few Instances it may have been the case, but I am far from thinking they are deserving the Charge in General;[3] besides which the Injury arising from a few abuses of this kind were they even more common, is triffling compared with that which the Army and Public suffers in the present State of things.

The Director General complains of the want of Medicine and says his stocks are but barely sufficient for the General Hospital. I can see no reason either from Policy or humanity that the Stores for the General Hospital should be preserved for Contingencies which may never happen, and the present regimental Sick left to perish for want of proper necessaries. It is wholly immaterial, in my opinion, either to the states or the Army whether a Man dies in the General or Regimental Hospital. The Platform of the General Hospital should be large enough to receive all the Sick that are unfit to continue in Quarters, or else to supply the Regimental Hospital with such medicines and necessaries as the State of the Sick requires. I am with due respect your obedient Servant

NATHANAEL GREENE

P S I do not mean to censure the conduct of the Director General nor to complain of his Activity, but I mean to point out the defect of the present establishment and to shew the necessity of giveing the Director some further powers and much more assistance to enable him to satisfy the numerous wants.[4]

N GREENE

LS (PCC: DNA); postscript in NG's hand.
1. For the background to this letter, see NG to Washington, 11 Aug. 1776, above.
2. Dr. John Morgan.
3. Washington was far more critical of the regimental surgeons. Two weeks earlier, in recommending to Congress more stringent control of the regimental surgeons by the director general, he charged that many "are very great Rascals, countenancing the Men in sham Complaints to exempt them from duty, and often receiving Bribes to Certifie Indispositions." He was persuaded, moreover, that they were aiming "to break up the Genl. Hospital, and have, in numberless Instances, drawn for Medicines, Stores &ca. in the most profuse and extravagant manner, for private purposes." (Fitzpatrick, GW, 6: 113)
4. As NG was writing this letter, Morgan arrived to consult on medical needs in New Jersey. On reading the letter, he was hurt, as he later wrote, by the fact that "not the least notice was taken of the unwearied pains I had bestowed to accomplish that purpose [relieving the suffering of the men]; which might lead Congress to imagine me very negligent of my duty, or inattentive to matters that so nearly concerned me." At Morgan's insistence NG added the postscript, although Morgan thought he "seemed barely to guard against reflexions upon me." (Morgan, Vindication, p. 107)
Neither of them could know that, only the day before, Congress had resolved on

drastic changes in the medical department which were counter to everything Morgan and Greene had recommended and which revealed, as Whitfield Bell has said, "an almost total want of understanding." (Bell, *Morgan*, p. 198) The resolves provided chiefly that in the future no regimental hospitals were to be "allowed in the neighbourhood of the general hospital, " that Morgan was to superintend a hospital for the army "posted on the east side of Hudson's river," and that Dr. William Shippen [Jr.] was to superintend a hospital in the state of New Jersey." (*JCC*, 6: 857–58) Shippen interpreted the resolves as placing him in charge of the medical department west of the Hudson and restricting Morgan to the east side, and over Morgan's strong objections, he gradually made his interpretation stick. He was the principal reason for Morgan's dismissal three months later, just as Morgan was responsible for Shippen's eventual removal. (The Shippen-Morgan controversy is fully treated in Bell, *Morgan*, pp. 197–239.)

## To Governor Nicholas Cooke of Rhode Island

Sir                              Fort Constitution [N.J.] Octob 11th, 1776

His Excellency General Washington will transmit you a list of Officers to constitute the two new Regiments to be raisd by your State.[1] The most of those officers are Gentlemen whose conduct has been approvd by those under whom they have servd. The success of the cause, the defeat of the Enemy, the Honnor of the State and the Reputation of the Army altogether depends upon the Establishing a good Core or Corps of Officers. My little experience has fully convinced me that without more attention is paid by the different States in the appointment of the Officers, the Troops never will Answer their expectation. I hope as everything that is dear and valueable is at Stake, that no popular prejudices nor family connexion will influence the House in the Election of the Officers for the new Army. I am sensible that America has as good materials to form an Army as any State in the World, but without a good set of Officers the Troops will be little better than a lawless Banditie or an ungovernable Mob. The Americans possess as much natural bravery as any People upon Earth, but habit must form the Soldier. He who expects men brought from the tender scenes of domestick life can meet danger and death with a becoming fortitude is a stranger to the Human Heart. There is nothing that can get the better of that active Principle of self Preservation but a proper Sentiment of Pride, or being often accustom'd to danger. As the Principle of Pride is not predominant enough in the minds of the common Soldiery, the force of habit must be called into its aid to get the better of our Natural fears ever alarmd at the Approach of danger.

There has been, it must be confest, some shameful conduct in this army this campaign, in a great measure oweing to the bad conduct of the Officers. I have neither seen nor heard of one instance of cowardice among the old Troops where they had good officers to lead them on. In the last Action every Regiment behavd with a becoming spirit, especially Col Hitchcocks and Col Varnums.² I dont wish to see an officer in the Army but such as has a regard for their Reputation, who feels a Sentiment of honnor and is ambitious of distinguishing himself. Such will answer the Publick expectation and be an honnor to the State that sent him.

Col Varnum from the treatment he has met with from Congress has taken the resolution of leaveing the army. The Colony are generally acquainted with his abillities, that he stands in no need of a recommendation. Perhaps the House may think proper to reelect him and give him the Opportunity to refuse the Appointment as a complement due to his past services.³ Col Cornwell [Cornell] and Col Carary [Crary] Youl observe are both left out in the Generals arrangement. They were both in the late action and behavd exceeding well, but as there is a reduction of Regiments tis not Possible to accomodate the whole, and there is a preference given by the under officers, tho they never have been consulted upon this occasion.⁴ His Excellency has put down only such as appears deserving without consulting them upon the subject to know whether they would serve or not. The House will appoint such and so many of those Recommended as they shall think proper and fill the Vacancies of their own choice; but I hope there will be none in the arrangement but men of Merit.⁵

The several Retreats and Evacuations that have taken place this Campaign without doubt has alarmd the fears of the timad [timid] and arousd their apprehension of an approaching ruin. The source of these misfortunes have originated from several causes. The strength of the Enemy far exceeded the expectations of Congress. The late season that they attempted to call in a reenforcement to our aid, the many delays that took place among the different States in furnishing their propotion, protracted the time of collecting the forces together to such a degree that when the Enimy had their whole Strength together, ours in different detachments were far inferior to theirs. With a force inferior to the Enemy in number, with Troops that were mostly raw and undiciplined, with Young and Ignorant Officers, What could be expected against old experienced officers with Veteran Troops to command, Short of what has taken place, Especially when you take in the Idea of the extent of ground we had to guard and the assistance the Enemy receivd from their Ships owing to the situation of the Posts we occupied. The Militia has come and gone in such Shoals that his Excellency could never tell scarcely two days together the strength he had at any one Post. If the different States compleats the establishment agreeable to the Resolve of Congress and the Troops come well officerd (for on that the whole depends) I have not the least doubt in my own mind but that in a few months we shall be able to seek the Enemy instead of they us. I know our men are more than equal to theirs and was our officers equal to our men, we should have nothing to fear from the best Troops in the World. I do not mean to derogate from the worth and merit of all the officers in the Army. We have many that are in the service deserveing the highest Applause; and has servd with Reputation and honnor to themselves; and the state that sent them; and I am happy that I have it to say that the Rhode Island Regiments hitherto are amongst this number.

Three of the Enemy Ships past the Cheveau de frise in the North River yesterday and went up to Tapan Bay. Our army are so strongly fortifyed and so much out of the Command of the Shiping[6] we have little more to fear this Campaign. The Troops have been and still are exceeding sickly. The same disorder rages in the Enemys camp as does in ours, but is much more mortal.

Nothing new from the Northern Army. I am with great esteem your obedient Servant

NATH GREENE

ALS (R-Ar).

1. Congress had authorized the states to appoint officers below the rank of general, reserving to itself their *commissioning*. At Cooke's request Washington sent a list (drawn up by NG) from which the assembly could select officers (Bartlett, *Records*, 8: 36). The Assembly, however, sidestepped its responsibility (see note 5, below).

2. The "Action" was at Harlem Heights, 16 Sept.

3. On Varnum's earlier threat to leave, see note NG to Washington, 12 Aug. 1776, above. NG recommended that Varnum's regiment be put under the command of Col. Christopher Greene (1737–81), a third cousin. He was still a prisoner in Canada, having been captured while serving with Arnold in the assault on Quebec, but Washington expected him to be exchanged soon. Christopher later won laurels as the defender of Ft. Mercer at Red Bank in 1777 and distinguished himself as commander of the famed R.I. Black Regiment. He was brutally killed by a group of DeLancey's Tories who surprised him at Croton River, N.Y., in May 1781. (*DAB*)

Despite his threats, Varnum was still serving as late as 7 Dec. (Lee to Cooke, Bartlett, *Records*, 8: 160). Three days later, however, when the R.I. Assembly was faced with the British occupation of Newport, they appointed him as brigadier general "of all the forces now raised, or to be raised, within this state" (ibid., p. 64). He remained in the militia until Feb. 1777, when he returned to the Continental army as a brigadier general (*JCC*, 7: 141).

4. The four old R.I. regiments (now called battalions) were to be reduced to two, which meant a corresponding reduction in officers.

5. Cooke wrote Washington on 5 Nov. that the Assembly could devise no better means of filling vacancies than to refer the task to "your Excellency and General Greene" (RIHS, *Coll.*, 6: 176). NG would be blamed later for the supposed inequities.

6. By being "so much out of the Command of the Shiping," NG meant that the height of Fts. Washington and Constitution (Lee) put them above the highest angle a ship's guns could be raised.

He gives scant space to a most important incident and ignores the obvious implications of the fact that the British ships not only sailed over the obstacles in the Hudson but, more importantly, ran past the batteries of the two forts, which had been greatly strengthened since HMS *Phoenix* and *Rose* had done the same thing in July and August. It is true that the ships suffered considerable damage (see Morgan, *Naval Docs.*, 6: 1178–83), but the question that should have suggested itself to NG was this: if the forts were constructed in order to stop the British from using this vital artery, what purpose do they now serve? He was not the only one, however, who failed to ask the question. Although Washington reported the incident fully to Congress, admitting his "surprize and mortification," he said nothing about the consequent uselessness of the forts for a month (see his letter to NG, 8 Nov., below). In the meantime he was almost as matter-of-fact as NG in reporting the incident to others. (His 9 Oct. letter to Congress is in Fitzpatrick, *GW*, 6: 184–85; the other references to the incident are on pp. 190, 193, 196, 198, and 205.)

## To George Washington

Fort Constitution [(Lee) N.J.]
Dear General                                         Octo 12th 5 oClock 1776
    I am informd a large body of the Enemies Troop have landed at Froggs Point.[1] If so I suppose the Troops here will be wanted there. I have three Brigades in readiness to reinforce you.[2] General Clintons Brigade will march first, General Nixons next, and then the Troops under the command of General Roberdeau. I dont apprehend any danger from this quarter at present. If the force on your side are insufficient I hope these three Brigades may be ordered over, and I with them, and leave General Ewings Brigade to guard the Post. If the Troops are wanted over your side or likely to be in the morning, they should be got over in the latter part of the Night as the Shiping may move up from below and impede if not totally stop the Troops from passing. I wait your Excellencys further commands. Should be glad to know where the Enemy has landed and their numbers. I am with great respect your Excellencys obedient Servant

N GREENE

N B The Tents upon Staten Island have been all struck as far as discovery has been made.

ALS (Washington Papers: DLC).
    1. After the battle at Harlem Heights, Gen. Howe waited almost a month before making a move against the Americans encamped there. Hesitant to assault fortified positions, he decided on an amphibious attack that would cut in behind Washington's forces to the north. Howe's first objective was Throg's Neck or Point (also Frog or Frogg) on Long Island Sound. A small American force was able to hold the British there for a week, giving Washington valuable time to retreat to White Plains (see below, NG to Cooke, 16 Oct.).
    2. NG's unsolicited offer, according to Freeman, "was so extraordinary a tender that it made the day notable." (Freeman, *GW*, 4: 215) The offer of Nixon's brigade was accepted by Washington, and it was ferried across the next night. (NG's order was in Nixon's orders of 13 Oct., Johnston, *NY 1776*, pt. 2, p. 144.) NG's offer to accompany his troops was ignored; Washington wished him to stay in command of the N.J. forces.

## General Greene's Orders

[Ft. Constitution (Lee), N.J.] October 13th 1776
General Nixon's and General Roberdeau's Brigade are to draw and

cook themselves 3 days provisions immediately.[1] The guard to be relieved from Col. Ewing's Brigade, the guards at Bergen to be excepted. The other two Brigades to hold themselves in readiness to march at a moment's warning. Captain Spurr from Col. Hitchcock's regiment is to oversee fatigue parties employed on Fortifications. The Company is desired to kill all the fat cattle brought from Bergen, that the inhabitants don't claim, take an account of all the marks and numbers and have their value estimated by 2 or 3 good men. The sheep that are fit are to be killed for the use of the Army. An exact account of their number and marks and value is to be kept.[2] The Quarter Master General is directed to take all horses brought from Bergen and not claimed and to employ such as are fit in the service; the rest to be disposed of at Public Vendue. Lest any should be injured that cannot claim his property, a record is to be kept describing the natural and artificial marks and the value of each.

Col. Moses Little Orderly Book, reprinted from Johnston, NY 1776, pt. 2, pp. 143–44.

1. See NG's offer of three brigades to Washington the previous day. Gen. Roberdeau stayed at Ft. Lee, but Nixon's brigade was ferried over that night.

2. Stock had been rounded up without the owners' permission. Whether the owners were recompensed is not recorded.

## To Governor Nicholas Cooke of Rhode Island

Sir                    Head Quarters Newyork Island Octo 16, 1776
    Yours of the 5th was deliverd me by Mr Hazzard the subject of which I had wrote upon before as fully as is necessary. The Anxiety I felt for the Honnor of the State and the good of the cause made me anticipate your wishes rellative to Recommendations. I had made a collection of the Officers belonging to the three Rhode Island Regiments;[1] and deliverd it into his Excellency General Washington to be forwarded to your state. That recommendation and arrangement of Officers is the best that I could make or recommend to the General, all circumstances considerd. The State will act their pleasure with respect to the Appointments. The General only wishes to have good men, such as will discharge their duty in every point of view; and maintain the Character of Gentlemen; he has no attachment to any Person farther than his merit recommends him. Men of merit he wishes to be appointed whether in or out of the Army.

    General How has landed at Frogs Point a place a few Miles East of Hell Gate; he is collecting his force together at that place with a design to cut of our Retreat.[2] His Excellency is makeing an Arrangement to counteract him. The Troops appear to be in good Spirits and I am in hopes if How Attacks us, he will meet with a defeat. A Battle is dayly, nay hourly expected. I shall come in for no share of the honnor or glory of the day if Victorious nor shame or disgrace if defeated, my command being in New Jersey. Hows designs evidently appears to be to get in our Rear to cut off our supplies and starve the Army out; this reduces us to the necessity of extending our left Wing out in the Country to preserve our communication with the Country from whence we get our support. A few days may produce some Events important to the American Interest. I was on Staten Island Night before last. The greatest part of the British Troops and Hessians are drawn off to support General Hows opperations at Frogs Point.

I am exceeding happy to hear of the safe recovery of your family from the small Pox. Present my Respects to them and to Mr [Henry] Ward the Secretary. I have carefully sent in the Letters sent me by the Flaggs. I am with great respect your obedient humble Servant

NATHANAEL GREENE

ALS (R-Ar).
1. There were four Rhode Island regiments, but Col. Richmond's regiment had never gotten to New York. For the background of this letter, see Cooke to NG, 5 Oct., above.
2. On Howe's landing, see above, NG to Washington, 12 Oct.

## From the New-York Committee of Safety[1]

Sir                            [                    16 Oct. 1776]
We have received your favour of the 7th instant, respecting the horse taken by William Bradford, Adjutant to Colonel Hitchcock's Regiment, which you inform us is the property of one Jacob Wyckoff, who has joined the enemy. As the horse is now in your possession, and you are in want of one, we desire you will have him appraised and kept in your service until some future determination of the Convention or future Legislature of this State relative to the disposition of the property of all such persons as have or hereafter may join the enemy, that may fall into our hands. The bravery of the Adjutant will then also be considered.

I am, with great respect, sir, your most obedient servant.

Reprinted from Force, *Archives* (5) 3: 251.
1. The letter was probably signed by Col. Peter R. Livingston, successor of Pres. Nathaniel Woodhull, who was killed in the battle of Long Island.

## To John Hancock, President of the Continental Congress

Camp at Fort Lee (lately Fort Constitution) [N.J.][1]
Sir                                                Octo 20, 1776
I was at Head Quarters near Kingsbridge with his Excellency General Washington last night[2] and on leaving him was desired to send by Express to acquaint you that the Army there are in great want

of a large Supply of Cartridges which no persons can be spared to make.[3] Therefore he requests that you will order all that are now made up at Philadelphia to be sent forward in light waggons that can travel with great Dispatch as they are realy very much wanted; and as none can be made up here, that persons be employ'd at Philadelphia to continue at that business, to furnish a full Supply for the Army.

Mr Commissary Lowry is in great want of supply of Salt which he begs may be sent to Trenton, to enable him to furnish Provisions for the Army at Kingsbridge which are much wanted, and the supplies from Connecticut may be shortly cut off, and I have great reason to apprehend the Evil will soon take place, if not wholy, in part. The article of salt is essentially necessary and must be procured, if possible.[4] Fresh provisions cannot be passed over without great Difficulty and the State of health of the Troops from a lapsed habit requires a supply of salt. Mr. Lowry mentions the Council of Safety of Pennsylvania having a quantity. I am Sir with great respect your obedient Servant

NATHANAEL GREENE

LS (PCC: DNA).
1. Fort Constitution, N.J., (often confused with a fort of the same name in New York) was renamed Ft. Lee in honor of Gen. Charles Lee, who had returned to Philadelphia two weeks earlier from his triumph in South Carolina (see note 2, NG to Cooke, 22 July 1776, above).
2. Washington was about to leave Kingsbridge to join his retreating army at White Plains. On 16 Oct. he had called a council of those officers who were east of the Hudson to consider whether Howe's landing at Throg's Neck endangered the army at Harlem and Kingsbridge. (See NG to Washington, 12 Oct., above.) The council had been enlarged by the release of Sullivan and Stirling from British imprisonment, by the addition of Benjamin Lincoln, and by the return of Charles Lee. They voted unanimously to have the principal part of the army that was then east of the river retreat to White Plains, leaving some two thousand troops behind to defend Ft. Washington. On 18 Oct., Howe moved his troops from Throg's Neck to Pells Point a few miles to the north. There Gen. John Glover's regiment of some 750 men were able to stop Howe's advance and thereby to delay him temporarily, which gave Washington further time to make a retreat to White Plains.
3. See below, Board of War to NG, 22 Oct.
4. Col. Thomas Lowry, assistant to Commissary Joseph Trumbull, had purchased large numbers of beef cattle, but without feed for them, it was necessary to butcher them and salt down the meat. Salt, however, was as scarce as hard money. A committee from Congress had reported on the need for salt in early Oct. (*JCC*, 5: 843), but Lowry was still without it in the middle of Nov., when he petitioned Congress directly. It was early Dec. before Wharton had two thousand barrels of beef ready for the army. (Lowry's petition is in Force, *Archives* (5) 3: 661–62.)

## From the Board of War

Sir,                    War Office, Philadelphia, Oct. 22, 1776.

The Congress having done the Board of War the Honour of referring to them your Letter for Consideration and execution, we beg Leave to inform you that we have ordered two hundred Thousand

Cartridges to be instantly forwarded to you.[1] Light Waggons have been got and are getting ready and you will receive the above supply by Tomorrow Evening or the next Morning. We have employed Persons to make up a Quantity for the use of the Army, which shall be forwarded to your Care as soon as a proper Number shall be compleated. We cannot however but wish that General Washington could procure such supplies of Ammunition as he may want, from the Eastern States, there being very little in this City, from whence alone every Demand to the Southward of Hudson's River must be answer'd. Every Assistance however that can be shall be afforded you as well as his Excellency the General from this Office.

⟨We have given orders about the purchase of salt, the result of which you shall hear so soon as we can write satisfactorily.[2]

With every wish for your success and honour, we, sir, are your very obedient, humble servants.

By order of the Board of War:⟩

EDWARD RUTLEDGE

Reprinted from Burnett, *Letters*, 2: 128, which was copied from the original then in the possession of Stan V. Henkels. The part in brackets is from Force, *Archives* (5) 2: 1185, where the letter is incorrectly addressed to Washington.

1. See NG's letter to Hancock, 20 Oct., above. His letter went by express to Philadelphia, where it was read in Congress the following day and immediately referred to the Board of War. The board was directed to "apply to the council of safety of Pennsylvania for the loan of as many cartridges as they can spare, which are to be sent, with all possible despatch, to General Washington; and . . . to take the most effectual measures to have a sufficient quantity of cartridges made up in Philadelphia, and forwarded to General Washington." (*JCC*, 6: 890) Swift as was the board's response, most of the wagons did not reach NG at Ft. Lee until 27 Oct.; there was not enough time to get them across the Hudson and north to Washington before the battle of White Plains on 28 Oct. (See below, NG to Mifflin, 27 Oct.)

2. See note 4, NG to Hancock, 20 Oct., above.

## To George Washington

Dear Sir                                    Fort Lee [N.J.] Octr 24, 1776

Inclosed you have a Copy of the Letter in answer to mine to Congress, relative to Cartridges.[1] As soon as the Cartridges comes up they shall be forwarded. Colonel Biddle has wrote to Amboy for Ninety thousand that are at that Post.

We have collected all the Waggons in our power and sent over. Our people have had extream hard duty; the common Guards, common fatigue, and the extraordinary Guards, and extraordinary fatigue for the removal of the Stores and forwarding the Provisions, has kept every man on duty.

General Putnam requested a party of men to reenforce them at Mount Washington. I sent between two and three Hundred of Colonel

Durkees Regiment.[2] Please to inform me whether your Excellency approves thereof.

We shall get a sufficient Quantity of Provisions over today for the Garrison at Fort Washington. General Mifflin thinks it not advisable to pull the Barracks down yet. He has hopes of our Armys returning to that Ground for *Winter Quarters*. I think this wou'd be runing too great a risque to have them standing in expectation of such an event, their being several strong Fortifications in and about Kings Bridge. If the Enemy should throw in a thousand or fifteen hundred men they could cut of[f] our communication effectually, and as the state of the Barracks are, they would find exceeding good cover for the men. But if we were to take the Barracks down,[3] if the Boards were not removed, it wou'd in a great measure deprive them of that advantage. However I have not had it in my power to do either as yet.

I have directed all the Waggons that are on the other side to be employ'd in picking up the scatterd boards about the encampment. I believe from what I saw yesterday, in riding over the Ground they will amount to many thousands. As soon as we have got these togather I purpose to begin upon the Barracks.[4] In the mean time shou'd be glad to know if your Excellency has any other orders to give respecting the business.

I have directed the Commissary and Quarter Master General of this department to lay in Provisions and Provinder upon the back Road to Philadelphia for twenty thousand Men for three Months. The principle Magazine will be at Equacanack. I shall Fortify it as soon as possible and secure that Post and the pass at the Bridge which is now repair'd and fit for an Army to pass over with the Baggage and Artillery.

I rejoice to hear of the Defeat of that vile Traytor Major Rogers and his party of Tories, Tho I am exceeding sorry to hear it cost us so brave an officer as Major Greene.[5] I am with great Respect your Excellencys Obedt Servt

NATHANAEL GREENE

LS (Washington Papers: DLC).
1. See Board of War to NG, 22 Oct., above.
2. Col. John Durkee's Conn. regiment. Gen. Israel Putnam was still in command of Ft. Washington.
3. The barracks along Harlem Heights near Ft. Washington, lately evacuated by Washington's main army.
4. The barracks at Ft. Lee.
5. The "Queen's Rangers" under Maj. John Rogers (a regiment of loyalists) were surprised at Mamaroneck, N.Y., during the night of 22 Oct. by Col. John Haslet and some seven hundred men. In the confused hand-to-hand fighting in the dark, Rogers was not defeated, but he was set back, and some thirty prisoners, sixty blankets, and a number of guns were taken. Maj. John Greene of Virginia was wounded, but not seriously. (Ward, *Delaware*, pp. 79–82)

## From Robert Harrison

[27 Oct. 1776. A much-damaged copy of a letter in which Harrison passes along Washington's request to NG concerning stores under his command. Cy (N) 1 p.]

## To General Thomas Mifflin[1]

Dear Sir                              Fort Lee [N.J.] Octo 27, 1776
    By Major Howel you will receive 119,000 Musket Cartridges.[2] Part arrived today and part last Night. As soon as the remainder comes up from Amboy and Philadelphia they shall be sent forward. I have been to view the roads again, and fixt upon Aquaianak [Aquacknock], Springfield, Bownsbrook [Boundbrook], Prince Town and Trenttown to establish the Magazines at. Trenttown and Equacanack [Aquacknock],[3] to be the principle ones, the others only to serve to support the Troops in passing from one to the other. They are all inland Posts and I hope the Stores will be secure. I have orderd all the Cannon from Amboy except two Eighteen pounders and two field pieces. I have directed them to be sent to Springfield, Bowns Brook [Bound Brook] and Equaianack to secure the Stores.[4]
    The People have been employed on the other side in geting the boards together at Fort Washington and the Ferry. Some have been brought from Kings Bridge. Today I sent up to Col Lasher to know what assistance he could give towards taking down the Barracks and bringing off the Boards, and had for Answer that he had orders to burn the barracks, quit the Post and join the army by the way of the North River at the White Plains.[5] We have had a considerable Skirmish on York Island today, the cannonade began in the morning and held until Evening, with very short intermissions. A Ship movd up opposite Fort No 1. Col Magaw got down an Eighteen pounder and fird 60 shot at her, 26 of which went into her. She slipt her Cable and left her Anchor and was towed off by four Boats. I think we must have kild a considerable number of their men for the confusion and distress exceeded all discription. Our Artillery behavd imcomparably well. Col Magaw is charmd with their conduct in firing at the Ship and in the Fields. I left the Island at three oClock this afternoon. [We] had lost but one Man, he was killed by a shell that fell upon his Head. We have brought off some of the Enemy off the field of Battle and more are still lying on the ground dead.[6]
    I am anxious to know the state of the Troops in the grand Army,[7] whether they are high or low spirited, whether well or ill Posted, whether a Battle is expected or not. We must govern our opperations by yours. The Troops here and on the other side are in good spirits,

but I fear quiting fort Independence will oblige Magaw to draw in his forces into the Garrison as the Enemy will have a passage open upon his back.[8] I fear it will damp the Spirits of his Troops. He did not expect it so soon. If the Barracks are not burnt in the morning and the Enemy dont press too hard ⟨upon us,⟩ we will try to get away some of the boards. I am dear General Your Obedient Servant

NATH GREENE

ALS (Washington Papers: DLC). The portion in angle brackets is from Greene, *Greene*, 1: 241–42.

1. Stephen Moylan, who succeeded Mifflin as quartermaster general in June, soon found the job beyond him. In Sept. a congressional committee persuaded Moylan to resign and Mifflin to take the post again. (Ellery to Cooke, 5 Oct. 1776, in Staples, *R.I.*, p. 89) Congress confirmed him in the office 1 Oct. (*JCC*, 5: 838).

2. For background, see Board of War to NG, 22 Oct., above.

3. Variously spelled.

4. The string of magazines lay to the west of the principal N.Y.–Philadelphia road. Aquacknock was on the west bank of the Passaic River, fourteen miles to the southwest of Ft. Lee; Springfield, Bound Brook, and Princeton were on a relatively straight line between Aquacknock and Trenton (see map, p. 357). For more on the stores cached there, see NG to Washington, 29 Oct., below, and Harrison to NG, 3 Nov., below.

5. Col. John Lasher commanded a regiment in the N.Y. militia. In recommending him for advancement two weeks later, the N.Y. Committee called him a good officer who "ought to be promoted, for he has lost his all, his four houses being burnt." (Force, *Archives* [5] 3: 953; see also Heitman, *Register*.)

6. For a more detailed account, which omits some of the particulars given here, see NG to Hancock, 28 Oct., below.

7. The "grand army" was Washington's main army east of the Hudson, which (unknown to NG) was in the midst of the battle of White Plains as he wrote this.

8. Ft. Independence was on the heights across Spuyten Duyvil to the north of Ft. Washington. Col. Robert Magaw, who had served in the Pennsylvania Rifle Regiment at Prospect Hill in 1775, was in command of the more than 1,500 men left to guard Ft. Washington. See below, NG to Knox, 17 Nov. 1776.

## To John Hancock

Sir                                          Fort Lee New Jersey Octo 28, 1776

This being a critical hour wherein the hopes and fears of the Country are continually alarm'd, and yesterday there being a considerable heavy cannonade most part of the day, I have thought it advisable to forward an express with the account of the action of the day. The communication between this and the grand Division of the army is in a great measure cut off. Therefore it will be some time before youl have any accounts from his Excellency General Washington.

A Ship movd up the River early in the morning above our lower lines right opposite to Fort No 1. near old Head Quarters at Morrises. She began a brisk Cannonade upon the Shore. Col Magaw who commands at Fort Washington got down an Eighteen pounder and fird Sixty rounds at her. Twenty Six went through her. The Gun was mostly loaded with two balls. She was annoyed considerably by his Eighteen pounders from this Shore. The confusion and distress that appeard on board the Ship exceeds all description. Without doubt she lost a great number of men. She was towed off by four Boats sent from the other Ships to her assistance. She slipt her Cable and left her anchor. Had the tide run flood one half hour longer, we should have sunk her. At the same time the fire from the Ships began the Enemy brought up their field Pieces and made a disposition to attack the lines, but Col Magaw had so happily disposd and arranged his men ⟨as to⟩ put them out of conceit of that manouver. A cannonade and fire with small arms continued almost all Day with very little intermission. We lost one man only. Several of the Enemy were kild. Two or three [of] our people got [shot?] and brought off the field, and several more were left there. The firing ceast last Evening and has not been renew'd this morning.[1]

General Washington and General How are very near Neighbours.[2] Some decisive stroke is hourly expected. God grant it may be a happy one. The Troops are in good Spirits and in every engagement since the Retreat from New York have given the Enimy a drubing. I have the honnor to be your most obedient humble Servant

NATHANAEL GREENE

ALS (PCC: DNA). Words in angle brackets from Force, *Archives* (5) 2: 1270.

1. Gen. Howe sent troops under Lord Percy to feel out the American lines at Ft. Washington. Lord Howe, who ordered the *Repulse* and *Pearl* to support Percy, minimized the damage to the ships, but the *Pearl*'s journal and Howe's own captain recorded considerable damage. (The action is described in Morgan, *Naval Docs.*, 6: 1429–30 and 1438.)

NG's account to Mifflin on 27 Oct., above, differs slightly. Another eyewitness was Thomas Paine, who had become an aide to NG a short time before. Paine published an unsigned account in the Philadelphia *Journal*. He stressed the British objective of cutting the ferry route between Fts. Washington and Lee, which may have been true. He also noted that it was very hazy and "impossible to see anything distinctly at a distance." (The letter is in Force, *Archives* [5] 2: 1266–67, the author unidentified. Alexander Graydon identified Paine in his *Memoirs*—pp. 187–88—as a witness who "gave us a handsome puff in one of the Philadelphia papers of the day." The style of the letter confirms Paine as the author. Graydon was a captain in a Pa. regiment stationed at Ft. Washington, where he was captured two weeks later.)

2. Washington's army was strongly entrenched at White Plains. At the moment NG wrote, Howe was launching an attack on Chatterton Hill to the west of Washington's main entrenchments. After sharp fighting, the British and Hessians took the hill, but at a cost of almost twice as many casualties as the Americans suffered. Although the hill commanded the American line, Howe hesitated to attack until he received reinforcements. With the addition of two brigades under Percy and Knyphausen's Hessians, he planned a frontal assault on 31 Oct., but a rainstorm delayed him, permitting Washington to retreat to a stronger position at North Castle above the Croton River. Howe could not call the battle of White Plains a victory.

# To George Washington

Dear Sir                                    Fort Lee [N.J., 29 October 1776]
Colo Lasher burnt the Barracks yesterday morning three oClock. He left all the Cannon in the Fort.[1] I went out to examin the ground and found between two and three hundred Stand of small arms (that were out of repair) about two miles beyound Kings Bridge, a great number of Spears, Shot, Shells &c. too numerous to mention.[2] I directed all the Waggons on the other side to be employd in geting the Stores away, and expect to get it compleated this morning. I forgot to mention five Tons of Bar Iron that was left. I am sorry the Barracks want [weren't] left Standing a few days longer. It would given us an opportunity to have got off some of the boards. I Think Fort Independance might kept the Enimy at Bay for several days, but the Troops here and on the other side are much fatigued that it must have been a work of time.

Col Magaw shew me a letter from Col Read[3] ordering the Rangers to march and join the Army. Major Coburn was wounded in the Sunday action. Col Magaw says the Rangers are the only security to his lines.[4] By keeping out constant patroles, their acquaintance with the ground enables them to discover the Enimies motions in every quarter. The Col Petitions very hard for their stay. I told him I would send an Express to learn your Excellencys further pleasure. The Col thinks if the Rangers leaves him he must draw the Garrison in from the lines. That would be a pity as the Redoubt is not yet in any great forwardness. From the Sunday affair I am more fully convinced that we can prevent any ships from stoping the communication.

I have forwarded Eighty thousand Musket Cartridges more, under the care of a Subbalterns Guard commanded by Lt Pempelton of Col Rollings Regiment.[5]

This moment heard of the Action of yesterday, can learn no particulars. God grant you protection and success. Col Crawford says he expects the Action to be renewed this morning. I hope to be commanded where ever I can be most useful. I am Dear General your most obedient and very humble Servant

N GREENE

ALS (Washington Papers: DLC).
1. On the burning of the barracks by Col. Lasher, see NG to Mifflin, 27 Oct., above. The fort was Ft. Washington.
2. The area in which military stores had been left was the encampment on Harlem Heights near Ft. Washington, which the army had evacuated ten days earlier.
3. Col. Robert Magaw, commander of Ft. Washington, and Col. Joseph Reed, Washington's adjutant general.
4. The rangers were volunteers, mostly from Conn. and other New England States, who had been handpicked by Thomas Knowlton to carry out advance reconnaissance missions. Knowlton, who was killed at Harlem Heights, was succeeded by

Maj. Andrew Colburn of N.H. Since the rangers were the only troops authorized to be behind enemy lines, they wore white armbands to distinguish them from wandering American soldiers or deserters. (Fitzpatrick, *GW*, 6: 68, 120, 146, 179)

5. Lieut. John Pendleton of Va. was in Col. Moses Rawlings's Md. and Va. Rifle Regiment. See below, note, NG to Knox, 17 Nov., on Rawlings's role at the battle of Ft. Washington.

# To George Washington

Dear Sir                                Fort Lee [N.J.] Octr. 29, 1776

Inclosed is an Estimate made of the Provisions and Provinder, necessary to be laid in, at the different Posts, between this and Philadelphia to form a communication; and for the support of the Troops, passing and repassing from the different States.[1]

Your excellency will please to examine it, and signafy your Pleasure.[2] Shoud the Estimate be larger than is necessary for the Consumption of the Army, very little or no loss can arise, as the Articles will be laid in at a season when the prises of things are at the lowest rates; and the situations will admit of an easy transportation to Market by Water.

The Ships have fallen down the North River and the Troops which advanced upon Harlem Plains, and on the Hill where the Monday Action was,[3] have drawn within their lines again.

I receiv'd the Prisoners taken, and have forwarded them to Philadelphia. I enclose you a Return of the Troops at this Post, who are chiefly raw and undisaplind.[4] I am with great Respect Your Excellencys Most Obedt humble Servt

NATHANAEL GREENE

ALS (Washington Papers: DLC). Enclosure of provisions to be placed in magazines is printed below; enclosure of troop returns is missing from the Washington papers (see note 4, below).

1. For background, see note 4, NG to Mifflin, 27 Oct., above.
2. Washington's response is found at Harrison to NG, 3 Nov., below.
3. The action was Sunday, 27 Oct.; see NG to Hancock, 28 Oct., above.
4. Force, *Archives* (5) 2: 1250, prints the return, which NG presumably enclosed, under the heading "Forces encamped on the Jersey Shore, under the command of Major-General Greene, Fort Lee, October 27, 1776." Brigades of Gen. Roberdeau and Gen. Ervin [Ewing] are listed as containing 1,163 and 1,122 rank and file; regiments of Col. McCallister and Col. Clotz (Klotz), 323 and 336 rank and file (Jacob Klotz and Richard McCallister commanded regiments of the Pennsylvania Flying Camp). Total officers and men were listed as 3,482, almost 500 of whom were sick. NG had already sent Durkee's regiment from Ft. Lee to Ft. Washington.

An Estimate of the Magazines To Be Laid In At the Following Posts for the Subsistance of the Troops and for the Horses In Waggons and Artillery[1]

| | bbls Flour | bbls Beef & Pork | Tons Hay | Bushls Grain |
|---|---|---|---|---|
| 2,000 men at Fort Lee for Five Months | 3,100 | 3,100 | 300 | 10,000 |
| At Hackinsack for the Use of the Hospital allowing fresh Provisions to supply the rest | 1,000 | 300 | 150 | 1,500 |
| At Equacanaugh [Aquacknock] to furnish the Troops at Elizabeth Town and Newark and to subsist the Main Army in passing to Philadelphia | 3,000 | 3,000 | 300 | 10,000 |
| At Springfield a Weeks Provision for 20,000 Men on their way to Philadelphia | 700 | 700 | 50 | 1,500 |
| At Boundbrook the Same | 700 | 700 | 50 | 1,500 |
| At Prince Town the Same | 700 | 700 | 50 | 1,500 |
| At Trentown to subsist 20,000 Men for three months | 3,000 | 3,000 | 300 | 10,000 |
| | 12,200 | 11,500 | 1,200 | 36,000 |

N. B. From Fort Lee to Hackinsack by new Bridge    9 Miles    Water Carriage from this place

from Hackinsack to Equacanaugh    5 Miles    Do

from Equacanaugh to Springfield    16 Miles    7 Miles to a Landing at Newark

from Springfield to Boundbrook    19 Miles    7 Miles to a Landing at Brunswick

from Boundbrook to Princetown    20 Miles    12 Miles Land Carriage to Dalaware River

from Prince Town to Trentown    12 Miles    Water Carriage to Philadelphia

NB. In the above calculation an Allowance is made for Supplying the Troops passing and Repassing from the the different States.[2]

N GREENE

DS (Washington Papers: DLC); enclosed in NG to Washington, 29 Oct., above.

1. This estimate is indicative of a principal weakness of NG at that time, as well as an underlying strength. The weakness was his unfounded optimism that foresaw (in the first line) the need to supply Ft. Lee for five months (in less than three weeks Fts. Washington and Lee were both in British hands). At the same time, he was not so optimistic that he did not consider an alternative—the retreat of a twenty-thousand-man army across N.J. to Philadelphia, which would need vast stores along the way. It was characteristic of his wartime career that he generally saw more than one possible consequence of a course of action, and he planned alternatives accordingly.

2. The Americans in N.J. kept few secrets from the British. On the same day that Washington received this report, loyalist Hugh Gaine, printer of the New York *Gazette*, reported to Lord Howe's secretary (among other bits of intelligence) that "the Rebels are removing their principal Stores and Magazines backwards into the Jerseys, to Aquacknock, Hackinsack & Newark." He also reported (correctly) that there were "not above 3 or 4000 at Fort Lee." (Serle, *Journal*, pp. 134–35)

## To George Washington

Dear Sir                                                Fort Lee [N.J.] Octr 31 1776

The Enemy have possession of Fort Independance on the Heights above Kings Bridge.[1] They made their appearance the night before last. We had got every thing of Value away. The Bridges are cutt down and I gave Colonel Magaw Orders to stop the Road between the Mountains.

I should be glad to know your Excellency's mind about holding all the ground from Kings Bridge to the lower lines.[2] If we attempt to hold the ground the Garrison must still be reinforced, but if the Garrison is to draw into Mount Washington and only keep that, the number of Troops on the Island is too large.

We are not able to determine with any certainty whether those Troops that have taken Post above Kings Bridge are the same Troops, or not that were in and about Harlem.[3] Several days past they disappear'd from below all at once, and some little time after about fifty Boats full of men was seen going up towards Hunts Point and that evening the Enemy were discovered at Fort Independance. We suspect them to be the same Troops that were engaged in the Sunday skirmish.

Six Officers belonging to Privateers that were taken by the Enemy made their escape last night. They inform me they were taken by the last Fleet that came in. They had about Six Thousand foreign Troops on board, one quarter of which had the black skurvy and died very fast.[4]

Seventy Sail of Transports and Ships fell down to Red Hook. They were bound for Rhode Island had on board about three thousand Troops.[5] They also inform that after the Sunday Action, an Officer of distinction was brought into the City, badly wounded.

The Ships have come up the River to their Station again, a little below their lines. Several deserters from powlers [Paulus] Hook have come over. They all report that General Howe is wounded as did those from the Fleet. It appears to be a prevailing opinion in the Land and Sea service.

I forwarded your Excellency a Return of the Troops at this Post and a Copy of a plan for establishing Magazines. I cou'd wish to know your pleasure as to the Magazines as soon as possible.

I shall Reinforce Col Magaw [at Ft. Washington] with Colo Ralling's [Rawlings] Regiment untill I hear from your Excellency respecting the matter.

The motions of the Grand Army will best determine the propriety of endeavouring to hold all the ground from Kings Bridge to the lower Lines. I shall be as much on the Island of York [Ft. Washington], as possible, so as not to neglect the duties of my own department.

I can learn no satisfactory accounts of the Action the other day. I am with great Respect your Excellency's Obedient Servt

NATHANAEL GREENE

ALS (Washington Papers: DLC).
1. Ft. Independence had been abandoned by Washington's troops a week before; see note 8, NG to Mifflin, 27 Oct., above.
2. The distance from Kings Bridge to the lower lines on the north side of Mt. Washington was more than a mile.
3. Lord Percy's troops who had been left by Gen. Howe to guard Manhattan.
4. The reference is to the convoy of some 120 sail which arrived in N.Y. on 18 and 19 Oct. and immediately joined Gen. Howe at New Rochelle. Ward reports about 4,000 Hessians, 670 Waldeckers, and a company of jaegers under Gen. Knyphausen. There were also 3,400 British troops. (Ward, *War*, 1: 261; also Serle, *Journal*, p. 125, and MacKenzie, *Diary*, 1: 82) The number NG reports as dying of "black skurvy" was exaggerated.
5. These are undoubtedly the vessels that Serle noted in his *Journal* on 28 Oct.: "Many Sail of Transports fell down the Harbor, in order to proceed in their Voyage homewards to Ireland" (p. 132). It would be late Nov. before a fleet set out to occupy Newport, R.I.

## To Catharine Greene

Camp New Jersey Fort Lee Nov 2d 1776

I embrace this opportunity to write you by Bill Hubbart who has got dismision from the service on account of his ill state of health. I am now very hearty and business enough. I am seperated from the grand Army 2nd Novr 1776 and can have no communication without going near seventy miles.[1] We had a little action on York Island on Sunday last. We drove the Enimy away and gave one of their Ships a severe drubing. There was an Engagement in the grand army of one Brigade.[2] Our Loss amounted to about ⟨400⟩ kild wounded and taken Prisoners. The Enimies unknown but it is Judged near as many again as ours. Our Troops are in good spirits and take a great number of the Enimy by Scouting Parties. I hold all the ground on York Island in spight of the Enimy.[3] Col Magaw commands the Garrison, a fine officer. The Enimy are at Kings Bridge and on the ground where you met with the insults from the Tavern keeper. Col Bedford lodges with me and wants you to come and go to Philadel, but as things are I cant advise it.[4] Col Biddle, a gentleman from Philadelphia Quarter Master General, is continually urging me to send for you to go to the city and spend some Weeks with his Lady. Was you here I should readily agree, but as you are at home in Peace I cannot recommend your coming to this troublesome part of America. Billy is Capt of my Guard.[5] I have recommended him to the assembly for a Lieutenancy in the new army. He has got hearty and well again, and is desireous of continueing in the service. Major Blodget is quite fat and laughs all Day. Common sense and Col Snarl or Cornwell are perpetually wrangling about Mathematical Problems. Major Livingston is sick and gone home.[6] I wish you well and happy and Am affectionately yours

N GREENE

I have but a moment to write. Pray is the family Coat of Arms drawn on your Carriage or at least the present one defaced and the two first letters of my name.

ALS (NjMoW). The casualty figures in angle brackets are taken from Greene, *Greene*, 1: 249.
1. Seventy miles was the round trip to White Plains.
2. See above, NG to Hancock, 28 Oct., for the action around Ft. Washington; for the engagement of the grand army at White Plains, see note 2 at that document.
3. This is a confusing sentence. Taken literally, one might assume that NG's troops held all of York Island—i.e., Manhattan. He meant that, in spite of Lord Percy's probing of Mt. Washington the previous Sunday, no ground was given up. The British, of course, held all of Manhattan except Mt. Washington.
4. Lieut. Col. Gunning Bedford (1742–97) of Haslet's Delaware Continentals had been wounded at White Plains a few days earlier, though not seriously. When Haslet was killed at Princeton, Bedford took command of the regiment. After the war he was governor of Delaware. He is often confused with a cousin of the same name, a prominent lawyer also involved in Delaware politics. (*DAB*) NG's lodging was a house near Burdett's Landing.
5. Catharine's brother William Littlefield.
6. Blodget's and Livingston were aides, as was "Common sense"—i.e., Thomas Paine. Col. Snarl was Ezekiel Cornell.

## From Colonel Robert H. Harrison

Dear Sir                                    White Plains [N.Y.] Nov 3d 1776
    I am directed by his Excellency to acknowledge his receipt of your favor of the 29th Ulto with its Inclosures. He has examined the

Estimate of provisions and provinder and approves not only of the Quantities but of the places you have fixed upon for 'em to be deposited at. He concurs entirely in your Observation, that no loss can arise tho' the Estimate should prove rather large, but of that there will be little doubt as our consumption and demands will be extremely great.[1]

Since my Letter of yesterday[2] no event of an interesting nature has turned up, but we have just received intelligence from Genl Parsons, who is stationed with his Brigade at the Saw Pits that a large body of the Enemy have advanced within a mile of him. He is on his march to meet 'em and requested some troops to be sent to maintain the Lines he has thrown up. I am etc

FC (Washington Papers: DLC).
　　1. Douglas Freeman thought it "entirely probable" that NG's alertness and zeal in establishing depots in New Jersey influenced Washington "particularly in Greene's favor" at that time. (Freeman, *GW*, 4: 245n) The implication is that Washington, therefore, may have relied too heavily on NG's opinion about holding Ft. Washington. See note, NG to Knox, 17 Nov. 1776, below.
　　2. Letter not found.

## To Colonel Robert Magaw

Dear Sir　　　　　　　　　　　　　　　　Fort Lee [N.J.] Nov 3, 1776
　　I am directed by his Excellency General Washington to remove Col Hutchinsons Regiment over to this Post and to send you another if necessary. I shall send you Col Backsters [Baxter's] Regiment in the place of Col Hutchinsons.[1]

Youl please to forward me Regimental Returns of the whole Strength under your command. I want to make a return to Congress and to General Washington.

Complaint was made to me tonight of some officers on your side abusing the Guard and the Barge Crew. The orders given the commanding officer of the Guards ought to govern his conduct. If he has obeyd his orders and has been ill treated doubtless he ought to be righted, and so ought the Barge Crew. Beg youl inquire into the matter, and see that right take place. A report prevails this Evening that General Gates had defeated Burgoyne and that the Enemy lost 2500 men. God grant it may be true.[2] Letters from General Washington came to hand this Evening but contain nothing material.[3] I expect to go up to Dobbs ferry in the morning. The situation of things there requires some better regulations than has taken place in the Commissarys department. If any thing appears in the Enemys Camp necessary for me to be Acquainted with beg youl forward an express to me. I am dear Sir with the greatest respect Your obed Servt

N GREENE

ALS (MH).
    1. Col. Israel Hutchinson of Mass. had served under NG in Boston immediately
after the British evacuation of the city (see NG's orders, 20–27 March 1776). His regiment had been assigned to Ft. Washington when NG was sent to New Jersey in
Sept. (Force, *Archives* [5] 2: 902, shows his regiment there 5 Oct. 1776.)
    Col. Baxter commanded a regiment of the Pa. Flying Camp. The exchange with
Hutchinson was fatal for Baxter, because he was killed two weeks later along the
Harlem River in defense of Ft. Washington. (Graydon, *Memoirs*, p. 201)
    2. It was of course a rumor without foundation, but it was strangely prophetic of
what was to happen a year later.
    3. Letters not found.

# From General Hugh Mercer[1]

Dear Sir                          Elize Town [N.J.] 4th Nov 1776
    Your favour of the 2d Instant which came to hand yesterday
Evening I shall pay the necessary attention to.[2] Col Tenyck[3] is to
march his Battalion of 250 men now on duty at New Ark immediately
to Acquaquconck [Acquaknock] to wait for your orders. An Engineer,
and Intrenching tools will be wanted. Hope last may perhaps be more
readily supplyed from Fort Lee than from this Quarter as what we
had to spare have been cheifly sent on. On examining Bound Brook
we can find no convenient Store houses nor accomodations. Att the
Landing two miles above Brunswick there are Store houses and more
accomodation for Troops than at Boundbrook. I am also assured by
Mr Mercereau that the distance from Springfield to Prince Town by
the Landing is not greater. On these considerations I have deposited
in Stores there sundrie things sent from Amboy. You will please to let
me know if this alteration in the Rout of the Army has your aproba-
tion. Some Troops from Virginia are on the way from Philadelphia.
Are they to be pushed forward to Fort Lee or would you not rather
attempt the driving the Hessians &c off Staten Island before those
Troops pass on from hence? I shall detain the Virginians about Brunswick till I have the pleasure to hear from you. I am most respectfully
your obed Sert

                                                    HUGH MERCER

ALS (MH).
    1. For background see letters, above, to Mifflin, 27 Oct.; to Washington, 29 Oct.
no. 1; and from Harrison, 3 Nov.
    2. Letter not found.
    3. Abraham Ten Eyck was a colonel in the N.J. militia (Heitman, *Register*).

# To the Pennsylvania Council of Safety[1]

Gentlemen                      Fort Lee [N.J.] November 4, 1776
    Your favor was deliverd me by Colonel Humpton.[2] You may

depend upon my doing everything in my power to promote the reinlisting the Troops.[3]

I shall be happy in concurring with your wishes in two respects, first to serve the *General Cause*, and secondly to oblige Colonel Humpton. I am Gentlemen with the greatest Respect Your Obedient Servt

NATHANAEL GREENE

ALS (PHi).
1. The letter was addressed to Thomas Wharton, Jr., president of the council.
2. Letter not found. Richard Humpton had just been made colonel of the Eleventh Pennsylvania Battalion.
3. For the problems encountered with Pa. recruiting at this time, see below, note 3, NG to Washington, 7 Nov., 1776.

## From Colonel Robert H. Harrison

Dear Sir           White Plains [N.Y.] November 5th 1776

Your favor of the 30th[1] Ultimo has been received by his Excellency, and I have it in charge to inform you, that the holding or not holding the Grounds between Kings bridge and the lower lines [on Mt. Washington] depends upon so many circumstances, that it is impossible for him to determine the points. He submits it intirely to your discretion and such Judgment as you will be enabld to form from the Enemy's movements and the whole complexion of things. He says you know the original design was to garrison the Works and preserve the lower Lines as long as they could be kept, that the communication across the river[2] might be open to us, at the same time that the Enemy should be prevented from having a passage up and down the River for their ships. The other parts of your Letter have been answered on former occasions. I am etc

R H H

FC (Washington Papers: DLC).
1. Harrison should have said "31st."
2. Harrison was apparently speaking of the Harlem River, which was connected with the Hudson by Spuyten Duyvil.

## To George Washington

Dear Sir           Kings Ferry [N.Y.] Nov 5, 1776[1]

Col Harrison wrote me you were in great want of flour. Tis attended with very great difficulty to bring it up from Fort Lee by land. Waggons ⟨can't be got⟩ to transport a sufficient supply for your Army. At Dobbs ferry there is Eight or Nine ⟨hundred⟩ barrels brought from the other side. I have directed Col Tupper to load a number of the Petty Augres and flat bottom Boats and send them on to Peeks Kill.[2] Our troops are so Arrangd along shore I am in hopes to keep a passage open for this mode of conveyance. If it can be done it will save an amazeing expence. I found every thing at this place in the utmost confusion, the Waggons and flour detaind for want of Boats and assistance to transport them over. I shall send Capt Pond hither as soon as I get back to take charge of the Publick Stores here and to transport the things across. Col Tupper is to convoy the Petty Augres by the Ships and if the Barges are mannd the Boats are to be run on shore and Major Clarke who commands a party opposite the Ships is to protect them.[3] I shall attempt to transport Publick stores from Burdetts Ferry if the Enemy make no ⟨new disposition⟩. The utmost care shall bee taken that nothing fall into the Enemys hands.

I am informd by Col Harrison that your Excellency approves of the plan for forming the Magizines. I have directed the Commissaries of this department to lay in the Provision as fast as possible. And the Quarter Master General [Mifflin] is exerting him self to lay in Provender.

Many of our People have got into Huts. The Tents are sent forward as fast as the People gets their Huts compleat.

Should this ferry [Kings Ferry] be wanted through the Winter the landing must be alterd. I can by altering the Road shorten the distance two Miles, one by land the other by Water. Where it now is, it freezes up very soon; where I propose it, it is open all Winter. I am now in the State of New York and am informd by Col Hawkes Hay that the Militia which he commands refuses to do duty.[4] They say General How has promised them *Peace Liberty and Safety*, and that is all they want. What is to be done with them? This spirit and temper should be checkt in its infancy. I purpose to send the Col about fifty men, and have directed the Col to acquaint them if they refuse to duty agreeable to the Order of the State, that I will send up a Regiment here and march them to Fort Lee to do duty there. I beg your Excellencys further Advice.

I am informd the Virginia Regiments are coming on.[5] I wish I could form a party sufficiently strong to make a little diversion in the rear of the Enimy by the way of Kings Bridge. The Hessians have relaid the Bridges and been across, but yesterday morning I believe they all went back again. What does your Excellency think of such a Manoever—is it practicable, has it the Appearance of being successful if attempted and well conducted?[6] We have a flying report that General Gates had defeated Burgoyne. We also hear that a party of Hessians has deserted over to us. I wish to know the truth of both reports. All things were quiet at Fort Lee and York Island yesterday at Noon.

The People seems to be much alarmd at Philadelphia from the

success of the Enimy. ⟨The country⟩ is greatly Alarmd at haveing their Grain and ⟨hay⟩ burnt. Yet I beleive it will answer a most valuable purpose. I wish it had been earlier agreed upon.

I am informd Hugh Gaine the Printer is gone into New York.[7] I have orderd all the Boats stores from Burdetts Ferry to Hobuck [Hoboken] and from Powleys [Paulus] Hook to Bergen Point to stop the communication. There is a vile generation here as well as with you. The Committee from Philadelphia for inquiring into the state of the Army complains the enlisting orders are not given out. Please to let me know your Pleasure. I am with the greatest respect Your Excell Obed Servt

N GREENE

ALS (Washington Papers: DLC). Document damaged; portions in angle brackets from Force, *Archives* (5) 3: 523.

1. King's Ferry is shown on maps as being on the east side of the Hudson, but ferries often gave their names to both sides of a river; from the content of the first paragraph, it is clear that NG was at the western terminus.

2. Col. Benjamin Tupper of Mass. had served as captain of the row galley *Washington* and commander of all row galleys that had attacked the *Phoenix* and *Rose* in the Hudson on 3 Aug. (Tupper's role is found in Tupper to Washington, 3 Aug. [Morgan, *Naval Docs.*, 6: 37–38], and Washington to Hancock, 5 Aug. [Fitzpatrick, *GW*, 5: 370].)

3. Maj. John Clark is identified in Clark to NG, 8 Nov., below.

4. Col. Ann Hawkes Hay of the N.Y. Militia had been ordered by the N.Y. Congress to guard the west side of the Hudson at Haverstraw Bay. On 15 Oct. he reported he was not able to muster more than thirty-eight of his regiment at one time. Some men refused to leave their families unprotected, some were needed to gather crops, but "the most numerous," he wrote, "declare that the Congress have rejected all overtures for a reconciliation inconsistent with independency; that all they desire is peace, liberty, and safety, and if they can procure that, they are contented." He had only eleven men to guard the shore between "Verdudigo Hook and Stony-Point" (Force, *Archives* [5] 2: 1067). Leiby reports similar disaffection among residents of the Hackensack Valley in the wake of the American setbacks after late Aug. (Leiby, *Hackensack*, p. 50).

5. See above, Mercer to NG, 4 Nov.

6. By the time Washington received the query, Howe was marching southward to Dobbs Ferry and was expected to continue on to Mt. Washington (as he did a week later).

7. See note 2, enclosure in NG to Washington, 29 Oct., no. 2, above.

## From Colonel Robert H. Harrison

Dear Sir                                     White Plains [N.Y.] Nov 7th 1776

His Excellency just now received Intelligence that three of the Enemy's Ships passed the Chivaux de frise yesterday or the day before.[1] When he considers this event with the present disposition of the Enemy who have advanced towards the North River, he apprehends that they have some thing in view that we are not apprized of. He wishes you to post parties of observation at every place on the Jersey side of the North River where they can land to watch their motions, and upon the least appearance of their collecting Boats or making any disposition to embark that they will give him the earliest notice. I am Dr Genl in haste yrs

ROBT H HARRISON

ALS (NjMoW).
1. Harrison's letter crossed with NG's to Washington of the same date reporting on the three ships; see below.

## From Colonel Robert Magaw

Dear Genl    Haarlem Heights [Ft. Washington, N.Y.] 7th Novr 1776
We have just now Discovered that the Enemy have brought down about 40 Sail to Morrissania Point, 10 of which are Ships.[1] By this I imagine they are Retreating and intend to Pay us a Visit. This forenoon we discovered several English Officers on the Plains on this side Kingsbridge. We Conjectured they had come from the Grand Army. We have made a bad exchange for Hutchisons Regiment at least in Point of Numbers and have great need of the 120 from them.[2] Perhaps you can Visit us in the Morning. The Hessians continue entrenching on the Heights on this Side Kingsbridge.[3] I am Dear Genl Yours Sincerely

ROBT MAGAW

Coll Cadwalader has discovered 23 Topsail Vessels.
[Written on address sheet] Coll Magaws Complim[en]ts to Genl Ewing and begs he'll furnish the Bearer with a Horse to ride to Genl Greenes.

ALS (MiU-C).
1. Morrisania was the area around the Roger Morris house, east of Mt. Washington on the Harlem River. Baurmeister noted that ships had landed provision there at this time for the impending attack on Mt. Washington. (Baurmeister, Revolution, p. 68)
2. On the exchange of regiments, see above, 3 Nov., NG to Magaw.
3. As early as 29 Oct., Howe had sent Gen. Knyphausen and his Hessian troops to Kings Bridge from New Rochelle (Baurmeister, Revolution, pp. 65–66). On 3 Nov., Knyphausen repaired the bridge the Americans had wrecked and crossed over to Manhattan with no resistance (MacKenzie, Diary, 1: 94). The Heights that they were entrenching was north of Mt. Washington.

## To George Washington

Dear Sir                                        Fort Lee [N.J.] Nov 7. 1776
By an Express from Major Clarke [John Clark] stationed at Dobbs ferry I find the Enemy are encamped right opposite, to the number of between three and five thousand and the Major adds from their disposition and search after Boats they design to cross the River.[1] A frigate and two transports or Provision Ships past the Chaveau de frize night before last. They were prodigiously shatterd from the fire

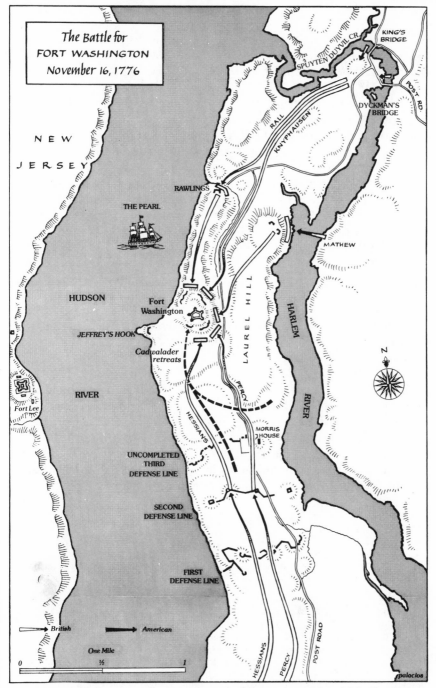

The Battle for
FORT WASHINGTON
November 16, 1776

KING'S
BRIDGE

SPUYTEN DUYVIL CR.

DYCKMAN'S
BRIDGE

POST RD.

N E W

J E R S E Y

RALL

KNYPHAUSEN

RAWLINGS

THE PEARL

MATHEW

HUDSON

Fort
Washington

JEFFREY'S HOOK

Cadwalader
retreats

L A U R E L   H I L L

HARLEM

N

RIVER

Fort Lee

PERCY

RIVER

HESSIANS

MORRIS
HOUSE

UNCOMPLETED
THIRD
DEFENSE LINE

SECOND
DEFENSE LINE

FIRST
DEFENSE LINE

British          American

HESSIANS          PERCY          POST ROAD

One Mile

0          ½          1

palacios

*From* The Winter Soldiers, *copyright © 1973 by Richard M. Ketchum.*
*Reproduced by permission of Doubleday & Company, Inc.*

of our Cannon.[2] The same Evening Col Tupper attemptd passing the Ships with the Pettie Augres loaded with flour. The Enemy mannd several Barges two Tenders and a Row Gallon [galley], and attackt them. Our People run the Petty Augres ashore and landed and defended them, the Enemy attempted to land several times, but were repulsed. The fire lasted about an hour and a half, and the Enemy movd off. Col Tupper still thinks he can transport the Provision in flat Boats. A second attempt shall be speedily made. We lost one man mortally wounded.

General Mercer writes me the Virgina Troops are coming on. They are now at Trent Town. He proposes an Attack on Staten Island, but the motions of the Enemy are such I think it necessary for them to come forward as fast as possible. On York Island the Enemy have taken Possession of the far Hill next to Spiteen Devil [Spuyten Duyvil]. I think they will not be able to penetrate any further. There appears to be about fifteen hundred of them, from the Enemys motions I should be apt to suspect they were retreating from your Army, or at least altering their opperations. Mr. Lovel who at last is enlarged from his confinement reports that Col Allen his fellow Prisoner was inform'd that Transports were geting in readiness to Sail at a moments warning sufficient to transport 15,000 Men.

The Officers of Col Hands Regiment are here with Enlisting orders. The Officers of the [other] Pensylvania Regiments thinks it a grievance (such of them as are Commisioned for the new Establishment) that the Officers of other Regiments should have the Priviledge of enlisting their men before they get orders. I have stopt it until I have your Excellencies pleasure. General Ewing is very much opposd to it. Youl please to favor me with a line on the subject.[3] I am with the greatest Respect your Excellency Obedient Servant

NATH GREENE

ALS (Washington Papers: DLC).
1. Howe's army had arrived from White Plains at Dobbs Ferry at noon on 6 Nov. (Kemble, *Journal*, p. 97).
2. Col. Kemble agreed that the three vessels were damaged (ibid.); the significance of the incident, however, was not the damage they sustained but the fact that they were again able to run past Fts. Lee and Washington as three ships had done in early Oct. NG again ignores the implications as he had done with the Oct. incident (NG to Cooke, 11 Oct., above). This time the significance of the British feat did not escape Washington; see below, his letter of 8 Nov.
3. The Pa. commissioners met with Washington, 8 Oct., on recruiting the new battalions. He then instructed Col. Hand to enlist troops and pay a bounty, but he authorized no others to do so, nor did he restrict Hand from invading other regiments. Faced with life-and-death decisions, he may have forgotten his instructions to Hand, for he told Congress on 6 Nov. that "not a single Officer is yet Commissioned to recruit." When the Pa. commissioners received complaints from Col. Magaw and Gen. Ewing, they asked Washington for an explanation. He answered rather brusquely and scarcely to the point—just one day before he received NG's complaints. (The

commissioners' letter is in Force, *Archives* [5] 2: 1202; Washington to Congress is in Fitzpatrick, *GW*, 6: 248–50, and his to the commissioners, ibid., pp. 251–52.)

## From George Washington

Dear Sir                                    White Plains [N.Y.] Nov 7th 1776

The Enemy after having Incamp'd in full view of us, and reconnoitring our Situation for several days thought proper on Tuesday Morning to decamp. They have bent their course to Dobbs Ferry Inclining towards Kings Bridge. What their real designs are, we, as yet are strangers to; but conjecturing that too little is yet done by General Howe to go into Winter Quarters, we conceive that Fort Washington will be an object for part of his Force whilst New Jersey may claim the Attention of the other part.

To guard against the evils ⟨arising⟩ from the first I must recommend to you to pay every attention in your power and give every assistance you can, to the Garrison opposite to you.[1] To guard against the latter, it has been determined (but this as much as possible under the rose) in a Council of War, to throw over a body of Troops so soon as we can with more precision ascertain the destination of the Enemy into the Jerseys.[2] To facilitate this move, the Quarter Master Genl has sent over for teams to meet the Troops at the Ferry above, and I should be glad to know your Sentiments of the place they should be March'd to as best for covering the Inhabitants and impeding their progress towards Philadelphia if such a Scheme is in contemplation. Would not Brunswick be the most likely place to answer this end? Or is it too far from New York? They can have no Capital object in view unless it is Philadelphia. Making excursions only into the Jerseys unless it is for Forage is playing no more than a small Game, but such a one as may be necessary for them and distressing to the Farmers, for which reason the Inhabitants should always be prepared to drive off their Waggons, Teams, and Stock that neither of them may fall into the hands of the Enemy. Impress this speedily, and forcibly upon them. They may rely upon it that the Enemy will leave nothing they find among them, nor do they discriminate between Whig and Tory. Woeful experience has convinced the latter in the movements of the Enemy in this State of this Truth.[3]

If you have not already sent my Boxes with Camp Tables and Chairs ⟨be so good as to let them remain with⟩ you, as I do not know but I shall move with the Troops designd for the Jerseys, persuaded as I am of their having turned their views that way.

I am of opinion that if your Magazines at Princeton were Increased and those in the Vicinity of New York lessened it would be better. We find great risque and Inconvenience arising from having Stores near Navigation, perhaps a Magazine at Brunswick might not be amiss.

The Barracks there should be got in order. I am very sincerely Dr Sir yr most Obed

GO:WASHINGTON

ALS (Greene Papers: DLC). Portions in angle brackets taken from a file copy in the Washington Papers: DLC.
1. That is, Ft. Washington. The commander in chief may have been purposely vague as to what kind of assistance NG was to render. Did he, for example, intend that more troops be sent to Col. Magaw?
2. Although the council agreed to "throw a body of troops into the Jerseys immediately," the number was not specified. They also decided that troops who "belonged" west of the river (i.e., who lived west or south of the Hudson) should be kept in or sent to N.J. if possible, and the same to apply to those who lived east of the river—mostly New Englanders. This was not possible for the two thousand men at Ft. Washington, many of whom were from the middle states. (The minutes of the council are printed in Force, *Archives* [5] 3: 543–44].)
3. Washington similarly warned Gov. Livingston of N.J. the same day, and the governor, in turn, strongly recommended to the committee of safety that the inhabitants comply. (Fitzpatrick, *GW*, 6: 255–56, and Force, *Archives* [5] 3: 617–18) NG relayed Washington's admonition to the Essex committee, which then recommended that those "who live near the water, or the great roads" remove all such items. Col. Kemble of the British army agreed with Washington on the threat to New Jersey: "Scandalous behavior [in Westchester] for British Troops: and the Hessians Outrageously Licentious, and Cruel. . . . Shudder for Jersey." (Kemble, *Journal*, p. 98) Although Howe threatened marauders with death and was "dismayed by the excesses of his men," as Ira D. Gruber has written, he "was apparently unable to stop them." (*Howe Bros.*, p. 146)

## From Major John Clark[1]

Sir          Mr Laurences Rockland [N.Y.] November 8th 1776
I received your agreeable Letter last Night.[2] I thank you for taking the state of this Place into consideration and hope (that eternal spring of the human heart) flatters me I will be able to defend it until the reinforcement arrives. Colo Tupper informs me per the same Express that a 20-Gun Ship and two Transports lay in the ferryway and requested me to reinforce the Guard at Taupaan landing, as he had ordered the Stores to be removed to that place, all which was completed late in the Night. At two in the morning I left Naiac and arrived at the Ferry by the dawn of Day. We held a little Counsel together and Concluded to give the Shipping a few Shot (tho' under every disadvantage). We manned the Battery and fired eleven Rounds, three of which went into the Man of War, one of which she received through her forecastle which happened to be full of Men. It did great execution you may depend, the other two, one in her Hull and t'other through her Rigging and the Transport next her received two in her Hull. They never returned the fire but appeared to be in great confusion. Had not the Wind blew so hard at North East and the Plat-

forms been laid I quere much if one shot wou'd have missed as nothing Saved them but the Springs on their Cables.[3]

Yesterday I viewed Slaughters landing where I found a few small Craft under no Guard and being informed of three Negroes going on board the Rose the Night before from this place I tho't proper to order all the Craft to be taken up the River to Haverstraw which I hope will merit your approbation. Should it be impractical to take the Stores now lying at Naiac by water past the Ship I wou'd advise to have them carried by land to the landing at Slaughters which is only 3 miles, from whence it may be taken to Kings Ferry by water safe, as 'tis out of sight of the Man of War.[4] This I believe Col Tupper will do. I intend to erect four small Batteries up the River in different places so as to twig the Gallies and Tenders when they move along shore and to prevent the Enemy from landing shou'd they dare to attempt it. They Militia or at least a Compy met yesterday. I attended. After having harangued them some time they assured me they were willing to afford every assistance in their power. Two of the above Negroes belong'd to Major Smith of Col Hays [N.Y. Militia] Battalion. I made use of this to prove the immediate necessity of their taking up Arms, a "lucky unlucky thing" as Church says in his Letter.

I wrote to Major Pain from Clarks Town several Days past to send me up 8 Tents and as many Cooking Kettles, as the late Reinforcement is in great distress for want of them but it has been disregarded or they're miscarried. Which of the two to impute it, I know not. If they are not sent before this reaches you pray send me the number of Tents and 20 Kettles, also 4 Barrells of Pork, a Barrell of Salt (if to spare) and I will be much obliged to you as the poor Soldiers suffer for want of them. I wrote to Colo Biddle to send a Waggon with my Baggage. Pray jog his memory.

I am sorry the Galley did not take one of the Store Ships. Had I known when they came up in the Night we might have taken one with ease as she lay at Anchor a League from the Rest. If any for the future shou'd pass the Chevaux de frise[5] I think a person ought to be dispatch'd along shore to watch them and give me intelligence. Shou'd any one come to, in the same manner, I'm sure of taking here a Cargo such as they have. I think wou'd be of infinite service.

I've Ordered a Fisherman to catch a few Pike. Hope to have the pleasure of presenting you with a Mess very soon. I Thank you for your good advice in reminding me of my duty, and hope I won't default from it when I send you the Fish and the service not injured. Pray tell Major Blodget there is a fine Pond to employ his Angling in and that I think an exercise of this kind will be conducive to his Health.

The Enemy I'm informed have left the Plains, their Encampment appears large enough to contain the greater part of the Army. They appear to be very busy. I take it some grand movement will soon take place as their camp is near 4 Miles in length. Every moment of my time shall be employ'd in watching their motions so as to be able to give you the earliest intelligence. I'm determined to dispute the Ground Inch by Inch while I've a Man it being such as will admit of it. I am your honors most obedt

JNO CLARK JUN

P S Pray dont forget to send for Beccaria on Crimes and Punishments for me and furnish me with Sternes Sentimental Journey.[6] I'll take care of it and Return it safe. Adieu.

JC

N B A few Axes, 20 if to spare as much wanting. I'd be glad they were sent with the above articles.

JC

ALS (NHi).
1. Two months later young Clark, a lawyer, became an aide to NG. His courage and dash in the battle of Long Island had advanced him to major in Mercer's Flying Camp. When assigned to the defense of the Hudson, he became acquainted with NG. His wit and his fondness for "fun and frolick" endeared him to NG's official family. In the fall of 1777, he won praise from Washington for his daring intelligence-gathering missions. An injury reduced him to the mundane job of auditor in Washington's army. During the War of 1812, he was again in uniform. (An autobiographical sketch is in *PMHB* 20 [1896]: 77–86. His exaggerated account should not blur his actual wartime exploits. His correspondence with Washington is in *Bull.* no. 1 of the Hist. Soc. of Pa. [1847] and vols. 9 and 10 of Fitzpatrick, *GW.* Heitman, *Register,* confuses him with another John Clark. See also Bakeless, *Turncoats,* pp. 191–205.)
2. Letter not found.
3. Baurmeister noted that the Americans had posted an eighteen-pounder behind an embankment across from Dobbs Ferry (*Revolution,* p. 67). The western terminus of the ferry was Snedens Landing, N.Y., near the N.J. line.
4. Slaughter's Landing was on the west side of the Hudson some ten miles north of Snedens Landing, where the river widens to form the Tappan Zee. Kings Ferry was several miles north in Haverstraw Bay. The supplies were for Washington's army on the east side of the river.
5. Between Fts. Lee and Washington.
6. Beccaria's *Essay on Crimes and Punishment* (translated into English in 1767) was an influential work that argued against cruel punishments.

## From George Washington

Sir                         Head Quarters [White Plains, N.Y.] Novr 8, 1776
    The late passage of the 3 Vessells up the North River (which we have just received advice of) is so plain a Proof of the inefficacy of all the obstructions we have thrown into it that I cannot but think it will fully Justify a Change in the Disposition which has been made. If we

cannot prevent Vessells passing up, and the Enemy are possessed of the surrounding Country, what valuable purpose can it answer to attempt to hold a post from which the expected Benefit cannot be had.[1] I am therefore inclined to think it will not be prudent to hazard the Men and Stores at Mount Washington, but as you are on the Spot, leave it to you to give such Orders as to evacuating Mount Washington as you judge best, and so far revoking the Order given Colo Magaw to defend it to the last.

The best Accounts obtained from the Enemy assure us of a considerable Movement among their Boats last Evening, and so far as can be collected from the various sources of Intelligence they must design a Penetration into Jersey and fall down upon your Post. You will therefore immediately have all the Stores &c removed which you do not deem necessary for your defence, and as the Enemy have drawn great relief from the Forage and Provisions they have found in the Country, and which our Tenderness spared, you will do well to prevent their receiving any fresh Supplies there by destroying it if the Inhabitants will not drive off their Stock and remove the Hay Grain &c in time.[2] Experience has shewn that a contrary Conduct is not of the least Advantage to the poor Inhabitants, from whom all their Effects of every kind are taken, without distinction and without the least Satisfaction.

Troops are filing off from hence as fast as our Circumstances and Situation will admit, in order to be transported over the River with all Expedition. I am Dr Sir Your Obedt Humble Servt

GO:WASHINGTON

I need not Suggest to you the necessity of giving General Mercer early Information of all Circumstances in Order that he may move up to your Relief with what Troops he has.[3]

A Letter inclosed to General Stevens is left open for your Perusal.[4]

Please to seal the Letter for General Stevens after you have read it. [*This sentence written on cover sheet.*]

LS (Greene Papers: DLC).

1. On Washington's failure to note the significance of the British ships that ran the American defenses in early Oct., see note 6, NG to Cooke, 11 Oct., above. On NG's failure to take Washington's sensible, if belated, advice, see below, NG to Knox, 17 Nov.

2. If force were necessary, NG had the blessing of Gov. Livingston, who told Washington that, while he would not act illegally, he did not doubt that "our magistrates will connive as much as possible at every thing done by the military, which bears the stamp of necessity, and cannot be impeached of wantonness or the causeless exertion of power. I think it is so absolutely necessary," he continued, "to remove the articles you mention, that I have already begun to set the example." (Force, *Archives* [5] 3: 618)

3. Gen. Hugh Mercer, of the Flying Camp, was at Perth Amboy. NG had written

him the previous day that "the motions of the Enemy discover an intention of crossing over" to N.J., and that Washington planned to move part of his army across the river. (NG's letter not found but is paraphrased in Mercer to the Board of War, 8 Nov. 1776, Force, *Archives* [5] 3: 600–601.) In response to NG's letter, Mercer had already ordered the Va. troops at Trenton to "move on with all possible expedition" to Amboy, where he would send those that could be spared to Ft. Lee.

4. The Board of War had ordered Gen. Adam Stephen (1718–91) and his Va. brigade to Trenton in late Oct. (*JCC*, 6: 901). Washington then asked Stephen to join NG at Ft. Lee and "remain under his command"—unless he got contrary orders from Congress. (Harrison cites Washington's request in a letter to Congress, Force, *Archives* [5] 3: 706) Washington may have countermanded the order in the enclosed letter that he left open for NG's "perusal" (which has not been found), for Stephen replaced Mercer at Amboy instead of joining NG (ibid.).

## To George Washington

Dear Sir                                             Fort Lee [N.J.] Nov 9 1776
     Your Excellency letters of the 8 this moment came to hand. I shall forward the letter to General Stevens [Stephen] by Express. The Stores at Dobbs ferry I had just given orders to the Quarter Master to prepare Waggons to remove them. I think the Enemy will meet with some difficulty in crossing the River at Dobbs ferry; however 'tis not safe to trust too much to the expected difficulties they may meet there. By the letter that will accompany this[1] and was to have gone last Night by Major Mifflin, Your Excellency will see what measures I took before your favor came to hand. The passing of the Ships up the River is, to be sure, full proof of the insufficiency of the Obstructions in the River to stop the Ships from going up but that Garrison employs double the number of men to Invest it, that we have to Occupy it. They must keep troops at Kings Bridge to prevent a communication with the Country, and they dare not leave a very small number for fear our people should attack them. Upon the whole I cannot help thinking the Garrison is of advantage, and I cannot conceive the Garrison to be in any great danger.[2] The men can be brought off at any time, but the stores may not be so easily removd. Yet I think they [the stores] can be got off in spight of them if matters grow desperate. This Post is off no importance only in conjunction with Mount Washington. I was over there last Evening the Enemy seems to be disposing matters to besiege the place, but Col Magaw thinks it will take them till December expires before they can carry it. If the Enemy dont find it an Object of importance they wont trouble themselves about it. If they do, its a full proof they fear an injury from our possessing it. Our giving it up will open a free communication with the Country by the Way of Kings bridge, that must be a great advantage to them and injury to us. If the Enemy cross the River I shall follow your Excellencys Advice respecting the Cattle and forage, those measures however cruel in appearance were

ever my Maxims of War in the defense of a Country; in attacking they would be very improper.[3]

By this Express several Packets from Congress are forwarded to you.

I shall collect our whole strength and watch the motions of the Enemy, and pursue such measures for the future as circumstances renders necessary.

As I have your Excellencys permission I shall order General Stevens on as far as Equacanack[4] at least, that is an important pass. I am fortifying it as fast as possible. I am dear Sir your most Obed and very humble Servt

NATH GREENE

ALS (Washington Papers: DLC).
1. His letter, presumably dated 8 Nov., has not been found.
2. NG's strong reassurances must have dispelled any doubts Washington had about either the ability or desirability of the garrison's holding Ft. Washington.
3. See Gov. Livingston's approval in note 2, Washington to NG, 8 Nov., above.
4. Aquacknock (modern Passaic) was on the Passaic River some fifteen miles inland from Ft. Lee. It was the site of one of the proposed magazines for stores.

## From George Washington

Dear Sir            White Plains [N.Y.] Novr 9th 1776

Since my Letters of yesterday two Deserters have got in from the Enemy (at Dobbs Ferry) who relate many circumstances in proof of the Enemy's Intention of crossing into the Jerseys at or near Dobbs Ferry under cover of a Cannonade from their Shipping.[1]

These Deserters say that Boats were to have been brought up (from New York, they add, but possibly they may be brought from the Sound by the way of Harlem River) as last night, and that their Troops were ordered to have five days Provisions ready dressed.

If there is a possibility of stopping these Boats it would be well to attempt it. A Reinforcement is by this time I expect on the West side the River marching to your assistance: other Troops are passing upon this side and will I hope be ready to act tomorrow. The Force on your own side under Genls Mercer and Stephen you will consider how best to employ. Keep an attentive watch upon the Enemy. I shall soon be with you; in the Interim I am Dr Sir Yr most Obedt and affect Servt

GO:WASHINGTON

ALS (Greene Papers: DLC).
1. It is doubtful if Howe intended to use the ships for a crossing into N.J. at this time. It is not surprising that Washington's intelligence was faulty, since a British officer said "the object of the expedition remains a profound secret" (MacKenzie, *Diary*, 1: 101).

## To George Washington

Dear Sir                                    Fort Lee [N.J.] Nov 10, 1776
     Your Excellencys favor by Col Harrison of the 8th came to hand
last Evening. I am taking every measure in my power to oppose the
Enemy's landing, if they attempt crossing the River into the Jerseys. I
have about 500 men posted at the different passes in the Mountains,
fortifying. About five hundred more are marching from Amboy directly for Dobbs Ferry.[1] General Mercer is with me now. I shall send
him up to take the command there immediately. I have directed the
General to have every thing removd out of the Enemies way, particularly Cattle, Carriages Hay and Grain. The flour at Dobbs Ferry is all
movd from that place, and I have directed Waggons to transport it to
Clarkes and Orange Towns. I was at Dobbs Ferry last Night, left it at
Sundown, ⟨saw no new⟩ movement of the Enemy. The Enemy landed
from on board the Ships many Bails of Goods, supposd to be cloathing. I am sure the Enemy cannot land at Dobbs Ferry, it will be so
hedged up by Night. The flats run off a great distance, they cant get
near the Shore with their Ships. If the Enemy intends to Effect a
landing at all, they will attempt it at Naiacs or Haverstraw Bay.[2]
     I wish these Intelligences may not be calculated to deceive us.
Methinks if the Enemy intended crossing the River they would not
given us several days to prepare to oppose them. They might have
taken their measures, lain conceald until they had got every thing in
readiness to cross the River, and then effected it at once. It might have
been so much easier accomplished that way than it can now, and so
many more advantages obtain in geting possession of the Grain,
Hay, Cattle Waggons, and Horses that I cannot help suspecting it to
be only a feint to lead our attention astray.[3] I wish it may not turn out
so. However I shall exert myself as much to be in readiness as if they
had actually landed, and make the same disposition to oppose them
as if I was certain they intended to cross. I shall keep a good intelli-
gent Officer at Bergen and another at Bulls Ferry to watch the motions
of the Ships.
     Your Excellencys letter to General Putnam this moment came to
hand.[4] I have orderd the Quarter Master General to send off all the
superfluous Stores, and the Commisary to hold themselves in readiness to provide for the troops at Dobbs Ferry and Haverstraw Bay. I
have wrote to Col Hawkes Hay to have the road altered at Kings
Ferry. I directed Col Tupper to send up to that ferry all the spare
Boats. I had given orders for collecting and scuttling all the Boats
before Your Excellencys letter came to hand on the subject. Our
numbers are small for the duty we have to go through, but I hope our
exertions may be in some propotion to your Excellencies expectation.[5]

Sixty or Seventy Sail of the Shiping from Froggs [Throgs] Point and Morrisania have fallen down the East River to New York. In my next I will inclose your Excellency a Return of the Stores of all kinds at this Post and take your further directions as to the dispositions of them. Believe me dear General to be Your most obedient and very humble Servant

NATH GREEN

ALS (Washington Papers: DLC). Portion in angle brackets from Force, *Archives* (5) 3: 630.
1. That is, to Snedens Landing opposite of Dobbs Ferry. On 14 Nov., NG had only five hundred rank and file left at Ft. Lee. (Force, *Archives* [5] 3: 663)
2. Nyack was on the west side of the river, halfway between Snedens Landing and Kings Ferry.
3. Whether the signs of an amphibious attack on the west bank of the Hudson were a deliberate feint or not, Howe at this time was concentrating on attacking Ft. Washington.
4. Letter not found.
5. The returns are confusing; some 2,600 effective rank and file are shown in Force as being "encamped" on the Jersey Shore under NG, but at least part of two regiments listed were on Mt. Washington (Rawlings's and Baxter's), so the figure was nearer 2,000. (Force, *Archives* [5] 3: 663–64)

## From General Charles Lee

Camp at North Caslte [Castle, N. Y.]

My [dear General]                                        Nov'r the 11th [1776]

If you shou'd be taken by the Enemy it woud be really a very serious affair, for I shoud have a chance of losing my horse and sulky. To prevent so melancholly an event I must request that you will send it to me by the Ser[vant] Who will deliver you this.[1]

I have just receiv'd a letter with the good news of the total defeat of the Cherokees. I begin to think my Friend Howe has lost the Campaign[2] and that his Most Gracious Majesty must request a Body of Russians to reestablish order, tranquility, happiness and good Government amongst his deluded Subjects of America. God bless you my Dr General, may You live long and reap twice a year an abundant crop of laurels. Yours most sincerely

CHARLES LEE

ALS (Greene Papers: DLC).
1. Lee had stopped at Ft. Lee to see NG on his way from Philadelphia to join Washington in the middle of Oct.
2. Only five days before Howe attacked Ft. Washington, Lee appears here no more fearful of its fall than NG. When he later blamed NG and Washington for not forseeing its capitulation he had apparently forgotten this letter. See below, NG to Knox, 17 Nov.

# To George Washington

Dear General                              Fort Lee [N.J.] Nov. 11, 1776
   By Justice Mercereau of Statten Island[1] I am informed that 10,000
Troops embarked on board of a number of Transports day before
yesterday. Lord Dunmore was to command and that they were bound
for South Carolina.[2] A large number of Transports were geting ready
to sail for England for Stores. Mercereau says that he saw a man from
York yesterday that informd him he had been employ'd in constructing a number of Gondolas to carry one Eighteen pounder, the Gondolas are to be employd in fetching Hay from the Newark Meadows.
The light Horse he says are perishing for want of Hay. Mercereau
further informs me by the way of General Williamson that our Prisoners in the City are Perishing for want of sustinance having only half
allowance of bread and Water. They are reduced to the necessity to
beg and instead of receiving any Charity are called damn Rebbels and
told their fare is good enough and that they had no business to burn
the Grain on Long Island.
   This moment came to hand a large Number of Letters from the
Prisoners of New York, several to your Excellency. They came out by
the way of Mount Washington. The Enemy remains quiet there this
afternoon. I am dear General your most obedient and very humble
Servt

NATH GREENE

ALS (Washington Papers: DLC).
   1. Several members of the Mersereau family of Staten Island served as informers
for Washington throughout the war (see Bakeless, *Turncoats*, pp. 177–81, 194–95).
   2. They were bound for Britain. MacKenzie reported "Near 200 sail of Vessels went
out this day for England and Ireland under Convoy of the Fowey and Active" (*Diary*, 1:
102). Lord Howe's secretary noted that Lord Dunmore was aboard the *Fowey* en route
to England (Serle, *Journal*, p. 138).

# To John Hancock, President of the Continental Congress

Sir                              Fort Lee [N.J.] Novem 12th 1776
   Your favor of the 4th and 5th of this instant came duly to hand.[1]
You may depend upon my transmitting to Congress every piece of
intelligence that comes to hand that is worthy their notice.
   By one Justice Mercereau a Gentleman that fled from Statten
Island I am informd that there are 10,000 Troops embark't for South
Carolina to be commanded by Lord Dunmore.[2] This intelligence he
obtaind by a Gentleman yesterday from the City of New York a man
of credit and truth. Mercereau is a very good friend to the cause and a
Sensible man, and he says from several ways this account is confirmed. Perhaps the numbers are not so great as reported. Mercereau

further informs that a large fleet are at the watering place on Long or Statten Island all ready to sail for England. It is reported the fleet consists of 100 Sail. By several accounts of different People from the City it appears our Prisoners are in a very suffering situation. Humanity requires that something should be done for them. They have only half allowance of bread and Water but this I Suppose is exaggerated.

The Enemy at Dobbs ferry where they have lain for several days past decamped this morning at nine oClock and took the Road towards Kings Bridge. They made an appearance at the ferry as if they intended to cross the River. I believe they are disappointed in their expectations and at a loss what measures to pursue.[3]

We have had several Skirmishes with the Hessians on York Island within a few days, kild and wounded between thirty and forty privates and one officer.[4] Day before yesterday our People had an Interview with the Hessians. They acknowledge they were greatly imposd upon by their Prince and Promised to desert that Night but none came over.

A considerable part of the Troops on the other side are coming over into the Jerseys and his Excellency General Washington with them. I expect General How will attempt to possess himself of Mount Washington but very much doubt whether he'll succeed in the attempt. Our Troops are much fatigued with the Amazeing duty, but are generally in good Spirits. The Hessians says they are on half allowance. The light Horse are said to be perishing for want of Provinder. I have the honnor to be your most obedient and very humble Servant

NATHANAEL GREENE

ALS (PCC: DNA).
    1. Letters not found.
    2. See note, NG to Washington, 11 Nov., above.
    3. Unfortunately for NG they were *not* at a loss about what measures to pursue; they were all headed directly toward Kings Bridge and Mt. Washington.
    4. The Hessians had occupied a hill between Mt. Washington and Kings Bridge. They were driven off briefly by advance American parties but soon returned. A long letter from Mt. Washington describing the skirmishes is in Force, *Archives* (5) 3: 601–2.

# John Hancock to George Washington, Governor Livingston, and "Commanding Officers in New Jersey"

[14 Nov. 1776. Encloses copy of a letter from James Searle. (Enclosure missing but it is printed in Force, *Archives* [5] 3: 669–70.) Searle sighted some one hundred British sail heading southward from Sandy Hook.[1] FC (PCC: DNA) 1 p.]

1. The following day Searle reported instead that they were sailing eastward (Wm. Ellery to Gov. Cooke, Staples, *R.I.*, p. 99). Note, NG to Washington, 11 Nov., above, confirms they were en route to England.

## From John Hancock, President of the Continental Congress

Dear General　　　　　　　　　　　　　　Philada 15th Novr 1776

I Rec'd your Letter of 12th Inst by Express, which I laid before Congress and in Consequence of your Intelligence have Dispatch'd our Express to Virginia and South Carolina acquainting them with the Reports, that they may be prepar'd in case the Enemy should visit that Quarter.

I shall be oblig'd to you at all times to give me the earliest Advice of the movements of the Enemy. I wish you very happy and am with Sentiments of Esteem Sir Your very humble Servt

JOHN HANCOCK

Tr. (G. W. Greene Transcripts, CSmH).

## To Colonel Robert Magaw

Sir　　　　　　　　　　　　　Fort Lee [N.J.] Novem 15, 1776

Yours of yesterday this moment came to hand.[1] The contents I have communicated to his Excellency General Washington, he being now at my Quarters and is on his way to Amboy or Brunswick. I had intelligence of the fleets being in readiness to sail. They are bound for Europe. Nothing material hath happened in the Army since my last.

The Enemy are retreating and its confidently asserted by the Inhabitants where the army has been, that they are going into Winter Quarters. We have intelligence of a Southern Expedition being in contemplation.[2] If that be true as I veryly believe it is, we shall have business for the Winter as well as Summer. His Excellency desires his love to be remembered to you. I am with respect your obt Sert

N GREENE

ALS (NjP).

1. Letter not found. It must have contained no hint of the impending British ultimatum (see Magaw's letter below) since in the second paragraph NG does not discount rumors of Howe's going into winter quarters.

2. On a possible southern expedition, see exchange above between NG and Hancock, 12–15 Nov.

## From Colonel Robert Magaw

Dear General　　　　　　　　Mt Washington [N.Y.] 15 Nov 1776

A flag of truce came out just now from Kingsbridge. The adjutant

Genl was at the head of it. I sent down Col Swoope.[1] The adjutant Genl would hardly give two hours for an alternative between surrendering *at discretion* or every man being put to the sword. He waits for an answer. I shall send a proper one.[2] You'll I dare say do what is best. We are determined to defend the post or die.

ROBT MAGAW

Cy (Washington Papers: DLC); copy enclosed in NG to Washington, below, same day.
    1. Howe's adjutant general was Col. James Patterson. Col. Michael Swope of York County, Pennsylvania, was serving as Magaw's adjutant in the place of William Demont, who had deserted to the enemy two weeks earlier (see below, NG to Knox, 17 Nov.). Col. Swope and fourteen of his officers were taken prisoner the next day. He was not paroled until 1778 (*PMHB* 32 [1908]: 489).
    2. In his answer to Col. Patterson, Magaw said the ultimatum was rather a "mistake than a settled resolution in General Howe to act a part so unworthy of himself and the British nation. But give me leave to assure his excellency that actuated by the most glorious cause that mankind ever fought in I am determined to defend the post to the very last extremity." (File copy, Washington Papers: DLC) Col. Thomas Bull, a fellow Pennsylvanian, crossed the Hudson immediately to take Magaw's letter to NG, along with a copy of Magaw's letter to the British adjutant. He, too, was captured the next day at Ft. Washington. (*PMHB* 10 [1886]: 459–60)

## To George Washington

Dear Sir                    Fort Lee [N.J.] 4 oclock [15 November 1776]
    Inclosd you have a letter from Col Magaw,[1] the contents will require your Excellencys attention. I have directed Col Magaw to defend the place until he hears from me. I have ordered General Herds Brigade to hasten on. I shall go to the Island soon. I am dear Sir your Excell[ency's] Obedient Servant

N GREENE

ALS (Washington Papers: DLC).
    1. See letter above.

## To Colonel Henry Knox

Dear Sir                          Fort Lee [N.J.] Nov [17], 1776
    Your favor of the 14th reacht me in a melancholy temper. The misfortune of loosing Fort Washington[1] with between two and three thousand men will reach you before this if it has not already. His Excellency General Washington has been with me for several days. The Evacuation or reinforcement of Fort Washington was under consideration, but finally nothing concluded on. Day before Yesterday about one oclock, Hows Adjutant General made a demand of the surrender of the Garrison in the Generals name but was answerd by the commanding officer that he should defend it to the last extremity. Yesterday morning General Washington, General Putnam, General

Mercer, and myself went to the Island to determine what was best to be done, but Just at the instant we stept on board the Boat the Enemy made their appearance on the Hill where the monday action was, and began a severe Cannonade with several field pieces. Our Guards soon fled, the Enemy advanced up to the second lines. This was done while we were crossing the River and geting upon the Hill. The Enemy made several marches to the right and to the left, I suppose to reconnoiter the fortifications and lines.

There we all stood in a very awkward situation; as the disposition was made and the Enemy advancing we durst not attempt to make any new disposition—indeed we saw nothing amiss. We all urged his Excellency to come off. I offerd to stay. General Putnam did the same and so did General Mercer, but his Excellency thought it best for us all to come off together, which we did about half an hour before the Enemy surrounded the fort. The Enemy came up Harlam River and landed a Party at Head Quarters which was upon the back of our People in the lines. A disorderly retreat soon took place without much fireing. The People retreated into the fort. On the north side of the fort there was a very heavy fire for a long while, and as they had the advantage of the ground I apprehend the Enemies loss must be great. After the Troops retreated in the fort very few Guns was fird. The Enemy approacht within small arm fire of the lines and sent in a flagg, and the Garrison cappitulated in an hour. I was afraid of the fort. The Redout you and I advisd to was not done, or little or nothing done to it. Had that been compleat I think the Garrison might have defended themselves a long while or been brought off. I feel mad, vext, sick and sorry. Never did I need the consoling voice of a friend more than now. Happy should I be to see you. This is a most terrible Event. Its consequences are justly to be dreaded. Pray what is said upon the Occasion.[2] A line from you will be very acceptable. I am dear Sir your obedient Servt.

N GREENE

No particulars of the Action as yet has come to my knowledge. I have not time to give you description of the battle.

ALS (MHi).
1. The terms Ft. Washington and Mt. Washington are often confused. Military historians have used both terms to identify the battle of 16 Nov. The battle took place on the slopes of Mt. Washington, where Americans defended themselves from behind various outworks or abatis, but their base was Ft. Washington, which stood on top of Mt. Washington, and it was the fort that formally surrendered. In the note that follows, the distinction has been followed where possible.
2. The surrender of Ft. Washington was the severest loss suffered by the Americans prior to the fall of Charleston, South Carolina, in May 1780. The 54 Americans killed and 100 wounded were considerably fewer than the American losses in the battle

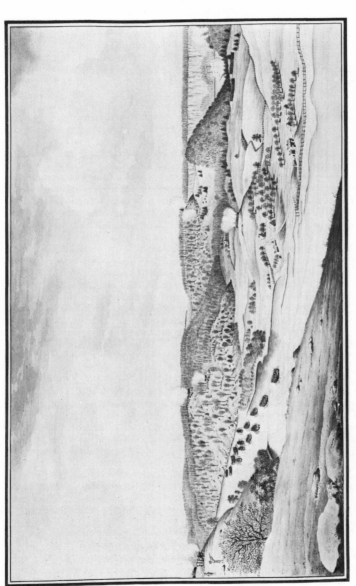

*Attack against Mount Washington, 16 November 1776, by Thomas Davies; Harlem River is in foreground; Hudson River and New Jersey Palisades shown at far right*
(Courtesy I. N. Phelps Stokes Collection, New York Public Library)

of Long Island, but at Ft. Washington more than 2,800 men were taken prisoner (Peckham, *Toll*, p. 26). It was small consolation that the British and Hessian losses were greater in killed and wounded. The defeat was the low point of NG's military career, and he had every reason to "feel mad, vext, sick and sorry." He would have felt far worse if he could have foreseen that, within a year and a half, two-thirds of the prisoners—jammed as they were into unheated warehouses or foul prison ships— would be dead from disease, exposure, or malnutrition.

Although his contemporaries and all but a few historians have held Washington ultimately responsible for the loss, most have blamed him primarily for being too easily swayed by NG's assurances that the garrison could hold out and for granting him too much discretionary power. One of NG's severest critics was Col. Lambert Cadwalader, commander of a Pennsylvania regiment that suffered greatly during imprisonment, although Cadwalader himself was soon paroled. Although he did not name NG, he undoubtedly had him foremost in mind when he wrote forty years later of the "Advisers and Abettors, of the fatal Measure of keeping the Troops on the Island, after General Washington had crossed, to the West Side of the North River, and whilst General Howe was marching his Army down to King's Bridge," saying that he "would not take a Feather from the Weight which must fall upon their Heads, however dignified, or however high they may have ranked in the Army." (*PMHB* 25 [1901]: 261)

There were other "Advisers and Abettors" besides NG. One undoubtedly was Cadwalader's fellow Pennsylvanian, Col. Robert Magaw, the senior colonel who was in command of the fort and who assured NG that the garrison could hold out until the end of Dec. (NG to Washington, 9 Nov., above). The other must have been Gen. Israel Putnam, who was nominally in command of the area. Because Putnam's enigmatic role has generally been overlooked, it is fitting to discuss it here. On 14 Oct., Washington placed Putnam in command of a division that was to remain on Manhattan Island with primary responsibility for the defensive works on the northern part of the island, particularly the "Works about Mount Washington" (Fitzpatrick, *GW*, 6: 206). Washington never rescinded the order, but after the appointment, he chose to ignore Putnam, addressing all communications concerning Mt. Washington directly to NG in New Jersey. His lack of respect for the old soldier was reflected in NG's relations with Putnam. When, for example, Putnam requested reinforcements for Mt. Washington on 23 Oct., NG sent half of Col. Durkee's regiment but immediately wrote Washington to ask "whether your Excellency approves thereof" (NG to Washington, 24 Oct., above). NG seems to have accepted the de facto command of Mt. Washington that had been unofficially assigned him, although he did have Putnam accompany him there on 15 Nov. to consult with Magaw about Howe's ultimatum. If Putnam bears no official responsibility for what was done or not done during the final week, he was not entirely blameless. His supreme confidence in the ability of the garrison to hold out reinforced NG's unfounded optimism—and indirectly influenced Washington. He probably remembered Bunker Hill (in which he also played an enigmatic role), when untrained militia, with nothing but stone walls and trees for protection, gave the British one of their biggest setbacks of the war. By comparison Mt. Washington must have appeared in his eyes as unconquerable.

NG never acknowledged deserving such harsh judgment as Cadwalader passed upon him, but neither did he absolve himself of the responsibility nor try to shift the blame to others. Washington, in his report to Congress, took responsibility for giving NG discretionary power, "directing him to govern himself by Circumstances, and to retain or evacuate the Post, as he should think best" (Fitzpatrick, *GW*, 6: 285), but while he underscored impelling reasons for NG's decision, he failed to mention his own arrival at Ft. Lee on 13 Nov. (three days before the battle) to consult with NG, only to decide against reversing his subordinate's decision. (Bernhard Knollenberg, *GW*, pp. 134–35 first stressed this.) The oversight did not mean that in his mind Washington had put all the blame on his subordinate. Three years later the burden was obviously still with him when he commented on his indecision in a letter to Joseph Reed. When he arrived at Ft. Lee, he told Reed, and found the evacuation had not started, he listened to others whose opinions were "co-incident" with NG's and began to weigh several considerations. "Lastly, when I considered that our policy led us to waste the

Campaign, without coming to a general action on the one hand, or to suffer the enemy to overrun the Country on the other I conceived that every impediment that stood in their way was a mean to answer these purposes, and when thrown into the scale with those opinions which were opposed to an evacuation caused that warfare in my mind and hesitation which ended in the loss of the Garrison." (Fitzpatrick, *GW*, 16: 151–52) Eight years later in a letter to the historian William Gordon, Washington mentions no such indecision and seems to shift more of the blame to NG. Knollenberg saw this as a perfidious omission (*GW*, pp. 138–39); others have more tolerantly accepted it as the memory's marvelous ability to gloss over the harsher realities.

Justified as the criticism has been of NG and Washington, their critics could have pointed out that their reluctance to give up Mt. Washington without a fight was based on a long train of misjudgments that were made by almost everyone associated with the fort, some of whom, after the surrender, were quick to blame Washington and NG. The list is lengthy. It includes the members of the N.Y. Committee of Safety (among the first to urge fortification); Col. Rufus Putnam, who laid out the defenses (Washington admitted that Putnam was "not a man of Scientific knowledge" but stressed that he was "indefatigable in business and possesses more practicable Knowledge in the Art of Engineering than any other we have in this Camp or Army" [Fitzpatrick, *GW*, 5: 348]); Col. Henry Knox, who assisted Putnam at times; Gen. Thomas Mifflin, the commander in charge of completing Putnam's plans; Cols. Robert Magaw and John Shee, whose Pennsylvania regiments carried out the toilsome work of fortification; and fifteen of Washington's general officers, including, as we have seen, Gen. Israel Putnam and others of less importance.

The truth is that, as it stood, Ft. Washington was incapable of withstanding a determined siege. In his ignorance of warfare, NG had trusted the judgment of others who were little more knowledgeable than he. So, apparently, had Washington.

Given the inexperience of the officers, the trouble lay primarily with Mt. Washington, on which Ft. Washington was built. In many ways it appeared ideally suited to the purpose for which it was chosen—that is, as a site for heavy artillery to prevent British ships from sailing up the Hudson River. First, it was at the narrowest part of the river within many miles. It had the height, moreover, that Knox needed for his artillery. To a reconnaissance party looking up at its height, it resembled an impregnable fortress just as it stood, towering 100 feet above the rest of Harlem Heights and some 230 feet above the Hudson River to the west and the Harlem River to the east (see map, p. 337). Its steep, tree-clad slopes would serve as natural obstacles to an attacking force. Heavy artillery mounted atop it could command more than half of the mile-wide stream, the rest being covered by another fort contemplated on the high New Jersey Palisades (the future Ft. Lee). Just below Mt. Washington was Jeffrey's Hook, a promontory in the river which would be highly suitable as the eastern anchor of a defensive chain across the river.

But beneath the thin covering of soil in which a thicket of trees had taken root, Mt. Washington was solid granite, impervious to every manner of entrenching tool in the army. In surveying the summit, Col. Rufus Putnam was soon aware of this. To build an effective fortification, vast quantities of powder would be needed to blast out ditches, casemates, bombproofs, and underground magazines for food and ammunition. Knowing there was not a pound of powder to be spared, the best the resourceful Putnam could do was to lay out an area of several acres to be surrounded by an earthen rampart—the dirt for which would have to be laboriously brought up from the lower slopes. Magaw's and Shee's men toiled through the hot dusty summer to complete a five-sided earthen work with bastions at each corner. It reached completion in October, but it was without a ditch along the ramparts, without bombproofs for the men, without underground storage for ammunition and other stores. Worst of all it was without water; and it was lack of water that made Mt. Washington especially defenseless against a siege. Early in the summer, a well had been started in the rock but had to be abandoned. During the entire summer, water had to be carried up the 230-foot elevation from the Hudson River; when Howe attacked on 16 Nov., water was still being brought up the same way, and there was no way of storing it in sizable amounts.

With such conditions it is difficult to understand the confidence the fort's builders placed in it. On 10 July, just two weeks after work began, Gen. Thomas Mifflin, who was overseeing the construction, wrote Elbridge Gerry: "We have erected a strong post—capable of containing about 1200 Men—It is in a State of Defence already." He would soon have thirty-one cannon, he said. "One Week will put us into most formidable Order." (Rossman, *Mifflin*, p. 59) Four months and thousands of man-hours later, it was still a dubious claim. (The quotation is in sharp contrast to a letter Mifflin wrote to Robert Morris a few days after the surrender. "I have talk'd heretofore about it & about it. I have abus'd the project and was never more surprised or shagrined than when I heard that post was reinforced instead of being dismantled and abandon'd" [ibid., p. 68].)

The early optimism of Mifflin seems to have infected most of those associated with the fort. Perhaps they saw it as another Dorchester Heights with its makeshift bulwarks—formidable enough to intimidate Gen. Howe by its very appearance, assuming that the memory of Bunker Hill still dulled Howe's ardor for attacking hills. And should he attack, the five-sided, earthen fort would withstand far more than the wooden chandeliers and bales of hay that Rufus Putnam had ordered to the frozen heights of Dorchester. By Oct., moreover, Ft. Washington boasted several outworks and abatis. Of the defense lines Washington had earlier had thrown across the encampment at Harlem Heights, one had been greatly strengthened, and redoubts had been built on the east and north slopes. The heights near Kingsbridge further north also had defense lines.

Some have said that the Americans must never have anticipated an attack by land and that, having pushed Howe's advance forces back at the battle of Harlem Heights in the middle of Sept., they assumed they could do it again if Howe should be so bold. At most they foresaw an attack on the Hudson River side of Mt. Washington by Lord Howe's warships, whose guns could not be raised high enough to do damage to the fort and which yet would be perfect targets, like sitting ducks, for the fort's heavy artillery. In such an attack, landing parties could be put ashore, but they would have rough going up the steep western slope. If indeed the defenders of Mt. Washington had consoled themselves by seeing this as the only British alternative, they should have changed their minds during the period of 9–13 Oct. On 9 Oct. three British ships ran the guns of Ft. Washington and Ft. Lee and crossed the cheveaux-de-frise (see note 6, NG to Cooke, 11 Oct., above); and on 12 Oct., Gen. Howe landed troops to the north of the American army at Throgs Neck.

Faced with these developments, Washington called a council of war on 16 Oct. at Gen. Lee's headquarters. Present were five major generals (including Lee, who had returned from the south in time to take command of the forces north of Kingsbridge), ten brigadier generals, and Col. Henry Knox (NG was at Ft. Lee and could not attend). The council wasted no time in agreeing with Lee that the rest of the army on Harlem Heights should withdraw at once and make its way north past Howe's army in West Chester. A tougher question was what was to be done with Ft. Washington. In view of the British ships having sailed past the forts the previous week, Washington asked whether the garrison at the fort should be maintained. It is not recorded what was discussed, but since (in the words of the minutes) there was "much consideration and debate," some time must have been devoted to two obvious questions: (1) Does the fort serve any purpose if it can no longer stop British ships sailing upriver, and (2) Can it be defended against a siege—a not unlikely prospect by the other half of Howe's army in Manhattan with the American army removed from Harlem Heights. The questions must have been answered to everyone's satisfaction in the affirmative—it still serves a purpose and it *can* withstand a siege—because they voted unanimously that "Fort Washington be retained as long as possible." (Force, *Archives* [5] 2: 1117–18) The council did not specify just how long that was. Col. Magaw could have truly said as he accepted Howe's surrender terms that he had carried out the council's instructions: he had maintained it "as long as possible."

Voting to retain the fort was Gen. Charles Lee. Although NG's erstwhile supporter and friend, he—like Mifflin—did not hesitate to blame NG for the loss of Ft. Washington later. In a letter to Washington three days after the surrender, he asked, "Oh, General, why would you be over-persuaded by men of inferiour judgment to

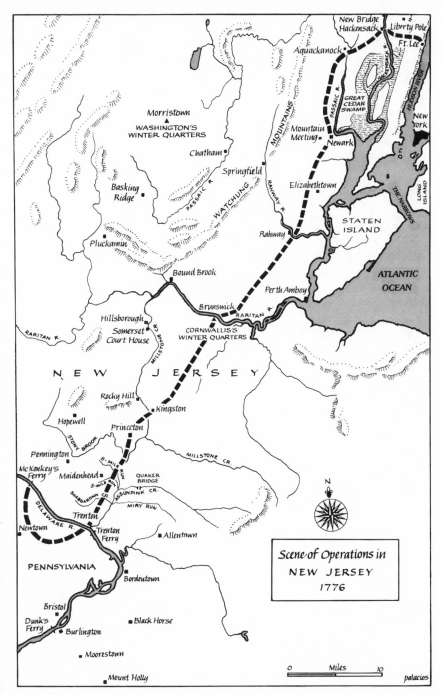

New Bridge
Hackensack
Liberty Pole
Ft. Lee

Aquackanock

GREAT
CEDAR
SWAMP

New York

Morristown
WASHINGTON'S
WINTER QUARTERS

Mountain
Meeting

Newark

Chatham

Springfield

Elizabethtown

Basking
Ridge

Rahway

STATEN
ISLAND

Pluckamin

THE NARROWS

LONG ISLAND

HUDSON RIVER

PASSAIC R.

WATCHUNG MOUNTAINS

PASSAIC R.

RAHWAY R.

Bound Brook

Perth Amboy

ATLANTIC
OCEAN

Hillsborough

Brunswick

RARITAN R.

Somerset
Court House

CORNWALLIS'S
WINTER QUARTERS

RARITAN R.

MILLSTONE CR.

N E W       J E R S E Y

Rocky Hill

Kingston

Hopewell

Princeton

MILLSTONE CR.

Pennington

STONY BROOK

8-MILE RUN

MILLSTONE CR.

McKonkey's
Ferry

Maidenhead

S-MILE RUN

QUAKER
BRIDGE

SHABBAKONK CR.

ASSUNPINK CR.

Trenton

MIRY RUN

DELAWARE R.

Newtown

Trenton
Ferry

Allentown

N

PENNSYLVANIA

Bordentown

Scene of Operations in
NEW JERSEY
1776

Bristol

Dunk's
Ferry

Black Horse

Burlington

Moorestown

0       Miles      10

Mount Holly

palacios

Adapted from The Winter Soldiers, copyright © 1973 by Richard M.
Ketchum, showing Washington's retreat across New Jersey, November–
December 1776. Reproduced by permission of Doubleday & Company, Inc.

your own? It was a cursed affair." (*Lee Papers*, 2: 288) In a letter to Benjamin Rush, he said the surrender "amazed and stunned me. I must entreat that you will keep what I say to yourself; but I foresaw, predicted, all that has happened; and urged the necessity of abandoning it; for could we have kept it, it was of little use." He admonished Rush to "let these few lines be thrown into the fire," possibly because they conflicted with earlier statements he had made. (Ibid.) Just ten days before Ft. Washington surrendered, he had told Benjamin Franklin that "we have by proper positions brought Mr. Howe to his *ne plus ultra* (ibid., p. 266), and only four days before the battle, when Howe's army was en route to Mt. Washington, he wrote NG, "I begin to think my friend Howe has lost the campaign and that his most Gracious Majesty must request a Body of Russians to reestablish order tranquillity happiness and good government amongst his deluded subjects of America. God bless you, my dr General May you live long and reap twice a year an abundant crop of laurels." (Ibid., p. 270)

Being on the east side of the Hudson, Lee was in a far better position than NG to anticipate Howe's attack, but his sources of intelligence were poor or he misinterpreted the reports he received on Howe's movements. Immediately after the battle of White Plains, for example, a full two weeks before Lee wrote to NG, he had ordered Gen. von Knyphausen's regiment to Kingsbridge. Two days later—on 31 Oct.—the Americans were forced to abandon nearby Ft. Independence. They crossed over to Manhattan Island, and although they destroyed the bridge behind them, within three days Knyphausen's men had repaired it and were pushing toward the heights to the north of Mt. Washington. On 4 Nov., Howe's main army marched out of White Plains toward Mt. Washington, setting up temporary camp at Dobbs Ferry. By this time Howe had apparently worked out his essential plan of attack. He may have altered his plans somewhat as the result of intelligence brought him by an American defector, William Demont of Magaw's staff, but it is clear that Howe did not owe his victory to the treasonable act. On 10 Nov. he ordered Col. Johann Rall and his Hessian regiment to reinforce Knyphausen, and on 12 Nov. the entire army left Dobbs Ferry for Mt. Washington—the same day that Washington crossed the Hudson en route to Ft. Lee. When Howe sent his ultimatum to Magaw on 15 Nov., his forces were poised for an attack.

Not until after the battle did anyone know how many Americans were then on Mt. Washington. From the documents printed above, it is evident that NG, acting under orders of Washington or Putnam or in response to requests by Magaw, had sent almost 1,000 additional men to Mt. Washington, including half of Durkee's regiment, some 250 Maryland and Virginia riflemen under Col. Moses Rawlings, and a comparable number of Pennsylvania militiamen under Col. William Baxter. With Magaw's and Cadwalader's regiments—and other reinforcements not documented—the total was approximately 2,900. (Cadwalader had taken over Col. John Shee's regiment when Shee, with no explanation, left for home—possibly, as some thought, because of a premonition of things to come.)

After defiantly vowing to Howe's adjutant that he would fight "to the last extremity," Magaw deployed most of his men outside the fort itself. To what extent NG participated in working out the deployment is not known. There is no doubt that, when NG and Putnam consulted with Magaw on 15 Nov., they both approved his plan. To the south, along the strongest of Washington's original defense lines across Harlem Heights, Magaw positioned his own regiment and Cadwalader's. On Laurel Hill to the east, which lay between Mt. Washington and the Harlem River, he placed Col. Baxter's militia regiment. His strongest defensive position was the steep northern slope, guarded by Rawlings's riflemen from behind makeshift redoubts and abatis of trees felled on the spot. Magaw assumed correctly there would be no manned assault on the even steeper western slope leading down to the Hudson.

Howe entrusted the attack against Rawlings's riflemen to some 4,000 Hessians and Waldeckers under Knyphausen, Col. Rall's regiment forming the right wing nearest the river. On the east Cornwallis (with Howe present) commanded some 2,000 select light-infantry and grenadier troops that were to make an amphibious attack across the Harlem River against Baxter's militia troops. To the south Earl Percy was ready to lead his strong brigade of more than 2,000 English and Hessians against Cadwalader.

Between Percy and Cornwallis, to the east of the Harlem River, the Forty-second Highlanders stood by as a feint to confuse the Americans. The only hitch in Howe's time schedule was the tide, which delayed Cornwallis's amphibious attack and in turn delayed Knyphausen and Percy. The opening guns were fired from HMS *Pearl* in the Hudson. At mid-morning Percy's brigade began their attack on Cadwalader's lines. After making initial headway, Percy had to stop his advance to await Cornwallis's attack. The Germans had not yet started their attack, also waiting Cornwallis's signal. When Cornwallis's crack troops finally landed on the west side of the Harlem at Laurel Hill, Baxter's militiamen proved to be no match for them. Baxter was killed and his disorganized troops made for the fort on top. The bitterest fighting was on the north. As Cornwallis landed Knyphausen launched his attack. Although outnumbering Rawlings's riflemen by eight to one, they could only inch their way up through the withering American fire, losing several hundred men in the process. As the Americans' rifles fouled and powder grew scarce, however, they were forced back up the slope toward the fort. On the southern slope, in the meantime, the feint by the Highlanders had turned into a full-fledged drive to cut off Cadwalader's forces, with Percy renewing his frontal assault on the Harlem Heights line.

The end was not long in coming. Almost two hundred of Cadwalader's men were captured, and the rest—soon overwhelmed by enemy numbers—withdrew hastily up the southern slope into the fort. Shortly thereafter Rawlings's men were also pushed back to the summit, and they too took refuge in the fort, where they could scarcely find room to stand. Knyphausen, whose brigade had paused outside the ramparts, now demanded the fort's surrender, giving Magaw only half an hour to comply. As the Germans had neared the fort, NG and Washington watched helplessly from Ft. Lee. Washington dispatched NG's friend John Gooch with a note to Magaw, saying he would try to withdraw the garrison if they could hold out till night. In a mission that was to become legendary, Gooch made it across the river and past German troops up to the fort, where he delivered Washington's note, then back down the rocky slope through murderous fire to the river, and back across. But there was no holding out by the garrison. For Magaw it was surrender or see the garrison slaughtered. Even after he capitulated, the Germans, who had suffered severe casualties, were ready to put all the Americans to the bayonet (as the rules of war then sanctioned) and were restrained only by the British officers.

The ordeal of the American prisoners started almost at once as they were jeered and herded off toward New York, and Ft. Washington was soon to be renamed Ft. Knyphausen.

The literature on the battle is extensive. The earliest scholarly study, which still has value, was made for the centennial of the battle by E. F. Delancey ("Mount Washington and Its Capture on the 16th of November, 1776," *Magazine of American History* 1 [1877]: 63–90). Since then letters, contemporary accounts, and memoirs have come to light to fill in many details. The fullest and most colorful account, soundly based on the pertinent literature, is Ketchum, *Winter Soldiers*, pp. 124–59.

## To George Washington

Dear Sir                              Fort Lee [N.J.] Nov 18th 1776

The much greater part of the Enimy marcht off from Fort Washington and above Kings Bridge this morning.[1] Their rout appeard to be towards New York. One of the Train of Artillery came across on the River last Night on a Raft. By his account the Enimy must have sufferd greatly on the North side of Fort Washington. Col Rollings [Rawlings] Regiment was Posted there, and behaved with great spirit. Col Magaw could not get the Men to man the lines, otherwise he would not have given up the Fort.

I am sending off the Stores as fast as I can get Waggons. I have sent three Expresses to Newark for Boats but can get no return of what Boats we may expect from that place. The Stores here are large, and the transportation by land will be almost endless. The Powder and fixt ammunition I have sent off first by land as it is an article too valuable to trust upon the Water.[2] Our Bergen Guard were alarmd last Night but believe with[out?] much reason. I am dear Sir your obedient Servant

NATHANAEL GREENE

ALS (Washington Papers: DLC).
1. On 17 Nov., Howe had ordered part of Knyphausen's Corps under Gen. Schmidt to occupy Ft. Washington. (Howe's Orders, *Kemble Papers*, 1: 410) In his orders of 21 Nov., he honored Gen. Knyphausen by renaming it Ft. Knyphausen (ibid., p. 413).
2. On the stores that were abandoned at Ft. Lee two days later, see NG to Cooke, 4 Dec., below.

## To Governor Nicholas Cooke of Rhode Island

Dear Sir                    Trenttown [N.J.] Decemb 4, 1776

I embrace this opportunity to write you by Capt. Skinner of the Conecticut light Horse, the Posts being uncertain, and sometimes the mails intercepted. I have not wrote you a History of the state of the army so early as I should otherwise have done—if those difficulties had not been in the way.

Upon the retreat of the Enemy at the White Plains his Excellency order'd over the North River the greatest part of the Southern Troops. The Enemy made a disposition at Dobbs Ferry as if they intended to cross the River also. I was there at Fort Lee opposite Fort Washington. The Enemy ⟨remained⟩ in that situation several days, and then decampt and marcht of for New York. By this [time?] his Excellency had arrivd at Fort Lee. In three or four days from the time his Excellency arrivd General How demanded a surrender of the Garrison of Fort Washington. It was refused. He attackd and carried it. The Garrison consisted of upwards of two thousand men. The lines were too extensive for that number to defend, and when they retreated into the Garrison so much confusion, disorder and dispiritedness prevaild that Col Magaw who commanded the Garrison could not get the Troops to man the outworks. We had very few kild, and those that were kild were principally from ⟨Col Rollings [Rawlings] Virginia⟩ Regiment that defended a point of ⟨a hill on⟩ which Mount Washington was situated. The loss of the Enemy we learn from several accounts was near 700 kild and as many wounded, but we have no accounts that are authentick.[1]

The loss of Fort Washington renderd Fort Lee useless. His Excel-

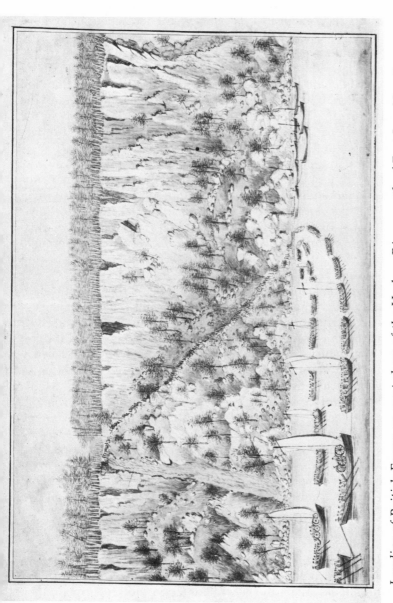

*Landing of British Forces on west shore of the Hudson River, north of Fort Lee, New Jersey, 20 November 1776, by Thomas Davies*

(Courtesy I. N. Phelps Stokes Collection, New York Public Library)

lency orderd it Evacuated accord[ing]ly. All the valuable Stores accord[ing]ly were sent off. The Enemy got intelligence of it and as
they were in possession of Harlam River brought their Boats through
that pass without our notice. They crost the river in a very rainy
night, and landed about five miles above the fort, about 6000, most
accounts say 8000. We had then at Fort Lee only between two and
three thousand effective men. His Excellency orderd a retreat immediately. We lost considerable baggage for want of Waggons, and a
considerable quantity of Stores. We had about Ninety or a hundred
Prisoners taken, but these were a set of rascals that Skulkt out of the
way, for fear of fighting. The Troops at Fort Lee were mostly of the
Flying Camp—irregular and undisciplind. Had they obeyed orders
not a man would have been taken.

I returnd to the Camp two hours after the troops marcht off. Col
Cornwell [Cornell] and myself got off several hundred. Yet notwithstanding all our endeavors still near a hundred remain hid above in
the Woods. We retreated to Hakensack; from Hakensack to Equacanock [Aquacknock]; from Equacanock to Newark; from Newark to
Brunswick; from Brunswick to this place. Here we are endeavoring to
collect an efficent force to give the Enemy battle or at least to stop
their progress.[2]

We have had another convincing proof of the folly of short
enlistments. The time for which the five months men were engagd
expird at this critical period. Two Brigades left us at Brunswick notwithstanding the Enemy were within two hours march and coming
on. The loss of these troops at this critical time reduced his Excellency
to the necessity to order retreat again. Here we are endeavoring to
draw our force together. The Philadelphia and Pennsylvania Militia
turn out with great Spirit but the Jersey Militia behaves scurvily and, I
fear, are not deserving the freedom we are contending for.[3] General
Lee is on his march for this place, and part of the Ticonderoga troops.
When we get collected together I am in hopes it will be a respectable
body of Troops.

The Enemy spread desolation wherever they go; the British and
Hessian Troops Plunder without distinction: Whig and Tory all fare
alike.[4]

I am in hopes the General will give orders to advance upon the
Enemy tomorrow. Our numbers are still small, not to exceed 5000,
but dayly increasing. When we left Brunswick we had not 3000 men,
a very pitiful army to trust the Liberties of America upon. The American States should establish their Militia upon the British plan; they
would be a much better body of Troops.[5] It would do less injury to
Husbandry, manufactories and commerce than upon the present
establishment. The distress of the People would be infinitely less, ⟨for

those to whose lot it fell to serve would naturally accomodate their business to their situation. A militia upon the British establishment are a respectable body of Troops and afford a great internal security to a State. They are subject to such a degree of decipline and order as renders them formidable and without that, numbers are useless, nay distressing, for you cannot bring them to act to any one point, and you have a great many useless and unprofitable mouths to feed.

The Vacancies you referd to His Excellency and me to fill up was referd to Hitchcock and Varnum.[6] How they have compleated the Corps of Officers, I have not learnt: I hope to their own satisfaction if to nobodies else. I wish the Enlisting may go on favorablely, but I fear the contrary: the success of Privateering has set all the Troops distracted. Tis impossible to oppose the Enimy successfully without a good firm body of Troops, subject to proper decipline and well Officerd. Our men are good, nothing is wanting, but Officers and dicipline are necessary to make the American Troops equal to any in the World. I have not time to look over the letter and must beg your excuse for any defects, for I have only a few moments to write. I did not know of the opportunity till within a few minutes. I am dear Sir with the greatest respect Your Obedient Servant

NATHANAEL GREENE$\rangle$

ALS (R-Ar); incomplete. Final portion in angle brackets are taken from G. W. Greene transcript (CSmH).

1. Although accurate figures were still not available to NG, the number of British and Germans killed was nearer seventy than seven hundred (Peckham, *Toll*, p. 26).

2. Although both he and Washington expected a British invasion of N.J., they were caught off guard by the alacrity with which the usually cautious Howe followed up his victory at Mt. Washington. In the early morning hours of 20 Nov., Cornwallis landed some five thousand troops at the only point along the western shore where NG had posted no guards—Closter Dock, some six miles upriver from Ft. Lee. A N.J. loyalist guided Cornwallis to the little-used landing. According to Thomas Paine, one of NG's sentries notified him of the enemy landing. In the time it took the British to get men and equipment to the top of the palisades, NG got word to Washington to ride posthaste the six miles from Hackensack, conferred with him on evacuating Ft. Lee (which Washington ordered at once), and headed most of his troops toward New Bridge with Washington in the lead. The men saved little more than their firearms and the clothes on their backs. Fortune did not abandon them completely, however: Cornwallis, instead of bottling up the Americans by cutting across to the Hackensack River, marched along the wooded palisades directly for Ft. Lee, in hopes it would be another Ft. Washington. His troops found breakfast fires still burning and took as prisoners the men NG here refers to as the "set of rascals that Skulkt out of the way." All the rest of the troops had crossed the river at New Bridge or had been taken by boat across the river to Hackensack Green.

American material losses were more severe than NG could bring himself to admit (see below, his letter to Cooke, 21 Dec.). Washington reported to Congress the loss of two or three hundred tents, all the baggage, "about a thousand Barrels of Flour and other stores," and all the cannon but two twelve-pounders. (Fitzpatrick, *GW*, 6: 295) Howe listed eighteen abandoned cannon at Ft. Lee and twelve on the road. From 16 to 20 Nov., American losses of arms and ammunition were catastrophic—in addition to cannon, almost 8,000 cannon shot, 4,000 cannon shells, 2,800 muskets, 400,000 cartridges, and such miscellaneous items as wheelbarrows, armorers' tools, and 500 entrenching tools—so many of the latter that the retreating troops could scarcely dig a shallow hole in the ground. (Howe's report is printed in Force, *Archives* [5] 3: 1058–59. In addition to accounts in the standard military histories, see Hall, "Ft. Lee," and Leiby, *Hackensack*, pp. 54–76.)

3. The terms of the Maryland and New Jersey brigades of the Flying Camp were up on 1 Dec. At Washington's request Gov. Livingston called out the N.J. militia, but the response was negligible. The farmers, as one historian has written, "preferred sitting by their comfortable firesides to joining a handful of bedraggled troops against a well trained and apparently invincible army." (Lundin, *Cockpit*, p. 143) NG scarcely hints in this letter at the black despair that settled down on the remnants of Washington's miserably clad army as it plodded along muddy roads from Hackensack to Aquacknock (Passaic) and then to Newark, where they camped for several days, too weak to oppose Cornwallis when he caught up with them. In their haste to get away, the few who had tents were forced to burn them and sleep in the rain and cold as the rest of the army was doing. Then on to Brunswick, Princeton, and finally Trenton, each day the number shrinking as the militia dropped off. Even the N.J. patriots began to look favorably upon Howe's offers of clemency.

NG's aide, Thomas Paine, marched beside him for eighty miles from Ft. Lee, turning over in his mind the words of the first *Crisis*, written in part (tradition has it) on a drumhead in one or another of NG's camps. "These are the times that try men's souls" went the memorable opening words. "The summer soldier and the sunshine patriot will, in this crisis, shrink from the service of their country." His words have rung down through the years, but they fall far short of conveying the horrors of the retreat. Two thoroughly researched and well-written accounts that do recapture the ordeal are Ketchum, *Winter Soldiers*, pp. 160 ff., and Fleming, *1776*, pp. 411–30.

4. On British and Hessian depredations, see below, NG to Catharine, 16 Dec. 1776.

5. The British Militia Act of 1757 was designed to release regular troops for assignment abroad during the Seven Years' War. It required that each county, in proportion to its population, choose men by lot to serve for three years. A sergeant from the regular army was assigned to each twenty men, an adjutant to each regiment. See Fortescue, *British Army*, 2: 307–8. A thorough study is J. R. Western, *The English Militia in the Eighteenth Century* (London: Routledge & Kegan Paul; Toronto: University of Toronto Press, 1965).

6. For their recommendations see above, Cooke to NG, 5 Oct., and NG to Cooke, 11 Oct. According to Gen. Charles Lee, Varnum and Hitchcock, who were now in Lee's brigade, did not remember making recommendations to NG and were thrown into a great "flame of discontent" when shown NG's list, accusing him of "partiality to his connections and townsmen." (Lee to Washington, 12 and 19 Nov., *Lee Papers*, 2: 273–74, 287–88) If Lee's account was accurate (by no means a certainty), they were unfair to NG. In his list of almost sixty officers, only three were his "connections." The listing of William Littlefield, his wife's brother, might have been a case of favoritism, but Christopher Greene, a distant relative who was then a prisoner of the British in Quebec and later one of Rhode Island's most celebrated heroes, was chosen for ability. The same could be said of Sammy Ward (his sister married NG's brother), who was also a prisoner in Quebec and had proved himself an able officer. In tiny Rhode Island, it would have been difficult for any public man to draw up such a list without including three "connections" and several townsmen. Varnum, moreover, who had refused to serve in the new army, should have had no concern over the appointments. NG's list is in Bartlett, *Records*, 8: 36. For later developments on this issue, see below, NG to Cooke, 1 Feb. 1777, and to Jacob, 2 Feb. 1777.

## To Catharine Greene

Trentown [N.J.] Decem 4, 1776

The situation this Army was in when I wrote you last[1] must naturally alarm your fears. The Enemy have since prest us very hard from place to place. The time for which our Troops were engaged expird and they went off by whole Brigades notwithstanding the Enemy lay within two or three hours march of us and our force [remaining] not near half equal to theirs. The Virtue of the Americans is put to a tryal. If they turn out with spirit all will go on well but if the Militia refuses their aid, the People must submit to the servitude they well deserve. But I think it impossible that the Americans can behave so Poltroonish. The Militia of Pennsylvania and Particularly Philadelphia are coming in by thousands. In a day or two I hope to advance upon the Enemy and drive them back as fast as they drove us on. We are makeing every disposition to advance upon the Enemy and by tomorrow I hope the General will issue his orders to move forward.

The Troops of Maryland and Virginia have orders to move forward, to stop the ravages of the Enemy; their footsteps are markt with destruction wherever they go. There is no difference made between the Whigs and Tories—all fare alike. They take the Cloaths off of the Peoples back. The distress they spread wherever they go exceeds all description.

I hope to God you have not set forward for this place from what I wrote you last. Continue at Home my Dear if you wish to enjoy the least share of Happiness. Seventy Sail of the Enemies fleet saild a few days past, their destination unknown; but tis suggested by many they were bound for Rhode Island; but I rather suppose them to be going to the Southward. The Climate will favor their opperations much more than the Northern States.[2]

What is the new amongst You? The loss of Fort Washington I suppose and the Enemies late movements weighd down the Spirits of the People. Tell Doctor Sentor to write me how recruiting goes on, and the temper of the People. The Success of the Privateers, and everything of an interesting Nature.

I am hearty and well amidst all the fatigues and hardships I endure. I hope you enjoy your health and the company of your friends about you. Be of good courage; dont be distressd. All things will turn out for the best. I wish you abundant happiness and am affectionately yours

N GREENE

ALS (NjP).

1. Since his last letter of 2 Nov. contained nothing to alarm her fears, the missing letter was undoubtedly written after Ft. Washington's fall.

2. The last of some seven thousand British troops had just left N.Y. for R.I. NG's thinking paralleled that of Gen. Clinton, commander of the force, who preferred a southern harbor; but the Howe brothers ignored Clinton's advice and upset NG's predictions. (Willcox, *Clinton*, pp. 120–22) On 7 Dec. the main body of troops landed

without opposition at Middletown, R.I., and the following day marched into Newport, which would not see the last of them for three years. Coming on top of Ft. Washington's loss, it was a blow to American morale—especially Rhode Island's; but in the long run, it was a gain for the Continental army. For any effect Clinton's brigades "produced upon the general result of the war," wrote the English historian Trevelyan, "they might have been as usefully, and much more agreeably, billeted in the town of the same name in the Isle of Wight." (Sir George Otto Trevelyan, *The American Revolution*, 4 vols. [New York, 1899–1907], 3: 20)

## To George Washington

Dear Sir                              Princetown [N.J.] Decemb 7, 1776
Lord Sterling will write by the same express that this comes by, and inclose to your Excellency several pieces of intelligence obtain'd of different People Yesterday. His Lordship thinks the Enemy are makeing a disposition to advance. For my part I am at a loss to determin whether their disposition is to advance, or for defence. The Enemy have got a party advanced about Seven Miles this side Brunswick; another at Boun[d]brook with an advance Guard two miles this side of the Town. Tis reported by some of the Country People that the Enemy intend to advance in two Columns—one this, the other Boun[d]brook road.[1] General Mercer is advanced upon this Road, and I should think the German Battallion[2] might advantageously [be] Posted on the other road.

Major Clarke reports General Lee is at the Heels of the Enimy. I should think he had better keep upon the flanks than the rear of the Enemy, unless it were possible to concert an Attack at the same instant of time in front and rear.

Our retreat should not be neglected for fear of consequences. The bottom of the River should be examined and see if the Boats can be anchord in the ferry way.[3] If there is no Anchor ground the bridge must be thrown over below. Colo Biddle had better make tryal immediately that we may not be in confusion. If a Bridge cannot be thrown over, forty Boats should be man'd under the care of a good officer, and held in readiness. With these boats prudently managed, the Troops could be thrown over in a very short time. Methinks all the cannon that dont com forward with the Army might be well Posted on the other side the river, to cover a retreat right above the ferry way.

I think General Lee must be confind within the Lines of some Genral Plan, or else his opperations will be independant of yours.[4] His own Troops, General Sinclairs [St. Clair] and the Militia must form a respectable body.

If General Dickinson[5] could engage the Militia for some given time, there might be some dependance upon them, but no opperations can be safely pland wherein they are to act apart unless they can be bound by some further tye than the common obligation of a militia man. I think if the General was to attempt to engage his Militia upon some such plan, Your Excellency might take your measures accordingly.

This moment a Capt has returnd that went to reconnoiter last Night and it is beyond a doubt the Enemy are advanceing, and my Lord Sterling thinks theyl be up here by 12 oclock.[6] I shall make the best disposition I can to oppose them. I am dear Sir Your obedient Servt

N GREENE

ALS (PCC: DNA).

1. Stirling's 1,200 troops served as a rear guard in the retreat. When Washington continued to Trenton, he left Stirling's brigade at Princeton, where they bivouacked in the college hall. NG had returned from Trenton the previous day.

2. Part of the recently recruited regiment of Pa. and Md. Germans had joined Washington on 5 Dec. in Trenton (Washington to Hancock, 6 Dec., Fitzpatrick, GW, 6: 333–34).

3. Washington had apparently discussed with NG the problem of getting troops across the Delaware. Considering the 2,800 who failed to get across the Hudson from Ft. Washington, it would be surprising if they had not given considerable thought to it. On 1 Dec., Washington had ordered all the boats on the river for seventy miles above Philadelphia to be commandeered. Those that could not be used were to be destroyed to keep them out of enemy hands (Fitzpatrick, GW, 6: 321–22, 397). On the flat-bottom Durham boats that he especially wanted, see note on the battle of Trenton in NG to Catharine, 30 Dec., below. There was no time to build a bridge of boats across the river as NG here suggests; see note 6, below.

4. NG's warning about Charles Lee was not without foundation. Washington had advised, then prodded, and finally entreated Lee (though never ordered him) to join the army west of the Hudson, but Lee put him off with real and contrived excuses. The truth seems to be that Lee acted independently in the hopes of reversing Howe's successes himself and perhaps, by so doing, becoming commander in chief. After the fall of Ft. Washington and the retreat across N.J., a number of men both inside and outside the army thought the salvation of the country was dependent on Lee. On Lee's capture see below, NG to Catharine, 16 Dec. On relations between Washington and Lee at this time, see Freeman, GW, 4: 260–90; Alden, Lee, pp. 146–56; and Shy, "Lee" in Billias, Washington's Generals, pp. 35–40. Both Alden and Shy are more sympathetic to Lee.

5. Philemon Dickinson (1739–1809), the brother of famed "Pennsylvania Farmer" John Dickinson, was a brigadier general in the N.J. militia. In June 1780, as a major general in the militia, he fought under NG at Springfield, N.J., where he won NG's praise. After the war he held several civil posts, including that of U.S. senator from N.J. (DAB)

6. Washington was en route from Trenton with 1,200 men to reinforce Stirling when he got NG's letter. He turned his troops back immediately toward Trenton, where he ordered them ferried across the Delaware, followed by Stirling's men. That evening they were safely on the Pa. side—the last of them just as the British reached the east bank.

## To Catharine Greene

⟨Coryells Ferry [Penn.] on the Delaware
40 Miles above Phila Dec 16, 1776⟩[1]

The last time I wrote you was at Trenton since which the enemy have reduced us to the necessity to pass the Delaware. We have been endeavoring to draw a force together to check General Howe's progress, but the militia of New Jersey have been so frighted, and the Pennsylvania militia so disaffected, that our endeavors have been ineffectual. The troops under the command of General Lee we expect to join us today, but without the General who had the misfortune to be made a prisoner on Friday last by a party of light-horse. The general, by some strange infatuation, was led from the army four miles; the Tories gave information of his situation and a party of light-horse came eighteen miles and seized and carried him off. This is a great loss to the American States, as he is a most consummate general.[2] Fortune seems to frown upon the cause of freedom; a combination of evils are pressing in upon us on all sides. However, I hope this is the dark part of the night, which generally is just before day. The Tories are the cursedest rascals amongst us, the most wicked, villainous, and oppressive. They lead the relentless foreigners to the houses of their neighbors and strip the poor women and children of everything they have to eat or wear; and after plundering them in this sort, the brutes often ravish the mothers and daughters, and compel the fathers and sons to behold their brutality; many have fallen sacrifices in this way.[3]

The Tories have done us more injury than they can repair during their generation. Beware of those miscreants; watch them narrowly.

I hear a fleet and army have made good their landing at Rhode Island. God forbid they should penetrate into the country with you as with us. But if the New England virtue is not greater than it is here, God knows what the consequence will be. The militia of the city of Philadelphia are the only people that have shown a disposition to support the cause.

The enemy are now retreating into winter quarters as they say; but perhaps 'tis only a feint to amuse, to try to surprise us. We must be on our guard, which I hope we shall.[4]

The Eastern delegates applied to his Excellency General Washington to permit me to go to New England to take the command there; but the General would not permit me to go.[5] I am impatient to hear how matters stand with you, what opposition is forming and how the recruiting service goes on.

We have pleasing accounts from Virginia and Maryland with respect to the recruiting service. The regiments are filling very fast.

We are fortifying the city of Philadelphia, and doubt not we shall be able to keep the enemy out this winter. The city is under martial law; the Quakers horridly frighted for fear the city should be burnt. The ravages of the Jerseys is shocking to behold.

I have no hope of coming to New England this winter. I enjoy my health perfectly well. I feel a great deal of anxiety for your sake. God bless you with health, and comfort you during our separation. Anything you want my brethern will furnish you; don't be afraid to apply. I should be happy to receive a line, if it can come by a safe hand; but if you cannot write by some safe hand don't write at all, for it's uncertain whose hands it may fall into. Remember my love to my brethren, and to all inquiring friends.

The Continental currency the Tories are endeavoring to destroy: the credit is almost lost in the Jerseys, and much injured in this State.⁶ However, a good army will soon repair the credit, and nothing else. Much depends upon New England this winter.

I must bid you adieu, being called in haste. Farewell, my dear. Kiss our ⟨little pledge of mutual affection, whom I long to see. I am affectionately

NATH GREENE⟩

Reprinted from Greene, *Greene*, 1: 281–83, except portions in angle brackets, which are taken from Nightingale transcripts (furnished by Bernard Nightingale, Brunswick, Ga.).

1. NG was quartered at the Merrick House, a stone dwelling that was not quite finished. It lay between Washington's headquarters and Coryells Ferry, and on Christmas eve it was the setting for a dinner at which Washington and his staff laid final plans for the attack on Trenton. (W. W. H. Davis, "Washington on the West Bank of the Delaware, 1776" *PMHB* 4 [1880]: 144–46)

2. Lee had been at Morristown for several days when he finally sent his army under John Sullivan to join Washington. After spending the night at White's Tavern at Basking Ridge, Lee was captured by a party under Col. William Harcourt, who, ironically, had served under him in Portugal. He would remain a prisoner until April 1778. If Lee were a serious threat to Washington (see note 4, NG to Washington, above, 7 Dec.), Harcourt had put an end to it. Great as his loss may have been, the victories at Trenton and Princeton would be planned and executed without him.

3. On plundering in N.J., see below, NG to Cooke, 10 Jan. 1777.

4. Howe had decided on 13 Dec. to go into winter quarters in N.Y. with the bulk of his army, leaving German regiments under Donop and Rall at Bordentown and Trenton, and British troops at Princeton, Brunswick, and Amboy. For most of Howe's army, winter quarters meant warmth and dryness; for Washington's troops it meant huddling along the western bank of the Delaware with little or nothing between them and the elements. They could, at least, for the first time in a month halt their flight before Howe's troops.

5. On 12 Dec., Samuel Adams and others had asked Washington, in view of the British landing in Rhode Island, if "Major General Green or Gates, who are greatly belovd in that Part of America, with a suitable Number of Brigadiers, could be spared for this Service." (Burnett, *Letters*, 2: 175) Instead, Washington sent Gen. Benedict Arnold, who was on his way from Ticonderoga, and Gen. Joseph Spencer to Rhode Island to help in the defense. (Freeman, *GW*, 4: 285; and Washington to Trumbull, 14 Dec. 1776, Fitzpatrick, *GW*, 6: 366)

6. Robert Morris, who noted the dollar was worth fifty cents in Philadelphia,

blamed internal enemies in part but also properly attributed much of the depreciation to meeting the enormous wartime expenses by "prodigious emissions of paper money" (Morris to Commissioners in France, Force, *Archives* [5] 3: 1332–34. A modern scholar finds the dollar was then worth an average of sixty-seven cents the country over (Bezanson, *Prices*, p. 71).

## To John Hancock, President of the Continental Congress

Sir                    Coryells Ferry [Pa.] on the Delaware Decemb 16, 1776

I take the liberty to recommend Doctor Warren to the Congress as a very suitable person to receive an Appointment of a Sub Director which I am informed they are about to create a number of. Doctor Warren has given great satisfaction where he has had the direction of business. He is a Young Gentleman of Abillity, Humanity and great Application to business.[1]

I feel a degree of happiness that the Congress are going to put the Hospital department upon a better establishment,[2] for the Sick, this Campaign, have sufferd beyonnd Description and Shocking to humanity. For my own part I have never felt any distress equal to what the sufferings of the Sick have occasion'd, and am confident that nothing will injure the recruiting services so much as the dissatisfaction ariseing upon that head. I am dear Sir your obedient Servt

NATHANAEL GREENE

ALS (PCC: DNA).

1. Dr. John Warren (1753–1815) had joined the army upon the death of his brother Joseph at Bunker Hill. At the age of twenty-two, he was made senior surgeon in a military hospital in Cambridge. In the summer of 1776, he set up the hospital that NG had requested for his camp on Long Island (see note, NG's orders for 11 July 1776, above). He returned to private practice in Boston in 1777 to become one of Boston's outstanding surgeons and the principal founder of Harvard Medical School. (*DAB*)

2. NG may not have been properly informed on the action Congress had taken concerning hospitals. Congress did nothing more than affirm Dr. Shippen's design of having himself placed in charge of the hospitals and surgeons on the west side of the Hudson. For the background, see NG to Hancock, 10 Oct., above.

## To John Hancock, President of the Continental Congress

Sir                    Corell's Ferry [Pa.] Decr 21st 1776

Altho I am far from thinking the American Cause desperate, yet I conceive it to be in a critical situation. The Enemy in the Heart of our Country; the disaffected dayly increasing; the Continental Money loosing its currency; the Time for which the Troops stand engaged almost ready to expire; very few enlisted upon the New Establishment; the Tide of publick Sentiment at a stand and ready to run thro different Channels; the People refusing to supply the Army under

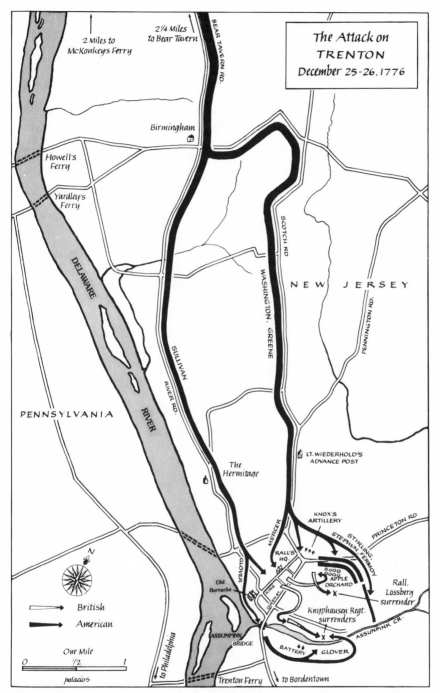

From The Winter Soldiers, copyright © 1973 by Richard M. Ketchum.
Reproduced by permission of Doubleday & Company, Inc.

various Pretenses, but evidently from a disaffection to the Cause and to the Currency, are combined evils calculated to pave the way for General Howe's Advances; who, having Canton'd his Troops advantageously, stands prepared to take Advantage of those Circumstances which (I am sorry to say) afford him but too favorable a Prospect.[1] It is necessary (in addition to this disagreeable Train of Evils) that the different Corps of Officers who are discontented and unsatisfied either from a real or supposed Injury in their Appointments from the different States should be reconciled, that recruiting may go on with Spirit that there should be an Augmentation of our Force and a longer Train of Artillery.

Effectually to remedy those Evils and oppose the Enemy, to put the Recruiting Service in a favorable Train, to establish the Artillery and Elabratory upon a proper footing, to check the disaffected, and call out Assistance, to give a Currency to the Continental Money and form the necessary Magazines, greater Powers must be lodged in the Hands of the General than he has ever yet exercised.[2] It is impossible in his present Situation and the short Time he has to prepare for the ensuing Campaign for him to be in Readiness so early as General Howe will take the Field unless you delegate to him full Power to take such Measures as he may find necessary to promote the Establishment of the New Army. Time will not admit nor Circumstance allow of a Reference to Congress.

I can see no Evil nor Danger to the States in delagating such Powers to the General, reserving to yourselves the Right of Confirming or repealing the Measures. The General should have Power to appoint Officers to enlist at large. This is no Time to be particular about Proportions or attentive to Oeconomy; the Measure of our Force should be the Extent of our Funds.

We have a formidable Enemy to oppose whose Progress can only be checked by a superior Force. And however disagreeable the reflections, tis a serious Truth that the present existance of the Civil depends upon the Military Powers. I am no advocate for the Extension of Military Power, neither would I advise it at present but from the fullest Conviction of its being absolutely necessary. Remember the Policy of the Romans (a People as tenacious of their Liberties as any on Earth) when their State was invaded they delagated full Powers to exert their whole Force. The Fate of War is so uncertain, dependant upon so many Contingencies. A Day, nay an Hour is so important in the Crisis of publick Affairs that it would be folly to wait for Relief from the deliberative Councils of Legislative Bodies. The Virtue of the People at such an Hour is not [to] be trusted, and I can assure you that the General will not exceed his Powers altho' he may sacrifice the Cause.

Capture of the Hessians at Trenton *by John Trumbull; Nathanael Greene on white horse at right; Washington on his horse at center*
(Courtesy Yale University Art Gallery)

There never was a man that might be more safely trusted nor a Time when there was a louder Call. If you intend to support your Independance you [must?] not be too delicate in the Choice of Means.

Examples are dayly made by General Howe of our Friends who fall in his Way while those who are disaffected to our Cause are suffered to remain in Peace and Quiet amongst us. Many who are now well affected will be induced from the Risque and Danger on the one side and the apparent Security on the other to change their Sentiments. A discretionary Power to punish the disaffected is necessary. The Militia have refused to turn out when there has been the greatest want of their Assistance and nothing but such a Power can ever Compel them. If the Refusal of the Continental Money and the withholding of the necessary supplies from the Army for want of such a Power in the General are to pass unpunished, the one will put it out of our Power to pay, and the other to support the Troops and consequently must Sap the Foundations of all Opposition. I am with all due respect your most obedient humble Servant

NATH GREENE

LS (PCC:DNA).
1. NG was warranted in most aspects of the bleak picture he drew, but he exaggerated the prospects of Howe's advancing. In truth both he and Washington had known for a week that Howe had gone into winter quarters and had left his outposts in a vulnerable position. The exaggeration was undoubtedly a prelude to his contention that Washington should be given dictatorial powers.
2. Before Congress left Philadelphia on 12 Dec., they rushed through a resolution giving vague temporary powers to Washington (*JCC*, 6: 1027). Although they reconvened in Baltimore on 20 Dec., it was not until they received NG's letter on 26 Dec. that they decided on more specific dictatorial powers. No doubt the victory at Trenton strengthened NG's arguments. The 27 Dec. resolution giving Washington vast powers for six months included most of the provisions in NG's letter above. The resolutions are printed in *JCC*, 6: 1043, 1045–46.

## To Governor Nicholas Cooke of Rhode Island

Dear Sir                    Coryells Ferry [Pa.] Decemb 21, 1776

By your letter to General Washington I find the British Troops have landed on Rhode Island.[1] Altho I am sorry my own Country should be subject to their ravages yet I rejoice that they are surrounded by a People who are United and firmly determind in opposition. You may be subject to a partial Evil but America cannot fail to reap the advantage. You think you are greatly infested with the Tories and disaffected but there is but the shadow of disaffection with you to what there is here. The friends or Quakers are almost to a man disaffected—many has the effrontery to refuse the Continental currency. This line of conduct cannot fail of drawing down the resentment of the People upon them. The fright and disaffection was so great in the Jerseys that in our retreat of one hundred and odd miles we were never joind by more than a hundred men. I dare say had that Army been in New England we should not been under the necessity of retreating twenty miles. We are now on the West side of the Delaware, our force tho small collected together, but small as it is I hope to give the Enimy a stroke in a few days.[2] Should fortune favor the Attack Perhaps it may put a stop to General Hows progress. His ravages in the Jerseys exceeds all description. Men slaughterd, Women ravisht, and Houses plundered, little Girls not ten Years old ravisht, Mothers and Daughters ravisht in presence of the Husband and Sons who were obligd to be spectators to their brutal conduct.[3]

I think notwithstanding the General disaffection of a certain order of People the army will fill up. Should that be the case nothing is to be feard. By a Vessel just arrivd from France with a valuable Cargo we learn a French War is inevitable.

Short enlistments has been in a great measure the Source of all the misfortunes that we labour under, tho thank God but few to what we at first expected. The Congress in the infancy of Politicks could not be brought to believe many serious truths; by attending to speculative principles rather than real life their maxims in War have been founded in folly. However, experience ripens Judgment and enables us to correct many an error in business that at first we could not conceive off, and I dont doubt the Congress in time will be as able Politicians in military matters as they are in civl Governmt.

The Eastern Delegates made application to General Washington for me to come to Rhode Island but the General would not consent.[4] He thinks more is to be trusted to the virtue of your People than to the force of this Country. As the Enemy have got possession of Rhode Island and done all the mischief they can, it will not be bad policy to let them remain in quiet until Spring. To attempt any [thing] against them unless you are sure of success will be a very dangerous manoeuvre. Tis an endless task to attempt to cover all the Country. You must drive back the Stock from the Shores and make a disposition to cover cappital Objects; by too great a division of your force youl be incapable of making any considerable opposition where ever they may think proper to make a descent. But its my oppinion they will be peaceable if you will, for from the best accounts we can get they consist of the Invalids of the army. They may attempt to plunder the Shores, but nothing more than that this Winter, for I am confident they have no hopes of penetrating into the Country. If they make any descent it will be against Providence to seize the Stores and burn the town. This is very probable as the Tories will endeavor in Newport to spirit them on to such an attempt, but unless it is already done you have nothing to fear.

I am told some malicious reports propagated industriously about me respecting the loss of the Baggage and Stores at Fort Lee. They are as malicious as they are untrue. I can bring very good vouchers for my conduct in every instance, and have the satisfaction to have it approvd by the General under whom I serve. Everything was got off from that place that could be with the Boats and Waggons we had to move the Stores with. The Evacuation of Fort Lee was determind upon several days before the Enemy landed above us, and happily all the most valueable Stores were away. The Enemies publiccation of the Cannon and Stores there taken is a grand falsehood. Not an article of military Stores was left there or nothing worth mentioning.[5]

The Congress have removd to Baltimore. General Spencer and General Arnold are coming to take the command at Rhode Island. Arnold is a fine spirited fellow, and an Active General.

I hope theyl keep the Enemy at Bay. My respects to your family and all my Providence friends. Believe me to be with the greatest respect your most obedient and very humble Servt

NATH GREENE

ALS (R-Ar).
    1. See note 2, NG to Catharine, 4 Dec., above.
    2. Despite the use of the first person singular, it is probable that he was speaking of the planned attack on Trenton in which Washington, as NG knew, planned to use every brigade available.
    3. On enemy depredations in N.J., see below, NG to Cooke, 10 Jan. 1777.
    4. See note 5, NG to Catharine, 16 Dec., above.
    5. NG had been goaded by the criticism into greatly understating the losses at Ft. Lee; see note 2, NG to Cooke, 4 Dec., above.

## To Colonel Clement Biddle

Dear Sir          Head Quarters [Coryells Ferry, Pa.] Decem 24, 1776

If your business at Newtown will permit I should be glad to see you here. There is some business of importance to communicate to you which I wish to do today.[1] No butter, No Chees, No Cyder. This is not for the honnor of Pensylvania. Col Griffin is at Mount Holley collecting great numbers of the Jersey Troops. They have drove the Hessians and high Landers many miles. Yesterday a great fireing was heard there, the consequence I have not learnt. Yours sincerely

N GREENE

ALS (MiU-C).
    1. Undoubtedly the attack on Trenton planned for Christmas day.

## To Catharine Greene

Trenton [N.J.] Decem 30, 1776

Before this reaches you doubtless you will hear of the Attack upon this place. We crost the River Delaware at McKonkees Ferry Eight miles above this place on the 25 of this instant and attackt the Town by Storm in the morning. It raind, haild and snowd and was a violent Storm. The Storm of nature and the Storm of the Town exhibited a Scene that fild the mind during the action with passions easier conceivd than describd. The Action lasted about three quarters of an hour. We kild, wounded and took Prisoners of the Enimy between Eleven and twelve hundred. Our Troops behavd with great Spirit. General Sullivan commanded the right Wing of the army and I the left.[1]

This is an important period to America, big with great events. God only knows what will be the issue of this Campaign, but everything wears a much better prospect than they have for some weeks past. The Enimy are collecting their force at Princeton; whether they mean to attack us or to act upon the defensive.[2]

I am well in health and hope to continue so. In a few Weeks I hope to have a fine army together. I observe the Enimy have got possession of Newport and Joseph Wanton proclaimd Govenor. I am sure the Enimy cannot penetrate the C[ountry] in N England as they have done here.

Should we get possession again of the Jerseys perhaps I may get liberty to come and see you. I pity your situation exceedingly. Your distress and anxiety must be very great; put on a good stock of fortitude. By the blessing of God I hope to meet again in the pleasures of wedlock. Adieu my love

N GREENE

ALS (MiU-C).

1. This is the only known account by NG of the battle of Trenton. Considering that it marked a dramatic turn in his own fortunes, as well as the nation's, it is extremely brief and matter-of-fact. His role in the battle largely erased the memory of Fts. Washington and Lee from the minds of his compatriots.

When Howe went into winter quarters in New York on 14 Dec., he left garrisons at five posts across New Jersey under the overall command of Gen. James Grant, the replacement for Cornwallis who was planning a trip back to England. In command of two German garrisons near the Delaware River was Col. von Donop; 1,500 men were directly under him in the vicinity of Bordentown and another 1,400 under his subordinate Col. Rall in Trenton, eight miles upriver. Washington, who feared that Donop would attack Philadelphia once the ice on the river would support his troops, contemplated an amphibious strike in the meantime at one or more posts if he could ever get Gen. Charles Lee and his 5,000 troops to join him. (See note 4, NG to Washington, 7 Dec., above.) Every day that Lee delayed was one day nearer the year's end, when the terms of enlistment for most of the army would be up. Washington would be lucky if by then he had 1,400 troops to oppose Donop's 3,000.

Lee's capture was a hard blow, but Washington did not abandon his plan for some kind of attack. Out of desperation, in fact, he seems to have drawn new hope and energy. The arrival of Sullivan on 20 Dec. with the remainder of Lee's forces (although now reduced to 2,000) strengthened Washington's resolve. With the addition of 600 men from Gates's army, a new Pennsylvania German unit, and the recently recruited Philadelphia Associators, he would have an army of some 6,000 effective troops—but only for ten days. In a now-or-never mood, he decided to attack Trenton, which a modern historian has called "his only really brilliant stroke of the war" (Higginbotham, *War*, p. 166). He discussed the plan with NG at length. In a letter to Gov. Cooke on 21 Dec. (above), NG said that "should fortune favor the Attack Perhaps it may put a stop to General Hows progress." The very audacity of the plan—to attack across the broad Delaware in the dead of winter with an army that was to be disbanded within a week—helped to assure its success, for neither Gen. Grant nor Col. Rall at Trenton took any steps to guard against what they considered most improbable.

Washington called a meeting of his officers at NG's headquarters in the Merrick House on Christmas eve to go over final details of his plan. Three separate crossings were to be made after dusk on Christmas day. Washington's main force of some 2,400 men under NG and Sullivan were to cross at McKonkey's Ferry, nine miles north of Trenton (now Washington's Crossing). If this first step could be completed by midnight, they should arrive at Trenton well before daylight. Downstream, opposite Trenton, some 700 militia under Gen. Ewing would be ferried over to block the Hessians from escaping across the Assunpink bridge. The third crossing would be made still further downstream by Col. John Cadwalader, temporarily in command of a brigade that was made up mostly of Daniel Hitchcock's veteran Rhode Islanders and the Philadelphia Associators. Their objective was to divert Donop's forces, which were then south of Bordentown.

Col. John Glover and his Marblehead mariners, who had saved the army on Long Island, were assigned the task of getting the main army across in the boats that Washington had earlier commandeered—especially the Durham boats that had been developed originally to carry iron ore. These shallow-draft vessels, forty to sixty feet long and eight feet wide, could carry a company of men or fifteen tons of equipment. They were generally poled and were steered by a sweep that could be fitted to either end of the boat.

Christmas day was a day that the participants would never forget. Snow from an earlier storm still lay on the ground, melted and refrozen in places. During the afternoon, as the men assembled behind the hills, a new storm moved in, bringing biting winds and later in the day a mixture of snow, sleet, and even hail. The river was covered by floating chunks of ice, swept along by a swift current. The poorly clad men made a pathetic picture as they marched to the point of embarkation. As Christopher Ward has written: "The story of ragged, shoeless men leaving bloody footprints in the snow has been told so often that it has become commonplace, and often fails to impress the reader" with what "was sufficiently real to the men." (Ward, *War*, 1: 295)

Although Glover's men performed near miracles in getting 2,400 men and Knox's eighteen cannon across the turbulent stream, it was three A.M. before the last unit landed on the Jersey shore, several hours behind schedule. Fortune, nevertheless, as NG had hoped, did favor them this time, because their landing and their march by early daylight went unnoticed and unreported to the Hessian garrison, most of whom were still sleeping off their Christmas celebrations. Halfway to Trenton, where the men stopped to rest and eat, NG's division, accompanied by Washington, split off in order to approach Trenton along a road that ran parallel to Sullivan's route and that would bring them into the north end of the town. In NG's division were the brigades of Gens. Stephen, Stirling, and Roche de Fermoy—a French nobleman who had been commissioned by Congress in Nov.

NG's advance column was within half a mile of Trenton before a German outpost took warning. For Rall's garrison the warning came too late, as the division advanced "pell mell" into town, keeping up as steady fire as their damp powder would permit. Sullivan miraculously arrived at the south end of town at almost the same moment and began an attack. The fierce Hessian victors of Mt. Washington poured out of their shelters half-dressed and but half-awake, utterly confused by the sound of the shooting. Col. Rall, aroused from a deep sleep, seemed the most confused of all. The fighting that ensued in the next hour and a half was all but indescribable. Knox thought that the "hurry, fright and confusion of the enemy, was not unlike that which will be when the last trumpet shall sound" (Callahan, *Knox*, p. 85). With NG's division sealing off any escape to the north and closing in on the bewildered foe in the center of town, and with Sullivan's division doing the same at the other end of town, Knox set up his artillery at the north end of two converging principal streets, directing a devastating fire down both. Gun smoke and driving sleet screened much of the action even from the participants. From behind buildings and from upstairs windows, American riflemen picked off German soldiers and officers, while those with muskets too wet to fire used their bayonets—much to the surprise of the Hessians.

The usually competent Rall tried hard to rally his troops, calling on the band to strike up some martial music. When his two field pieces were put out of action, his men retreated to an apple orchard at the east edge of town. One hitch in Washington's plan, which allowed some to escape, was the failure of Gen. Ewing's militia to protect the Assunpink bridge. Lacking Washington's determination and Glover's mariners, Ewing had not even ventured to cross the river during the night. Before Sullivan reached the creek, more than 400 Hessians escaped, but they were the last to do so.

In the meantime Rall was fatally wounded in an attempt to launch a counterattack. Soon thereafter, with all escape cut off, the garrison surrendered. More than twenty of their countrymen were dead and ninety lay wounded, many so severely that they could not be moved. Although some 500 had escaped, 918 were taken prisoner—30 of them officers. Of the Americans none was killed in battle, and but few were wounded.

Besides Ewing's failure one other hitch had developed in Washington's plans. With great difficulty Cadwalader had gotten a third of his troops across the river during the night, but when he was unable to load his artillery, and believing Washington still on the Pennsylvania side, he had brought the men back across. Thus there was no one to block Donop. Fortunately Donop had not learned about the battle in time to come to Rall's aid. But now that he was free to attack the exhausted American troops, Washington ordered them back across the river, along with the prisoners that NG had entrusted to Lord Stirling's care. The crossing was even worse than the previous night; several American soldiers froze to death. But victory lifted the spirits of the weary men as news of it did for all Americans. Hope replaced the despair that had settled on the new nation in the month after Ft. Washington's fall.

The British were shaken by the American victory. Gen. James Grant, who had thought the Americans along the Delaware could be contained by a corporals guard, admitted that he "did not think that all the Rebels in America would have taken that Brigade Prisoners." For Gen. Howe, it was a terrible ending to a year that had brought him a knighthood for his victories at Long Island and Ft. Washington. His superior, Lord George Germain, would never forget it; two years later he told Parliament that all his hopes for an early ending to the war had been "blasted by that unhappy affair at Trenton." (Quotations from Ketchum, *Winter Soldiers*, pp. 323, 325.)

The battle of Trenton has been retold many times. The classic account, thorough and still useful, is by William S. Stryker in *The Battles of Trenton and Princeton* (Boston, 1898). Ketchum makes use of sources not available to Stryker and does so most compellingly; Trenton is covered in pp. 269–327 and the battle of Princeton in pp. 328–79.

2. Although the campaign of 1776 is generally considered to end with the battle of Princeton in early Jan., that battle is described in a letter from NG of 10 Jan. to be printed and annotated in volume two. Suffice it to say here that, on 30 Dec., Washington crossed back over the Delaware in the hope of taking Princeton and possibly New Brunswick, only to find to his great surprise that Cornwallis, his trip to England canceled, had reached Princeton by forced marches with 8,000 men. Washington marched to Trenton, where NG wrote the above letter, and then began entrenching south of Assunpink Creek. On 2 Jan., Cornwallis left for Trenton, where Washington's inferior forces seemed trapped. NG's division slowed the advance enough to delay their arrival at Trenton until nightfall—giving Washington's army an opportunity to withdraw along a back road to Princeton during the night, muffling their gun-carriage

wheels to mask their retreat and leaving a unit behind to deceive the British with busy sounds of fortification.

When Cornwallis discovered the ruse, the Americans had already engaged a surprised British garrison at Princeton. Although the British succeeded at first in driving back the advance unit, they soon gave way in a rout that cost them 28 killed, 58 wounded, and 129 captured. American losses were 23 killed and 20 wounded. Among the killed was NG's good friend Gen. Hugh Mercer, and among the wounded was his old regimental commander Daniel Hitchcock, who died a week later from injuries and exposure.

NG pursued the British part of the way to New Brunswick, but with Cornwallis close behind, all the officers agreed to head for the hills of Morristown where a camp had been prepared. The British, now confined to eastern New Jersey, would be no threat to the American army for some months.

# INDEX

Richard K. Showman has been associated with the Rhode Island Historical Society as editor of these volumes since 1972. He is assistant editor of *The Harvard Guide to American History*.

Margaret Cobb assisted in the publication of *The Susquehannah Company Papers*.

Robert E. McCarthy is special lecturer in history at Providence College and assisted in organizing bibliographies for *The Harvard Guide to American History*.